BATMAN ODYSSEY

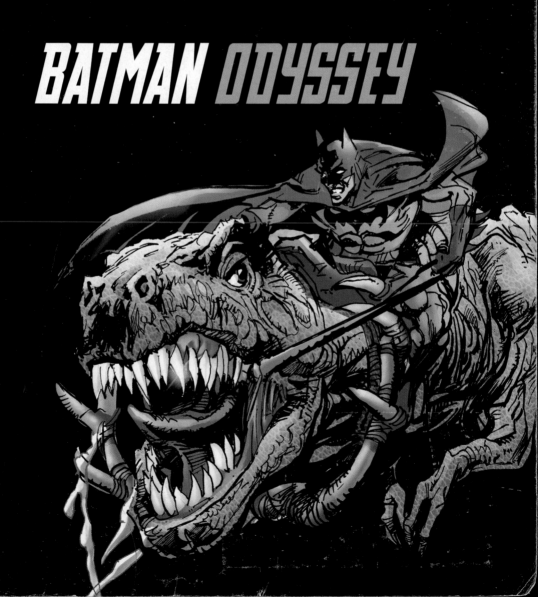

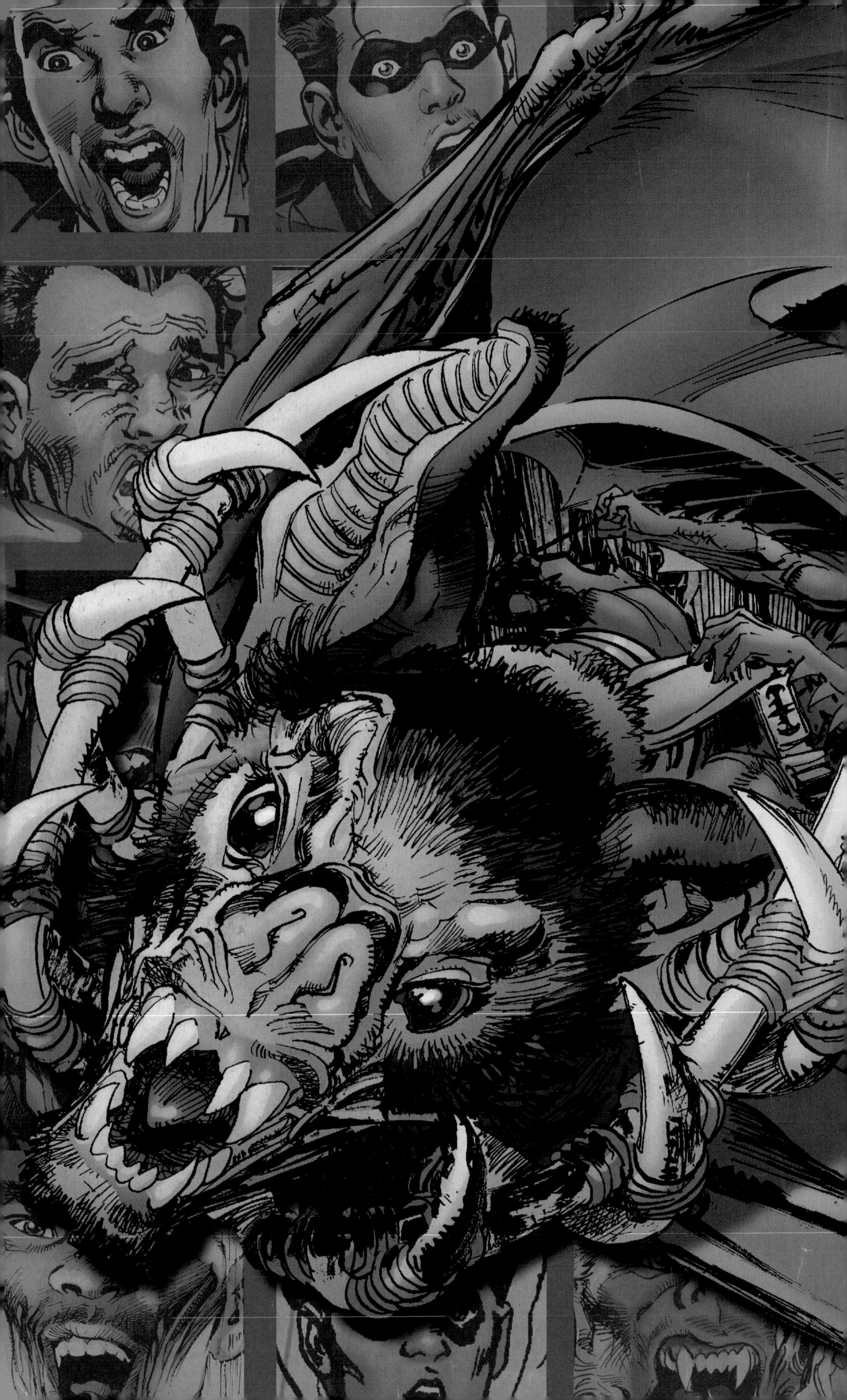

BATMAN ODYSSEY

NEAL ADAMS
story and art

MICHAEL GOLDEN
SCOTT WILLIAMS
BILL SIENKIEWICZ
PAUL NEARY
JOSH ADAMS
KEVIN NOWLAN
inkers

CONTINUITY STUDIOS
GINGER KARALEXAS
CORY ADAMS
MOOSE BAUMANN
GUY MAJOR
colorists

ROB LEIGH
KEN LOPEZ
DAVE SHARPE
letterers

NEAL ADAMS
series and collection
cover artist

Batman created by
BOB KANE

MIKE MARTS
MIKE CARLIN
JOEY CAVALIERI
EDITORS – ORIGINAL SERIES

RACHEL GLUCKSTERN
CHRIS CONROY
ASSOCIATE EDITORS – ORIGINAL SERIES

JANELLE SIEGEL
ASSISTANT EDITOR – ORIGINAL SERIES

ROWENA YOW
EDITOR

ROBBIN BROSTERMAN
DESIGN DIRECTOR – BOOKS

DAMIAN RYLAND
PUBLICATION DESIGN

BOB HARRAS *SENIOR VP – EDITOR-IN-CHIEF, DC COMICS*

DIANE NELSON *PRESIDENT*
DAN DIDIO AND JIM LEE *CO-PUBLISHERS*
GEOFF JOHNS *CHIEF CREATIVE OFFICER*
JOHN ROOD *EXECUTIVE VP – SALES, MARKETING AND BUSINESS DEVELOPMENT*
AMY GENKINS *SENIOR VP – BUSINESS AND LEGAL AFFAIRS*
NAIRI GARDINER *SENIOR VP – FINANCE*
JEFF BOISON *VP – PUBLISHING PLANNING*
MARK CHIARELLO *VP – ART DIRECTION AND DESIGN*
JOHN CUNNINGHAM *VP – MARKETING*
TERRI CUNNINGHAM *VP – EDITORIAL ADMINISTRATION*
ALISON GILL *SENIOR VP – MANUFACTURING AND OPERATIONS*
HANK KANALZ *SENIOR VP – VERTIGO & INTEGRATED PUBLISHING*
JAY KOGAN *VP – BUSINESS AND LEGAL AFFAIRS, PUBLISHING*
JACK MAHAN *VP – BUSINESS AFFAIRS, TALENT*
NICK NAPOLITANO *VP – MANUFACTURING ADMINISTRATION*
SUE POHJA *VP – BOOK SALES*
COURTNEY SIMMONS *SENIOR VP – PUBLICITY*
BOB WAYNE *SENIOR VP – SALES*

BATMAN: ODYSSEY

Published by DC Comics. Cover and compilation Copyright © 2012 DC
Comics. All Rights Reserved.

Originally published in single magazine form in BATMAN ODYSSEY 1-6
(VOL. 1), BATMAN ODYSSEY 1-7 (VOL. 2) © 2010, 2011, 2012,
DC Comics. All Rights Reserved. All characters, their distinctive
likenesses and related elements featured in this publication are
trademarks of DC Comics. The stories, characters and incidents
featured in this publication are entirely fictional. DC Comics
does not read or accept unsolicited ideas, stories or artwork.

DC Comics, 1700 Broadway, New York, NY 10019
A Warner Bros. Entertainment Company.
Printed by RR Donnelley, Salem, VA, USA. 8/30/13.
First Printing.
ISBN: 978-1-4012-3684-7

Library of Congress Cataloging-in-Publication Data

Adams, Neal, 1941-
Batman : odyssey / Neal Adams.
p. cm.
"Originally published in single magazine form in BATMAN
ODYSSEY (VOL. 1) 1-6, BATMAN: ODYSSEY (VOL. 2) 1-7."
ISBN 978-1-4012-3683-0
1. Graphic novels. I. Title.
PN6728.B36A35 2012
741.5'973--dc23
2012019981

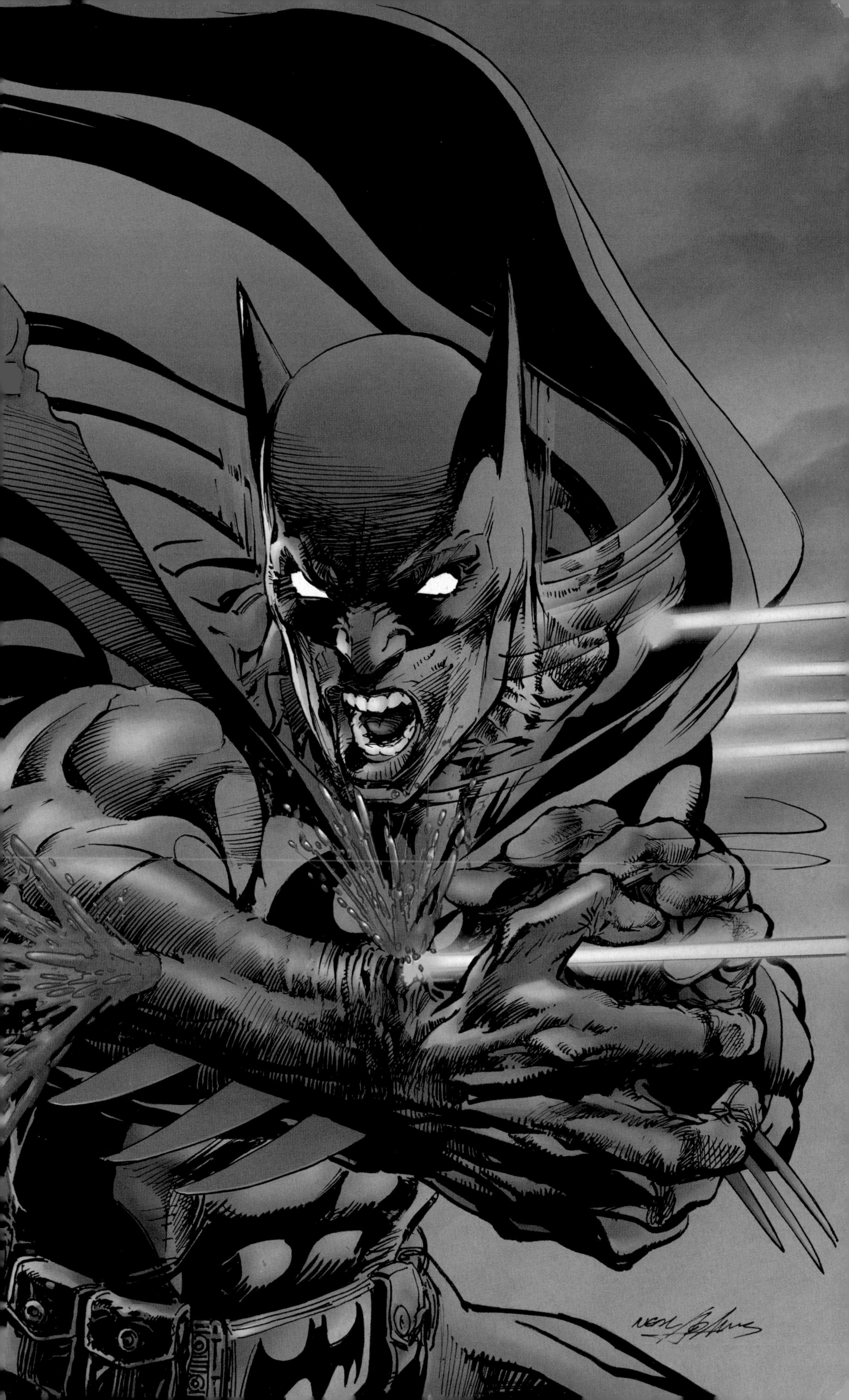

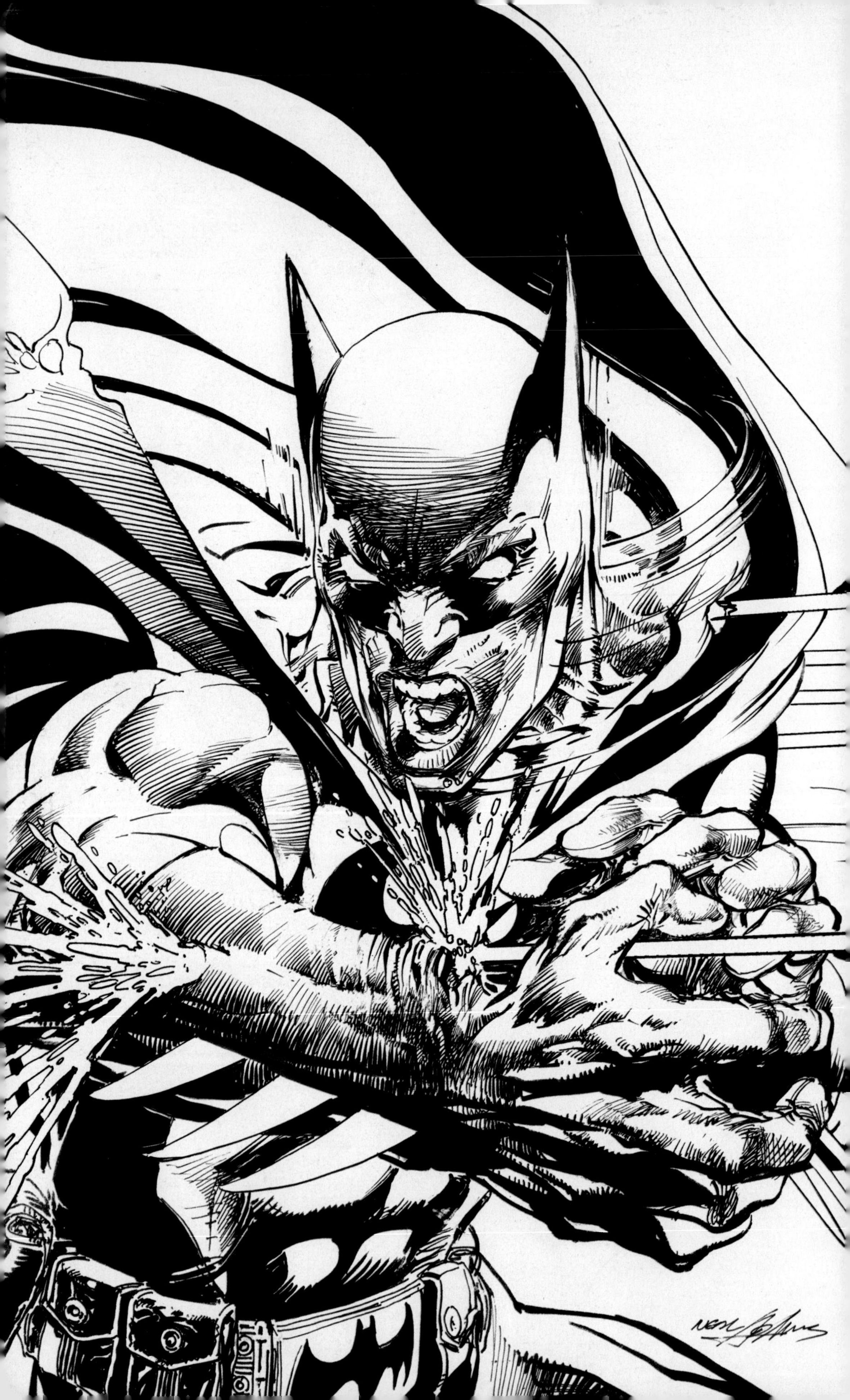

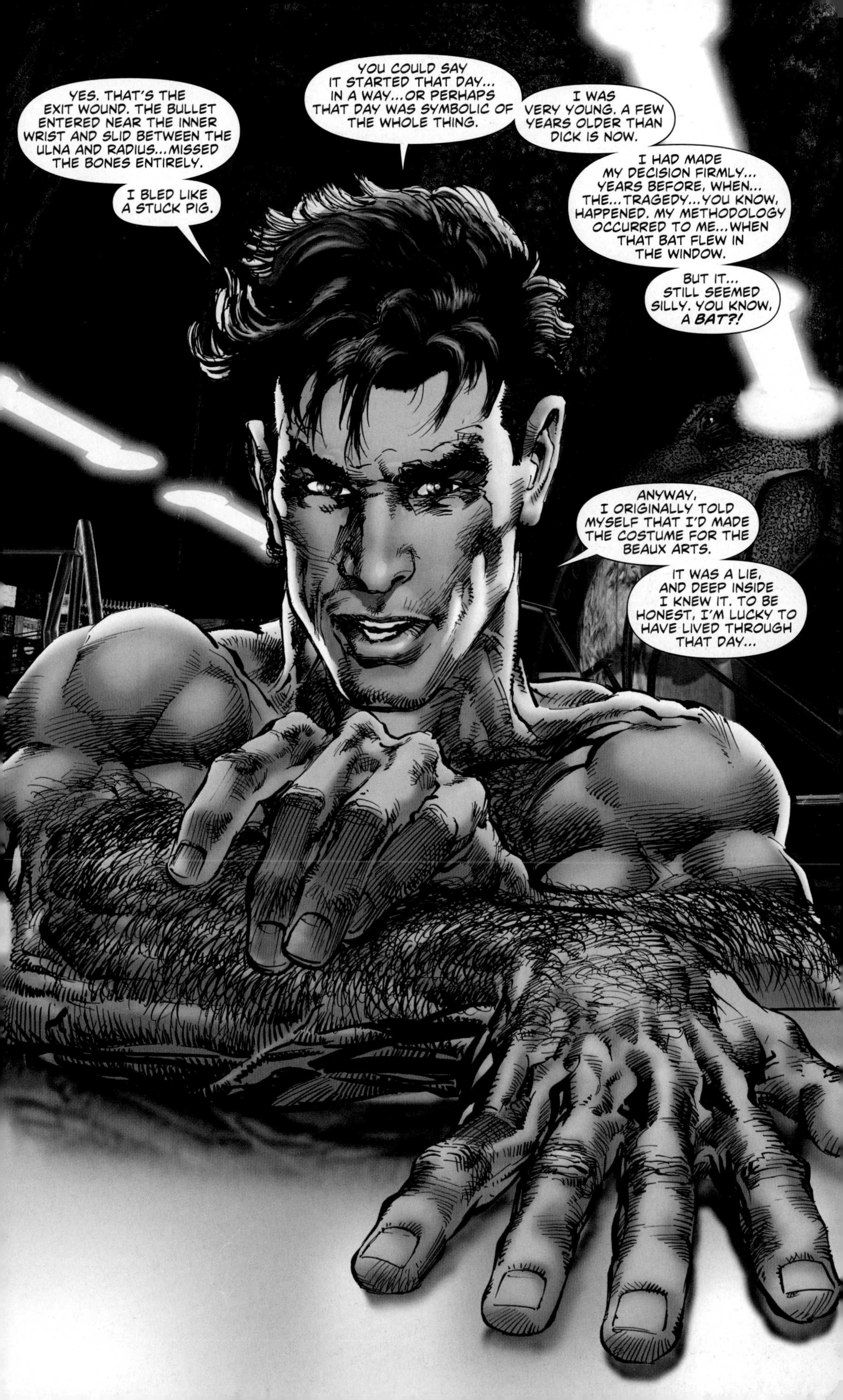
YES. THAT'S THE EXIT WOUND. THE BULLET ENTERED NEAR THE INNER WRIST AND SLID BETWEEN THE ULNA AND RADIUS...MISSED THE BONES ENTIRELY.
I BLED LIKE A STUCK PIG.
YOU COULD SAY IT STARTED THAT DAY... IN A WAY...OR PERHAPS THAT DAY WAS SYMBOLIC OF THE WHOLE THING.
I WAS VERY YOUNG. A FEW YEARS OLDER THAN DICK IS NOW.
I HAD MADE MY DECISION FIRMLY... YEARS BEFORE, WHEN... THE...TRAGEDY...YOU KNOW, HAPPENED. MY METHODOLOGY OCCURRED TO ME...WHEN THAT BAT FLEW IN THE WINDOW.
BUT IT... STILL SEEMED SILLY. YOU KNOW, A *BAT?!*
ANYWAY, I ORIGINALLY TOLD MYSELF THAT I'D MADE THE COSTUME FOR THE BEAUX ARTS.
IT WAS A LIE, AND DEEP INSIDE I KNEW IT. TO BE HONEST, I'M LUCKY TO HAVE LIVED THROUGH THAT DAY...

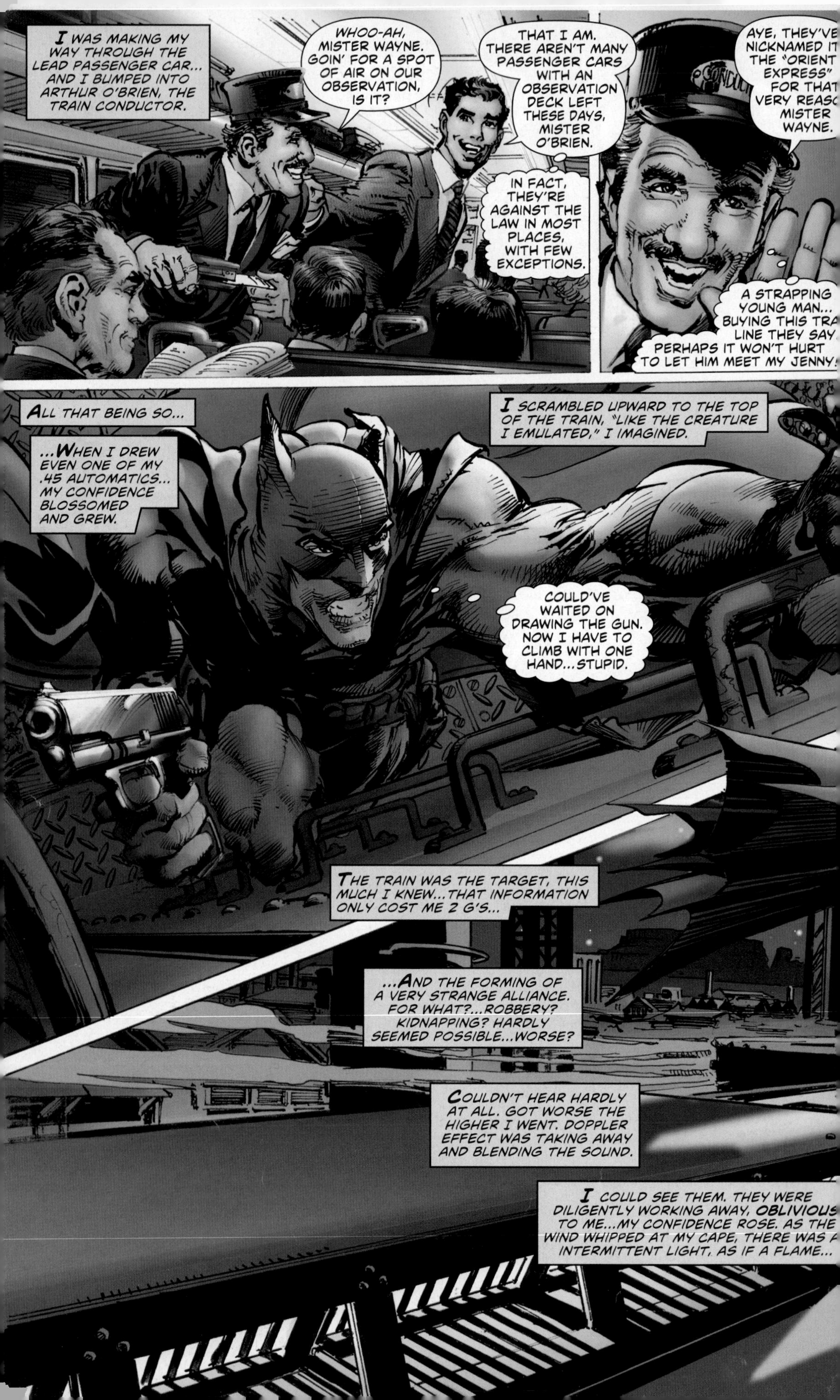
I WAS MAKING MY WAY THROUGH THE LEAD PASSENGER CAR... AND I BUMPED INTO ARTHUR O'BRIEN, THE TRAIN CONDUCTOR.
WHOO-AH, MISTER WAYNE. GOIN' FOR A SPOT OF AIR ON OUR OBSERVATION, IS IT?
THAT I AM. THERE AREN'T MANY PASSENGER CARS WITH AN OBSERVATION DECK LEFT THESE DAYS, MISTER O'BRIEN.
IN FACT, THEY'RE AGAINST THE LAW IN MOST PLACES, WITH FEW EXCEPTIONS.
AYE, THEY'VE NICKNAMED IT THE "ORIENT EXPRESS" FOR THAT VERY REASO MISTER WAYNE.
A STRAPPING YOUNG MAN... BUYING THIS TRA LINE THEY SAY. PERHAPS IT WON'T HURT TO LET HIM MEET MY JENNY.
ALL THAT BEING SO...
...WHEN I DREW EVEN ONE OF MY .45 AUTOMATICS... MY CONFIDENCE BLOSSOMED AND GREW.
I SCRAMBLED UPWARD TO THE TOP OF THE TRAIN, "LIKE THE CREATURE I EMULATED," I IMAGINED.
COULD'VE WAITED ON DRAWING THE GUN. NOW I HAVE TO CLIMB WITH ONE HAND...STUPID.
THE TRAIN WAS THE TARGET, THIS MUCH I KNEW...THAT INFORMATION ONLY COST ME 2 G'S...
...AND THE FORMING OF A VERY STRANGE ALLIANCE. FOR WHAT?...ROBBERY? KIDNAPPING? HARDLY SEEMED POSSIBLE...WORSE?
COULDN'T HEAR HARDLY AT ALL. GOT WORSE THE HIGHER I WENT. DOPPLER EFFECT WAS TAKING AWAY AND BLENDING THE SOUND.
I COULD SEE THEM. THEY WERE DILIGENTLY WORKING AWAY, OBLIVIOUS TO ME...MY CONFIDENCE ROSE. AS THE WIND WHIPPED AT MY CAPE, THERE WAS A INTERMITTENT LIGHT, AS IF A FLAME...

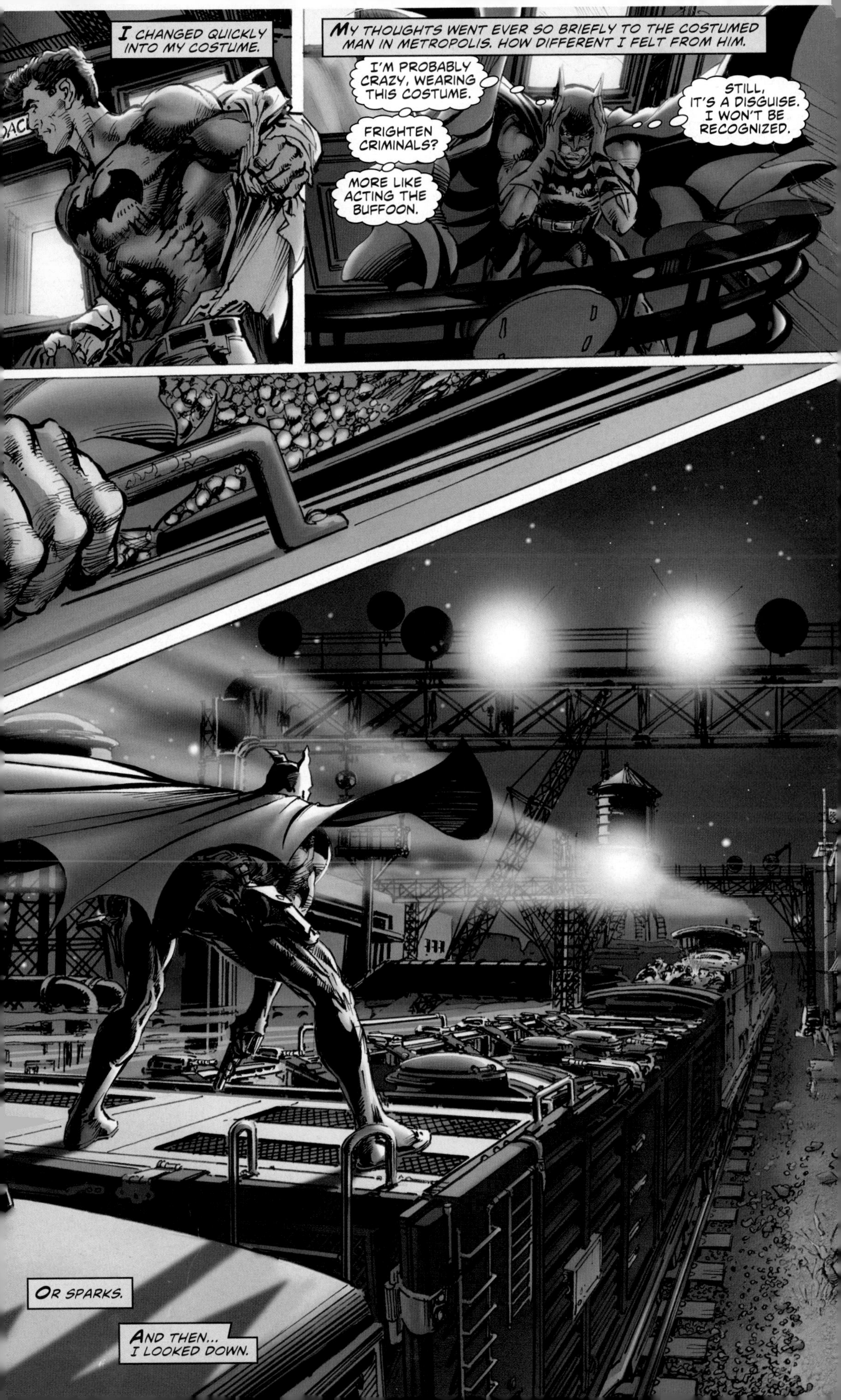
I CHANGED QUICKLY INTO MY COSTUME.
MY THOUGHTS WENT EVER SO BRIEFLY TO THE COSTUMED MAN IN METROPOLIS. HOW DIFFERENT I FELT FROM HIM.
I'M PROBABLY CRAZY, WEARING THIS COSTUME.
FRIGHTEN CRIMINALS?
MORE LIKE ACTING THE BUFFOON.
STILL, IT'S A DISGUISE. I WON'T BE RECOGNIZED.
OR SPARKS.
AND THEN... I LOOKED DOWN.

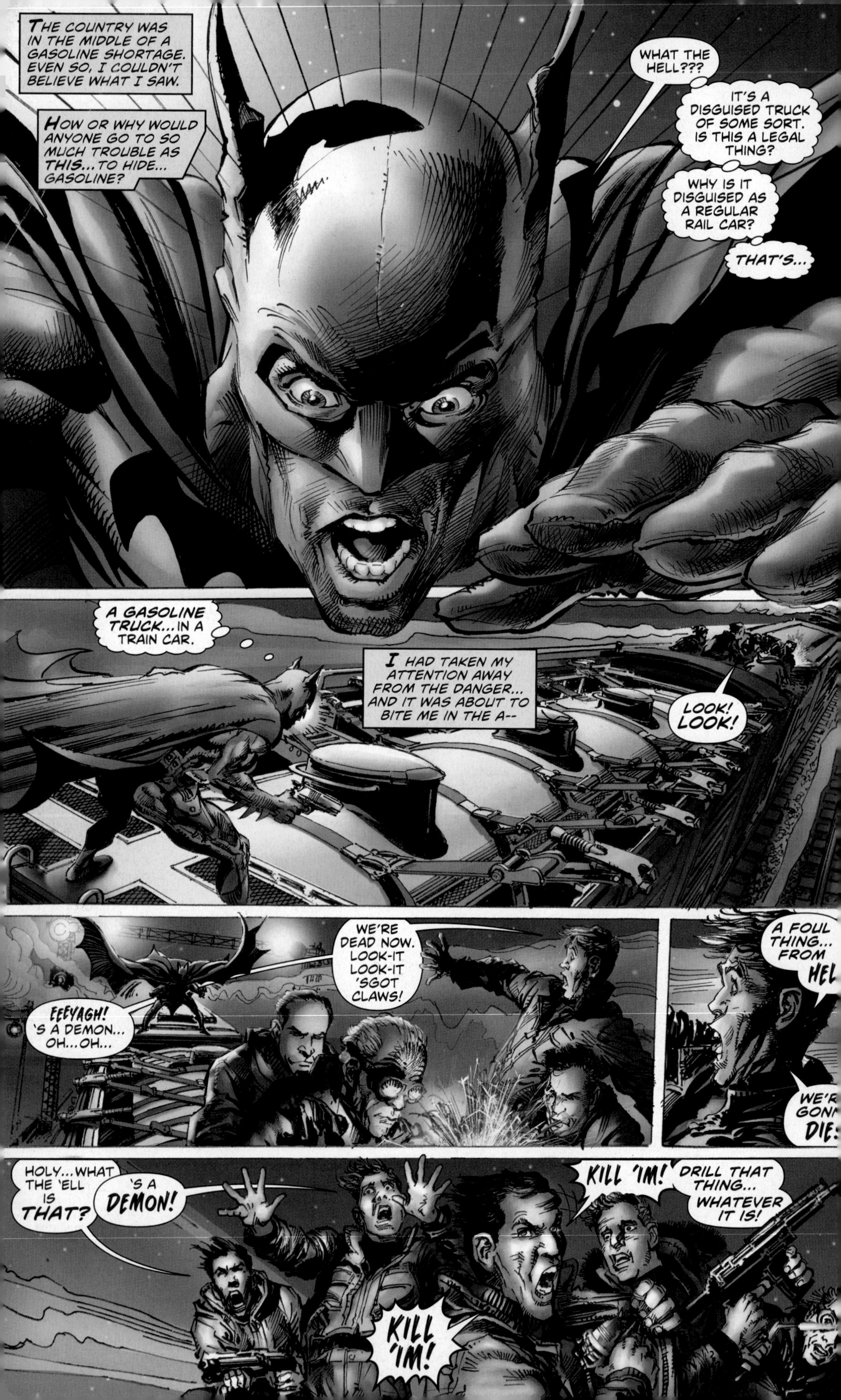
THE COUNTRY WAS IN THE MIDDLE OF A GASOLINE SHORTAGE. EVEN SO, I COULDN'T BELIEVE WHAT I SAW.
HOW OR WHY WOULD ANYONE GO TO SO MUCH TROUBLE AS THIS...TO HIDE... GASOLINE?
WHAT THE HELL???
IT'S A DISGUISED TRUCK OF SOME SORT. IS THIS A LEGAL THING?
WHY IS IT DISGUISED AS A REGULAR RAIL CAR?
THAT'S...
A GASOLINE TRUCK...IN A TRAIN CAR.
I HAD TAKEN MY ATTENTION AWAY FROM THE DANGER... AND IT WAS ABOUT TO BITE ME IN THE A--
LOOK! LOOK!
WE'RE DEAD NOW. LOOK-IT LOOK-IT 'SGOT CLAWS!
EEEYAGH! 'S A DEMON... OH...OH...
A FOUL THING... FROM HEL
WE'R GON DIE
HOLY...WHAT THE 'ELL IS THAT?
'S A DEMON!
KILL 'IM!
DRILL THAT THING... WHATEVER IT IS!
KILL 'IM!

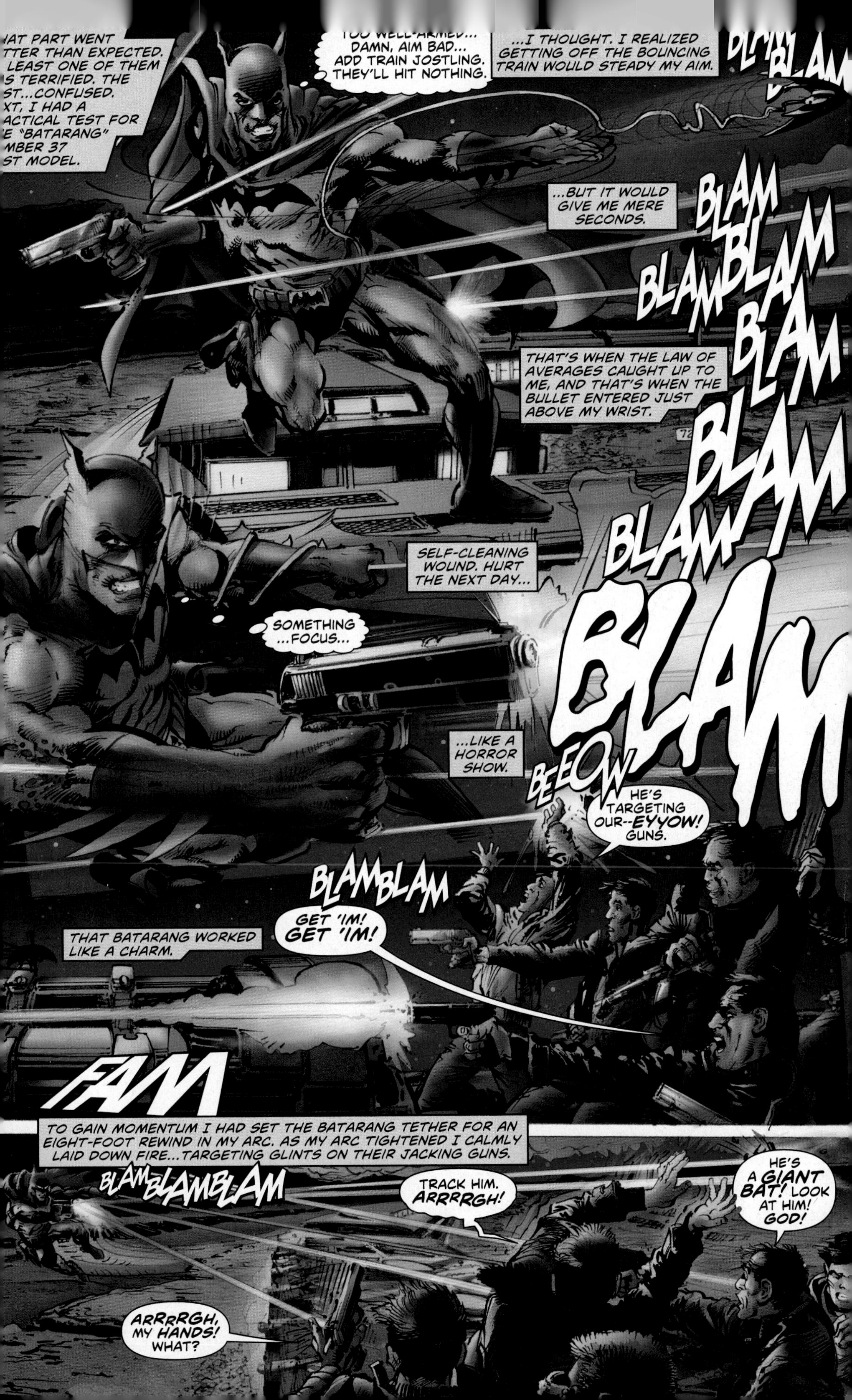

...HAT PART WENT ...TTER THAN EXPECTED. ...LEAST ONE OF THEM ...S TERRIFIED. THE ...ST...CONFUSED. ...XT, I HAD A ...ACTICAL TEST FOR ...E "BATARANG" ...MBER 37 ...ST MODEL.
TOO WELL-ARMED... DAMN, AIM BAD... ADD TRAIN JOSTLING. THEY'LL HIT NOTHING.
...I THOUGHT. I REALIZED GETTING OFF THE BOUNCING TRAIN WOULD STEADY MY AIM.
BLAM BLAM
...BUT IT WOULD GIVE ME MERE SECONDS.
BLAM BLAMBLAM BLAM BLAM
THAT'S WHEN THE LAW OF AVERAGES CAUGHT UP TO ME, AND THAT'S WHEN THE BULLET ENTERED JUST ABOVE MY WRIST.
BLAM BLAM
SELF-CLEANING WOUND. HURT THE NEXT DAY...
SOMETHING ...FOCUS...
BLAM
...LIKE A HORROR SHOW.
BEEEOW
HE'S TARGETING OUR--EYYOW! GUNS.
BLAMBLAM
GET 'IM! GET 'IM!
THAT BATARANG WORKED LIKE A CHARM.
FAM
TO GAIN MOMENTUM I HAD SET THE BATARANG TETHER FOR AN EIGHT-FOOT REWIND IN MY ARC. AS MY ARC TIGHTENED I CALMLY LAID DOWN FIRE...TARGETING GLINTS ON THEIR JACKING GUNS.
BLAMBLAMBLAM
TRACK HIM. ARRRRGH!
HE'S A GIANT BAT! LOOK AT HIM! GOD!
ARRRRGH, MY HANDS! WHAT?

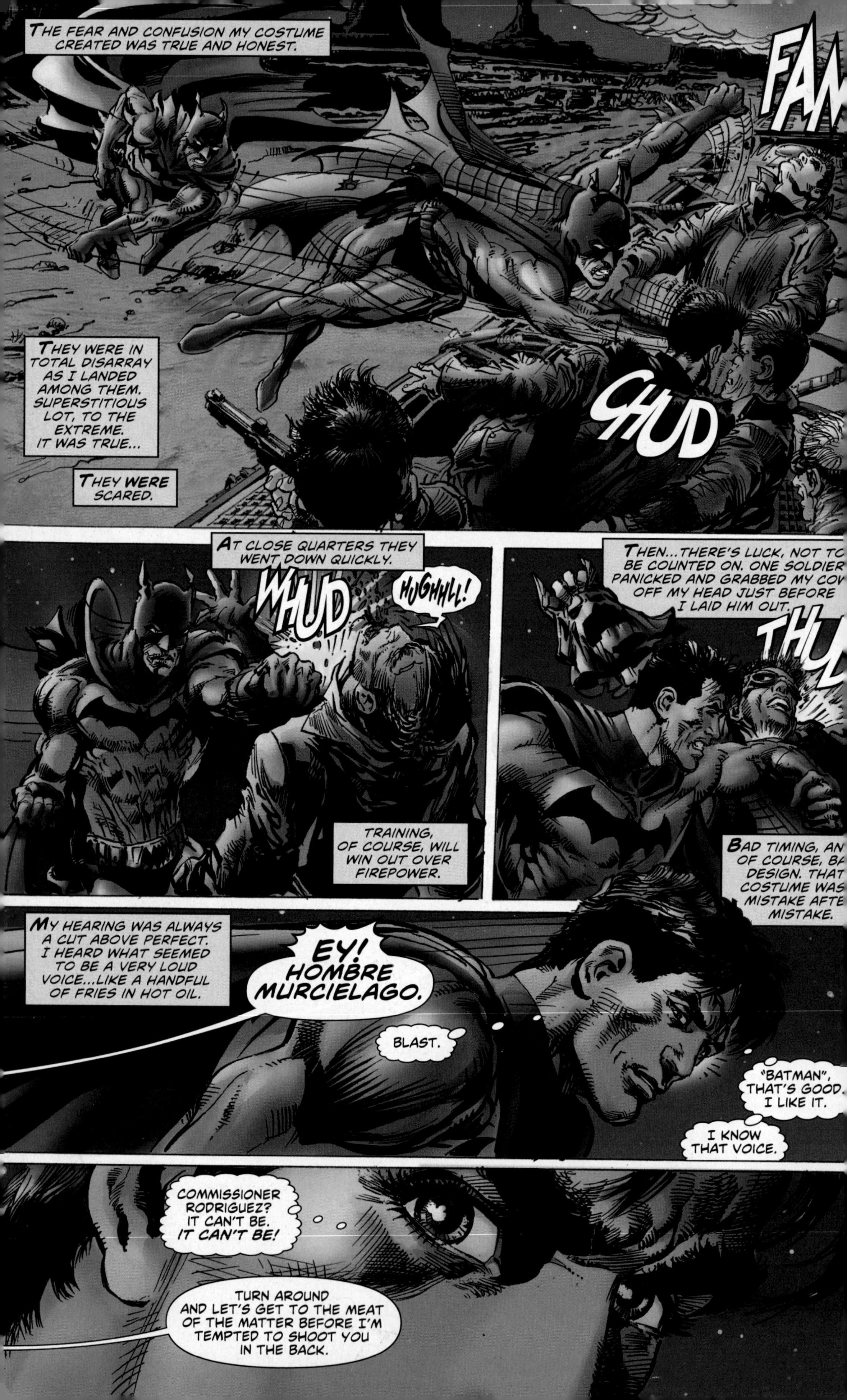
THE FEAR AND CONFUSION MY COSTUME CREATED WAS TRUE AND HONEST.
FAM
THEY WERE IN TOTAL DISARRAY AS I LANDED AMONG THEM. SUPERSTITIOUS LOT, TO THE EXTREME. IT WAS TRUE...
THEY WERE SCARED.
CHUD
AT CLOSE QUARTERS THEY WENT DOWN QUICKLY.
WHUD
HUGHHLL!
TRAINING, OF COURSE, WILL WIN OUT OVER FIREPOWER.
THEN...THERE'S LUCK, NOT TO BE COUNTED ON. ONE SOLDIER PANICKED AND GRABBED MY COW OFF MY HEAD JUST BEFORE I LAID HIM OUT.
THU
BAD TIMING, AN OF COURSE, BA DESIGN. THAT COSTUME WAS MISTAKE AFTE MISTAKE.
MY HEARING WAS ALWAYS A CUT ABOVE PERFECT. I HEARD WHAT SEEMED TO BE A VERY LOUD VOICE...LIKE A HANDFUL OF FRIES IN HOT OIL.
EY! HOMBRE MURCIELAGO.
BLAST.
"BATMAN", THAT'S GOOD. I LIKE IT.
I KNOW THAT VOICE.
COMMISSIONER RODRIGUEZ? IT CAN'T BE. IT CAN'T BE!
TURN AROUND AND LET'S GET TO THE MEAT OF THE MATTER BEFORE I'M TEMPTED TO SHOOT YOU IN THE BACK.

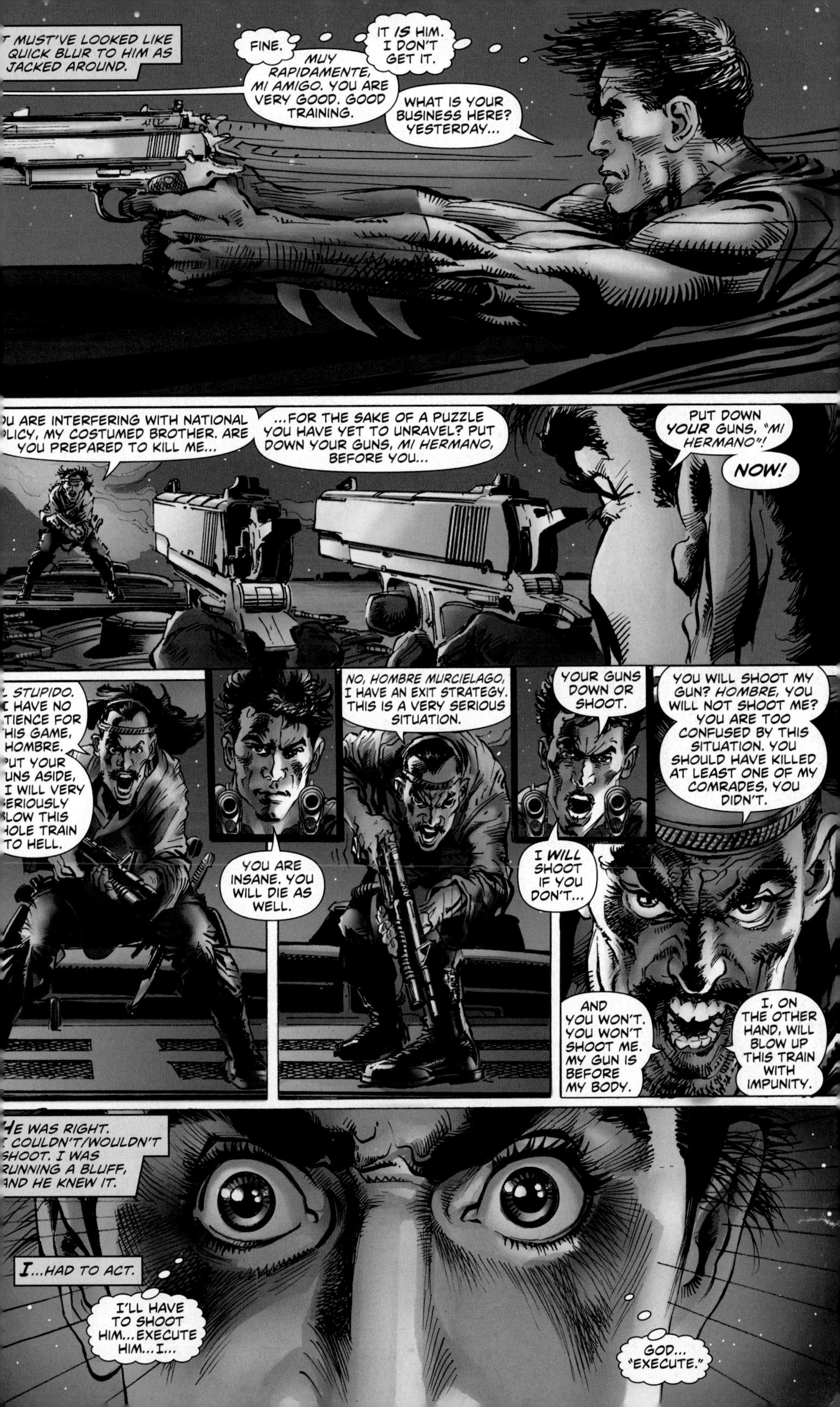
T MUST'VE LOOKED LIKE QUICK BLUR TO HIM AS JACKED AROUND.
FINE.
IT IS HIM. I DON'T GET IT.
MUY RAPIDAMENTE, MI AMIGO. YOU ARE VERY GOOD. GOOD TRAINING.
WHAT IS YOUR BUSINESS HERE? YESTERDAY...
U ARE INTERFERING WITH NATIONAL LICY, MY COSTUMED BROTHER. ARE YOU PREPARED TO KILL ME...
...FOR THE SAKE OF A PUZZLE YOU HAVE YET TO UNRAVEL? PUT DOWN YOUR GUNS, MI HERMANO, BEFORE YOU...
PUT DOWN YOUR GUNS, "MI HERMANO"!
NOW!
STUPIDO. HAVE NO TIENCE FOR THIS GAME, HOMBRE. PUT YOUR UNS ASIDE, I WILL VERY ERIOUSLY LOW THIS HOLE TRAIN TO HELL.
YOU ARE INSANE. YOU WILL DIE AS WELL.
NO, HOMBRE MURCIELAGO, I HAVE AN EXIT STRATEGY. THIS IS A VERY SERIOUS SITUATION.
YOUR GUNS DOWN OR SHOOT.
I WILL SHOOT IF YOU DON'T...
YOU WILL SHOOT MY GUN? HOMBRE, YOU WILL NOT SHOOT ME? YOU ARE TOO CONFUSED BY THIS SITUATION. YOU SHOULD HAVE KILLED AT LEAST ONE OF MY COMRADES. YOU DIDN'T.
AND YOU WON'T. YOU WON'T SHOOT ME. MY GUN IS BEFORE MY BODY.
I, ON THE OTHER HAND, WILL BLOW UP THIS TRAIN WITH IMPUNITY.
HE WAS RIGHT. COULDN'T/WOULDN'T SHOOT. I WAS RUNNING A BLUFF, AND HE KNEW IT.
I...HAD TO ACT.
I'LL HAVE TO SHOOT HIM...EXECUTE HIM...I...
GOD... "EXECUTE."

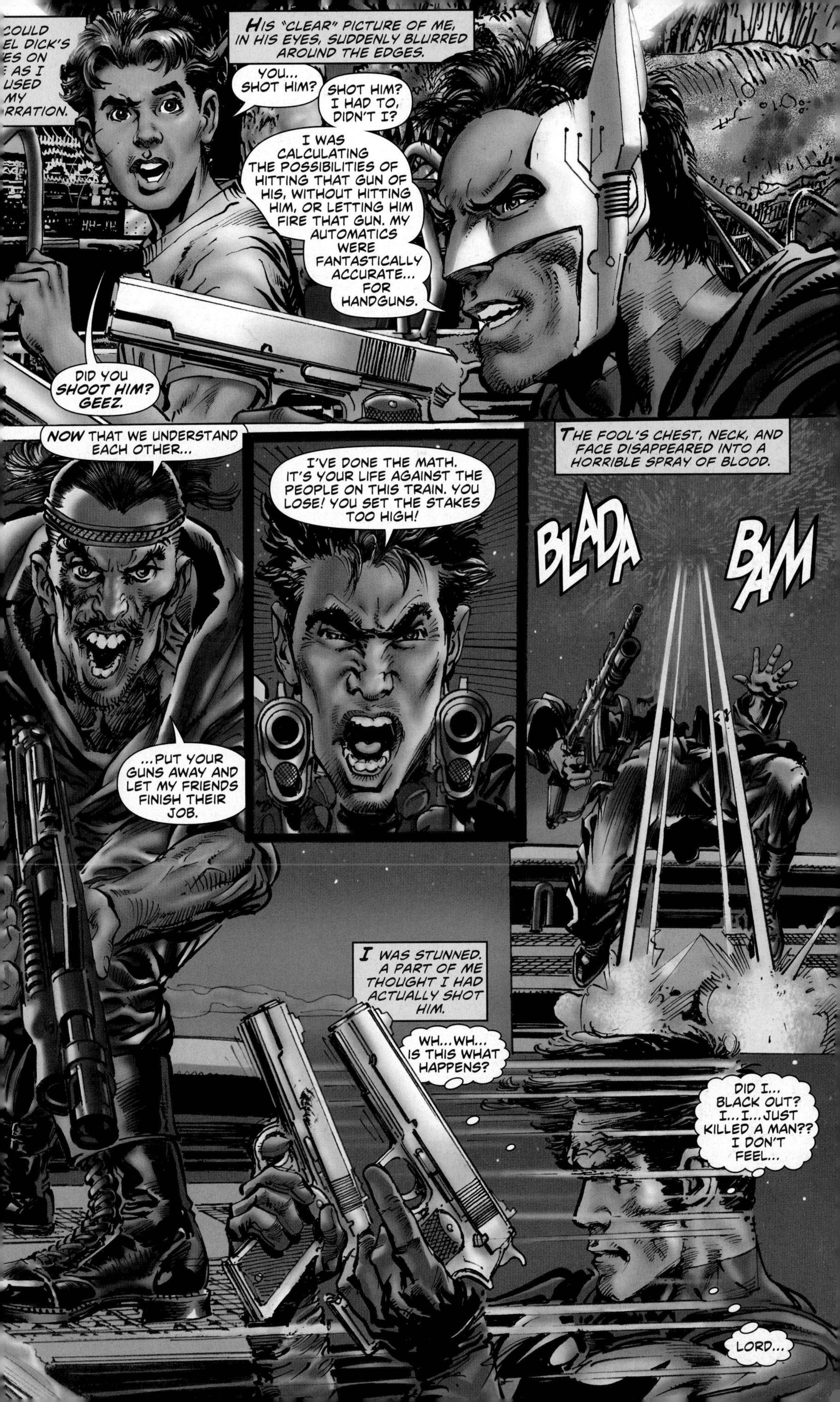

COULD
EL DICK'S
ES ON
AS I
USED
MY
RRATION.
HIS "CLEAR" PICTURE OF ME, IN HIS EYES, SUDDENLY BLURRED AROUND THE EDGES.
YOU... SHOT HIM?
SHOT HIM? I HAD TO, DIDN'T I?
I WAS CALCULATING THE POSSIBILITIES OF HITTING THAT GUN OF HIS, WITHOUT HITTING HIM, OR LETTING HIM FIRE THAT GUN. MY AUTOMATICS WERE FANTASTICALLY ACCURATE... FOR HANDGUNS.
DID YOU SHOOT HIM? GEEZ.
NOW THAT WE UNDERSTAND EACH OTHER...
...PUT YOUR GUNS AWAY AND LET MY FRIENDS FINISH THEIR JOB.
I'VE DONE THE MATH. IT'S YOUR LIFE AGAINST THE PEOPLE ON THIS TRAIN. YOU LOSE! YOU SET THE STAKES TOO HIGH!
THE FOOL'S CHEST, NECK, AND FACE DISAPPEARED INTO A HORRIBLE SPRAY OF BLOOD.
BLADA
BAM
I WAS STUNNED. A PART OF ME THOUGHT I HAD ACTUALLY SHOT HIM.
WH...WH... IS THIS WHAT HAPPENS?
DID I... BLACK OUT? I...I...JUST KILLED A MAN?? I DON'T FEEL...
LORD...

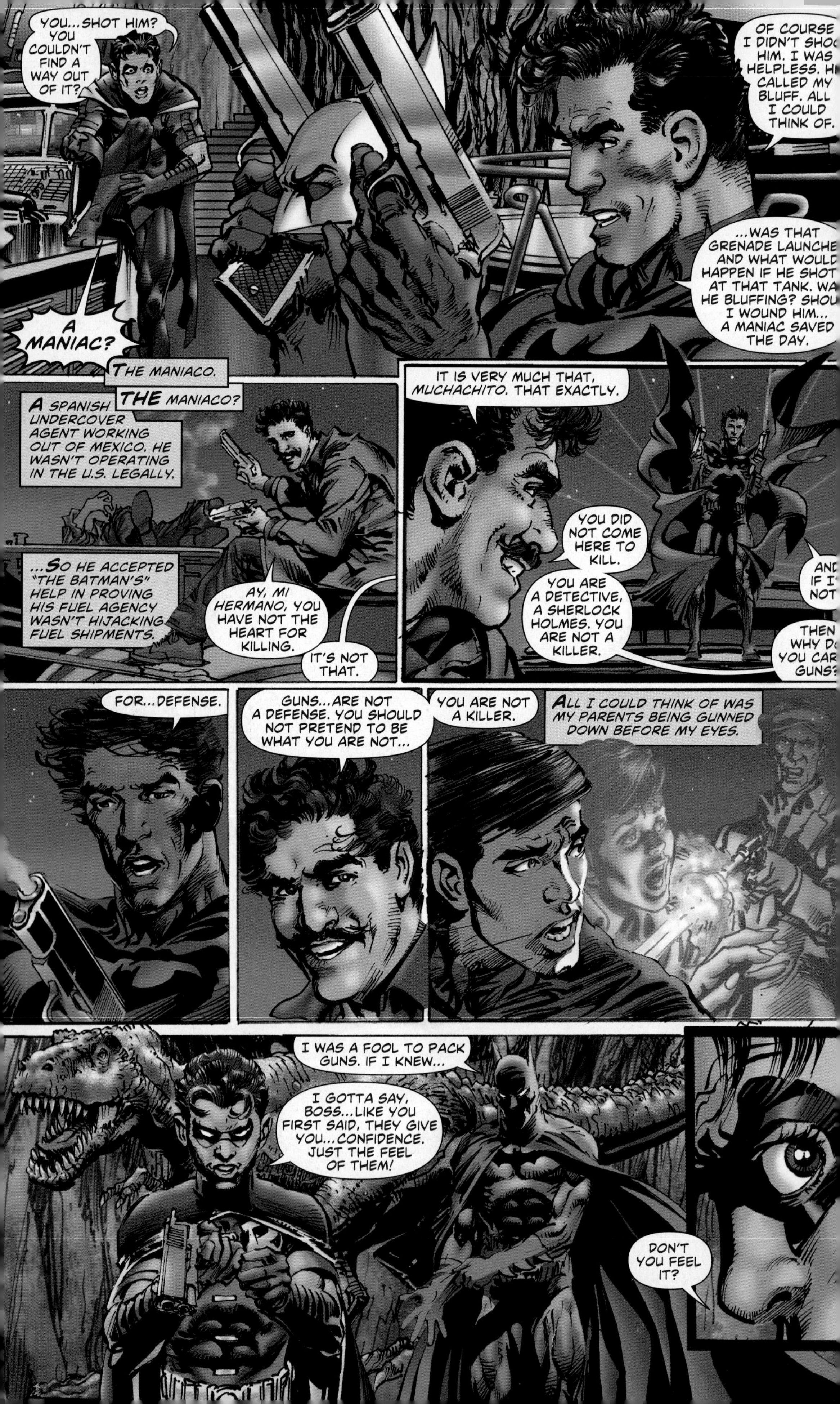

YOU...SHOT HIM? YOU COULDN'T FIND A WAY OUT OF IT?
OF COURSE I DIDN'T SHOO HIM. I WAS HELPLESS. H CALLED MY BLUFF. ALL I COULD THINK OF...
...WAS THAT GRENADE LAUNCHE AND WHAT WOULD HAPPEN IF HE SHOT AT THAT TANK. WA HE BLUFFING? SHOU I WOUND HIM... A MANIAC SAVED THE DAY.
A MANIAC?
THE MANIACO.
THE MANIACO?
A SPANISH UNDERCOVER AGENT WORKING OUT OF MEXICO. HE WASN'T OPERATING IN THE U.S. LEGALLY.
...SO HE ACCEPTED "THE BATMAN'S" HELP IN PROVING HIS FUEL AGENCY WASN'T HIJACKING FUEL SHIPMENTS.
AY, MI HERMANO, YOU HAVE NOT THE HEART FOR KILLING.
IT'S NOT THAT.
IT IS VERY MUCH THAT, MUCHACHITO. THAT EXACTLY.
YOU DID NOT COME HERE TO KILL.
YOU ARE A DETECTIVE, A SHERLOCK HOLMES. YOU ARE NOT A KILLER.
AND IF I' NOT
THEN WHY DO YOU CAR GUNS?
FOR...DEFENSE.
GUNS...ARE NOT A DEFENSE. YOU SHOULD NOT PRETEND TO BE WHAT YOU ARE NOT...
YOU ARE NOT A KILLER.
ALL I COULD THINK OF WAS MY PARENTS BEING GUNNED DOWN BEFORE MY EYES.
I WAS A FOOL TO PACK GUNS. IF I KNEW...
I GOTTA SAY, BOSS...LIKE YOU FIRST SAID, THEY GIVE YOU...CONFIDENCE. JUST THE FEEL OF THEM!
DON'T YOU FEEL IT?

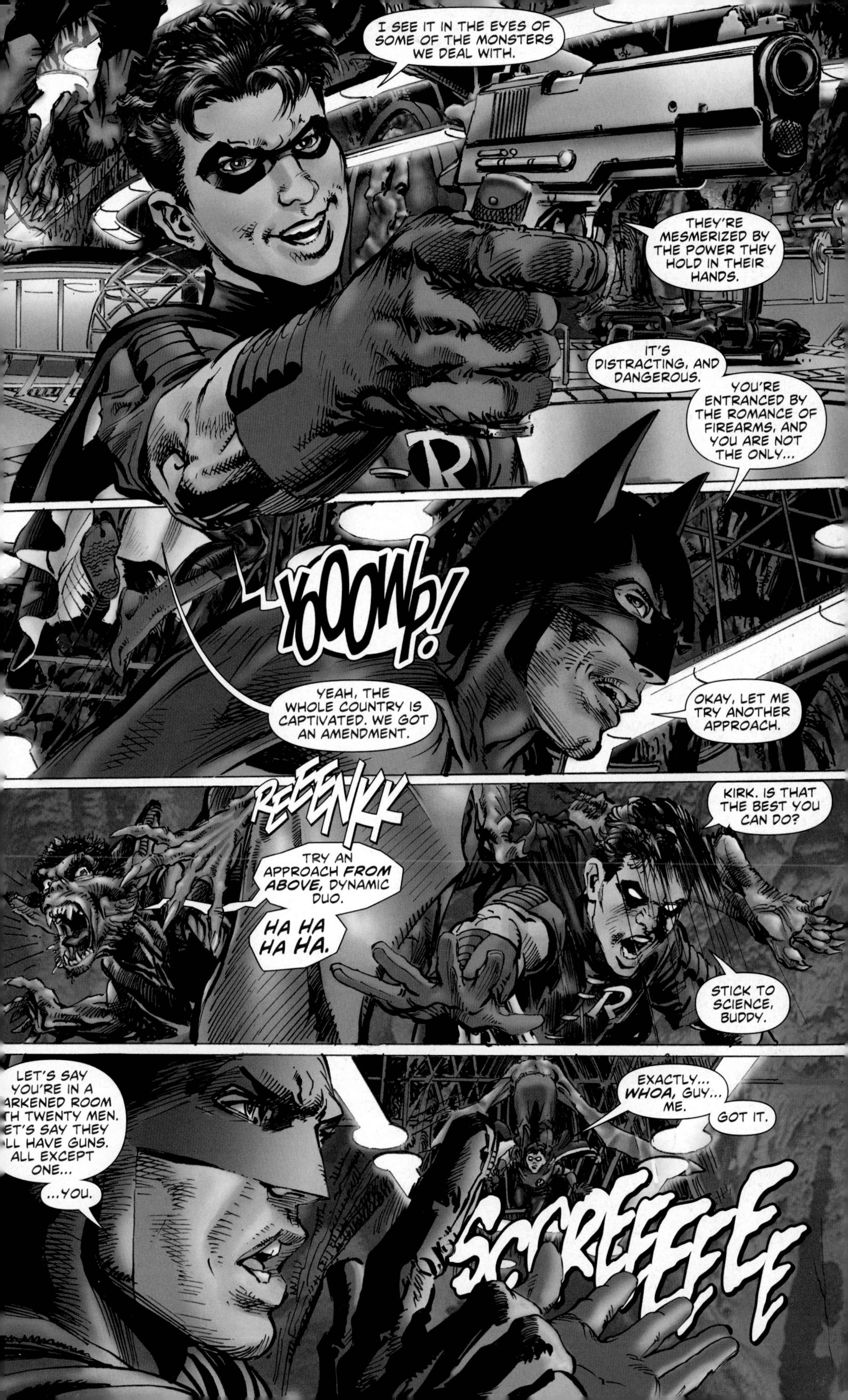
I SEE IT IN THE EYES OF SOME OF THE MONSTERS WE DEAL WITH.
THEY'RE MESMERIZED BY THE POWER THEY HOLD IN THEIR HANDS.
IT'S DISTRACTING, AND DANGEROUS.
YOU'RE ENTRANCED BY THE ROMANCE OF FIREARMS, AND YOU ARE NOT THE ONLY...
YOOOWP!
YEAH, THE WHOLE COUNTRY IS CAPTIVATED. WE GOT AN AMENDMENT.
OKAY, LET ME TRY ANOTHER APPROACH.
REEEENKK
TRY AN APPROACH *FROM ABOVE*, DYNAMIC DUO.
HA HA HA HA.
KIRK. IS THAT THE BEST YOU CAN DO?
STICK TO SCIENCE, BUDDY.
LET'S SAY YOU'RE IN A ARKENED ROOM TH TWENTY MEN. ET'S SAY THEY LL HAVE GUNS. ALL EXCEPT ONE...
...YOU.
EXACTLY... *WHOA*, GUY... ME.
GOT IT.
SCREEEEEE

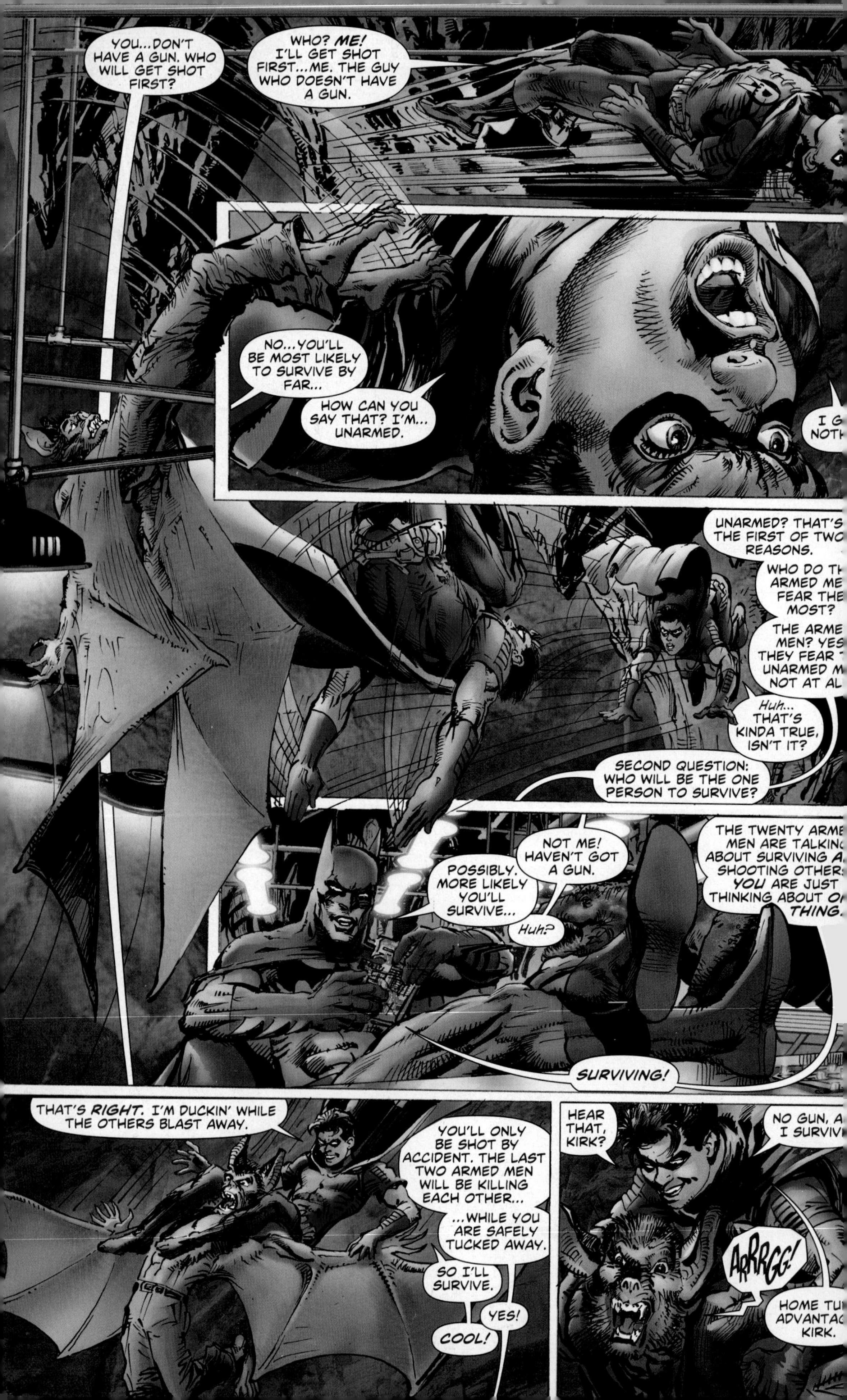
YOU...DON'T HAVE A GUN. WHO WILL GET SHOT FIRST?
WHO? ME! I'LL GET SHOT FIRST...ME. THE GUY WHO DOESN'T HAVE A GUN.
NO...YOU'LL BE MOST LIKELY TO SURVIVE BY FAR...
HOW CAN YOU SAY THAT? I'M... UNARMED.
UNARMED? THAT'S THE FIRST OF TWO REASONS.
Huh... THAT'S KINDA TRUE, ISN'T IT?
SECOND QUESTION: WHO WILL BE THE ONE PERSON TO SURVIVE?
NOT ME! HAVEN'T GOT A GUN.
POSSIBLY. MORE LIKELY YOU'LL SURVIVE...
Huh?
SURVIVING!
THAT'S RIGHT. I'M DUCKIN' WHILE THE OTHERS BLAST AWAY.
YOU'LL ONLY BE SHOT BY ACCIDENT. THE LAST TWO ARMED MEN WILL BE KILLING EACH OTHER...
...WHILE YOU ARE SAFELY TUCKED AWAY.
SO I'LL SURVIVE.
YES!
COOL!
HEAR THAT, KIRK?
ARRRGG!

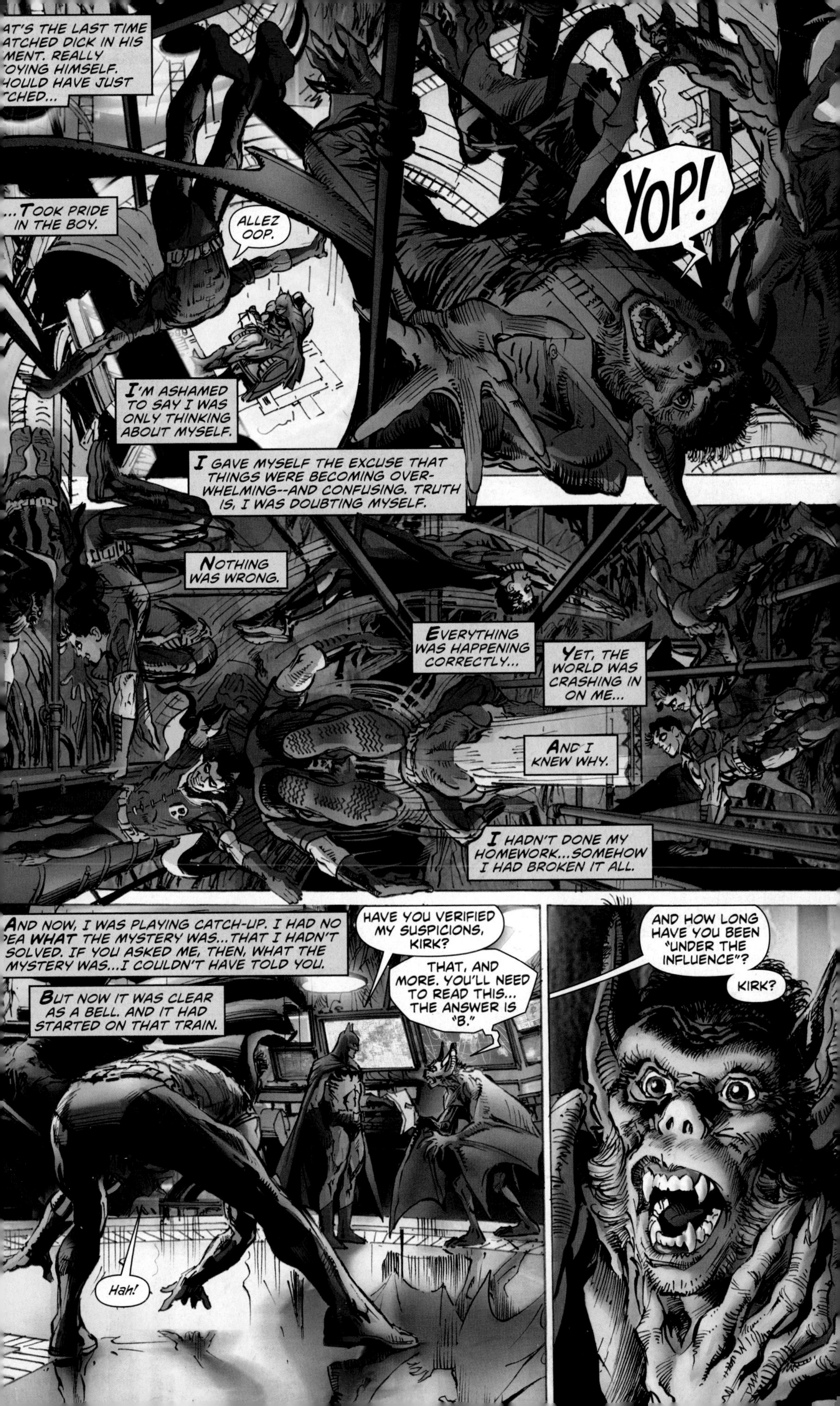
AT'S THE LAST TIME
ATCHED DICK IN HIS
MENT. REALLY
OYING HIMSELF.
HOULD HAVE JUST
TCHED...
...TOOK PRIDE IN THE BOY.
ALLEZ OOP.
YOP!
I'M ASHAMED TO SAY I WAS ONLY THINKING ABOUT MYSELF.
I GAVE MYSELF THE EXCUSE THAT THINGS WERE BECOMING OVER-WHELMING--AND CONFUSING. TRUTH IS, I WAS DOUBTING MYSELF.
NOTHING WAS WRONG.
EVERYTHING WAS HAPPENING CORRECTLY...
YET, THE WORLD WAS CRASHING IN ON ME...
AND I KNEW WHY.
I HADN'T DONE MY HOMEWORK...SOMEHOW I HAD BROKEN IT ALL.
AND NOW, I WAS PLAYING CATCH-UP. I HAD NO
EA WHAT THE MYSTERY WAS...THAT I HADN'T SOLVED. IF YOU ASKED ME, THEN, WHAT THE MYSTERY WAS...I COULDN'T HAVE TOLD YOU.
BUT NOW IT WAS CLEAR AS A BELL. AND IT HAD STARTED ON THAT TRAIN.
HAVE YOU VERIFIED MY SUSPICIONS, KIRK?
THAT, AND MORE. YOU'LL NEED TO READ THIS... THE ANSWER IS "B."
Hah!
AND HOW LONG HAVE YOU BEEN "UNDER THE INFLUENCE"?
KIRK?

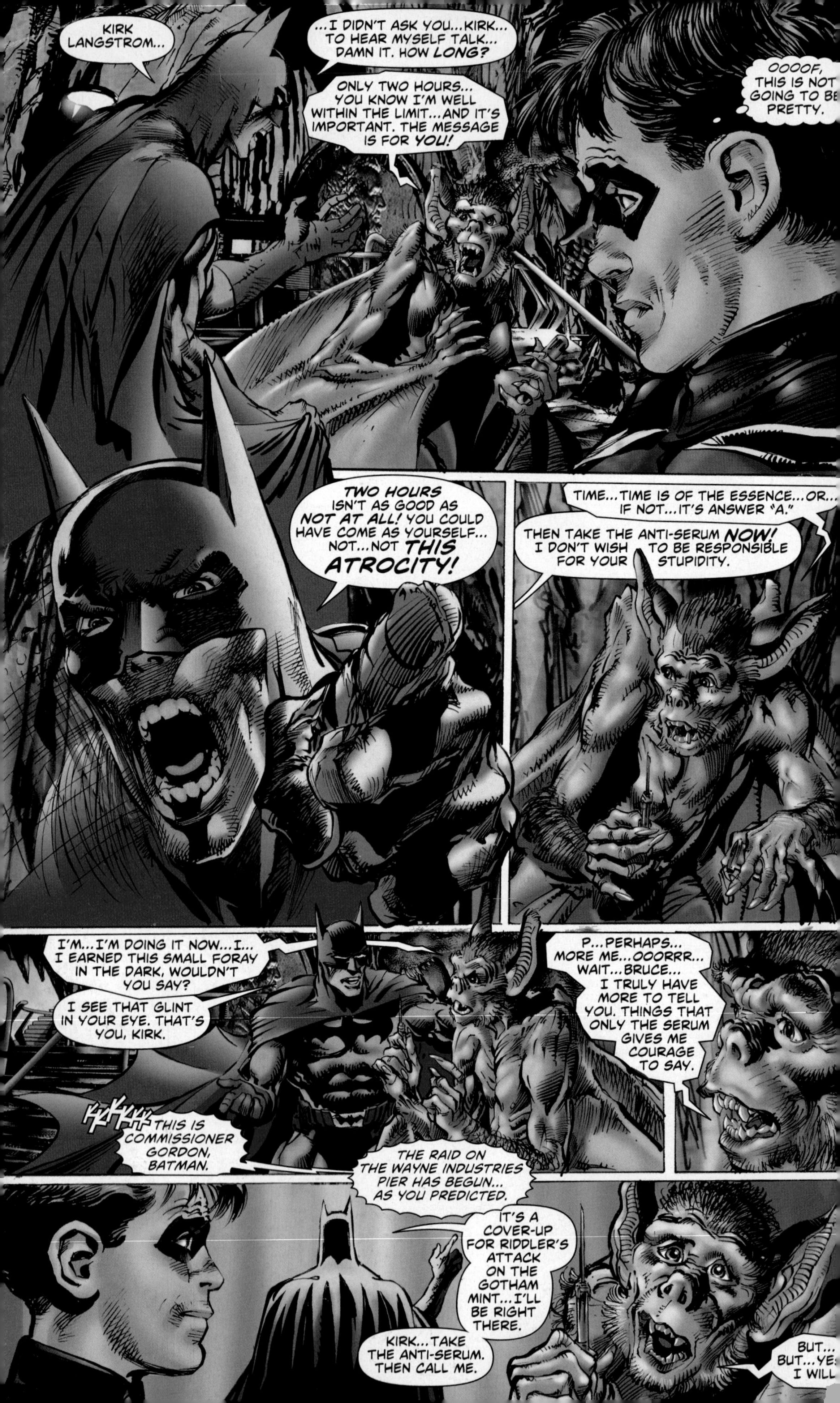

KIRK LANGSTROM...
...I DIDN'T ASK YOU...KIRK... TO HEAR MYSELF TALK... DAMN IT. HOW LONG?
ONLY TWO HOURS... YOU KNOW I'M WELL WITHIN THE LIMIT...AND IT'S IMPORTANT. THE MESSAGE IS FOR YOU!
OOOOF, THIS IS NOT GOING TO BE PRETTY.
TWO HOURS ISN'T AS GOOD AS NOT AT ALL! YOU COULD HAVE COME AS YOURSELF... NOT...NOT THIS ATROCITY!
TIME...TIME IS OF THE ESSENCE...OR... IF NOT...IT'S ANSWER "A."
THEN TAKE THE ANTI-SERUM NOW! I DON'T WISH TO BE RESPONSIBLE FOR YOUR STUPIDITY.
I'M...I'M DOING IT NOW...I... I EARNED THIS SMALL FORAY IN THE DARK, WOULDN'T YOU SAY?
I SEE THAT GLINT IN YOUR EYE. THAT'S YOU, KIRK.
P...PERHAPS... MORE ME...OOORRR... WAIT...BRUCE... I TRULY HAVE MORE TO TELL YOU. THINGS THAT ONLY THE SERUM GIVES ME COURAGE TO SAY.
KKKKKK
THIS IS COMMISSIONER GORDON, BATMAN.
THE RAID ON THE WAYNE INDUSTRIES PIER HAS BEGUN... AS YOU PREDICTED.
IT'S A COVER-UP FOR RIDDLER'S ATTACK ON THE GOTHAM MINT...I'LL BE RIGHT THERE.
KIRK...TAKE THE ANTI-SERUM. THEN CALL ME.
BUT... BUT...YES I WILL.

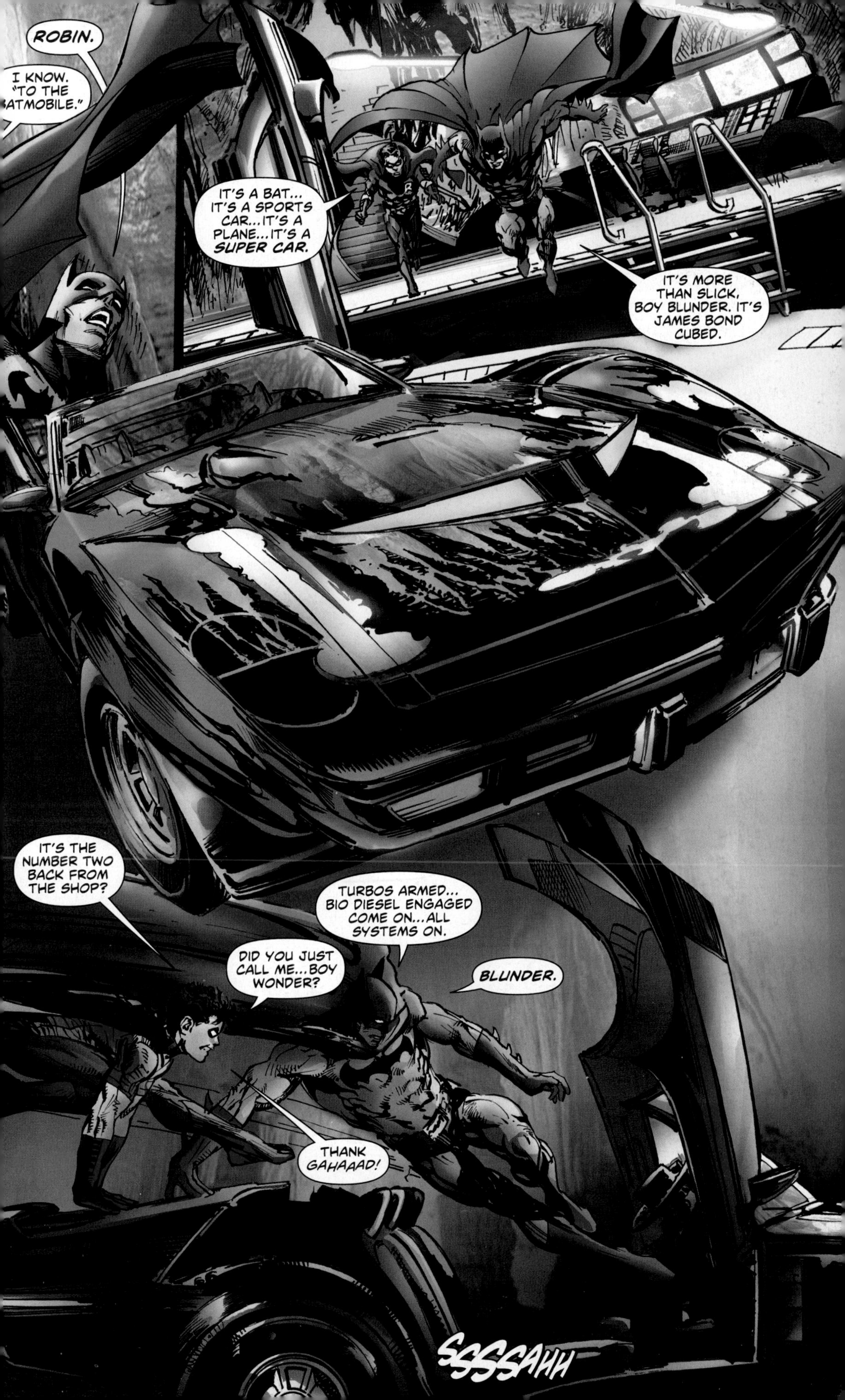
ROBIN.
I KNOW. "TO THE ATMOBILE."
IT'S A BAT... IT'S A SPORTS CAR...IT'S A PLANE...IT'S A SUPER CAR.
IT'S MORE THAN SLICK, BOY BLUNDER. IT'S JAMES BOND CUBED.
IT'S THE NUMBER TWO BACK FROM THE SHOP?
TURBOS ARMED... BIO DIESEL ENGAGED COME ON...ALL SYSTEMS ON.
DID YOU JUST CALL ME...BOY WONDER?
BLUNDER.
THANK GAHAAAD!
SSSSAHH

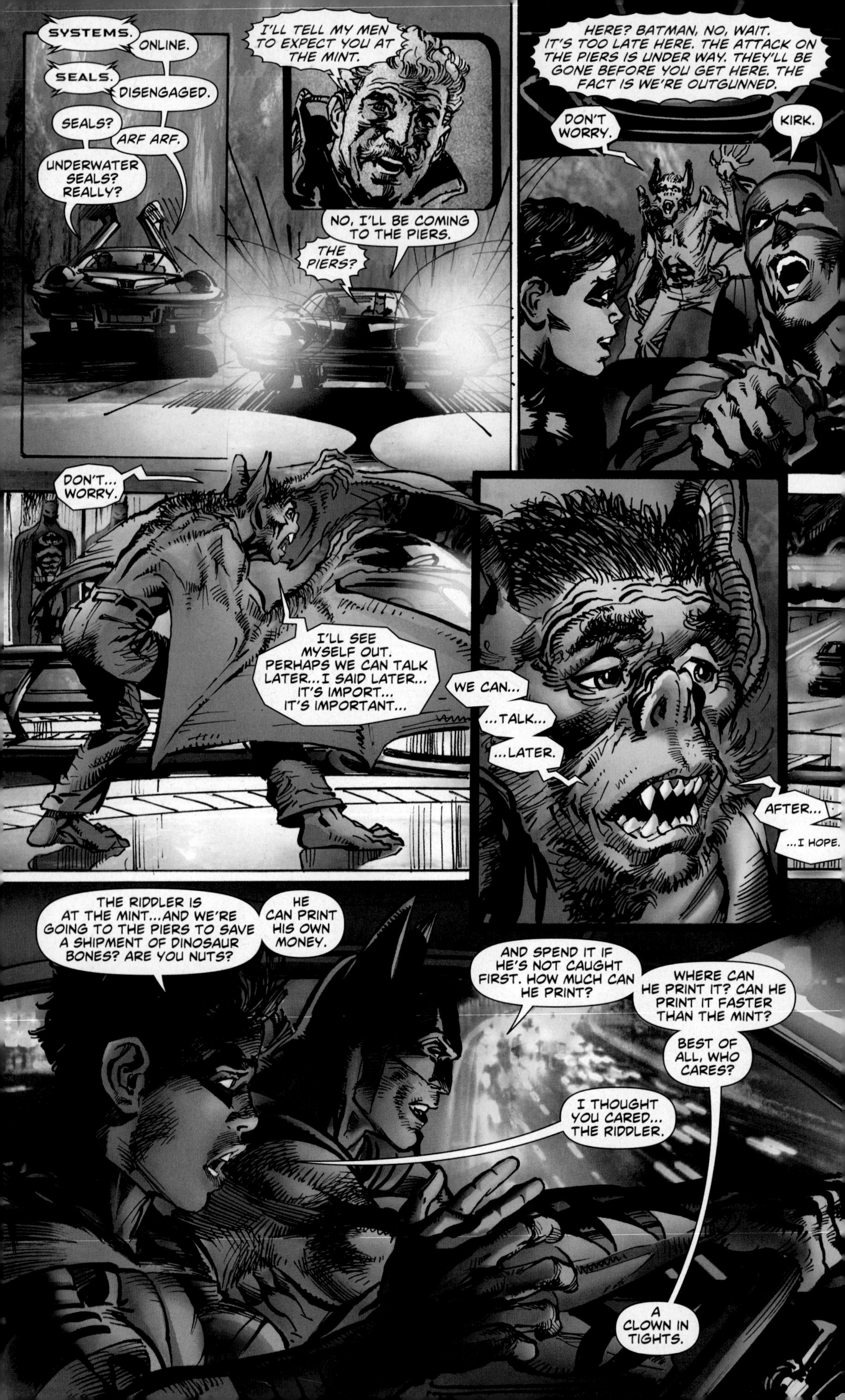
SYSTEMS.
ONLINE.
SEALS.
DISENGAGED.
SEALS?
ARF ARF.
UNDERWATER SEALS? REALLY?
I'LL TELL MY MEN TO EXPECT YOU AT THE MINT.
NO, I'LL BE COMING TO THE PIERS.
THE PIERS?
HERE? BATMAN, NO, WAIT. IT'S TOO LATE HERE. THE ATTACK ON THE PIERS IS UNDER WAY. THEY'LL BE GONE BEFORE YOU GET HERE. THE FACT IS WE'RE OUTGUNNED.
DON'T WORRY.
KIRK.
DON'T... WORRY.
I'LL SEE MYSELF OUT. PERHAPS WE CAN TALK LATER...I SAID LATER... IT'S IMPORT... IT'S IMPORTANT...
WE CAN...
...TALK...
...LATER.
AFTER...
...I HOPE.
THE RIDDLER IS AT THE MINT...AND WE'RE GOING TO THE PIERS TO SAVE A SHIPMENT OF DINOSAUR BONES? ARE YOU NUTS?
HE CAN PRINT HIS OWN MONEY.
AND SPEND IT IF HE'S NOT CAUGHT FIRST. HOW MUCH CAN HE PRINT?
WHERE CAN HE PRINT IT? CAN HE PRINT IT FASTER THAN THE MINT?
BEST OF ALL, WHO CARES?
I THOUGHT YOU CARED... THE RIDDLER.
A CLOWN IN TIGHTS.

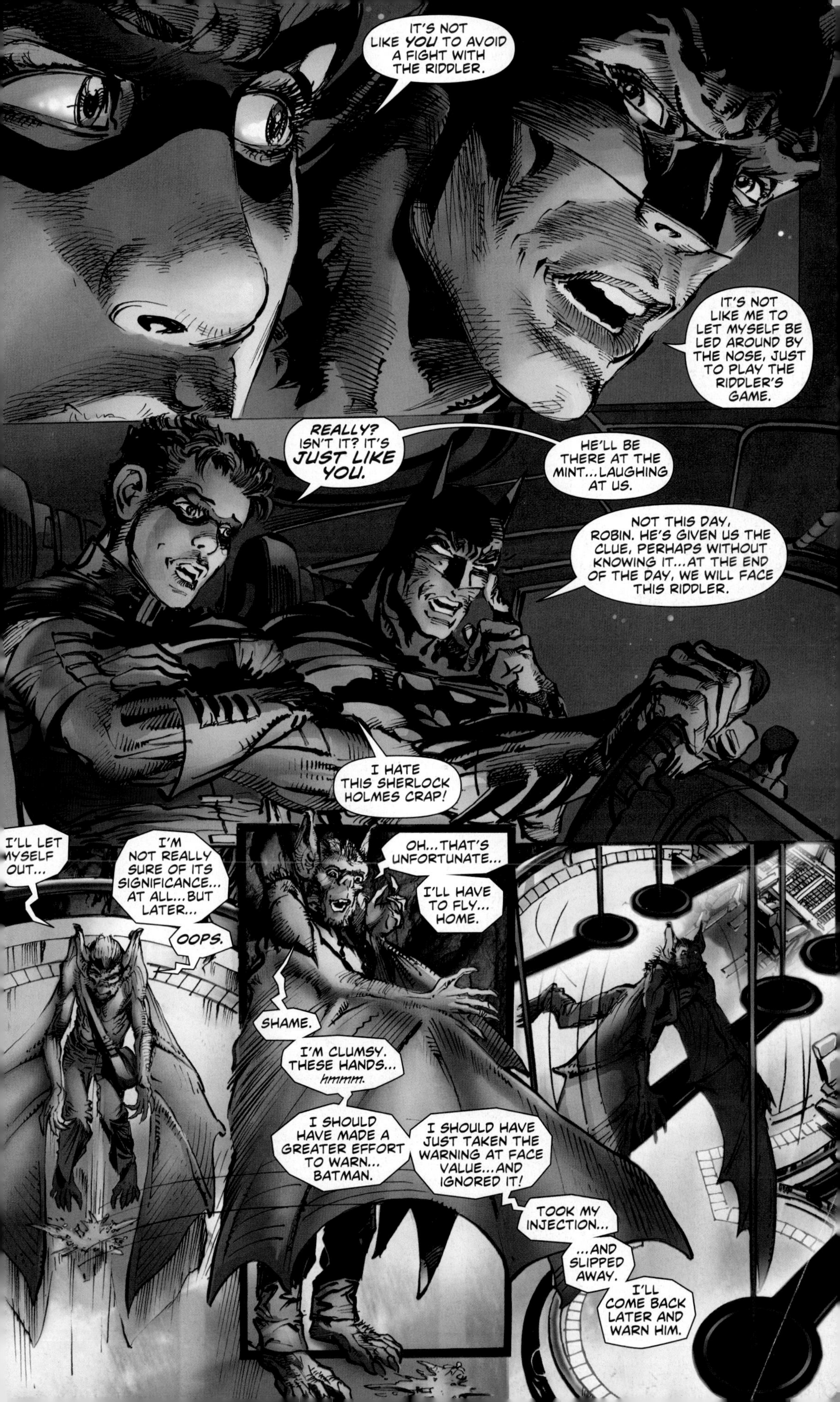
IT'S NOT LIKE YOU TO AVOID A FIGHT WITH THE RIDDLER.
IT'S NOT LIKE ME TO LET MYSELF BE LED AROUND BY THE NOSE, JUST TO PLAY THE RIDDLER'S GAME.
REALLY? ISN'T IT? IT'S JUST LIKE YOU.
HE'LL BE THERE AT THE MINT... LAUGHING AT US.
NOT THIS DAY, ROBIN. HE'S GIVEN US THE CLUE, PERHAPS WITHOUT KNOWING IT... AT THE END OF THE DAY, WE WILL FACE THIS RIDDLER.
I HATE THIS SHERLOCK HOLMES CRAP!
I'LL LET MYSELF OUT...
I'M NOT REALLY SURE OF ITS SIGNIFICANCE... AT ALL... BUT LATER...
OOPS.
OH... THAT'S UNFORTUNATE...
I'LL HAVE TO FLY... HOME.
SHAME.
I'M CLUMSY. THESE HANDS... hmmm.
I SHOULD HAVE MADE A GREATER EFFORT TO WARN... BATMAN.
I SHOULD HAVE JUST TAKEN THE WARNING AT FACE VALUE... AND IGNORED IT!
TOOK MY INJECTION...
...AND SLIPPED AWAY.
I'LL COME BACK LATER AND WARN HIM.

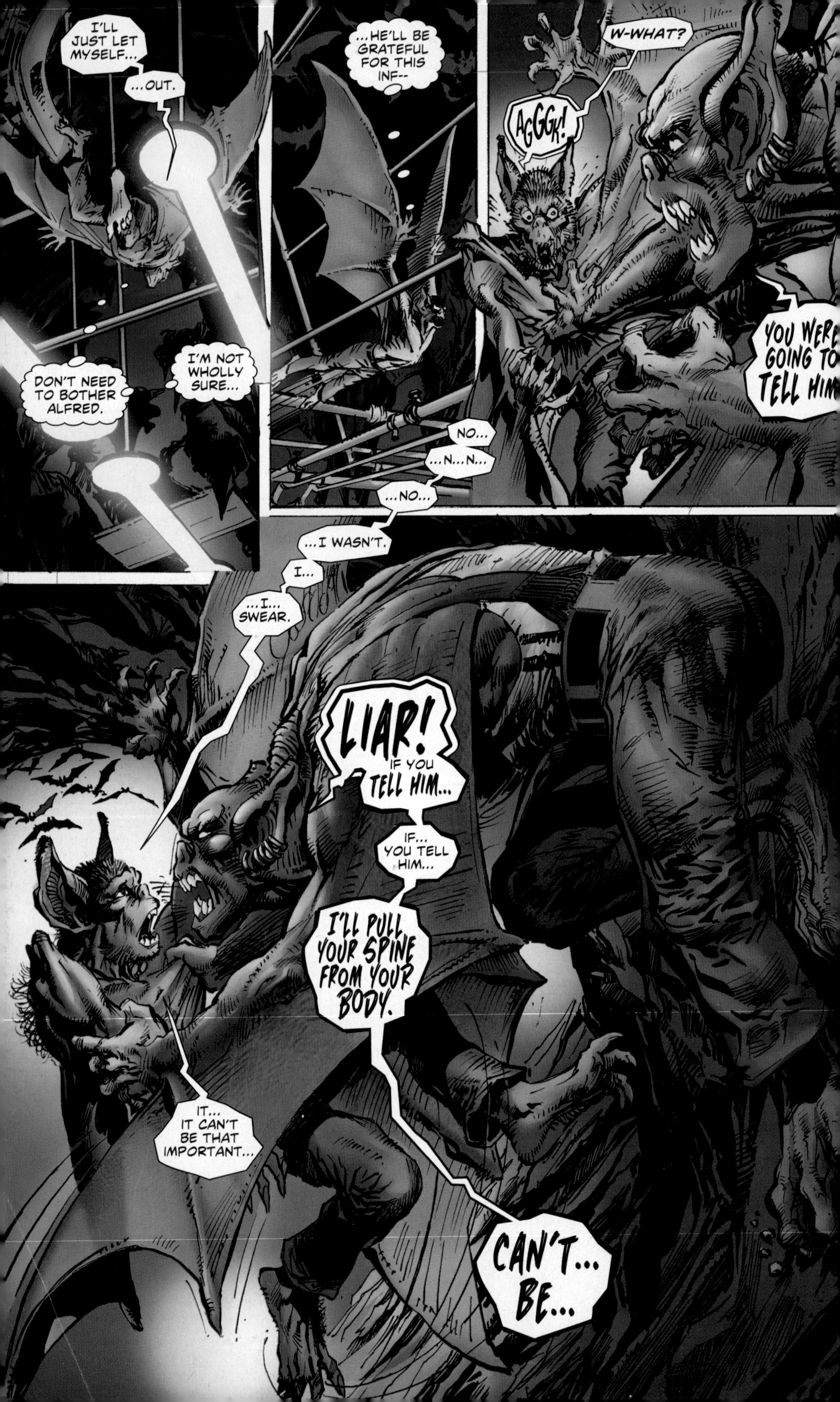

I'LL JUST LET MYSELF...
...OUT.
DON'T NEED TO BOTHER ALFRED.
I'M NOT WHOLLY SURE...
...HE'LL BE GRATEFUL FOR THIS INF--
W-WHAT?
AGGGK!
YOU WERE GOING TO TELL HIM
NO...
...N...N...
...NO...
...I WASN'T.
I...
...I... SWEAR.
LIAR! IF YOU TELL HIM...
IF... YOU TELL HIM...
I'LL PULL YOUR SPINE FROM YOUR BODY.
IT... IT CAN'T BE THAT IMPORTANT...
CAN'T... BE...

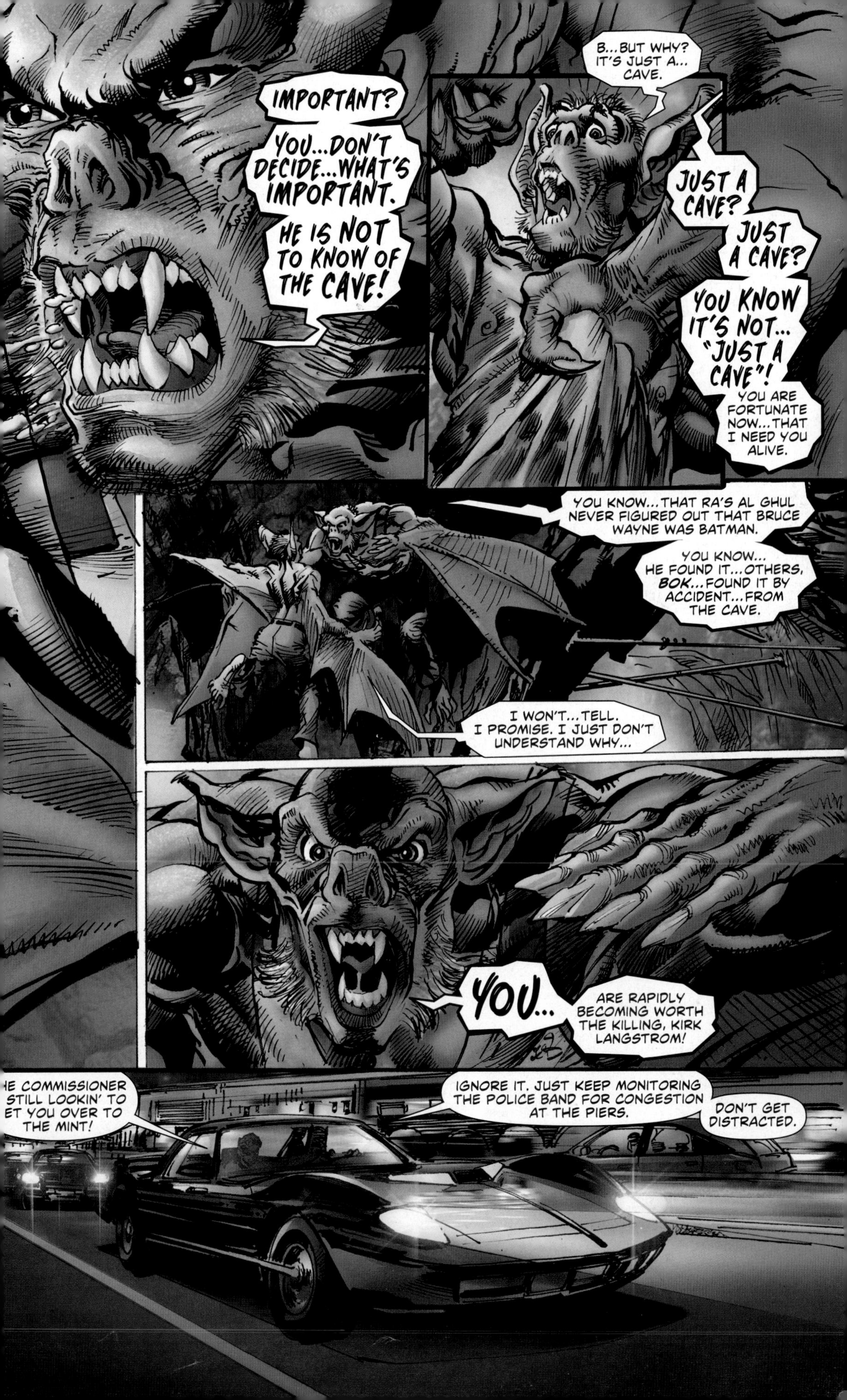
IMPORTANT?
YOU...DON'T DECIDE...WHAT'S IMPORTANT.
HE IS NOT TO KNOW OF THE CAVE!
B...BUT WHY? IT'S JUST A... CAVE.
JUST A CAVE? JUST A CAVE?
YOU KNOW IT'S NOT... "JUST A CAVE"!
YOU ARE FORTUNATE NOW...THAT I NEED YOU ALIVE.
YOU KNOW...THAT RA'S AL GHUL NEVER FIGURED OUT THAT BRUCE WAYNE WAS BATMAN.
YOU KNOW... HE FOUND IT...OTHERS, BOK...FOUND IT BY ACCIDENT...FROM THE CAVE.
I WON'T...TELL. I PROMISE. I JUST DON'T UNDERSTAND WHY...
YOU...
ARE RAPIDLY BECOMING WORTH THE KILLING, KIRK LANGSTROM!
HE COMMISSIONER STILL LOOKIN' TO ET YOU OVER TO THE MINT!
IGNORE IT. JUST KEEP MONITORING THE POLICE BAND FOR CONGESTION AT THE PIERS.
DON'T GET DISTRACTED.

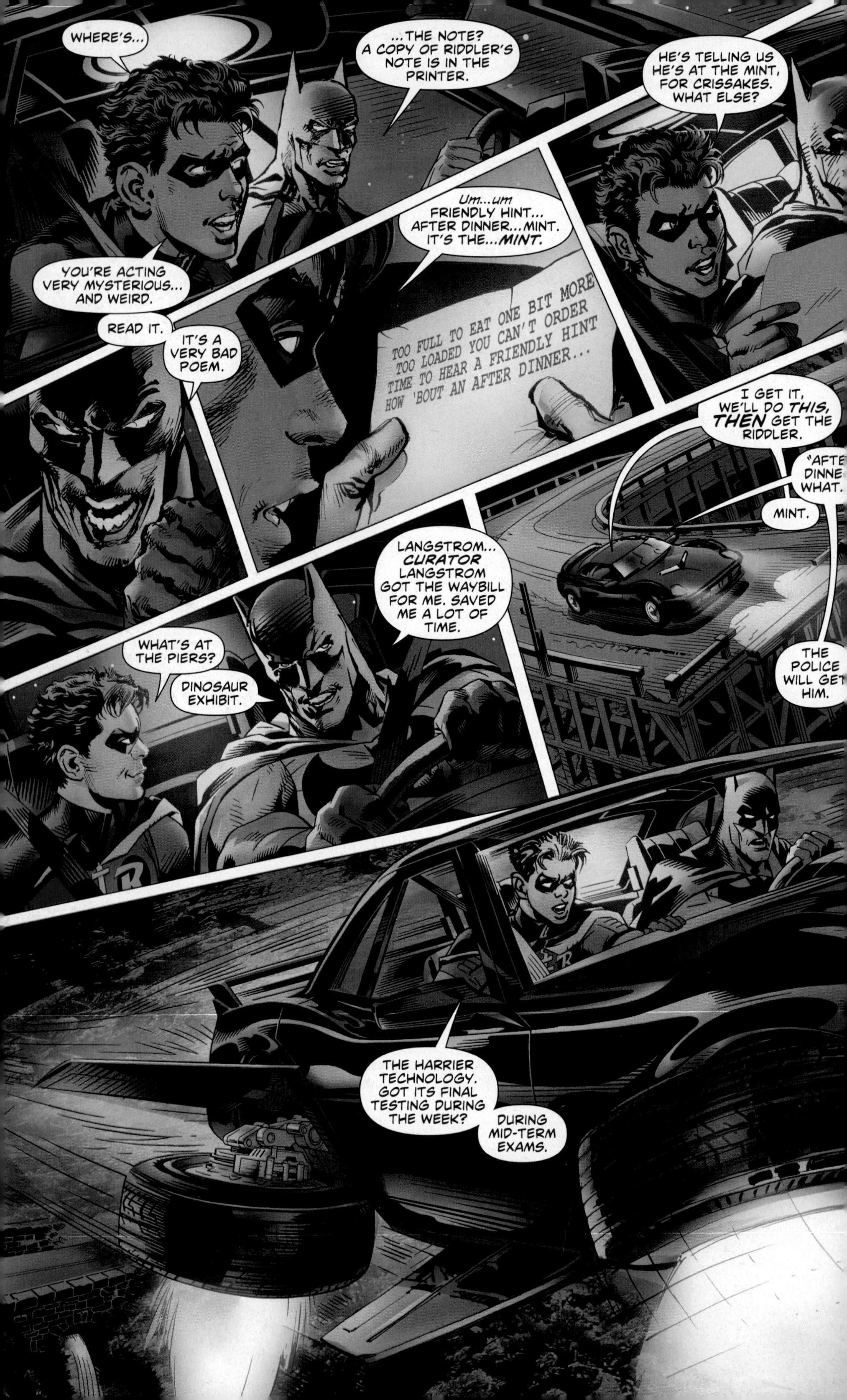
WHERE'S...
...THE NOTE? A COPY OF RIDDLER'S NOTE IS IN THE PRINTER.
HE'S TELLING US HE'S AT THE MINT, FOR CRISSAKES. WHAT ELSE?
Um...um FRIENDLY HINT... AFTER DINNER...MINT. IT'S THE...MINT.
YOU'RE ACTING VERY MYSTERIOUS... AND WEIRD.
READ IT.
IT'S A VERY BAD POEM.
TOO FULL TO EAT ONE BIT MORE
TOO LOADED YOU CAN'T ORDER
TIME TO HEAR A FRIENDLY HINT
HOW 'BOUT AN AFTER DINNER...
I GET IT, WE'LL DO THIS, THEN GET THE RIDDLER.
MINT.
THE POLICE WILL GET HIM.
LANGSTROM... CURATOR LANGSTROM GOT THE WAYBILL FOR ME. SAVED ME A LOT OF TIME.
WHAT'S AT THE PIERS?
DINOSAUR EXHIBIT.
THE HARRIER TECHNOLOGY. GOT ITS FINAL TESTING DURING THE WEEK?
DURING MID-TERM EXAMS.

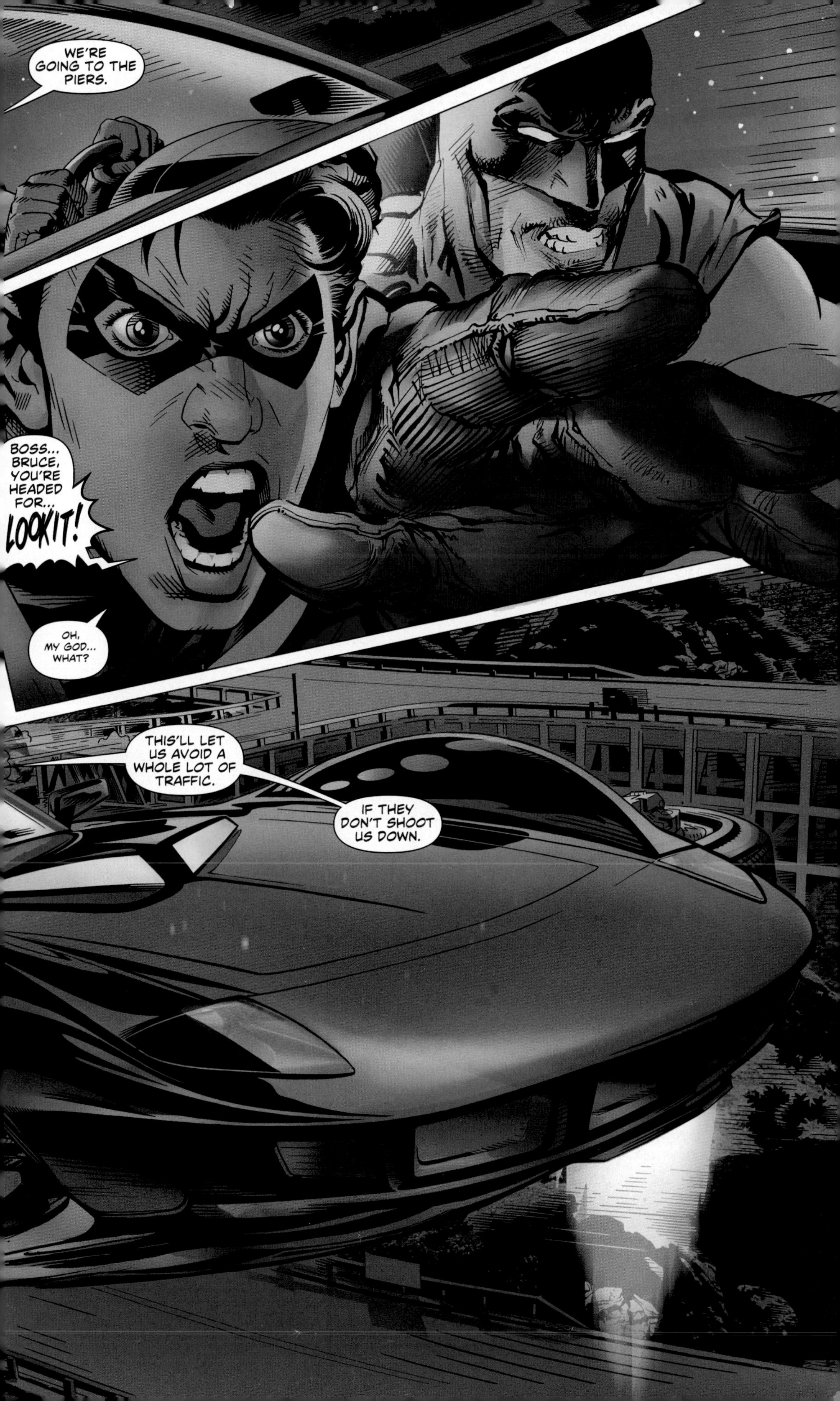
WE'RE GOING TO THE PIERS.
BOSS... BRUCE, YOU'RE HEADED FOR... LOOKIT!
OH, MY GOD... WHAT?
THIS'LL LET US AVOID A WHOLE LOT OF TRAFFIC.
IF THEY DON'T SHOOT US DOWN.

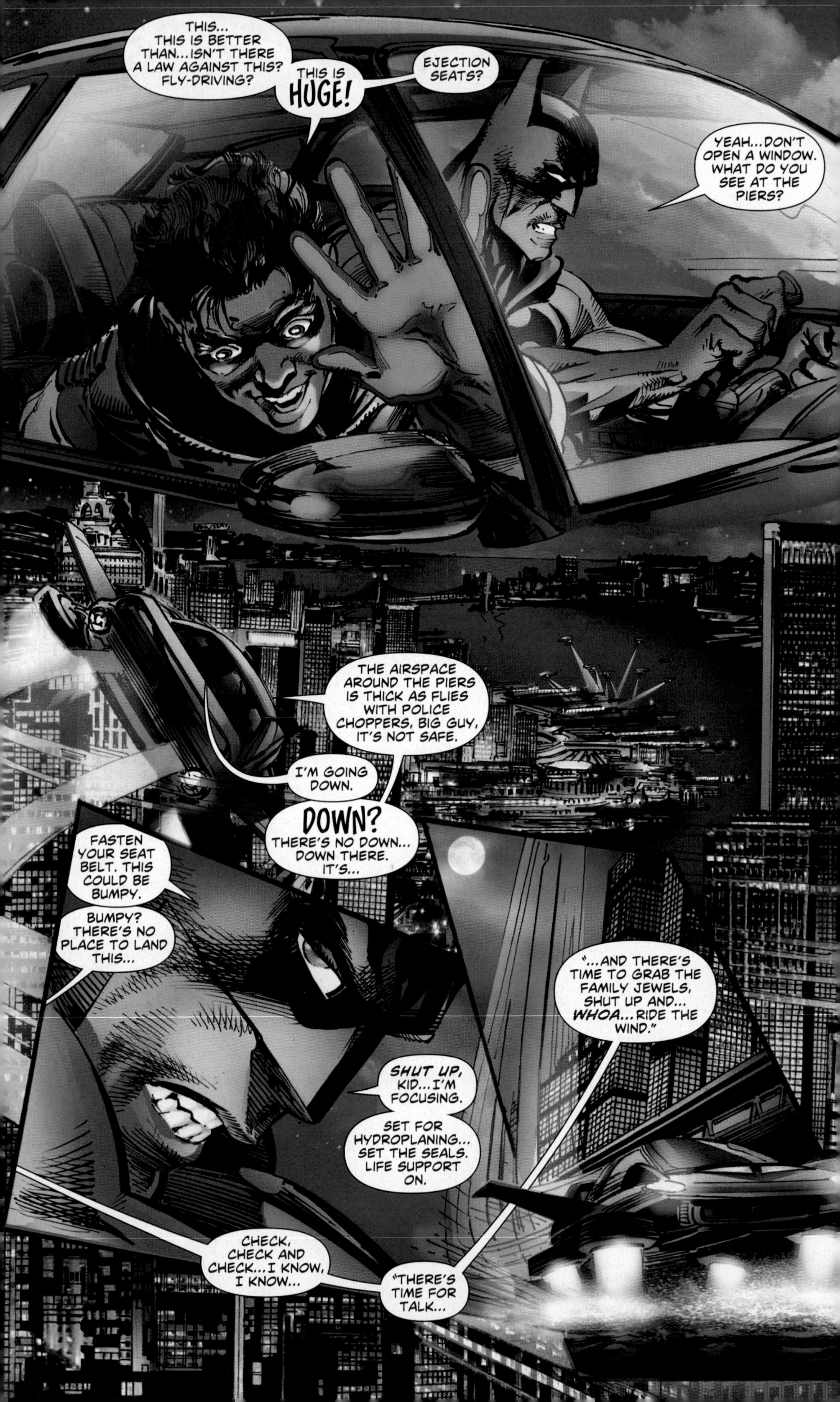
THIS... THIS IS BETTER THAN...ISN'T THERE A LAW AGAINST THIS? FLY-DRIVING?
THIS IS HUGE!
EJECTION SEATS?
YEAH...DON'T OPEN A WINDOW. WHAT DO YOU SEE AT THE PIERS?
THE AIRSPACE AROUND THE PIERS IS THICK AS FLIES WITH POLICE CHOPPERS, BIG GUY, IT'S NOT SAFE.
I'M GOING DOWN.
DOWN? THERE'S NO DOWN... DOWN THERE. IT'S...
FASTEN YOUR SEAT BELT. THIS COULD BE BUMPY.
BUMPY? THERE'S NO PLACE TO LAND THIS...
SHUT UP, KID...I'M FOCUSING.
SET FOR HYDROPLANING... SET THE SEALS. LIFE SUPPORT ON.
CHECK, CHECK AND CHECK...I KNOW, I KNOW...
"THERE'S TIME FOR TALK...
"...AND THERE'S TIME TO GRAB THE FAMILY JEWELS, SHUT UP AND... WHOA...RIDE THE WIND."

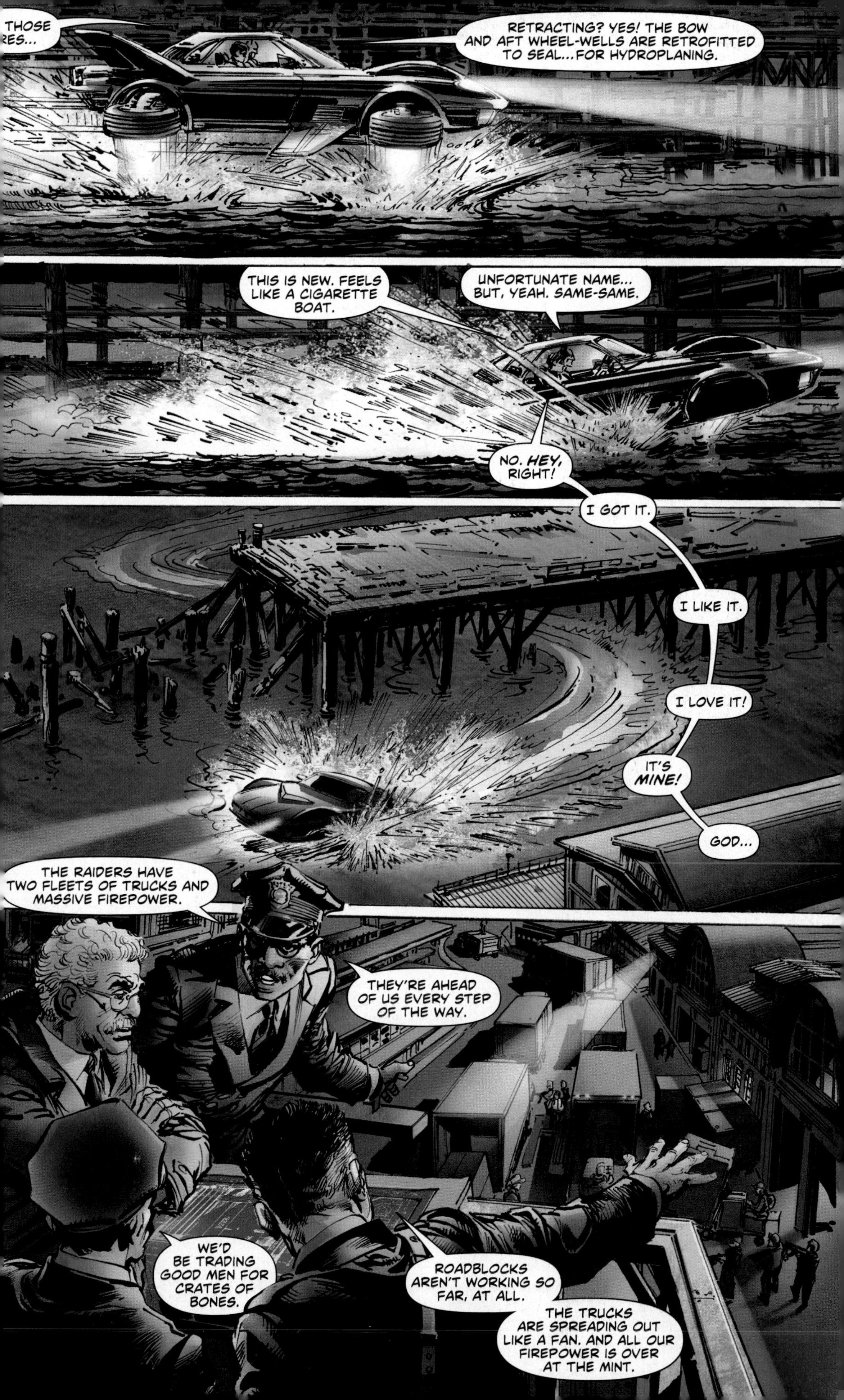
THOSE
RES...
RETRACTING? YES! THE BOW AND AFT WHEEL-WELLS ARE RETROFITTED TO SEAL...FOR HYDROPLANING.
THIS IS NEW. FEELS LIKE A CIGARETTE BOAT.
UNFORTUNATE NAME... BUT, YEAH. SAME-SAME.
NO. HEY, RIGHT!
I GOT IT.
I LIKE IT.
I LOVE IT!
IT'S MINE!
GOD...
THE RAIDERS HAVE TWO FLEETS OF TRUCKS AND MASSIVE FIREPOWER.
THEY'RE AHEAD OF US EVERY STEP OF THE WAY.
WE'D BE TRADING GOOD MEN FOR CRATES OF BONES.
ROADBLOCKS AREN'T WORKING SO FAR, AT ALL.
THE TRUCKS ARE SPREADING OUT LIKE A FAN. AND ALL OUR FIREPOWER IS OVER AT THE MINT.

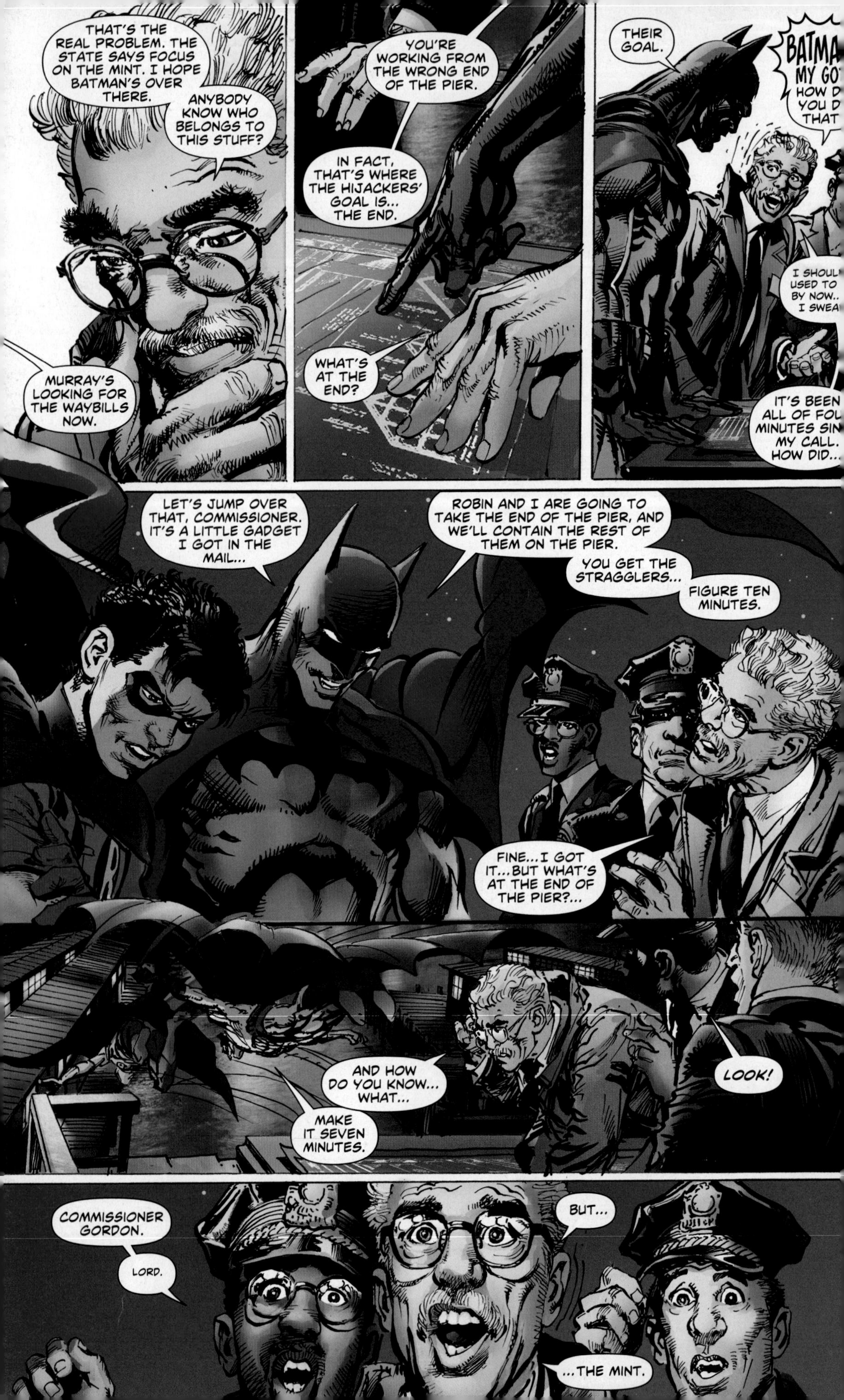
THAT'S THE REAL PROBLEM. THE STATE SAYS FOCUS ON THE MINT. I HOPE BATMAN'S OVER THERE.
ANYBODY KNOW WHO BELONGS TO THIS STUFF?
MURRAY'S LOOKING FOR THE WAYBILLS NOW.
YOU'RE WORKING FROM THE WRONG END OF THE PIER.
IN FACT, THAT'S WHERE THE HIJACKERS' GOAL IS... THE END.
WHAT'S AT THE END?
THEIR GOAL.
BATMA
MY GO
HOW D
YOU D
THAT
I SHOUL
USED TO
BY NOW..
I SWEA
IT'S BEEN
ALL OF FOU
MINUTES SIN
MY CALL.
HOW DID...
LET'S JUMP OVER THAT, COMMISSIONER. IT'S A LITTLE GADGET I GOT IN THE MAIL...
ROBIN AND I ARE GOING TO TAKE THE END OF THE PIER, AND WE'LL CONTAIN THE REST OF THEM ON THE PIER.
YOU GET THE STRAGGLERS...
FIGURE TEN MINUTES.
FINE...I GOT IT...BUT WHAT'S AT THE END OF THE PIER?...
AND HOW DO YOU KNOW... WHAT...
MAKE IT SEVEN MINUTES.
LOOK!
COMMISSIONER GORDON.
LORD.
BUT...
...THE MINT.

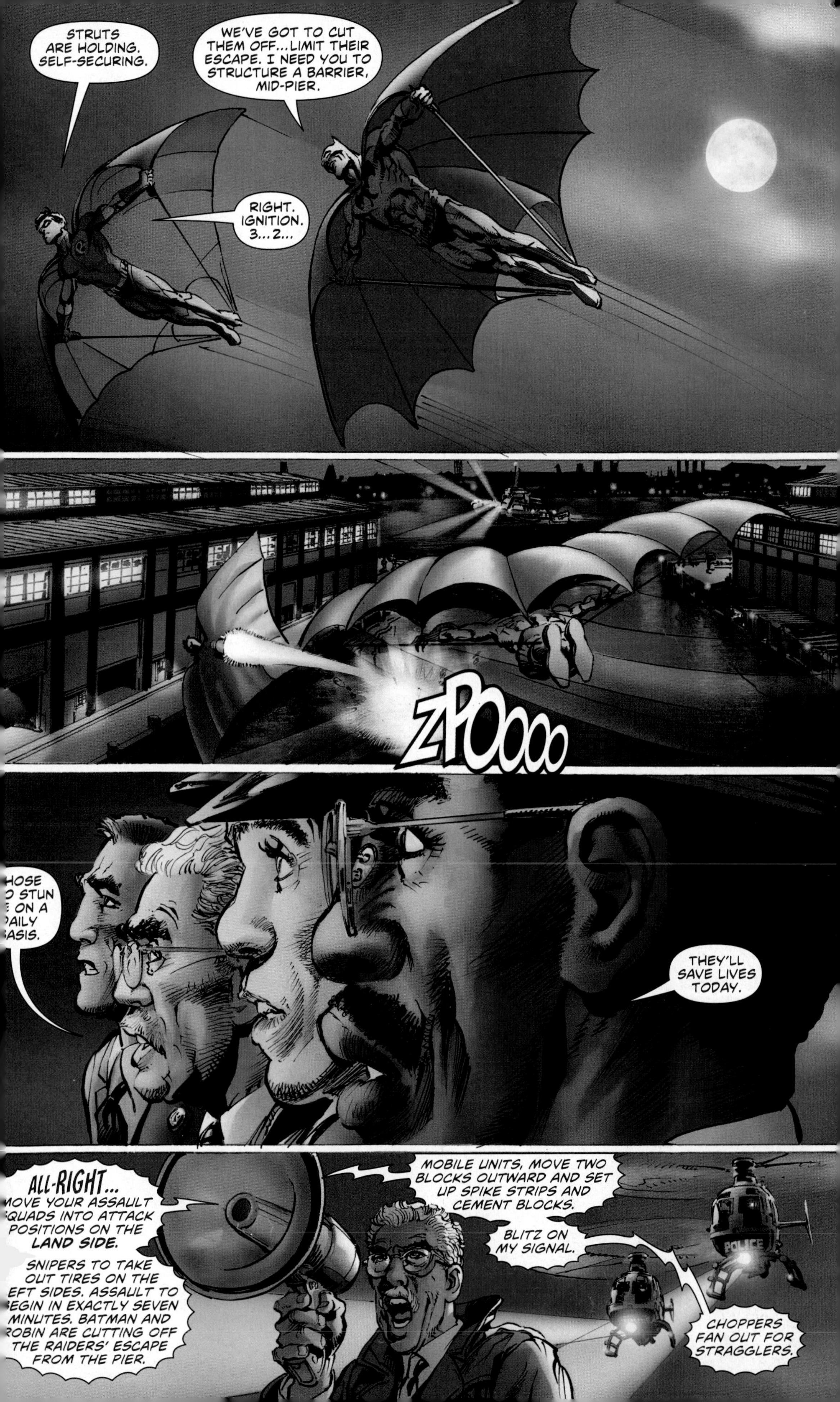

STRUTS ARE HOLDING. SELF-SECURING.
WE'VE GOT TO CUT THEM OFF...LIMIT THEIR ESCAPE. I NEED YOU TO STRUCTURE A BARRIER, MID-PIER.
RIGHT. IGNITION. 3...2...
ZPOOOO
HOSE O STUN E ON A AILY ASIS.
THEY'LL SAVE LIVES TODAY.
ALL-RIGHT... MOVE YOUR ASSAULT QUADS INTO ATTACK POSITIONS ON THE LAND SIDE.
SNIPERS TO TAKE OUT TIRES ON THE EFT SIDES. ASSAULT TO EGIN IN EXACTLY SEVEN MINUTES. BATMAN AND ROBIN ARE CUTTING OFF THE RAIDERS' ESCAPE FROM THE PIER.
MOBILE UNITS, MOVE TWO BLOCKS OUTWARD AND SET UP SPIKE STRIPS AND CEMENT BLOCKS.
BLITZ ON MY SIGNAL.
CHOPPERS FAN OUT FOR STRAGGLERS.
POLICE

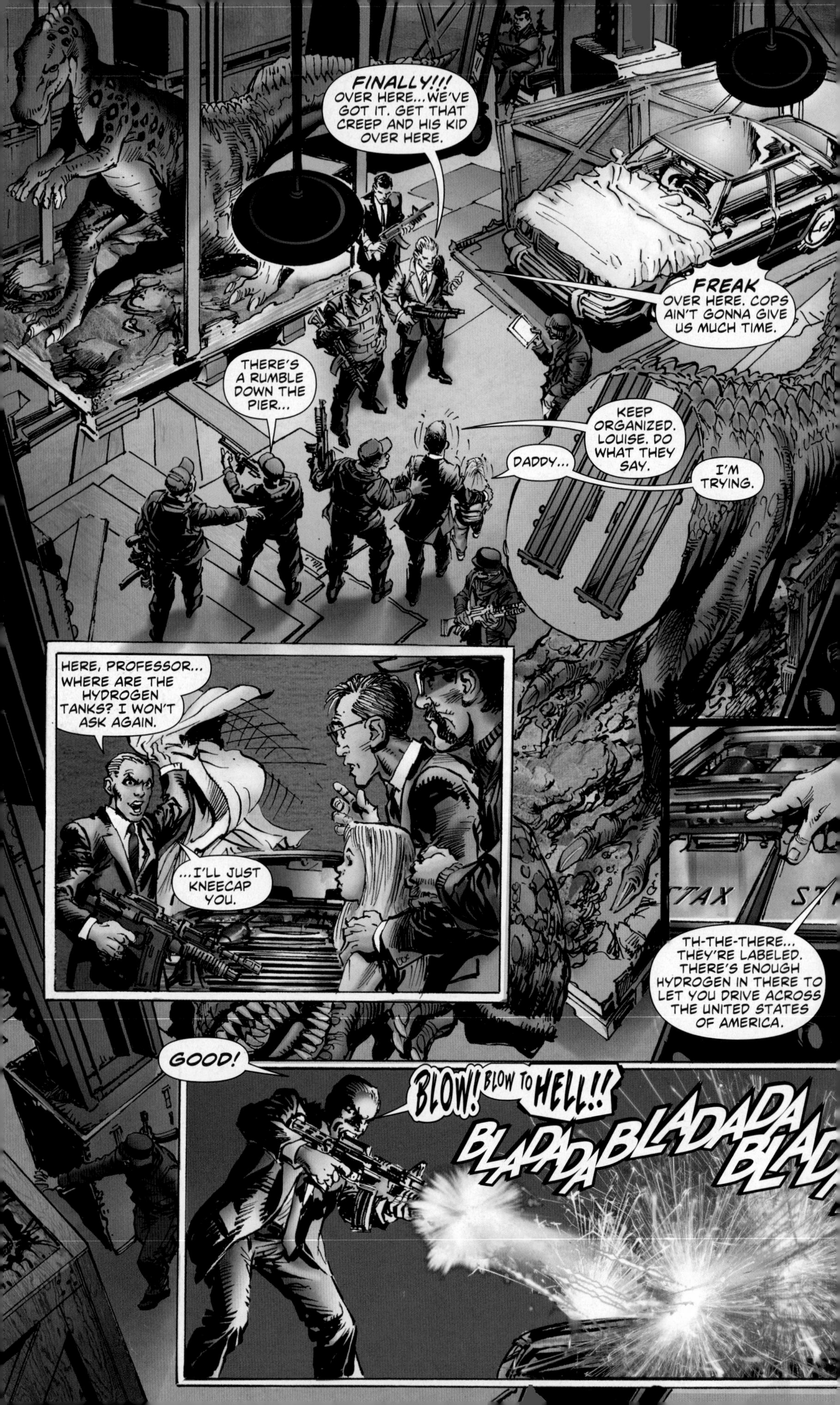
FINALLY!!! OVER HERE...WE'VE GOT IT. GET THAT CREEP AND HIS KID OVER HERE.
FREAK OVER HERE. COPS AIN'T GONNA GIVE US MUCH TIME.
THERE'S A RUMBLE DOWN THE PIER...
KEEP ORGANIZED. LOUISE. DO WHAT THEY SAY.
DADDY...
I'M TRYING.
HERE, PROFESSOR... WHERE ARE THE HYDROGEN TANKS? I WON'T ASK AGAIN.
...I'LL JUST KNEECAP YOU.
TH-THE-THERE... THEY'RE LABELED. THERE'S ENOUGH HYDROGEN IN THERE TO LET YOU DRIVE ACROSS THE UNITED STATES OF AMERICA.
GOOD!
BLOW! BLOW TO HELL!!
BLADADA BLADADA BLAD

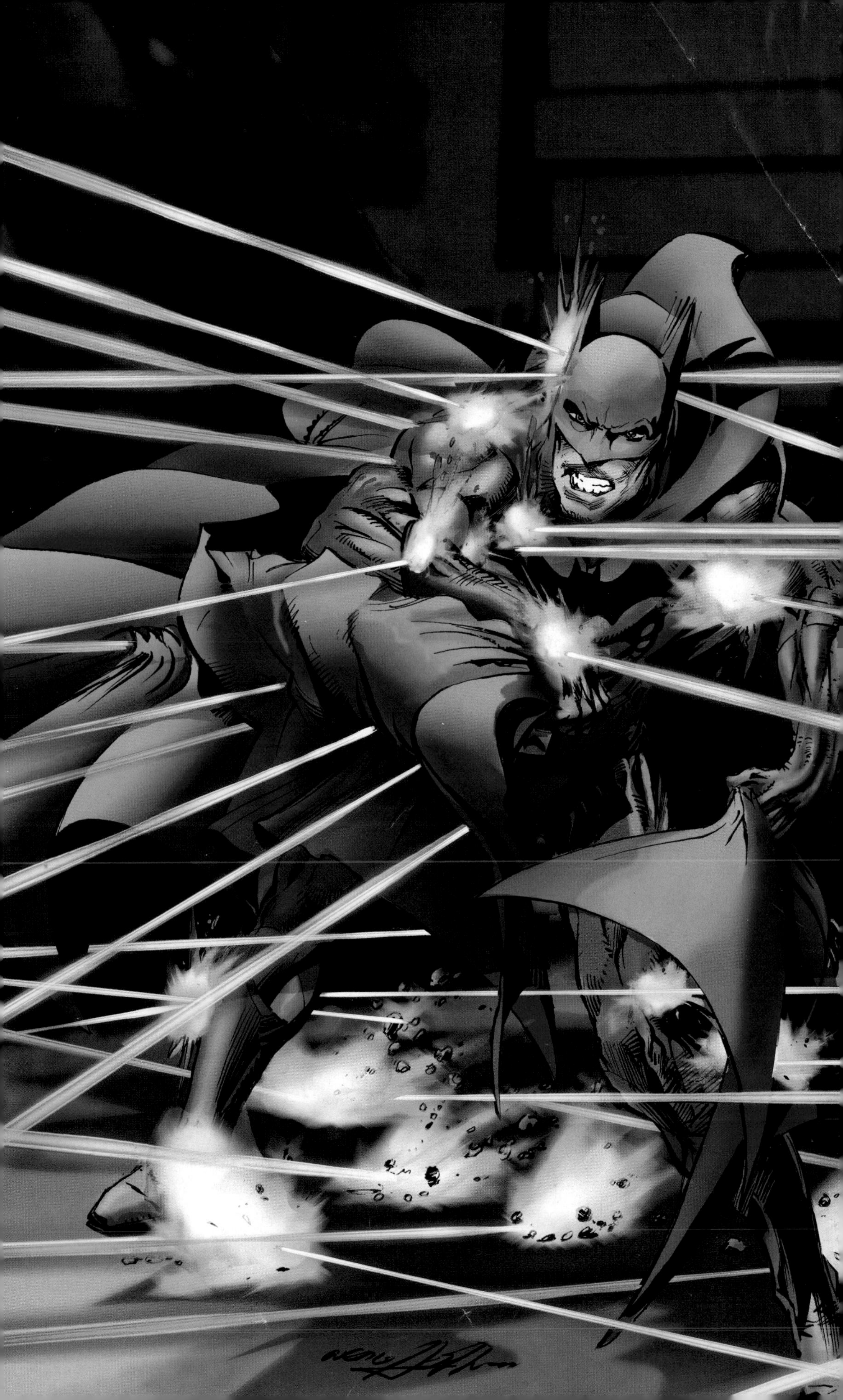

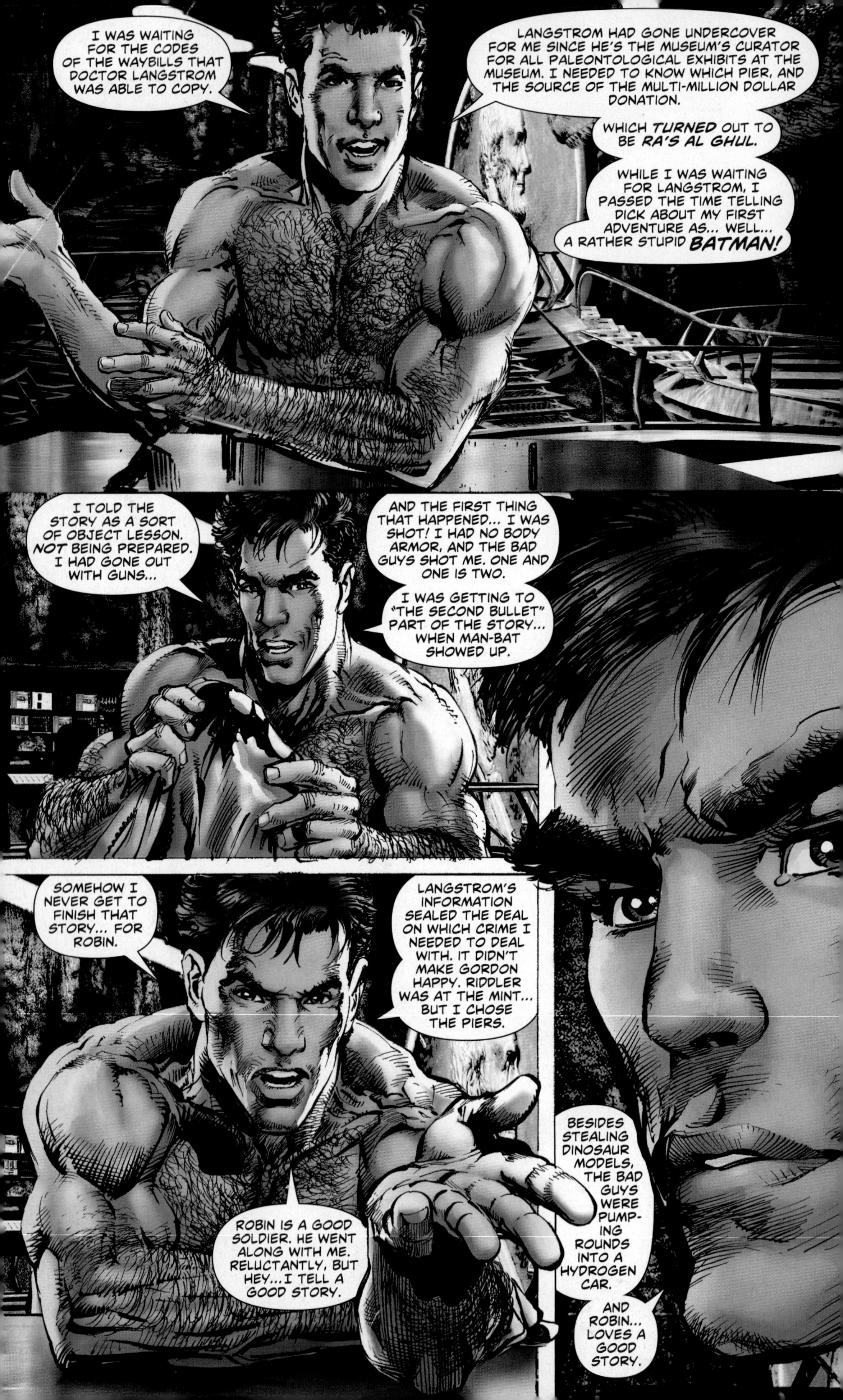

I WAS WAITING FOR THE CODES OF THE WAYBILLS THAT DOCTOR LANGSTROM WAS ABLE TO COPY.
LANGSTROM HAD GONE UNDERCOVER FOR ME SINCE HE'S THE MUSEUM'S CURATOR FOR ALL PALEONTOLOGICAL EXHIBITS AT THE MUSEUM. I NEEDED TO KNOW WHICH PIER, AND THE SOURCE OF THE MULTI-MILLION DOLLAR DONATION.
WHICH *TURNED* OUT TO BE *RA'S AL GHUL.*
WHILE I WAS WAITING FOR LANGSTROM, I PASSED THE TIME TELLING DICK ABOUT MY FIRST ADVENTURE AS... WELL... A RATHER STUPID **BATMAN!**
I TOLD THE STORY AS A SORT OF OBJECT LESSON. *NOT* BEING PREPARED. I HAD GONE OUT WITH GUNS...
AND THE FIRST THING THAT HAPPENED... I WAS SHOT! I HAD NO BODY ARMOR, AND THE BAD GUYS SHOT ME. ONE AND ONE IS TWO.
I WAS GETTING TO "THE SECOND BULLET" PART OF THE STORY... WHEN MAN-BAT SHOWED UP.
SOMEHOW I NEVER GET TO FINISH THAT STORY... FOR ROBIN.
LANGSTROM'S INFORMATION SEALED THE DEAL ON WHICH CRIME I NEEDED TO DEAL WITH. IT DIDN'T MAKE GORDON HAPPY. RIDDLER WAS AT THE MINT... BUT I CHOSE THE PIERS.
ROBIN IS A GOOD SOLDIER. HE WENT ALONG WITH ME. RELUCTANTLY, BUT HEY... I TELL A GOOD STORY.
BESIDES STEALING DINOSAUR MODELS, THE BAD GUYS WERE PUMPING ROUNDS INTO A HYDROGEN CAR.
AND ROBIN... LOVES A GOOD STORY.

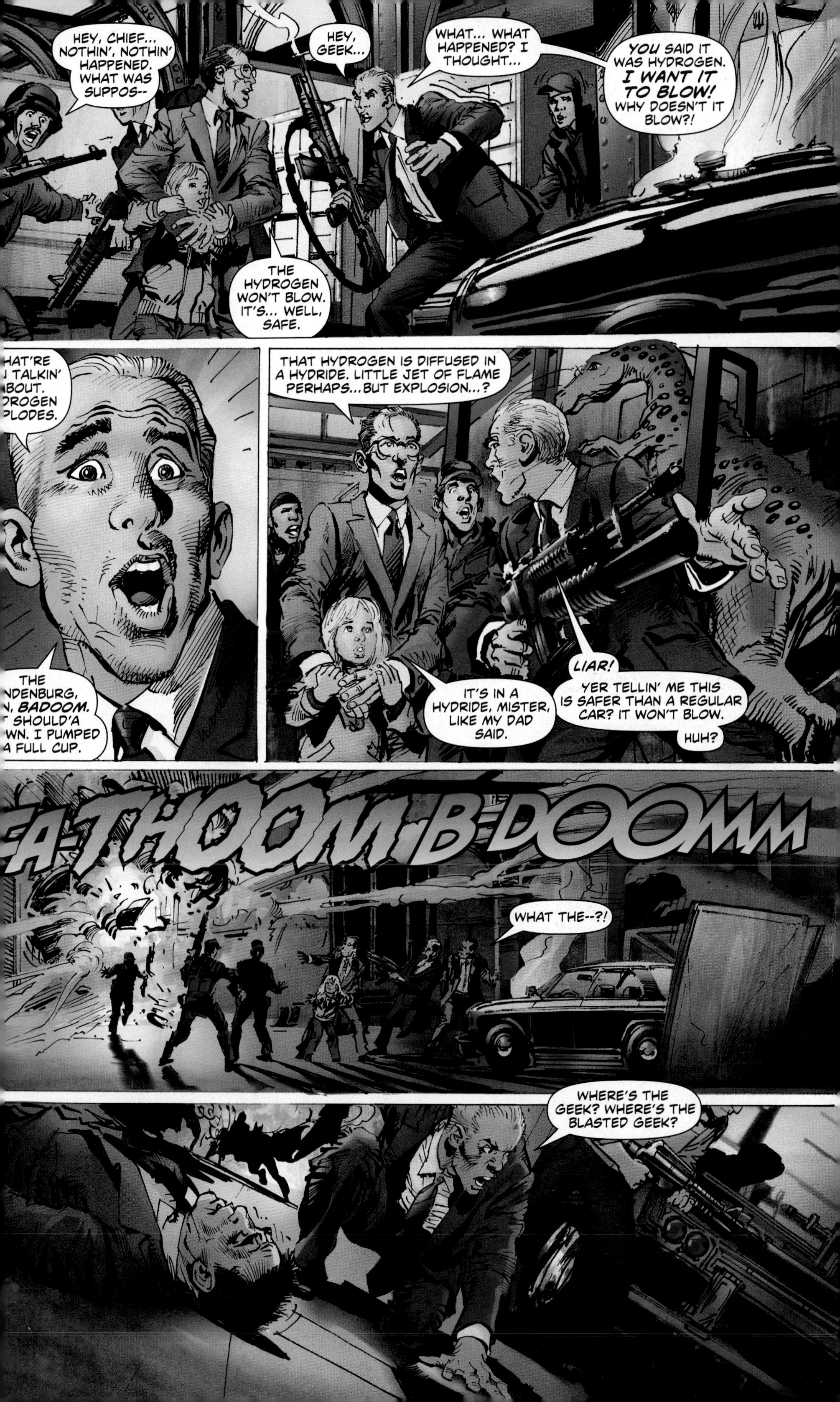
HEY, CHIEF... NOTHIN', NOTHIN' HAPPENED. WHAT WAS SUPPOS--
HEY, GEEK...
WHAT... WHAT HAPPENED? I THOUGHT...
YOU SAID IT WAS HYDROGEN. I WANT IT TO BLOW! WHY DOESN'T IT BLOW?!
THE HYDROGEN WON'T BLOW. IT'S... WELL, SAFE.
HAT'RE
TALKIN'
BOUT.
DROGEN
PLODES.
THE
NDENBURG,
N, BADOOM.
SHOULD'A
WN. I PUMPED
A FULL CUP.
THAT HYDROGEN IS DIFFUSED IN A HYDRIDE. LITTLE JET OF FLAME PERHAPS...BUT EXPLOSION...?
IT'S IN A HYDRIDE, MISTER, LIKE MY DAD SAID.
LIAR!
YER TELLIN' ME THIS IS SAFER THAN A REGULAR CAR? IT WON'T BLOW.
HUH?
A-THOOM-B-DOOMM
WHAT THE--?!
WHERE'S THE GEEK? WHERE'S THE BLASTED GEEK?

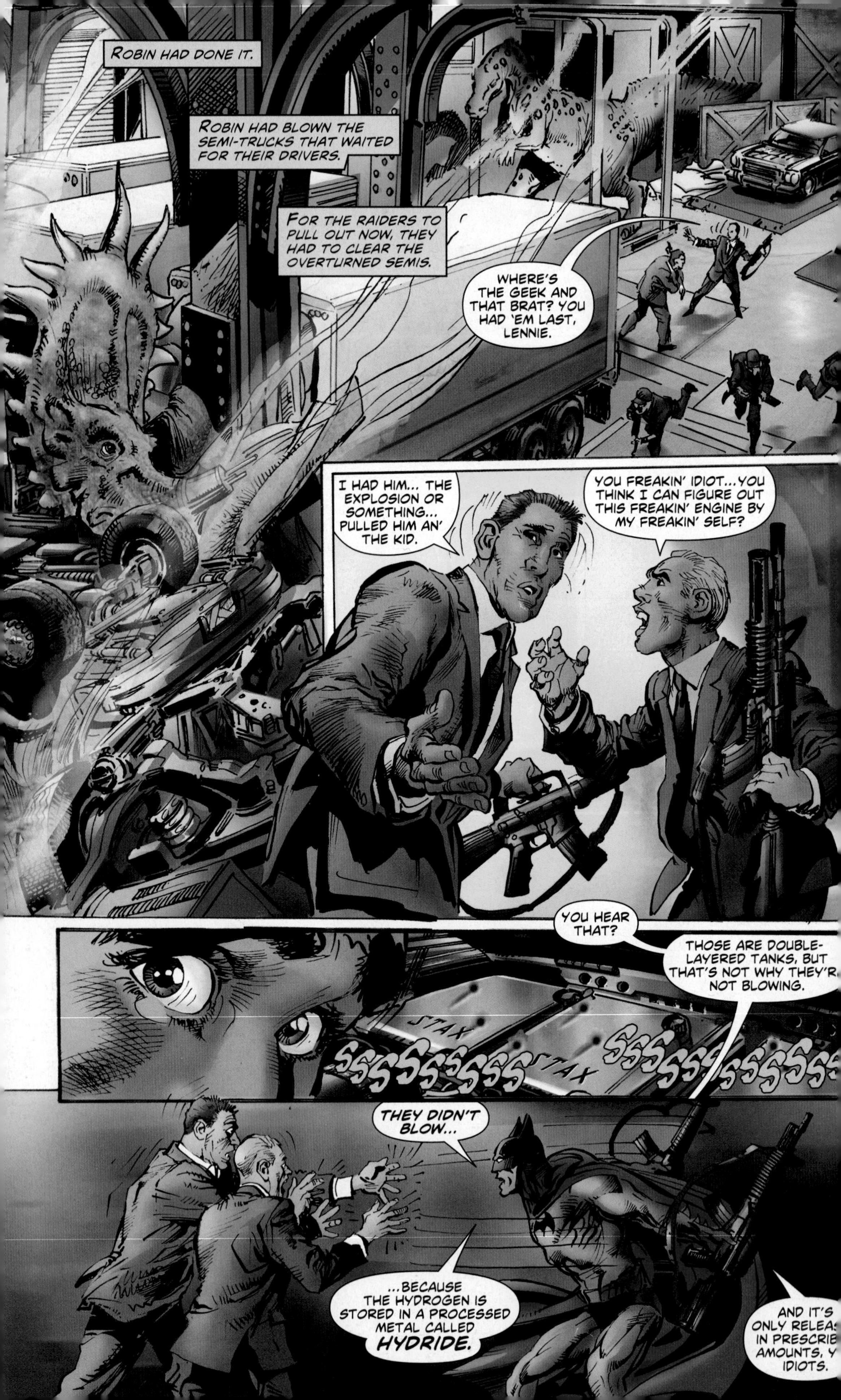
ROBIN HAD DONE IT.
ROBIN HAD BLOWN THE SEMI-TRUCKS THAT WAITED FOR THEIR DRIVERS.
FOR THE RAIDERS TO PULL OUT NOW, THEY HAD TO CLEAR THE OVERTURNED SEMIS.
WHERE'S THE GEEK AND THAT BRAT? YOU HAD 'EM LAST, LENNIE.
I HAD HIM... THE EXPLOSION OR SOMETHING... PULLED HIM AN' THE KID.
YOU FREAKIN' IDIOT...YOU THINK I CAN FIGURE OUT THIS FREAKIN' ENGINE BY MY FREAKIN' SELF?
YOU HEAR THAT?
THOSE ARE DOUBLE-LAYERED TANKS, BUT THAT'S NOT WHY THEY'R NOT BLOWING.
STAX
SSSSSSSSSSS
SSSSSSSSSSSSS
THEY DIDN'T BLOW...
...BECAUSE THE HYDROGEN IS STORED IN A PROCESSED METAL CALLED HYDRIDE.
AND IT'S ONLY RELEA IN PRESCRIB AMOUNTS, Y IDIOTS.

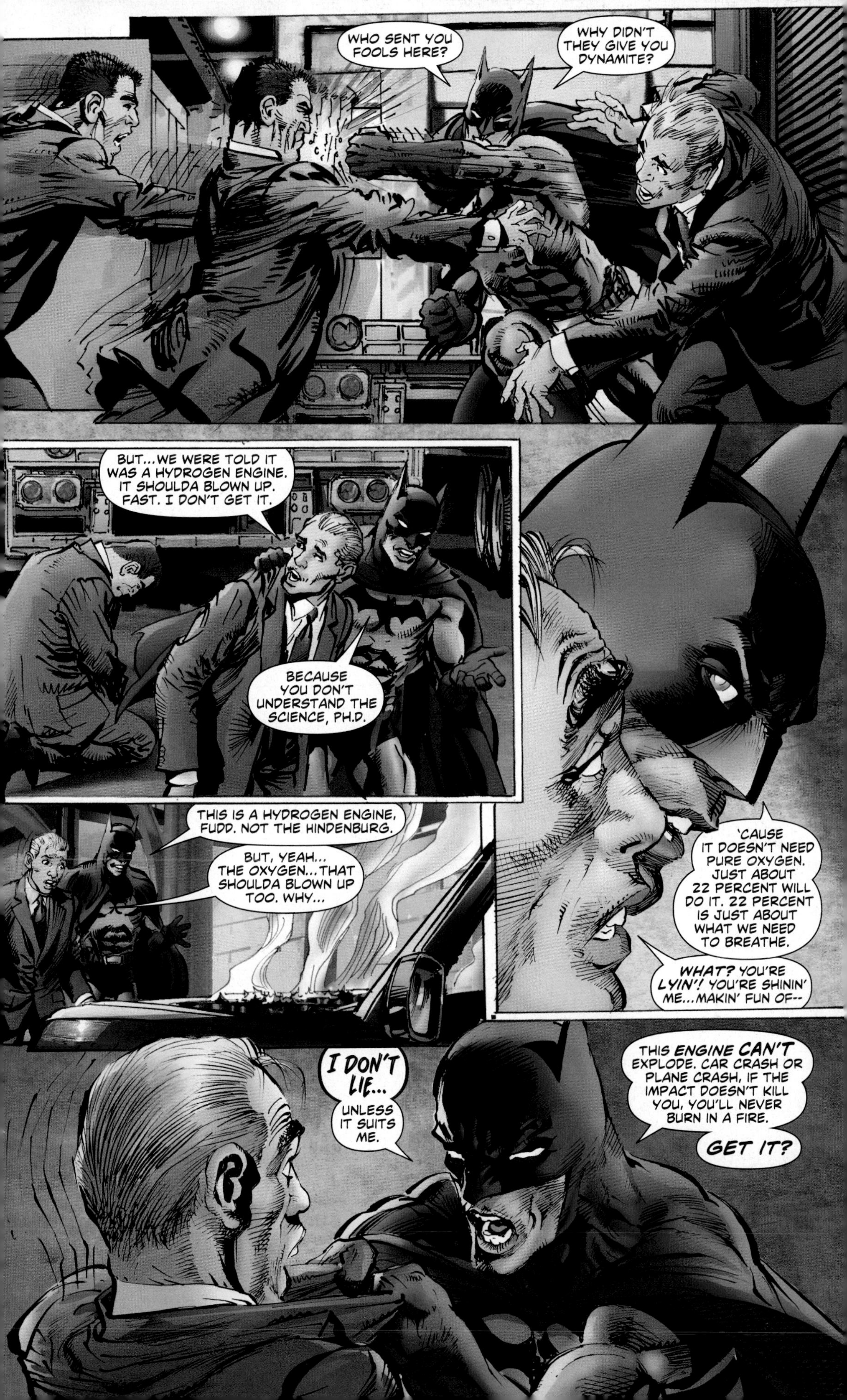
WHO SENT YOU FOOLS HERE?
WHY DIDN'T THEY GIVE YOU DYNAMITE?
BUT...WE WERE TOLD IT WAS A HYDROGEN ENGINE. IT SHOULDA BLOWN UP. FAST. I DON'T GET IT.
BECAUSE YOU DON'T UNDERSTAND THE SCIENCE, PH.D.
THIS IS A HYDROGEN ENGINE, FUDD. NOT THE HINDENBURG.
BUT, YEAH... THE OXYGEN...THAT SHOULDA BLOWN UP TOO. WHY...
'CAUSE IT DOESN'T NEED PURE OXYGEN. JUST ABOUT 22 PERCENT WILL DO IT. 22 PERCENT IS JUST ABOUT WHAT WE NEED TO BREATHE.
WHAT? YOU'RE *LYIN'!* YOU'RE SHININ' ME...MAKIN' FUN OF--
I DON'T LIE... UNLESS IT SUITS ME.
THIS *ENGINE CAN'T* EXPLODE. CAR CRASH OR PLANE CRASH, IF THE IMPACT DOESN'T KILL YOU, YOU'LL NEVER BURN IN A FIRE.
GET IT?

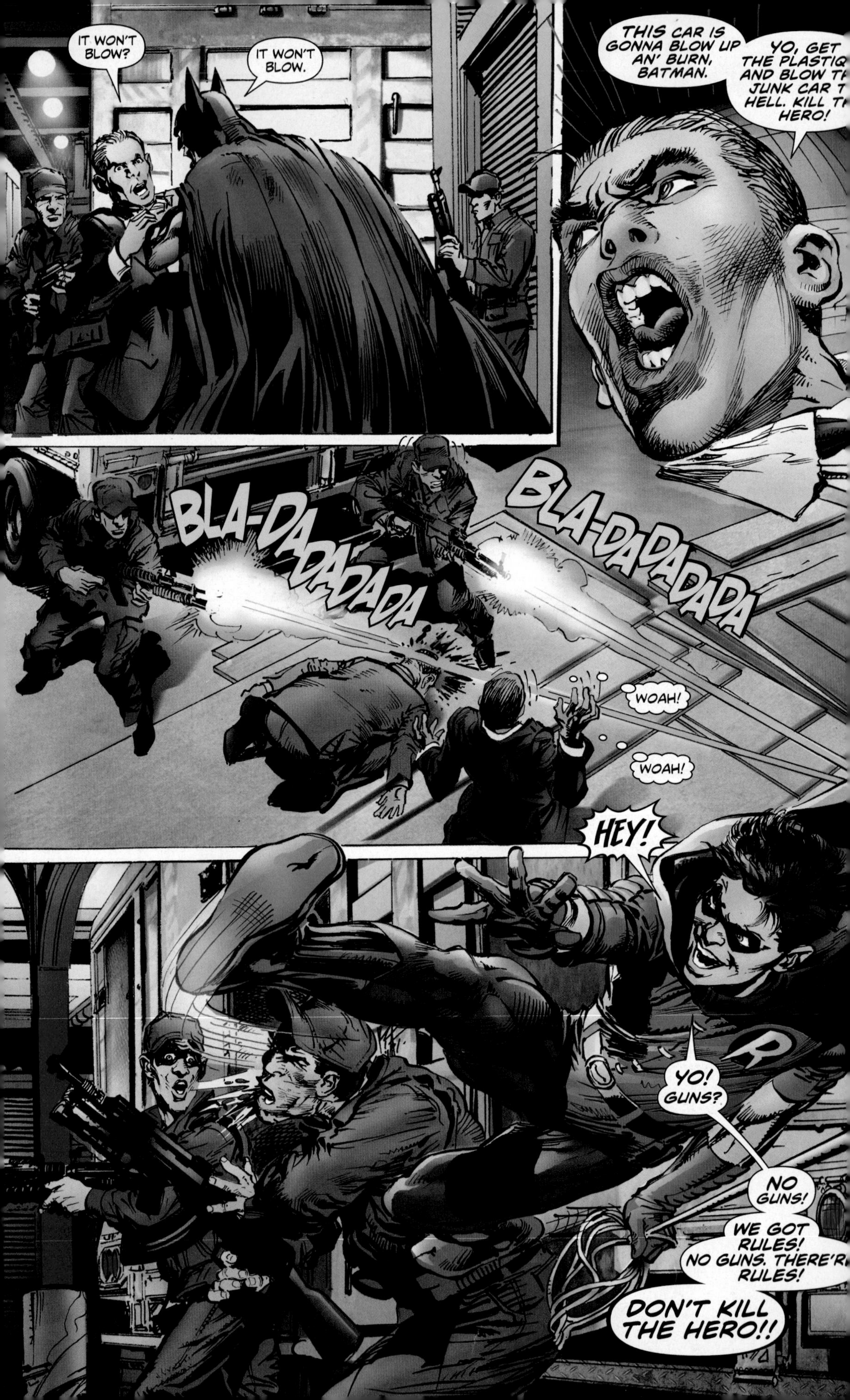
IT WON'T BLOW?
IT WON'T BLOW.
THIS CAR IS GONNA BLOW UP AN' BURN, BATMAN.
YO, GET THE PLASTIQ AND BLOW TH JUNK CAR T HELL. KILL TH HERO!
BLA-DADADADA
BLA-DADADADA
WOAH!
WOAH!
HEY!
YO! GUNS?
NO GUNS!
WE GOT RULES! NO GUNS. THERE'R RULES!
DON'T KILL THE HERO!!

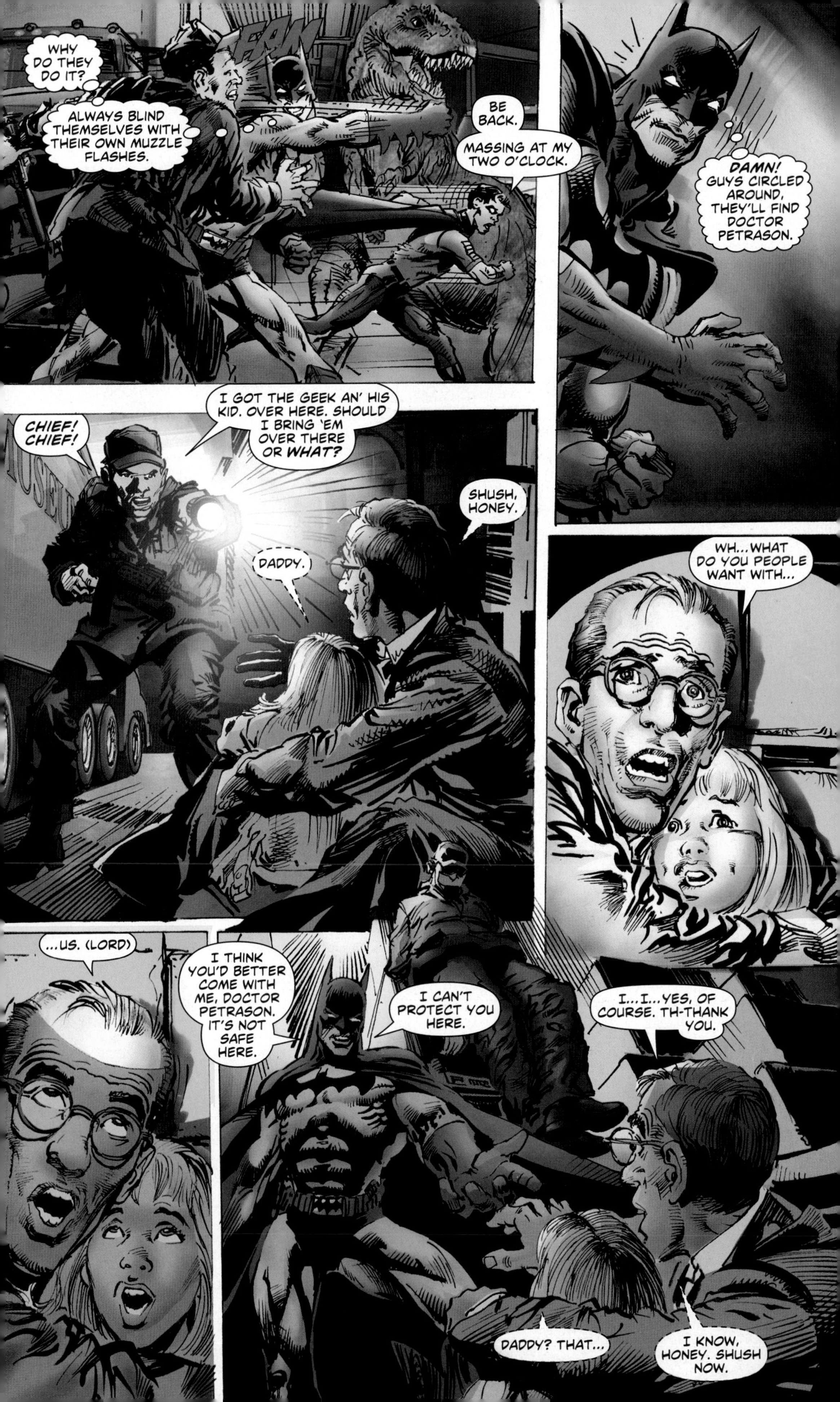

WHY DO THEY DO IT?
ALWAYS BLIND THEMSELVES WITH THEIR OWN MUZZLE FLASHES.
BE BACK.
MASSING AT MY TWO O'CLOCK.
DAMN! GUYS CIRCLED AROUND, THEY'LL FIND DOCTOR PETRASON.
CHIEF! CHIEF!
I GOT THE GEEK AN' HIS KID. OVER HERE. SHOULD I BRING 'EM OVER THERE OR WHAT?
SHUSH, HONEY.
DADDY.
WH...WHAT DO YOU PEOPLE WANT WITH...
...US. (LORD)
I THINK YOU'D BETTER COME WITH ME, DOCTOR PETRASON. IT'S NOT SAFE HERE.
I CAN'T PROTECT YOU HERE.
I...I...YES, OF COURSE. TH-THANK YOU.
DADDY? THAT...
I KNOW, HONEY. SHUSH NOW.

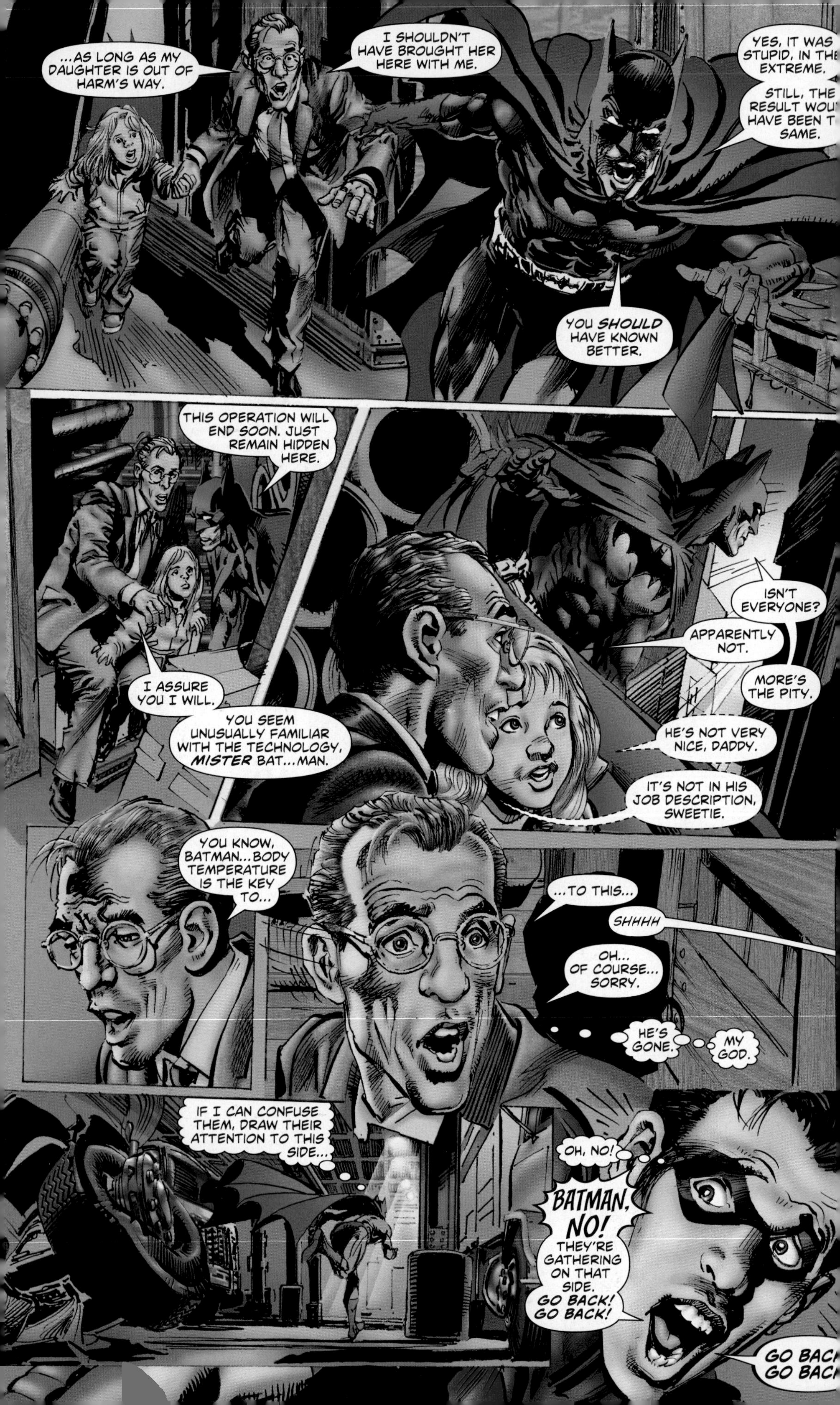

...AS LONG AS MY DAUGHTER IS OUT OF HARM'S WAY.
I SHOULDN'T HAVE BROUGHT HER HERE WITH ME.
YES, IT WAS STUPID, IN THE EXTREME.
STILL, THE RESULT WOU HAVE BEEN T SAME.
YOU SHOULD HAVE KNOWN BETTER.
THIS OPERATION WILL END SOON. JUST REMAIN HIDDEN HERE.
I ASSURE YOU I WILL.
YOU SEEM UNUSUALLY FAMILIAR WITH THE TECHNOLOGY, MISTER BAT...MAN.
ISN'T EVERYONE?
APPARENTLY NOT.
MORE'S THE PITY.
HE'S NOT VERY NICE, DADDY.
IT'S NOT IN HIS JOB DESCRIPTION, SWEETIE.
YOU KNOW, BATMAN...BODY TEMPERATURE IS THE KEY TO...
...TO THIS...
SHHHH
OH... OF COURSE... SORRY.
HE'S GONE.
MY GOD.
IF I CAN CONFUSE THEM, DRAW THEIR ATTENTION TO THIS SIDE...
OH, NO!
BATMAN, NO! THEY'RE GATHERING ON THAT SIDE. GO BACK! GO BACK!
GO BAC GO BAC

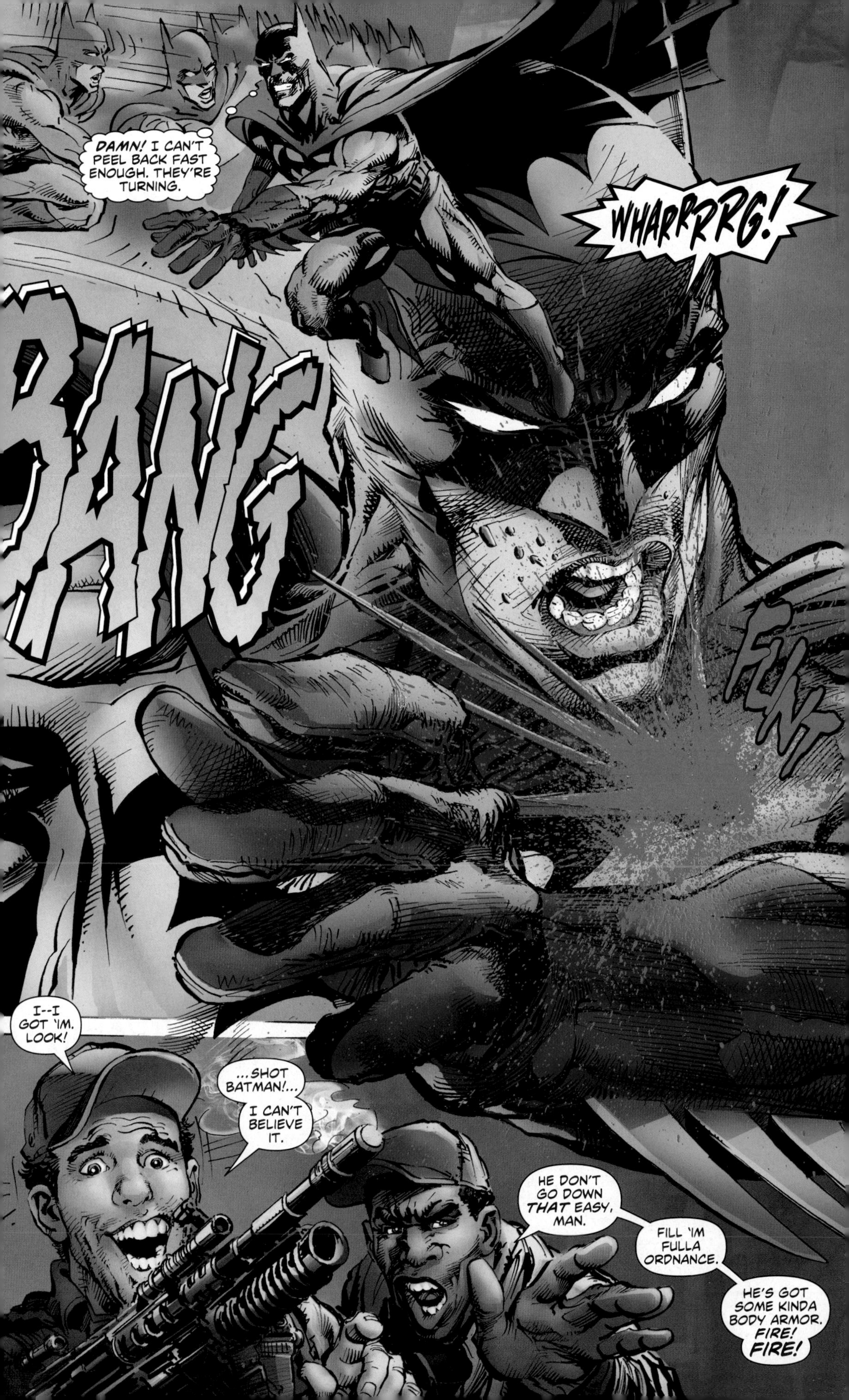
DAMN! I CAN'T PEEL BACK FAST ENOUGH. THEY'RE TURNING.
WHARRRRG!
BANG
FLNT
I--I GOT 'IM. LOOK!
...SHOT BATMAN!...
I CAN'T BELIEVE IT.
HE DON'T GO DOWN THAT EASY, MAN.
FILL 'IM FULLA ORDNANCE.
HE'S GOT SOME KINDA BODY ARMOR. FIRE! FIRE!

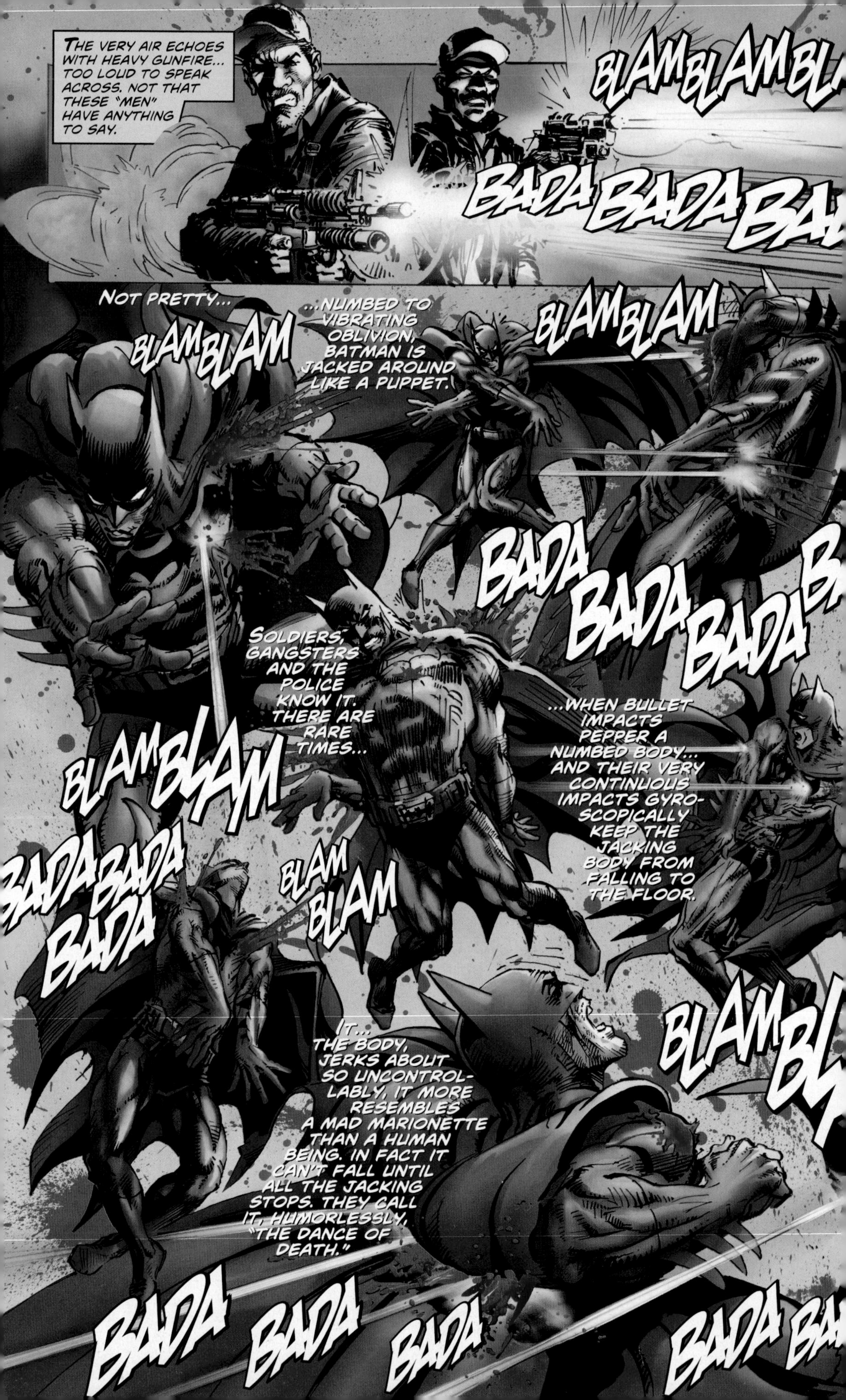
THE VERY AIR ECHOES WITH HEAVY GUNFIRE... TOO LOUD TO SPEAK ACROSS. NOT THAT THESE "MEN" HAVE ANYTHING TO SAY.
BLAMBLAMBL
BADA BADA BA
NOT PRETTY...
BLAMBLAM
...NUMBED TO VIBRATING OBLIVION, BATMAN IS JACKED AROUND LIKE A PUPPET.
BLAMBLAM
BADA BADA BADA B
SOLDIERS, GANGSTERS AND THE POLICE KNOW IT. THERE ARE RARE TIMES...
...WHEN BULLET IMPACTS PEPPER A NUMBED BODY... AND THEIR VERY CONTINUOUS IMPACTS GYRO-SCOPICALLY KEEP THE JACKING BODY FROM FALLING TO THE FLOOR.
BLAMBLAM
BADA BADA BADA
BLAM BLAM
IT... THE BODY, JERKS ABOUT SO UNCONTROL-LABLY, IT MORE RESEMBLES A MAD MARIONETTE THAN A HUMAN BEING. IN FACT IT CAN'T FALL UNTIL ALL THE JACKING STOPS. THEY CALL IT, HUMORLESSLY, "THE DANCE OF DEATH."
BLAMBL
BADA BADA BADA BADA BA

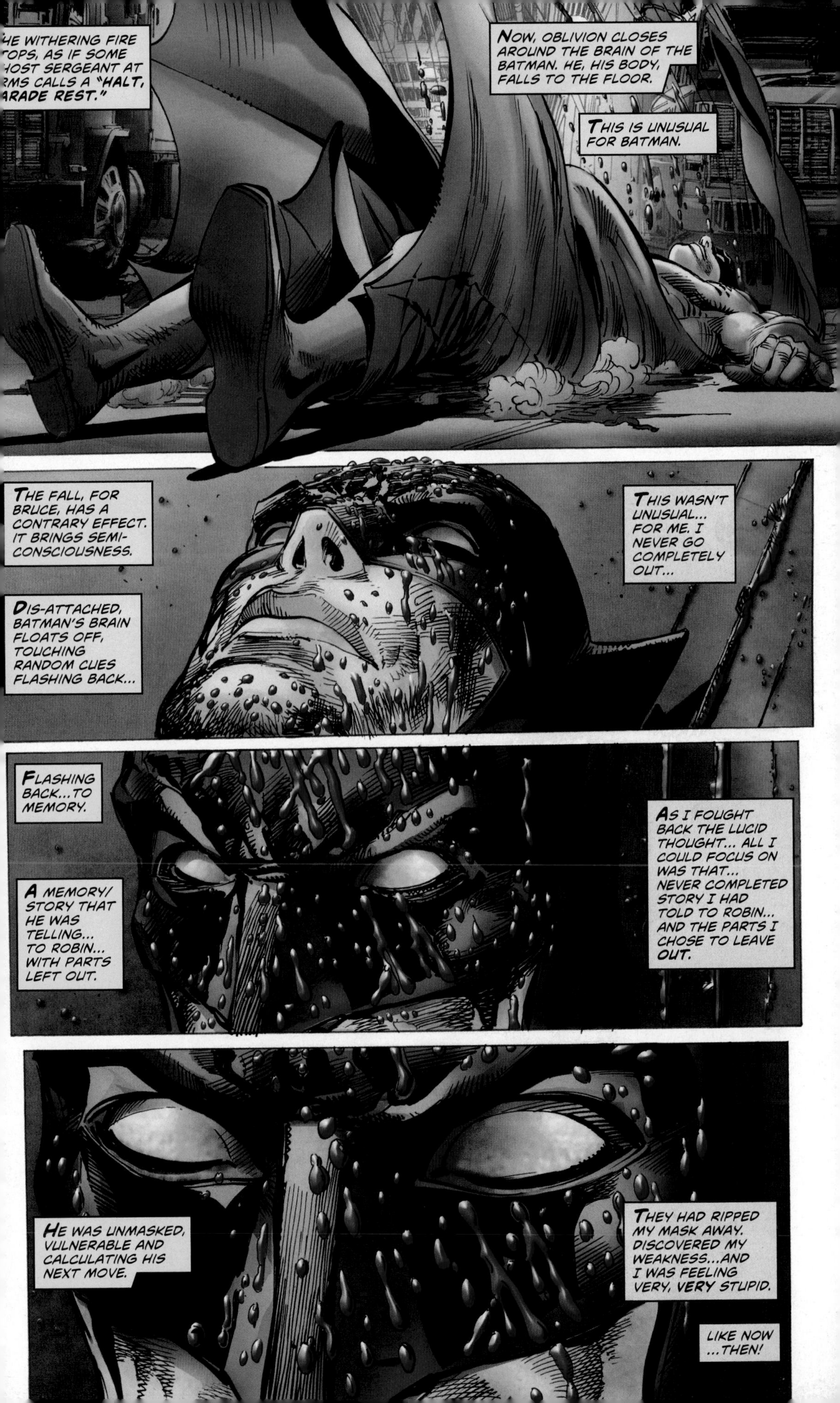

HE WITHERING FIRE TOPS, AS IF SOME HOST SERGEANT AT RMS CALLS A "HALT, ARADE REST."
NOW, OBLIVION CLOSES AROUND THE BRAIN OF THE BATMAN. HE, HIS BODY, FALLS TO THE FLOOR.
THIS IS UNUSUAL FOR BATMAN.
THE FALL, FOR BRUCE, HAS A CONTRARY EFFECT. IT BRINGS SEMI-CONSCIOUSNESS.
THIS WASN'T UNUSUAL... FOR ME. I NEVER GO COMPLETELY OUT...
DIS-ATTACHED, BATMAN'S BRAIN FLOATS OFF, TOUCHING RANDOM CUES FLASHING BACK...
FLASHING BACK...TO MEMORY.
AS I FOUGHT BACK THE LUCID THOUGHT... ALL I COULD FOCUS ON WAS THAT... NEVER COMPLETED STORY I HAD TOLD TO ROBIN... AND THE PARTS I CHOSE TO LEAVE OUT.
A MEMORY/ STORY THAT HE WAS TELLING... TO ROBIN... WITH PARTS LEFT OUT.
HE WAS UNMASKED, VULNERABLE AND CALCULATING HIS NEXT MOVE.
THEY HAD RIPPED MY MASK AWAY. DISCOVERED MY WEAKNESS...AND I WAS FEELING VERY, VERY STUPID.
LIKE NOW ...THEN!

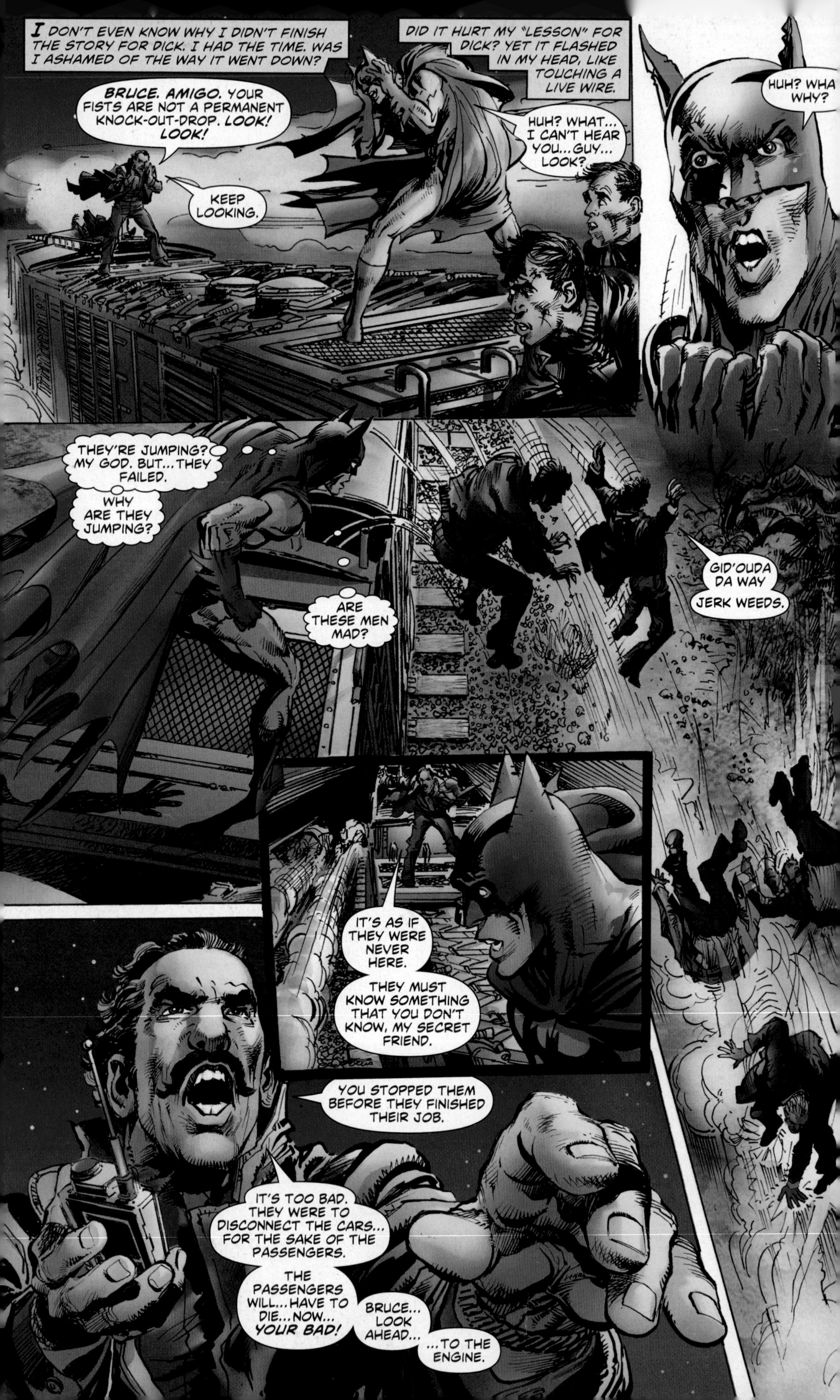
I DON'T EVEN KNOW WHY I DIDN'T FINISH THE STORY FOR DICK. I HAD THE TIME. WAS I ASHAMED OF THE WAY IT WENT DOWN?
DID IT HURT MY "LESSON" FOR DICK? YET IT FLASHED IN MY HEAD, LIKE TOUCHING A LIVE WIRE.
BRUCE. AMIGO. YOUR FISTS ARE NOT A PERMANENT KNOCK-OUT-DROP. LOOK! LOOK!
HUH? WHAT... I CAN'T HEAR YOU...GUY... LOOK?
KEEP LOOKING.
HUH? WHA WHY?
THEY'RE JUMPING? MY GOD. BUT...THEY FAILED.
WHY ARE THEY JUMPING?
ARE THESE MEN MAD?
GID'OUDA DA WAY JERK WEEDS.
IT'S AS IF THEY WERE NEVER HERE.
THEY MUST KNOW SOMETHING THAT YOU DON'T KNOW, MY SECRET FRIEND.
YOU STOPPED THEM BEFORE THEY FINISHED THEIR JOB.
IT'S TOO BAD. THEY WERE TO DISCONNECT THE CARS... FOR THE SAKE OF THE PASSENGERS.
THE PASSENGERS WILL...HAVE TO DIE...NOW... YOUR BAD!
BRUCE... LOOK AHEAD...
...TO THE ENGINE.

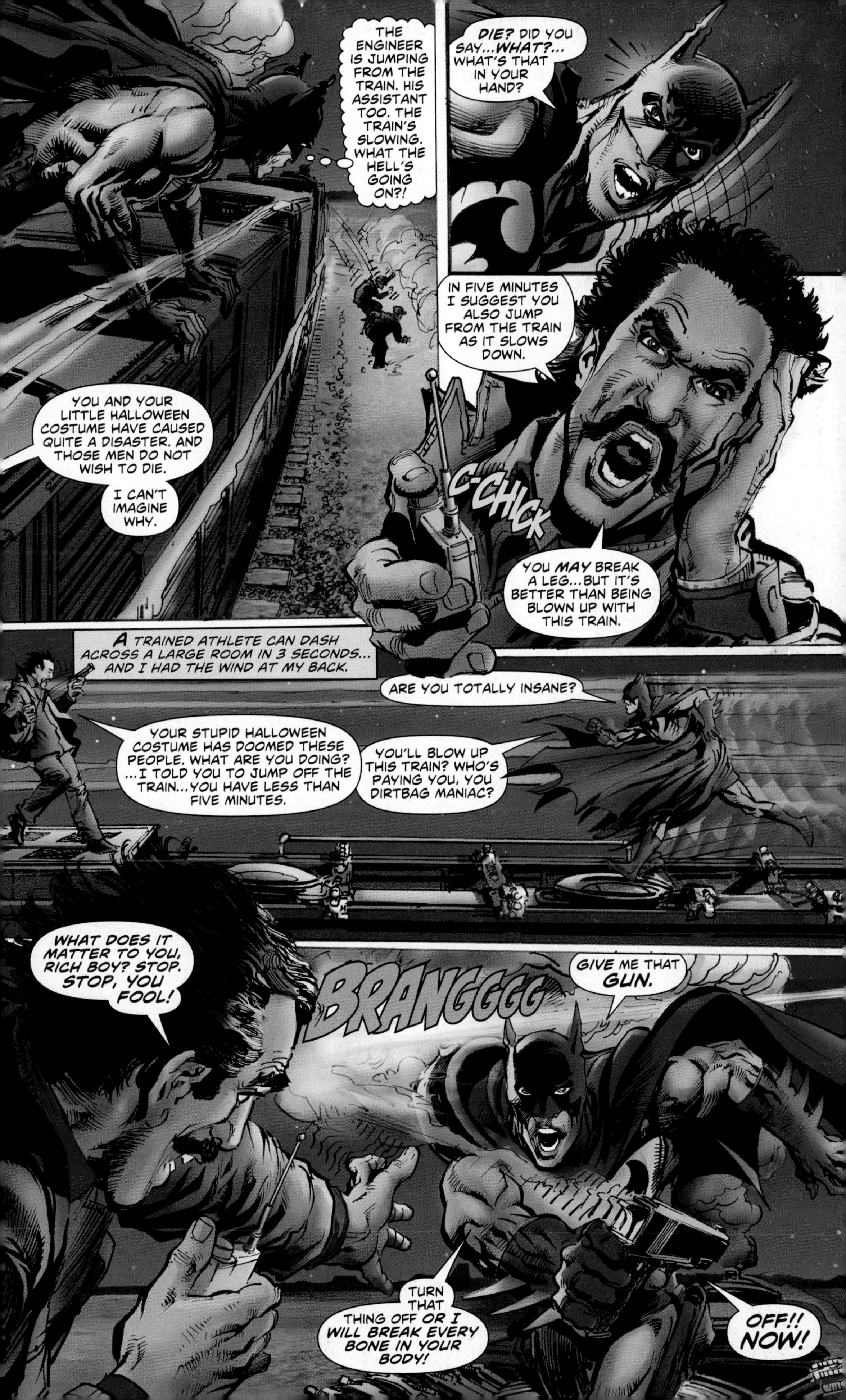
THE ENGINEER IS JUMPING FROM THE TRAIN. HIS ASSISTANT TOO. THE TRAIN'S SLOWING. WHAT THE HELL'S GOING ON?!
DIE? DID YOU SAY...WHAT?... WHAT'S THAT IN YOUR HAND?
YOU AND YOUR LITTLE HALLOWEEN COSTUME HAVE CAUSED QUITE A DISASTER. AND THOSE MEN DO NOT WISH TO DIE.
I CAN'T IMAGINE WHY.
IN FIVE MINUTES I SUGGEST YOU ALSO JUMP FROM THE TRAIN AS IT SLOWS DOWN.
C-CHICK
YOU MAY BREAK A LEG...BUT IT'S BETTER THAN BEING BLOWN UP WITH THIS TRAIN.
A TRAINED ATHLETE CAN DASH ACROSS A LARGE ROOM IN 3 SECONDS... AND I HAD THE WIND AT MY BACK.
ARE YOU TOTALLY INSANE?
YOUR STUPID HALLOWEEN COSTUME HAS DOOMED THESE PEOPLE. WHAT ARE YOU DOING? ...I TOLD YOU TO JUMP OFF THE TRAIN...YOU HAVE LESS THAN FIVE MINUTES.
YOU'LL BLOW UP THIS TRAIN? WHO'S PAYING YOU, YOU DIRTBAG MANIAC?
WHAT DOES IT MATTER TO YOU, RICH BOY? STOP. STOP, YOU FOOL!
BRANGGGG
GIVE ME THAT GUN.
TURN THAT THING OFF OR I WILL BREAK EVERY BONE IN YOUR BODY!
OFF!! NOW!

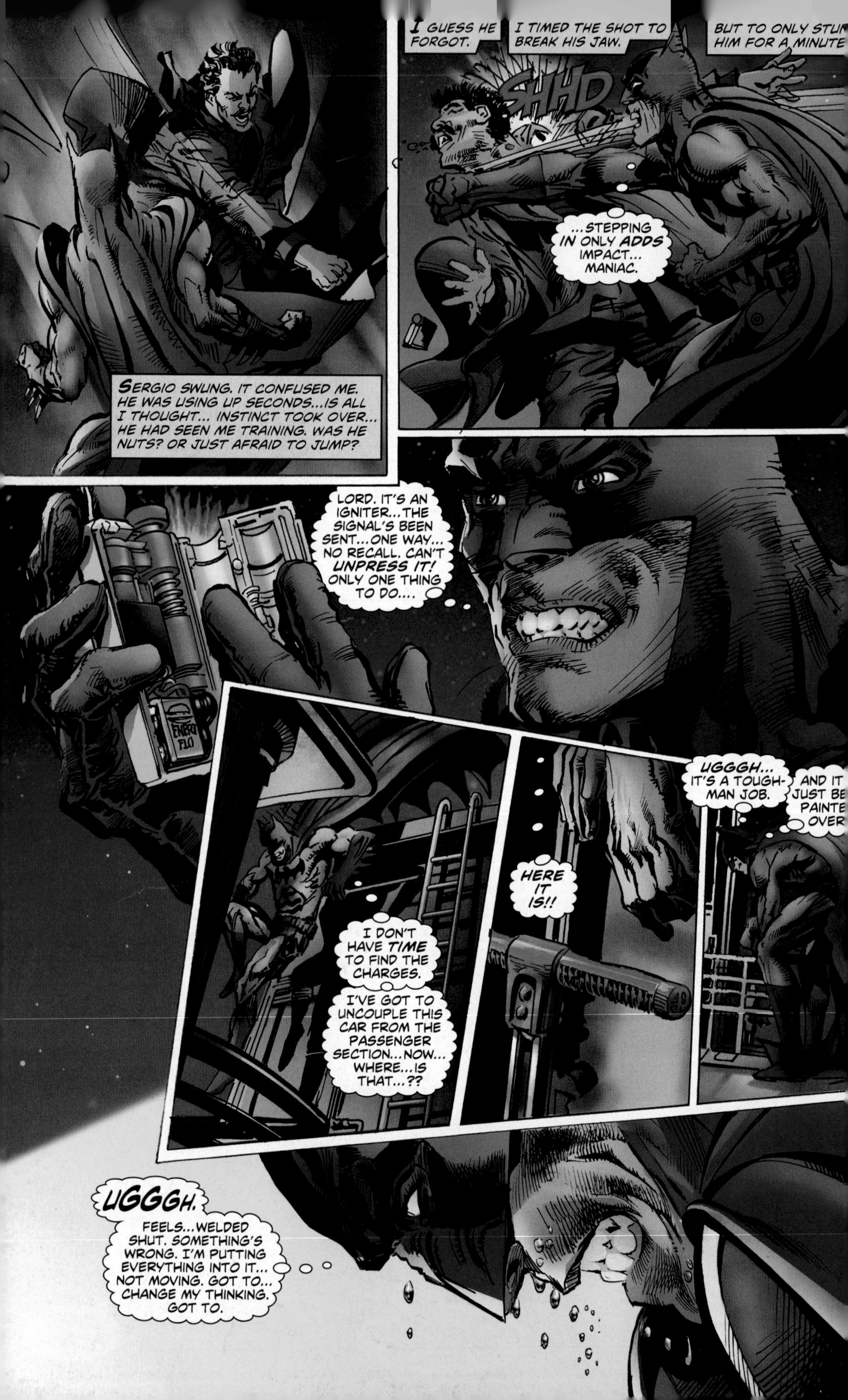
SERGIO SWUNG. IT CONFUSED ME. HE WAS USING UP SECONDS...IS ALL I THOUGHT... INSTINCT TOOK OVER... HE HAD SEEN ME TRAINING. WAS HE NUTS? OR JUST AFRAID TO JUMP?
I GUESS HE FORGOT.
I TIMED THE SHOT TO BREAK HIS JAW.
BUT TO ONLY STUN HIM FOR A MINUTE
SHHD
...STEPPING IN ONLY ADDS IMPACT... MANIAC.
LORD. IT'S AN IGNITER...THE SIGNAL'S BEEN SENT...ONE WAY... NO RECALL. CAN'T UNPRESS IT! ONLY ONE THING TO DO....
ENERG FLO
I DON'T HAVE TIME TO FIND THE CHARGES.
I'VE GOT TO UNCOUPLE THIS CAR FROM THE PASSENGER SECTION...NOW... WHERE...IS THAT...??
HERE IT IS!!
UGGGH... IT'S A TOUGH-MAN JOB.
AND IT JUST BE PAINTE OVER
UGGGH.
FEELS...WELDED SHUT. SOMETHING'S WRONG. I'M PUTTING EVERYTHING INTO IT... NOT MOVING. GOT TO... CHANGE MY THINKING. GOT TO.

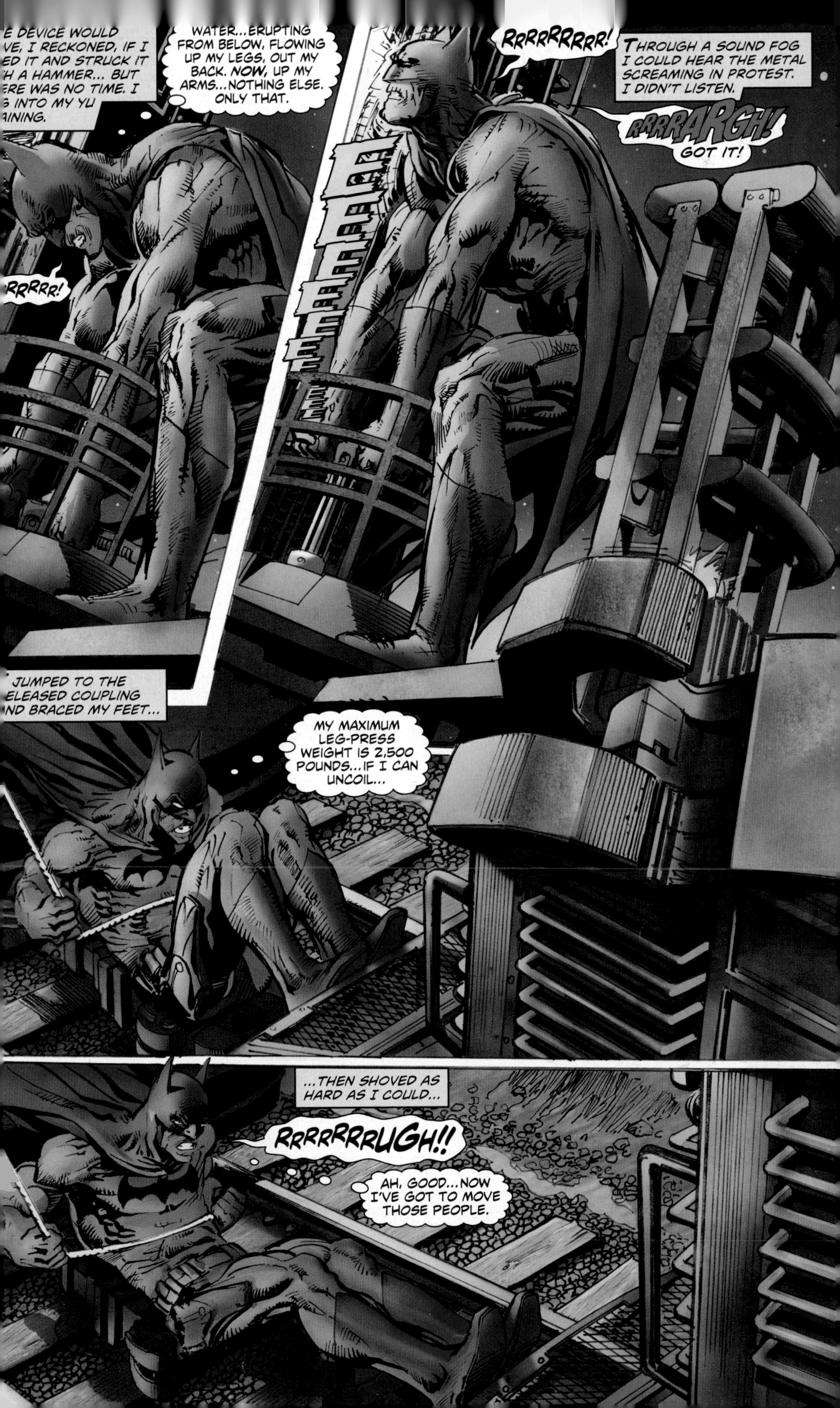
E DEVICE WOULD
VE, I RECKONED, IF I
ED IT AND STRUCK IT
H A HAMMER... BUT
ERE WAS NO TIME. I
G INTO MY YU
AINING.
RRRRR!
WATER...ERUPTING FROM BELOW, FLOWING UP MY LEGS, OUT MY BACK. NOW, UP MY ARMS...NOTHING ELSE. ONLY THAT.
EEEEEEEE
RRRRRRRRR!
THROUGH A SOUND FOG I COULD HEAR THE METAL SCREAMING IN PROTEST. I DIDN'T LISTEN.
RRRRARGH!
GOT IT!
JUMPED TO THE
ELEASED COUPLING
ND BRACED MY FEET...
MY MAXIMUM LEG-PRESS WEIGHT IS 2,500 POUNDS...IF I CAN UNCOIL...
...THEN SHOVED AS HARD AS I COULD...
RRRRRRRUGH!!
AH, GOOD...NOW I'VE GOT TO MOVE THOSE PEOPLE.

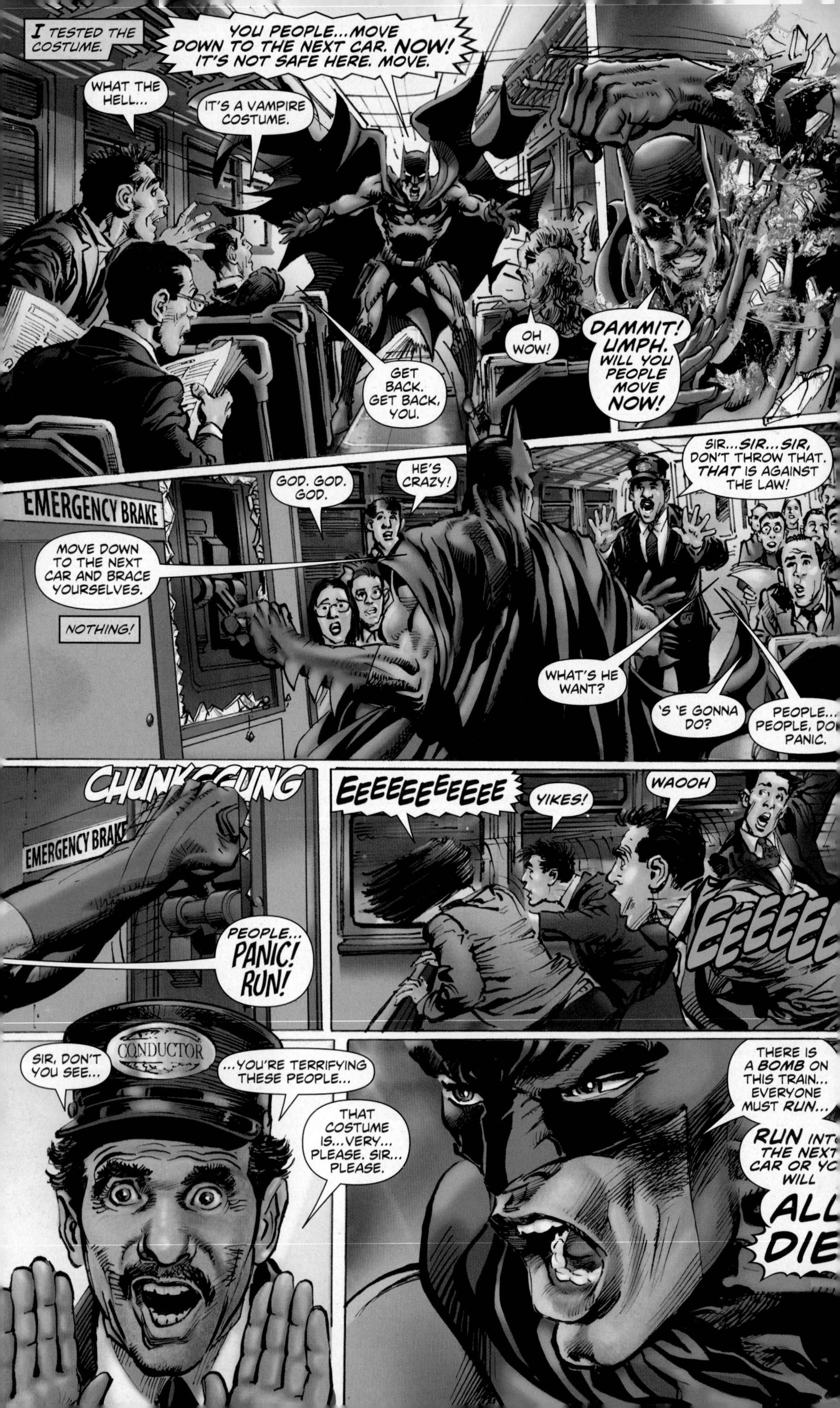
I TESTED THE COSTUME.
YOU PEOPLE...MOVE DOWN TO THE NEXT CAR. NOW! IT'S NOT SAFE HERE. MOVE.
WHAT THE HELL...
IT'S A VAMPIRE COSTUME.
GET BACK. GET BACK, YOU.
OH WOW!
DAMMIT! UMPH. WILL YOU PEOPLE MOVE NOW!
GOD. GOD. GOD.
HE'S CRAZY!
SIR...SIR...SIR, DON'T THROW THAT. THAT IS AGAINST THE LAW!
EMERGENCY BRAKE
MOVE DOWN TO THE NEXT CAR AND BRACE YOURSELVES.
NOTHING!
WHAT'S HE WANT?
'S 'E GONNA DO?
PEOPLE... PEOPLE, DO PANIC.
EMERGENCY BRAKE
PEOPLE... PANIC! RUN!
EEEEEEEEEEE
YIKES!
WAOOH
EEEEEE
CONDUCTOR
SIR, DON'T YOU SEE...
...YOU'RE TERRIFYING THESE PEOPLE...
THAT COSTUME IS...VERY... PLEASE. SIR... PLEASE.
THERE IS A BOMB ON THIS TRAIN... EVERYONE MUST RUN...
RUN INTO THE NEXT CAR OR YO WILL
ALL DIE

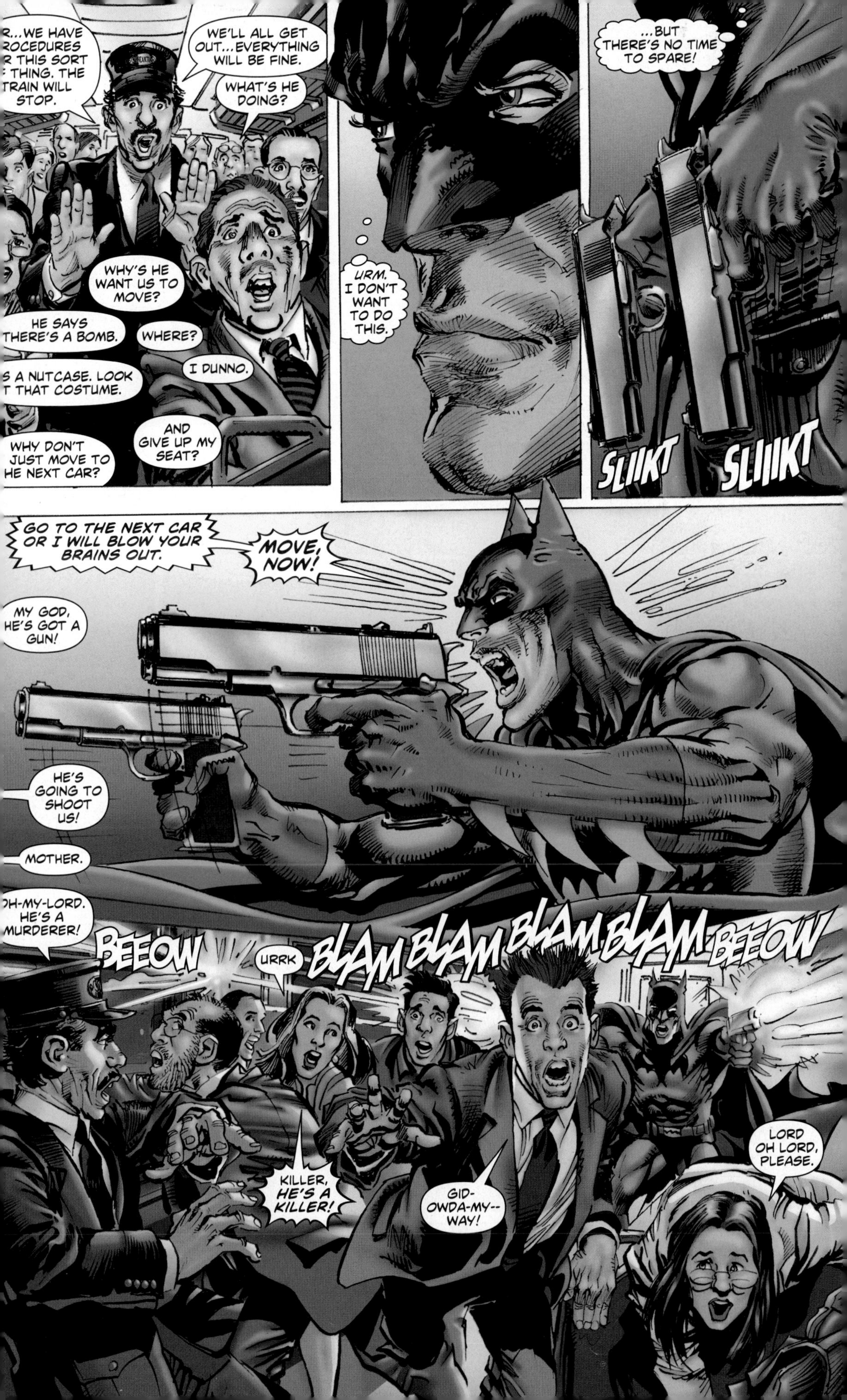

R...WE HAVE
ROCEDURES
R THIS SORT
F THING. THE
TRAIN WILL
STOP.
WE'LL ALL GET
OUT...EVERYTHING
WILL BE FINE.
WHAT'S HE
DOING?
WHY'S HE
WANT US TO
MOVE?
HE SAYS
THERE'S A BOMB.
WHERE?
I DUNNO.
S A NUTCASE. LOOK
T THAT COSTUME.
WHY DON'T
JUST MOVE TO
HE NEXT CAR?
AND
GIVE UP MY
SEAT?
URM.
I DON'T
WANT
TO DO
THIS.
...BUT
THERE'S NO TIME
TO SPARE!
SLIIKT
SLIIIKT
GO TO THE NEXT CAR
OR I WILL BLOW YOUR
BRAINS OUT.
MOVE,
NOW!
MY GOD,
HE'S GOT A
GUN!
HE'S
GOING TO
SHOOT
US!
MOTHER.
OH-MY-LORD.
HE'S A
MURDERER!
BEEOW
URRK
BLAM BLAM BLAM BLAM BEEOW
KILLER,
HE'S A
KILLER!
GID-
OWDA-MY--
WAY!
LORD
OH LORD,
PLEASE.

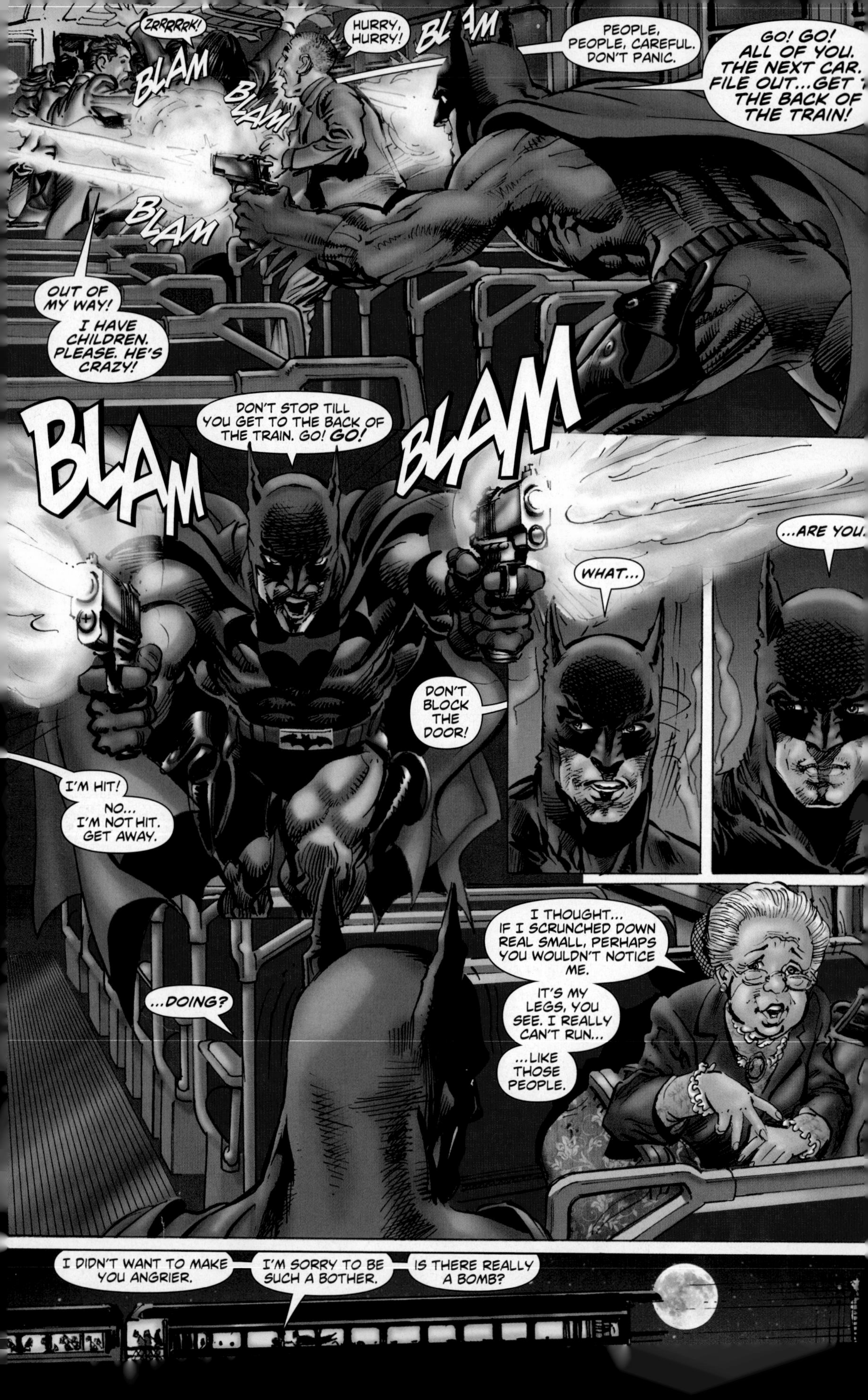
ZRRRRRK!
HURRY, HURRY!
BLAM
PEOPLE, PEOPLE, CAREFUL. DON'T PANIC.
GO! GO! ALL OF YOU. THE NEXT CAR. FILE OUT...GET T THE BACK OF THE TRAIN!
BLAM
BLAM
BLAM
OUT OF MY WAY!
I HAVE CHILDREN. PLEASE. HE'S CRAZY!
BLAM
DON'T STOP TILL YOU GET TO THE BACK OF THE TRAIN. GO! GO!
BLAM
DON'T BLOCK THE DOOR!
I'M HIT!
NO... I'M NOT HIT. GET AWAY.
WHAT...
...ARE YOU...
...DOING?
I THOUGHT... IF I SCRUNCHED DOWN REAL SMALL, PERHAPS YOU WOULDN'T NOTICE ME.
IT'S MY LEGS, YOU SEE. I REALLY CAN'T RUN...
...LIKE THOSE PEOPLE.
I DIDN'T WANT TO MAKE YOU ANGRIER.
I'M SORRY TO BE SUCH A BOTHER.
IS THERE REALLY A BOMB?

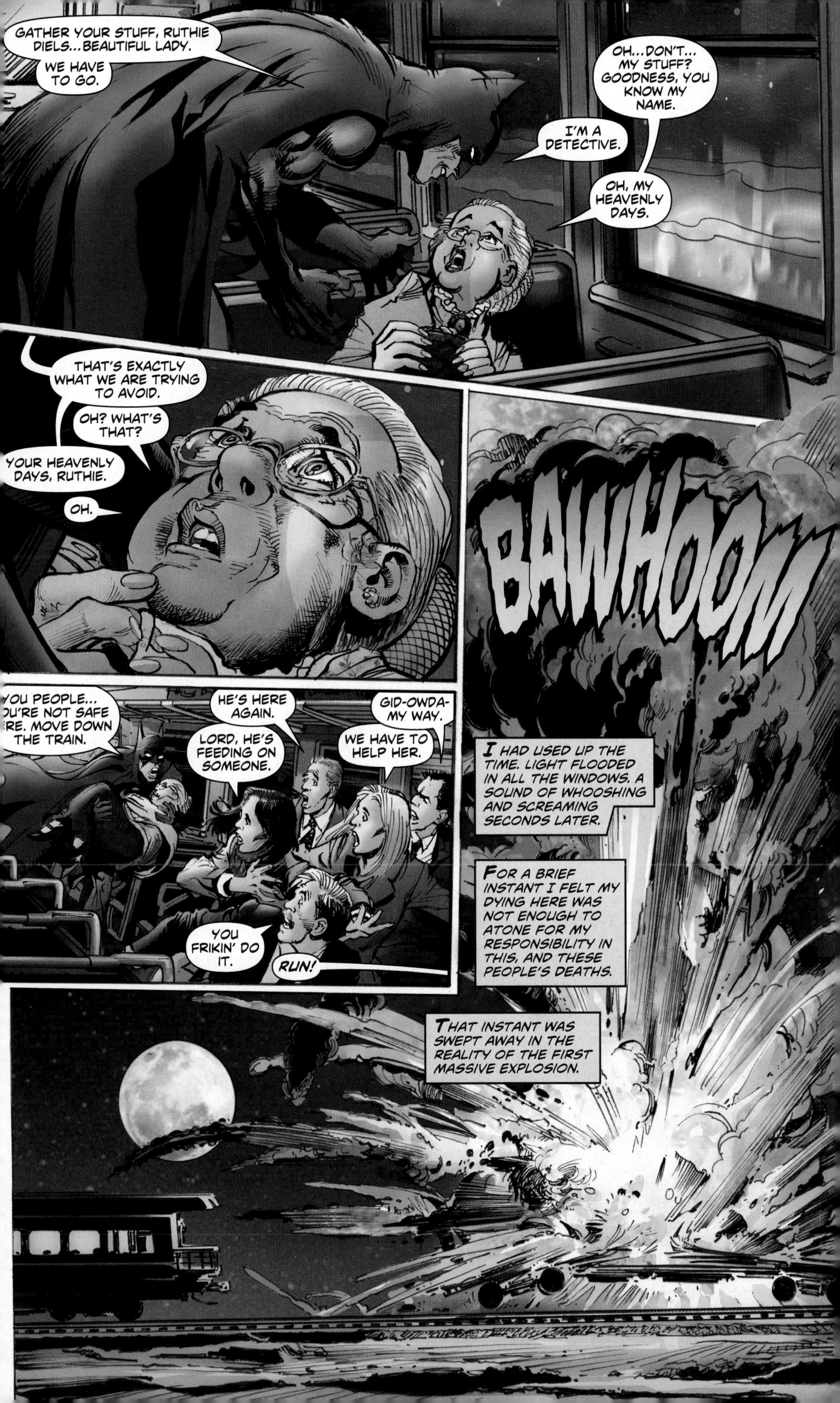
GATHER YOUR STUFF, RUTHIE DIELS...BEAUTIFUL LADY.
WE HAVE TO GO.
OH...DON'T... MY STUFF? GOODNESS, YOU KNOW MY NAME.
I'M A DETECTIVE.
OH, MY HEAVENLY DAYS.
THAT'S EXACTLY WHAT WE ARE TRYING TO AVOID.
OH? WHAT'S THAT?
YOUR HEAVENLY DAYS, RUTHIE.
OH.
BAWHOOM
YOU PEOPLE... YOU'RE NOT SAFE HERE. MOVE DOWN THE TRAIN.
HE'S HERE AGAIN.
LORD, HE'S FEEDING ON SOMEONE.
GID-OWDA-MY WAY.
WE HAVE TO HELP HER.
YOU FRIKIN' DO IT.
RUN!
I HAD USED UP THE TIME. LIGHT FLOODED IN ALL THE WINDOWS. A SOUND OF WHOOSHING AND SCREAMING SECONDS LATER.
FOR A BRIEF INSTANT I FELT MY DYING HERE WAS NOT ENOUGH TO ATONE FOR MY RESPONSIBILITY IN THIS, AND THESE PEOPLE'S DEATHS.
THAT INSTANT WAS SWEPT AWAY IN THE REALITY OF THE FIRST MASSIVE EXPLOSION.

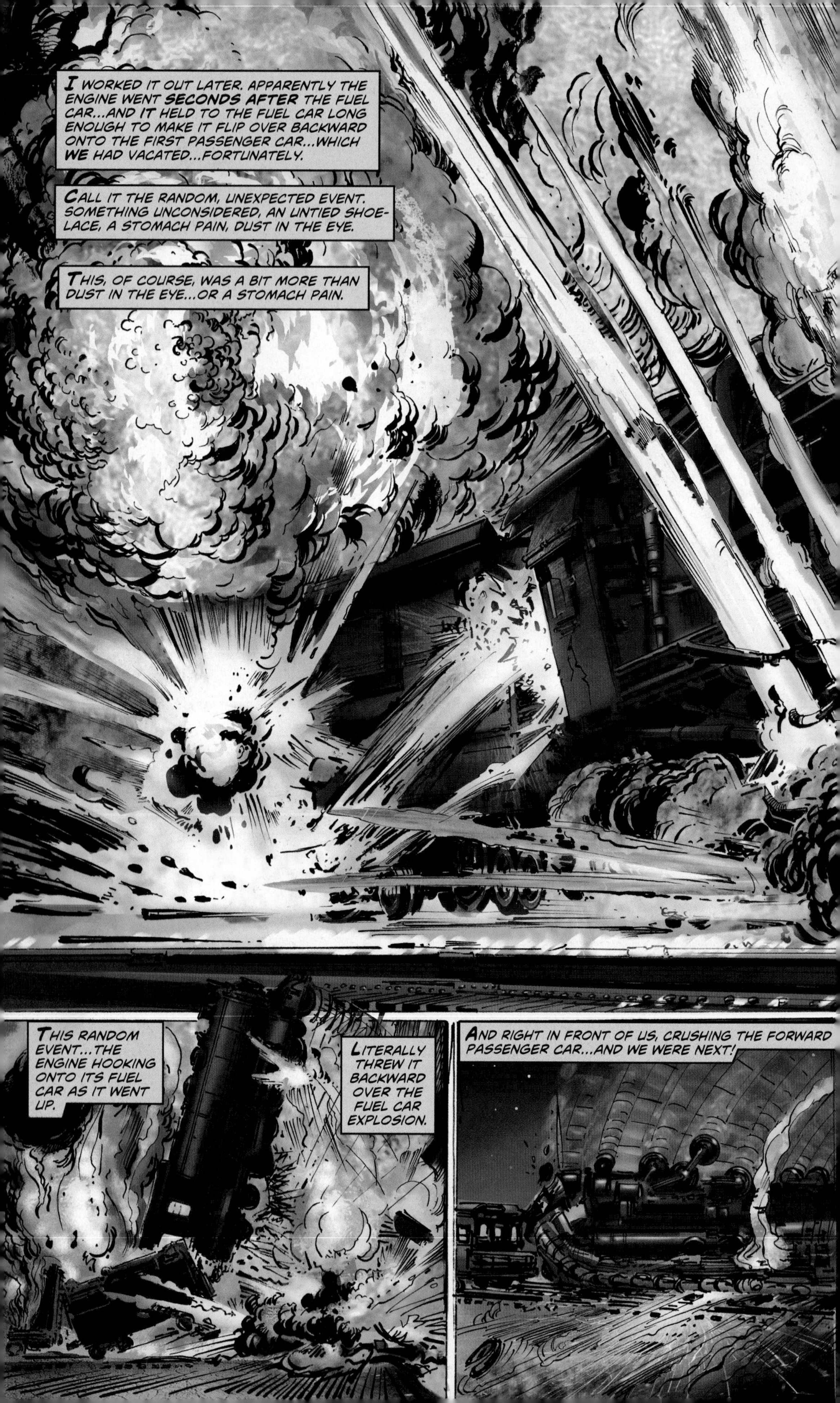
I WORKED IT OUT LATER. APPARENTLY THE ENGINE WENT SECONDS AFTER THE FUEL CAR...AND IT HELD TO THE FUEL CAR LONG ENOUGH TO MAKE IT FLIP OVER BACKWARD ONTO THE FIRST PASSENGER CAR...WHICH WE HAD VACATED...FORTUNATELY.
CALL IT THE RANDOM, UNEXPECTED EVENT. SOMETHING UNCONSIDERED, AN UNTIED SHOE-LACE, A STOMACH PAIN, DUST IN THE EYE.
THIS, OF COURSE, WAS A BIT MORE THAN DUST IN THE EYE...OR A STOMACH PAIN.
THIS RANDOM EVENT...THE ENGINE HOOKING ONTO ITS FUEL CAR AS IT WENT UP.
LITERALLY THREW IT BACKWARD OVER THE FUEL CAR EXPLOSION.
AND RIGHT IN FRONT OF US, CRUSHING THE FORWARD PASSENGER CAR...AND WE WERE NEXT!

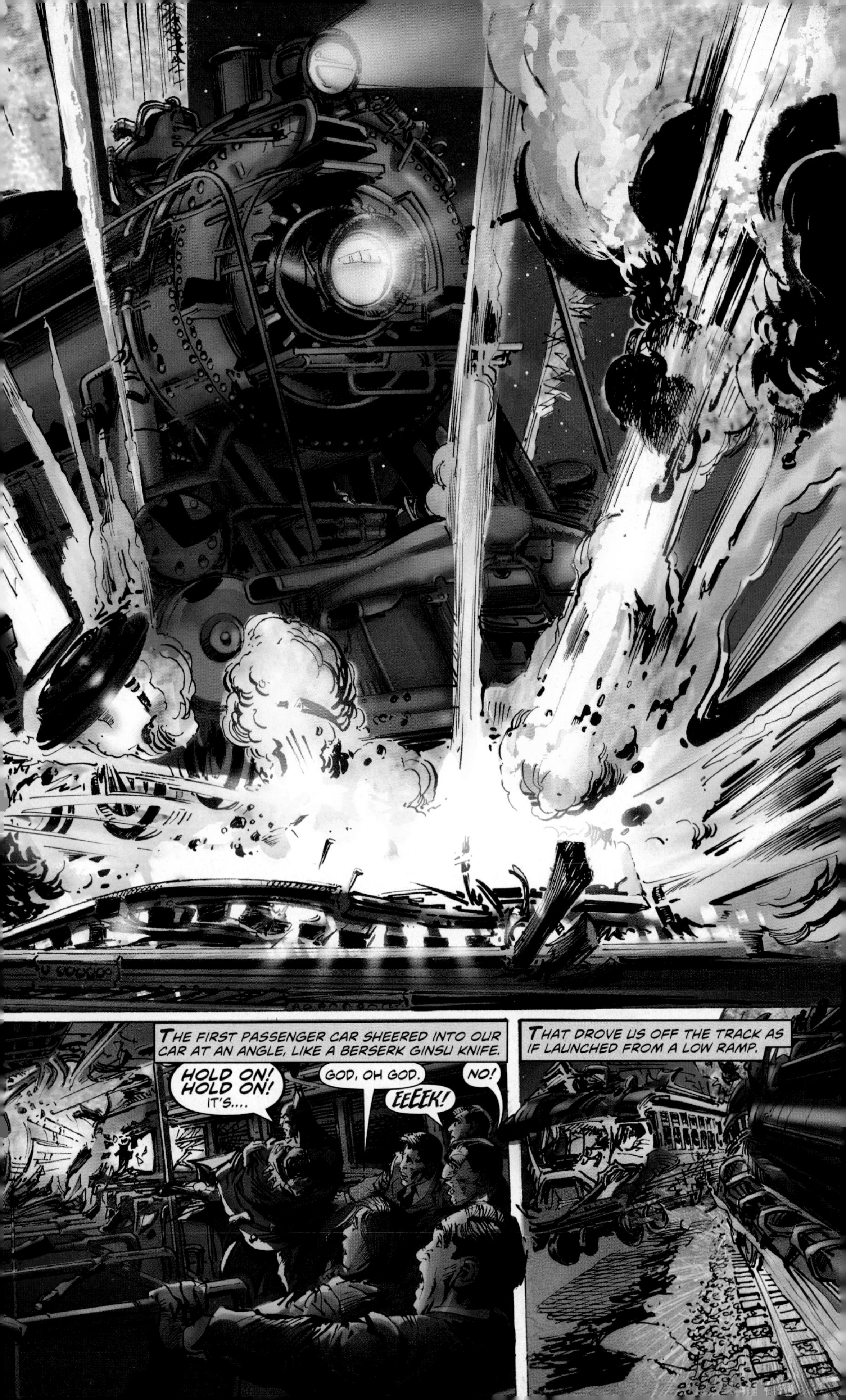
THE FIRST PASSENGER CAR SHEERED INTO OUR CAR AT AN ANGLE, LIKE A BERSERK GINSU KNIFE.
HOLD ON! HOLD ON! IT'S....
GOD, OH GOD.
EEEEK!
NO!
THAT DROVE US OFF THE TRACK AS IF LAUNCHED FROM A LOW RAMP.

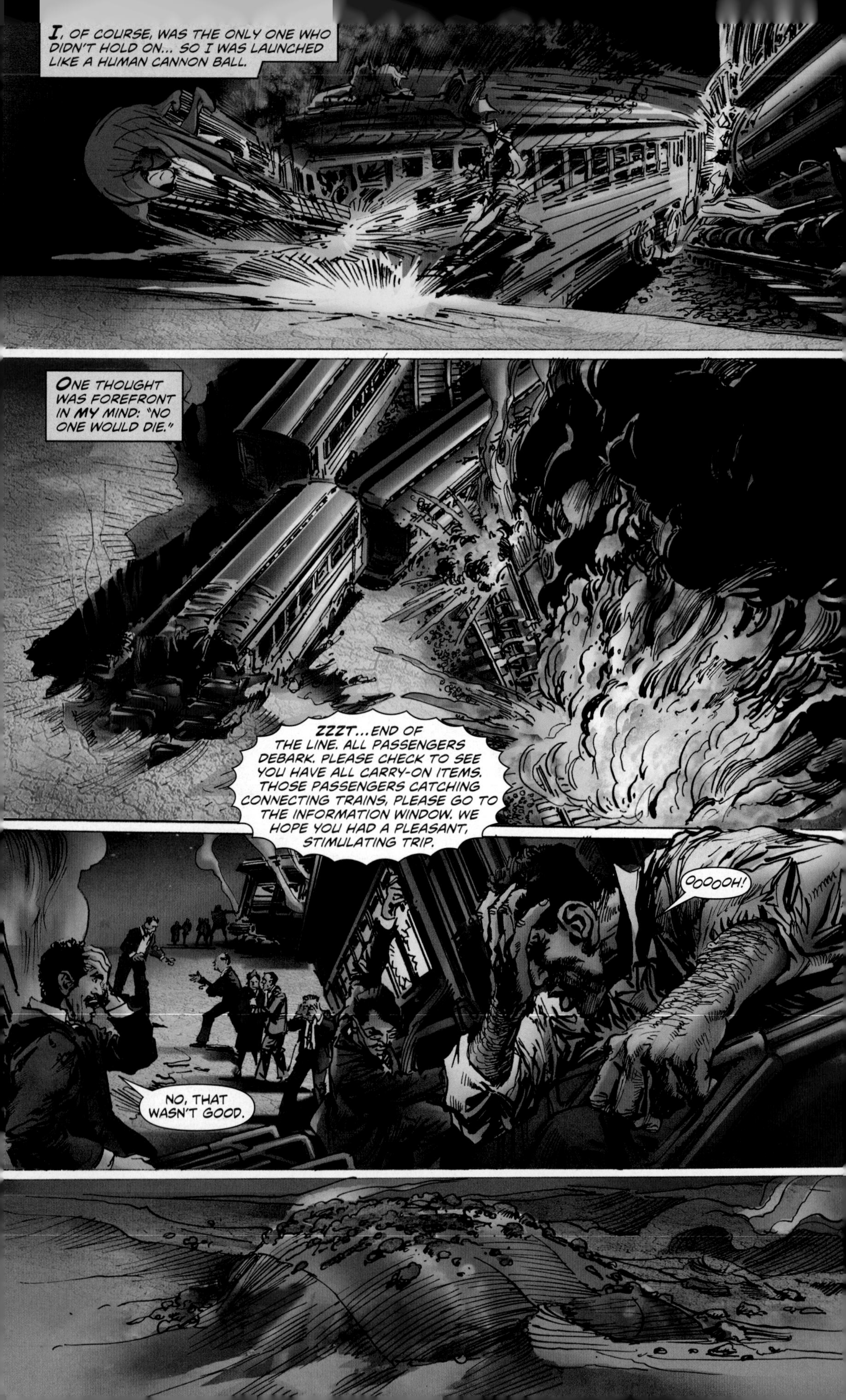
I, OF COURSE, WAS THE ONLY ONE WHO DIDN'T HOLD ON... SO I WAS LAUNCHED LIKE A HUMAN CANNON BALL.
ONE THOUGHT WAS FOREFRONT IN MY MIND: "NO ONE WOULD DIE."
ZZZT...END OF THE LINE. ALL PASSENGERS DEBARK. PLEASE CHECK TO SEE YOU HAVE ALL CARRY-ON ITEMS. THOSE PASSENGERS CATCHING CONNECTING TRAINS, PLEASE GO TO THE INFORMATION WINDOW. WE HOPE YOU HAD A PLEASANT, STIMULATING TRIP.
OOOOOH!
NO, THAT WASN'T GOOD.

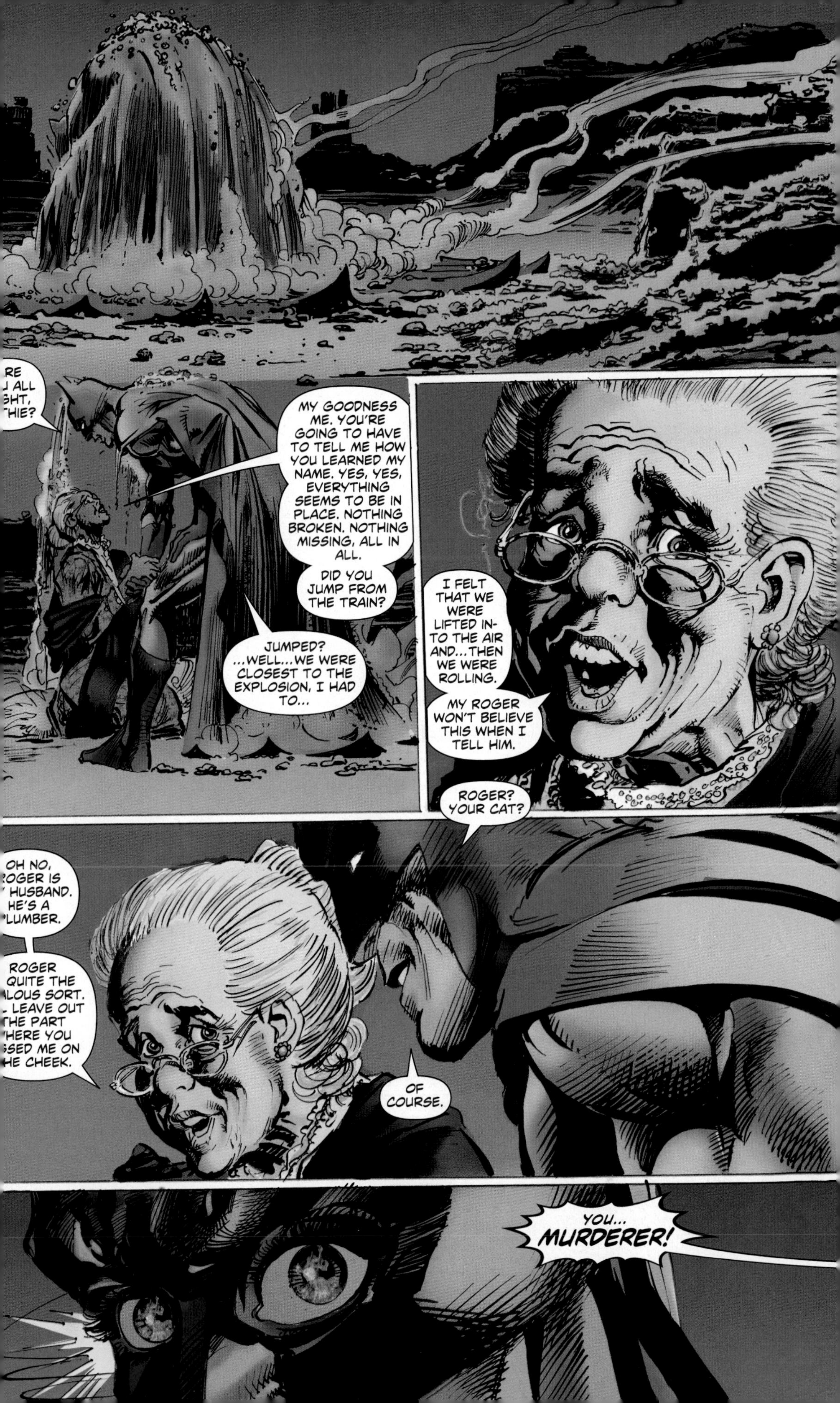
RE U ALL GHT, THIE?
MY GOODNESS ME. YOU'RE GOING TO HAVE TO TELL ME HOW YOU LEARNED MY NAME. YES, YES, EVERYTHING SEEMS TO BE IN PLACE. NOTHING BROKEN. NOTHING MISSING, ALL IN ALL.
DID YOU JUMP FROM THE TRAIN?
JUMPED? ...WELL...WE WERE CLOSEST TO THE EXPLOSION, I HAD TO...
I FELT THAT WE WERE LIFTED IN-TO THE AIR AND...THEN WE WERE ROLLING.
MY ROGER WON'T BELIEVE THIS WHEN I TELL HIM.
ROGER? YOUR CAT?
OH NO, OGER IS HUSBAND. HE'S A LUMBER.
ROGER QUITE THE LOUS SORT. LEAVE OUT THE PART HERE YOU SED ME ON HE CHEEK.
OF COURSE.
YOU... MURDERER!

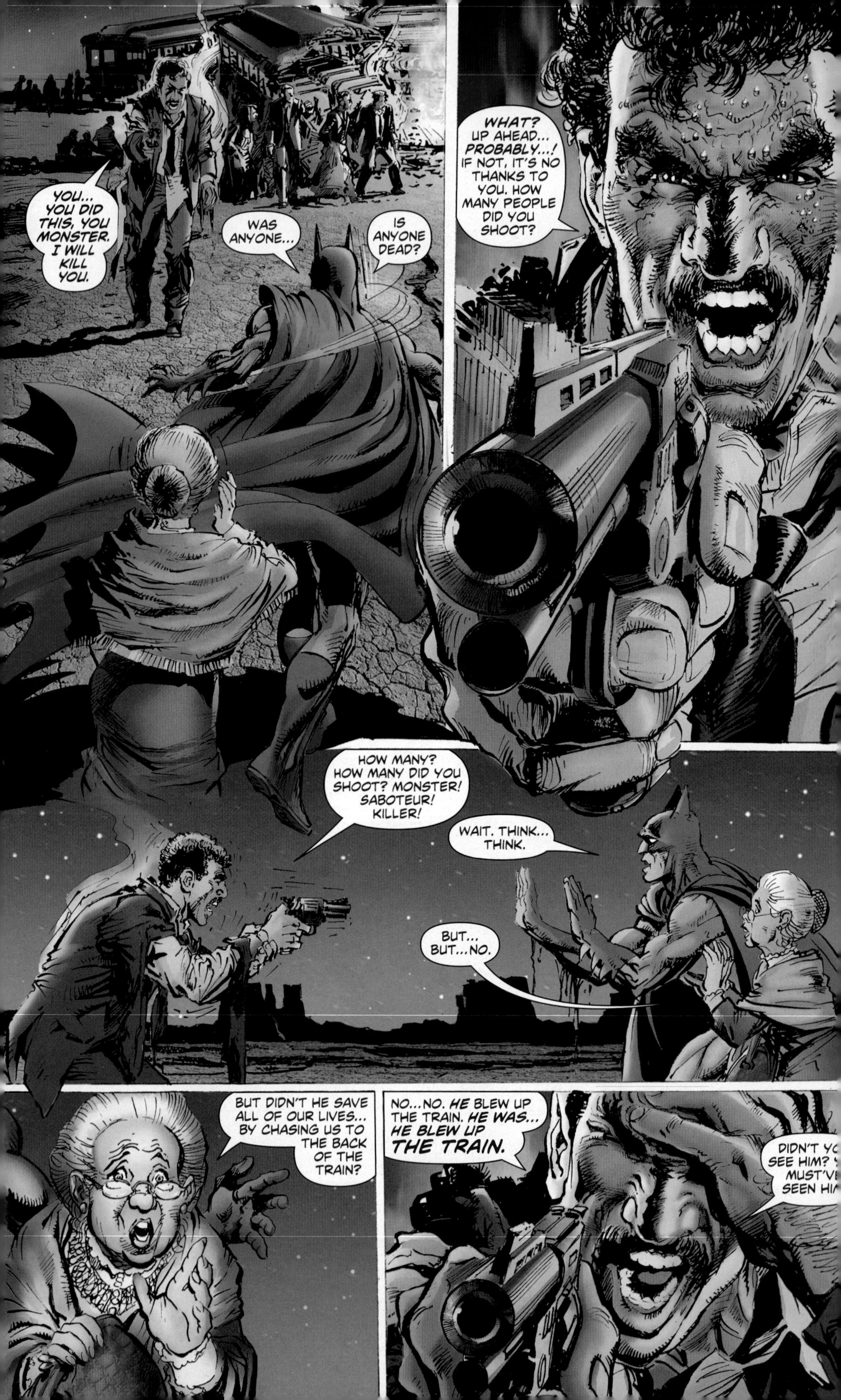

YOU... YOU DID THIS, YOU MONSTER. I WILL KILL YOU.
WAS ANYONE...
IS ANYONE DEAD?
WHAT? UP AHEAD... PROBABLY...! IF NOT, IT'S NO THANKS TO YOU. HOW MANY PEOPLE DID YOU SHOOT?
HOW MANY? HOW MANY DID YOU SHOOT? MONSTER! SABOTEUR! KILLER!
WAIT. THINK... THINK.
BUT... BUT...NO.
BUT DIDN'T HE SAVE ALL OF OUR LIVES... BY CHASING US TO THE BACK OF THE TRAIN?
NO...NO. HE BLEW UP THE TRAIN. HE WAS... HE BLEW UP THE TRAIN.

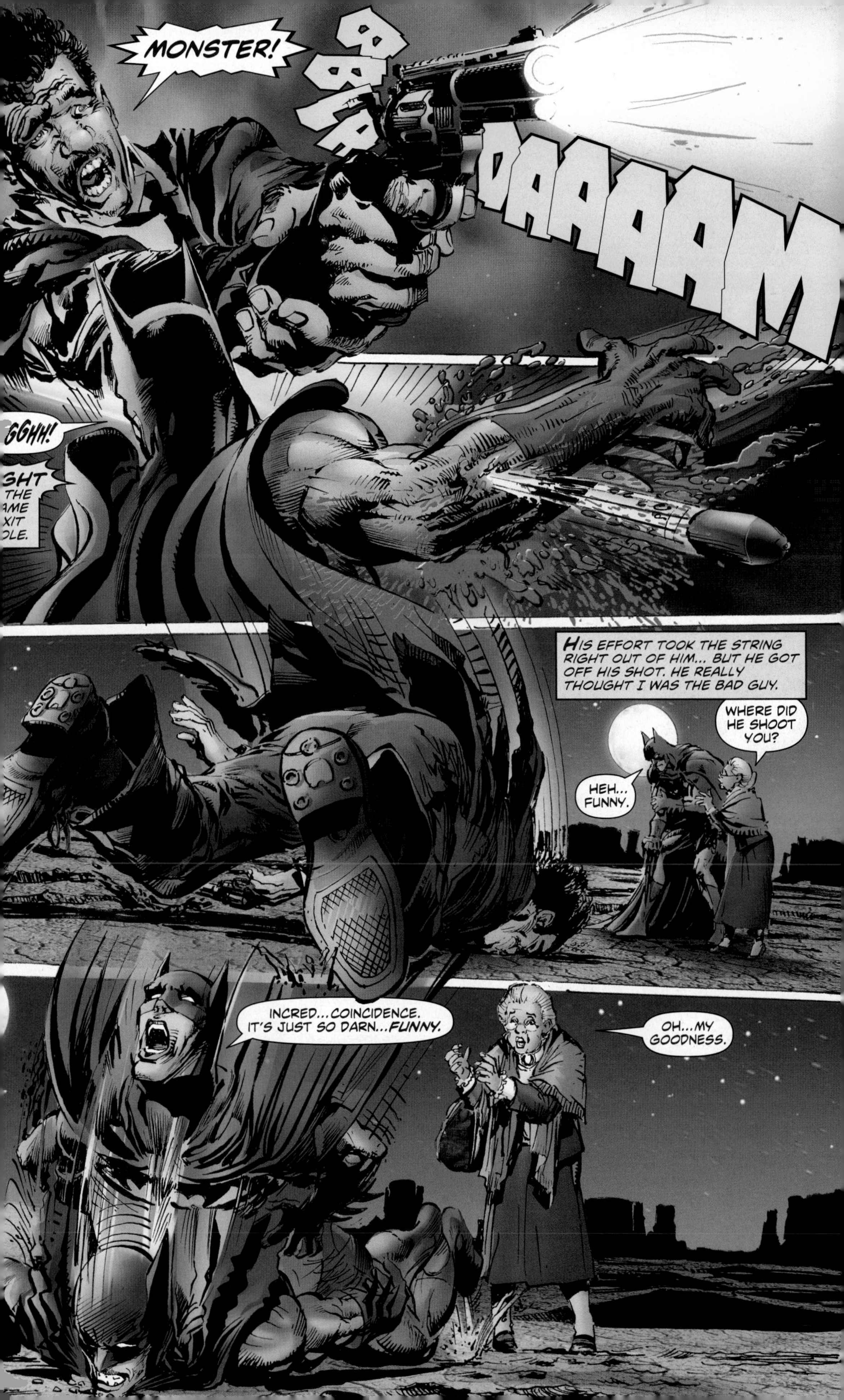
MONSTER!
BBLA
DAAAAAM
GGHH!
GHT THE AME XIT OLE.
HIS EFFORT TOOK THE STRING RIGHT OUT OF HIM... BUT HE GOT OFF HIS SHOT. HE REALLY THOUGHT I WAS THE BAD GUY.
WHERE DID HE SHOOT YOU?
HEH... FUNNY.
INCRED...COINCIDENCE. IT'S JUST SO DARN...FUNNY.
OH...MY GOODNESS.

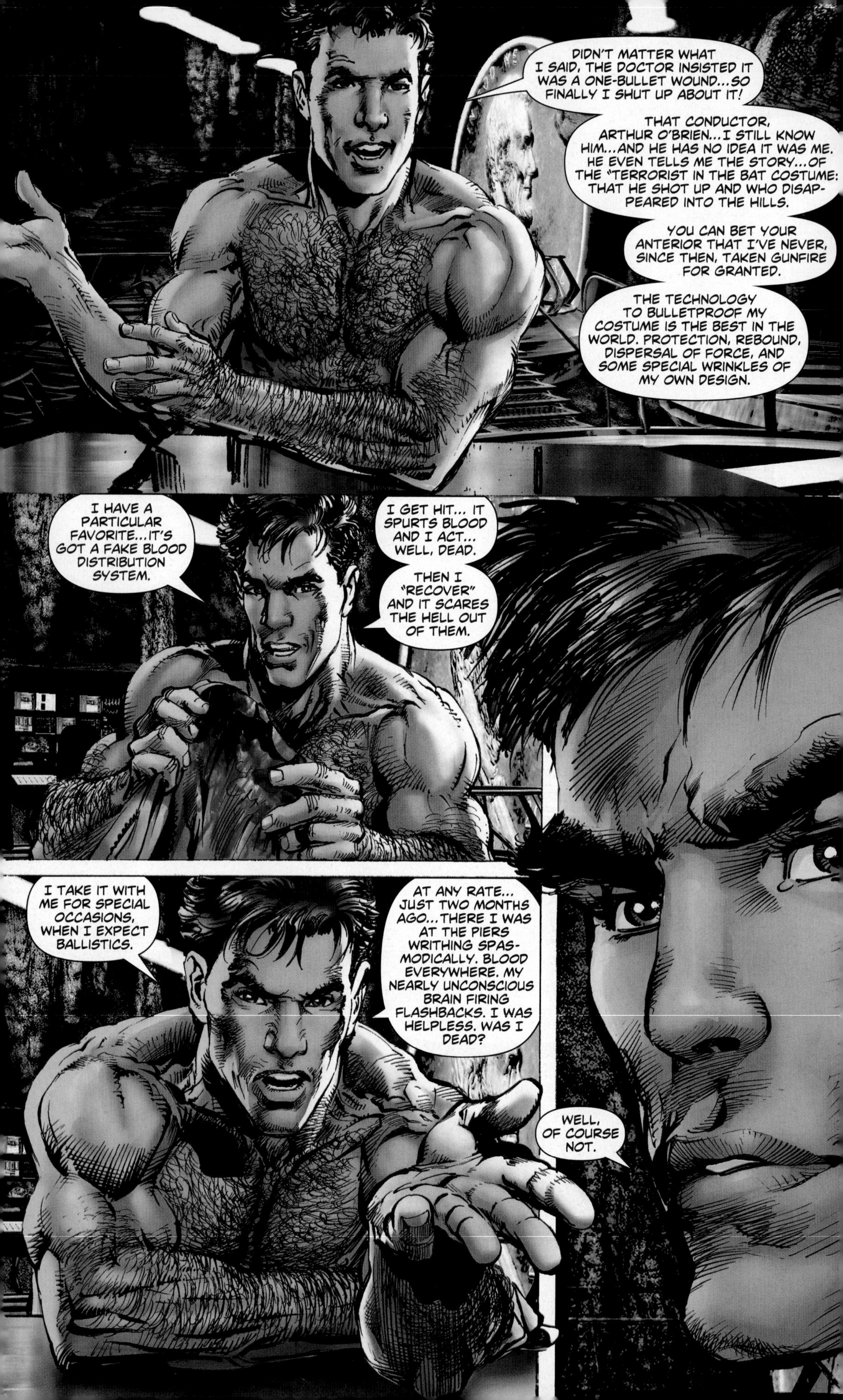
DIDN'T MATTER WHAT I SAID, THE DOCTOR INSISTED IT WAS A ONE-BULLET WOUND...SO FINALLY I SHUT UP ABOUT IT!
THAT CONDUCTOR, ARTHUR O'BRIEN...I STILL KNOW HIM...AND HE HAS NO IDEA IT WAS ME. HE EVEN TELLS ME THE STORY...OF THE "TERRORIST IN THE BAT COSTUME: THAT HE SHOT UP AND WHO DISAPPEARED INTO THE HILLS.
YOU CAN BET YOUR ANTERIOR THAT I'VE NEVER, SINCE THEN, TAKEN GUNFIRE FOR GRANTED.
THE TECHNOLOGY TO BULLETPROOF MY COSTUME IS THE BEST IN THE WORLD. PROTECTION, REBOUND, DISPERSAL OF FORCE, AND SOME SPECIAL WRINKLES OF MY OWN DESIGN.
I HAVE A PARTICULAR FAVORITE...IT'S GOT A FAKE BLOOD DISTRIBUTION SYSTEM.
I GET HIT... IT SPURTS BLOOD AND I ACT... WELL, DEAD.
THEN I "RECOVER" AND IT SCARES THE HELL OUT OF THEM.
I TAKE IT WITH ME FOR SPECIAL OCCASIONS, WHEN I EXPECT BALLISTICS.
AT ANY RATE... JUST TWO MONTHS AGO...THERE I WAS AT THE PIERS WRITHING SPASMODICALLY. BLOOD EVERYWHERE. MY NEARLY UNCONSCIOUS BRAIN FIRING FLASHBACKS. I WAS HELPLESS. WAS I DEAD?
WELL, OF COURSE NOT.

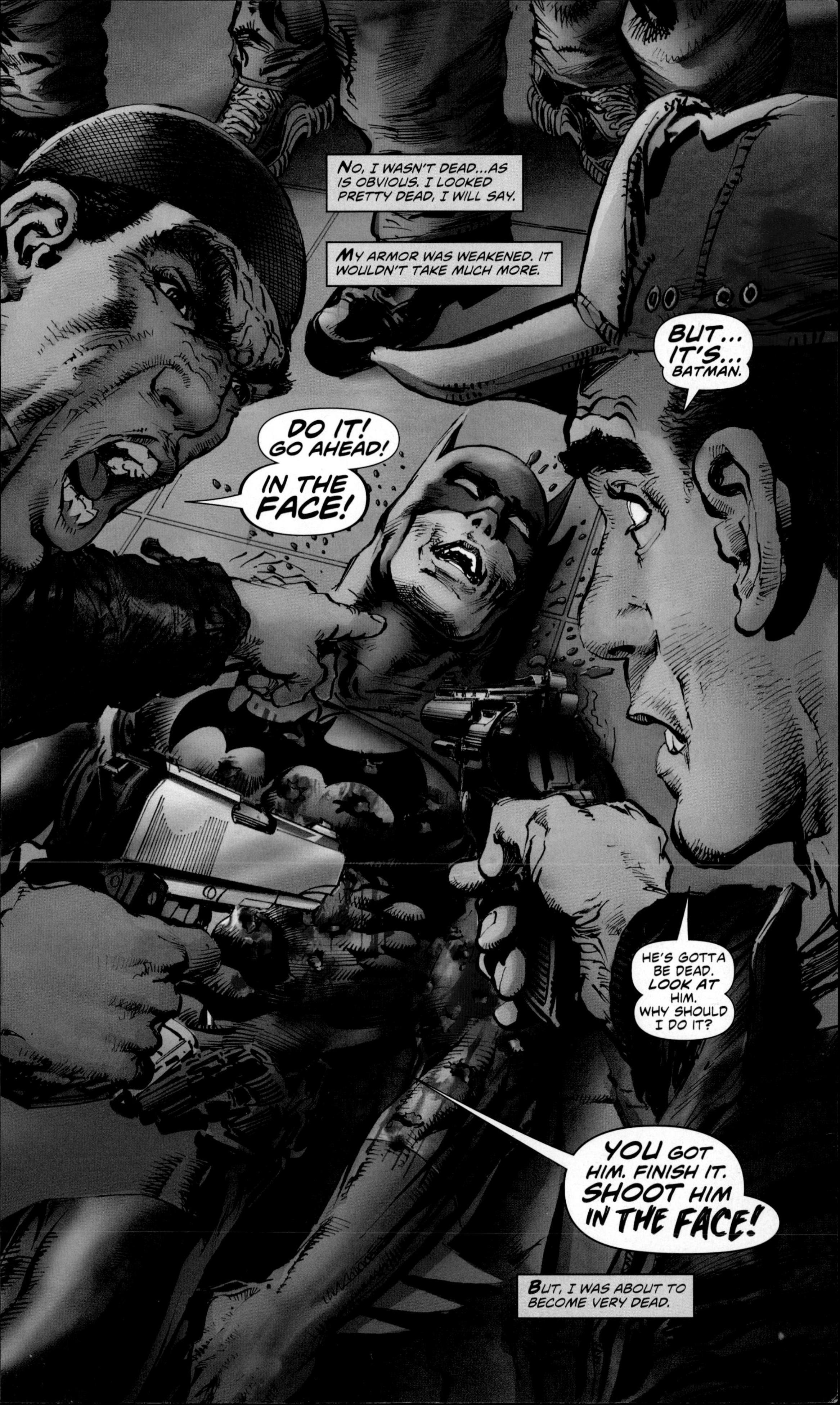
NO, I WASN'T DEAD...AS IS OBVIOUS. I LOOKED PRETTY DEAD, I WILL SAY.
MY ARMOR WAS WEAKENED. IT WOULDN'T TAKE MUCH MORE.
BUT... IT'S... BATMAN.
DO IT! GO AHEAD!
IN THE FACE!
HE'S GOTTA BE DEAD. LOOK AT HIM. WHY SHOULD I DO IT?
YOU GOT HIM. FINISH IT. SHOOT HIM IN THE FACE!
BUT, I WAS ABOUT TO BECOME VERY DEAD.

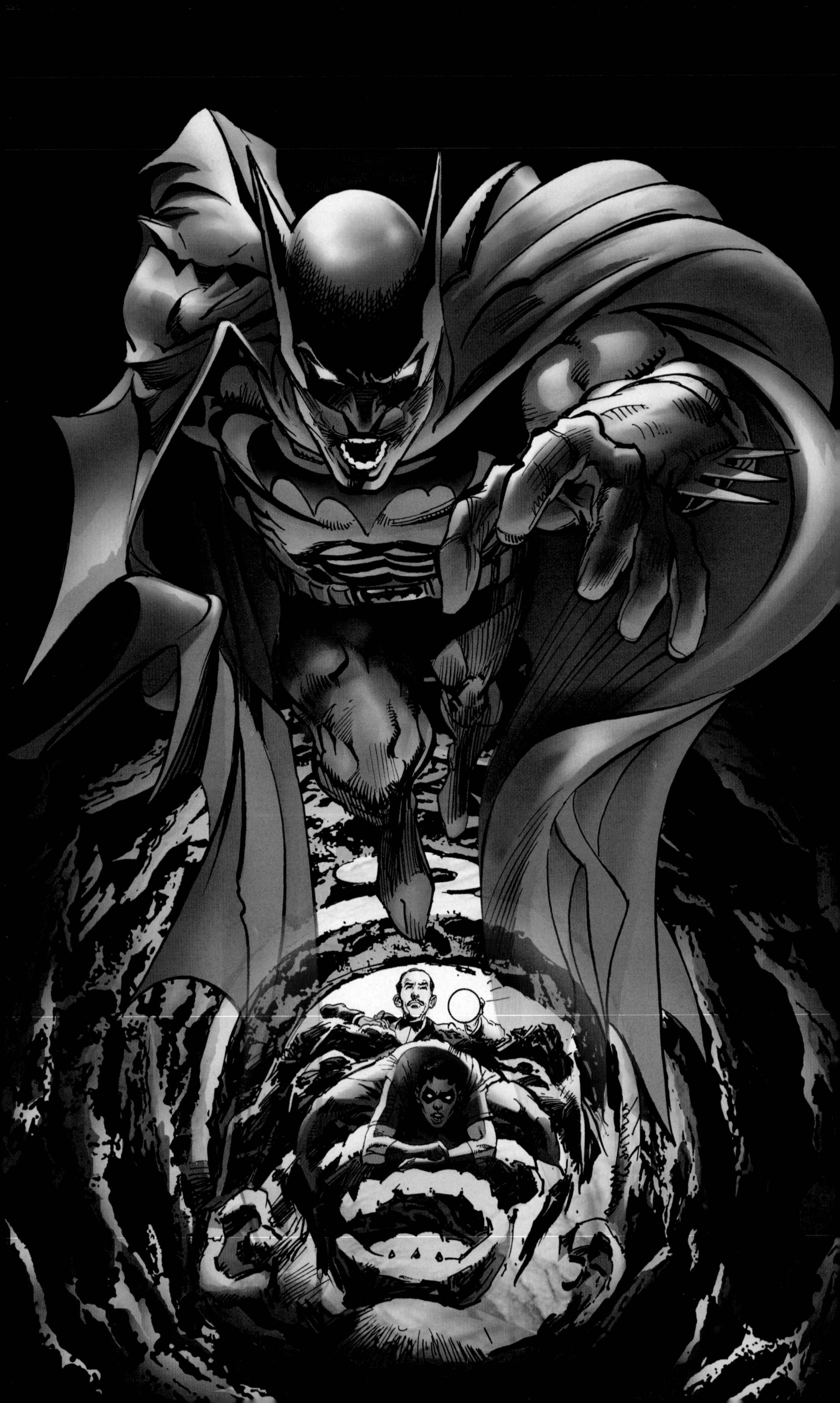

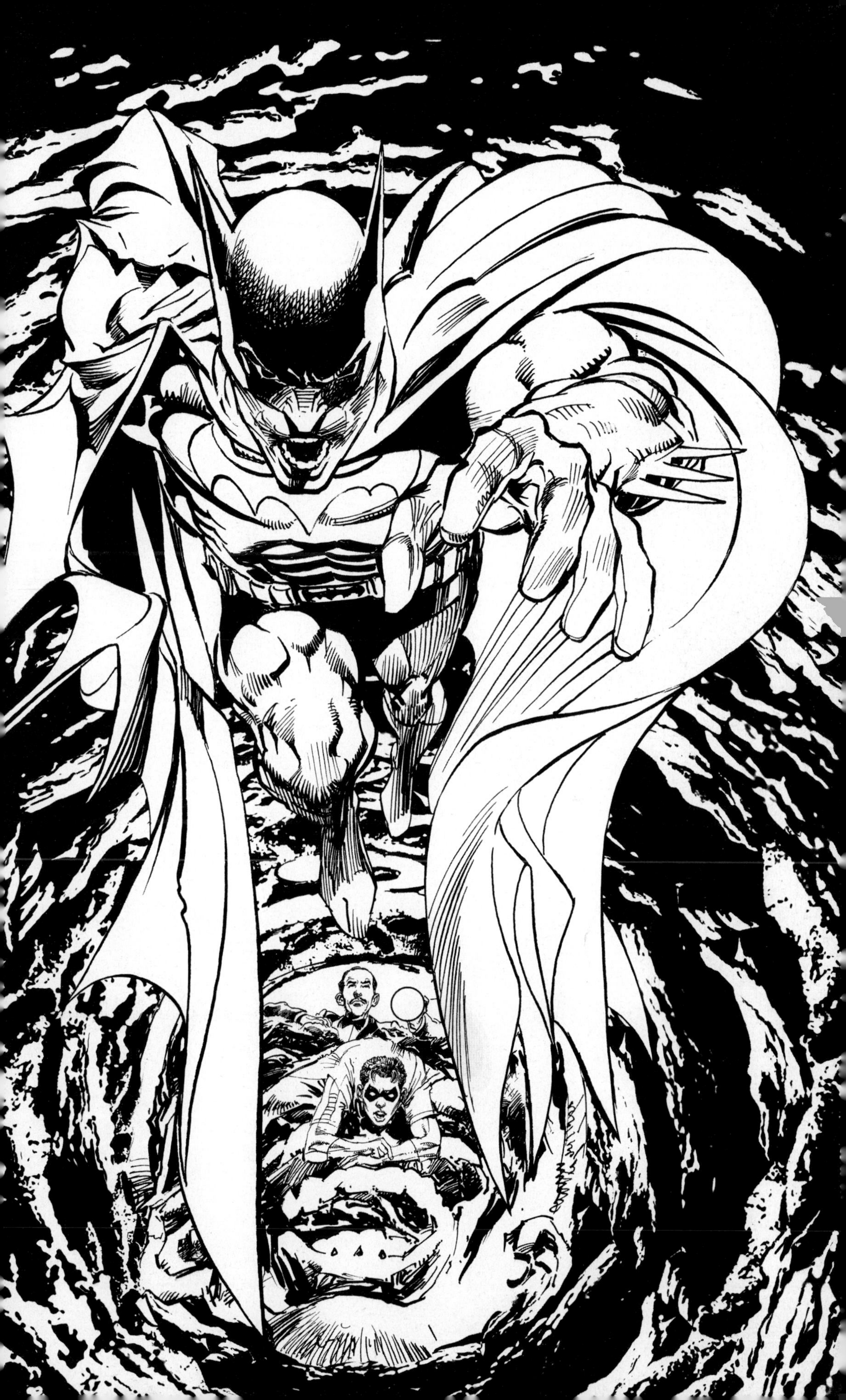

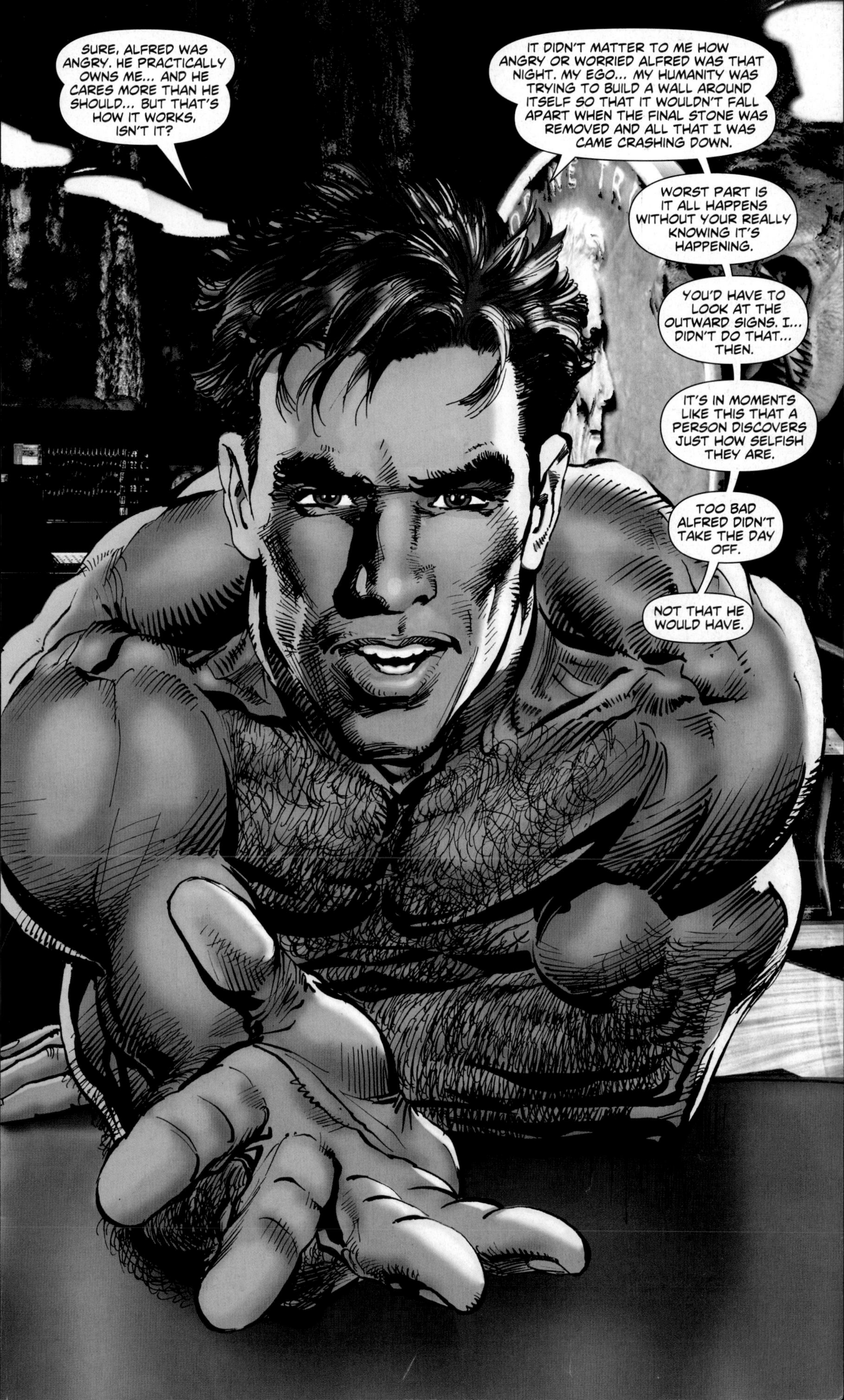

SURE, ALFRED WAS ANGRY. HE PRACTICALLY OWNS ME... AND HE CARES MORE THAN HE SHOULD... BUT THAT'S HOW IT WORKS, ISN'T IT?
IT DIDN'T MATTER TO ME HOW ANGRY OR WORRIED ALFRED WAS THAT NIGHT. MY EGO... MY HUMANITY WAS TRYING TO BUILD A WALL AROUND ITSELF SO THAT IT WOULDN'T FALL APART WHEN THE FINAL STONE WAS REMOVED AND ALL THAT I WAS CAME CRASHING DOWN.
WORST PART IS IT ALL HAPPENS WITHOUT YOUR REALLY KNOWING IT'S HAPPENING.
YOU'D HAVE TO LOOK AT THE OUTWARD SIGNS. I... DIDN'T DO THAT... THEN.
IT'S IN MOMENTS LIKE THIS THAT A PERSON DISCOVERS JUST HOW SELFISH THEY ARE.
TOO BAD ALFRED DIDN'T TAKE THE DAY OFF.
NOT THAT HE WOULD HAVE.

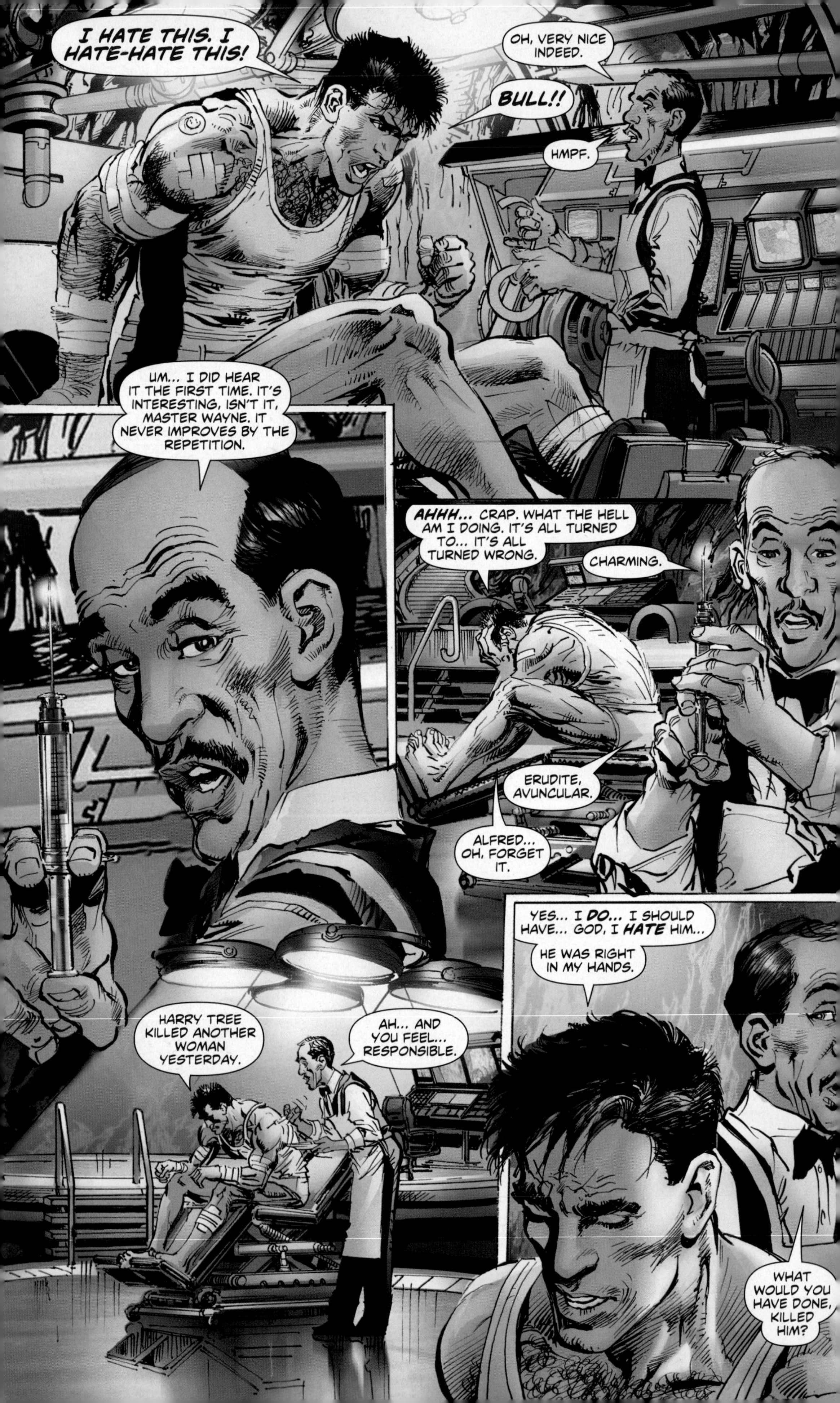

I HATE THIS. I HATE-HATE THIS!
OH, VERY NICE INDEED.
BULL!!
HMPF.
UM... I DID HEAR IT THE FIRST TIME. IT'S INTERESTING, ISN'T IT, MASTER WAYNE. IT NEVER IMPROVES BY THE REPETITION.
AHHH... CRAP. WHAT THE HELL AM I DOING. IT'S ALL TURNED TO... IT'S ALL TURNED WRONG.
CHARMING.
ERUDITE, AVUNCULAR.
ALFRED... OH, FORGET IT.
HARRY TREE KILLED ANOTHER WOMAN YESTERDAY.
AH... AND YOU FEEL... RESPONSIBLE.
YES... I DO... I SHOULD HAVE... GOD, I HATE HIM...
HE WAS RIGHT IN MY HANDS.
WHAT WOULD YOU HAVE DONE, KILLED HIM?

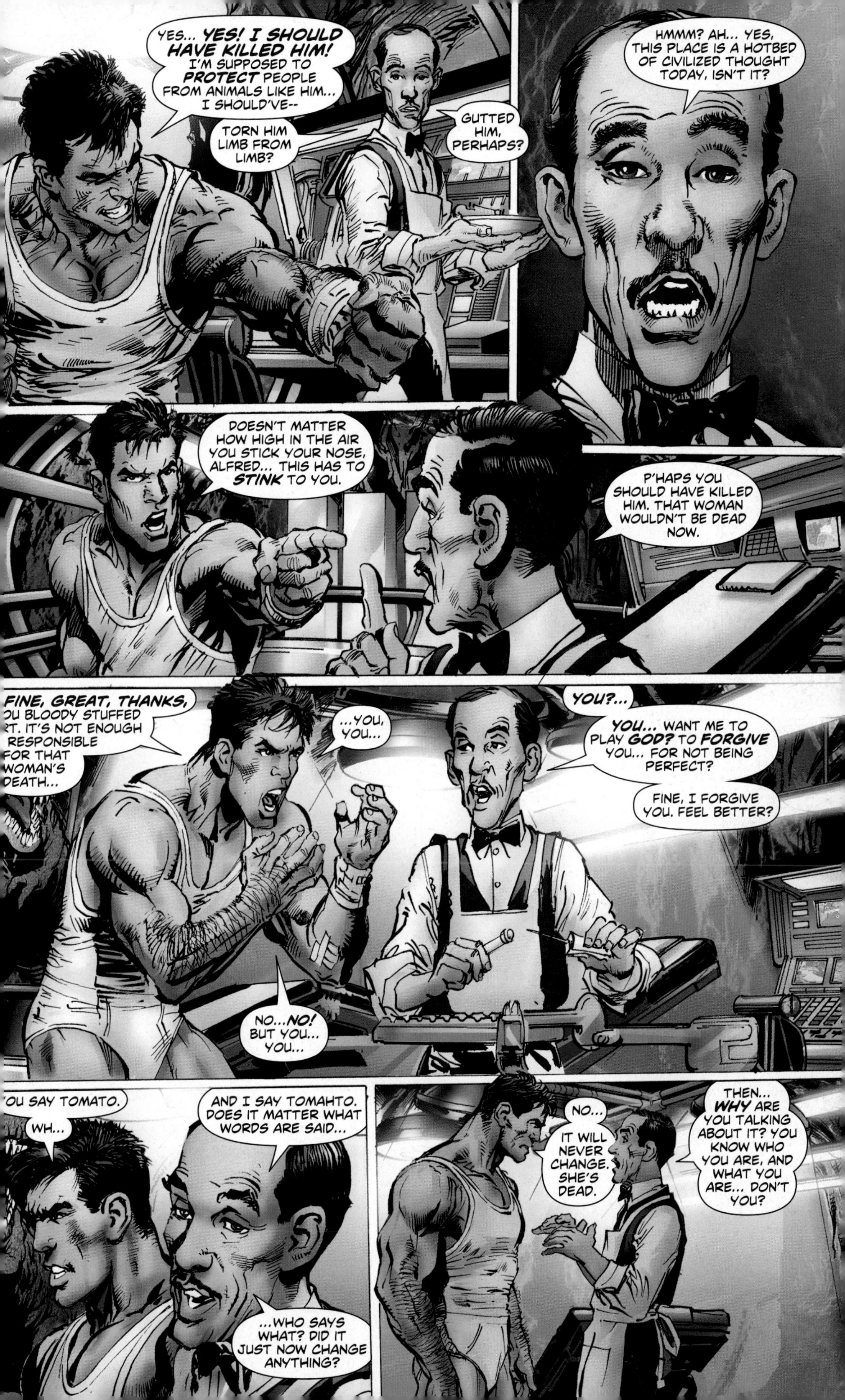

YES... YES! I SHOULD HAVE KILLED HIM! I'M SUPPOSED TO PROTECT PEOPLE FROM ANIMALS LIKE HIM... I SHOULD'VE--
TORN HIM LIMB FROM LIMB?
GUTTED HIM, PERHAPS?
HMMM? AH... YES, THIS PLACE IS A HOTBED OF CIVILIZED THOUGHT TODAY, ISN'T IT?
DOESN'T MATTER HOW HIGH IN THE AIR YOU STICK YOUR NOSE, ALFRED... THIS HAS TO STINK TO YOU.
P'HAPS YOU SHOULD HAVE KILLED HIM. THAT WOMAN WOULDN'T BE DEAD NOW.
FINE, GREAT, THANKS,
OU BLOODY STUFFED RT. IT'S NOT ENOUGH RESPONSIBLE FOR THAT WOMAN'S DEATH...
...YOU, YOU...
YOU?...
YOU... WANT ME TO PLAY GOD? TO FORGIVE YOU... FOR NOT BEING PERFECT?
FINE, I FORGIVE YOU. FEEL BETTER?
NO...NO! BUT YOU... YOU...
OU SAY TOMATO.
WH...
AND I SAY TOMAHTO. DOES IT MATTER WHAT WORDS ARE SAID...
...WHO SAYS WHAT? DID IT JUST NOW CHANGE ANYTHING?
NO...
IT WILL NEVER CHANGE. SHE'S DEAD.
THEN... WHY ARE YOU TALKING ABOUT IT? YOU KNOW WHO YOU ARE, AND WHAT YOU ARE... DON'T YOU?

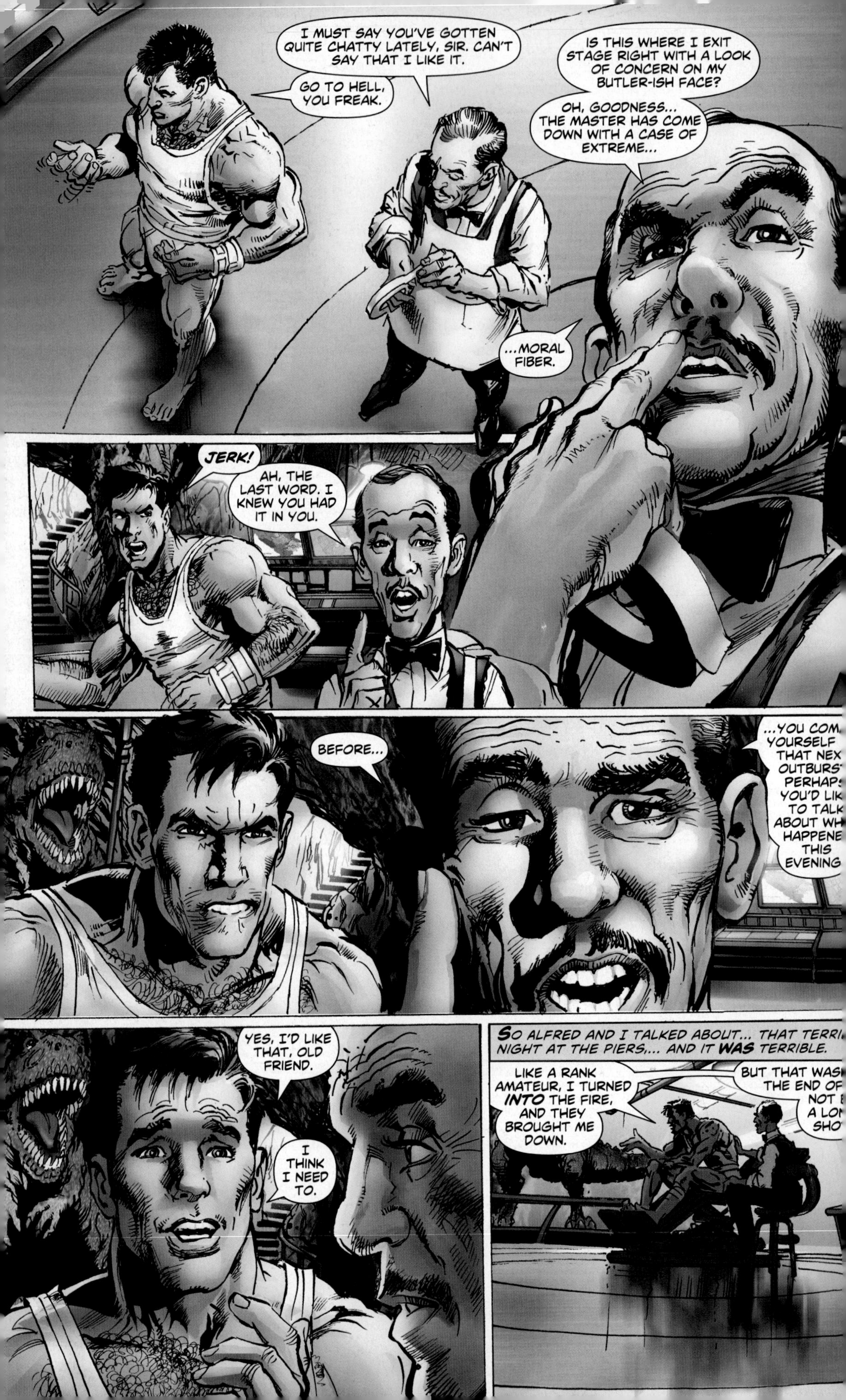
I MUST SAY YOU'VE GOTTEN QUITE CHATTY LATELY, SIR. CAN'T SAY THAT I LIKE IT.
GO TO HELL, YOU FREAK.
IS THIS WHERE I EXIT STAGE RIGHT WITH A LOOK OF CONCERN ON MY BUTLER-ISH FACE?
OH, GOODNESS... THE MASTER HAS COME DOWN WITH A CASE OF EXTREME...
...MORAL FIBER.
JERK!
AH, THE LAST WORD. I KNEW YOU HAD IT IN YOU.
BEFORE...
...YOU COM
YOURSELF
THAT NEX
OUTBURS
PERHAP
YOU'D LIK
TO TALK
ABOUT WH
HAPPENE
THIS
EVENING
YES, I'D LIKE THAT, OLD FRIEND.
I THINK I NEED TO.
SO ALFRED AND I TALKED ABOUT... THAT TERRI
NIGHT AT THE PIERS,... AND IT WAS TERRIBLE.
LIKE A RANK AMATEUR, I TURNED INTO THE FIRE, AND THEY BROUGHT ME DOWN.
BUT THAT WAS
THE END OF
NOT
A LON
SHO

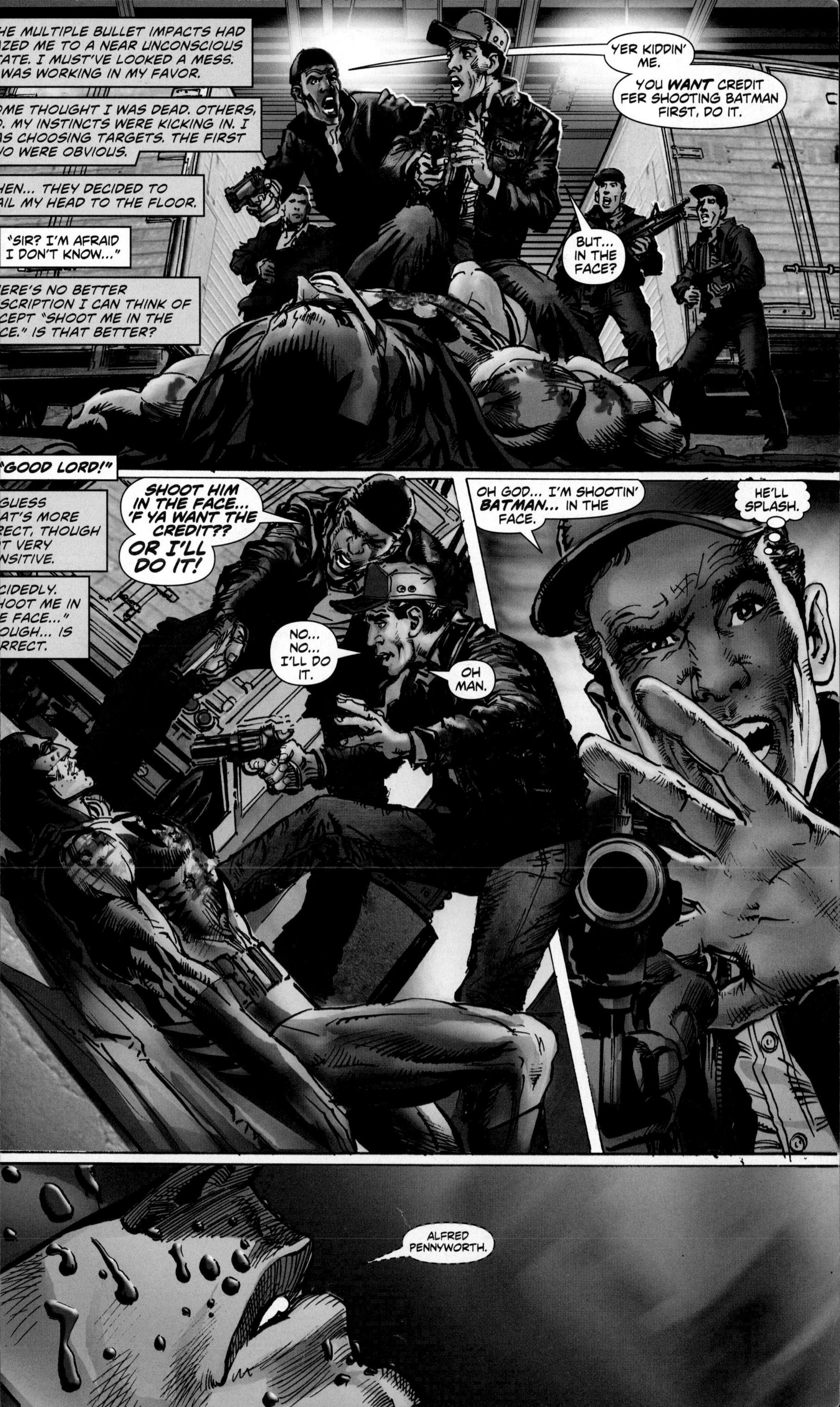

HE MULTIPLE BULLET IMPACTS HAD ZED ME TO A NEAR UNCONSCIOUS TATE. I MUST'VE LOOKED A MESS. WAS WORKING IN MY FAVOR.
YER KIDDIN' ME.
YOU WANT CREDIT FER SHOOTING BATMAN FIRST, DO IT.
OME THOUGHT I WAS DEAD. OTHERS, O. MY INSTINCTS WERE KICKING IN. I AS CHOOSING TARGETS. THE FIRST WO WERE OBVIOUS.
HEN... THEY DECIDED TO AIL MY HEAD TO THE FLOOR.
"SIR? I'M AFRAID I DON'T KNOW..."
BUT... IN THE FACE?
ERE'S NO BETTER SCRIPTION I CAN THINK OF CEPT "SHOOT ME IN THE CE." IS THAT BETTER?
"GOOD LORD!"
GUESS AT'S MORE RECT, THOUGH T VERY NSITIVE.
SHOOT HIM IN THE FACE... 'F YA WANT THE CREDIT?? OR I'LL DO IT!
CIDEDLY. HOOT ME IN E FACE..." OUGH... IS RRECT.
NO... NO... I'LL DO IT.
OH MAN.
OH GOD... I'M SHOOTIN' BATMAN... IN THE FACE.
HE'LL SPLASH.
ALFRED PENNYWORTH.

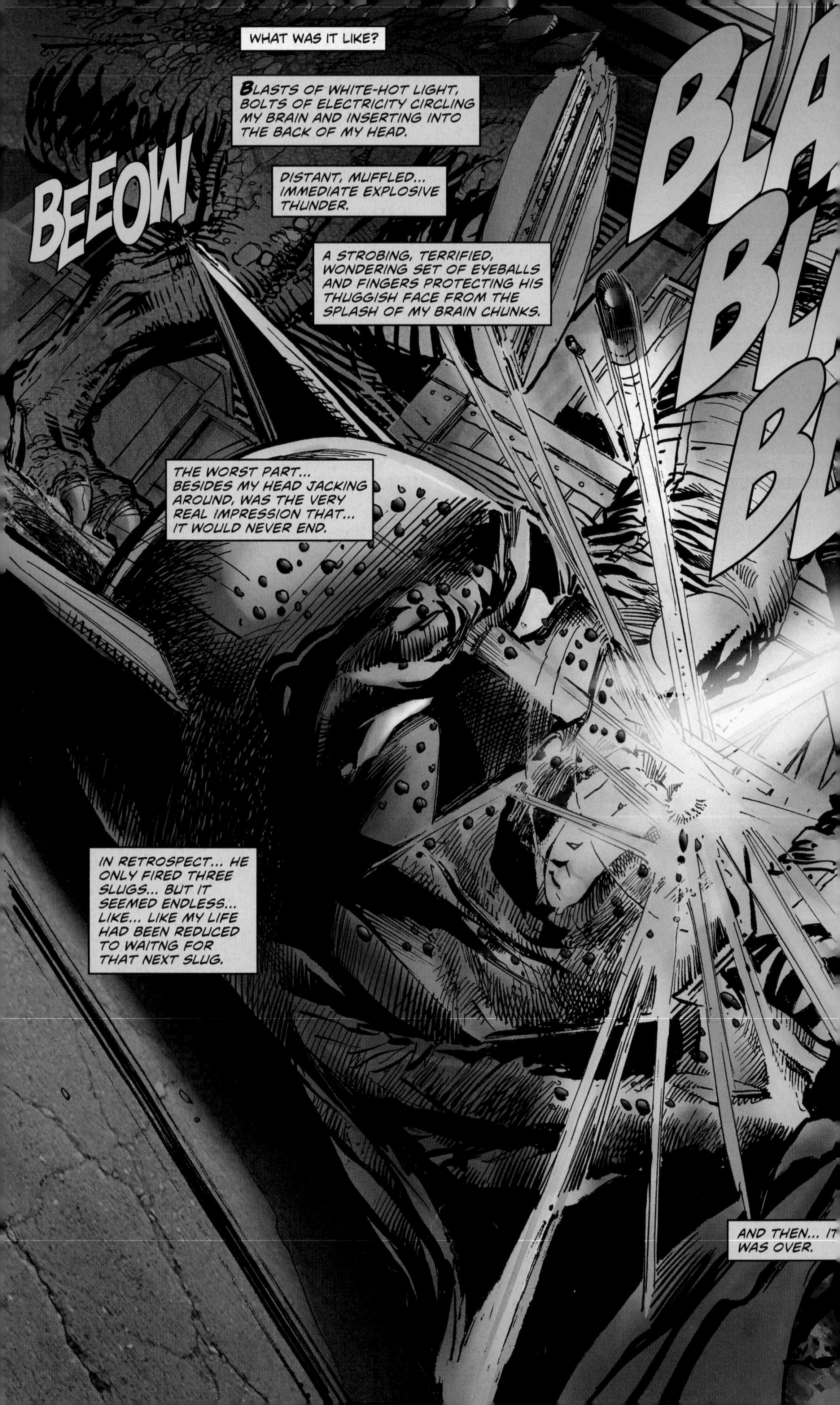

WHAT WAS IT LIKE?
BLASTS OF WHITE-HOT LIGHT, BOLTS OF ELECTRICITY CIRCLING MY BRAIN AND INSERTING INTO THE BACK OF MY HEAD.
BEEOW
DISTANT, MUFFLED... IMMEDIATE EXPLOSIVE THUNDER.
A STROBING, TERRIFIED, WONDERING SET OF EYEBALLS AND FINGERS PROTECTING HIS THUGGISH FACE FROM THE SPLASH OF MY BRAIN CHUNKS.
THE WORST PART... BESIDES MY HEAD JACKING AROUND, WAS THE VERY REAL IMPRESSION THAT... IT WOULD NEVER END.
IN RETROSPECT... HE ONLY FIRED THREE SLUGS... BUT IT SEEMED ENDLESS... LIKE... LIKE MY LIFE HAD BEEN REDUCED TO WAITNG FOR THAT NEXT SLUG.
AND THEN... IT WAS OVER.

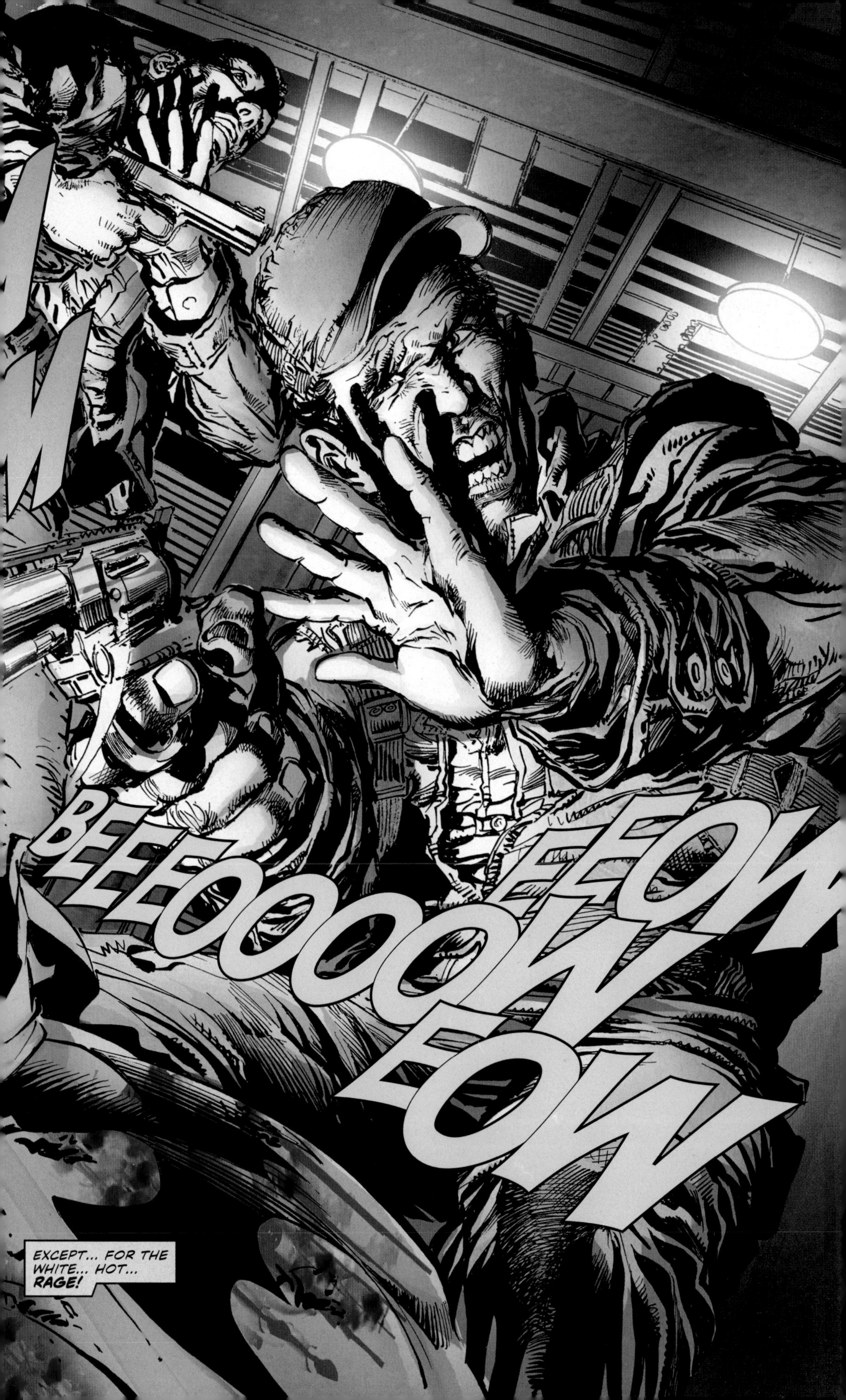
BEEEOOOOOOWEEOW
EOW
EXCEPT... FOR THE WHITE... HOT... **RAGE!**

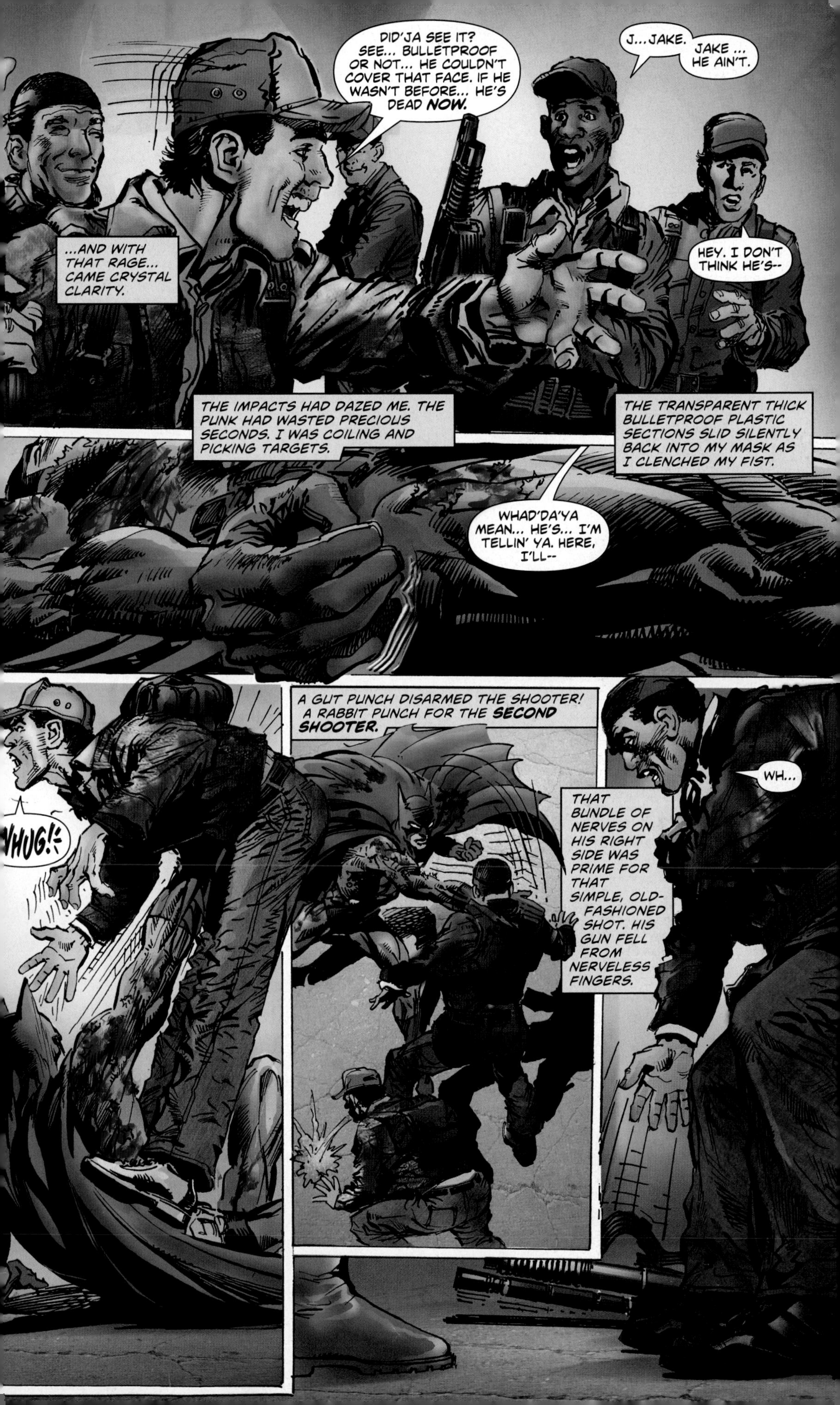
DID'JA SEE IT? SEE... BULLETPROOF OR NOT... HE COULDN'T COVER THAT FACE. IF HE WASN'T BEFORE... HE'S DEAD NOW.
J... JAKE.
JAKE ... HE AIN'T.
...AND WITH THAT RAGE... CAME CRYSTAL CLARITY.
HEY. I DON'T THINK HE'S--
THE IMPACTS HAD DAZED ME. THE PUNK HAD WASTED PRECIOUS SECONDS. I WAS COILING AND PICKING TARGETS.
THE TRANSPARENT THICK BULLETPROOF PLASTIC SECTIONS SLID SILENTLY BACK INTO MY MASK AS I CLENCHED MY FIST.
WHAD'DA'YA MEAN... HE'S... I'M TELLIN' YA. HERE, I'LL--
A GUT PUNCH DISARMED THE SHOOTER! A RABBIT PUNCH FOR THE SECOND SHOOTER.
WH...
THAT BUNDLE OF NERVES ON HIS RIGHT SIDE WAS PRIME FOR THAT SIMPLE, OLD-FASHIONED SHOT. HIS GUN FELL FROM NERVELESS FINGERS.

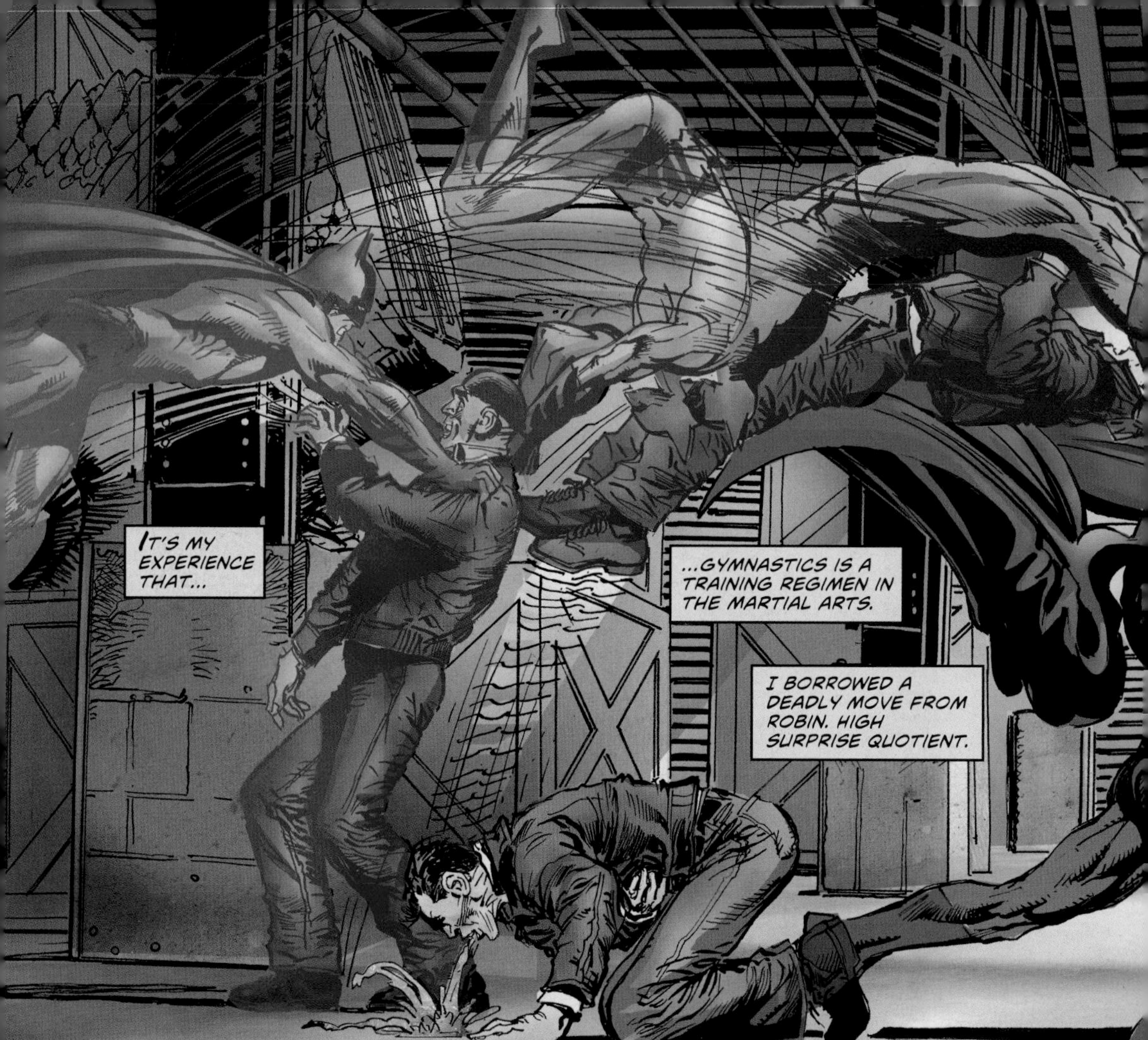
IT'S MY EXPERIENCE THAT...
...GYMNASTICS IS A TRAINING REGIMEN IN THE MARTIAL ARTS.
I BORROWED A DEADLY MOVE FROM ROBIN. HIGH SURPRISE QUOTIENT.

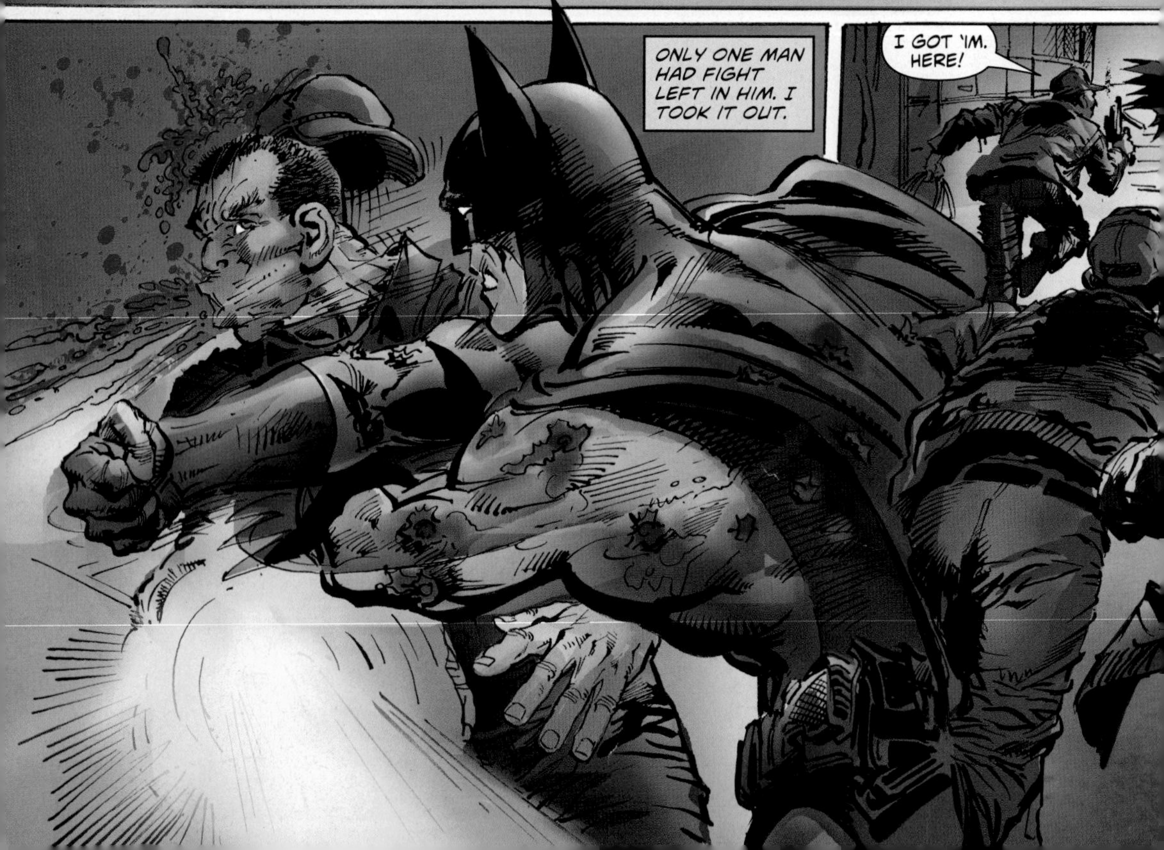
ONLY ONE MAN HAD FIGHT LEFT IN HIM. I TOOK IT OUT.
I GOT 'IM. HERE!

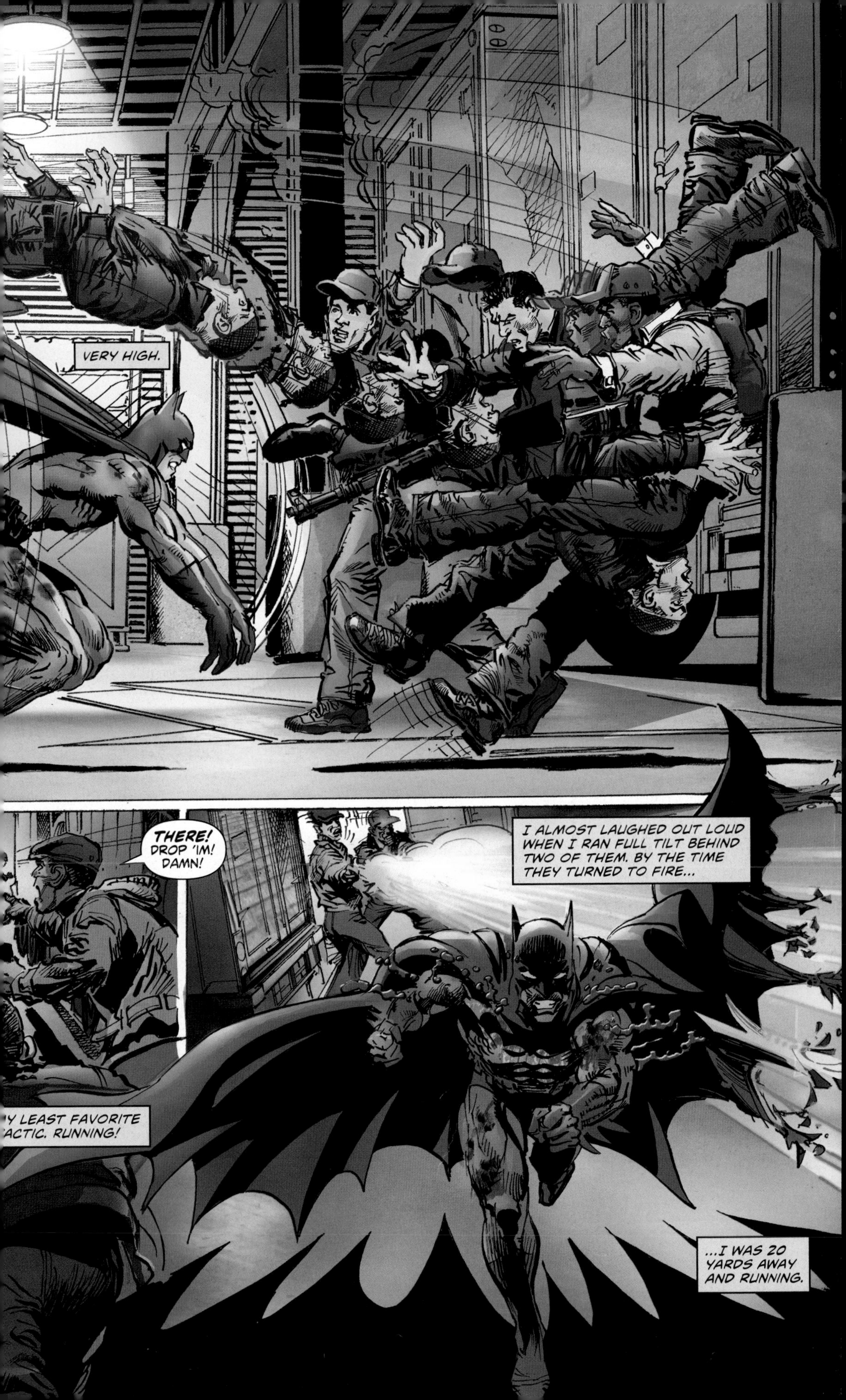
VERY HIGH.
THERE! DROP 'IM! DAMN!
I ALMOST LAUGHED OUT LOUD WHEN I RAN FULL TILT BEHIND TWO OF THEM. BY THE TIME THEY TURNED TO FIRE...
Y LEAST FAVORITE ACTIC. RUNNING!
...I WAS 20 YARDS AWAY AND RUNNING.

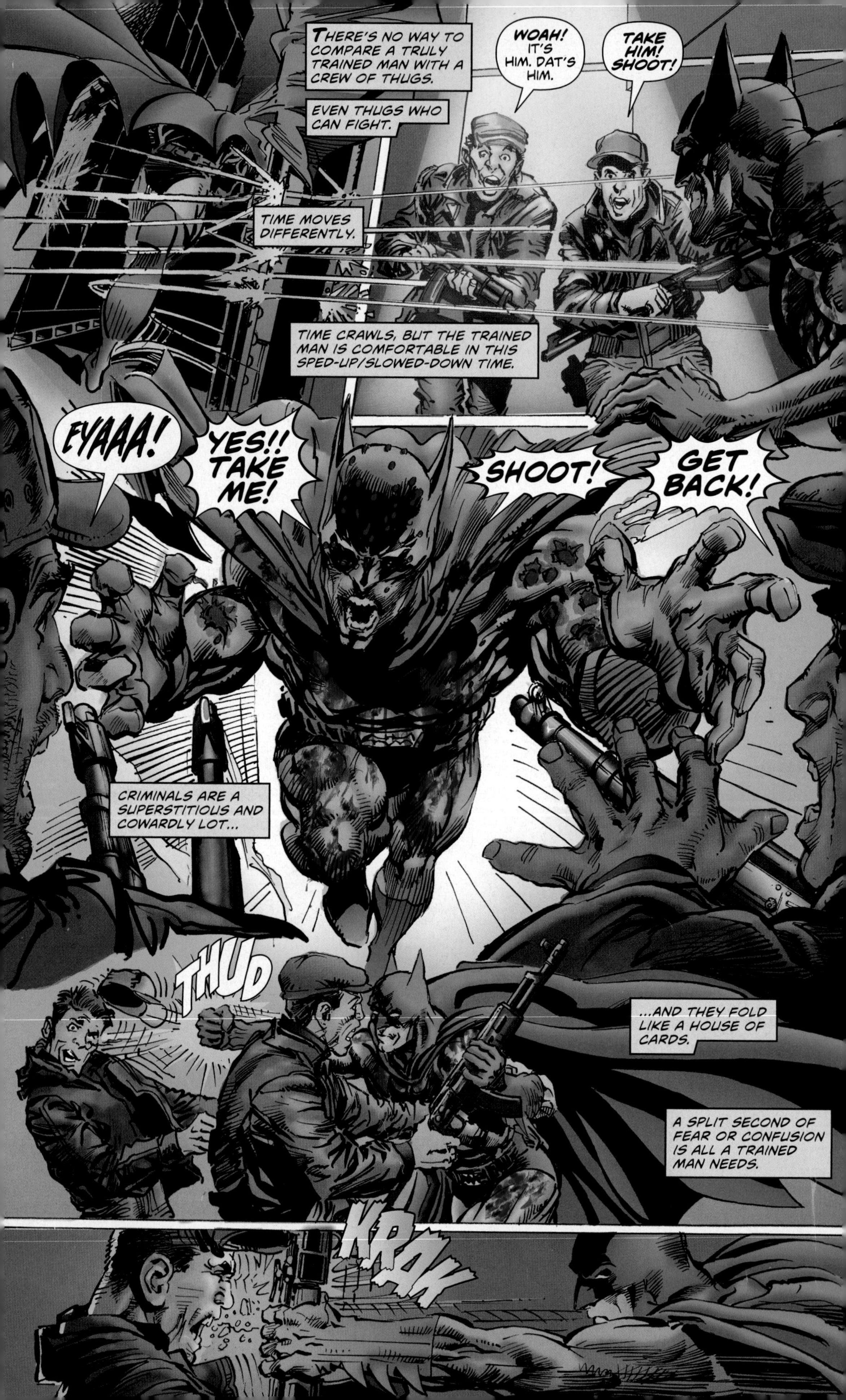
THERE'S NO WAY TO COMPARE A TRULY TRAINED MAN WITH A CREW OF THUGS.
EVEN THUGS WHO CAN FIGHT.
WOAH! IT'S HIM. DAT'S HIM.
TAKE HIM! SHOOT!
TIME MOVES DIFFERENTLY.
TIME CRAWLS, BUT THE TRAINED MAN IS COMFORTABLE IN THIS SPED-UP/SLOWED-DOWN TIME.
EYAAA!
YES!! TAKE ME!
SHOOT!
GET BACK!
CRIMINALS ARE A SUPERSTITIOUS AND COWARDLY LOT...
THUD
...AND THEY FOLD LIKE A HOUSE OF CARDS.
A SPLIT SECOND OF FEAR OR CONFUSION IS ALL A TRAINED MAN NEEDS.
KRAK

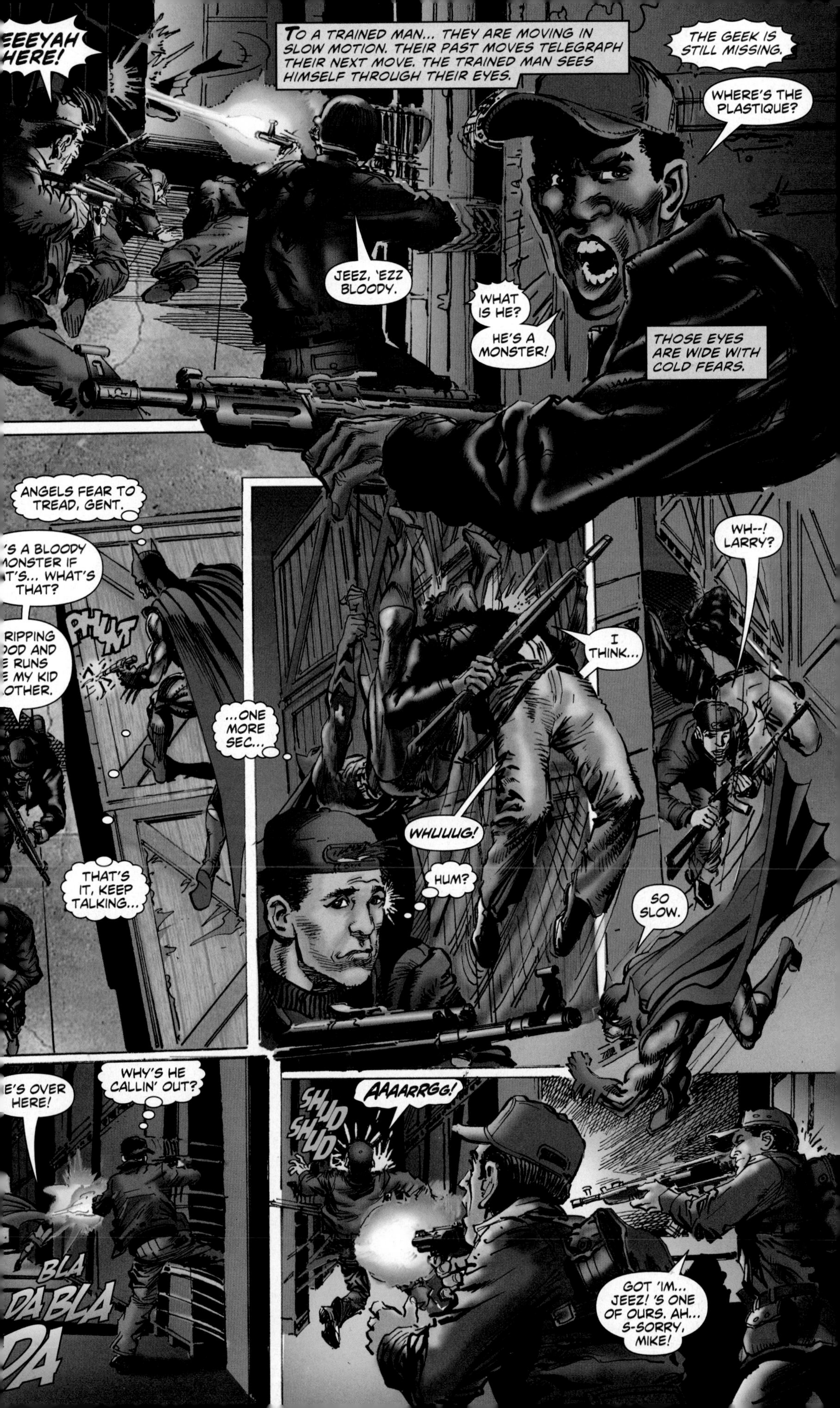
EEEYAH
HERE!
TO A TRAINED MAN... THEY ARE MOVING IN SLOW MOTION. THEIR PAST MOVES TELEGRAPH THEIR NEXT MOVE. THE TRAINED MAN SEES HIMSELF THROUGH THEIR EYES.
THE GEEK IS STILL MISSING.
WHERE'S THE PLASTIQUE?
JEEZ, 'EZZ BLOODY.
WHAT IS HE?
HE'S A MONSTER!
THOSE EYES ARE WIDE WITH COLD FEARS.
ANGELS FEAR TO TREAD, GENT.
'S A BLOODY MONSTER IF T'S... WHAT'S THAT?
RIPPING OOD AND E RUNS E MY KID OTHER.
PHUNT
...ONE MORE SEC...
THAT'S IT, KEEP TALKING...
I THINK...
WHUUUG!
HUM?
WH--! LARRY?
SO SLOW.
E'S OVER HERE!
WHY'S HE CALLIN' OUT?
BLA
DA BLA
DA
SHUD
SHUD
AAAARRGG!
GOT 'IM... JEEZ! 'S ONE OF OURS. AH... S-SORRY, MIKE!

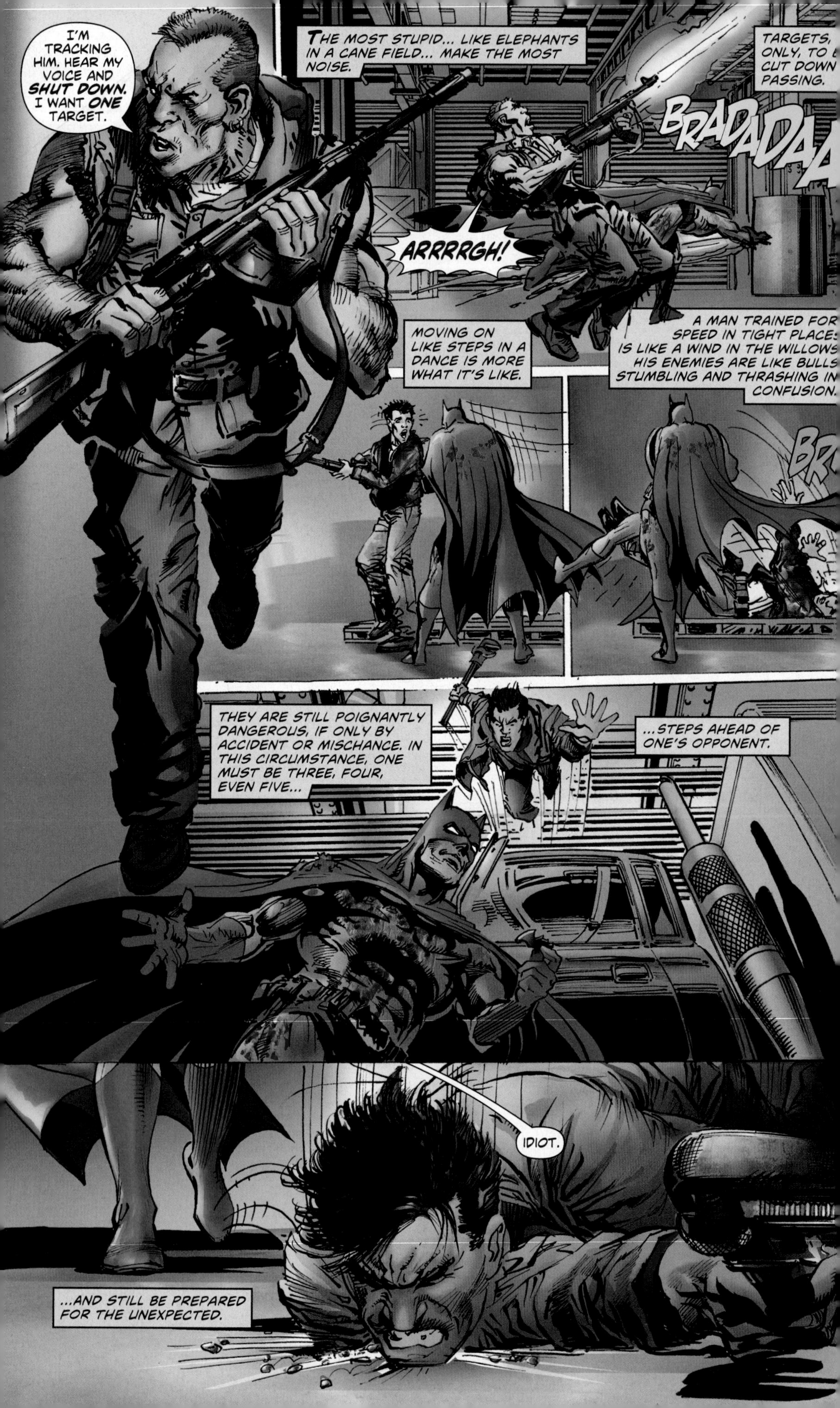

I'M TRACKING HIM. HEAR MY VOICE AND SHUT DOWN. I WANT ONE TARGET.
THE MOST STUPID... LIKE ELEPHANTS IN A CANE FIELD... MAKE THE MOST NOISE.
TARGETS, ONLY, TO CUT DOWN PASSING.
BRADADAA
ARRRRGH!
MOVING ON LIKE STEPS IN A DANCE IS MORE WHAT IT'S LIKE.
A MAN TRAINED FOR SPEED IN TIGHT PLACES IS LIKE A WIND IN THE WILLOWS. HIS ENEMIES ARE LIKE BULLS STUMBLING AND THRASHING IN CONFUSION.
THEY ARE STILL POIGNANTLY DANGEROUS, IF ONLY BY ACCIDENT OR MISCHANCE. IN THIS CIRCUMSTANCE, ONE MUST BE THREE, FOUR, EVEN FIVE...
...STEPS AHEAD OF ONE'S OPPONENT.
IDIOT.
...AND STILL BE PREPARED FOR THE UNEXPECTED.

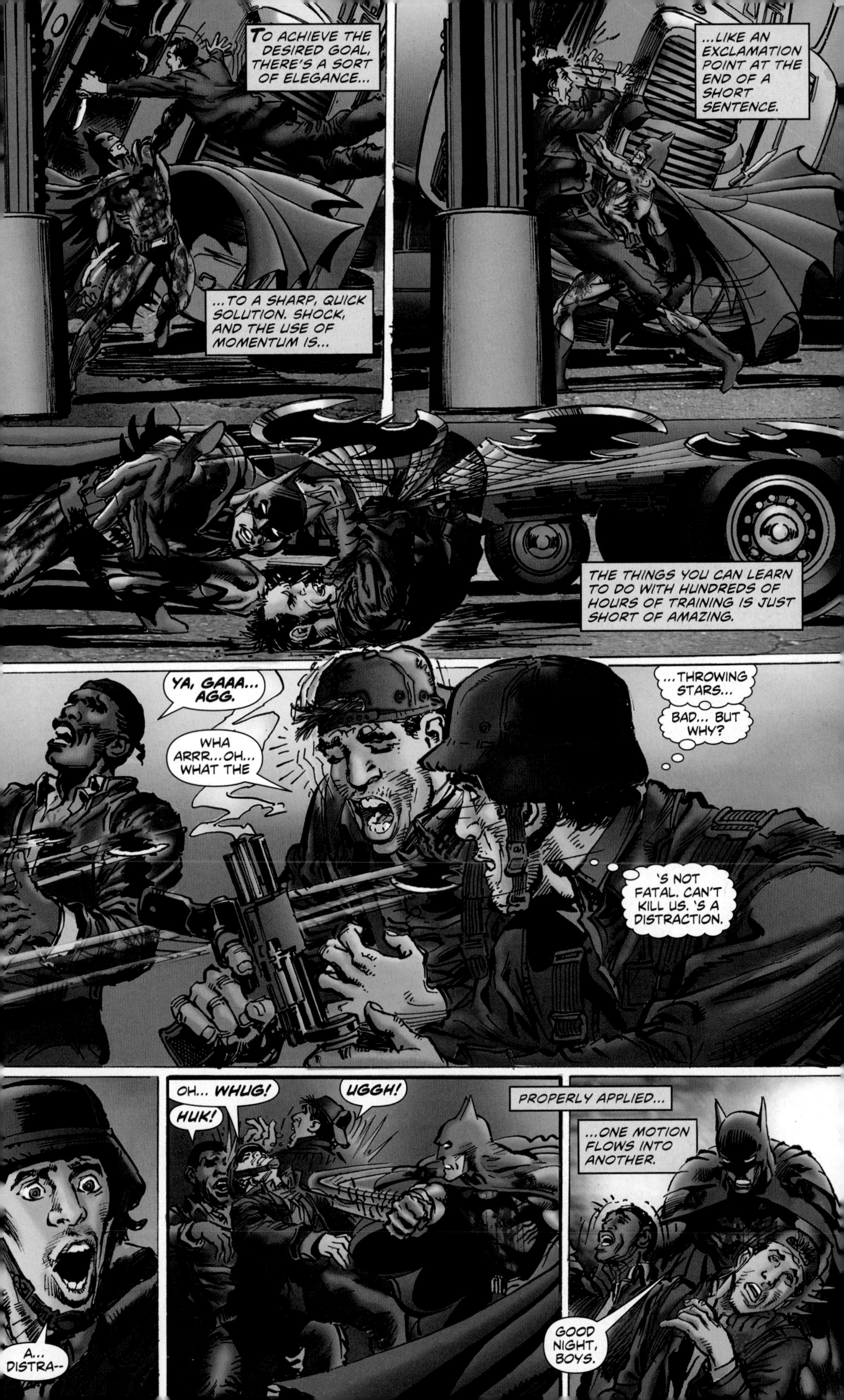
TO ACHIEVE THE DESIRED GOAL, THERE'S A SORT OF ELEGANCE...
...TO A SHARP, QUICK SOLUTION. SHOCK, AND THE USE OF MOMENTUM IS...
...LIKE AN EXCLAMATION POINT AT THE END OF A SHORT SENTENCE.
THE THINGS YOU CAN LEARN TO DO WITH HUNDREDS OF HOURS OF TRAINING IS JUST SHORT OF AMAZING.
YA, GAAA... AGG.
WHA ARRR...OH... WHAT THE
...THROWING STARS...
BAD... BUT WHY?
'S NOT FATAL. CAN'T KILL US. 'S A DISTRACTION.
A... DISTRA--
OH... WHUG!
HUK!
UGGH!
PROPERLY APPLIED...
...ONE MOTION FLOWS INTO ANOTHER.
GOOD NIGHT, BOYS.

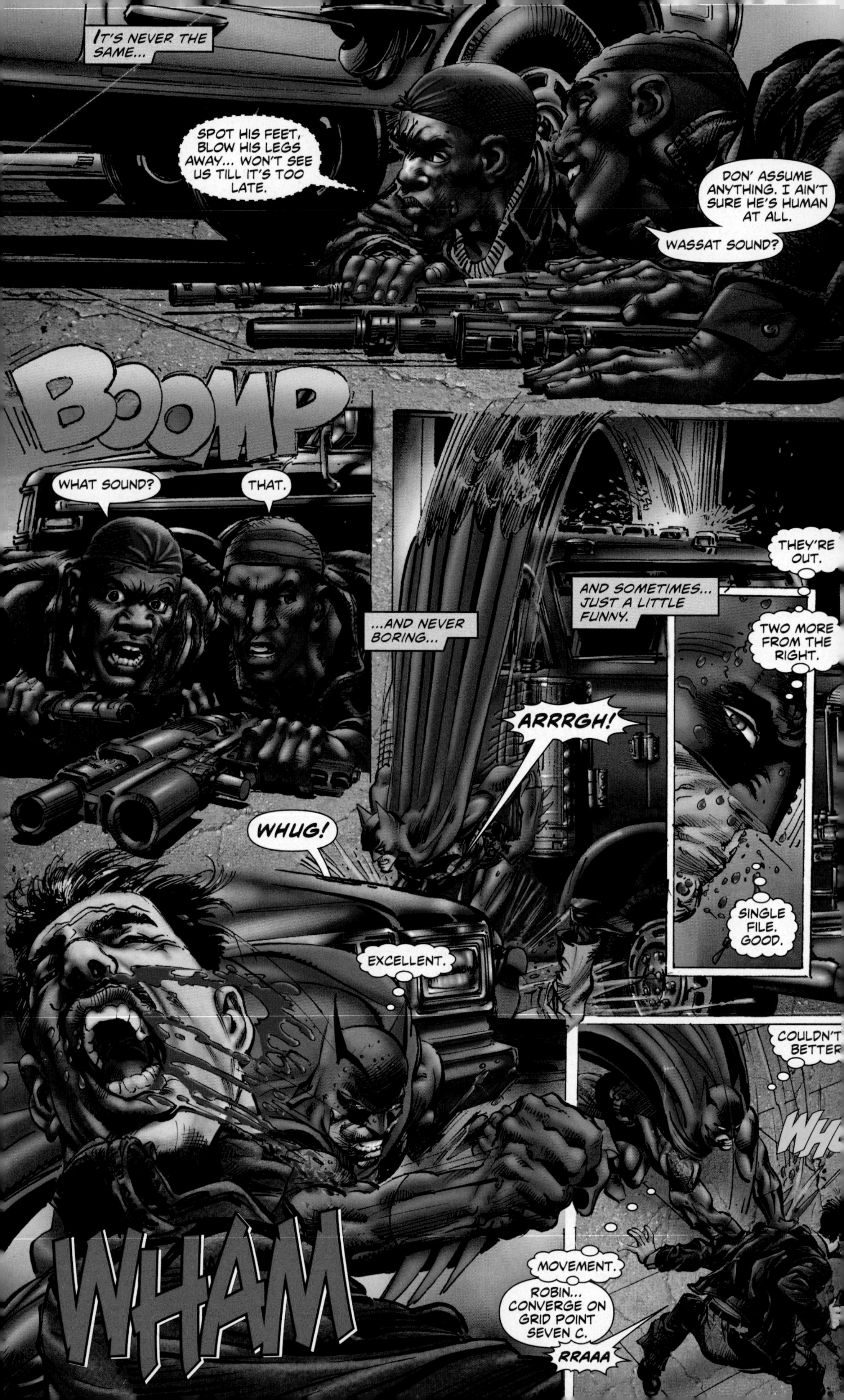
IT'S NEVER THE SAME...
SPOT HIS FEET, BLOW HIS LEGS AWAY... WON'T SEE US TILL IT'S TOO LATE.
DON' ASSUME ANYTHING. I AIN'T SURE HE'S HUMAN AT ALL.
WASSAT SOUND?
BOOMP
WHAT SOUND?
THAT.
...AND NEVER BORING...
AND SOMETIMES... JUST A LITTLE FUNNY.
THEY'RE OUT.
TWO MORE FROM THE RIGHT.
ARRRGH!
WHUG!
SINGLE FILE. GOOD.
EXCELLENT.
COULDN'T BETTER
WHAM
MOVEMENT.
ROBIN... CONVERGE ON GRID POINT SEVEN C.
RRAAA

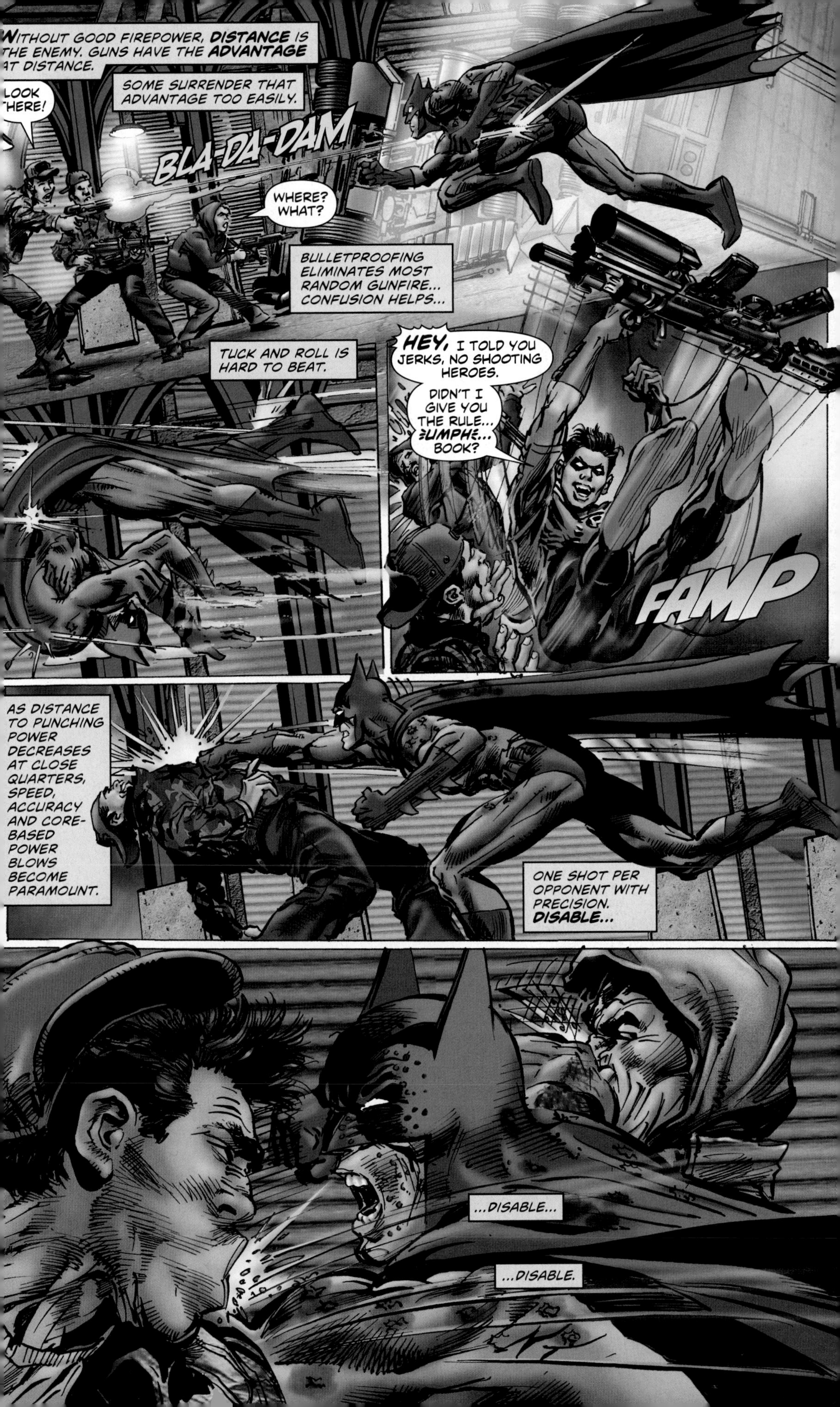
WITHOUT GOOD FIREPOWER, DISTANCE IS THE ENEMY. GUNS HAVE THE ADVANTAGE AT DISTANCE.
LOOK THERE!
SOME SURRENDER THAT ADVANTAGE TOO EASILY.
BLA-DA-DAM
WHERE? WHAT?
BULLETPROOFING ELIMINATES MOST RANDOM GUNFIRE... CONFUSION HELPS...
TUCK AND ROLL IS HARD TO BEAT.
HEY, I TOLD YOU JERKS, NO SHOOTING HEROES.
DIDN'T I GIVE YOU THE RULE... UMPH... BOOK?
FAMP
AS DISTANCE TO PUNCHING POWER DECREASES AT CLOSE QUARTERS, SPEED, ACCURACY AND CORE-BASED POWER BLOWS BECOME PARAMOUNT.
ONE SHOT PER OPPONENT WITH PRECISION. DISABLE...
...DISABLE...
...DISABLE.

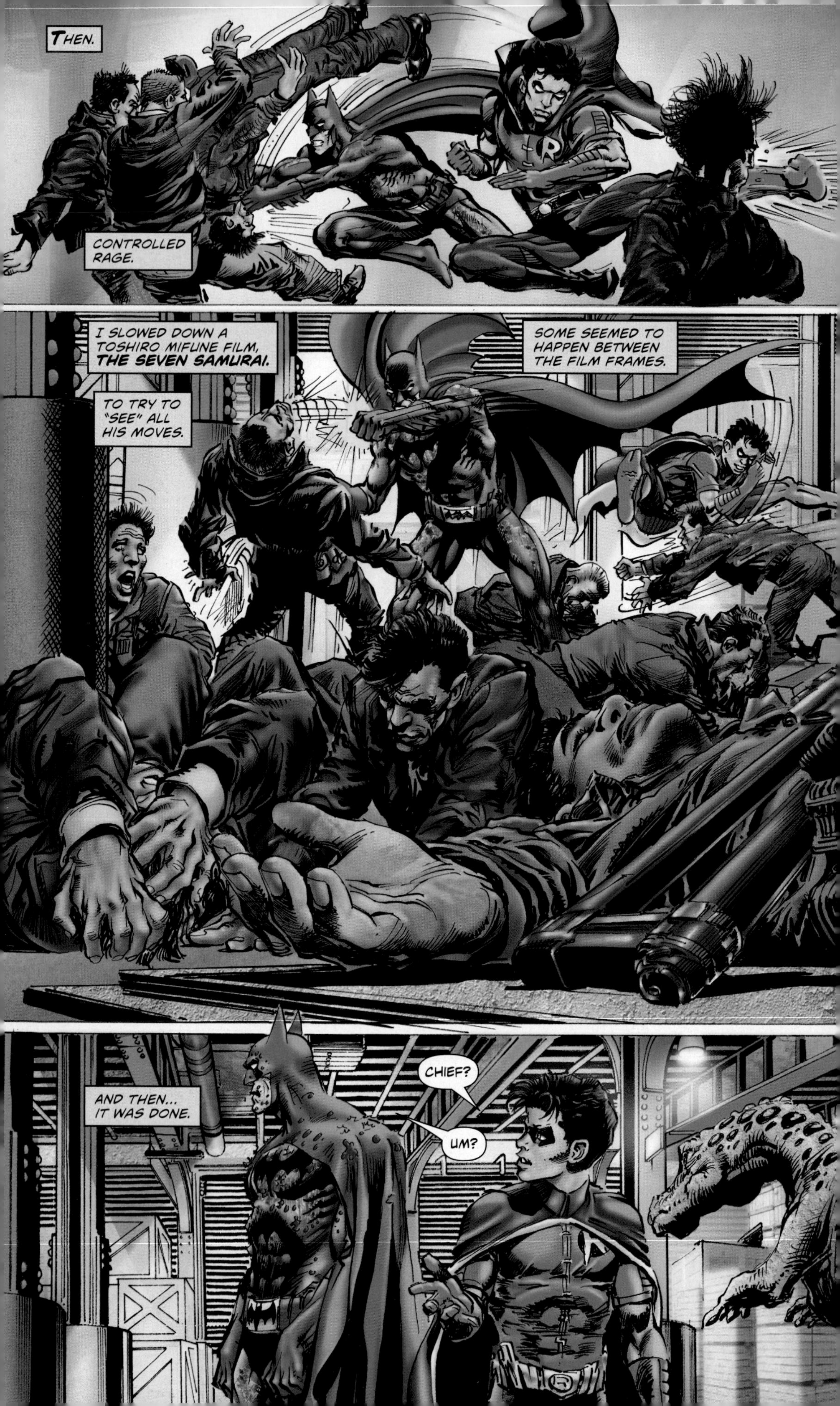
THEN.
CONTROLLED RAGE.
I SLOWED DOWN A TOSHIRO MIFUNE FILM, THE SEVEN SAMURAI.
TO TRY TO "SEE" ALL HIS MOVES.
SOME SEEMED TO HAPPEN BETWEEN THE FILM FRAMES.
AND THEN... IT WAS DONE.
CHIEF?
UM?

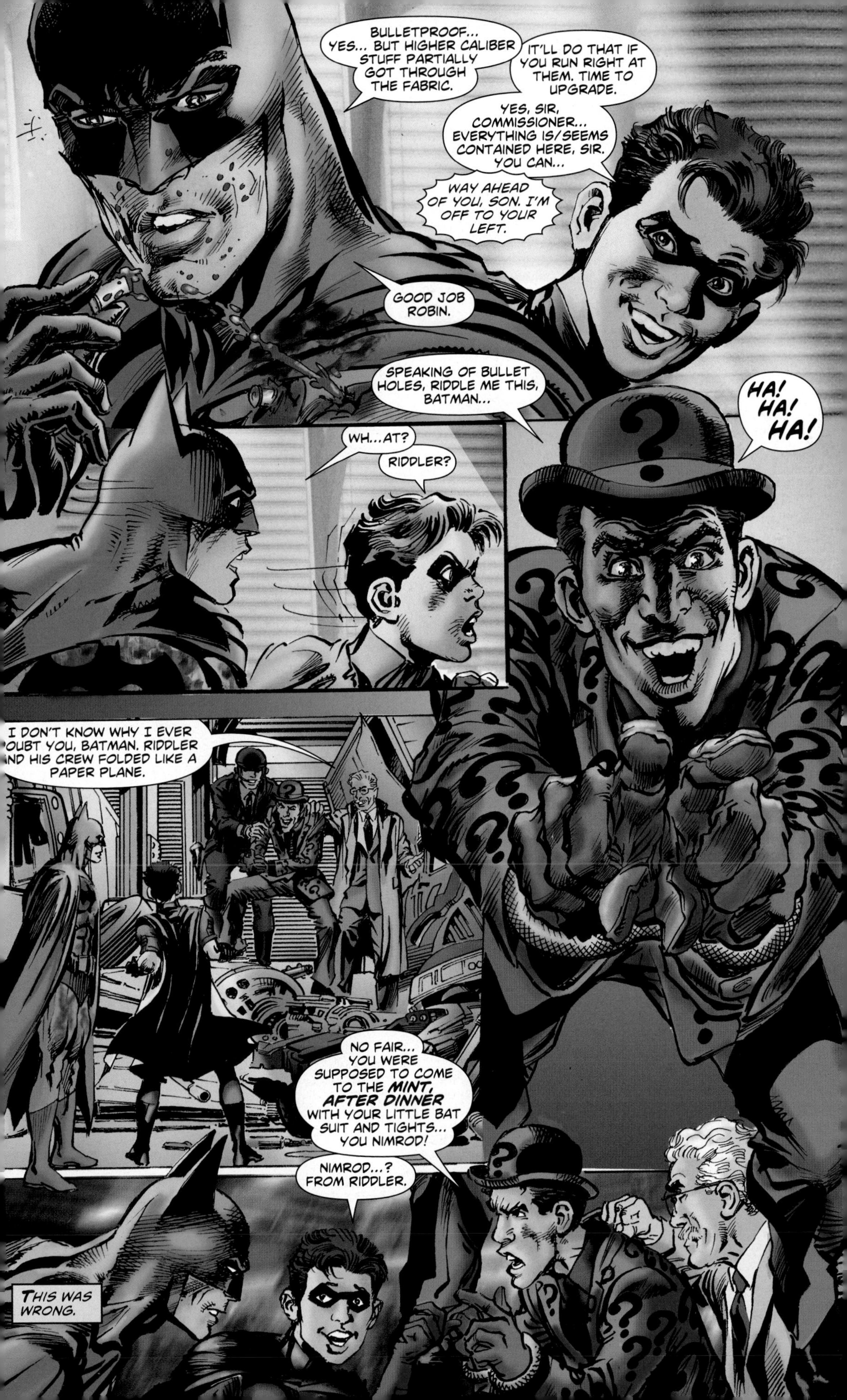

BULLETPROOF... YES... BUT HIGHER CALIBER STUFF PARTIALLY GOT THROUGH THE FABRIC.
IT'LL DO THAT IF YOU RUN RIGHT AT THEM. TIME TO UPGRADE.
YES, SIR, COMMISSIONER... EVERYTHING IS/SEEMS CONTAINED HERE, SIR. YOU CAN...
WAY AHEAD OF YOU, SON. I'M OFF TO YOUR LEFT.
GOOD JOB ROBIN.
SPEAKING OF BULLET HOLES, RIDDLE ME THIS, BATMAN...
HA! HA! HA!
WH...AT?
RIDDLER?
I DON'T KNOW WHY I EVER OUBT YOU, BATMAN. RIDDLER ND HIS CREW FOLDED LIKE A PAPER PLANE.
NO FAIR... YOU WERE SUPPOSED TO COME TO THE MINT, AFTER DINNER WITH YOUR LITTLE BAT SUIT AND TIGHTS... YOU NIMROD!
NIMROD...? FROM RIDDLER.
THIS WAS WRONG.

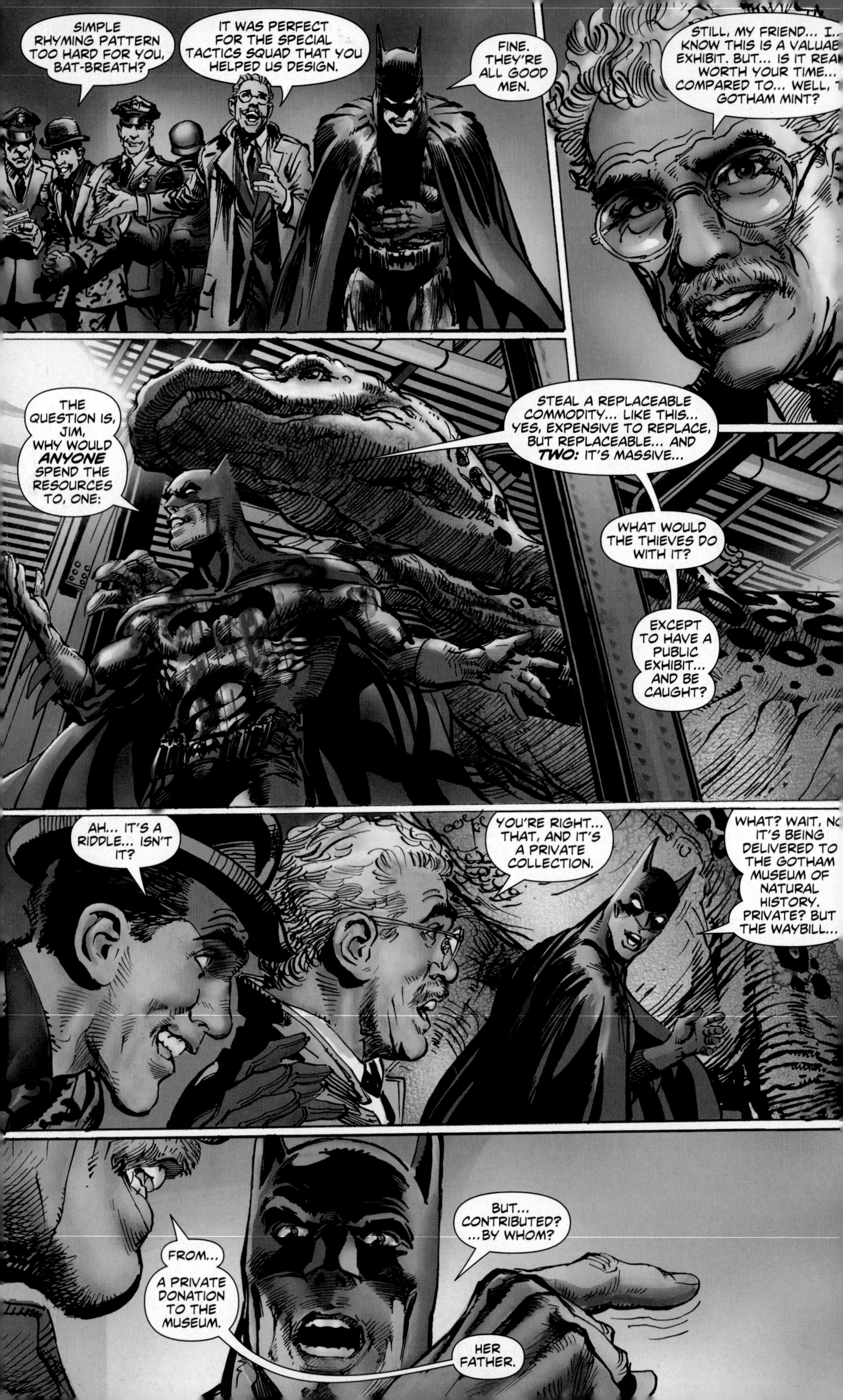
SIMPLE RHYMING PATTERN TOO HARD FOR YOU, BAT-BREATH?
IT WAS PERFECT FOR THE SPECIAL TACTICS SQUAD THAT YOU HELPED US DESIGN.
FINE. THEY'RE ALL GOOD MEN.
STILL, MY FRIEND... I... KNOW THIS IS A VALUAB EXHIBIT. BUT... IS IT REA WORTH YOUR TIME... COMPARED TO... WELL, T GOTHAM MINT?
THE QUESTION IS, JIM, WHY WOULD ***ANYONE*** SPEND THE RESOURCES TO, ONE:
STEAL A REPLACEABLE COMMODITY... LIKE THIS... YES, EXPENSIVE TO REPLACE, BUT REPLACEABLE... AND ***TWO:*** IT'S MASSIVE...
WHAT WOULD THE THIEVES DO WITH IT?
EXCEPT TO HAVE A PUBLIC EXHIBIT... AND BE CAUGHT?
AH... IT'S A RIDDLE... ISN'T IT?
YOU'RE RIGHT... THAT, AND IT'S A PRIVATE COLLECTION.
WHAT? WAIT, N IT'S BEING DELIVERED TO THE GOTHAM MUSEUM OF NATURAL HISTORY. PRIVATE? BUT THE WAYBILL...
FROM... A PRIVATE DONATION TO THE MUSEUM.
BUT... CONTRIBUTED? ...BY WHOM?
HER FATHER.

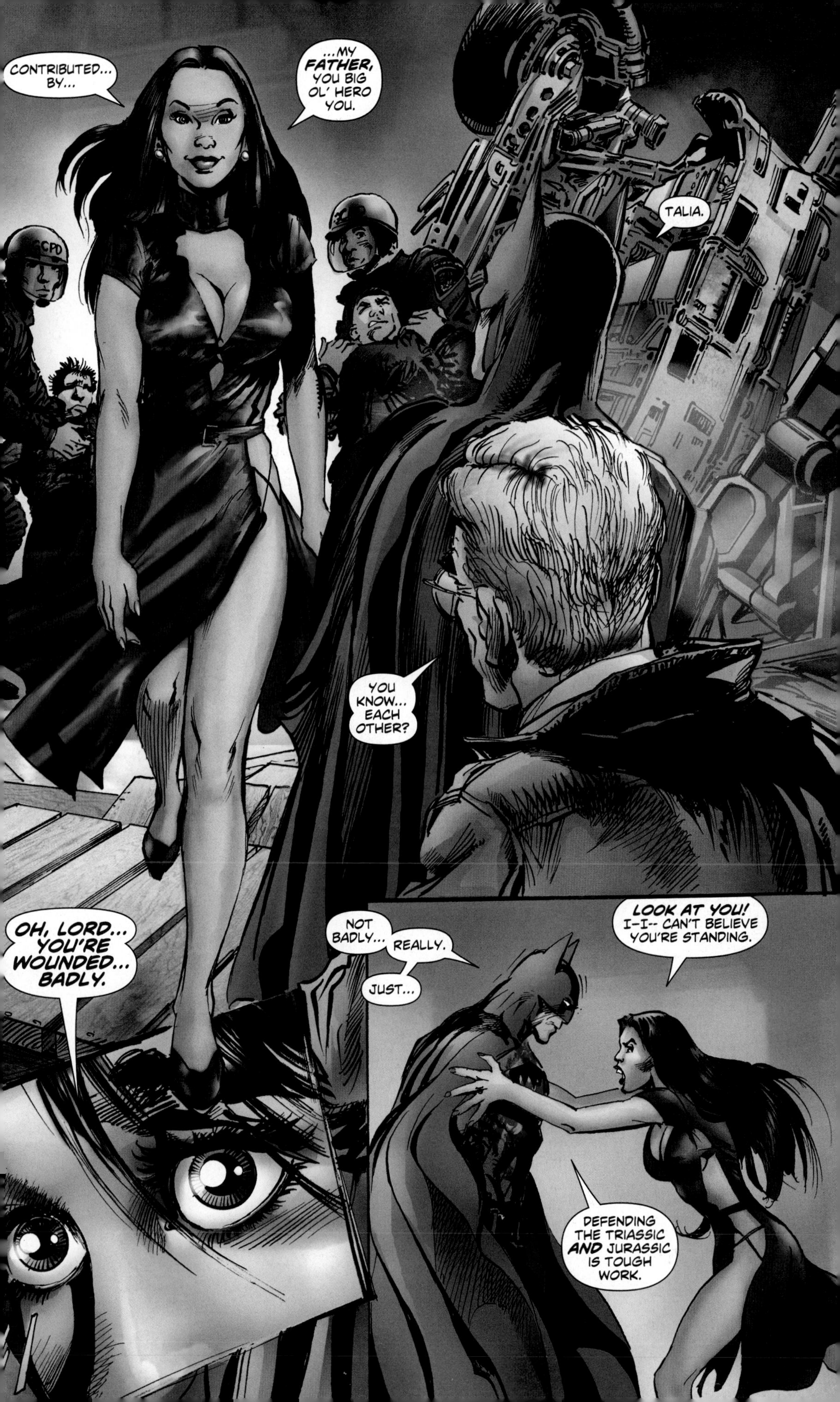
CONTRIBUTED... BY...
...MY *FATHER,* YOU BIG OL' HERO YOU.
TALIA.
YOU KNOW... EACH OTHER?
OH, LORD... YOU'RE WOUNDED... BADLY.
NOT BADLY...
REALLY.
JUST...
LOOK AT YOU! I-I-- CAN'T BELIEVE YOU'RE STANDING.
DEFENDING THE TRIASSIC *AND* JURASSIC IS TOUGH WORK.

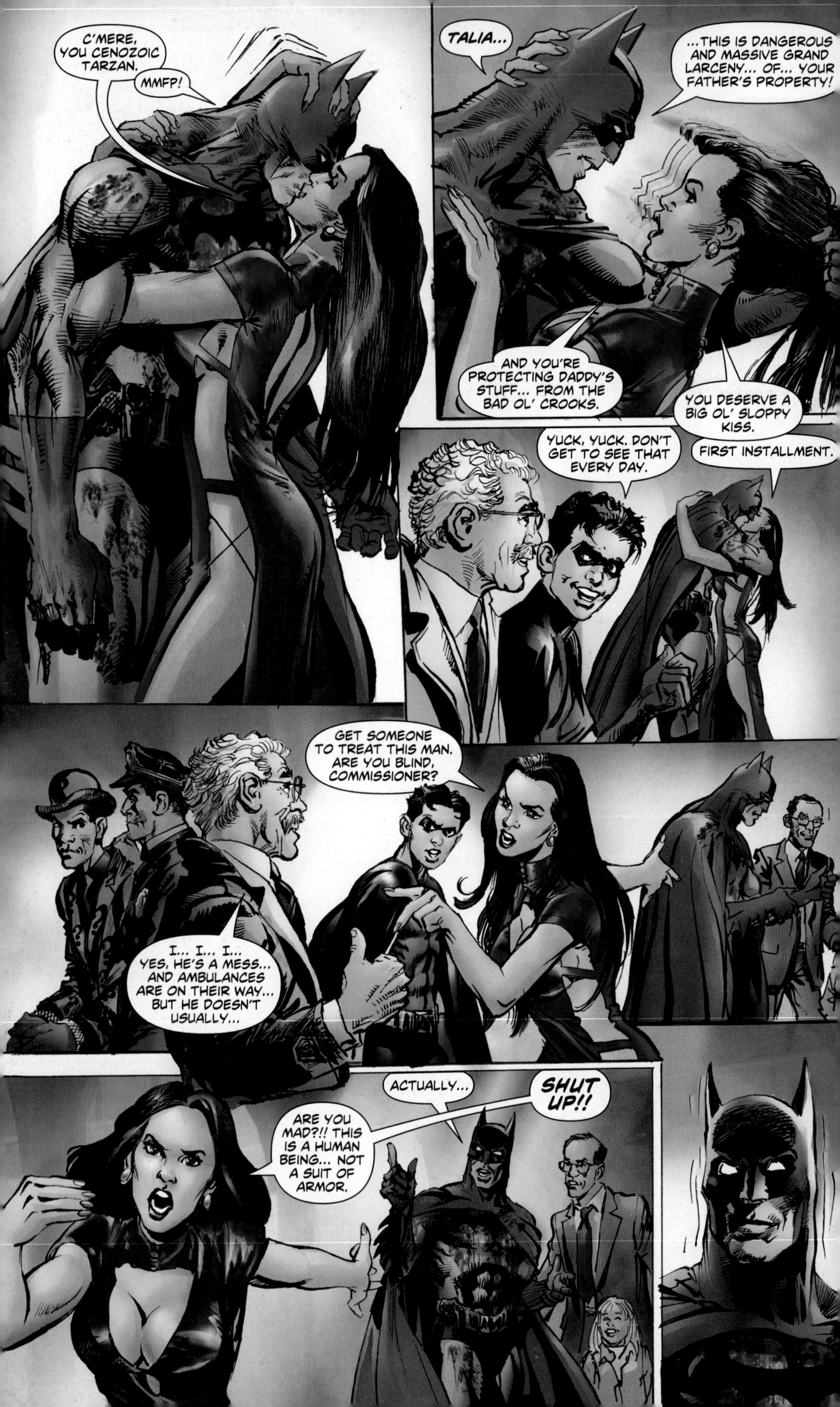

C'MERE, YOU CENOZOIC TARZAN.
MMFP!
TALIA...
...THIS IS DANGEROUS AND MASSIVE GRAND LARCENY... OF... YOUR FATHER'S PROPERTY!
AND YOU'RE PROTECTING DADDY'S STUFF... FROM THE BAD OL' CROOKS.
YOU DESERVE A BIG OL' SLOPPY KISS.
FIRST INSTALLMENT.
YUCK, YUCK. DON'T GET TO SEE THAT EVERY DAY.
GET SOMEONE TO TREAT THIS MAN. ARE YOU BLIND, COMMISSIONER?
I... I... I... YES, HE'S A MESS... AND AMBULANCES ARE ON THEIR WAY... BUT HE DOESN'T USUALLY...
ACTUALLY...
SHUT UP!!
ARE YOU MAD?!! THIS IS A HUMAN BEING... NOT A SUIT OF ARMOR.

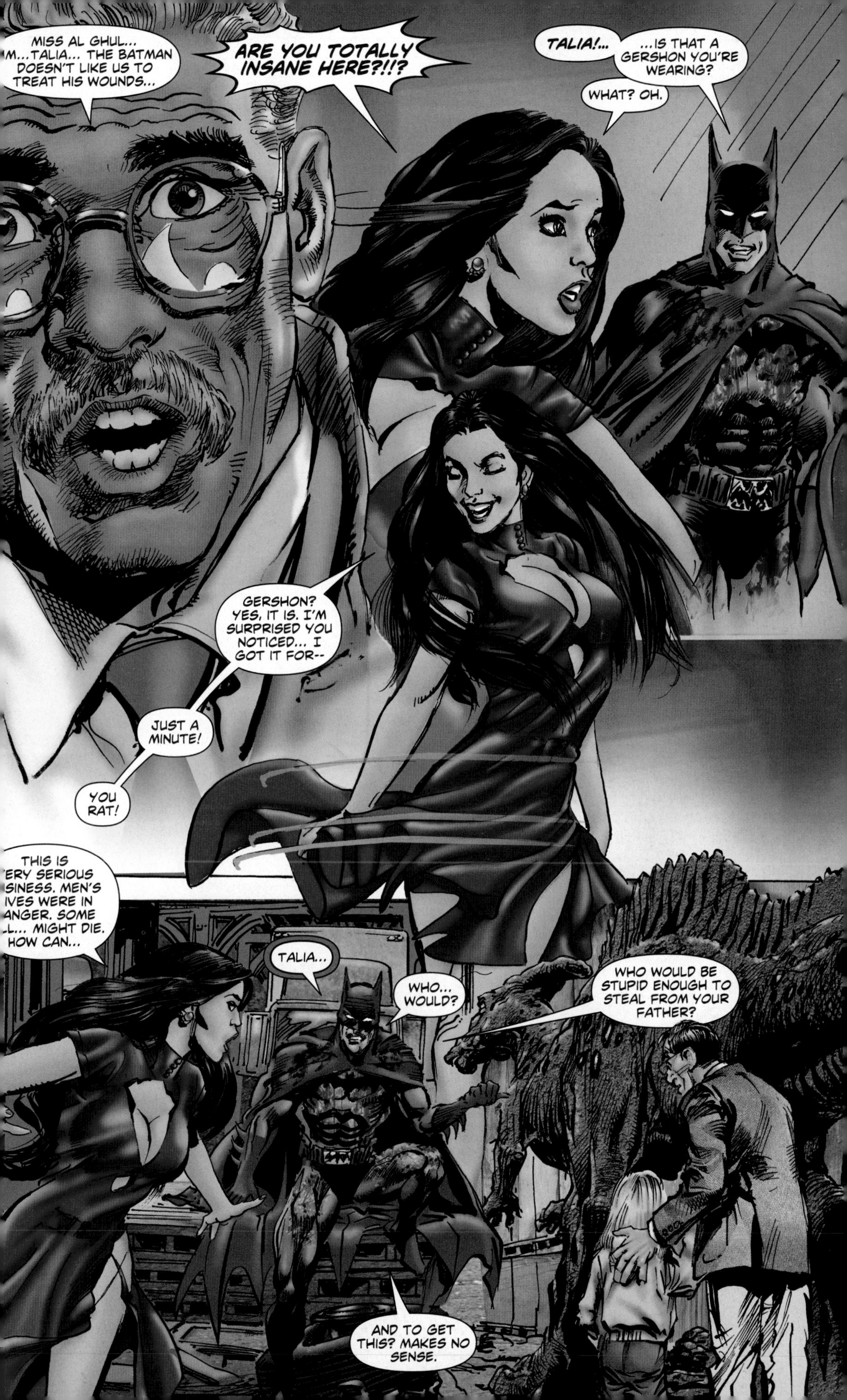
MISS AL GHUL... M...TALIA... THE BATMAN DOESN'T LIKE US TO TREAT HIS WOUNDS...
ARE YOU TOTALLY INSANE HERE?!!?
TALIA!...
...IS THAT A GERSHON YOU'RE WEARING?
WHAT? OH.
GERSHON? YES, IT IS. I'M SURPRISED YOU NOTICED... I GOT IT FOR--
JUST A MINUTE!
YOU RAT!
THIS IS 'ERY SERIOUS SINESS. MEN'S IVES WERE IN ANGER. SOME L... MIGHT DIE. HOW CAN...
TALIA...
WHO... WOULD?
WHO WOULD BE STUPID ENOUGH TO STEAL FROM YOUR FATHER?
AND TO GET THIS? MAKES NO SENSE.

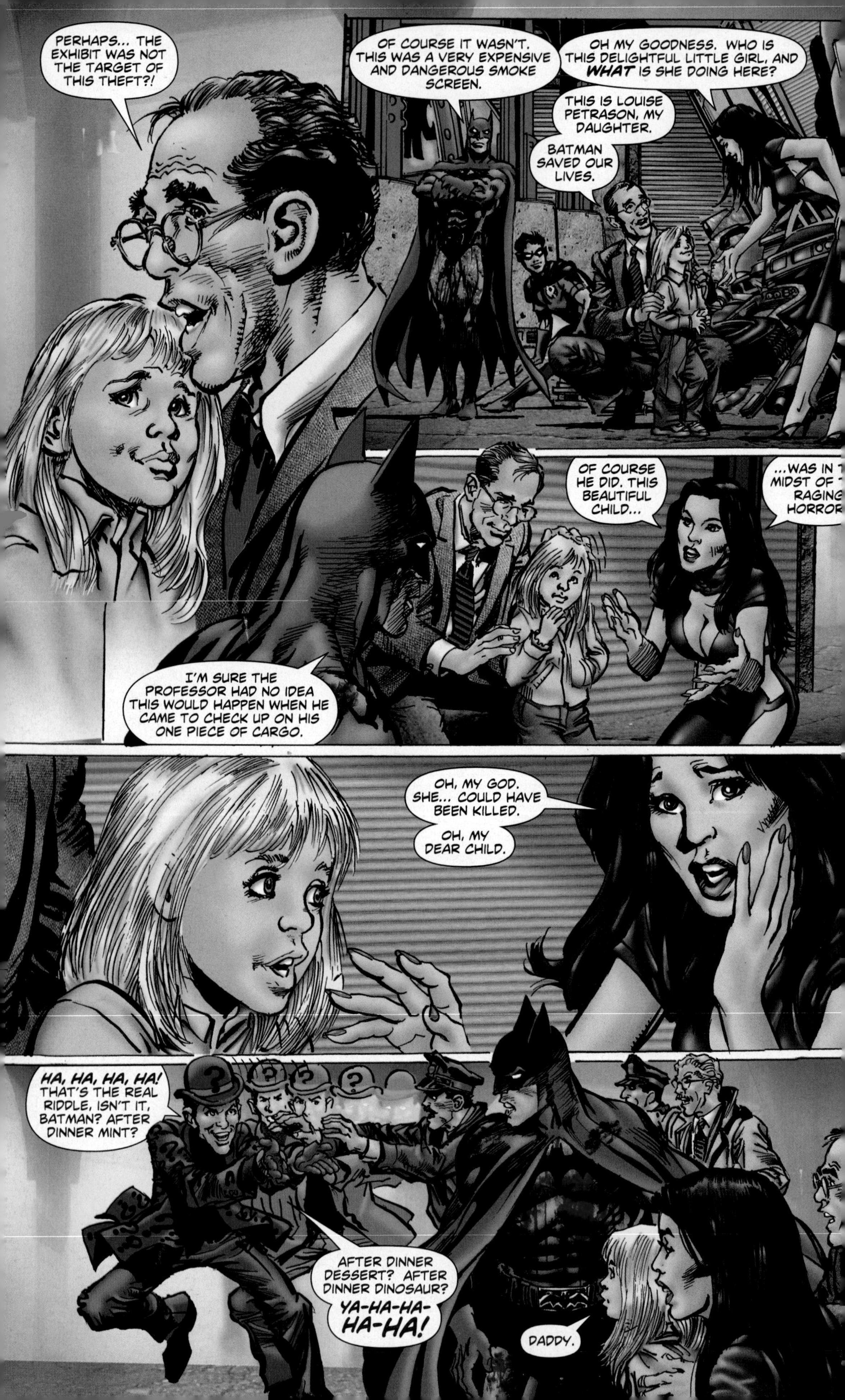
PERHAPS... THE EXHIBIT WAS NOT THE TARGET OF THIS THEFT?!
OF COURSE IT WASN'T. THIS WAS A VERY EXPENSIVE AND DANGEROUS SMOKE SCREEN.
OH MY GOODNESS. WHO IS THIS DELIGHTFUL LITTLE GIRL, AND ***WHAT*** IS SHE DOING HERE?
THIS IS LOUISE PETRASON, MY DAUGHTER.
BATMAN SAVED OUR LIVES.
I'M SURE THE PROFESSOR HAD NO IDEA THIS WOULD HAPPEN WHEN HE CAME TO CHECK UP ON HIS ONE PIECE OF CARGO.
OF COURSE HE DID. THIS BEAUTIFUL CHILD...
OH, MY GOD. SHE... COULD HAVE BEEN KILLED.
OH, MY DEAR CHILD.
HA, HA, HA, HA! THAT'S THE REAL RIDDLE, ISN'T IT, BATMAN? AFTER DINNER MINT?
AFTER DINNER DESSERT? AFTER DINNER DINOSAUR? ***YA-HA-HA-HA-HA-HA!***
DADDY.

UMPHHH

BACK OFF, JERK, WITH YOUR AFTER DINNER... ... ... AFTER DINNER, ...

WHAT?

"HOW ABOUT AN AFTER DINNER..."

MINT.

WATER.

RHYMING PATTERN.

WATER.

BUT THE MINT. HE WAS ROBBING THE MINT!

QUOTE, "CAN'T EAT ONE BIT MORE." IF YOU CAN'T EAT ONE BIT MORE," YOU CAN'T EAT A MINT. YOU CAN HAVE... WHAT RHYMES WITH "ORDER?" IT'S WATER! H_2O!

WATER.

THAT'S WHAT S WHOLE THING'S OUT. THE RIDDLER HAD TO... WAS MPELLED TO GIVE HE REAL CLUE DE THE FAKE CLUE. ORDER RHYMES WITH WATER.

DIFFERENT RHYMING PATTERN.

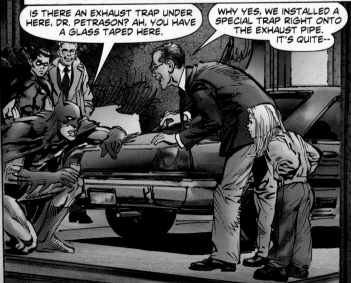

IS THERE AN EXHAUST TRAP UNDER HERE, DR. PETRASON? AH, YOU HAVE A GLASS TAPED HERE.

WHY YES, WE INSTALLED A SPECIAL TRAP RIGHT ONTO THE EXHAUST PIPE. IT'S QUITE--

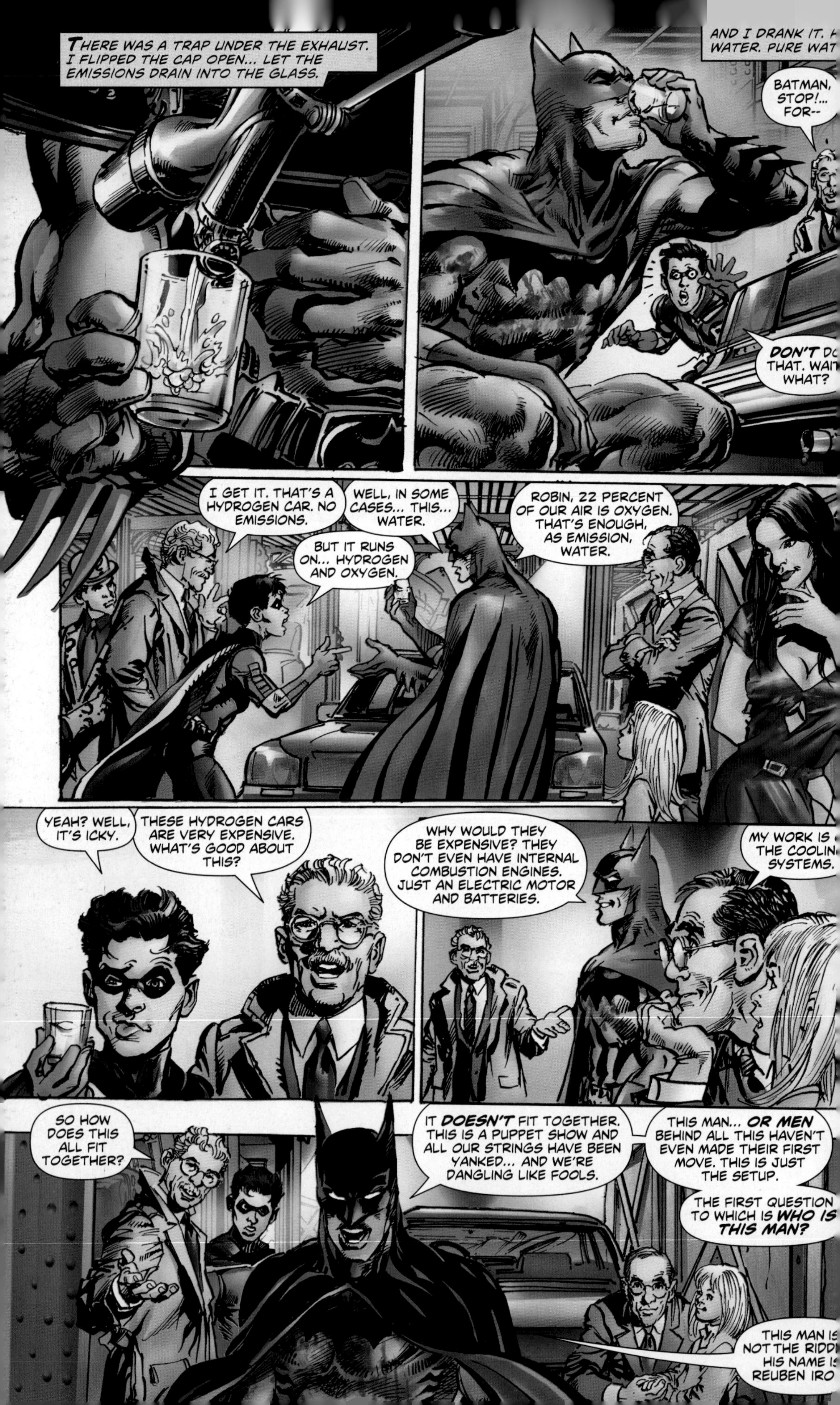

THERE WAS A TRAP UNDER THE EXHAUST. I FLIPPED THE CAP OPEN... LET THE EMISSIONS DRAIN INTO THE GLASS.
AND I DRANK IT.
WATER. PURE WAT
BATMAN, STOP!... FOR--
DON'T D
THAT. WAI
WHAT?
I GET IT. THAT'S A HYDROGEN CAR. NO EMISSIONS.
WELL, IN SOME CASES... THIS... WATER.
BUT IT RUNS ON... HYDROGEN AND OXYGEN.
ROBIN, 22 PERCENT OF OUR AIR IS OXYGEN. THAT'S ENOUGH, AS EMISSION, WATER.
YEAH? WELL, IT'S ICKY.
THESE HYDROGEN CARS ARE VERY EXPENSIVE. WHAT'S GOOD ABOUT THIS?
WHY WOULD THEY BE EXPENSIVE? THEY DON'T EVEN HAVE INTERNAL COMBUSTION ENGINES. JUST AN ELECTRIC MOTOR AND BATTERIES.
MY WORK IS
THE COOLIN
SYSTEMS.
SO HOW DOES THIS ALL FIT TOGETHER?
IT DOESN'T FIT TOGETHER. THIS IS A PUPPET SHOW AND ALL OUR STRINGS HAVE BEEN YANKED... AND WE'RE DANGLING LIKE FOOLS.
THIS MAN... OR MEN BEHIND ALL THIS HAVEN'T EVEN MADE THEIR FIRST MOVE. THIS IS JUST THE SETUP.
THE FIRST QUESTION TO WHICH IS WHO IS THIS MAN?
THIS MAN IS
NOT THE RIDD
HIS NAME IS
REUBEN IRO

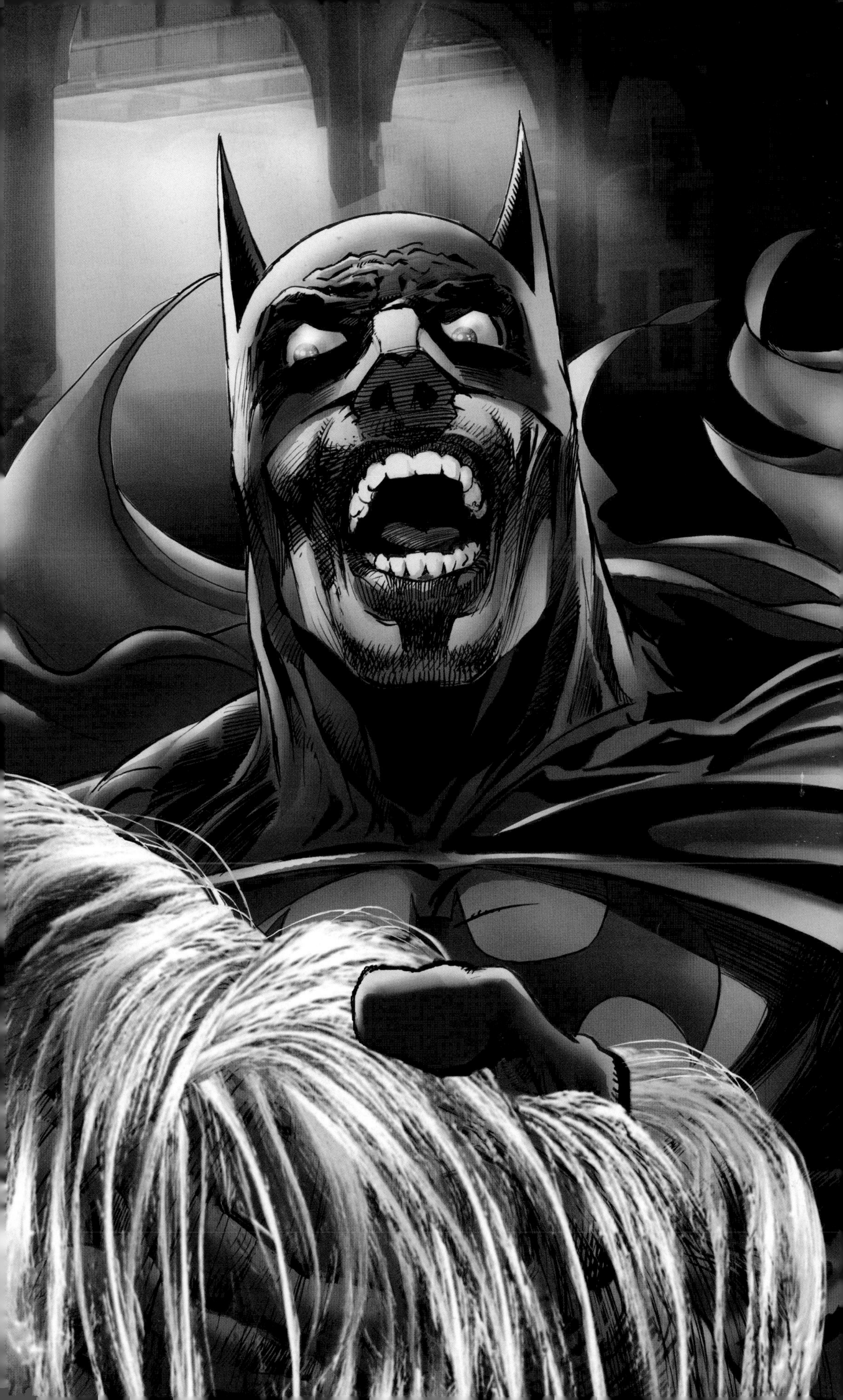

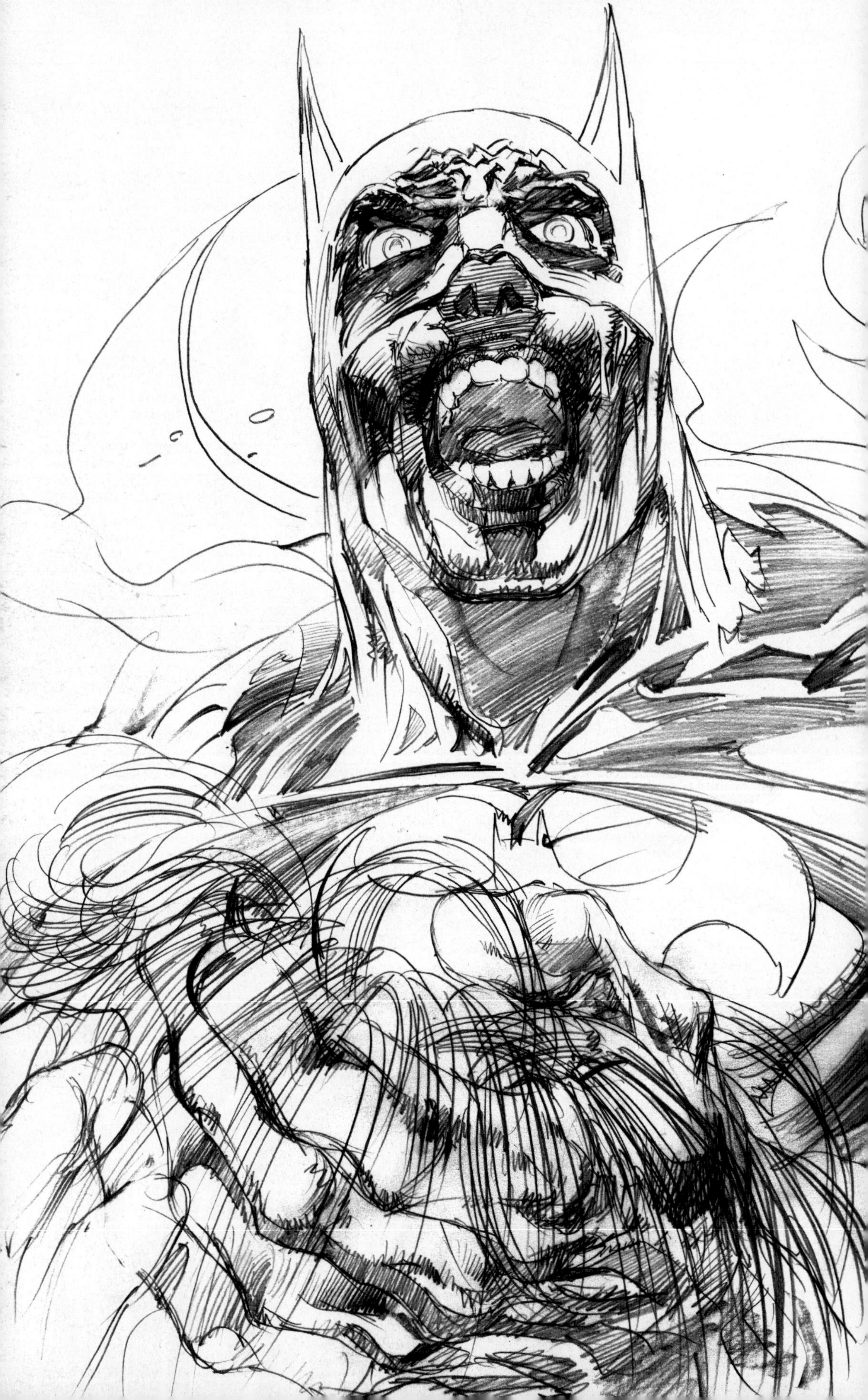

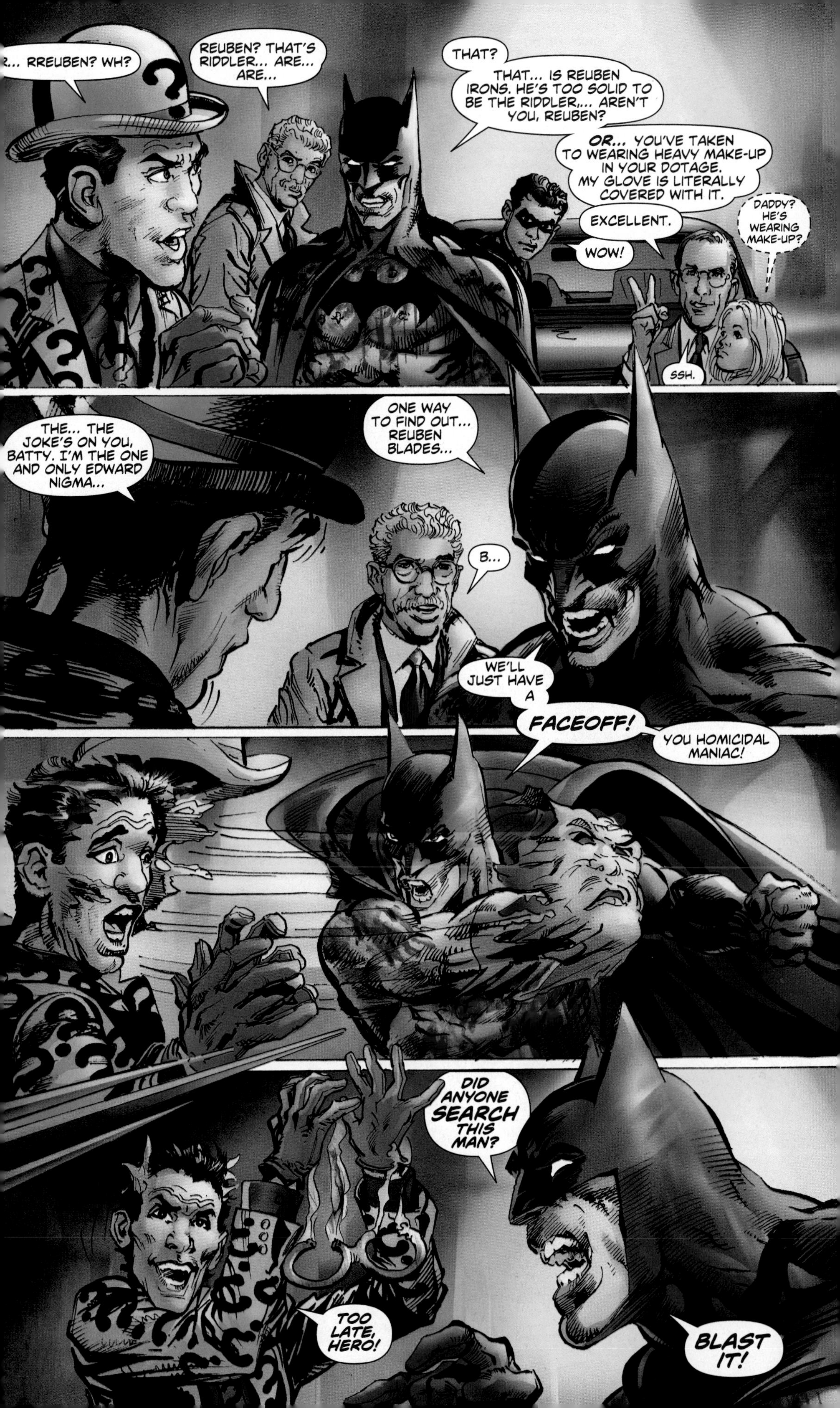
R... RREUBEN? WH?
REUBEN? THAT'S RIDDLER... ARE... ARE...
THAT?
THAT... IS REUBEN IRONS. HE'S TOO SOLID TO BE THE RIDDLER,... AREN'T YOU, REUBEN?
OR... YOU'VE TAKEN TO WEARING HEAVY MAKE-UP IN YOUR DOTAGE. MY GLOVE IS LITERALLY COVERED WITH IT.
EXCELLENT.
WOW!
DADDY? HE'S WEARING MAKE-UP?
SSH.
THE... THE JOKE'S ON YOU, BATTY. I'M THE ONE AND ONLY EDWARD NIGMA...
ONE WAY TO FIND OUT... REUBEN BLADES...
B...
WE'LL JUST HAVE A FACEOFF!
YOU HOMICIDAL MANIAC!
DID ANYONE SEARCH THIS MAN?
TOO LATE, HERO!
BLAST IT!

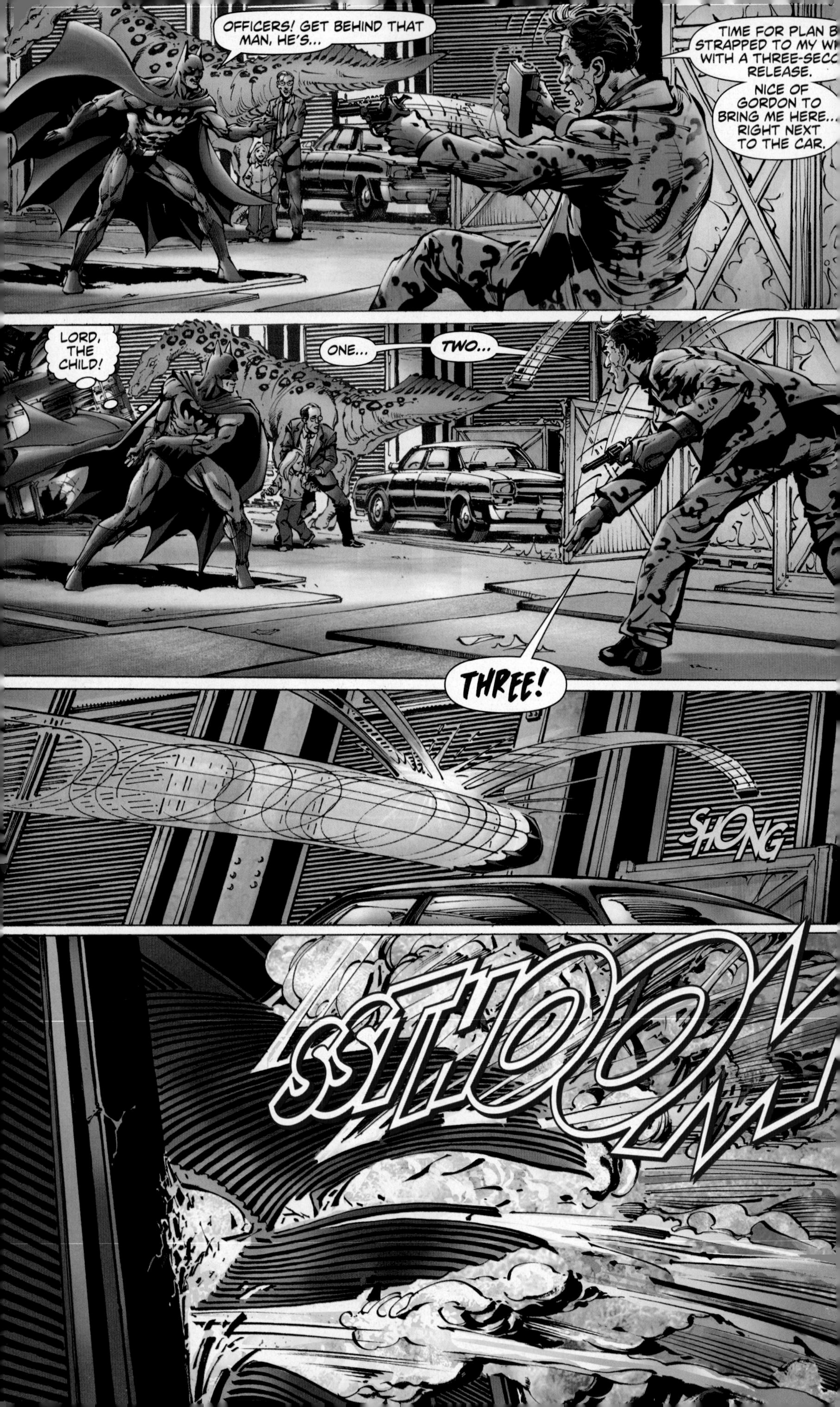

OFFICERS! GET BEHIND THAT MAN, HE'S...
TIME FOR PLAN B STRAPPED TO MY WI WITH A THREE-SECO RELEASE.
NICE OF GORDON TO BRING ME HERE... RIGHT NEXT TO THE CAR.
LORD, THE CHILD!
ONE...
TWO...
THREE!
SHONG
SSHOOM

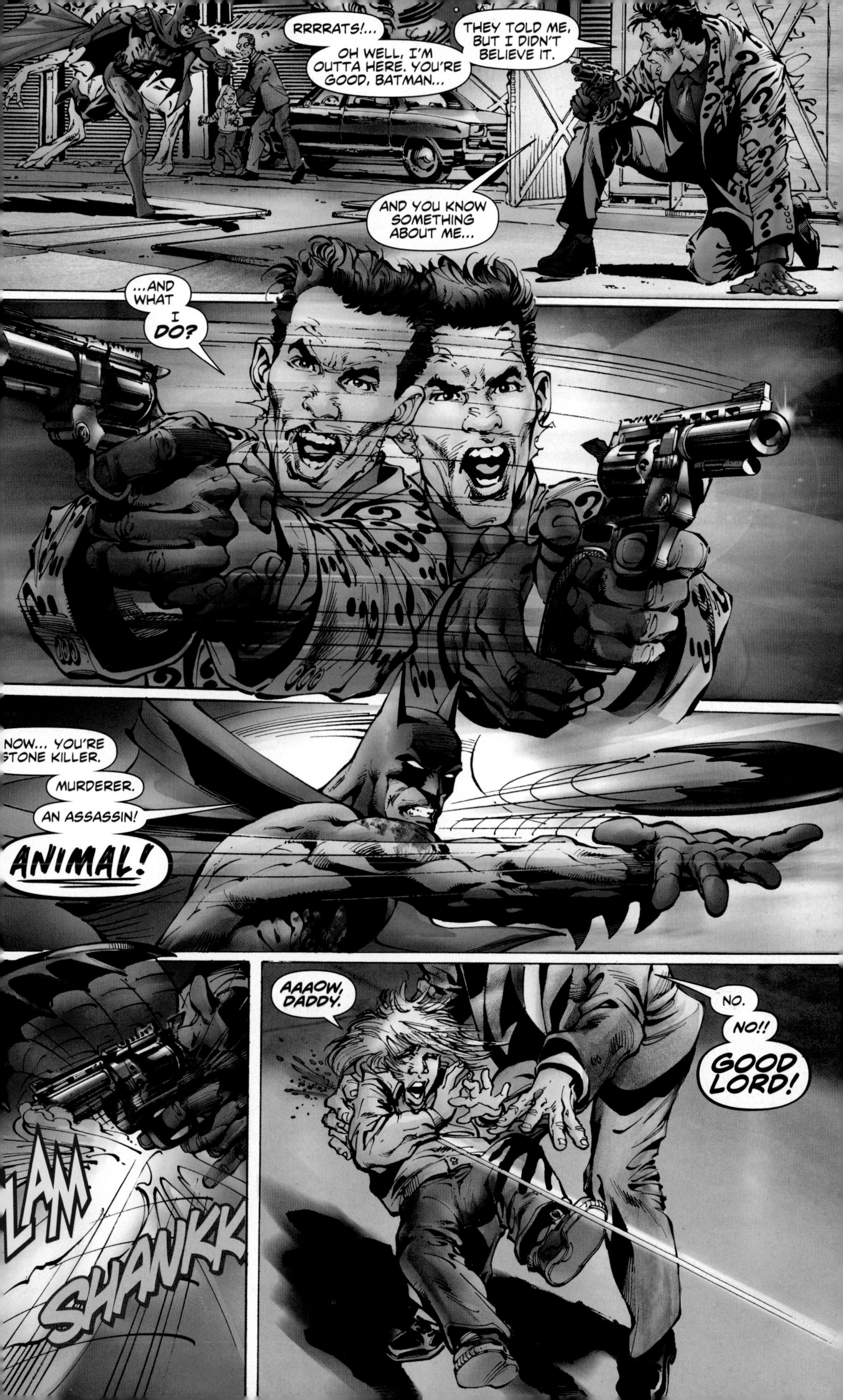
RRRRATS!...
OH WELL, I'M OUTTA HERE. YOU'RE GOOD, BATMAN...
THEY TOLD ME, BUT I DIDN'T BELIEVE IT.
AND YOU KNOW SOMETHING ABOUT ME...
...AND WHAT I DO?
NOW... YOU'RE
STONE KILLER.
MURDERER.
AN ASSASSIN!
ANIMAL!
LAM
SHANKK
AAAOW, DADDY.
NO.
NO!!
GOOD LORD!

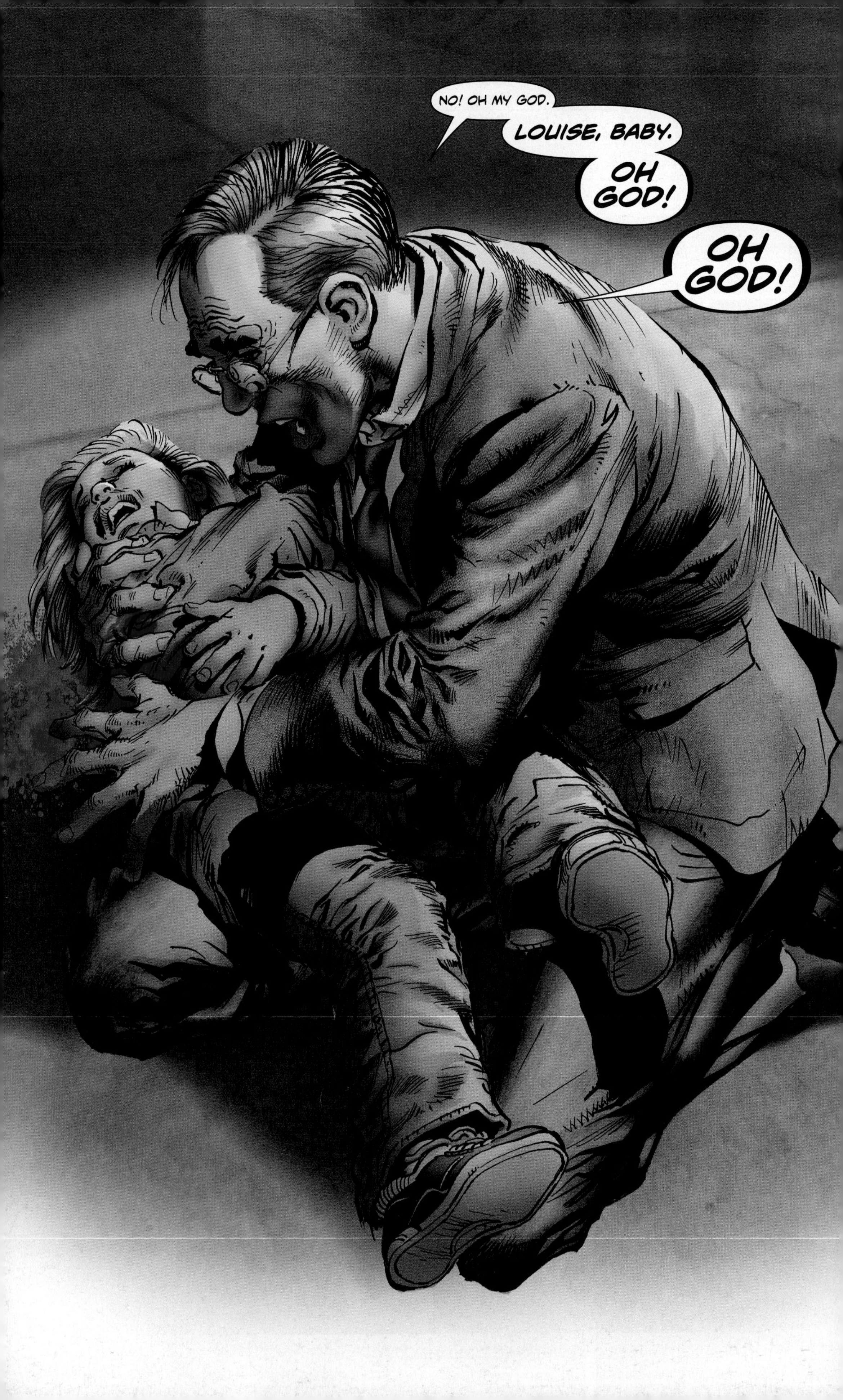
NO! OH MY GOD.
LOUISE, BABY.
OH GOD!
OH GOD!

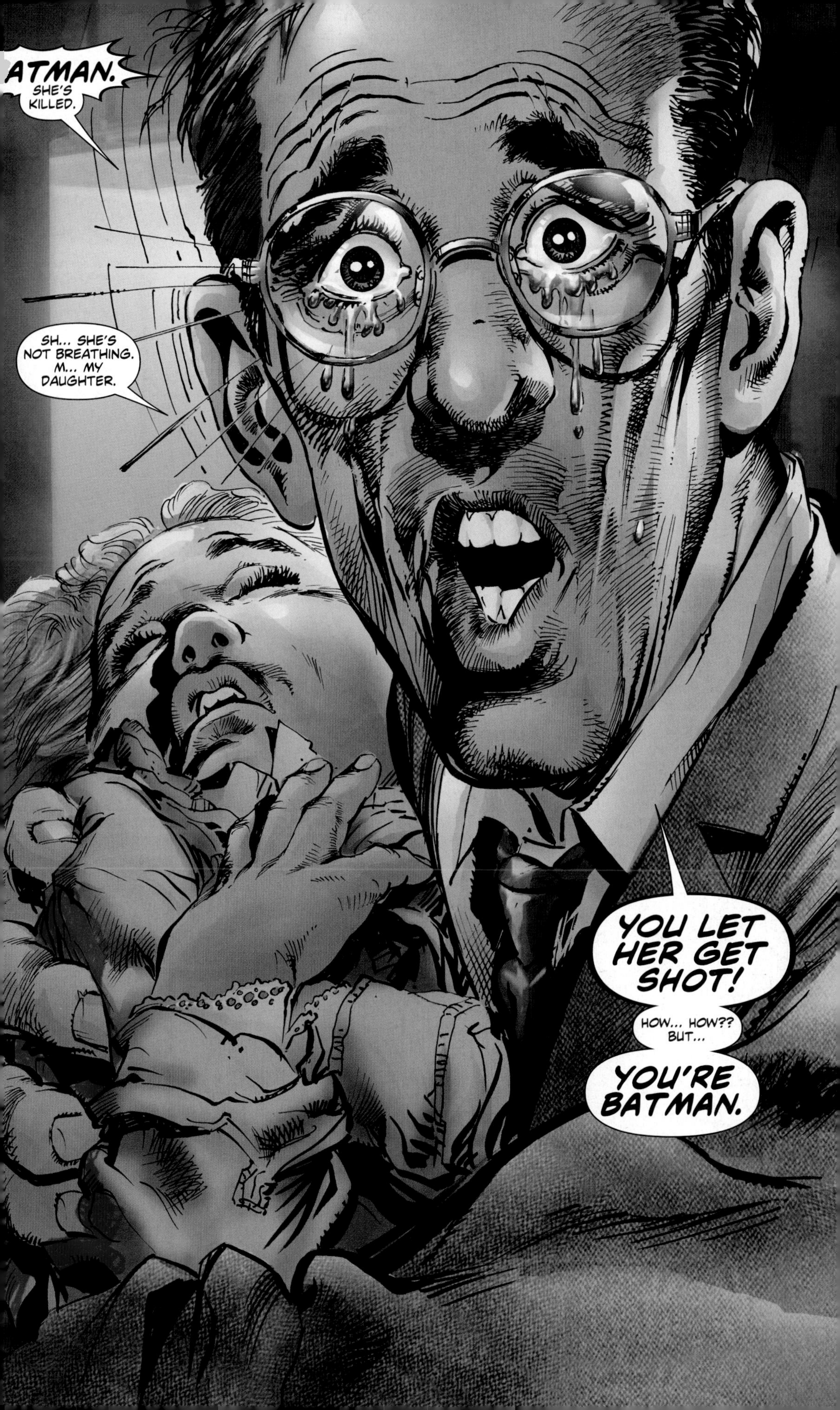
ATMAN.
SHE'S KILLED.
SH... SHE'S NOT BREATHING. M... MY DAUGHTER.
YOU LET HER GET SHOT!
HOW... HOW?? BUT...
YOU'RE BATMAN.

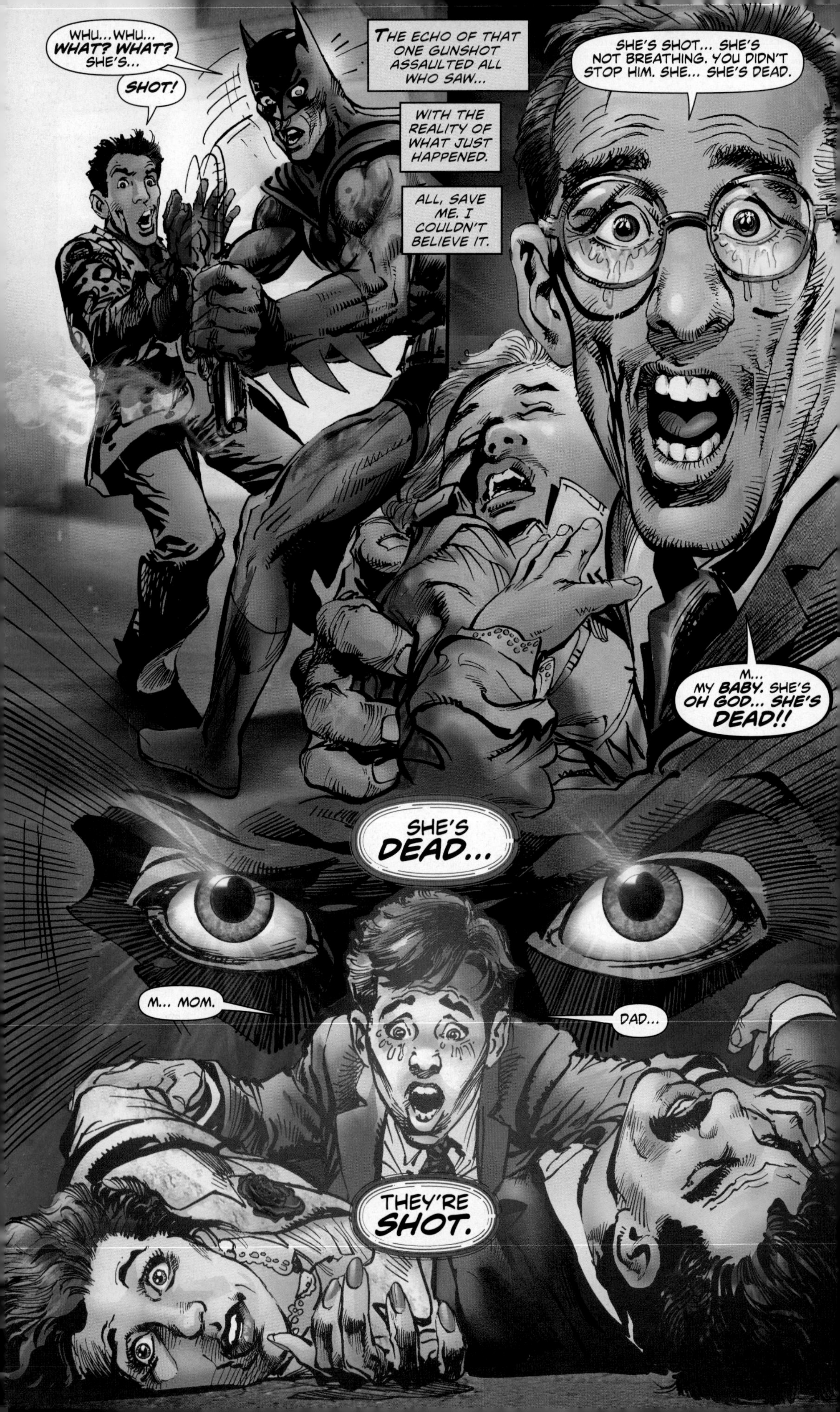

WHU...WHU... WHAT? WHAT? SHE'S...
SHOT!
THE ECHO OF THAT ONE GUNSHOT ASSAULTED ALL WHO SAW...
WITH THE REALITY OF WHAT JUST HAPPENED.
ALL, SAVE ME. I COULDN'T BELIEVE IT.
SHE'S SHOT... SHE'S NOT BREATHING. YOU DIDN'T STOP HIM. SHE... SHE'S DEAD.
M... MY BABY. SHE'S OH GOD... SHE'S DEAD!!
SHE'S DEAD...
M... MOM.
DAD...
THEY'RE SHOT.

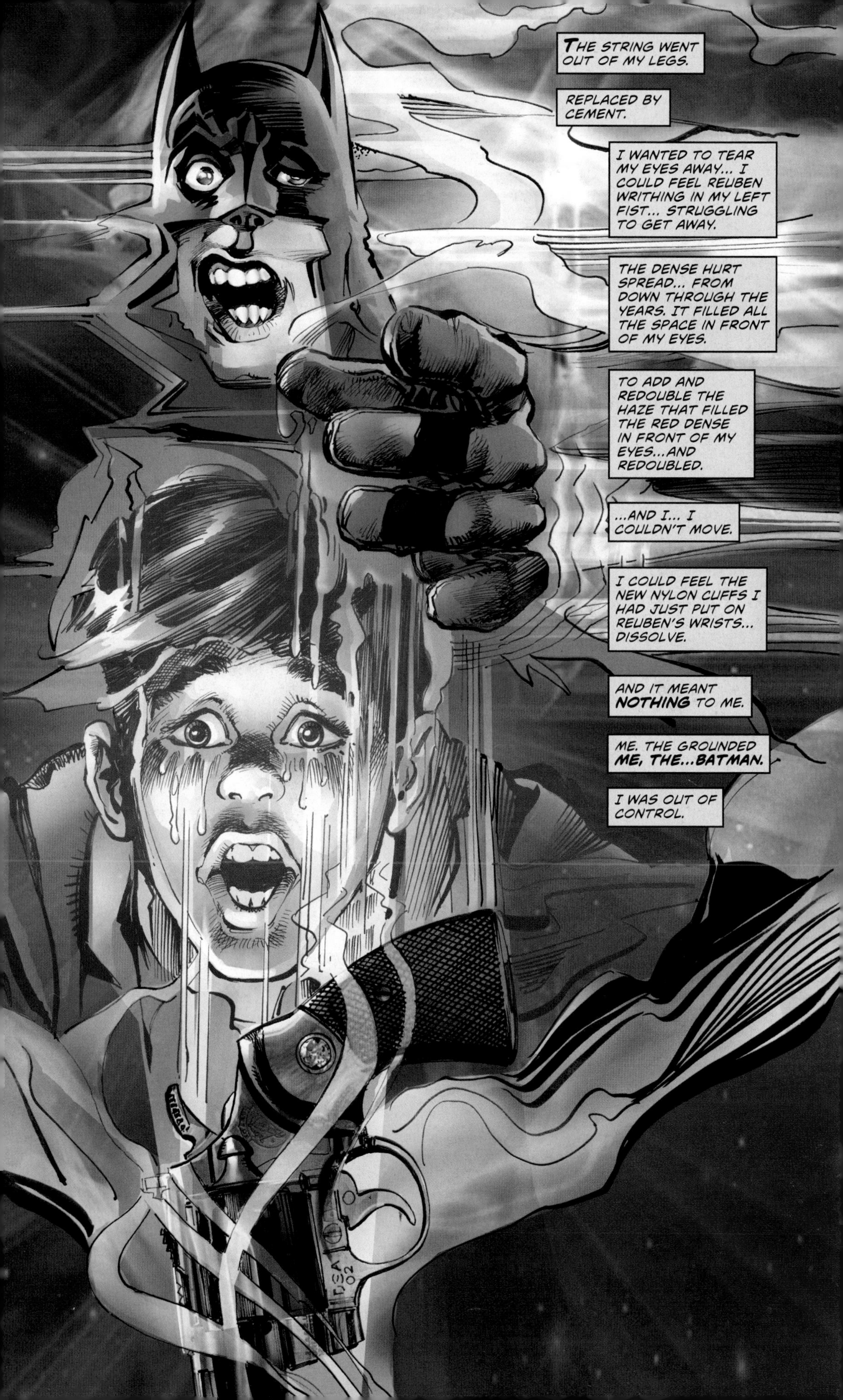
THE STRING WENT OUT OF MY LEGS.
REPLACED BY CEMENT.
I WANTED TO TEAR MY EYES AWAY... I COULD FEEL REUBEN WRITHING IN MY LEFT FIST... STRUGGLING TO GET AWAY.
THE DENSE HURT SPREAD... FROM DOWN THROUGH THE YEARS. IT FILLED ALL THE SPACE IN FRONT OF MY EYES.
TO ADD AND REDOUBLE THE HAZE THAT FILLED THE RED DENSE IN FRONT OF MY EYES...AND REDOUBLED.
...AND I... I COULDN'T MOVE.
I COULD FEEL THE NEW NYLON CUFFS I HAD JUST PUT ON REUBEN'S WRISTS... DISSOLVE.
AND IT MEANT NOTHING TO ME.
ME. THE GROUNDED ME, THE...BATMAN.
I WAS OUT OF CONTROL.

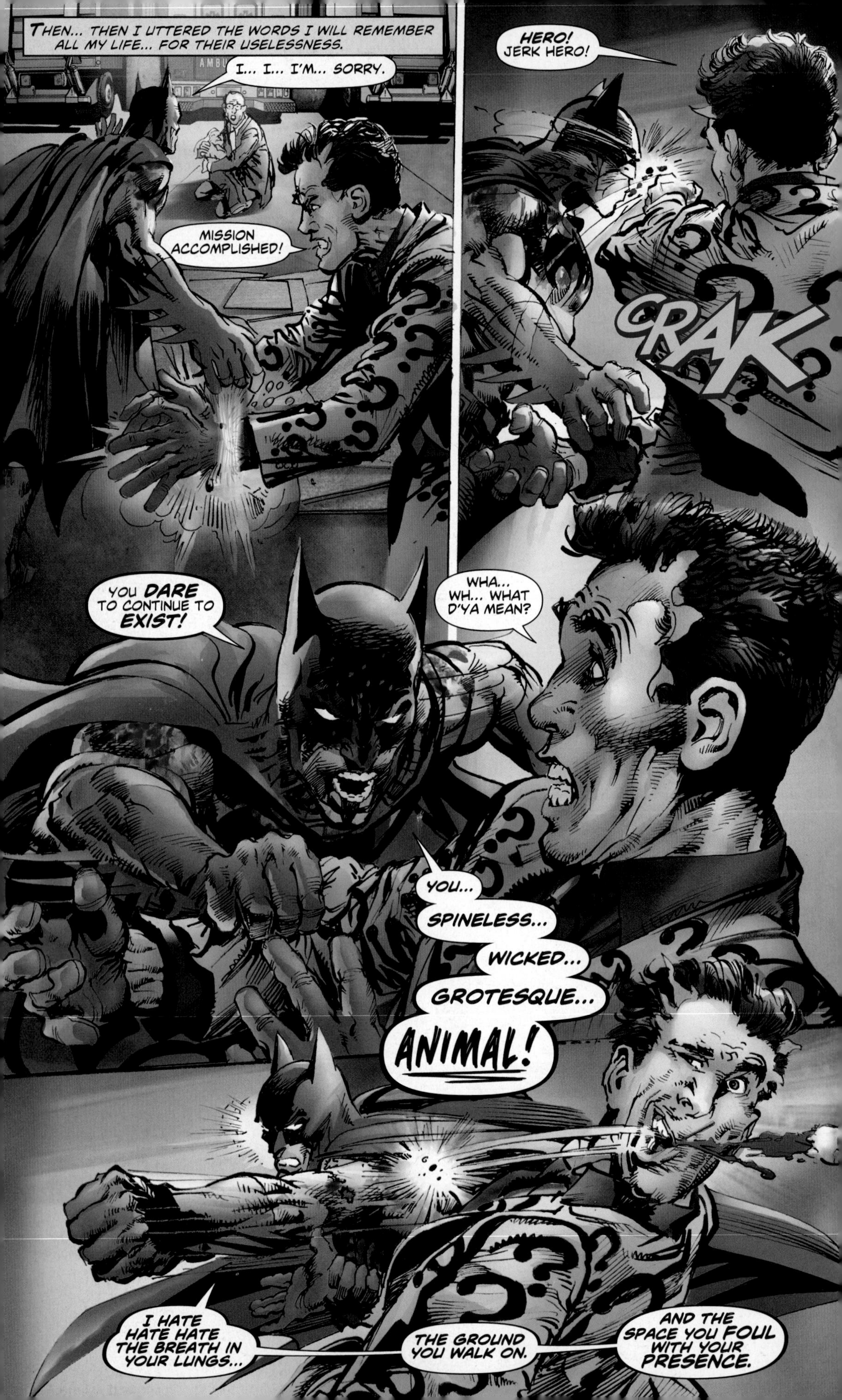
THEN... THEN I UTTERED THE WORDS I WILL REMEMBER ALL MY LIFE... FOR THEIR USELESSNESS.
I... I... I'M... SORRY.
MISSION ACCOMPLISHED!
HERO! JERK HERO!
CRAK!
YOU DARE TO CONTINUE TO EXIST!
WHA... WH... WHAT D'YA MEAN?
YOU...
SPINELESS...
WICKED...
GROTESQUE...
ANIMAL!
I HATE HATE HATE THE BREATH IN YOUR LUNGS...
THE GROUND YOU WALK ON.
AND THE SPACE YOU FOUL WITH YOUR PRESENCE.

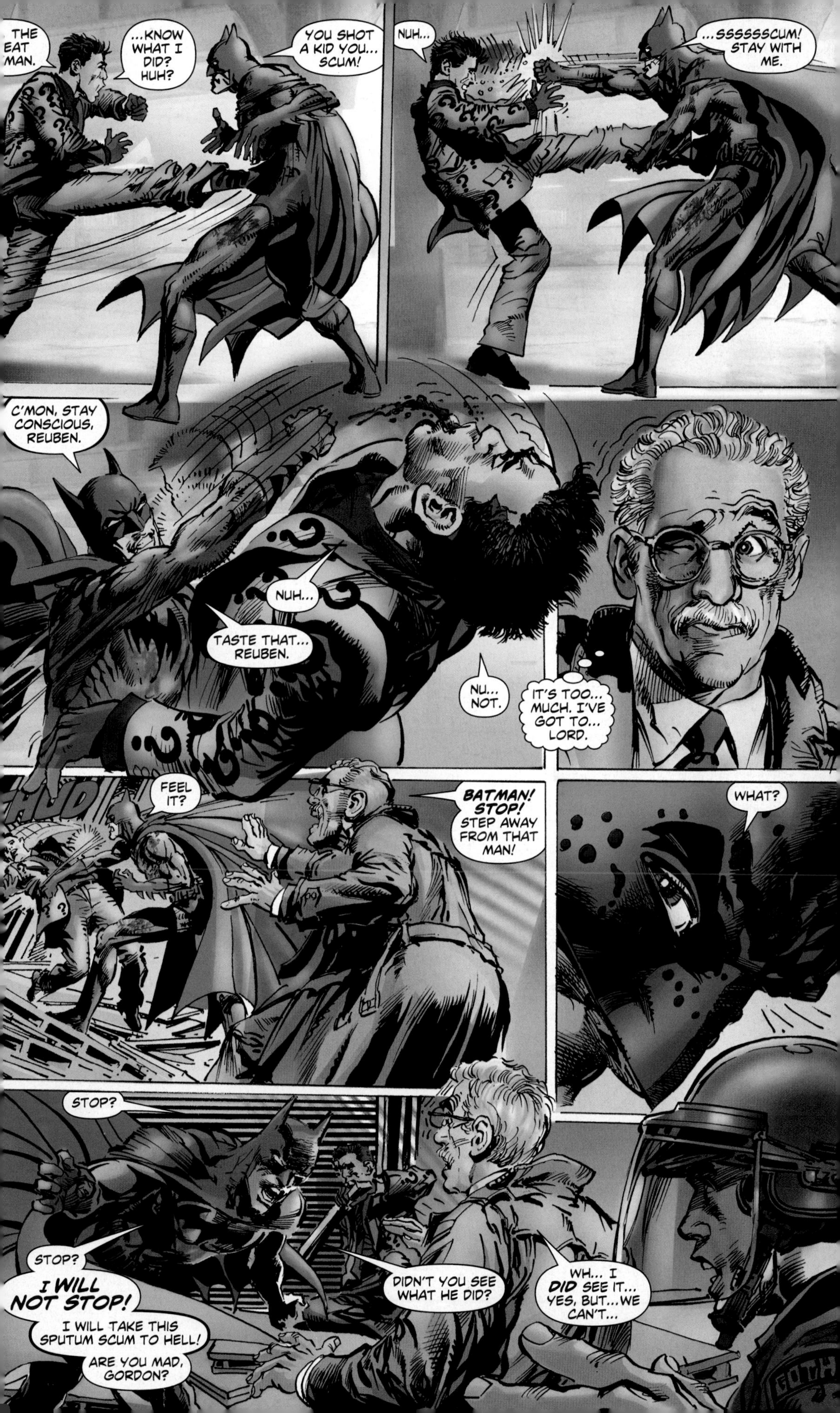
THE
EAT
MAN.
...KNOW WHAT I DID? HUH?
YOU SHOT A KID YOU... SCUM!
NUH...
...SSSSSSCUM! STAY WITH ME.
C'MON, STAY CONSCIOUS, REUBEN.
NUH...
TASTE THAT... REUBEN.
NU... NOT.
IT'S TOO... MUCH. I'VE GOT TO... LORD.
FEEL IT?
BATMAN! STOP! STEP AWAY FROM THAT MAN!
WHAT?
STOP?
STOP? I WILL NOT STOP!
I WILL TAKE THIS SPUTUM SCUM TO HELL!
ARE YOU MAD, GORDON?
DIDN'T YOU SEE WHAT HE DID?
WH... I DID SEE IT... YES, BUT... WE CAN'T...

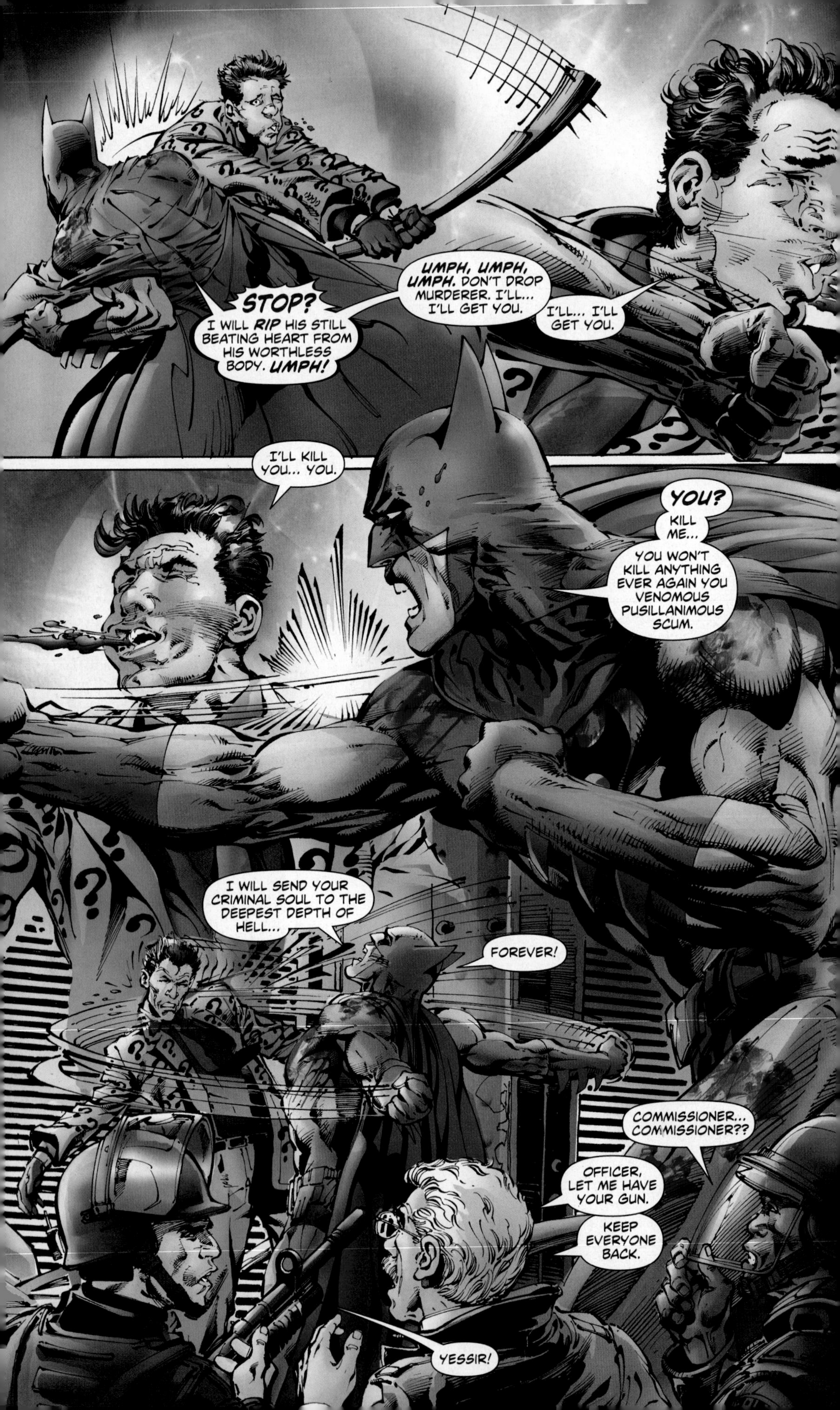
STOP? I WILL RIP HIS STILL BEATING HEART FROM HIS WORTHLESS BODY. UMPH!
UMPH, UMPH, UMPH. DON'T DROP MURDERER. I'LL... I'LL GET YOU.
I'LL... I'LL GET YOU.
I'LL KILL YOU... YOU.
YOU?
KILL ME...
YOU WON'T KILL ANYTHING EVER AGAIN YOU VENOMOUS PUSILLANIMOUS SCUM.
I WILL SEND YOUR CRIMINAL SOUL TO THE DEEPEST DEPTH OF HELL...
FOREVER!
COMMISSIONER... COMMISSIONER??
OFFICER, LET ME HAVE YOUR GUN.
KEEP EVERYONE BACK.
YESSIR!

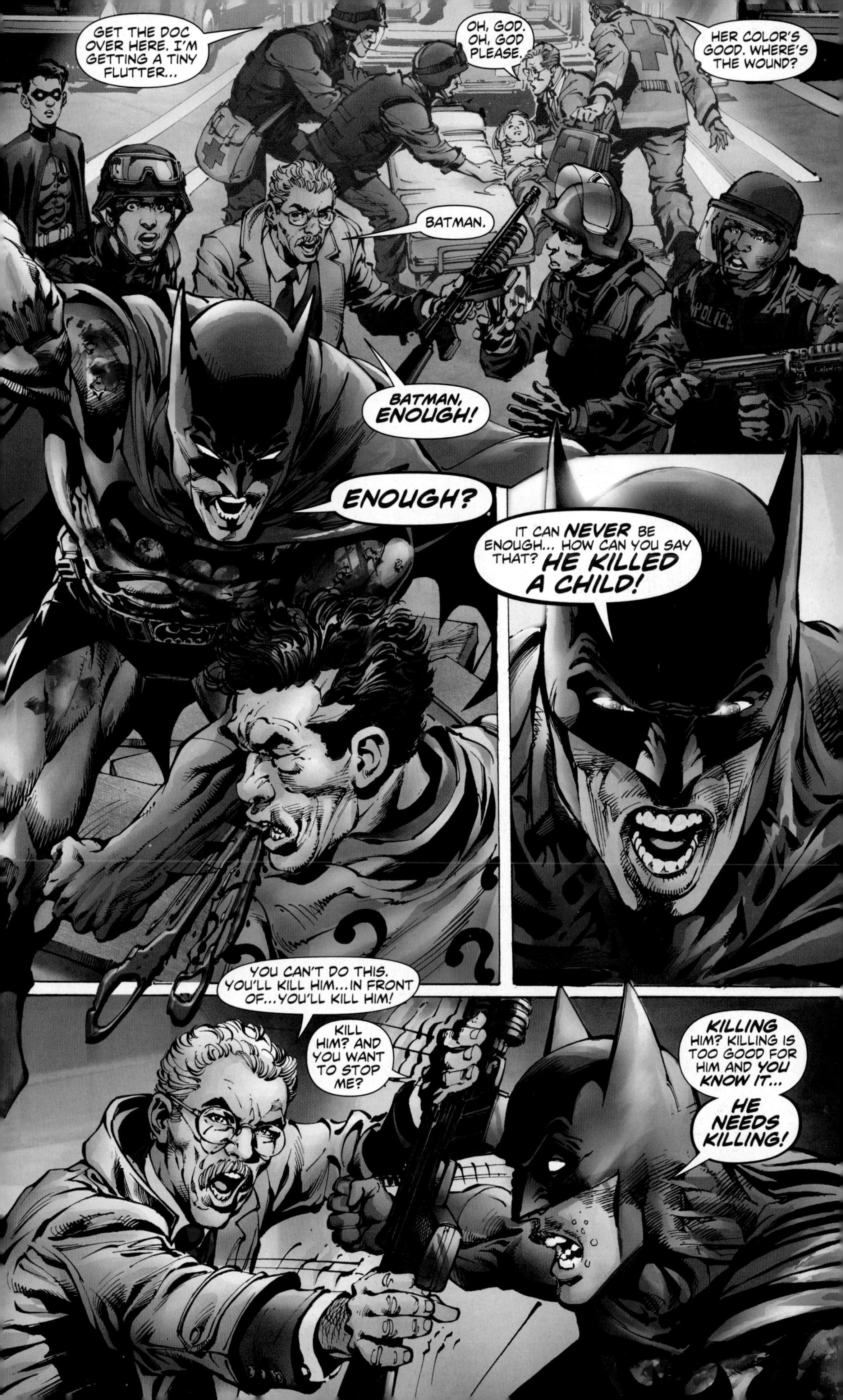
GET THE DOC OVER HERE. I'M GETTING A TINY FLUTTER...
OH, GOD. OH, GOD PLEASE.
HER COLOR'S GOOD. WHERE'S THE WOUND?
BATMAN.
BATMAN, ENOUGH!
ENOUGH?
IT CAN NEVER BE ENOUGH... HOW CAN YOU SAY THAT? HE KILLED A CHILD!
YOU CAN'T DO THIS. YOU'LL KILL HIM...IN FRONT OF...YOU'LL KILL HIM!
KILL HIM? AND YOU WANT TO STOP ME?
KILLING HIM? KILLING IS TOO GOOD FOR HIM AND YOU KNOW IT...
HE NEEDS KILLING!

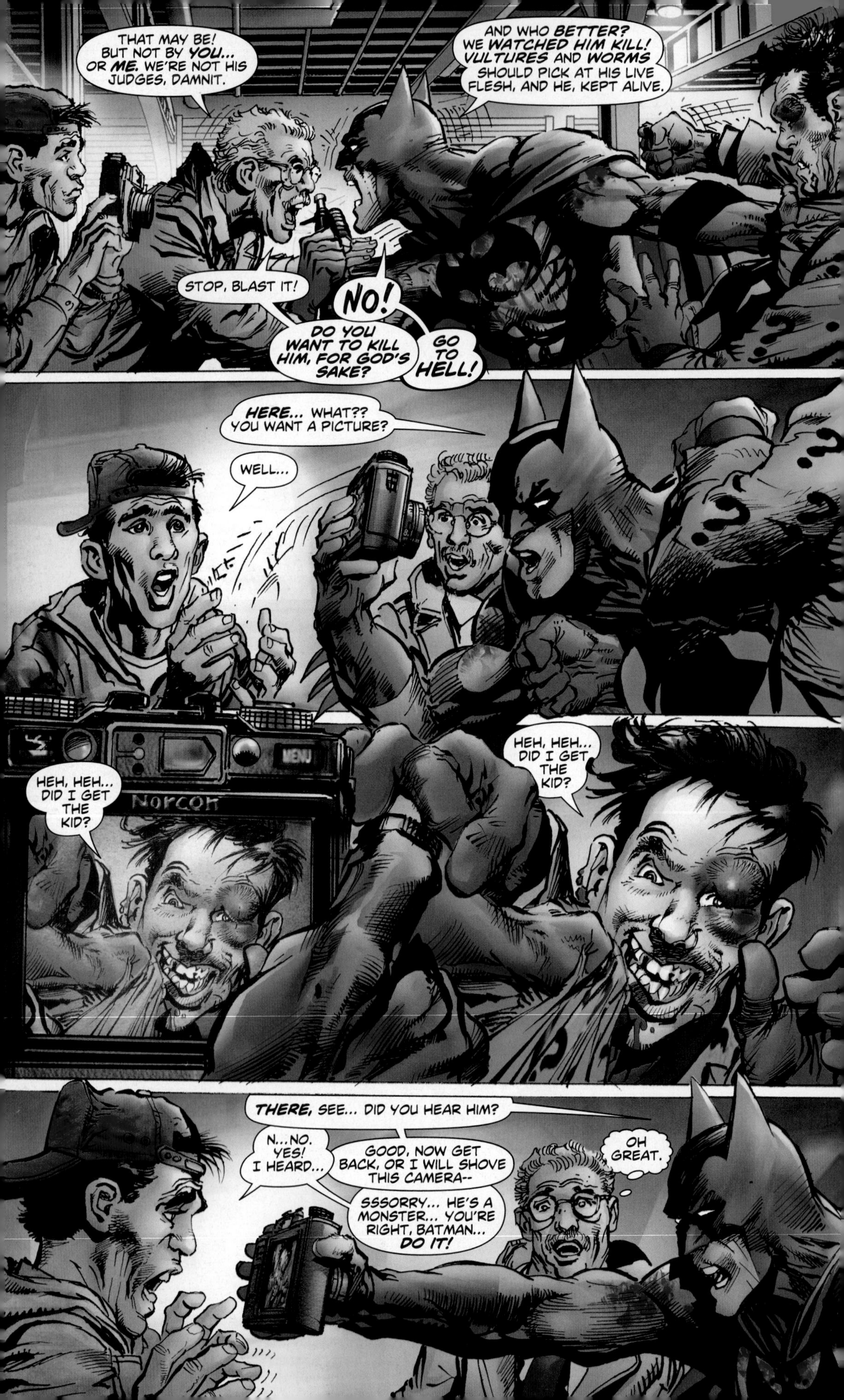
THAT MAY BE! BUT NOT BY YOU... OR ME. WE'RE NOT HIS JUDGES, DAMNIT.
AND WHO BETTER? WE WATCHED HIM KILL! VULTURES AND WORMS SHOULD PICK AT HIS LIVE FLESH, AND HE, KEPT ALIVE.
STOP, BLAST IT!
NO!
DO YOU WANT TO KILL HIM, FOR GOD'S SAKE?
GO TO HELL!
HERE... WHAT?? YOU WANT A PICTURE?
WELL...
MENU
NORCON
HEH, HEH... DID I GET THE KID?
HEH, HEH... DID I GET THE KID?
THERE, SEE... DID YOU HEAR HIM?
N...NO. YES! I HEARD...
GOOD, NOW GET BACK, OR I WILL SHOVE THIS CAMERA--
SSSORRY... HE'S A MONSTER... YOU'RE RIGHT, BATMAN... DO IT!
OH GREAT.

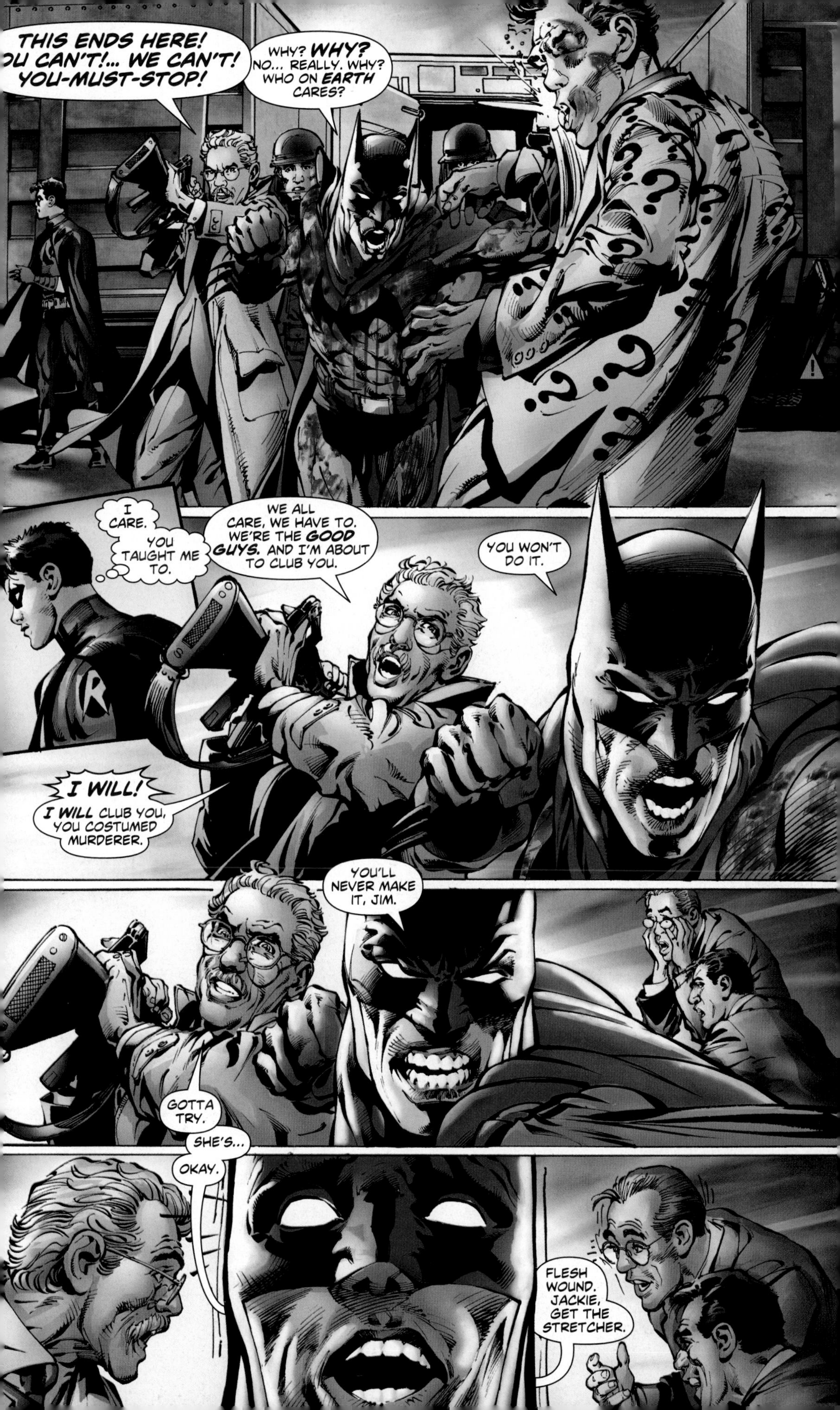
THIS ENDS HERE! YOU CAN'T!... WE CAN'T! YOU-MUST-STOP!
WHY? WHY? NO... REALLY. WHY? WHO ON EARTH CARES?
I CARE. YOU TAUGHT ME TO.
WE ALL CARE, WE HAVE TO. WE'RE THE GOOD GUYS. AND I'M ABOUT TO CLUB YOU.
YOU WON'T DO IT.
I WILL! I WILL CLUB YOU, YOU COSTUMED MURDERER.
YOU'LL NEVER MAKE IT, JIM.
GOTTA TRY.
SHE'S...
OKAY.
FLESH WOUND. JACKIE, GET THE STRETCHER.

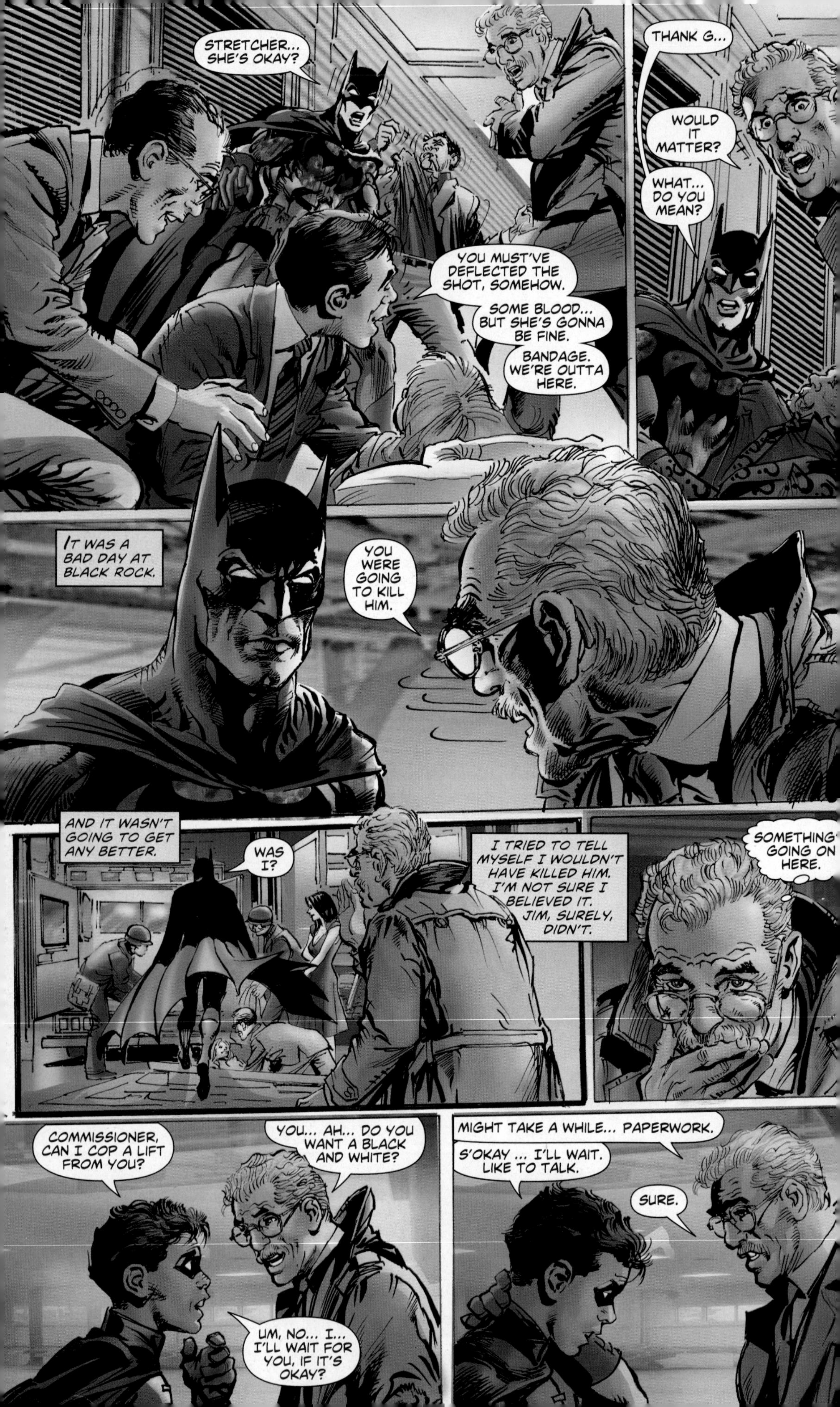

STRETCHER... SHE'S OKAY?
YOU MUST'VE DEFLECTED THE SHOT, SOMEHOW.
SOME BLOOD... BUT SHE'S GONNA BE FINE.
BANDAGE. WE'RE OUTTA HERE.
THANK G...
WOULD IT MATTER?
WHAT... DO YOU MEAN?
IT WAS A BAD DAY AT BLACK ROCK.
YOU WERE GOING TO KILL HIM.
AND IT WASN'T GOING TO GET ANY BETTER.
WAS I?
I TRIED TO TELL MYSELF I WOULDN'T HAVE KILLED HIM. I'M NOT SURE I BELIEVED IT. JIM, SURELY, DIDN'T.
SOMETHING GOING ON HERE.
COMMISSIONER, CAN I COP A LIFT FROM YOU?
YOU... AH... DO YOU WANT A BLACK AND WHITE?
UM, NO... I... I'LL WAIT FOR YOU, IF IT'S OKAY?
MIGHT TAKE A WHILE... PAPERWORK.
S'OKAY ... I'LL WAIT. LIKE TO TALK.
SURE.

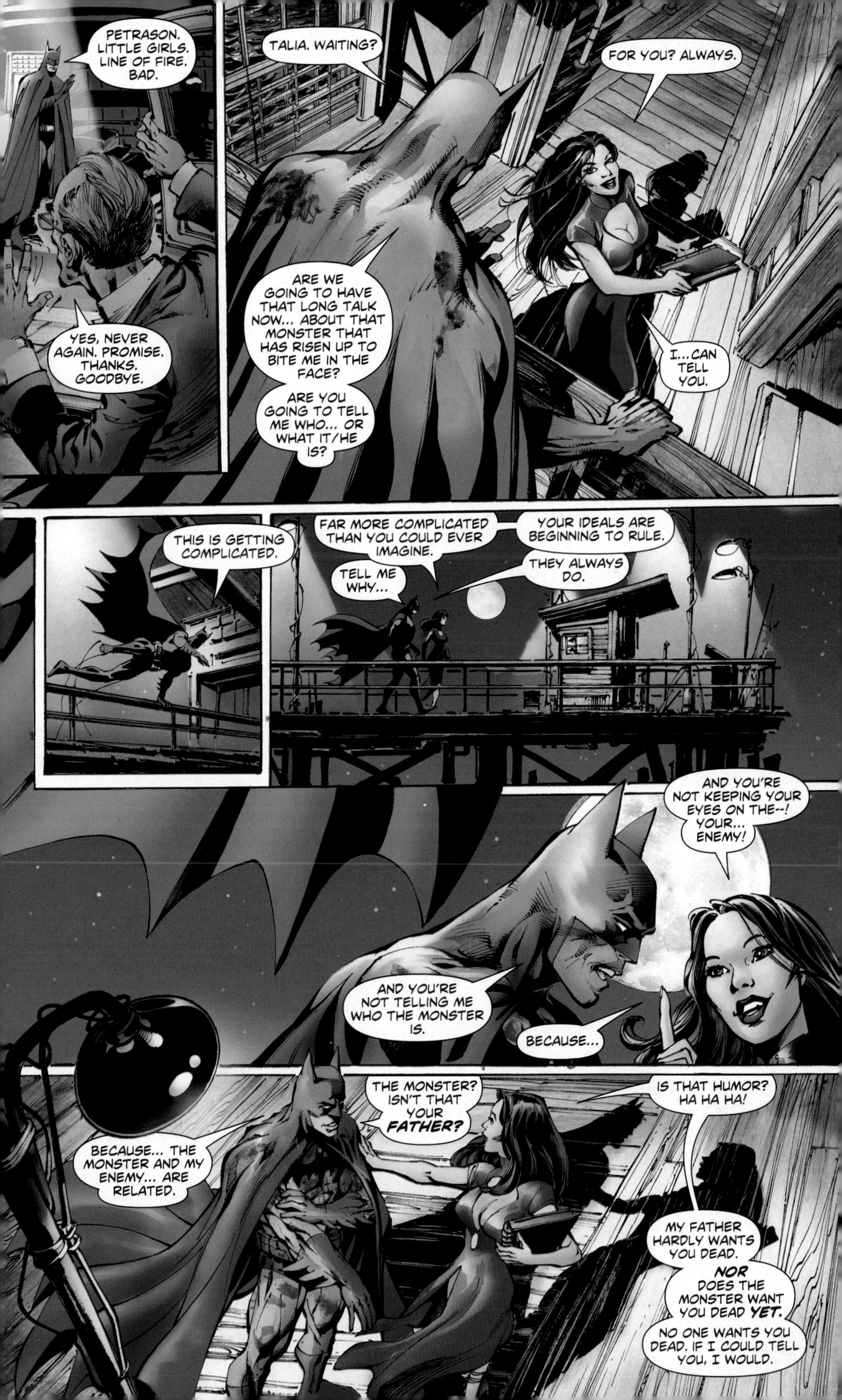
PETRASON. LITTLE GIRLS. LINE OF FIRE. BAD.
YES, NEVER AGAIN. PROMISE. THANKS. GOODBYE.
TALIA. WAITING?
FOR YOU? ALWAYS.
ARE WE GOING TO HAVE THAT LONG TALK NOW... ABOUT THAT MONSTER THAT HAS RISEN UP TO BITE ME IN THE FACE?
ARE YOU GOING TO TELL ME WHO... OR WHAT IT/HE IS?
I...CAN TELL YOU.
THIS IS GETTING COMPLICATED.
FAR MORE COMPLICATED THAN YOU COULD EVER IMAGINE.
TELL ME WHY...
YOUR IDEALS ARE BEGINNING TO RULE.
THEY ALWAYS DO.
AND YOU'RE NOT KEEPING YOUR EYES ON THE--! YOUR... ENEMY!
AND YOU'RE NOT TELLING ME WHO THE MONSTER IS.
BECAUSE...
BECAUSE... THE MONSTER AND MY ENEMY... ARE RELATED.
THE MONSTER? ISN'T THAT YOUR FATHER?
IS THAT HUMOR? HA HA HA!
MY FATHER HARDLY WANTS YOU DEAD.
NOR DOES THE MONSTER WANT YOU DEAD YET.
NO ONE WANTS YOU DEAD. IF I COULD TELL YOU, I WOULD.

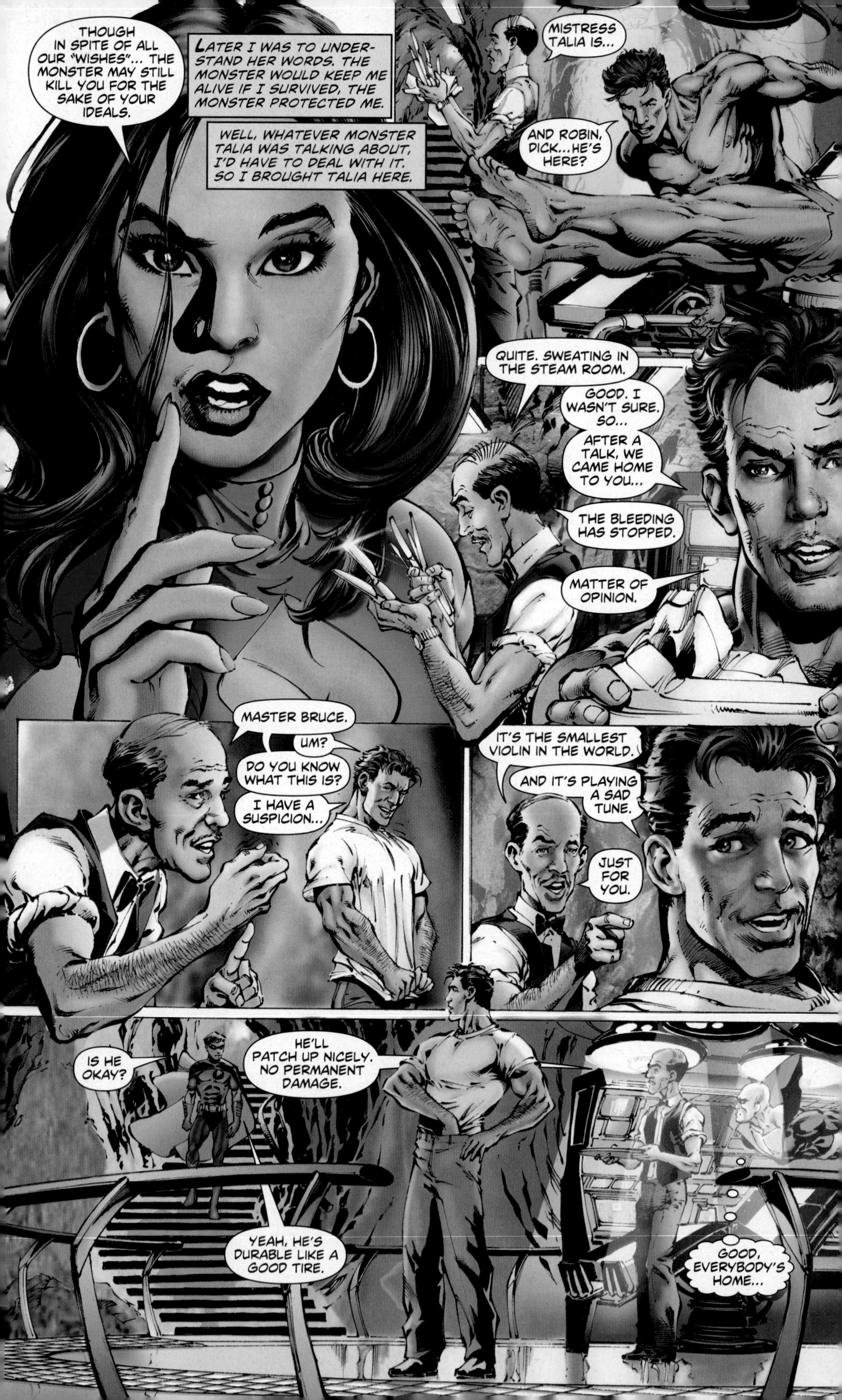
THOUGH IN SPITE OF ALL OUR "WISHES"... THE MONSTER MAY STILL KILL YOU FOR THE SAKE OF YOUR IDEALS.
LATER I WAS TO UNDERSTAND HER WORDS. THE MONSTER WOULD KEEP ME ALIVE IF I SURVIVED, THE MONSTER PROTECTED ME.
WELL, WHATEVER MONSTER TALIA WAS TALKING ABOUT, I'D HAVE TO DEAL WITH IT. SO I BROUGHT TALIA HERE.
MISTRESS TALIA IS...
AND ROBIN, DICK...HE'S HERE?
QUITE. SWEATING IN THE STEAM ROOM.
GOOD. I WASN'T SURE. SO...
AFTER A TALK, WE CAME HOME TO YOU...
THE BLEEDING HAS STOPPED.
MATTER OF OPINION.
MASTER BRUCE.
UM?
DO YOU KNOW WHAT THIS IS?
I HAVE A SUSPICION...
IT'S THE SMALLEST VIOLIN IN THE WORLD.
AND IT'S PLAYING A SAD TUNE.
JUST FOR YOU.
IS HE OKAY?
HE'LL PATCH UP NICELY. NO PERMANENT DAMAGE.
YEAH, HE'S DURABLE LIKE A GOOD TIRE.
GOOD, EVERYBODY'S HOME...

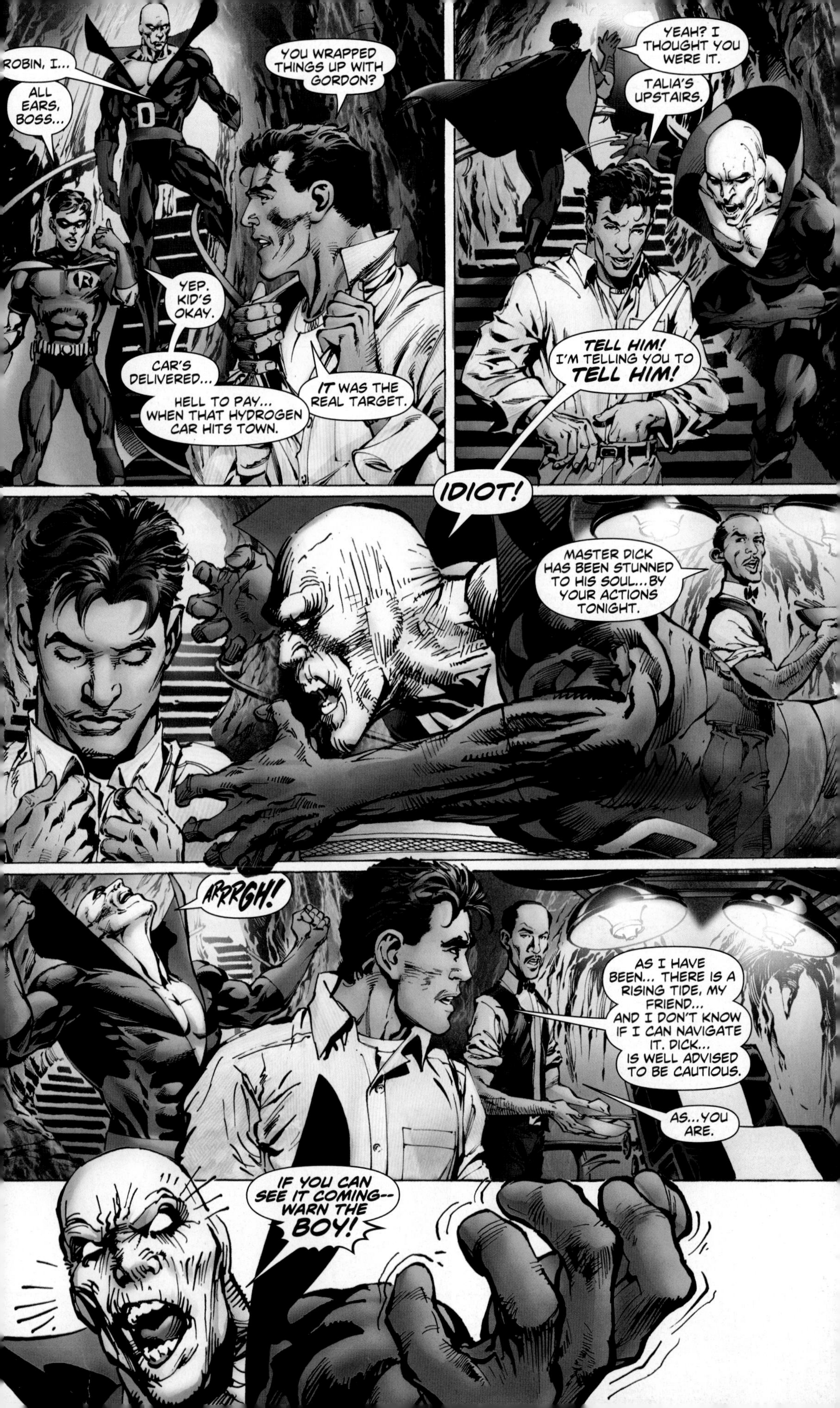
ROBIN, I...
ALL EARS, BOSS...
YOU WRAPPED THINGS UP WITH GORDON?
YEP. KID'S OKAY.
CAR'S DELIVERED...
HELL TO PAY... WHEN THAT HYDROGEN CAR HITS TOWN.
IT WAS THE REAL TARGET.
YEAH? I THOUGHT YOU WERE IT.
TALIA'S UPSTAIRS.
TELL HIM! I'M TELLING YOU TO TELL HIM!
IDIOT!
MASTER DICK HAS BEEN STUNNED TO HIS SOUL... BY YOUR ACTIONS TONIGHT.
ARRRGH!
AS I HAVE BEEN... THERE IS A RISING TIDE, MY FRIEND...
AND I DON'T KNOW IF I CAN NAVIGATE IT. DICK...
IS WELL ADVISED TO BE CAUTIOUS.
AS...YOU ARE.
IF YOU CAN SEE IT COMING-- WARN THE BOY!

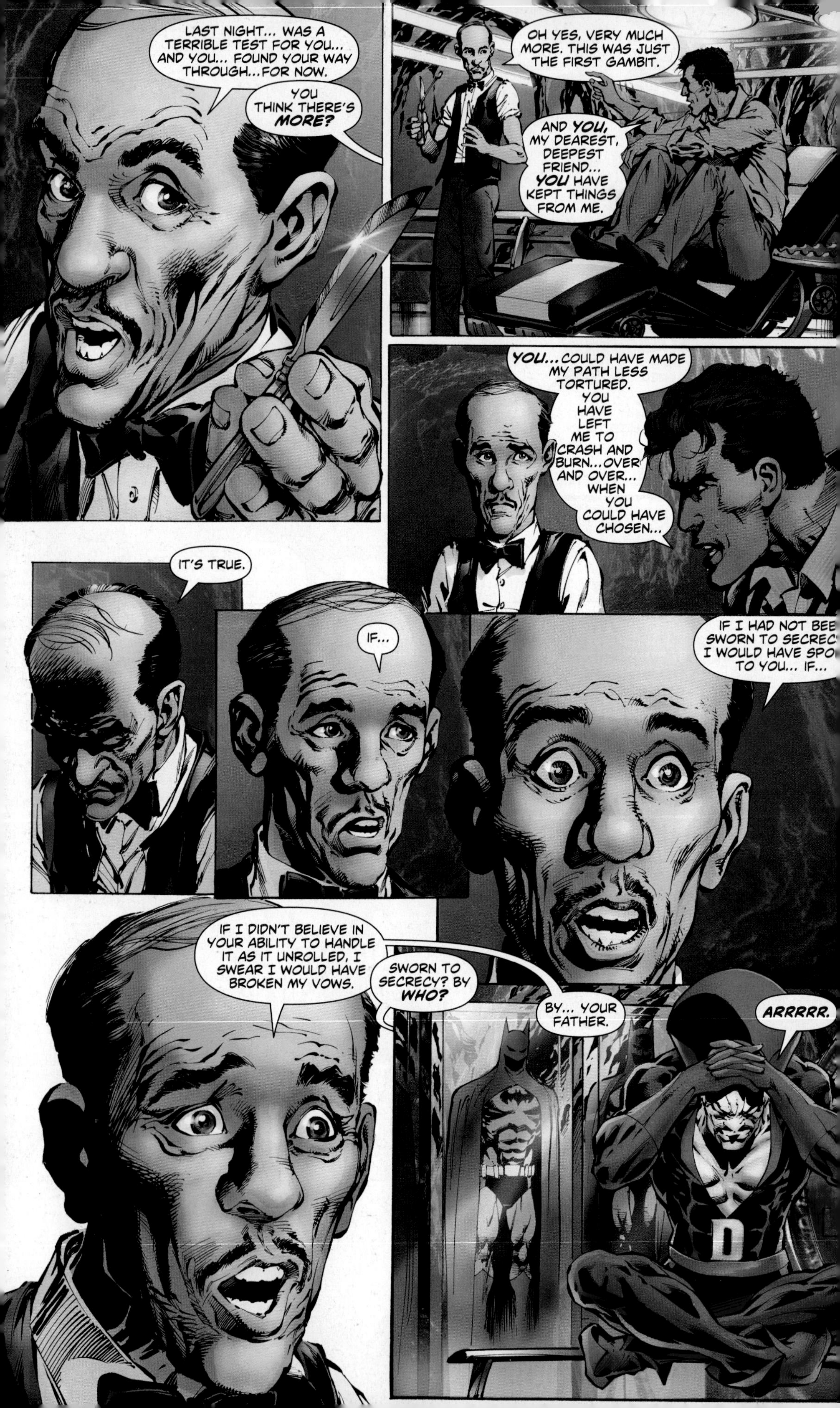
LAST NIGHT... WAS A TERRIBLE TEST FOR YOU... AND YOU... FOUND YOUR WAY THROUGH...FOR NOW.
YOU THINK THERE'S MORE?
OH YES, VERY MUCH MORE. THIS WAS JUST THE FIRST GAMBIT.
AND YOU, MY DEAREST, DEEPEST FRIEND... YOU HAVE KEPT THINGS FROM ME.
YOU...COULD HAVE MADE MY PATH LESS TORTURED. YOU HAVE LEFT ME TO CRASH AND BURN...OVER AND OVER... WHEN YOU COULD HAVE CHOSEN...
IT'S TRUE.
IF...
IF I HAD NOT BEE SWORN TO SECREC I WOULD HAVE SPO TO YOU... IF...
IF I DIDN'T BELIEVE IN YOUR ABILITY TO HANDLE IT AS IT UNROLLED, I SWEAR I WOULD HAVE BROKEN MY VOWS.
SWORN TO SECRECY? BY WHO?
BY... YOUR FATHER.
ARRRRR.

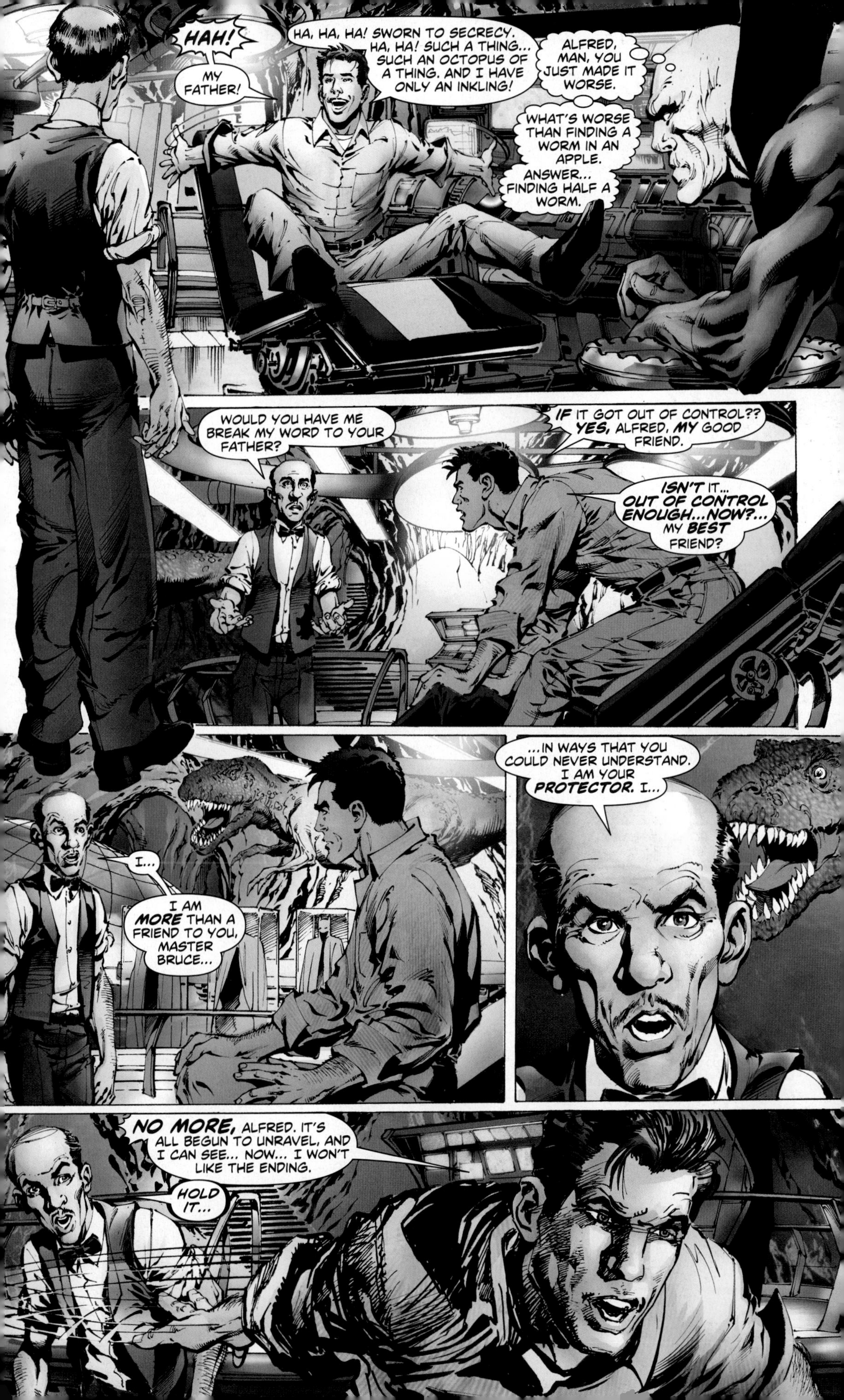
HAH!
MY FATHER!
HA, HA, HA! SWORN TO SECRECY. HA, HA! SUCH A THING... SUCH AN OCTOPUS OF A THING. AND I HAVE ONLY AN INKLING!
ALFRED, MAN, YOU JUST MADE IT WORSE.
WHAT'S WORSE THAN FINDING A WORM IN AN APPLE. ANSWER... FINDING HALF A WORM.
WOULD YOU HAVE ME BREAK MY WORD TO YOUR FATHER?
IF IT GOT OUT OF CONTROL?? YES, ALFRED, MY GOOD FRIEND.
ISN'T IT... OUT OF CONTROL ENOUGH...NOW?... MY BEST FRIEND?
I...
I AM MORE THAN A FRIEND TO YOU, MASTER BRUCE...
...IN WAYS THAT YOU COULD NEVER UNDERSTAND. I AM YOUR PROTECTOR. I...
NO MORE, ALFRED. IT'S ALL BEGUN TO UNRAVEL, AND I CAN SEE... NOW... I WON'T LIKE THE ENDING.
HOLD IT...

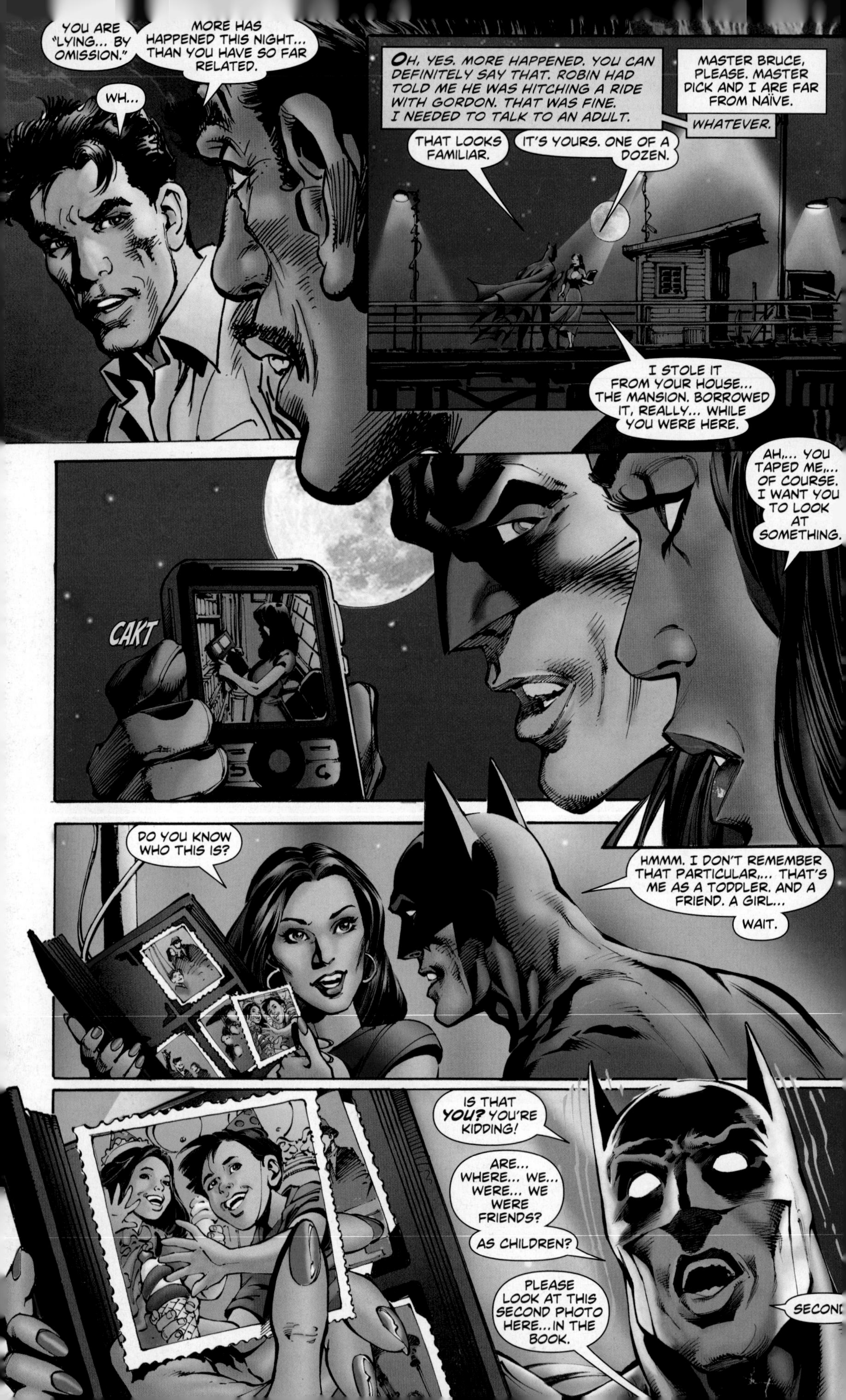

YOU ARE "LYING... BY OMISSION."
MORE HAS HAPPENED THIS NIGHT... THAN YOU HAVE SO FAR RELATED.
WH...
OH, YES. MORE HAPPENED. YOU CAN DEFINITELY SAY THAT. ROBIN HAD TOLD ME HE WAS HITCHING A RIDE WITH GORDON. THAT WAS FINE. I NEEDED TO TALK TO AN ADULT.
MASTER BRUCE, PLEASE. MASTER DICK AND I ARE FAR FROM NAÏVE.
WHATEVER.
THAT LOOKS FAMILIAR.
IT'S YOURS. ONE OF A DOZEN.
I STOLE IT FROM YOUR HOUSE... THE MANSION. BORROWED IT, REALLY... WHILE YOU WERE HERE.
AH,... YOU TAPED ME,... OF COURSE. I WANT YOU TO LOOK AT SOMETHING.
CAKT
DO YOU KNOW WHO THIS IS?
HMMM. I DON'T REMEMBER THAT PARTICULAR,... THAT'S ME AS A TODDLER. AND A FRIEND. A GIRL...
WAIT.
IS THAT YOU? YOU'RE KIDDING!
ARE... WHERE... WE... WERE... WE WERE FRIENDS?
AS CHILDREN?
PLEASE LOOK AT THIS SECOND PHOTO HERE...IN THE BOOK.
SECOND

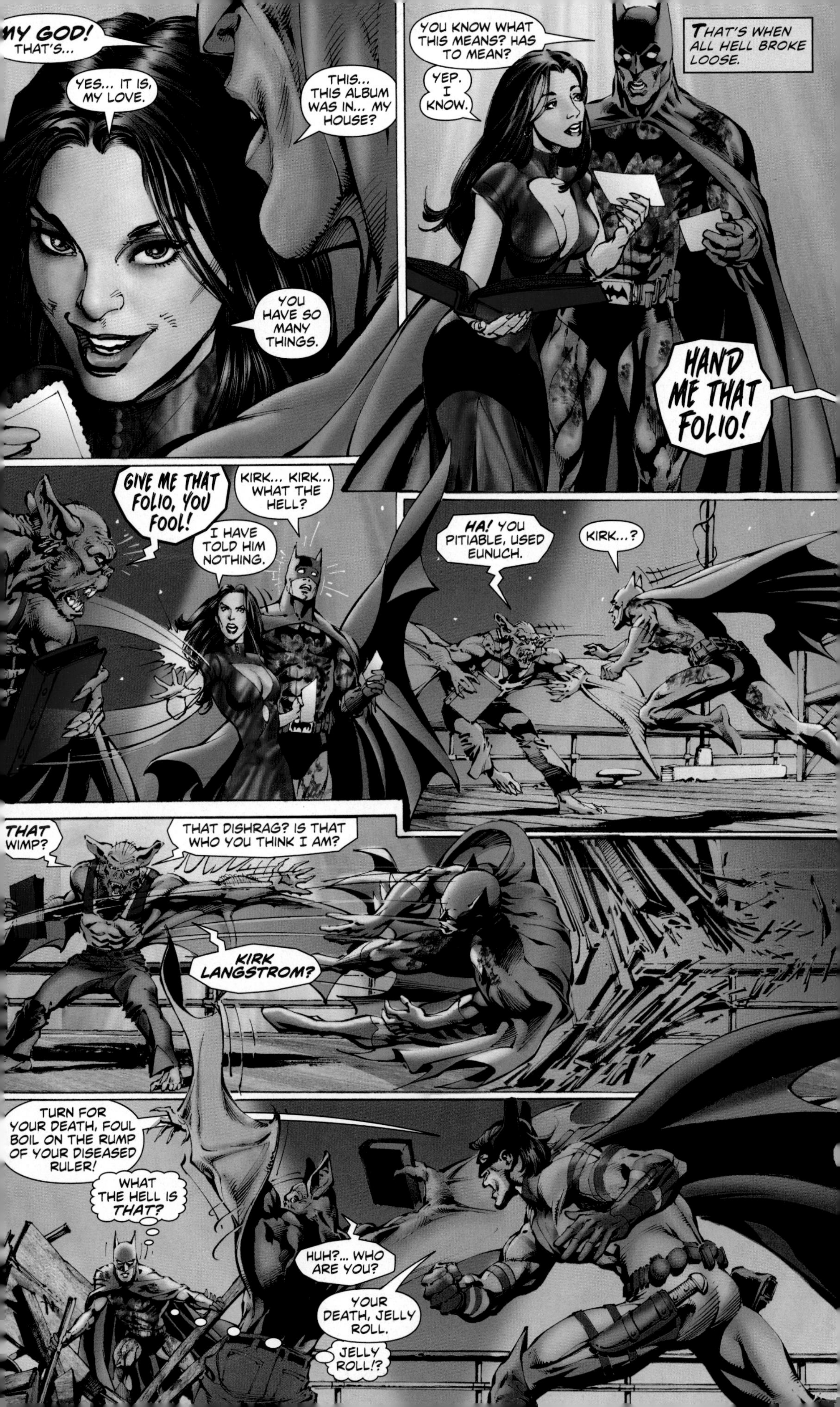
MY GOD! THAT'S...
YES... IT IS, MY LOVE.
THIS... THIS ALBUM WAS IN... MY HOUSE?
YOU HAVE SO MANY THINGS.
YOU KNOW WHAT THIS MEANS? HAS TO MEAN?
YEP. I KNOW.
THAT'S WHEN ALL HELL BROKE LOOSE.
HAND ME THAT FOLIO!
GIVE ME THAT FOLIO, YOU FOOL!
KIRK... KIRK... WHAT THE HELL?
I HAVE TOLD HIM NOTHING.
HA! YOU PITIABLE, USED EUNUCH.
KIRK...?
THAT WIMP?
THAT DISHRAG? IS THAT WHO YOU THINK I AM?
KIRK LANGSTROM?
TURN FOR YOUR DEATH, FOUL BOIL ON THE RUMP OF YOUR DISEASED RULER!
WHAT THE HELL IS THAT?
HUH?... WHO ARE YOU?
YOUR DEATH, JELLY ROLL.
JELLY ROLL!?

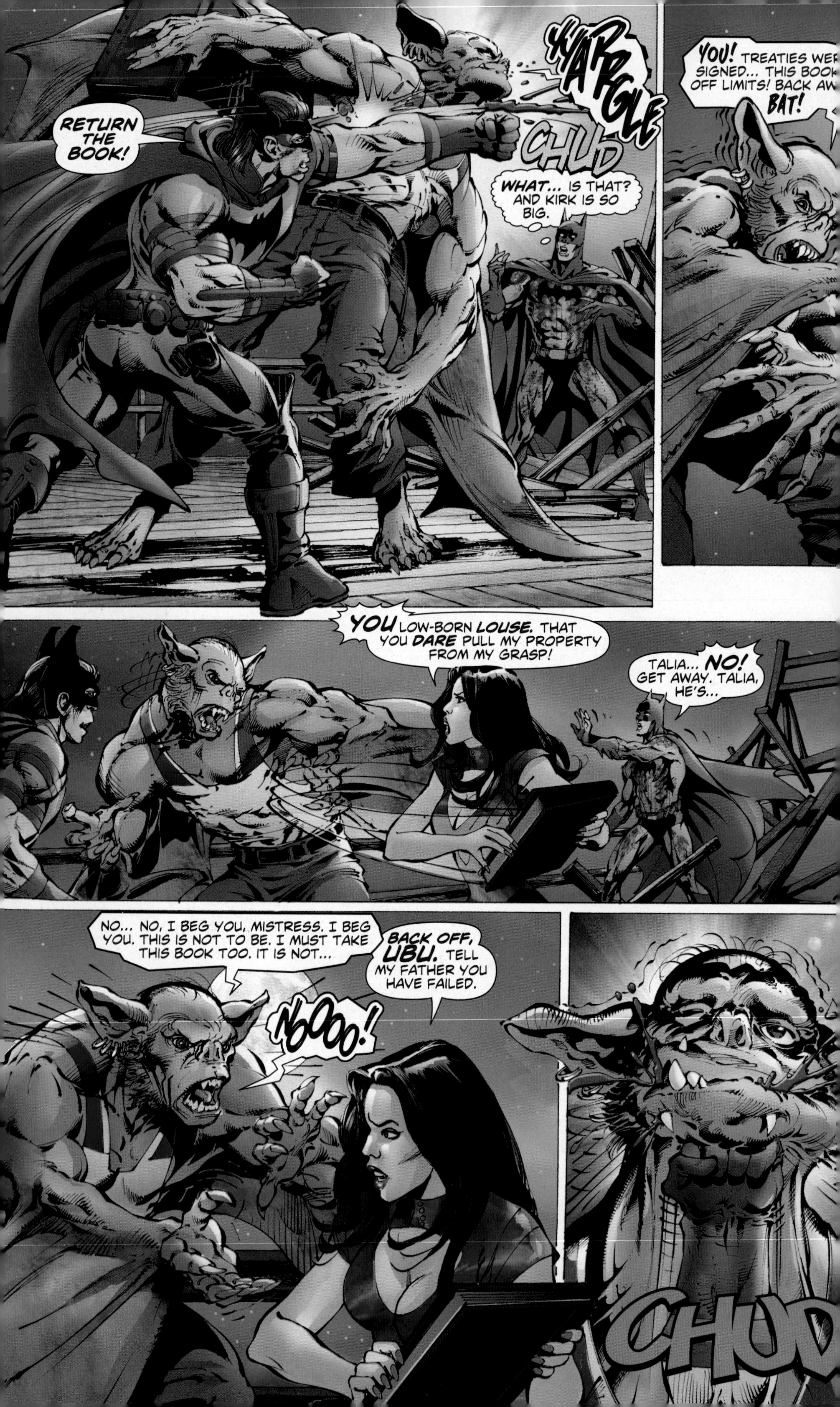
RETURN THE BOOK!
GYYARGGLE
CHUD
WHAT... IS THAT? AND KIRK IS SO BIG.
YOU! TREATIES WER SIGNED... THIS BOOK OFF LIMITS! BACK AW BAT!
YOU LOW-BORN LOUSE. THAT YOU DARE PULL MY PROPERTY FROM MY GRASP!
TALIA... NO! GET AWAY. TALIA, HE'S...
NO... NO, I BEG YOU, MISTRESS. I BEG YOU. THIS IS NOT TO BE. I MUST TAKE THIS BOOK TOO. IT IS NOT...
BACK OFF, UBU. TELL MY FATHER YOU HAVE FAILED.
NOOOO!
CHUD

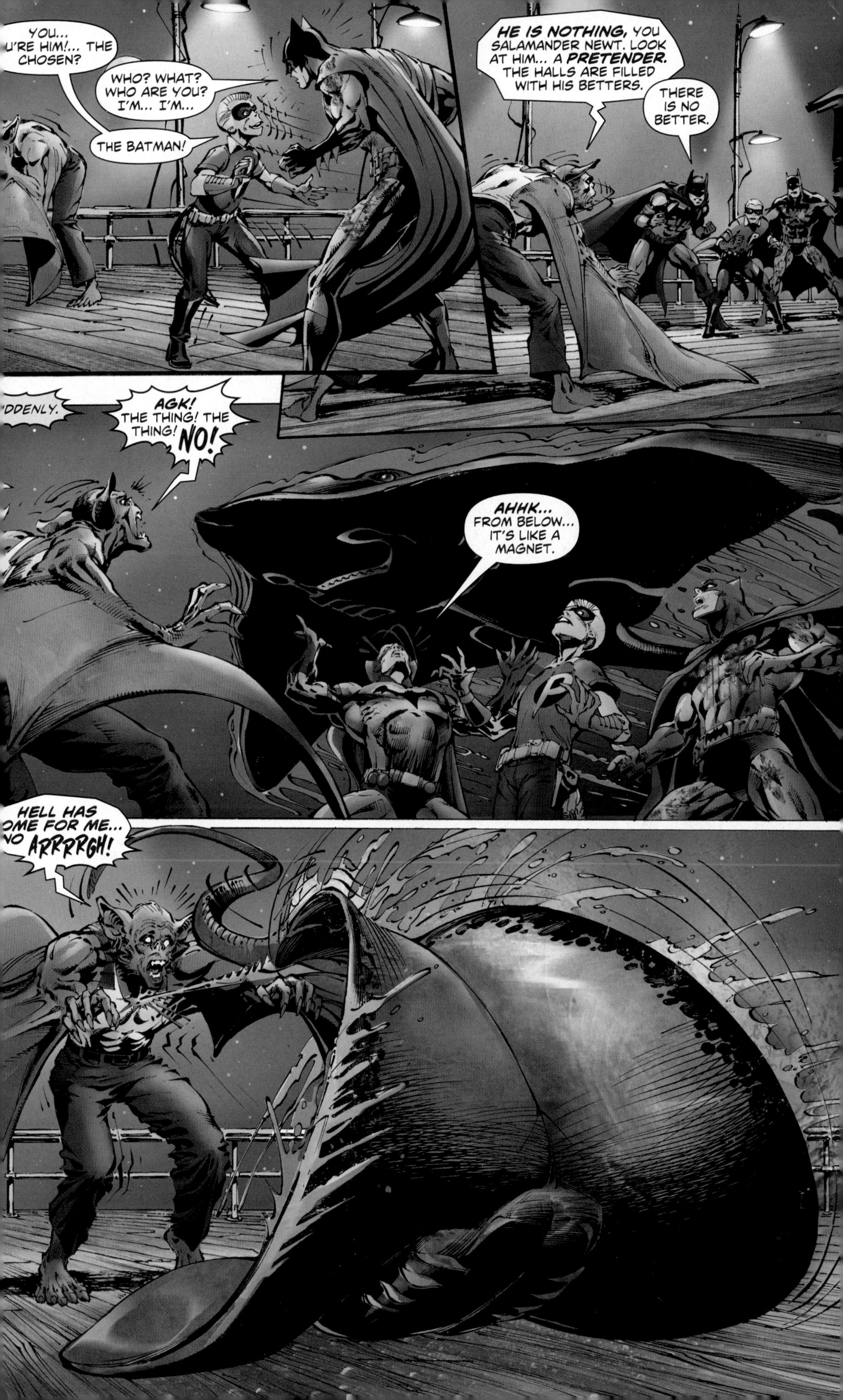
YOU... U'RE HIM!... THE CHOSEN?
WHO? WHAT? WHO ARE YOU? I'M... I'M...
THE BATMAN!
HE IS NOTHING, YOU SALAMANDER NEWT. LOOK AT HIM... A PRETENDER. THE HALLS ARE FILLED WITH HIS BETTERS.
THERE IS NO BETTER.
DDENLY.
AGK! THE THING! THE THING! NO!
AHHK... FROM BELOW... IT'S LIKE A MAGNET.
HELL HAS OME FOR ME... NO ARRRRGH!

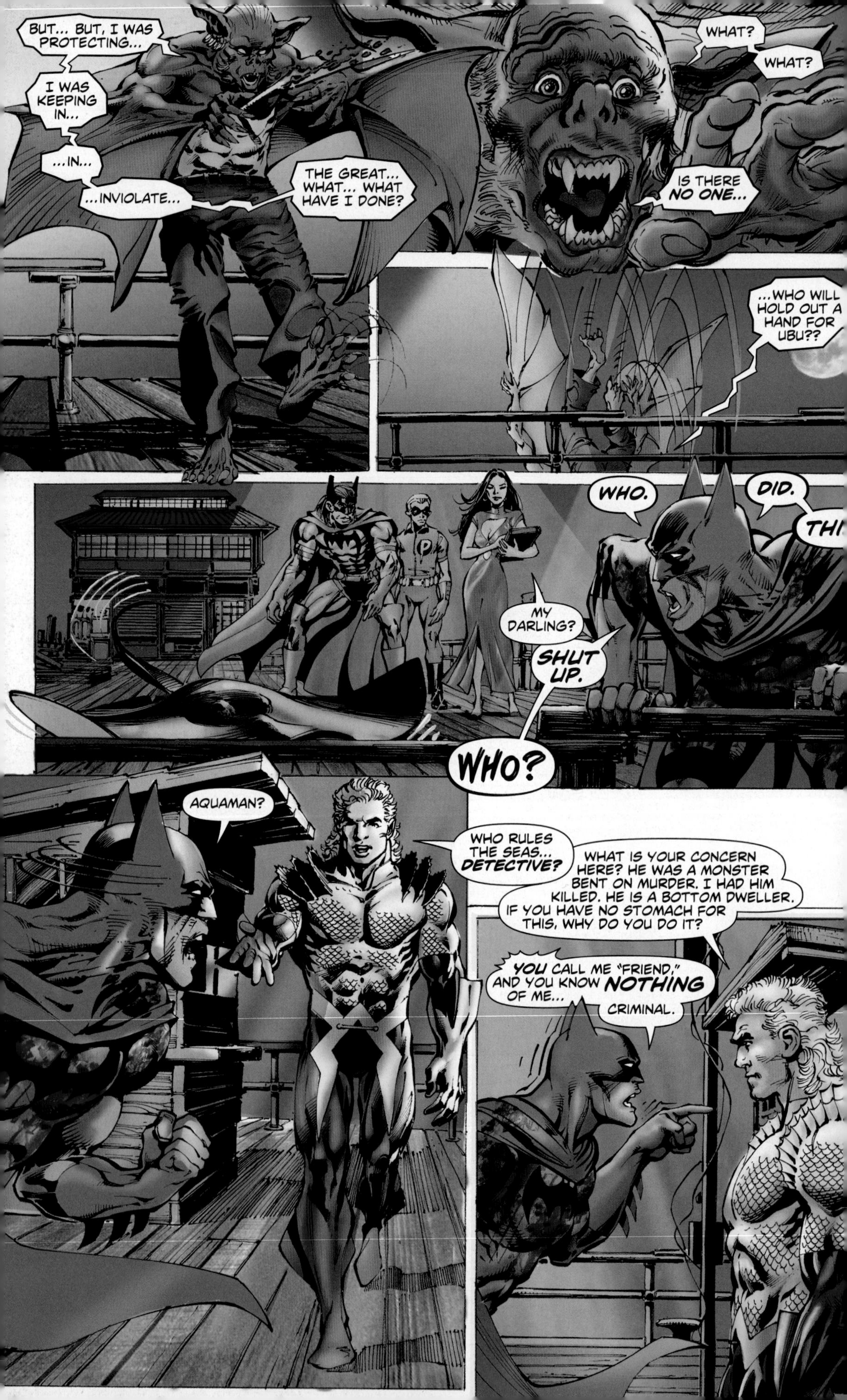
BUT... BUT, I WAS PROTECTING...
I WAS KEEPING IN...
...IN...
...INVIOLATE...
THE GREAT... WHAT... WHAT HAVE I DONE?
WHAT?
WHAT?
IS THERE NO ONE...
...WHO WILL HOLD OUT A HAND FOR UBU??
WHO.
DID.
THI
MY DARLING?
SHUT UP.
WHO?
AQUAMAN?
WHO RULES THE SEAS... DETECTIVE?
WHAT IS YOUR CONCERN HERE? HE WAS A MONSTER BENT ON MURDER. I HAD HIM KILLED. HE IS A BOTTOM DWELLER. IF YOU HAVE NO STOMACH FOR THIS, WHY DO YOU DO IT?
YOU CALL ME "FRIEND," AND YOU KNOW NOTHING OF ME...
CRIMINAL.

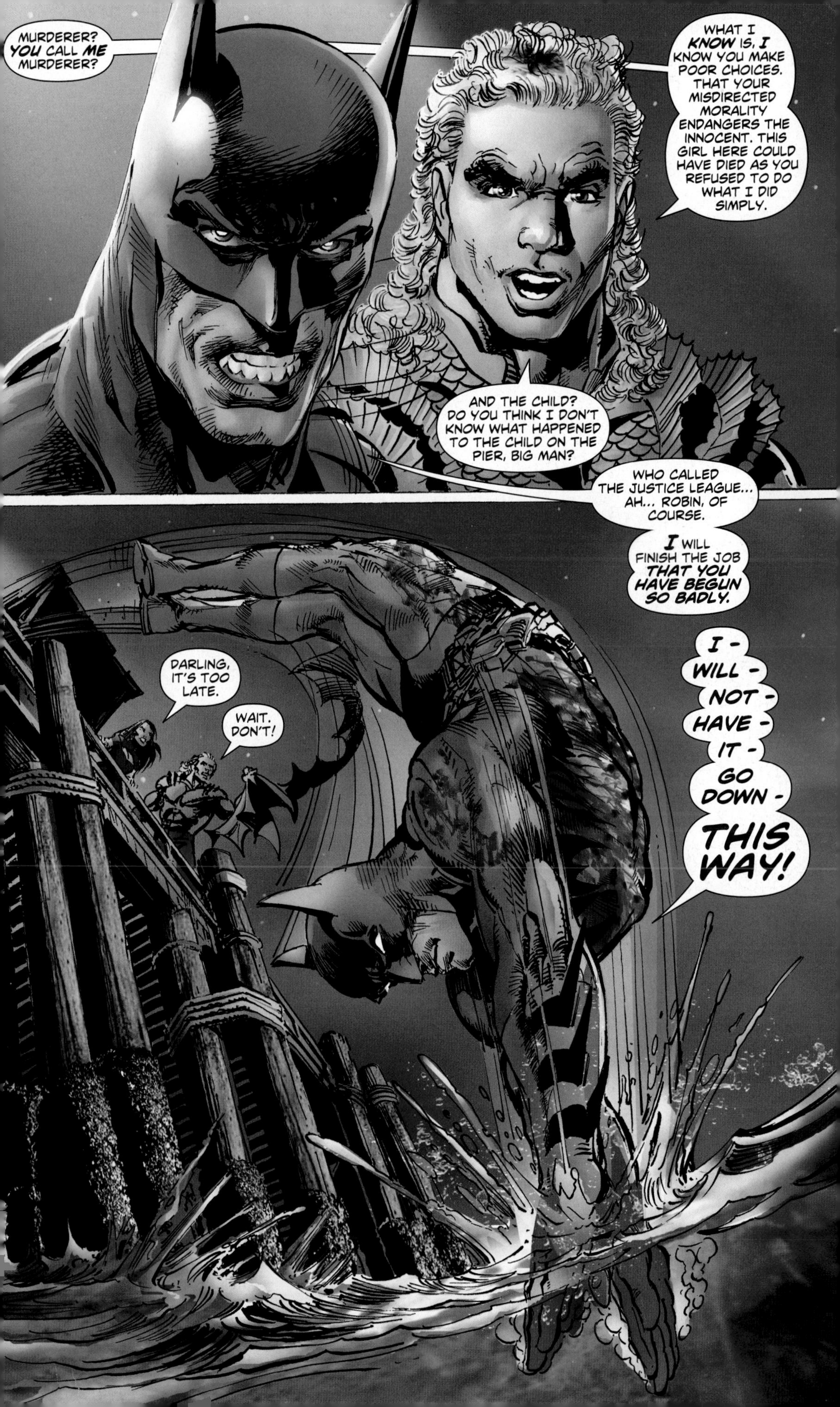
MURDERER? YOU CALL ME MURDERER?
WHAT I KNOW IS, I KNOW YOU MAKE POOR CHOICES. THAT YOUR MISDIRECTED MORALITY ENDANGERS THE INNOCENT. THIS GIRL HERE COULD HAVE DIED AS YOU REFUSED TO DO WHAT I DID SIMPLY.
AND THE CHILD? DO YOU THINK I DON'T KNOW WHAT HAPPENED TO THE CHILD ON THE PIER, BIG MAN?
WHO CALLED THE JUSTICE LEAGUE... AH... ROBIN, OF COURSE.
I WILL FINISH THE JOB THAT YOU HAVE BEGUN SO BADLY.
I - WILL - NOT - HAVE - IT - GO DOWN - THIS WAY!
DARLING, IT'S TOO LATE.
WAIT. DON'T!

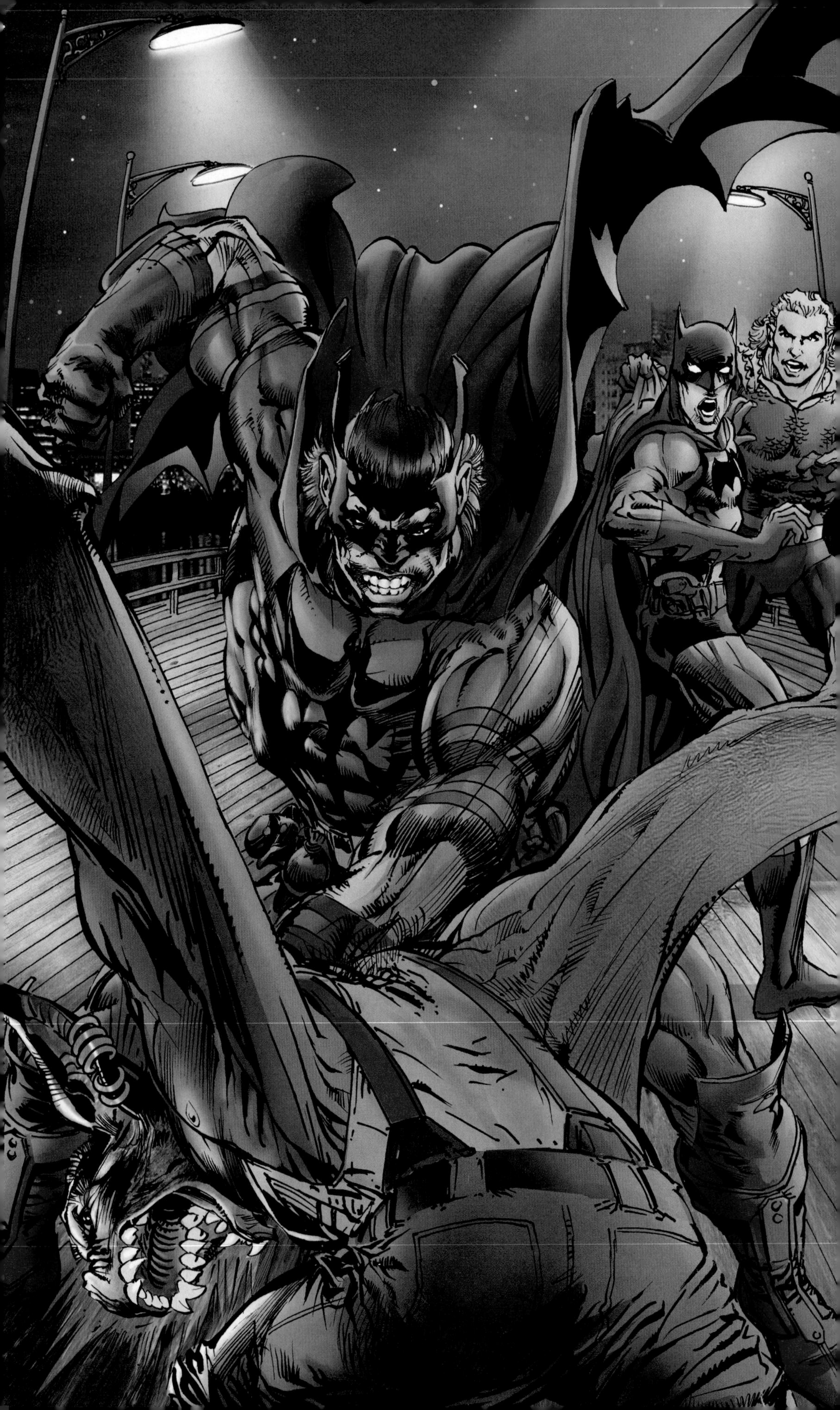

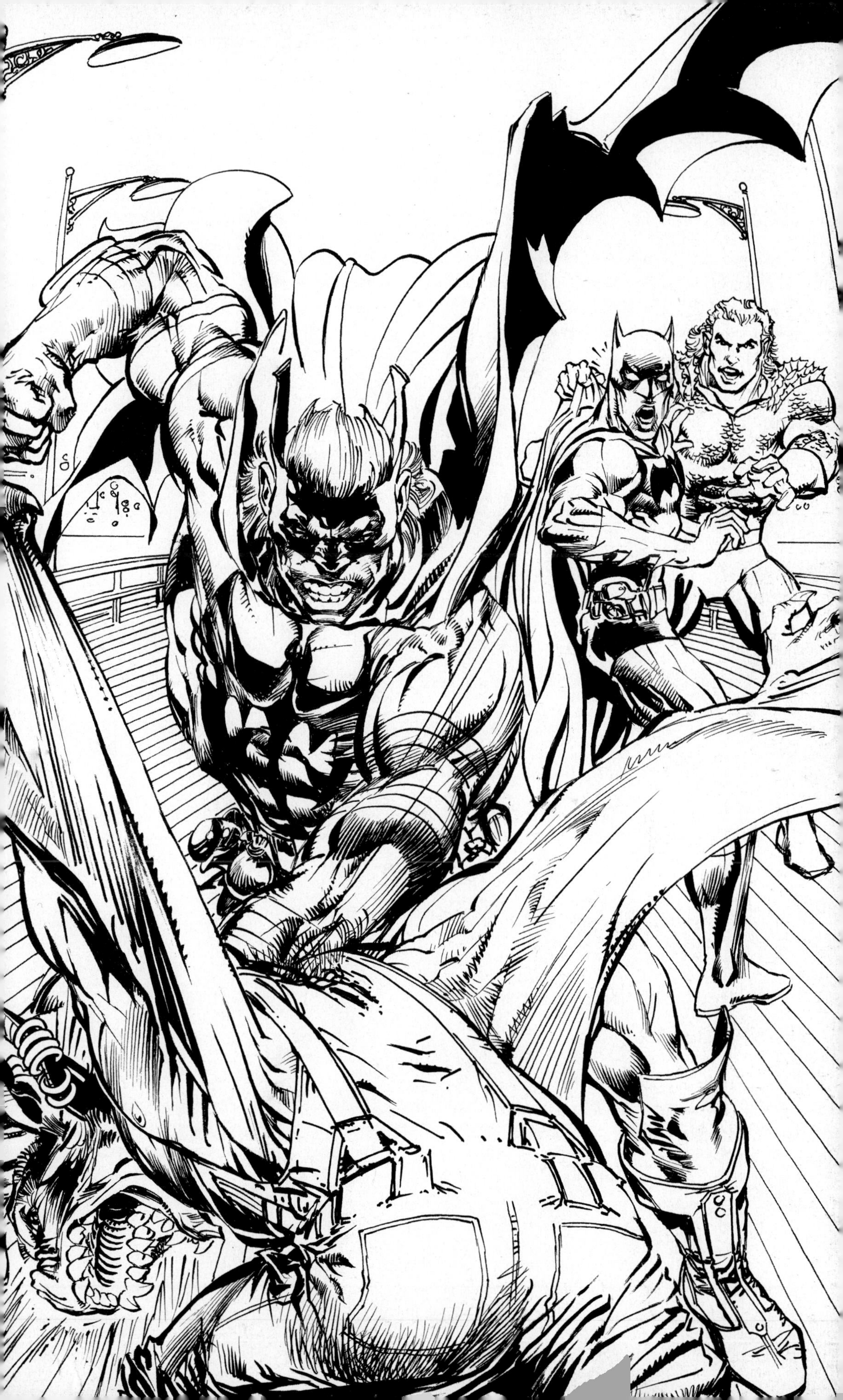

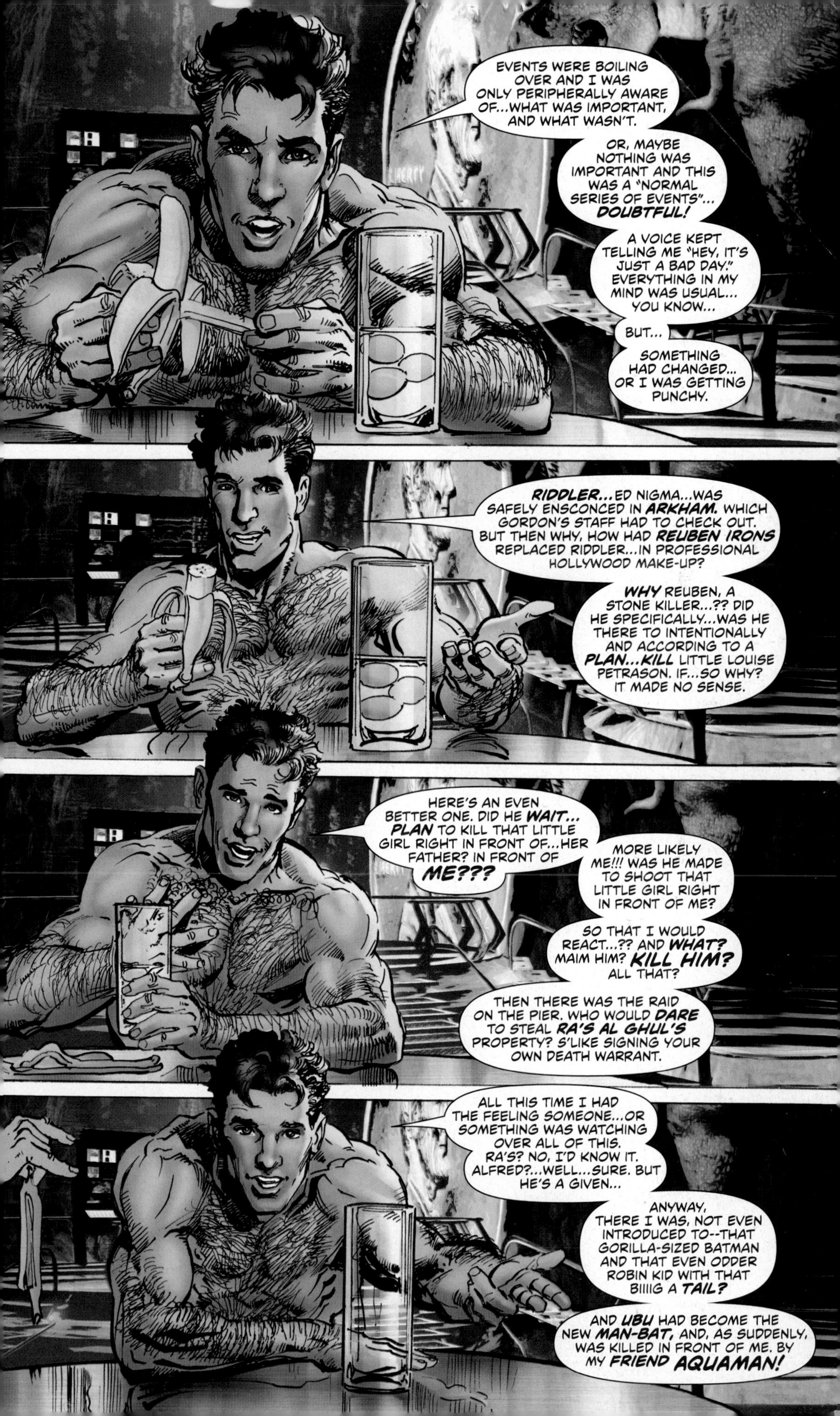

EVENTS WERE BOILING OVER AND I WAS ONLY PERIPHERALLY AWARE OF...WHAT WAS IMPORTANT, AND WHAT WASN'T.
OR, MAYBE NOTHING WAS IMPORTANT AND THIS WAS A "NORMAL SERIES OF EVENTS"... DOUBTFUL!
A VOICE KEPT TELLING ME "HEY, IT'S JUST A BAD DAY." EVERYTHING IN MY MIND WAS USUAL... YOU KNOW...
BUT...
SOMETHING HAD CHANGED... OR I WAS GETTING PUNCHY.
RIDDLER...ED NIGMA...WAS SAFELY ENSCONCED IN ARKHAM. WHICH GORDON'S STAFF HAD TO CHECK OUT. BUT THEN WHY, HOW HAD REUBEN IRONS REPLACED RIDDLER...IN PROFESSIONAL HOLLYWOOD MAKE-UP?
WHY REUBEN, A STONE KILLER...?? DID HE SPECIFICALLY...WAS HE THERE TO INTENTIONALLY AND ACCORDING TO A PLAN...KILL LITTLE LOUISE PETRASON. IF...SO WHY? IT MADE NO SENSE.
HERE'S AN EVEN BETTER ONE. DID HE WAIT... PLAN TO KILL THAT LITTLE GIRL RIGHT IN FRONT OF...HER FATHER? IN FRONT OF ME???
MORE LIKELY ME!!! WAS HE MADE TO SHOOT THAT LITTLE GIRL RIGHT IN FRONT OF ME?
SO THAT I WOULD REACT...?? AND WHAT? MAIM HIM? KILL HIM? ALL THAT?
THEN THERE WAS THE RAID ON THE PIER. WHO WOULD DARE TO STEAL RA'S AL GHUL'S PROPERTY? S'LIKE SIGNING YOUR OWN DEATH WARRANT.
ALL THIS TIME I HAD THE FEELING SOMEONE...OR SOMETHING WAS WATCHING OVER ALL OF THIS. RA'S? NO, I'D KNOW IT. ALFRED?...WELL...SURE. BUT HE'S A GIVEN...
ANYWAY, THERE I WAS, NOT EVEN INTRODUCED TO--THAT GORILLA-SIZED BATMAN AND THAT EVEN ODDER ROBIN KID WITH THAT BIIIIG A TAIL?
AND UBU HAD BECOME THE NEW MAN-BAT, AND, AS SUDDENLY, WAS KILLED IN FRONT OF ME. BY MY FRIEND AQUAMAN!

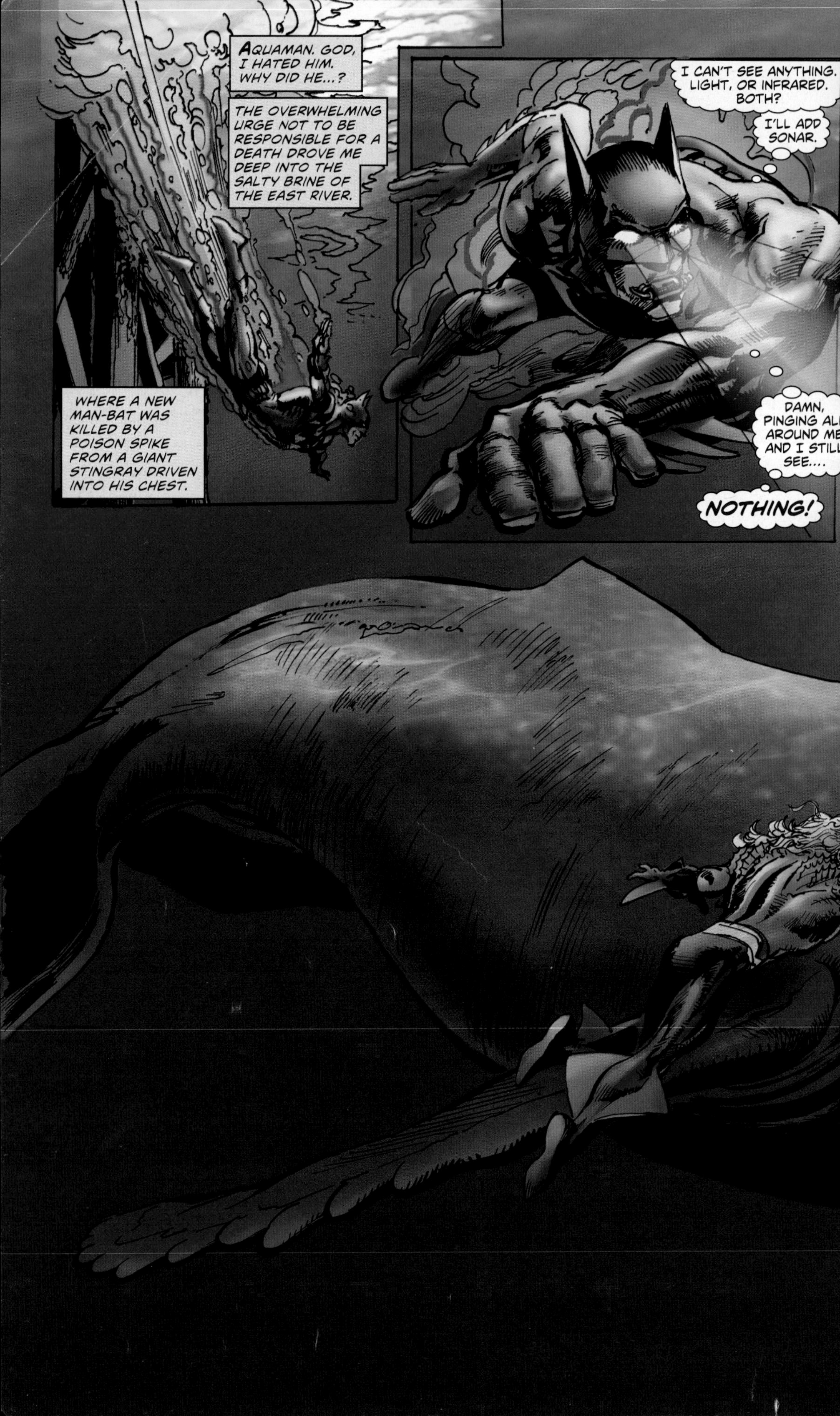
AQUAMAN. GOD, I HATED HIM. WHY DID HE...?
THE OVERWHELMING URGE NOT TO BE RESPONSIBLE FOR A DEATH DROVE ME DEEP INTO THE SALTY BRINE OF THE EAST RIVER.
WHERE A NEW MAN-BAT WAS KILLED BY A POISON SPIKE FROM A GIANT STINGRAY DRIVEN INTO HIS CHEST.
I CAN'T SEE ANYTHING. LIGHT, OR INFRARED. BOTH?
I'LL ADD SONAR.
NOTHING!

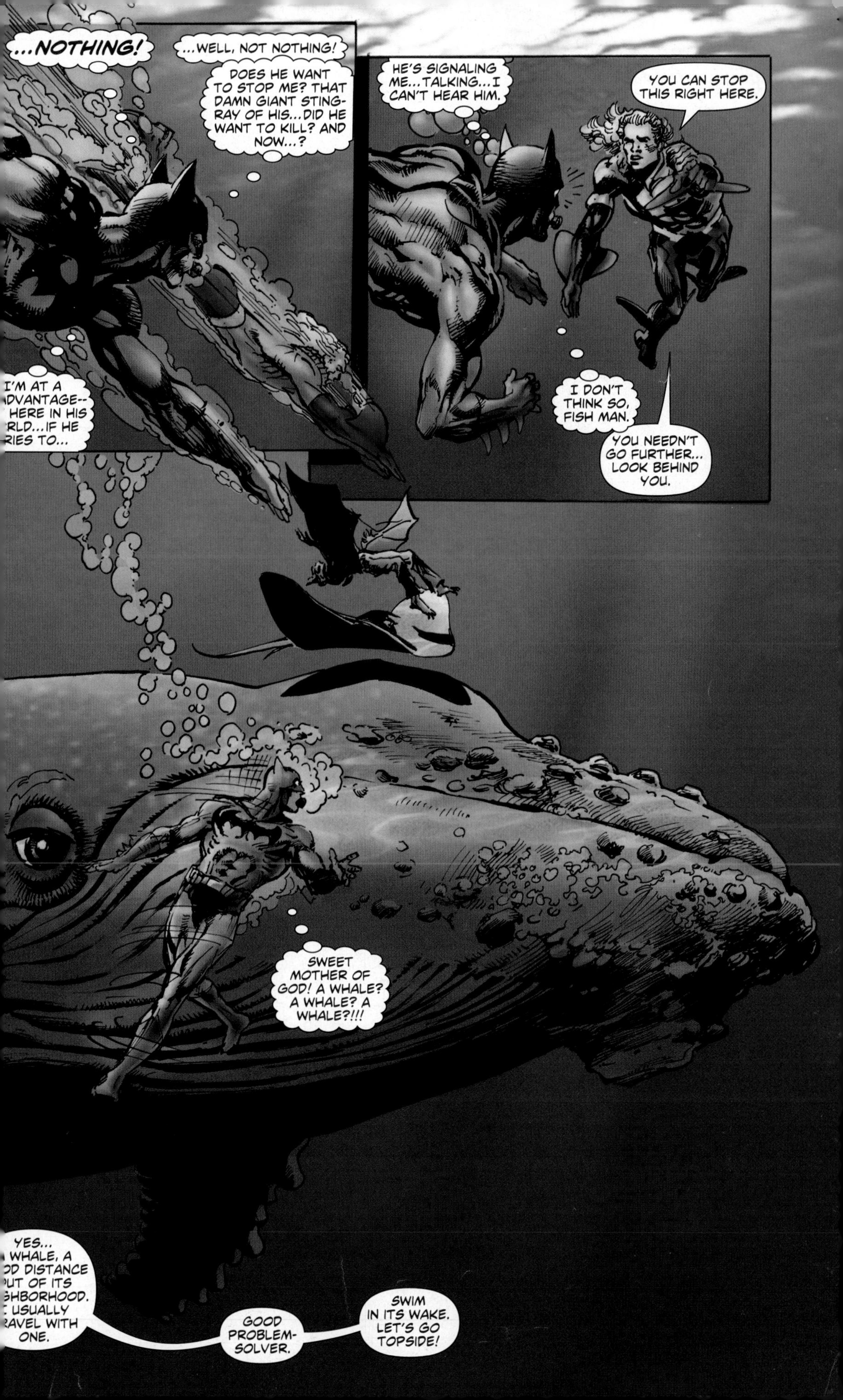
...NOTHING!
...WELL, NOT NOTHING!
DOES HE WANT TO STOP ME? THAT DAMN GIANT STING-RAY OF HIS...DID HE WANT TO KILL? AND NOW...?
I'M AT A DVANTAGE-- HERE IN HIS RLD...IF HE RIES TO...
HE'S SIGNALING ME...TALKING...I CAN'T HEAR HIM.
YOU CAN STOP THIS RIGHT HERE.
I DON'T THINK SO, FISH MAN.
YOU NEEDN'T GO FURTHER... LOOK BEHIND YOU.
SWEET MOTHER OF GOD! A WHALE? A WHALE? A WHALE?!!!
YES... WHALE, A OD DISTANCE UT OF ITS GHBORHOOD. USUALLY RAVEL WITH ONE.
GOOD PROBLEM-SOLVER.
SWIM IN ITS WAKE. LET'S GO TOPSIDE!

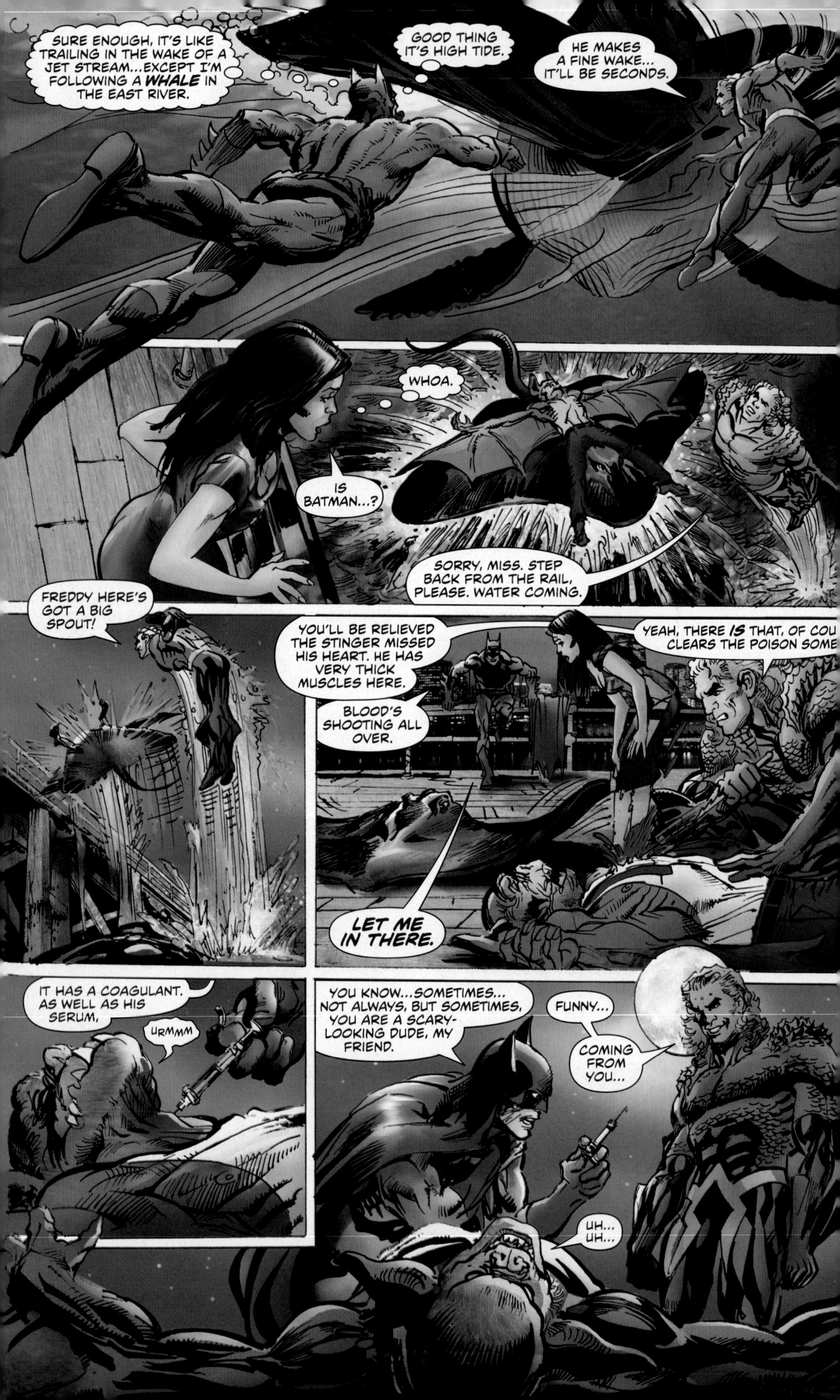
SURE ENOUGH, IT'S LIKE TRAILING IN THE WAKE OF A JET STREAM...EXCEPT I'M FOLLOWING A WHALE IN THE EAST RIVER.
GOOD THING IT'S HIGH TIDE.
HE MAKES A FINE WAKE... IT'LL BE SECONDS.
WHOA.
IS BATMAN...?
SORRY, MISS. STEP BACK FROM THE RAIL, PLEASE. WATER COMING.
FREDDY HERE'S GOT A BIG SPOUT!
YOU'LL BE RELIEVED THE STINGER MISSED HIS HEART. HE HAS VERY THICK MUSCLES HERE.
BLOOD'S SHOOTING ALL OVER.
YEAH, THERE IS THAT, OF COU
CLEARS THE POISON SOME
LET ME IN THERE.
IT HAS A COAGULANT. AS WELL AS HIS SERUM.
URMMM
YOU KNOW...SOMETIMES... NOT ALWAYS, BUT SOMETIMES, YOU ARE A SCARY-LOOKING DUDE, MY FRIEND.
FUNNY...
COMING FROM YOU...
UH... UH...

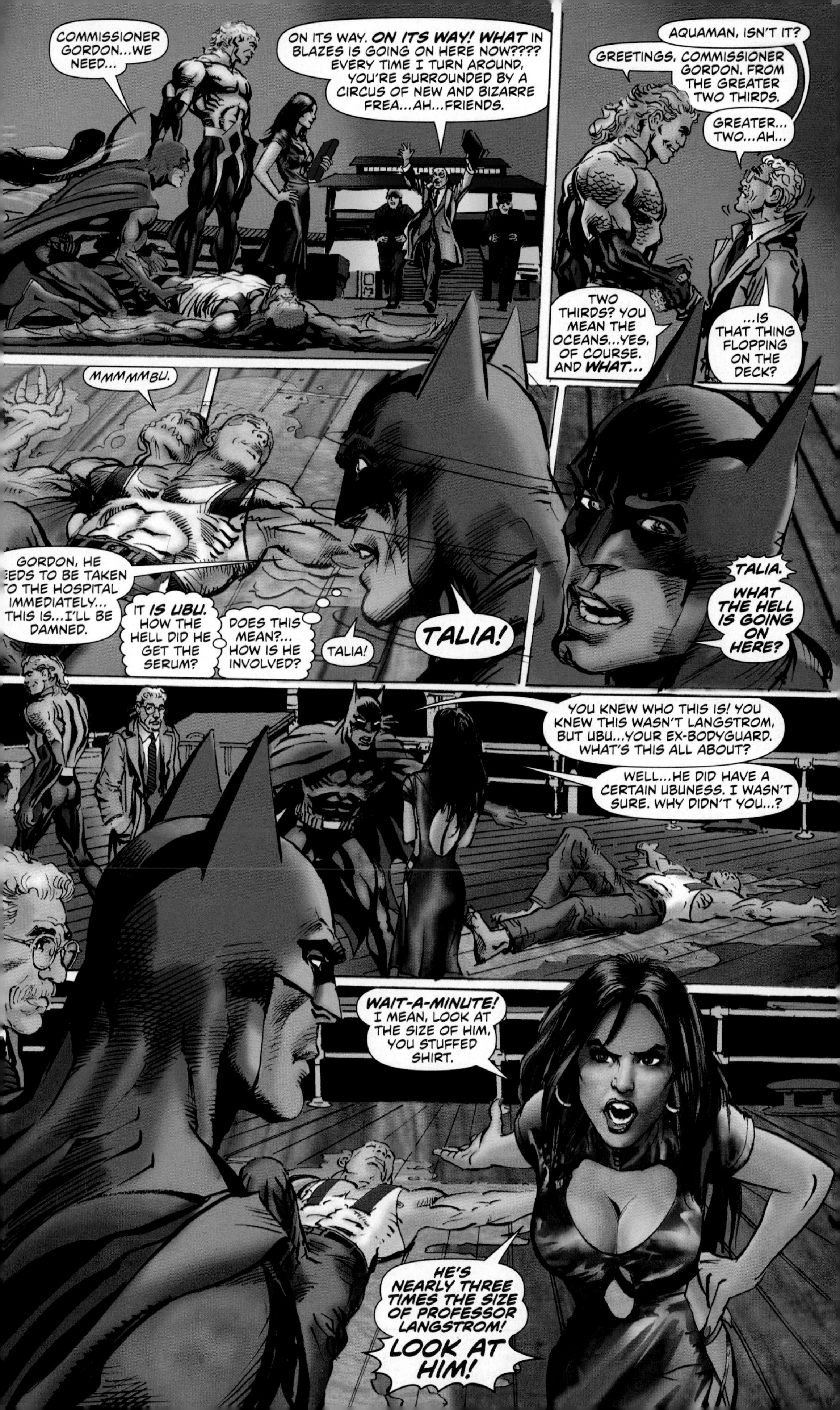
COMMISSIONER GORDON...WE NEED...
ON ITS WAY. ON ITS WAY! WHAT IN BLAZES IS GOING ON HERE NOW???? EVERY TIME I TURN AROUND, YOU'RE SURROUNDED BY A CIRCUS OF NEW AND BIZARRE FREA...AH...FRIENDS.
GREETINGS, COMMISSIONER GORDON. FROM THE GREATER TWO THIRDS.
AQUAMAN, ISN'T IT?
GREATER... TWO...AH...
TWO THIRDS? YOU MEAN THE OCEANS...YES, OF COURSE. AND WHAT...
...IS THAT THING FLOPPING ON THE DECK?
MMMMMBU.
GORDON, HE NEEDS TO BE TAKEN TO THE HOSPITAL IMMEDIATELY... THIS IS...I'LL BE DAMNED.
IT IS UBU. HOW THE HELL DID HE GET THE SERUM?
DOES THIS MEAN?... HOW IS HE INVOLVED?
TALIA!
TALIA!
TALIA. WHAT THE HELL IS GOING ON HERE?
YOU KNEW WHO THIS IS! YOU KNEW THIS WASN'T LANGSTROM, BUT UBU...YOUR EX-BODYGUARD. WHAT'S THIS ALL ABOUT?
WELL...HE DID HAVE A CERTAIN UBUNESS. I WASN'T SURE. WHY DIDN'T YOU...?
WAIT-A-MINUTE! I MEAN, LOOK AT THE SIZE OF HIM, YOU STUFFED SHIRT.
HE'S NEARLY THREE TIMES THE SIZE OF PROFESSOR LANGSTROM! LOOK AT HIM!

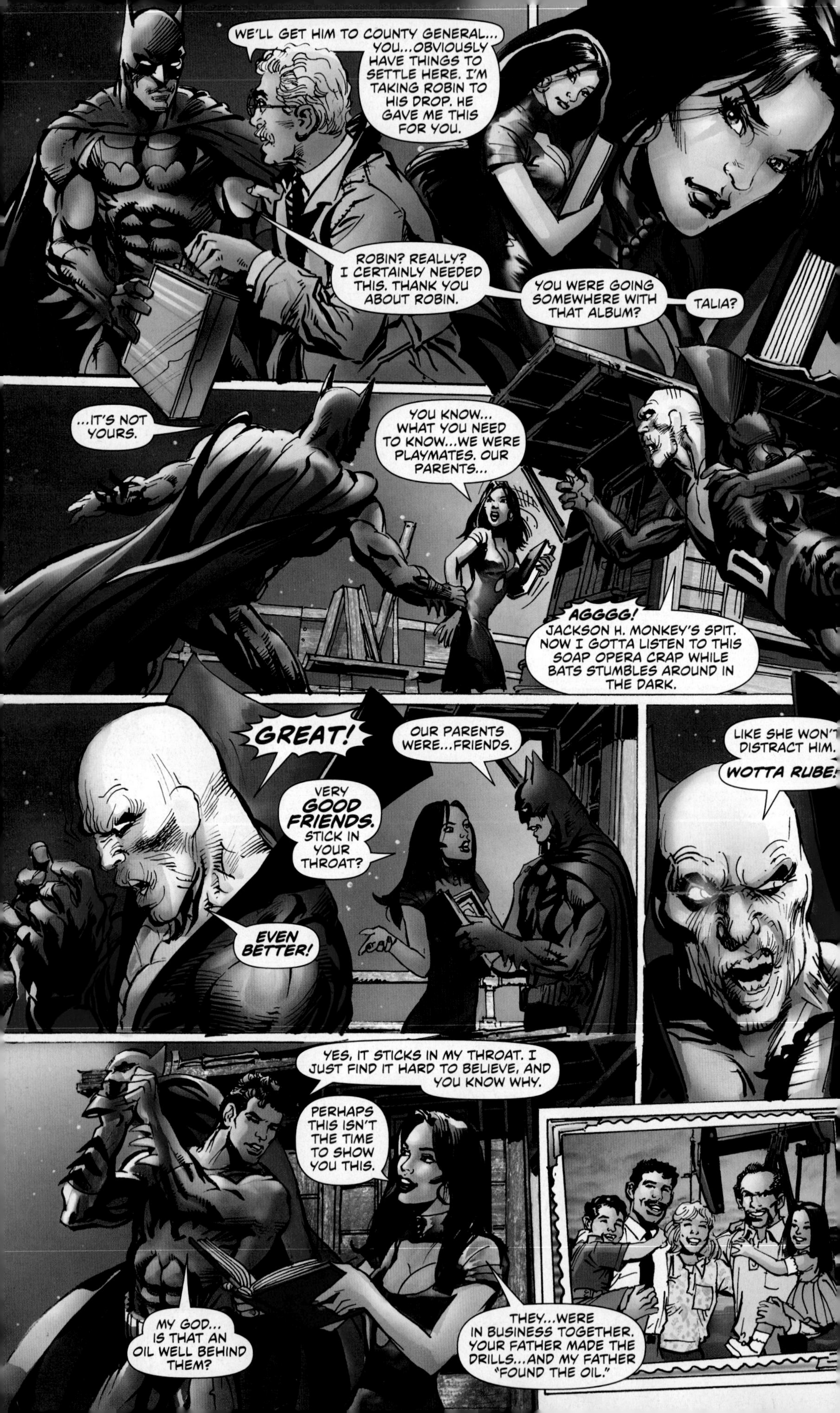
WE'LL GET HIM TO COUNTY GENERAL... YOU...OBVIOUSLY HAVE THINGS TO SETTLE HERE. I'M TAKING ROBIN TO HIS DROP. HE GAVE ME THIS FOR YOU.
ROBIN? REALLY? I CERTAINLY NEEDED THIS. THANK YOU ABOUT ROBIN.
YOU WERE GOING SOMEWHERE WITH THAT ALBUM?
TALIA?
...IT'S NOT YOURS.
YOU KNOW... WHAT YOU NEED TO KNOW...WE WERE PLAYMATES. OUR PARENTS...
AGGGG! JACKSON H. MONKEY'S SPIT. NOW I GOTTA LISTEN TO THIS SOAP OPERA CRAP WHILE BATS STUMBLES AROUND IN THE DARK.
GREAT!
OUR PARENTS WERE...FRIENDS.
VERY GOOD FRIENDS. STICK IN YOUR THROAT?
EVEN BETTER!
LIKE SHE WON'T DISTRACT HIM.
WOTTA RUBE!
YES, IT STICKS IN MY THROAT. I JUST FIND IT HARD TO BELIEVE, AND YOU KNOW WHY.
PERHAPS THIS ISN'T THE TIME TO SHOW YOU THIS.
MY GOD... IS THAT AN OIL WELL BEHIND THEM?
THEY...WERE IN BUSINESS TOGETHER. YOUR FATHER MADE THE DRILLS...AND MY FATHER "FOUND THE OIL."

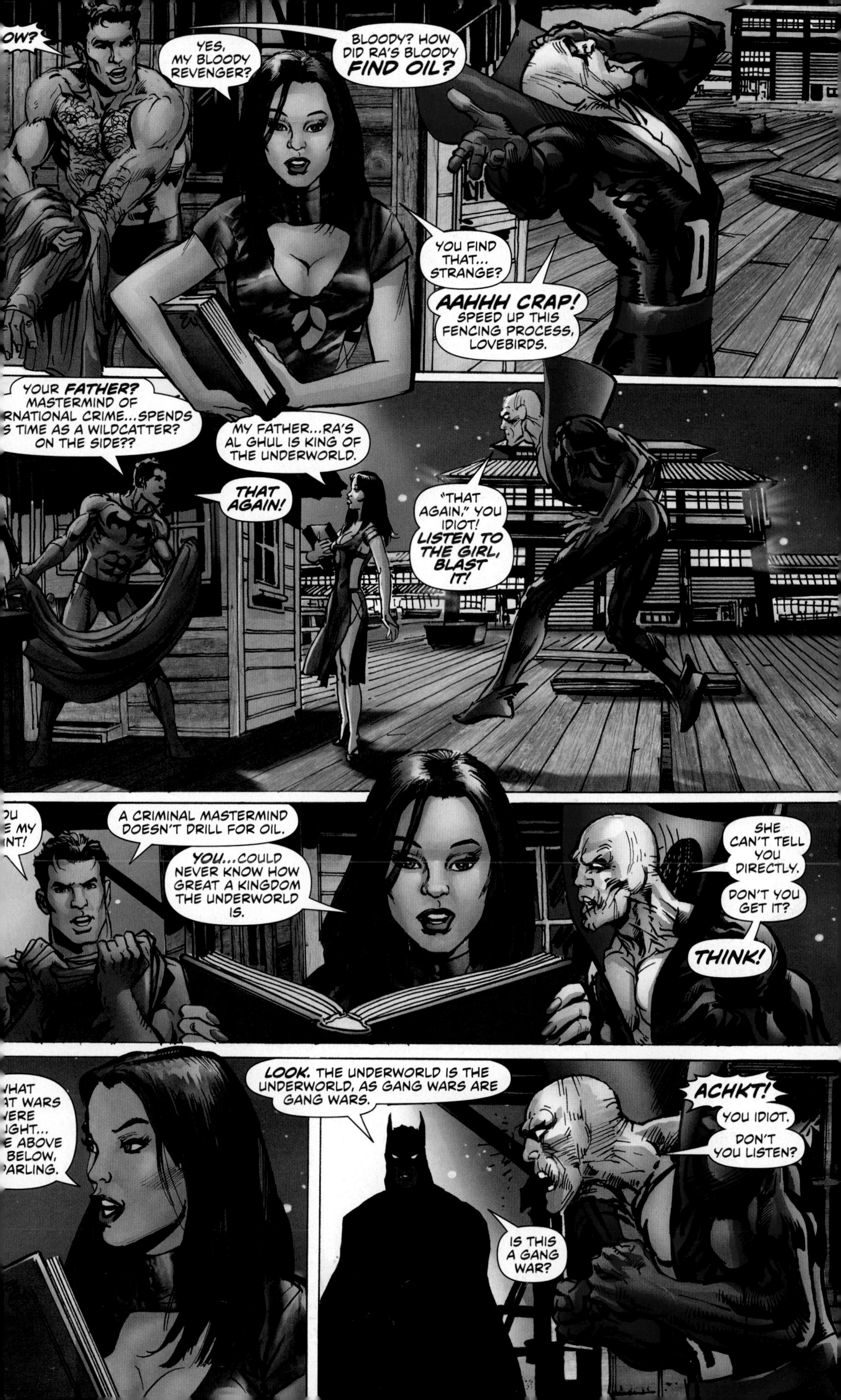
OW?
YES, MY BLOODY REVENGER?
BLOODY? HOW DID RA'S BLOODY FIND OIL?
YOU FIND THAT... STRANGE?
AAHHH CRAP! SPEED UP THIS FENCING PROCESS, LOVEBIRDS.
YOUR FATHER? MASTERMIND OF RNATIONAL CRIME...SPENDS S TIME AS A WILDCATTER? ON THE SIDE??
MY FATHER...RA'S AL GHUL IS KING OF THE UNDERWORLD.
THAT AGAIN!
"THAT AGAIN," YOU IDIOT! LISTEN TO THE GIRL, BLAST IT!
A CRIMINAL MASTERMIND DOESN'T DRILL FOR OIL.
YOU...COULD NEVER KNOW HOW GREAT A KINGDOM THE UNDERWORLD IS.
SHE CAN'T TELL YOU DIRECTLY.
DON'T YOU GET IT?
THINK!
LOOK. THE UNDERWORLD IS THE UNDERWORLD, AS GANG WARS ARE GANG WARS.
IS THIS A GANG WAR?
ACHKT!
YOU IDIOT.
DON'T YOU LISTEN?

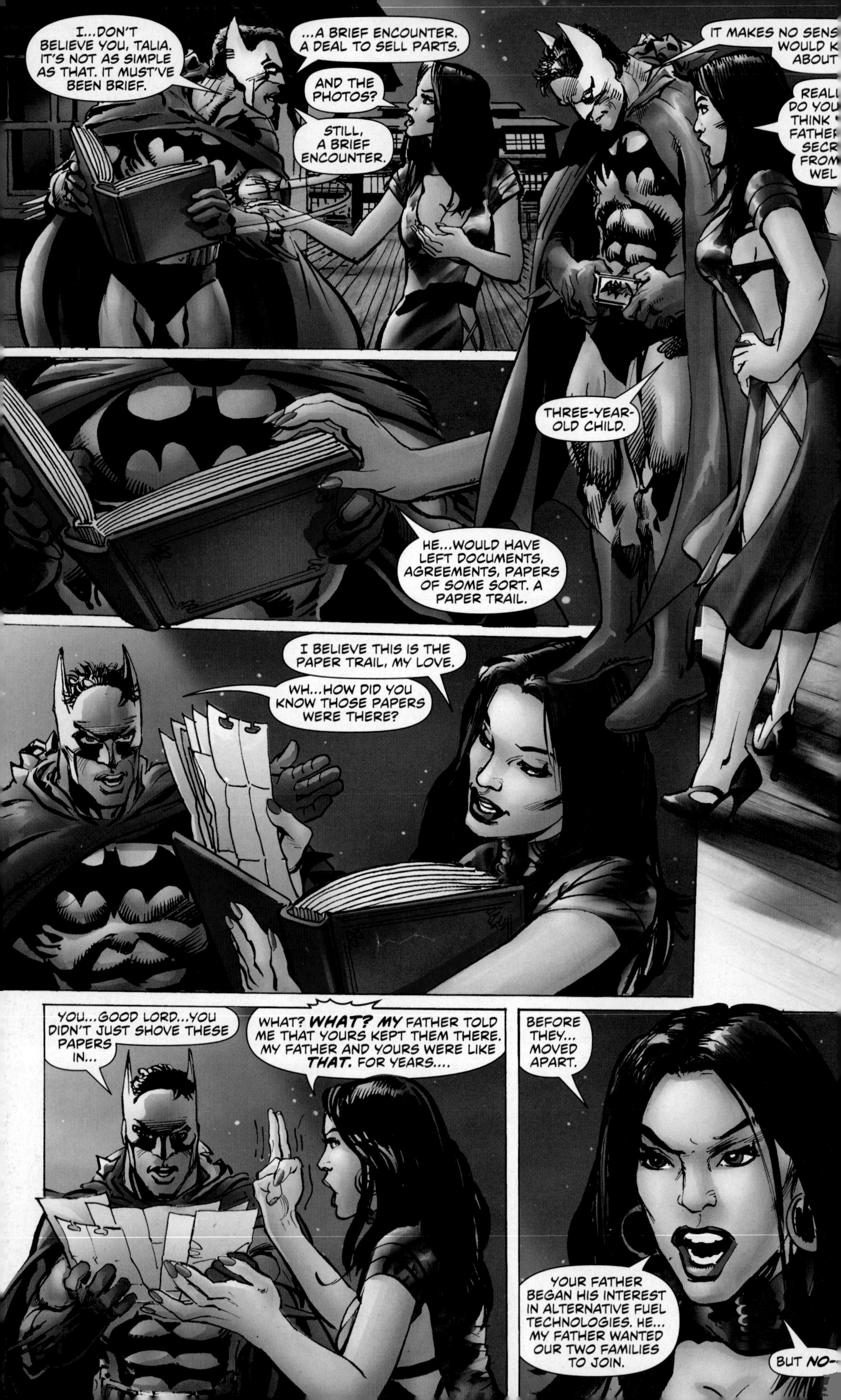

I...DON'T BELIEVE YOU, TALIA. IT'S NOT AS SIMPLE AS THAT. IT MUST'VE BEEN BRIEF.
...A BRIEF ENCOUNTER. A DEAL TO SELL PARTS.
AND THE PHOTOS?
STILL, A BRIEF ENCOUNTER.
THREE-YEAR-OLD CHILD.
HE...WOULD HAVE LEFT DOCUMENTS, AGREEMENTS, PAPERS OF SOME SORT. A PAPER TRAIL.
I BELIEVE THIS IS THE PAPER TRAIL, MY LOVE.
WH...HOW DID YOU KNOW THOSE PAPERS WERE THERE?
YOU...GOOD LORD...YOU DIDN'T JUST SHOVE THESE PAPERS IN...
WHAT? WHAT? MY FATHER TOLD ME THAT YOURS KEPT THEM THERE. MY FATHER AND YOURS WERE LIKE THAT. FOR YEARS....
BEFORE THEY... MOVED APART.
YOUR FATHER BEGAN HIS INTEREST IN ALTERNATIVE FUEL TECHNOLOGIES. HE... MY FATHER WANTED OUR TWO FAMILIES TO JOIN.
BUT NO—

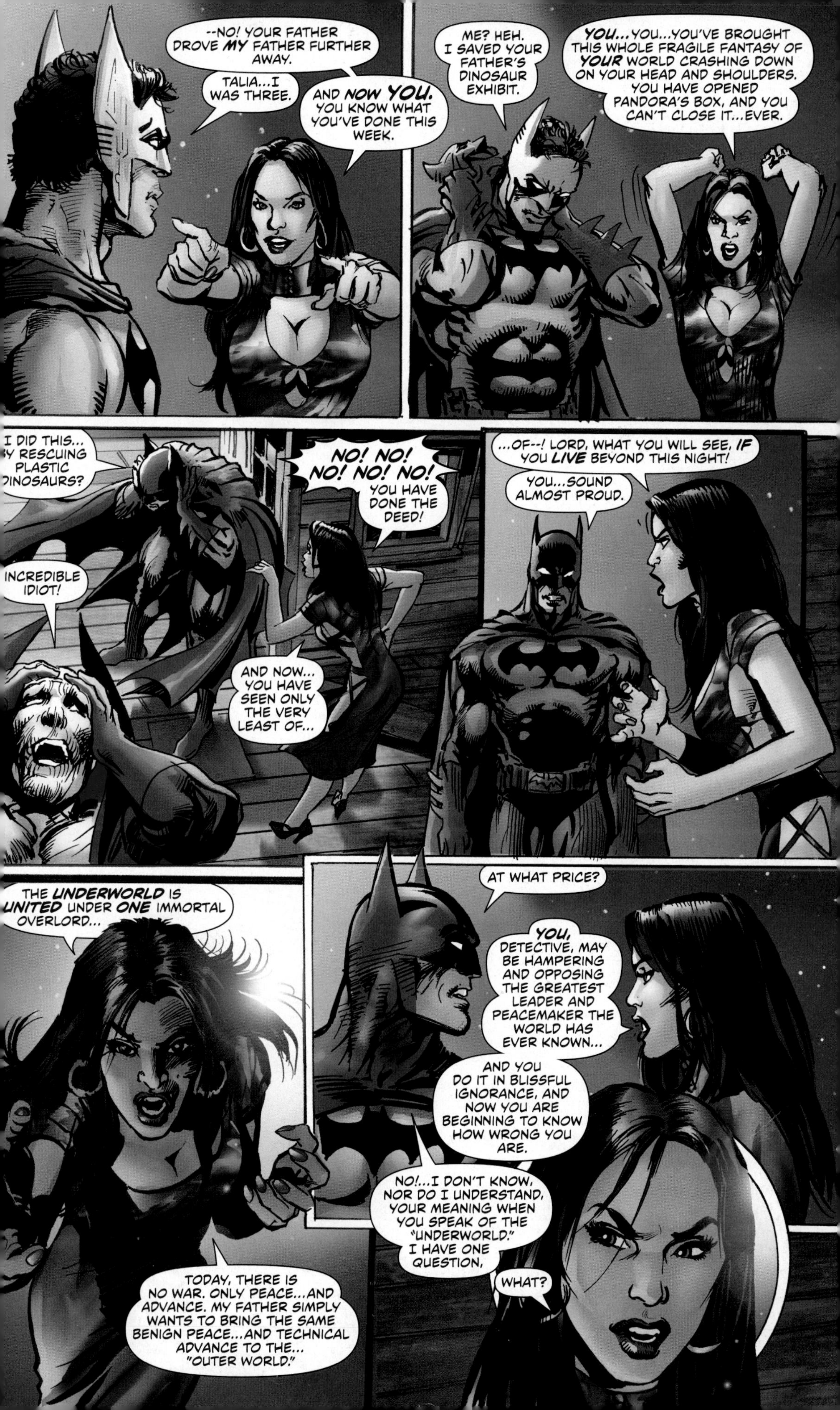
--NO! YOUR FATHER DROVE MY FATHER FURTHER AWAY.
TALIA...I WAS THREE.
AND NOW YOU. YOU KNOW WHAT YOU'VE DONE THIS WEEK.
ME? HEH. I SAVED YOUR FATHER'S DINOSAUR EXHIBIT.
YOU...YOU...YOU'VE BROUGHT THIS WHOLE FRAGILE FANTASY OF YOUR WORLD CRASHING DOWN ON YOUR HEAD AND SHOULDERS. YOU HAVE OPENED PANDORA'S BOX, AND YOU CAN'T CLOSE IT...EVER.
I DID THIS... BY RESCUING PLASTIC DINOSAURS?
NO! NO! NO! NO! NO! YOU HAVE DONE THE DEED!
INCREDIBLE IDIOT!
AND NOW... YOU HAVE SEEN ONLY THE VERY LEAST OF...
...OF--! LORD, WHAT YOU WILL SEE, IF YOU LIVE BEYOND THIS NIGHT!
YOU...SOUND ALMOST PROUD.
THE UNDERWORLD IS UNITED UNDER ONE IMMORTAL OVERLORD...
TODAY, THERE IS NO WAR. ONLY PEACE...AND ADVANCE. MY FATHER SIMPLY WANTS TO BRING THE SAME BENIGN PEACE...AND TECHNICAL ADVANCE TO THE... "OUTER WORLD."
AT WHAT PRICE?
YOU, DETECTIVE, MAY BE HAMPERING AND OPPOSING THE GREATEST LEADER AND PEACEMAKER THE WORLD HAS EVER KNOWN...
AND YOU DO IT IN BLISSFUL IGNORANCE, AND NOW YOU ARE BEGINNING TO KNOW HOW WRONG YOU ARE.
NO!...I DON'T KNOW, NOR DO I UNDERSTAND, YOUR MEANING WHEN YOU SPEAK OF THE "UNDERWORLD." I HAVE ONE QUESTION,
WHAT?

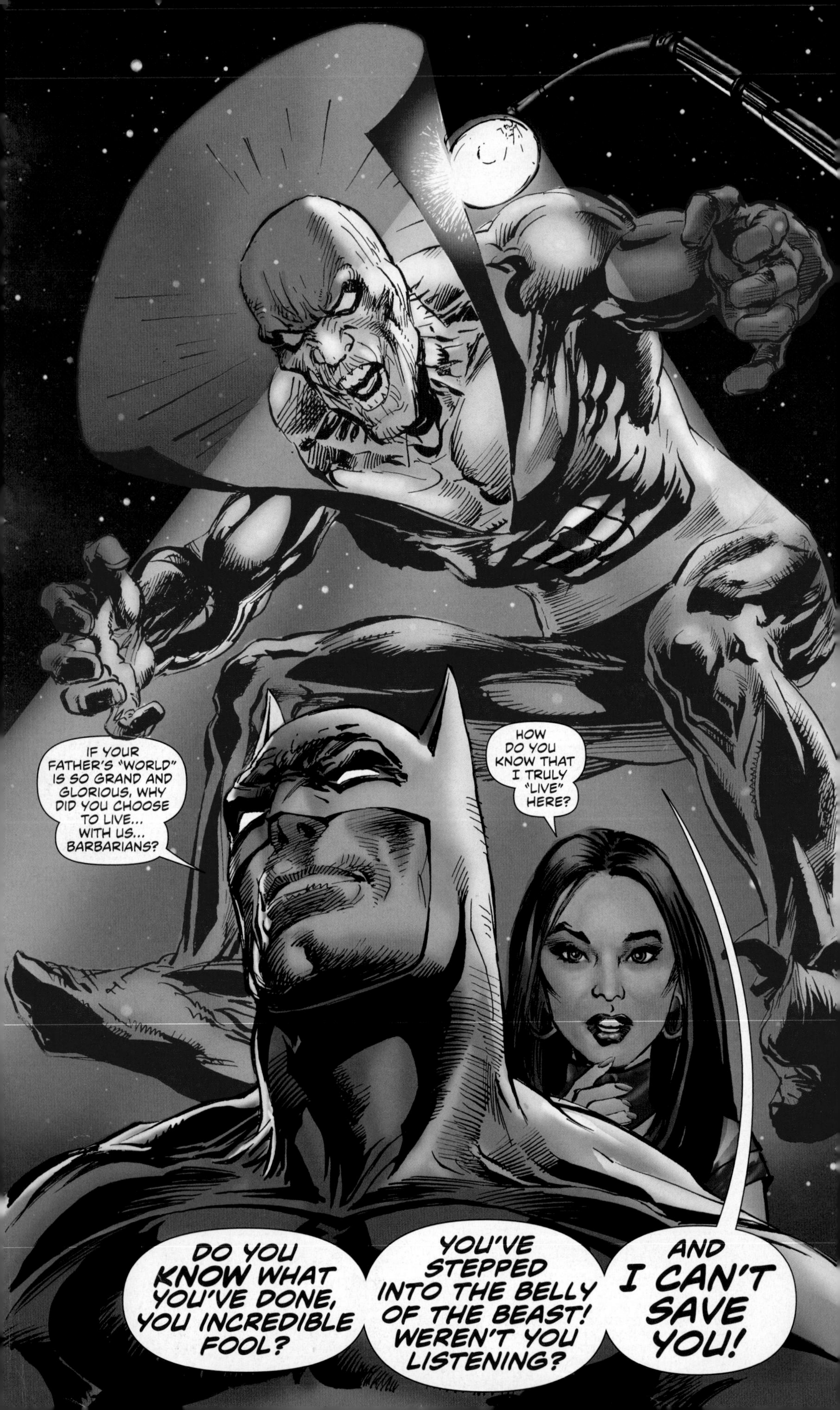
IF YOUR FATHER'S "WORLD" IS SO GRAND AND GLORIOUS, WHY DID YOU CHOOSE TO LIVE... WITH US... BARBARIANS?
HOW DO YOU KNOW THAT I TRULY "LIVE" HERE?
DO YOU KNOW WHAT YOU'VE DONE, YOU INCREDIBLE FOOL?
YOU'VE STEPPED INTO THE BELLY OF THE BEAST! WEREN'T YOU LISTENING?
AND I CAN'T SAVE YOU!

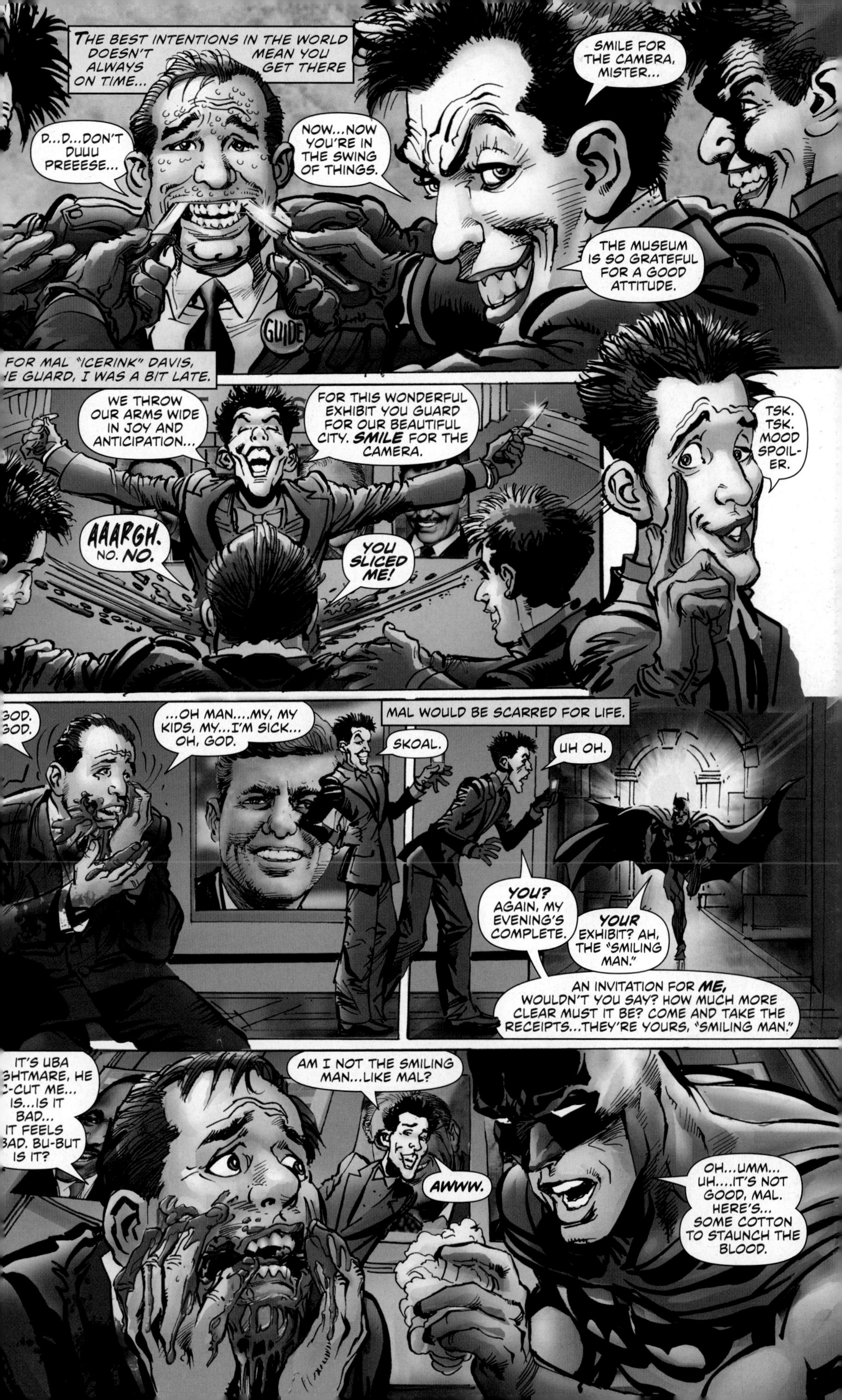
THE BEST INTENTIONS IN THE WORLD DOESN'T ALWAYS MEAN YOU GET THERE ON TIME...
D...D...DON'T DUUU PREEESE...
NOW...NOW YOU'RE IN THE SWING OF THINGS.
SMILE FOR THE CAMERA, MISTER...
THE MUSEUM IS SO GRATEFUL FOR A GOOD ATTITUDE.
GUIDE
FOR MAL "ICERINK" DAVIS, HE GUARD, I WAS A BIT LATE.
WE THROW OUR ARMS WIDE IN JOY AND ANTICIPATION...
FOR THIS WONDERFUL EXHIBIT YOU GUARD FOR OUR BEAUTIFUL CITY. SMILE FOR THE CAMERA.
TSK. TSK. MOOD SPOIL-ER.
AAARGH. NO. NO.
YOU SLICED ME!
GOD. GOD.
...OH MAN....MY, MY KIDS, MY...I'M SICK... OH, GOD.
MAL WOULD BE SCARRED FOR LIFE.
SKOAL.
UH OH.
YOU? AGAIN, MY EVENING'S COMPLETE.
YOUR EXHIBIT? AH, THE "SMILING MAN."
AN INVITATION FOR ME, WOULDN'T YOU SAY? HOW MUCH MORE CLEAR MUST IT BE? COME AND TAKE THE RECEIPTS...THEY'RE YOURS, "SMILING MAN."
IT'S UBA GHTMARE, HE C-CUT ME... IS...IS IT BAD... IT FEELS BAD. BU-BUT IS IT?
AM I NOT THE SMILING MAN...LIKE MAL?
AWWW.
OH...UMM... UH....IT'S NOT GOOD, MAL. HERE'S... SOME COTTON TO STAUNCH THE BLOOD.

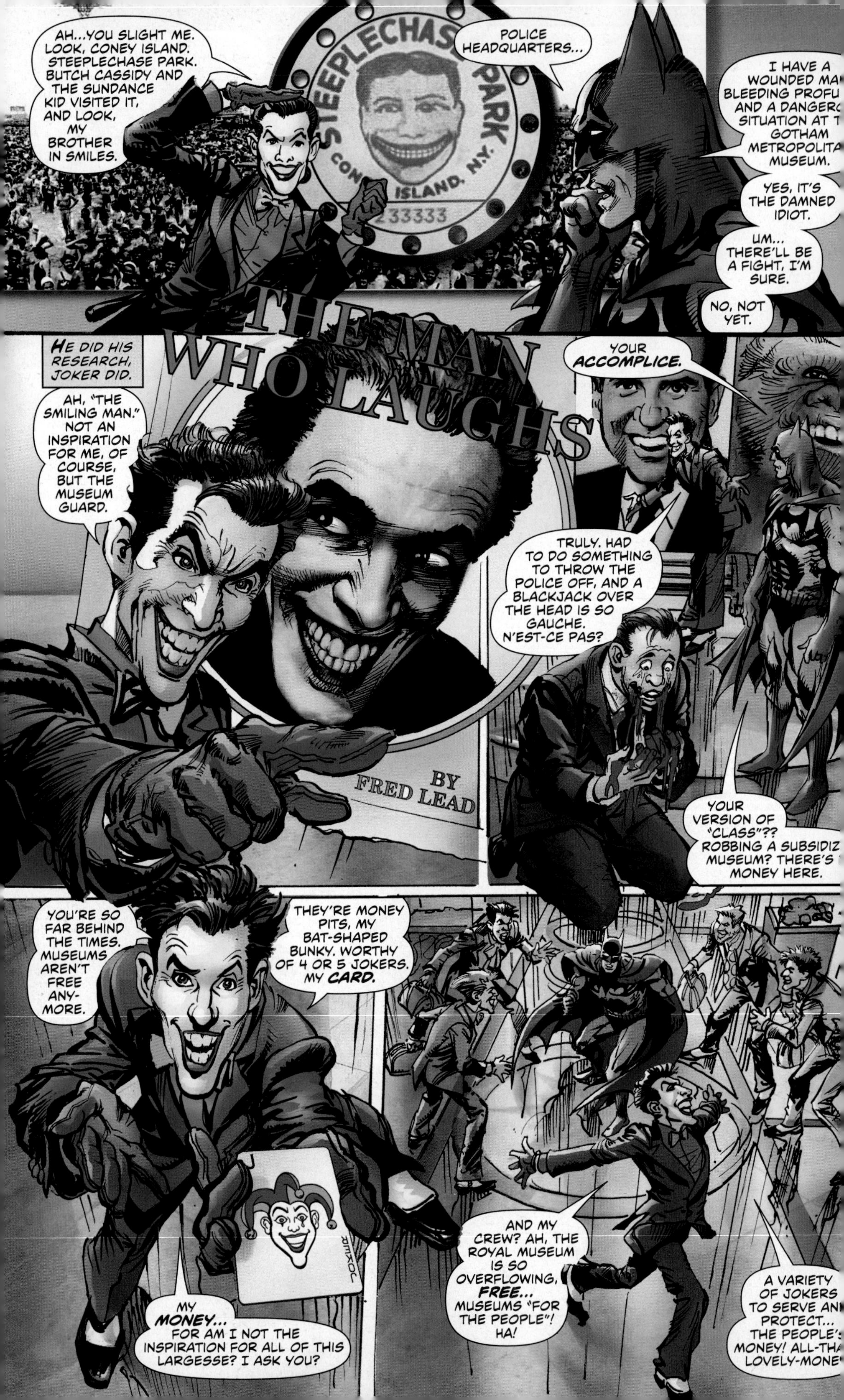
AH...YOU SLIGHT ME. LOOK, CONEY ISLAND. STEEPLECHASE PARK. BUTCH CASSIDY AND THE SUNDANCE KID VISITED IT, AND LOOK, MY BROTHER IN SMILES.
STEEPLECHASE PARK CONEY ISLAND, N.Y.
233333
POLICE HEADQUARTERS...
I HAVE A WOUNDED MA BLEEDING PROFU AND A DANGER SITUATION AT T GOTHAM METROPOLITA MUSEUM.
YES, IT'S THE DAMNED IDIOT.
UM... THERE'LL BE A FIGHT, I'M SURE.
NO, NOT YET.
THE MAN WHO LAUGHS
BY FRED LEAD
HE DID HIS RESEARCH, JOKER DID.
AH, "THE SMILING MAN." NOT AN INSPIRATION FOR ME, OF COURSE, BUT THE MUSEUM GUARD.
YOUR ACCOMPLICE.
TRULY. HAD TO DO SOMETHING TO THROW THE POLICE OFF, AND A BLACKJACK OVER THE HEAD IS SO GAUCHE. N'EST-CE PAS?
YOUR VERSION OF "CLASS"?? ROBBING A SUBSIDIZ MUSEUM? THERE'S MONEY HERE.
YOU'RE SO FAR BEHIND THE TIMES. MUSEUMS AREN'T FREE ANY-MORE.
THEY'RE MONEY PITS, MY BAT-SHAPED BUNKY. WORTHY OF 4 OR 5 JOKERS. MY CARD.
JOKER
MY MONEY... FOR AM I NOT THE INSPIRATION FOR ALL OF THIS LARGESSE? I ASK YOU?
AND MY CREW? AH, THE ROYAL MUSEUM IS SO OVERFLOWING, FREE... MUSEUMS "FOR THE PEOPLE"! HA!
A VARIETY OF JOKERS TO SERVE AN PROTECT... THE PEOPLE' MONEY! ALL-TH LOVELY-MONE

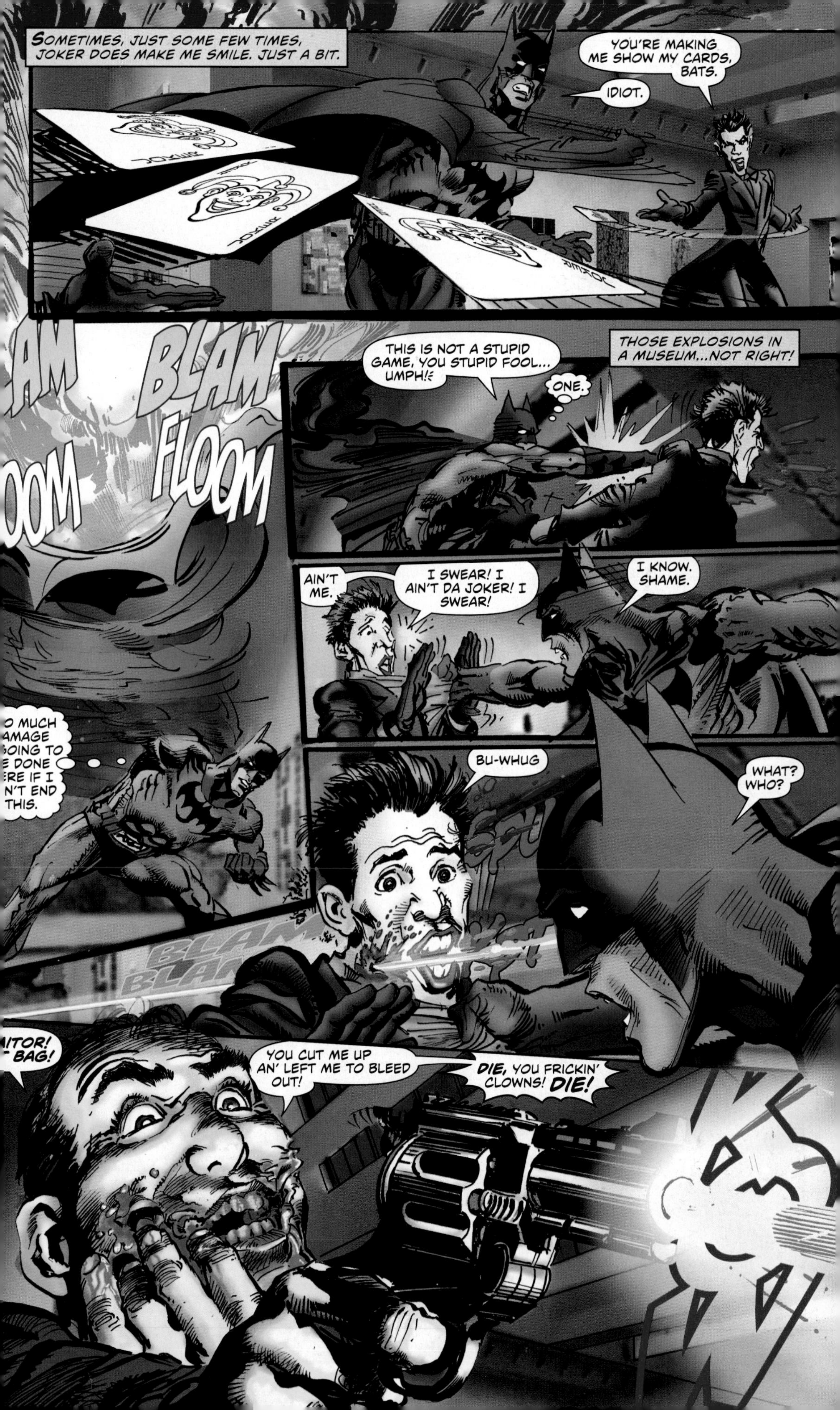
SOMETIMES, JUST SOME FEW TIMES, JOKER DOES MAKE ME SMILE. JUST A BIT.
YOU'RE MAKING ME SHOW MY CARDS, BATS.
IDIOT.
BLAM
BLAM
FLOOM
FLOOM
THIS IS NOT A STUPID GAME, YOU STUPID FOOL... UMPH!
THOSE EXPLOSIONS IN A MUSEUM...NOT RIGHT!
ONE.
AIN'T ME.
I SWEAR! I AIN'T DA JOKER! I SWEAR!
I KNOW. SHAME.
BU-WHUG
WHAT? WHO?
BLAM
YOU CUT ME UP AN' LEFT ME TO BLEED OUT!
DIE, YOU FRICKIN' CLOWNS! DIE!

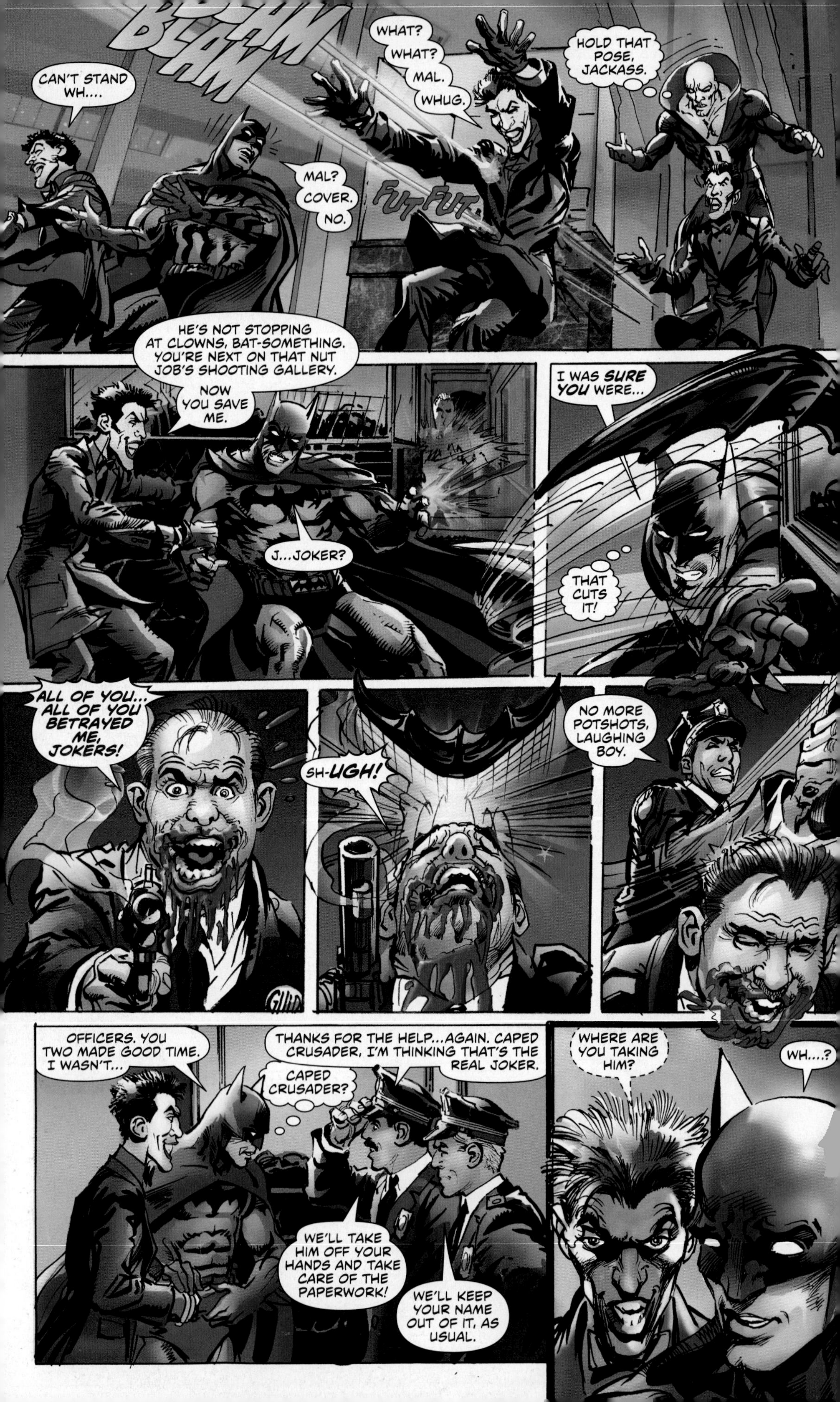
BLAM
CAN'T STAND WH....
WHAT?
WHAT?
MAL.
WHUG.
HOLD THAT POSE, JACKASS.
MAL?
COVER.
NO.
FUT FUT
HE'S NOT STOPPING AT CLOWNS, BAT-SOMETHING. YOU'RE NEXT ON THAT NUT JOB'S SHOOTING GALLERY.
NOW YOU SAVE ME.
J...JOKER?
I WAS SURE YOU WERE...
THAT CUTS IT!
ALL OF YOU... ALL OF YOU BETRAYED ME, JOKERS!
SH-UGH!
NO MORE POTSHOTS, LAUGHING BOY.
OFFICERS. YOU TWO MADE GOOD TIME. I WASN'T...
THANKS FOR THE HELP...AGAIN. CAPED CRUSADER, I'M THINKING THAT'S THE REAL JOKER.
CAPED CRUSADER?
WE'LL TAKE HIM OFF YOUR HANDS AND TAKE CARE OF THE PAPERWORK!
WE'LL KEEP YOUR NAME OUT OF IT, AS USUAL.
WHERE ARE YOU TAKING HIM?
WH...?

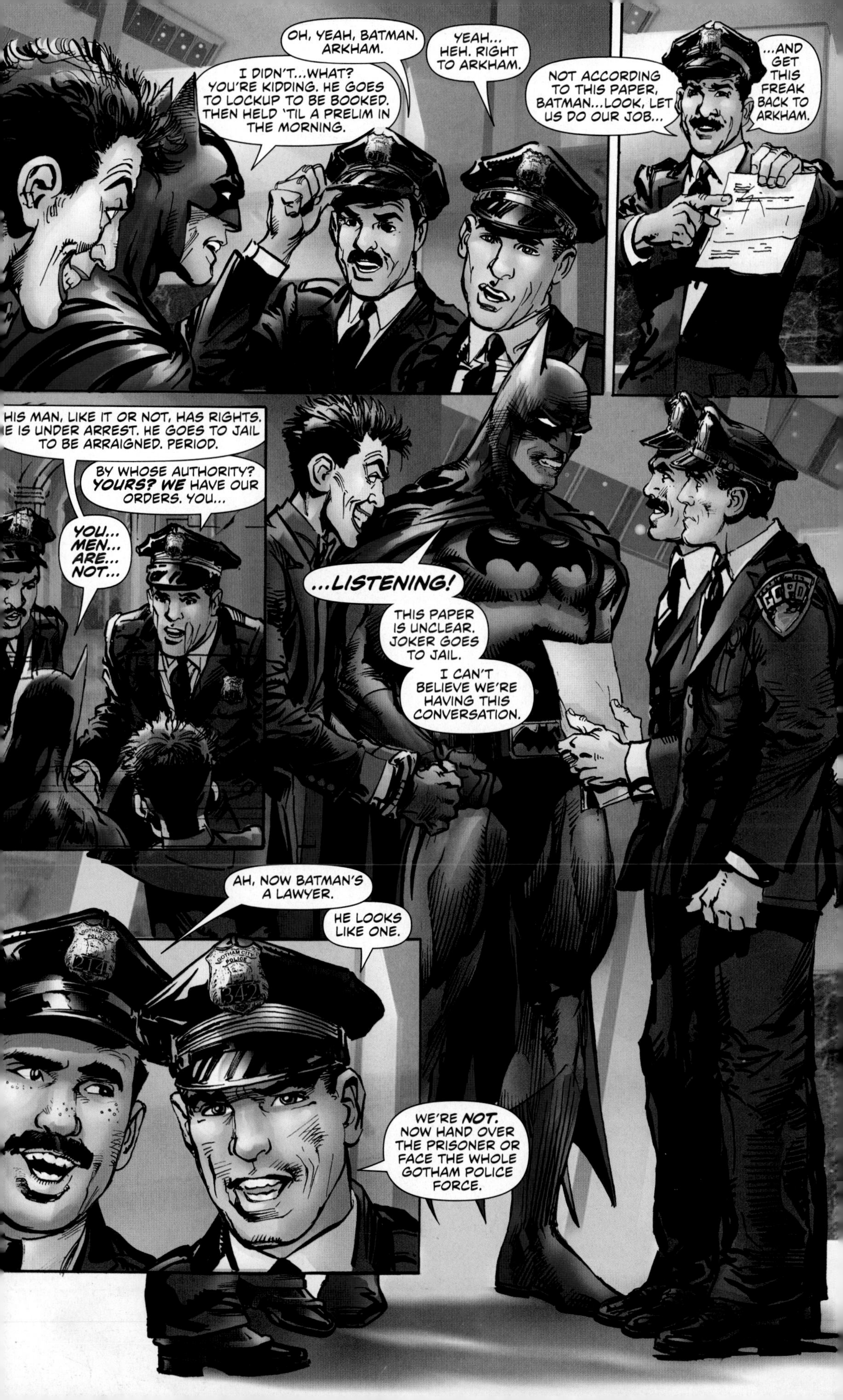
I DIDN'T...WHAT? YOU'RE KIDDING. HE GOES TO LOCKUP TO BE BOOKED. THEN HELD 'TIL A PRELIM IN THE MORNING.
OH, YEAH, BATMAN. ARKHAM.
YEAH... HEH. RIGHT TO ARKHAM.
NOT ACCORDING TO THIS PAPER, BATMAN...LOOK, LET US DO OUR JOB...
...AND GET THIS FREAK BACK TO ARKHAM.
HIS MAN, LIKE IT OR NOT, HAS RIGHTS. E IS UNDER ARREST. HE GOES TO JAIL TO BE ARRAIGNED. PERIOD.
BY WHOSE AUTHORITY? YOURS? WE HAVE OUR ORDERS. YOU...
YOU... MEN... ARE... NOT...
...LISTENING!
THIS PAPER IS UNCLEAR. JOKER GOES TO JAIL.
I CAN'T BELIEVE WE'RE HAVING THIS CONVERSATION.
AH, NOW BATMAN'S A LAWYER.
HE LOOKS LIKE ONE.
WE'RE NOT. NOW HAND OVER THE PRISONER OR FACE THE WHOLE GOTHAM POLICE FORCE.

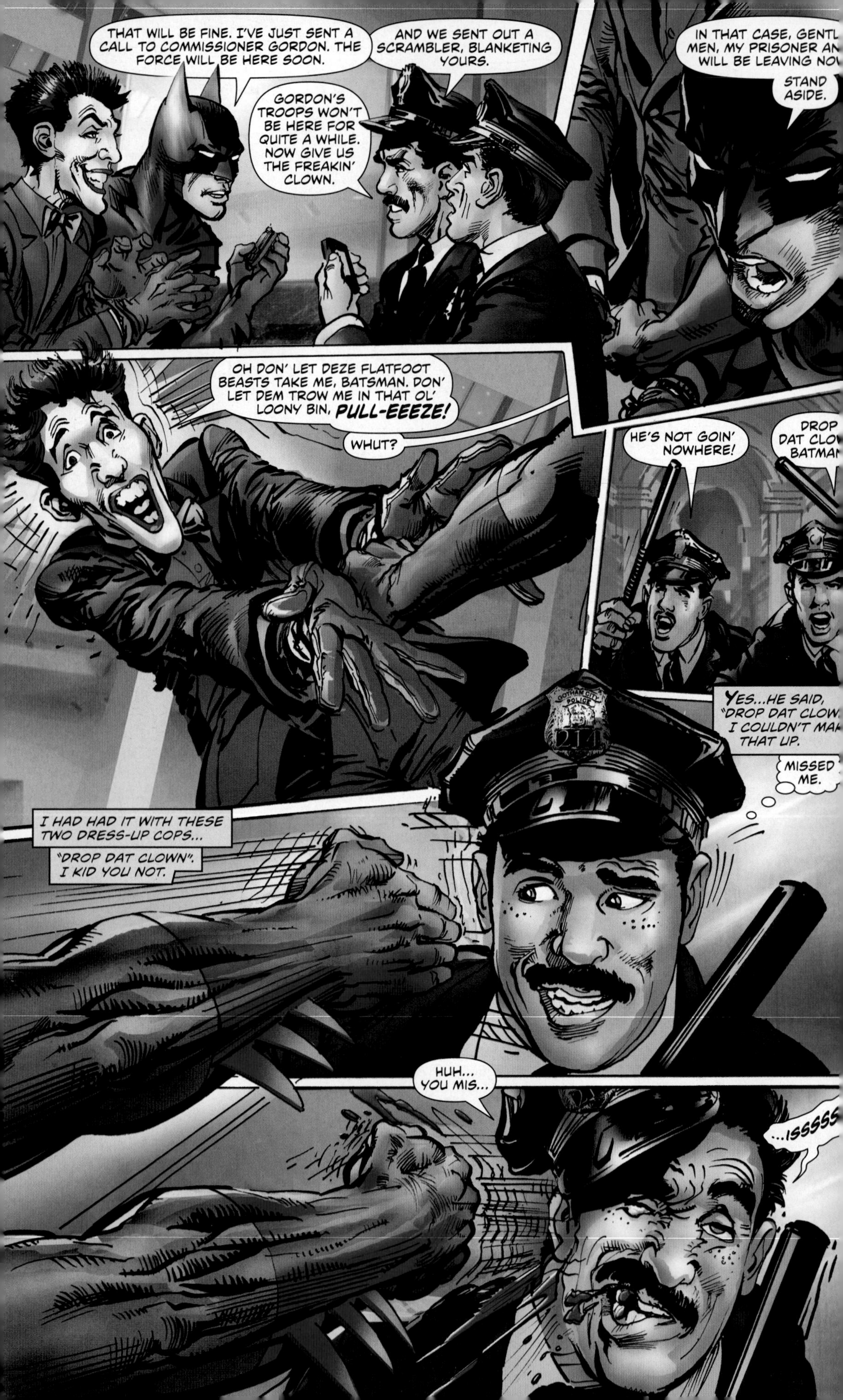
THAT WILL BE FINE. I'VE JUST SENT A CALL TO COMMISSIONER GORDON. THE FORCE WILL BE HERE SOON.
AND WE SENT OUT A SCRAMBLER, BLANKETING YOURS.
GORDON'S TROOPS WON'T BE HERE FOR QUITE A WHILE. NOW GIVE US THE FREAKIN' CLOWN.
IN THAT CASE, GENTL MEN, MY PRISONER AN WILL BE LEAVING NOW
STAND ASIDE.
OH DON' LET DEZE FLATFOOT BEASTS TAKE ME, BATSMAN. DON' LET DEM TROW ME IN THAT OL' LOONY BIN, PULL-EEEZE!
WHUT?
HE'S NOT GOIN' NOWHERE!
DROP DAT CLOW BATMAN
YES...HE SAID, "DROP DAT CLOWN I COULDN'T MA THAT UP.
MISSED ME.
I HAD HAD IT WITH THESE TWO DRESS-UP COPS...
"DROP DAT CLOWN". I KID YOU NOT.
HUH... YOU MIS...
...ISSSSS

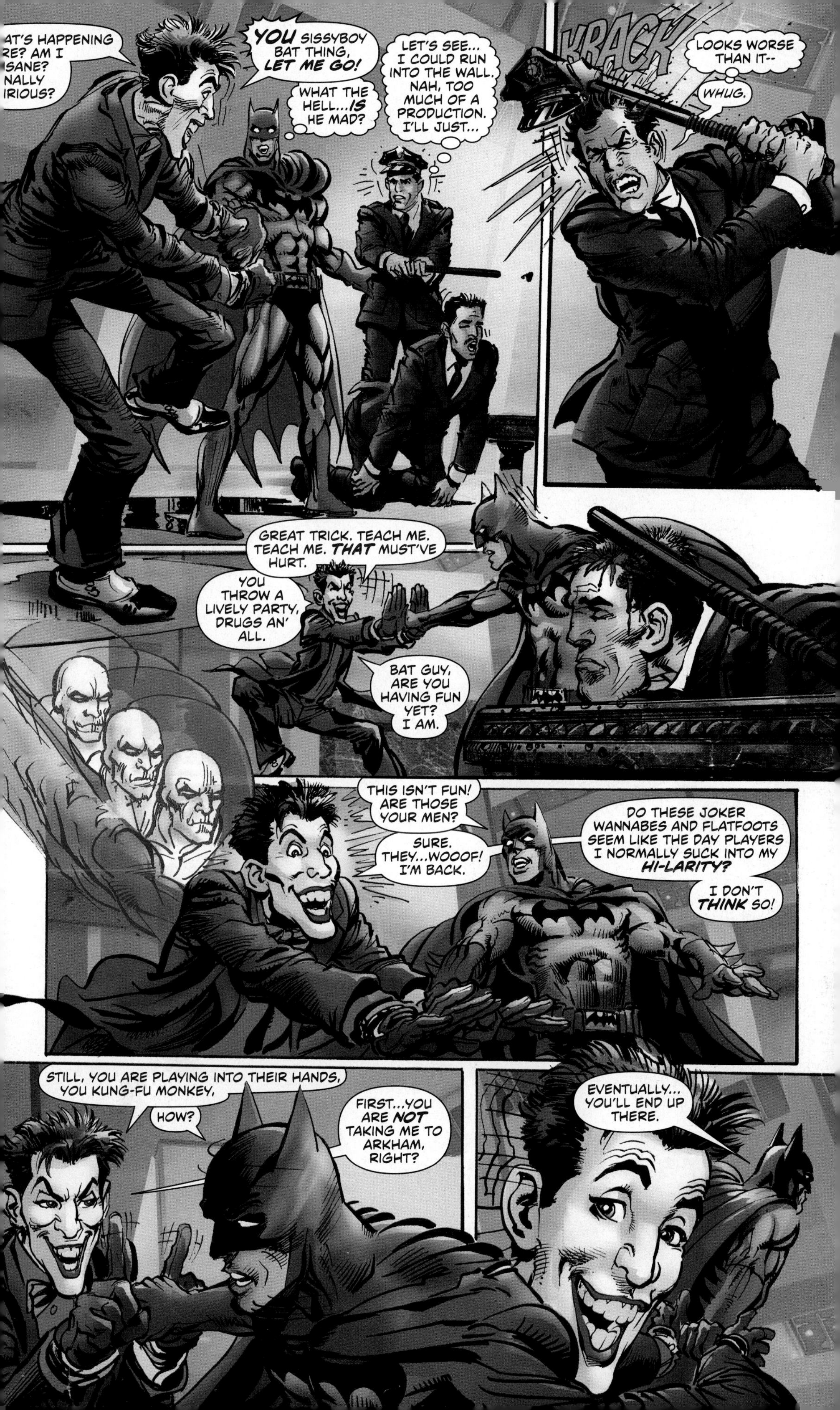

AT'S HAPPENING
RE? AM I
SANE?
NALLY
IRIOUS?
YOU SISSYBOY BAT THING, LET ME GO!
WHAT THE HELL...IS HE MAD?
LET'S SEE... I COULD RUN INTO THE WALL. NAH, TOO MUCH OF A PRODUCTION. I'LL JUST...
KRACK
LOOKS WORSE THAN IT--
WHUG.
GREAT TRICK. TEACH ME. TEACH ME. THAT MUST'VE HURT.
YOU THROW A LIVELY PARTY, DRUGS AN' ALL.
BAT GUY, ARE YOU HAVING FUN YET? I AM.
THIS ISN'T FUN! ARE THOSE YOUR MEN?
SURE. THEY...WOOOF! I'M BACK.
DO THESE JOKER WANNABES AND FLATFOOTS SEEM LIKE THE DAY PLAYERS I NORMALLY SUCK INTO MY HI-LARITY?
I DON'T THINK SO!
STILL, YOU ARE PLAYING INTO THEIR HANDS, YOU KUNG-FU MONKEY.
HOW?
FIRST...YOU ARE NOT TAKING ME TO ARKHAM, RIGHT?
EVENTUALLY... YOU'LL END UP THERE.

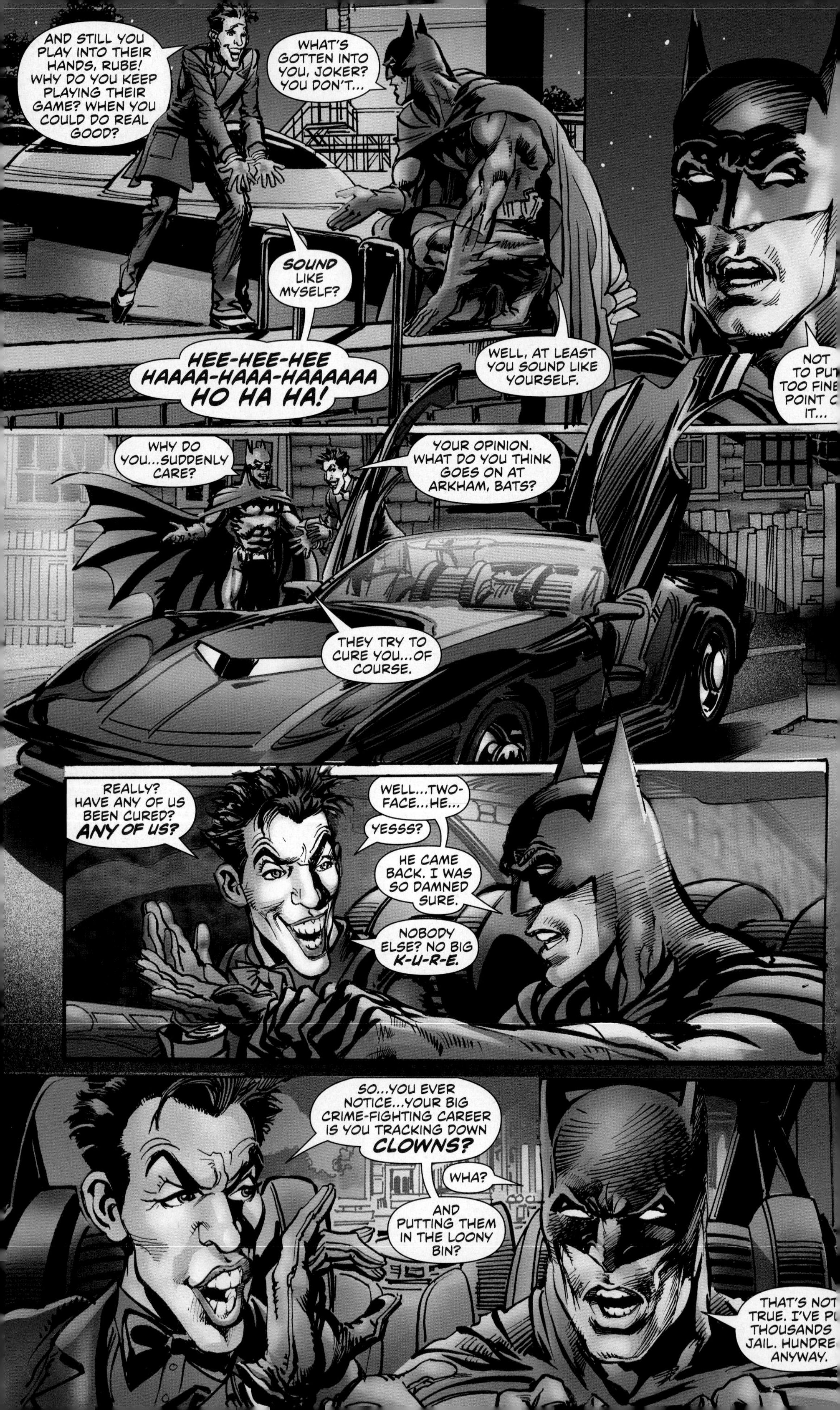

AND STILL YOU PLAY INTO THEIR HANDS, RUBE! WHY DO YOU KEEP PLAYING THEIR GAME? WHEN YOU COULD DO REAL GOOD?
WHAT'S GOTTEN INTO YOU, JOKER? YOU DON'T...
SOUND LIKE MYSELF?
HEE-HEE-HEE HAAAA-HAAA-HAAAAAA HO HA HA!
WELL, AT LEAST YOU SOUND LIKE YOURSELF.
NOT TO PUT TOO FINE POINT C IT...
WHY DO YOU...SUDDENLY CARE?
YOUR OPINION. WHAT DO YOU THINK GOES ON AT ARKHAM, BATS?
THEY TRY TO CURE YOU...OF COURSE.
REALLY? HAVE ANY OF US BEEN CURED? ANY OF US?
WELL...TWO-FACE...HE...
YESSS?
HE CAME BACK. I WAS SO DAMNED SURE.
NOBODY ELSE? NO BIG K-U-R-E.
SO...YOU EVER NOTICE...YOUR BIG CRIME-FIGHTING CAREER IS YOU TRACKING DOWN CLOWNS?
WHA?
AND PUTTING THEM IN THE LOONY BIN?
THAT'S NOT TRUE. I'VE PU THOUSANDS JAIL. HUNDRE ANYWAY.

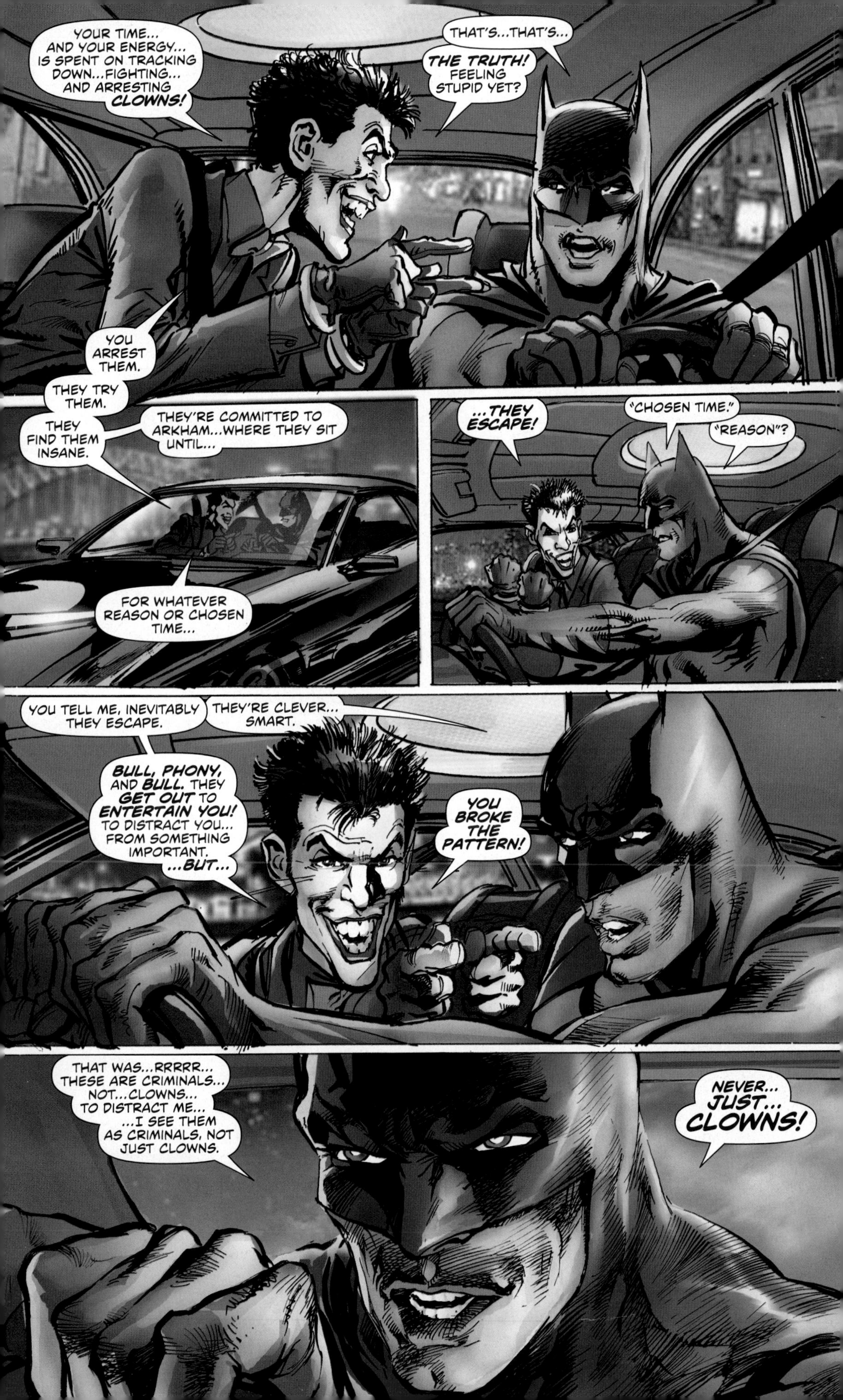

YOUR TIME... AND YOUR ENERGY... IS SPENT ON TRACKING DOWN...FIGHTING... AND ARRESTING CLOWNS!
THAT'S...THAT'S...
THE TRUTH! FEELING STUPID YET?
YOU ARREST THEM.
THEY TRY THEM.
THEY FIND THEM INSANE.
THEY'RE COMMITTED TO ARKHAM...WHERE THEY SIT UNTIL...
FOR WHATEVER REASON OR CHOSEN TIME...
...THEY ESCAPE!
"CHOSEN TIME."
"REASON"?
YOU TELL ME, INEVITABLY THEY ESCAPE.
THEY'RE CLEVER... SMART.
BULL, PHONY, AND BULL. THEY GET OUT TO ENTERTAIN YOU! TO DISTRACT YOU... FROM SOMETHING IMPORTANT. ...BUT...
YOU BROKE THE PATTERN!
THAT WAS...RRRRR... THESE ARE CRIMINALS... NOT...CLOWNS... TO DISTRACT ME... ...I SEE THEM AS CRIMINALS, NOT JUST CLOWNS.
NEVER... JUST... CLOWNS!

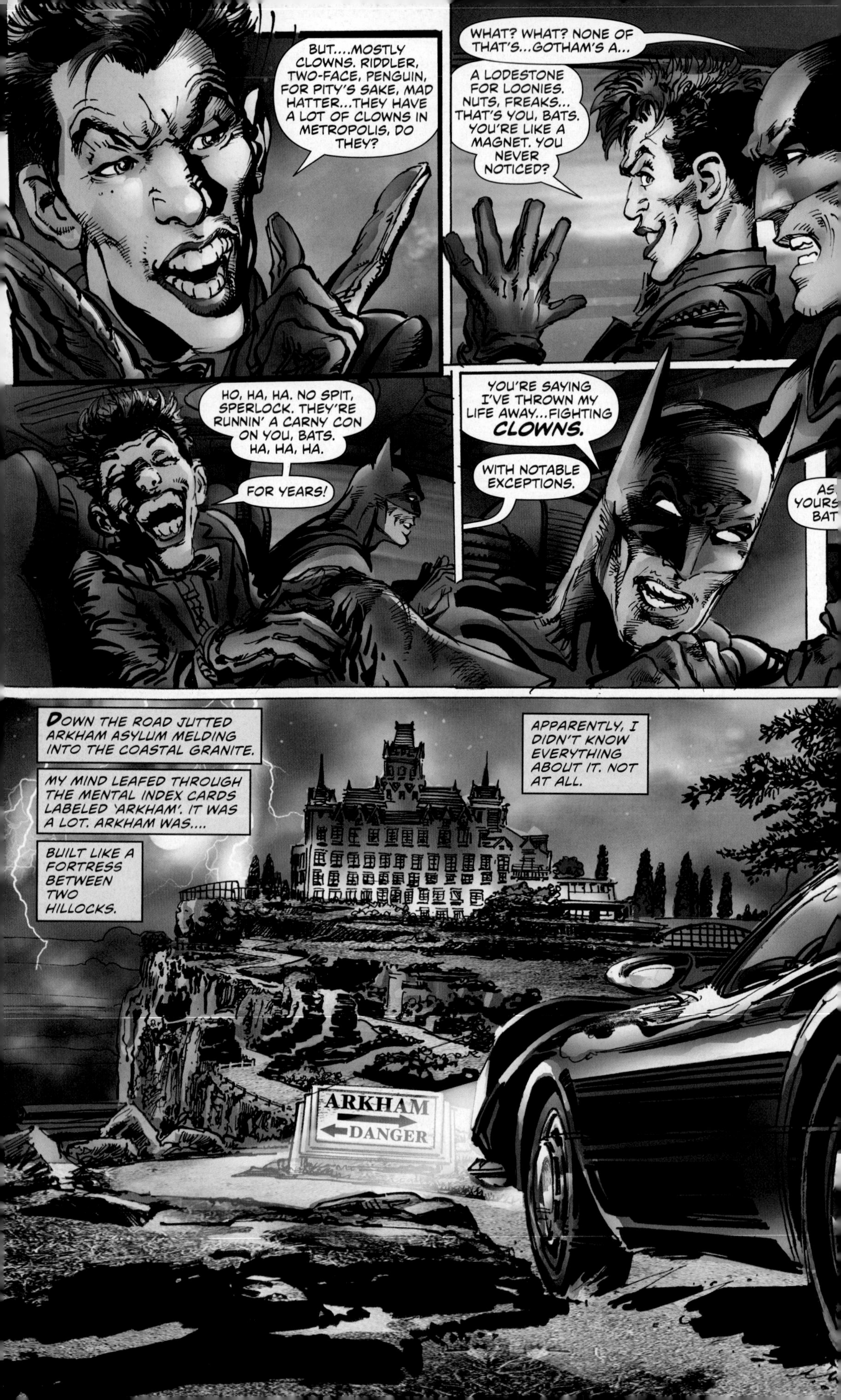

BUT....MOSTLY CLOWNS. RIDDLER, TWO-FACE, PENGUIN, FOR PITY'S SAKE, MAD HATTER...THEY HAVE A LOT OF CLOWNS IN METROPOLIS, DO THEY?
WHAT? WHAT? NONE OF THAT'S...GOTHAM'S A...
A LODESTONE FOR LOONIES. NUTS, FREAKS... THAT'S YOU, BATS. YOU'RE LIKE A MAGNET. YOU NEVER NOTICED?
HO, HA, HA. NO SPIT, SPERLOCK. THEY'RE RUNNIN' A CARNY CON ON YOU, BATS. HA, HA, HA.
FOR YEARS!
YOU'RE SAYING I'VE THROWN MY LIFE AWAY...FIGHTING CLOWNS.
WITH NOTABLE EXCEPTIONS.
DOWN THE ROAD JUTTED ARKHAM ASYLUM MELDING INTO THE COASTAL GRANITE.
MY MIND LEAFED THROUGH THE MENTAL INDEX CARDS LABELED 'ARKHAM'. IT WAS A LOT. ARKHAM WAS....
BUILT LIKE A FORTRESS BETWEEN TWO HILLOCKS.
APPARENTLY, I DIDN'T KNOW EVERYTHING ABOUT IT. NOT AT ALL.
ARKHAM
DANGER

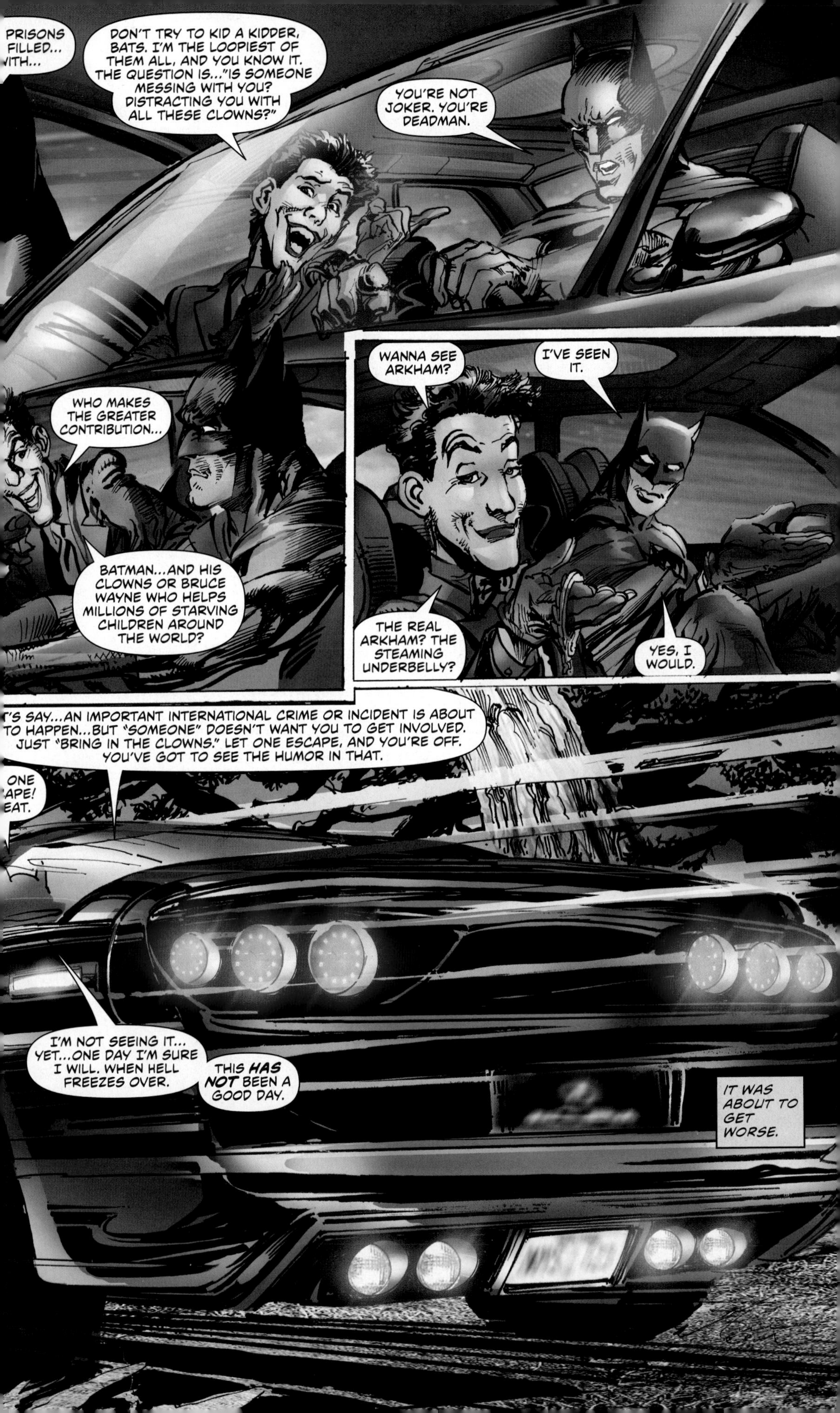
PRISONS FILLED... WITH...
DON'T TRY TO KID A KIDDER, BATS. I'M THE LOOPIEST OF THEM ALL, AND YOU KNOW IT. THE QUESTION IS..."IS SOMEONE MESSING WITH YOU? DISTRACTING YOU WITH ALL THESE CLOWNS?"
YOU'RE NOT JOKER. YOU'RE DEADMAN.
WHO MAKES THE GREATER CONTRIBUTION...
BATMAN...AND HIS CLOWNS OR BRUCE WAYNE WHO HELPS MILLIONS OF STARVING CHILDREN AROUND THE WORLD?
WANNA SEE ARKHAM?
I'VE SEEN IT.
THE REAL ARKHAM? THE STEAMING UNDERBELLY?
YES, I WOULD.
'S SAY...AN IMPORTANT INTERNATIONAL CRIME OR INCIDENT IS ABOUT TO HAPPEN...BUT "SOMEONE" DOESN'T WANT YOU TO GET INVOLVED. JUST "BRING IN THE CLOWNS." LET ONE ESCAPE, AND YOU'RE OFF. YOU'VE GOT TO SEE THE HUMOR IN THAT.
ONE APE! EAT.
I'M NOT SEEING IT... YET...ONE DAY I'M SURE I WILL. WHEN HELL FREEZES OVER.
THIS **HAS NOT** BEEN A GOOD DAY.
IT WAS ABOUT TO GET WORSE.

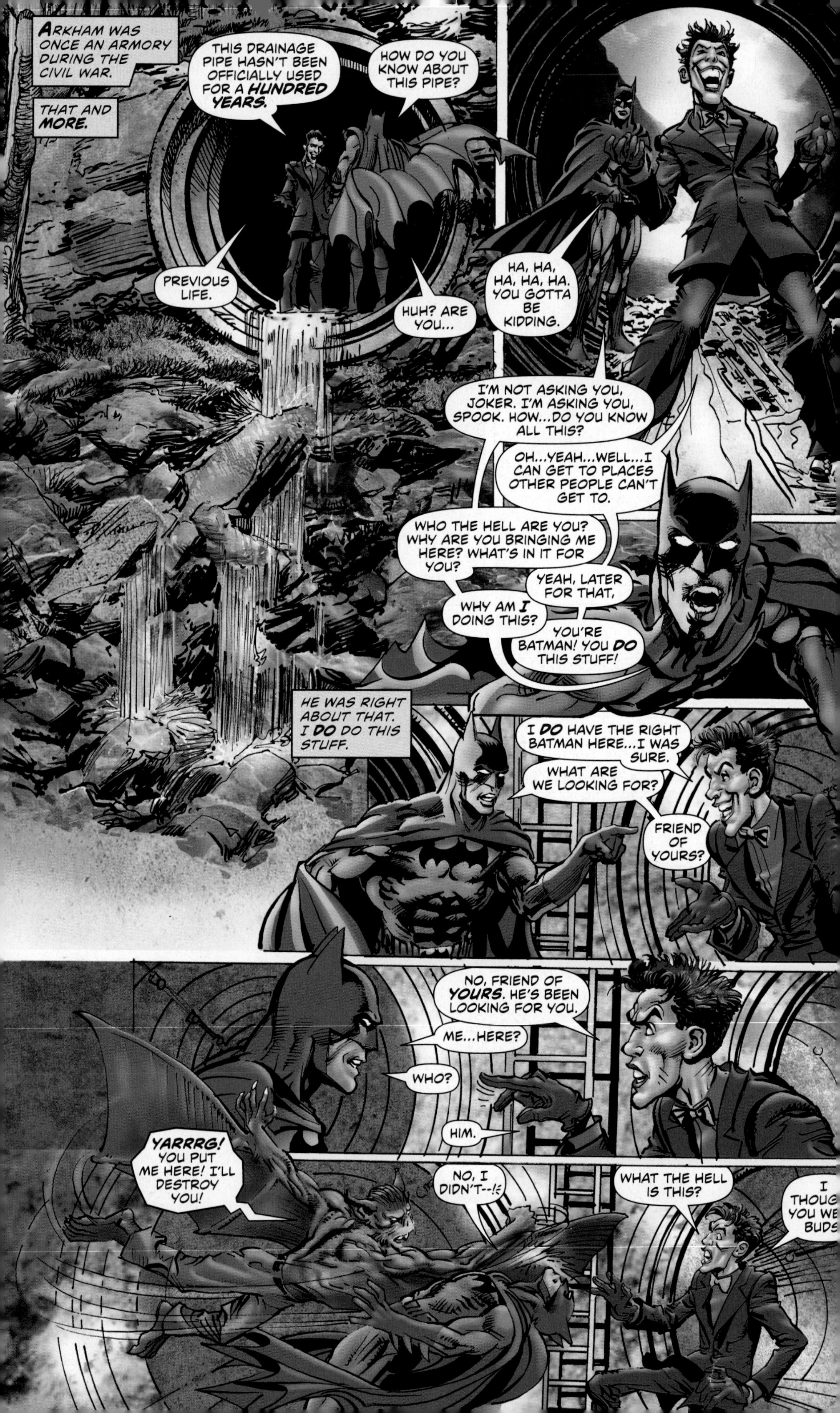
ARKHAM WAS ONCE AN ARMORY DURING THE CIVIL WAR.
THAT AND MORE.
THIS DRAINAGE PIPE HASN'T BEEN OFFICIALLY USED FOR A HUNDRED YEARS.
HOW DO YOU KNOW ABOUT THIS PIPE?
PREVIOUS LIFE.
HUH? ARE YOU...
HA, HA, HA, HA, HA. YOU GOTTA BE KIDDING.
I'M NOT ASKING YOU, JOKER. I'M ASKING YOU, SPOOK. HOW...DO YOU KNOW ALL THIS?
OH...YEAH...WELL...I CAN GET TO PLACES OTHER PEOPLE CAN'T GET TO.
WHO THE HELL ARE YOU? WHY ARE YOU BRINGING ME HERE? WHAT'S IN IT FOR YOU?
WHY AM I DOING THIS?
YEAH, LATER FOR THAT,
YOU'RE BATMAN! YOU DO THIS STUFF!
HE WAS RIGHT ABOUT THAT. I DO DO THIS STUFF.
I DO HAVE THE RIGHT BATMAN HERE...I WAS SURE.
WHAT ARE WE LOOKING FOR?
FRIEND OF YOURS?
NO, FRIEND OF YOURS. HE'S BEEN LOOKING FOR YOU.
ME...HERE?
WHO?
HIM.
YARRRG! YOU PUT ME HERE! I'LL DESTROY YOU!
NO, I DIDN'T--!?
WHAT THE HELL IS THIS?

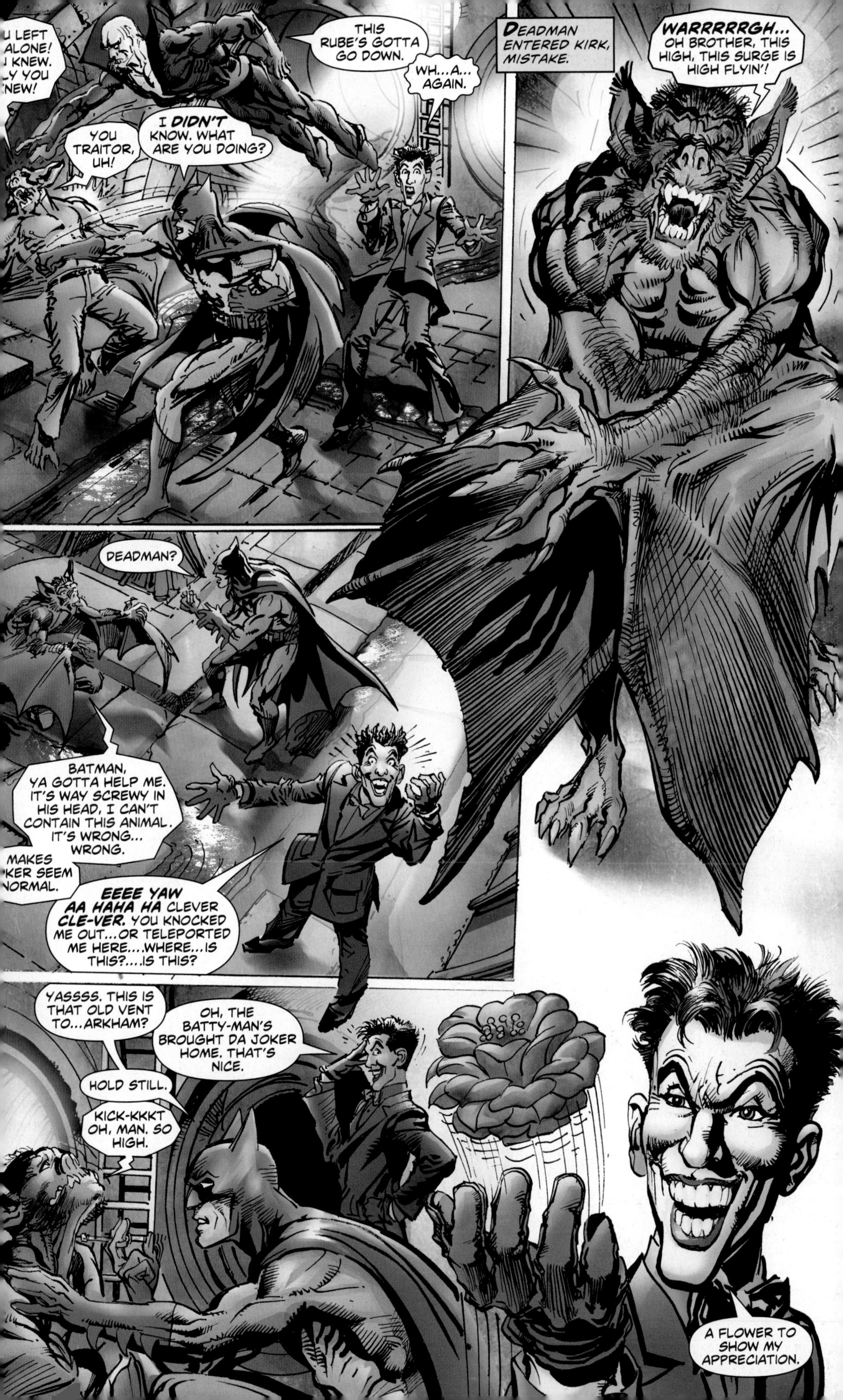

U LEFT
ALONE!
I KNEW.
LY YOU
NEW!
THIS RUBE'S GOTTA GO DOWN.
WH...A... AGAIN.
YOU TRAITOR, UH!
I DIDN'T KNOW. WHAT ARE YOU DOING?
DEADMAN ENTERED KIRK, MISTAKE.
WARRRRRGH... OH BROTHER, THIS HIGH, THIS SURGE IS HIGH FLYIN'!
DEADMAN?
BATMAN, YA GOTTA HELP ME. IT'S WAY SCREWY IN HIS HEAD, I CAN'T CONTAIN THIS ANIMAL. IT'S WRONG... WRONG.
MAKES
KER SEEM
NORMAL.
EEEE YAW AA HAHA HA CLEVER CLE-VER. YOU KNOCKED ME OUT...OR TELEPORTED ME HERE....WHERE...IS THIS?....IS THIS?
YASSSS. THIS IS THAT OLD VENT TO...ARKHAM?
OH, THE BATTY-MAN'S BROUGHT DA JOKER HOME. THAT'S NICE.
HOLD STILL.
KICK-KKKT OH, MAN. SO HIGH.
A FLOWER TO SHOW MY APPRECIATION.

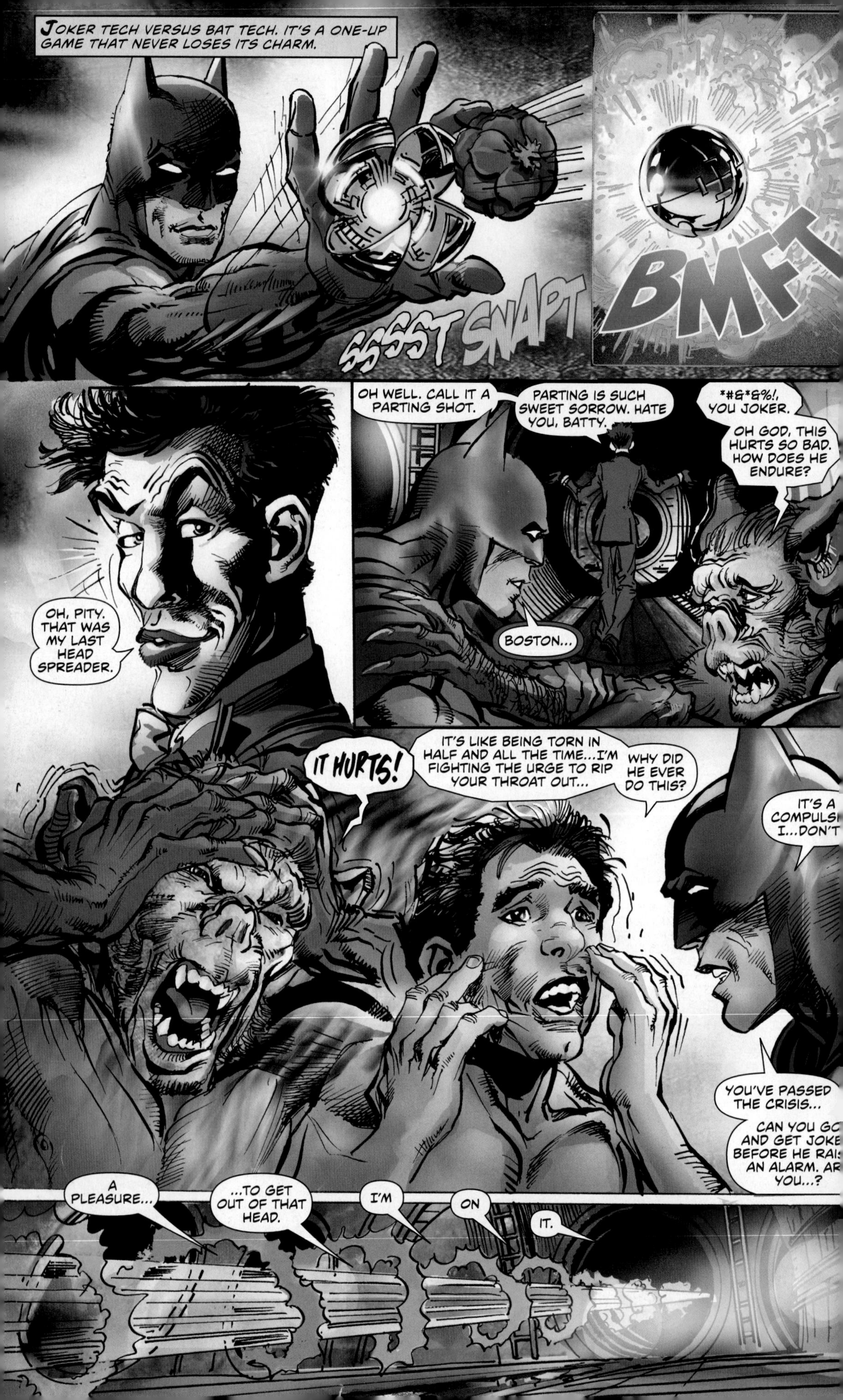
JOKER TECH VERSUS BAT TECH. IT'S A ONE-UP GAME THAT NEVER LOSES ITS CHARM.
SSSST SNAPT
BMFT
OH, PITY. THAT WAS MY LAST HEAD SPREADER.
OH WELL. CALL IT A PARTING SHOT.
PARTING IS SUCH SWEET SORROW. HATE YOU, BATTY.
BOSTON...
#&&%!, YOU JOKER.
OH GOD, THIS HURTS SO BAD. HOW DOES HE ENDURE?
IT HURTS!
IT'S LIKE BEING TORN IN HALF AND ALL THE TIME...I'M FIGHTING THE URGE TO RIP YOUR THROAT OUT...
WHY DID HE EVER DO THIS?
IT'S A COMPULS I...DON'T
YOU'VE PASSED THE CRISIS...
CAN YOU GO AND GET JOKE BEFORE HE RAI AN ALARM. AR YOU...?
A PLEASURE...
...TO GET OUT OF THAT HEAD.
I'M
ON
IT.

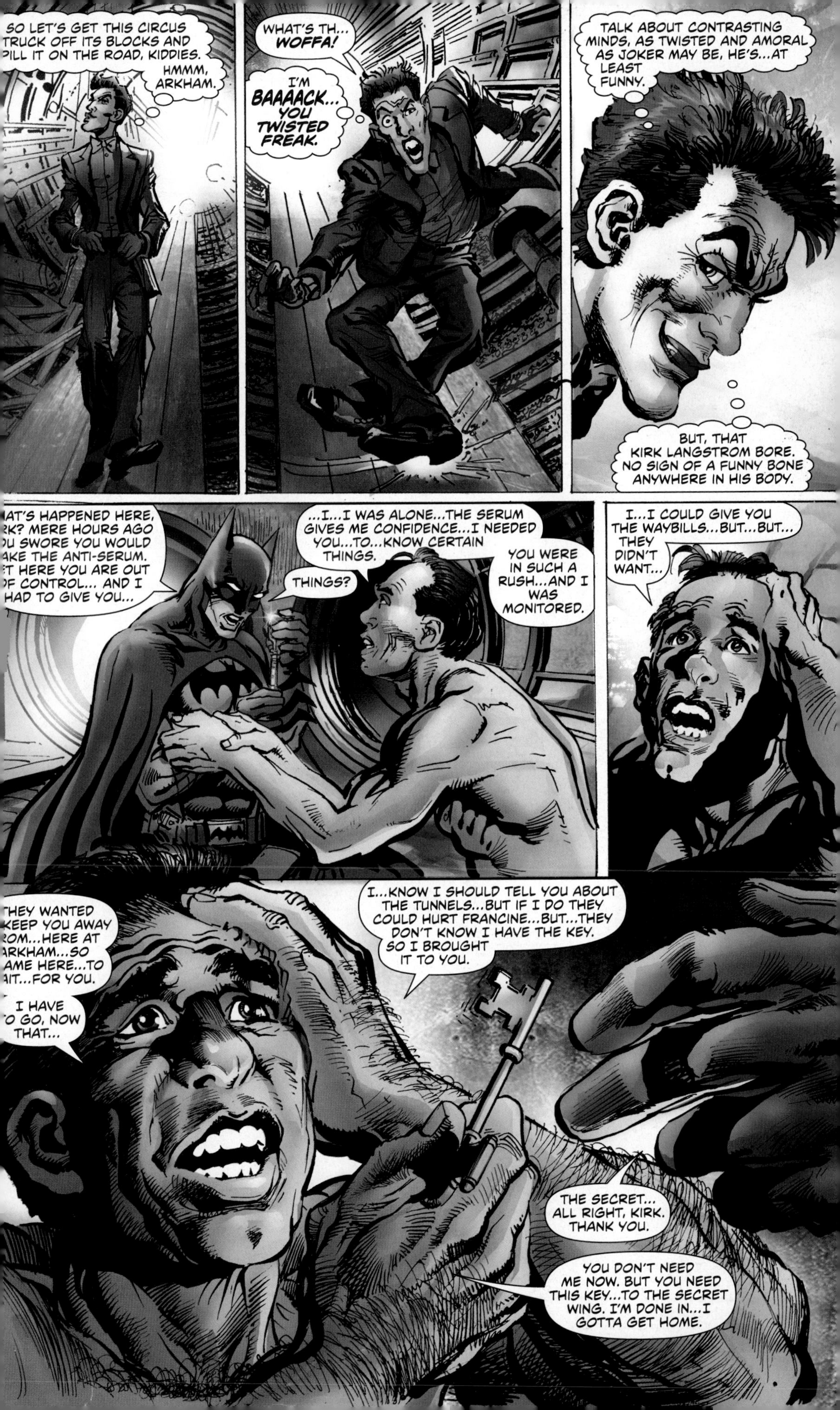
SO LET'S GET THIS CIRCUS TRUCK OFF ITS BLOCKS AND PILL IT ON THE ROAD, KIDDIES.
HMMM, ARKHAM.
WHAT'S TH... WOFFA!
I'M BAAAACK... YOU TWISTED FREAK.
TALK ABOUT CONTRASTING MINDS, AS TWISTED AND AMORAL AS JOKER MAY BE, HE'S...AT LEAST FUNNY.
BUT, THAT KIRK LANGSTROM BORE. NO SIGN OF A FUNNY BONE ANYWHERE IN HIS BODY.
AT'S HAPPENED HERE, RK? MERE HOURS AGO U SWORE YOU WOULD AKE THE ANTI-SERUM. T HERE YOU ARE OUT F CONTROL... AND I HAD TO GIVE YOU...
...I...I WAS ALONE...THE SERUM GIVES ME CONFIDENCE...I NEEDED YOU...TO...KNOW CERTAIN THINGS.
THINGS?
YOU WERE IN SUCH A RUSH...AND I WAS MONITORED.
I...I COULD GIVE YOU THE WAYBILLS...BUT...BUT... THEY DIDN'T WANT...
THEY WANTED KEEP YOU AWAY ROM...HERE AT ARKHAM...SO AME HERE...TO AIT...FOR YOU.
I HAVE O GO, NOW THAT...
I...KNOW I SHOULD TELL YOU ABOUT THE TUNNELS...BUT IF I DO THEY COULD HURT FRANCINE...BUT...THEY DON'T KNOW I HAVE THE KEY. SO I BROUGHT IT TO YOU.
THE SECRET... ALL RIGHT, KIRK. THANK YOU.
YOU DON'T NEED ME NOW. BUT YOU NEED THIS KEY...TO THE SECRET WING. I'M DONE IN...I GOTTA GET HOME.

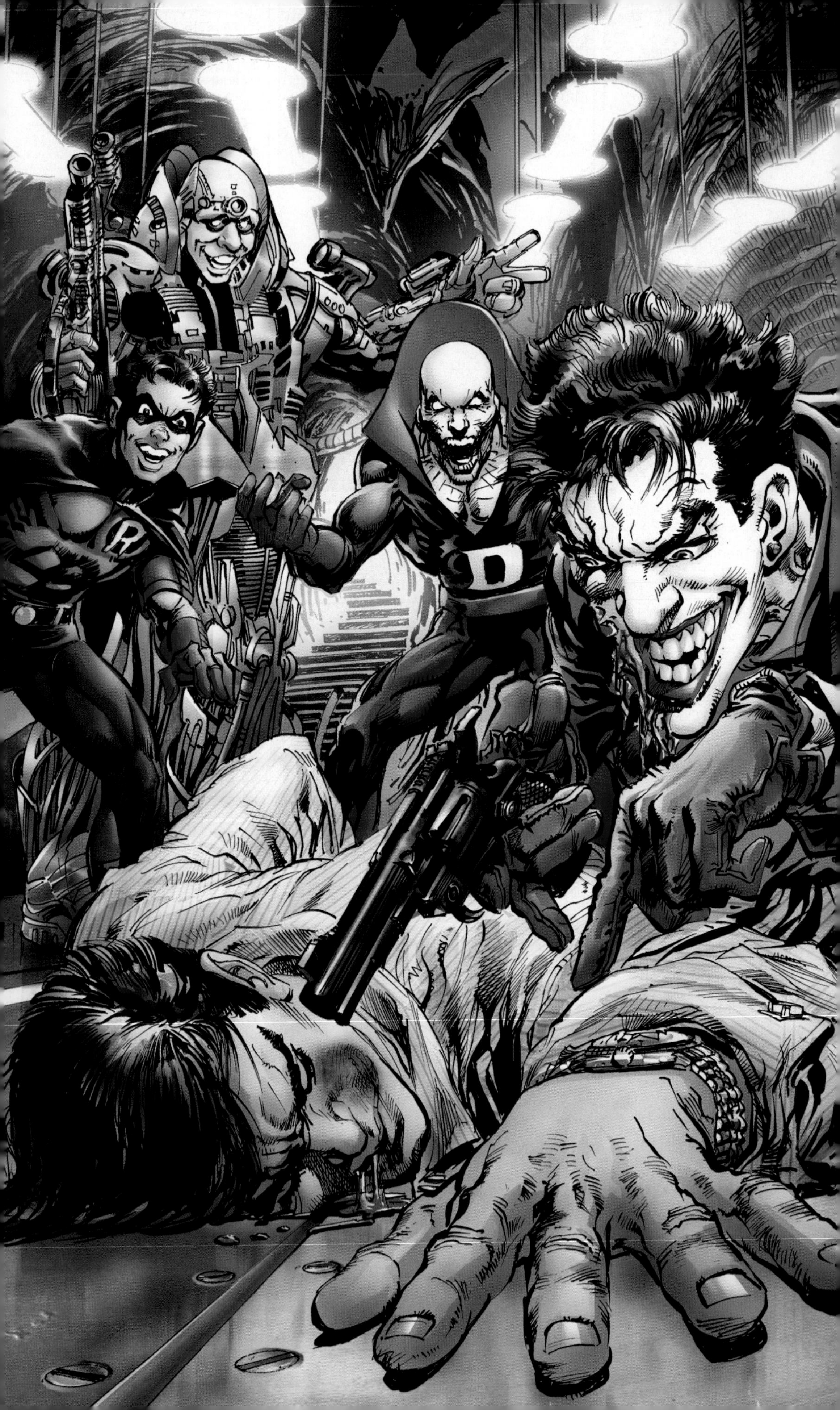

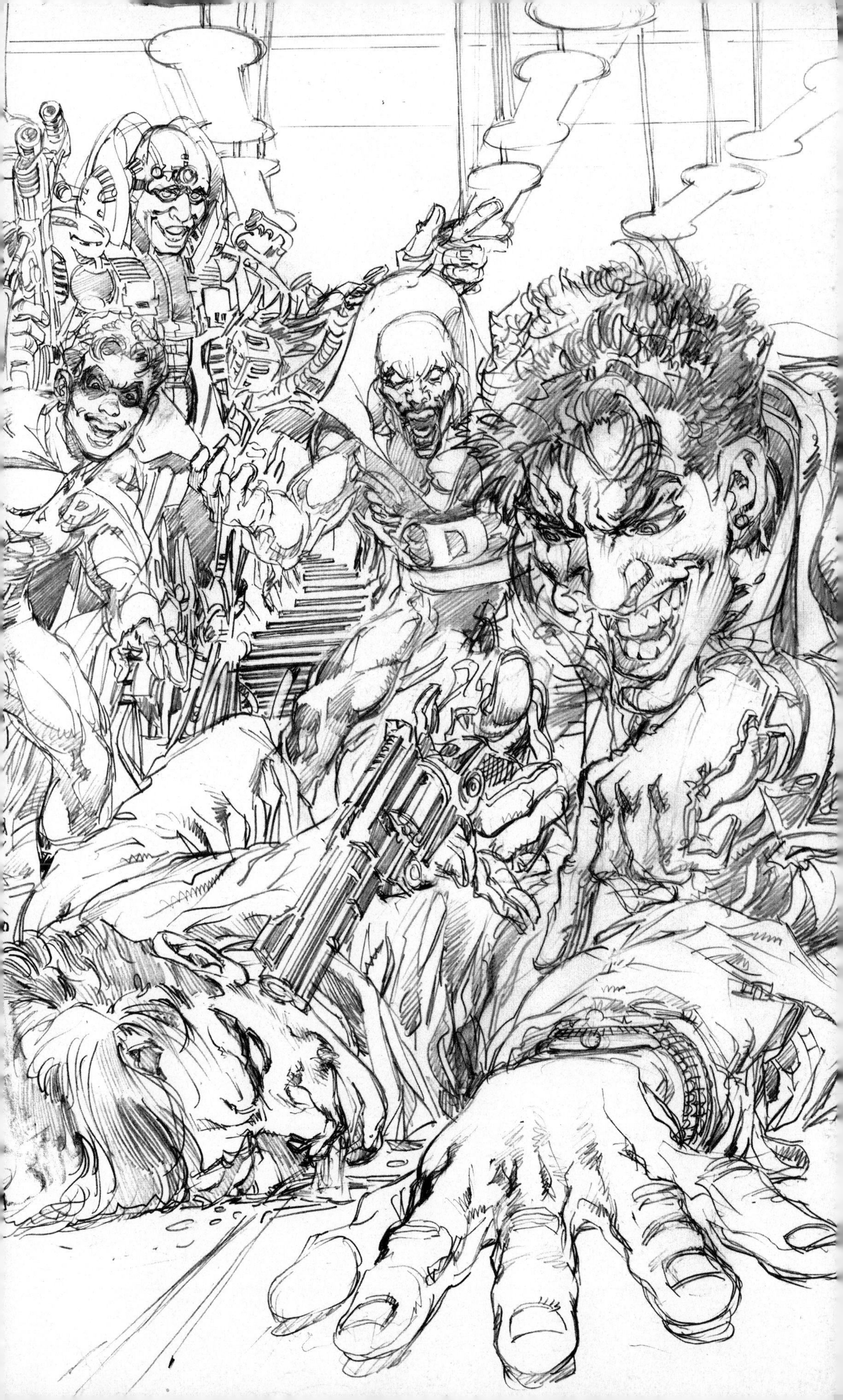

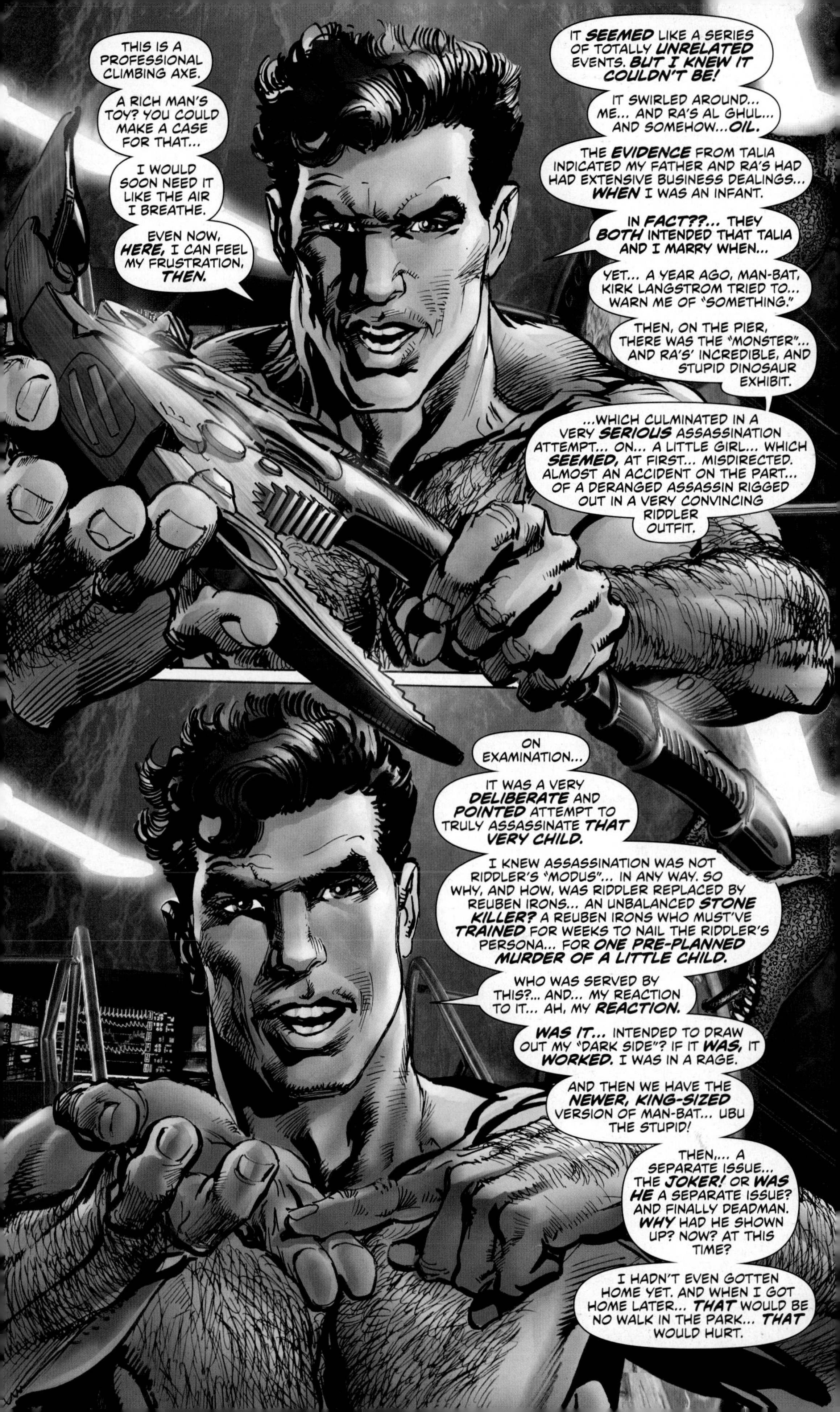
THIS IS A PROFESSIONAL CLIMBING AXE.
A RICH MAN'S TOY? YOU COULD MAKE A CASE FOR THAT...
I WOULD SOON NEED IT LIKE THE AIR I BREATHE.
EVEN NOW, HERE, I CAN FEEL MY FRUSTRATION, THEN.
IT SEEMED LIKE A SERIES OF TOTALLY UNRELATED EVENTS. BUT I KNEW IT COULDN'T BE!
IT SWIRLED AROUND... ME... AND RA'S AL GHUL... AND SOMEHOW... OIL.
THE EVIDENCE FROM TALIA INDICATED MY FATHER AND RA'S HAD HAD EXTENSIVE BUSINESS DEALINGS... WHEN I WAS AN INFANT.
IN FACT??... THEY BOTH INTENDED THAT TALIA AND I MARRY WHEN...
YET... A YEAR AGO, MAN-BAT, KIRK LANGSTROM TRIED TO... WARN ME OF "SOMETHING."
THEN, ON THE PIER, THERE WAS THE "MONSTER"... AND RA'S' INCREDIBLE, AND STUPID DINOSAUR EXHIBIT.
...WHICH CULMINATED IN A VERY SERIOUS ASSASSINATION ATTEMPT... ON... A LITTLE GIRL... WHICH SEEMED, AT FIRST... MISDIRECTED. ALMOST AN ACCIDENT ON THE PART... OF A DERANGED ASSASSIN RIGGED OUT IN A VERY CONVINCING RIDDLER OUTFIT.
ON EXAMINATION...
IT WAS A VERY DELIBERATE AND POINTED ATTEMPT TO TRULY ASSASSINATE THAT VERY CHILD.
I KNEW ASSASSINATION WAS NOT RIDDLER'S "MODUS"... IN ANY WAY. SO WHY, AND HOW, WAS RIDDLER REPLACED BY REUBEN IRONS... AN UNBALANCED STONE KILLER? A REUBEN IRONS WHO MUST'VE TRAINED FOR WEEKS TO NAIL THE RIDDLER'S PERSONA... FOR ONE PRE-PLANNED MURDER OF A LITTLE CHILD.
WHO WAS SERVED BY THIS?... AND... MY REACTION TO IT... AH, MY REACTION.
WAS IT... INTENDED TO DRAW OUT MY "DARK SIDE"? IF IT WAS, IT WORKED. I WAS IN A RAGE.
AND THEN WE HAVE THE NEWER, KING-SIZED VERSION OF MAN-BAT... UBU THE STUPID!
THEN,... A SEPARATE ISSUE... THE JOKER! OR WAS HE A SEPARATE ISSUE? AND FINALLY DEADMAN. WHY HAD HE SHOWN UP? NOW? AT THIS TIME?
I HADN'T EVEN GOTTEN HOME YET. AND WHEN I GOT HOME LATER... THAT WOULD BE NO WALK IN THE PARK... THAT WOULD HURT.

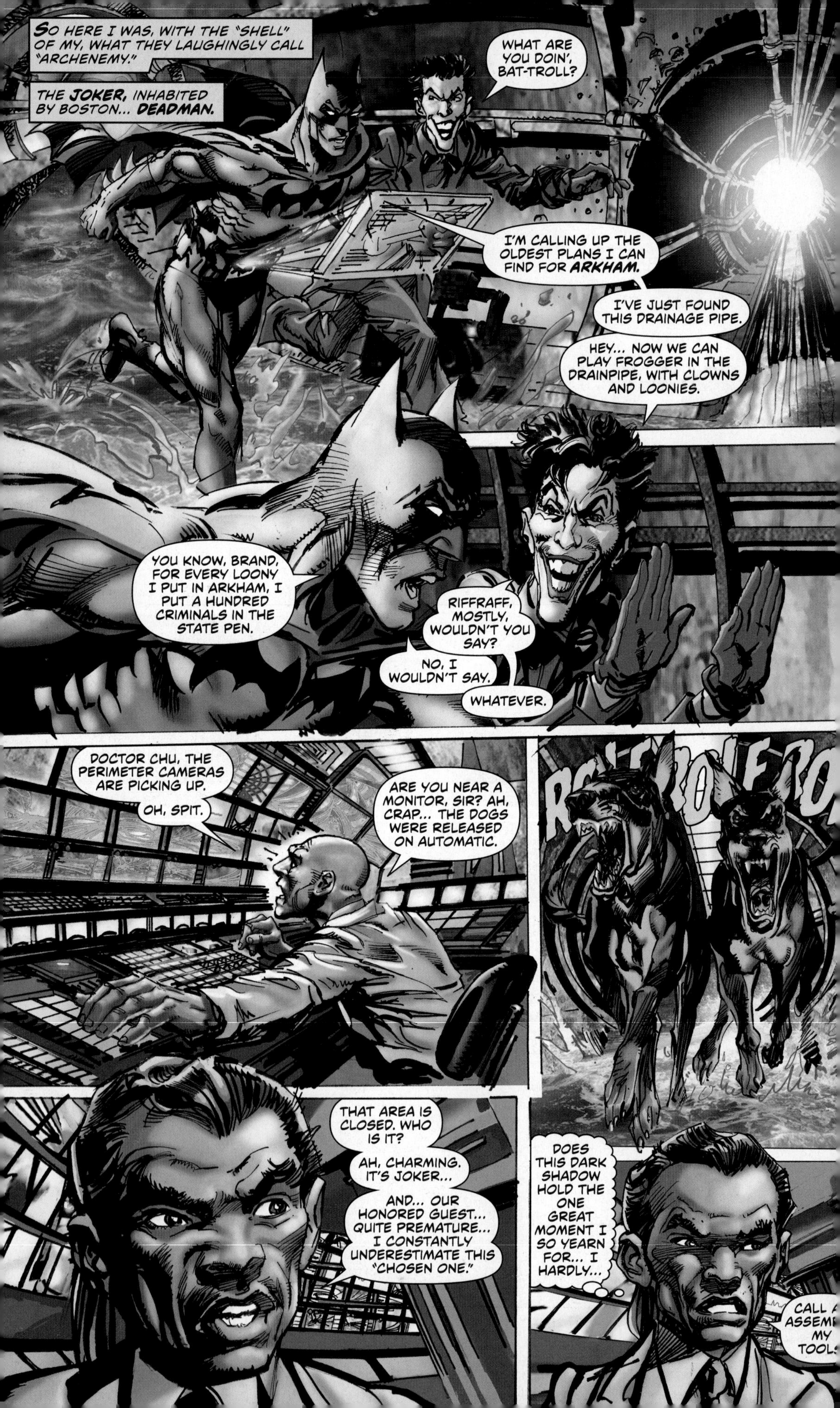

SO HERE I WAS, WITH THE "SHELL" OF MY, WHAT THEY LAUGHINGLY CALL "ARCHENEMY."
THE JOKER, INHABITED BY BOSTON... DEADMAN.
WHAT ARE YOU DOIN', BAT-TROLL?
I'M CALLING UP THE OLDEST PLANS I CAN FIND FOR ARKHAM.
I'VE JUST FOUND THIS DRAINAGE PIPE.
HEY... NOW WE CAN PLAY FROGGER IN THE DRAINPIPE, WITH CLOWNS AND LOONIES.
YOU KNOW, BRAND, FOR EVERY LOONY I PUT IN ARKHAM, I PUT A HUNDRED CRIMINALS IN THE STATE PEN.
RIFFRAFF, MOSTLY, WOULDN'T YOU SAY?
NO, I WOULDN'T SAY.
WHATEVER.
DOCTOR CHU, THE PERIMETER CAMERAS ARE PICKING UP.
OH, SPIT.
ARE YOU NEAR A MONITOR, SIR? AH, CRAP... THE DOGS WERE RELEASED ON AUTOMATIC.
THAT AREA IS CLOSED. WHO IS IT?
AH, CHARMING. IT'S JOKER...
AND... OUR HONORED GUEST... QUITE PREMATURE... I CONSTANTLY UNDERESTIMATE THIS "CHOSEN ONE."
DOES THIS DARK SHADOW HOLD THE ONE GREAT MOMENT I SO YEARN FOR... I HARDLY...
CALL
ASSEM
MY
TOOLS

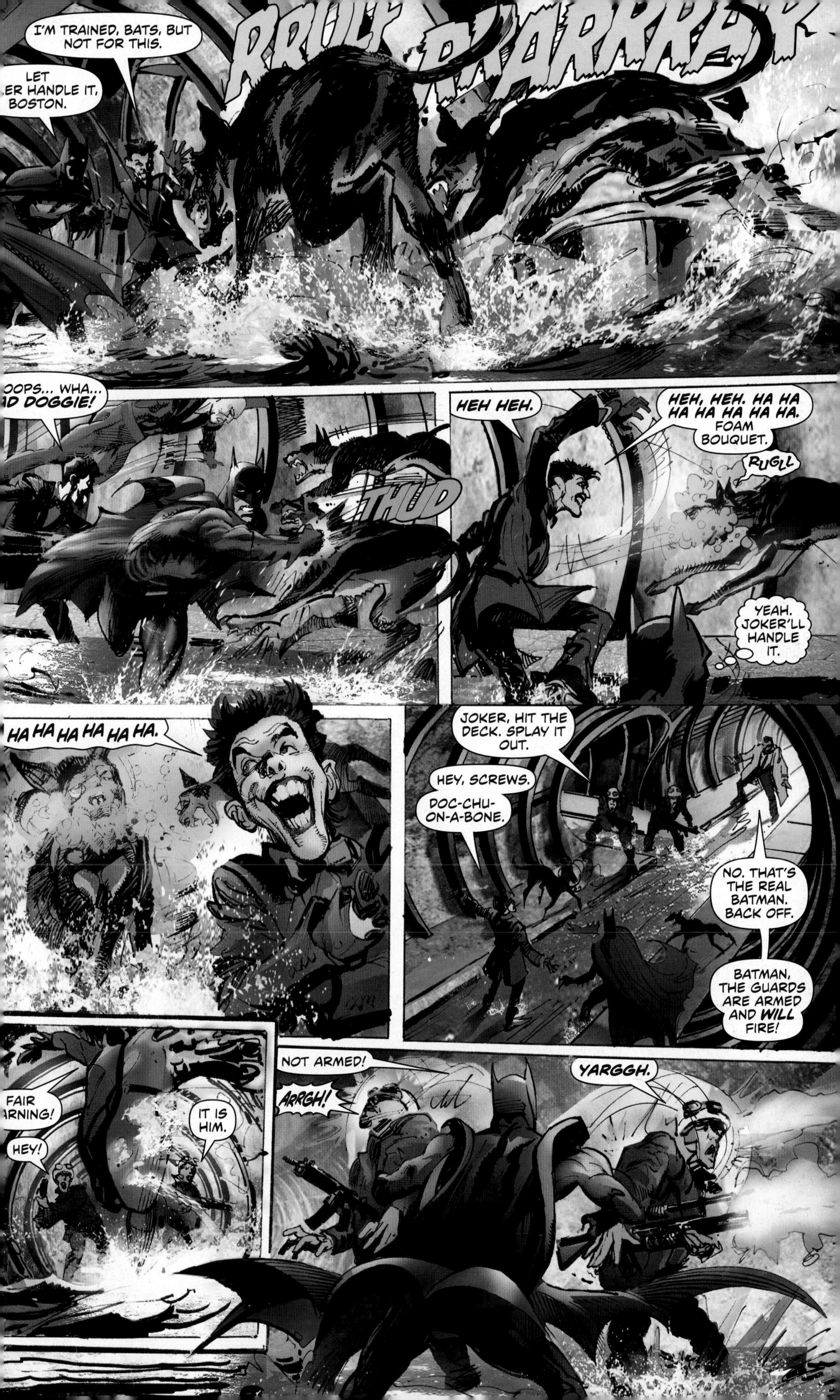
I'M TRAINED, BATS, BUT NOT FOR THIS.
LET ER HANDLE IT, BOSTON.
RRULL RWARRRAH
OOPS... WHA... D DOGGIE!
THUD
HEH HEH.
HEH, HEH. HA HA HA HA HA HA HA. FOAM BOUQUET.
RUGLL
YEAH. JOKER'LL HANDLE IT.
HA HA HA HA HA HA HA.
JOKER, HIT THE DECK. SPLAY IT OUT.
HEY, SCREWS.
DOC-CHU-ON-A-BONE.
NO. THAT'S THE REAL BATMAN. BACK OFF.
BATMAN, THE GUARDS ARE ARMED AND WILL FIRE!
FAIR ARNING!
HEY!
IT IS HIM.
NOT ARMED!
ARRGH!
YARGGH.

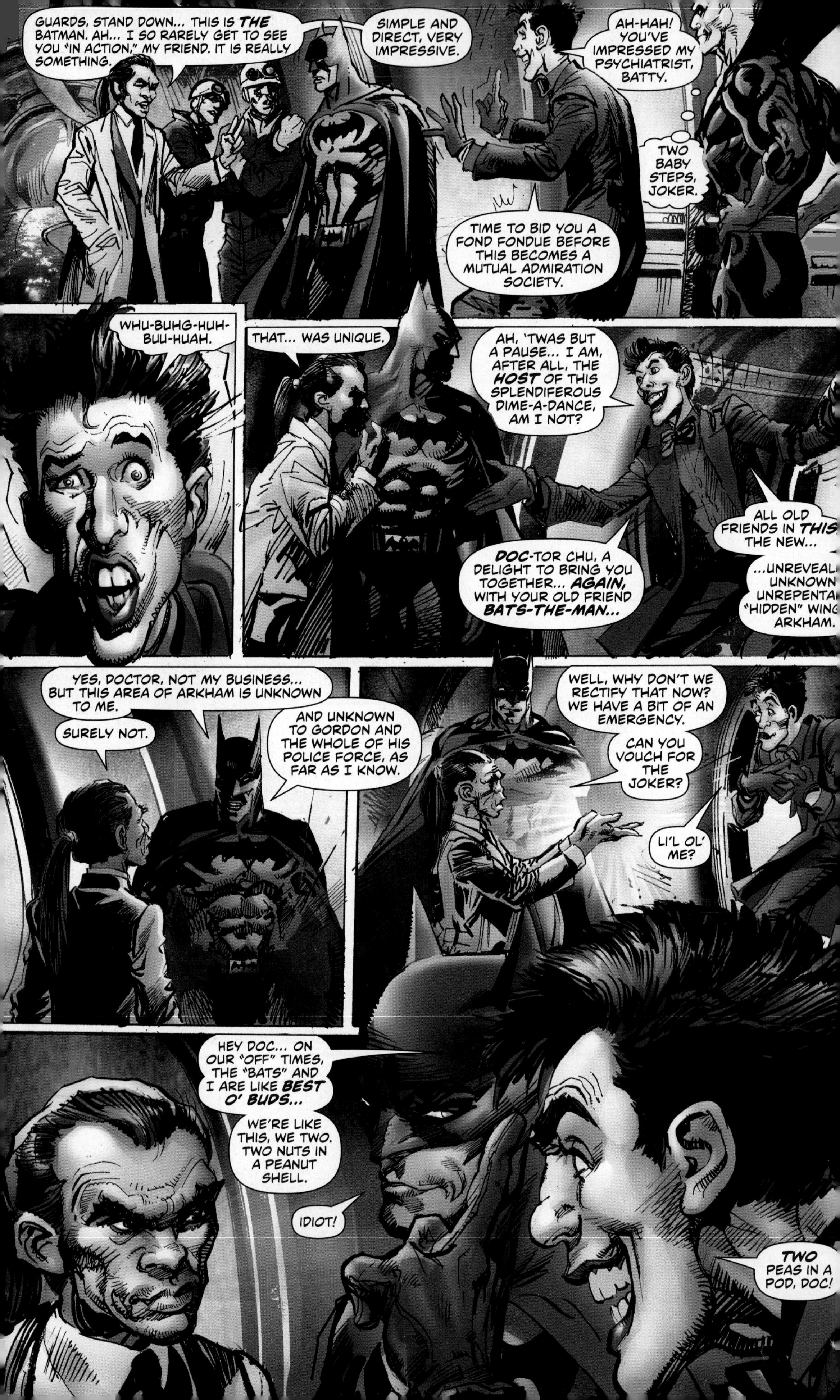

GUARDS, STAND DOWN... THIS IS THE BATMAN. AH... I SO RARELY GET TO SEE YOU "IN ACTION," MY FRIEND. IT IS REALLY SOMETHING.
SIMPLE AND DIRECT, VERY IMPRESSIVE.
AH-HAH! YOU'VE IMPRESSED MY PSYCHIATRIST, BATTY.
TWO BABY STEPS, JOKER.
TIME TO BID YOU A FOND FONDUE BEFORE THIS BECOMES A MUTUAL ADMIRATION SOCIETY.
WHU-BUHG-HUH-BUU-HUAH.
THAT... WAS UNIQUE.
AH, 'TWAS BUT A PAUSE... I AM, AFTER ALL, THE HOST OF THIS SPLENDIFEROUS DIME-A-DANCE, AM I NOT?
DOC-TOR CHU, A DELIGHT TO BRING YOU TOGETHER... AGAIN, WITH YOUR OLD FRIEND BATS-THE-MAN...
ALL OLD FRIENDS IN THIS THE NEW...
...UNREVEAL UNKNOWN UNREPENTA "HIDDEN" WING ARKHAM.
YES, DOCTOR, NOT MY BUSINESS... BUT THIS AREA OF ARKHAM IS UNKNOWN TO ME.
SURELY NOT.
AND UNKNOWN TO GORDON AND THE WHOLE OF HIS POLICE FORCE, AS FAR AS I KNOW.
WELL, WHY DON'T WE RECTIFY THAT NOW? WE HAVE A BIT OF AN EMERGENCY.
CAN YOU VOUCH FOR THE JOKER?
LI'L OL' ME?
HEY DOC... ON OUR "OFF" TIMES, THE "BATS" AND I ARE LIKE BEST O' BUDS...
WE'RE LIKE THIS, WE TWO. TWO NUTS IN A PEANUT SHELL.
IDIOT!
TWO PEAS IN A POD, DOC!

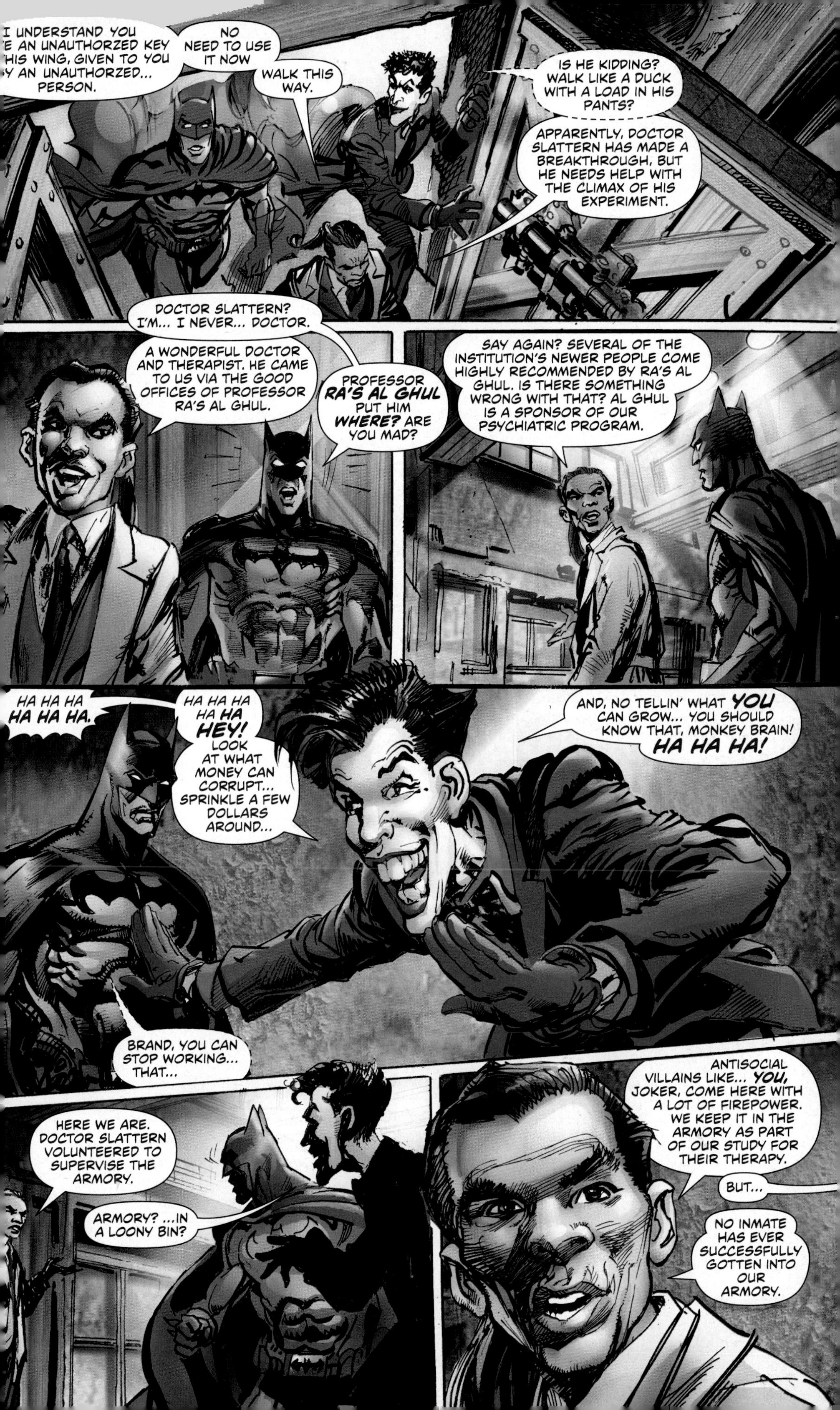
I UNDERSTAND YOU
E AN UNAUTHORZED KEY
HIS WING, GIVEN TO YOU
Y AN UNAUTHORZED...
PERSON.
NO NEED TO USE IT NOW
WALK THIS WAY.
IS HE KIDDING? WALK LIKE A DUCK WITH A LOAD IN HIS PANTS?
APPARENTLY, DOCTOR SLATTERN HAS MADE A BREAKTHROUGH, BUT HE NEEDS HELP WITH THE CLIMAX OF HIS EXPERIMENT.
DOCTOR SLATTERN? I'M... I NEVER... DOCTOR.
A WONDERFUL DOCTOR AND THERAPIST. HE CAME TO US VIA THE GOOD OFFICES OF PROFESSOR RA'S AL GHUL.
PROFESSOR RA'S AL GHUL PUT HIM WHERE? ARE YOU MAD?
SAY AGAIN? SEVERAL OF THE INSTITUTION'S NEWER PEOPLE COME HIGHLY RECOMMENDED BY RA'S AL GHUL. IS THERE SOMETHING WRONG WITH THAT? AL GHUL IS A SPONSOR OF OUR PSYCHIATRIC PROGRAM.
HA HA HA HA HA HA.
HA HA HA HA HA HEY! LOOK AT WHAT MONEY CAN CORRUPT... SPRINKLE A FEW DOLLARS AROUND...
AND, NO TELLIN' WHAT YOU CAN GROW... YOU SHOULD KNOW THAT, MONKEY BRAIN! HA HA HA!
BRAND, YOU CAN STOP WORKING... THAT...
HERE WE ARE. DOCTOR SLATTERN VOLUNTEERED TO SUPERVISE THE ARMORY.
ARMORY? ...IN A LOONY BIN?
ANTISOCIAL VILLAINS LIKE... YOU, JOKER, COME HERE WITH A LOT OF FIREPOWER. WE KEEP IT IN THE ARMORY AS PART OF OUR STUDY FOR THEIR THERAPY.
BUT...
NO INMATE HAS EVER SUCCESSFULLY GOTTEN INTO OUR ARMORY.

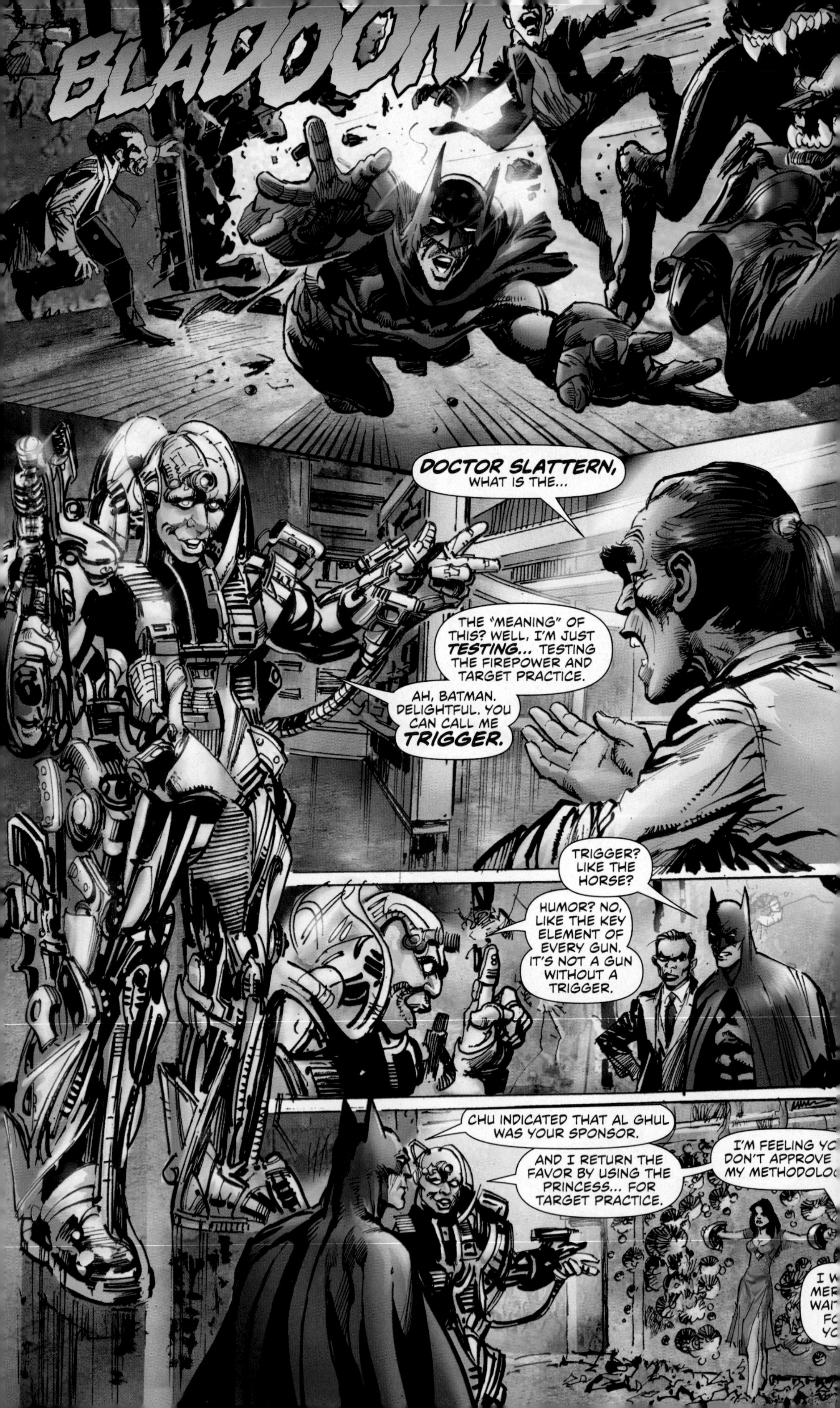
BLADOOM
DOCTOR SLATTERN, WHAT IS THE...
THE "MEANING" OF THIS? WELL, I'M JUST TESTING... TESTING THE FIREPOWER AND TARGET PRACTICE.
AH, BATMAN. DELIGHTFUL. YOU CAN CALL ME TRIGGER.
TRIGGER? LIKE THE HORSE?
HUMOR? NO, LIKE THE KEY ELEMENT OF EVERY GUN. IT'S NOT A GUN WITHOUT A TRIGGER.
CHU INDICATED THAT AL GHUL WAS YOUR SPONSOR.
AND I RETURN THE FAVOR BY USING THE PRINCESS... FOR TARGET PRACTICE.

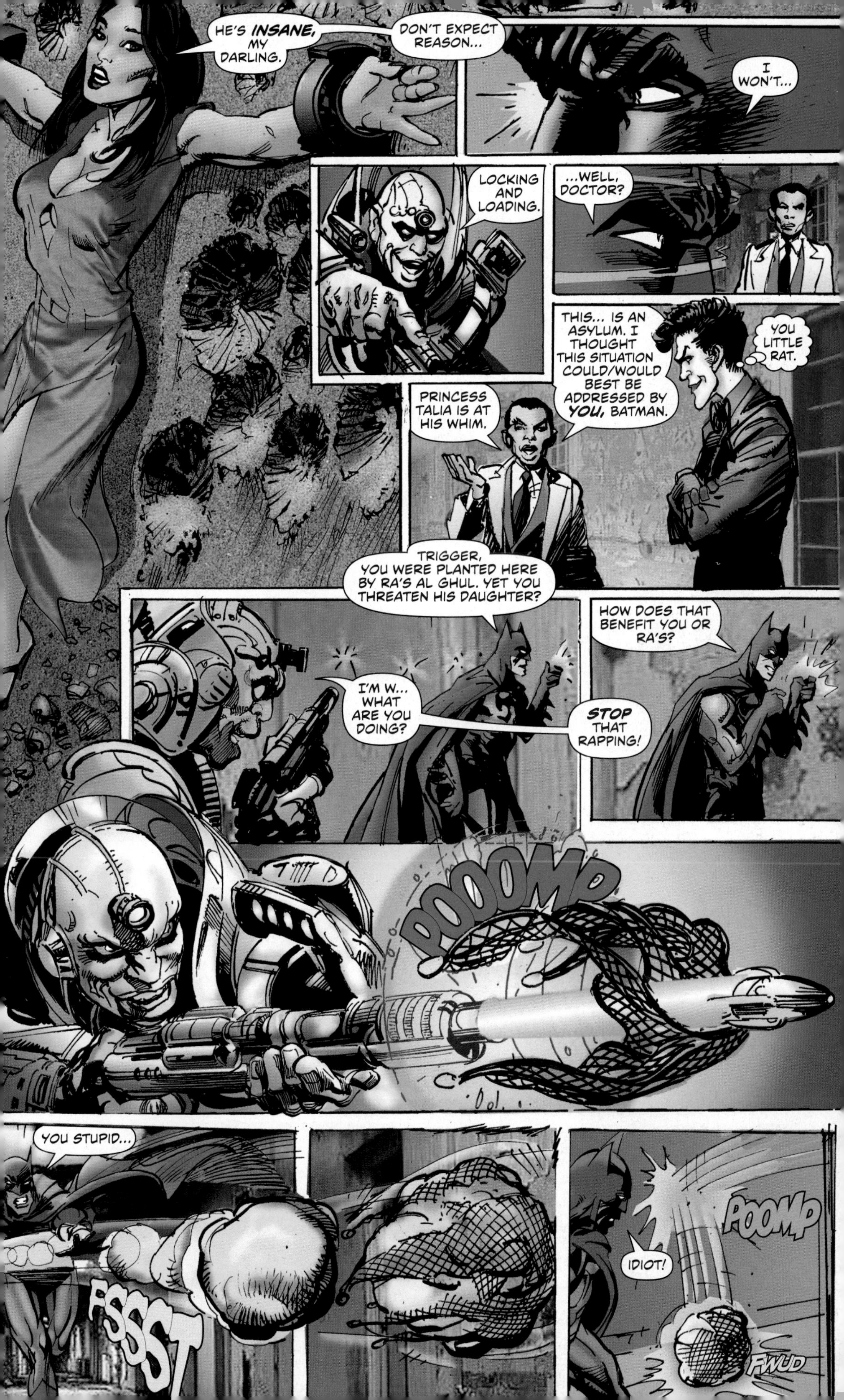
HE'S INSANE, MY DARLING.
DON'T EXPECT REASON...
I WON'T...
LOCKING AND LOADING.
...WELL, DOCTOR?
THIS... IS AN ASYLUM. I THOUGHT THIS SITUATION COULD/WOULD BEST BE ADDRESSED BY YOU, BATMAN.
YOU LITTLE RAT.
PRINCESS TALIA IS AT HIS WHIM.
TRIGGER, YOU WERE PLANTED HERE BY RA'S AL GHUL. YET YOU THREATEN HIS DAUGHTER?
HOW DOES THAT BENEFIT YOU OR RA'S?
I'M W... WHAT ARE YOU DOING?
STOP THAT RAPPING!
POOOMP
YOU STUPID...
FSSST
POOMP
IDIOT!
FWUD

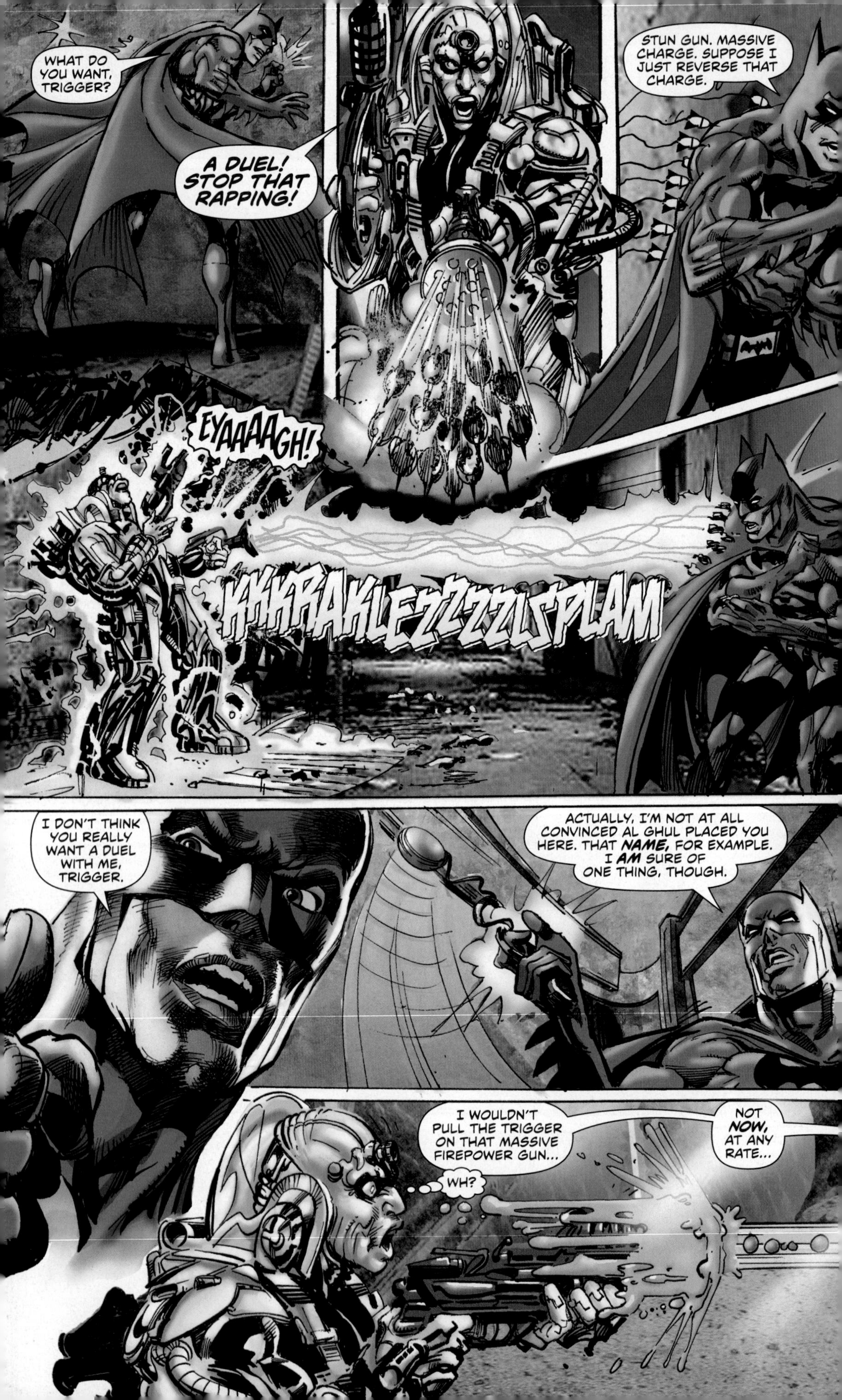
WHAT DO YOU WANT, TRIGGER?
A DUEL! STOP THAT RAPPING!
STUN GUN. MASSIVE CHARGE. SUPPOSE I JUST REVERSE THAT CHARGE.
EYAAAAGH!
KKKRAKLEZZZZLSPLAM
I DON'T THINK YOU REALLY WANT A DUEL WITH ME, TRIGGER.
ACTUALLY, I'M NOT AT ALL CONVINCED AL GHUL PLACED YOU HERE. THAT NAME, FOR EXAMPLE. I AM SURE OF ONE THING, THOUGH.
I WOULDN'T PULL THE TRIGGER ON THAT MASSIVE FIREPOWER GUN...
NOT NOW, AT ANY RATE...
WH?

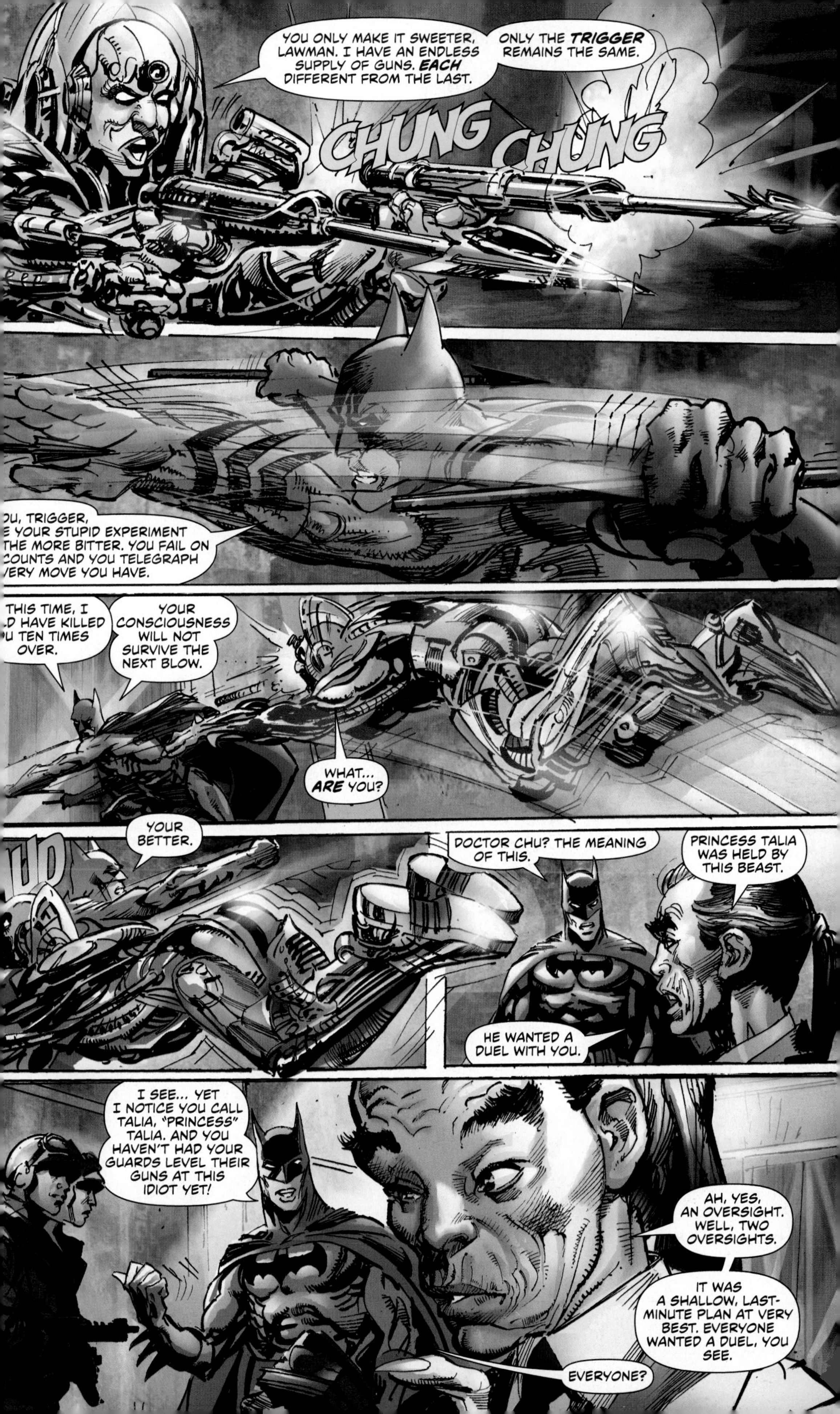

YOU ONLY MAKE IT SWEETER, LAWMAN. I HAVE AN ENDLESS SUPPLY OF GUNS. **EACH** DIFFERENT FROM THE LAST.
ONLY THE **TRIGGER** REMAINS THE SAME.
CHUNG CHUNG
OU, TRIGGER,
E YOUR STUPID EXPERIMENT
THE MORE BITTER. YOU FAIL ON
COUNTS AND YOU TELEGRAPH
VERY MOVE YOU HAVE.
THIS TIME, I
D HAVE KILLED
U TEN TIMES
OVER.
YOUR CONSCIOUSNESS WILL NOT SURVIVE THE NEXT BLOW.
WHAT... **ARE** YOU?
YOUR BETTER.
DOCTOR CHU? THE MEANING OF THIS.
PRINCESS TALIA WAS HELD BY THIS BEAST.
HE WANTED A DUEL WITH YOU.
I SEE... YET I NOTICE YOU CALL TALIA, "PRINCESS" TALIA. AND YOU HAVEN'T HAD YOUR GUARDS LEVEL THEIR GUNS AT THIS IDIOT YET!
AH, YES, AN OVERSIGHT. WELL, TWO OVERSIGHTS.
IT WAS A SHALLOW, LAST-MINUTE PLAN AT VERY BEST. EVERYONE WANTED A DUEL, YOU SEE.
EVERYONE?

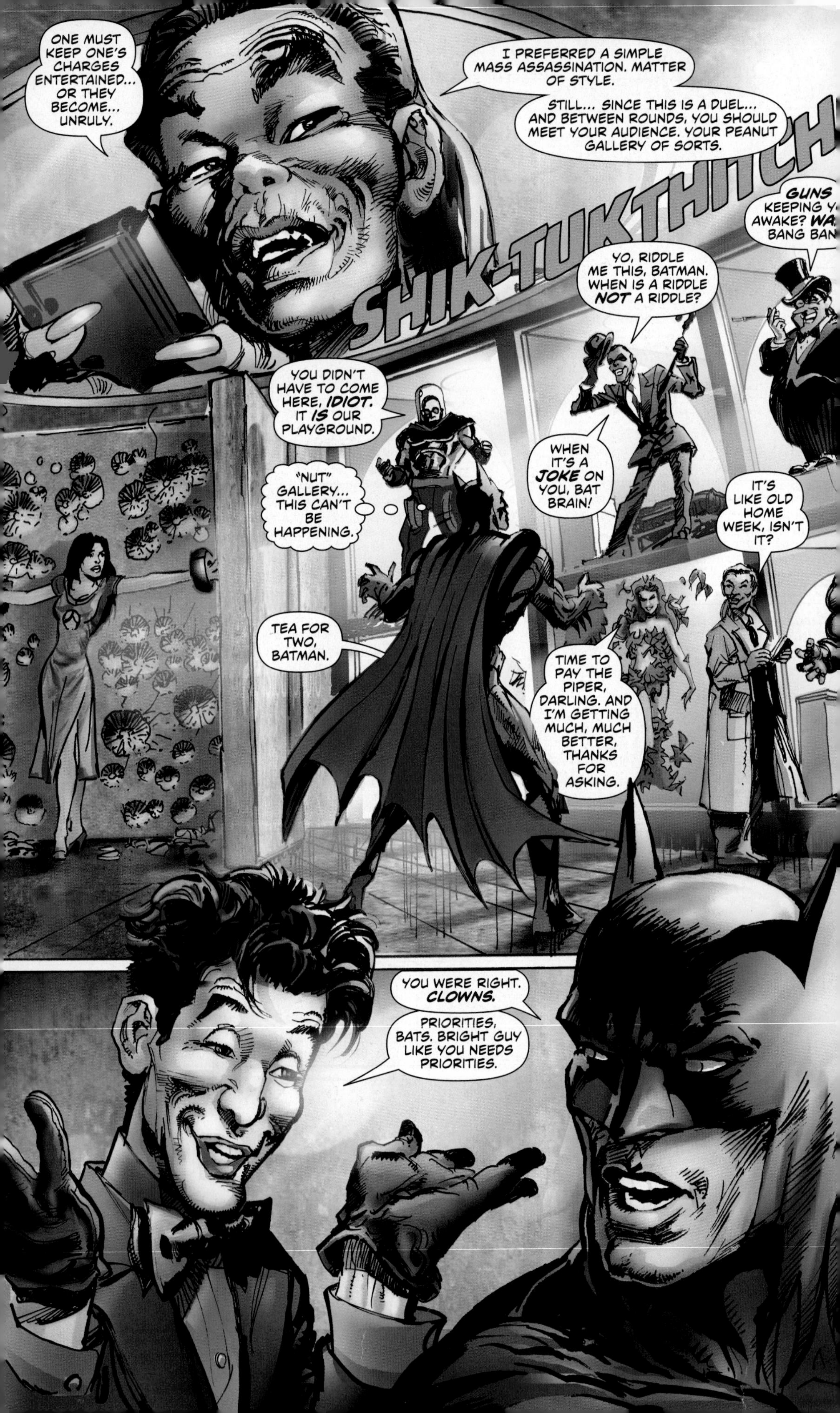
ONE MUST KEEP ONE'S CHARGES ENTERTAINED... OR THEY BECOME... UNRULY.
I PREFERRED A SIMPLE MASS ASSASSINATION. MATTER OF STYLE.
STILL... SINCE THIS IS A DUEL... AND BETWEEN ROUNDS, YOU SHOULD MEET YOUR AUDIENCE. YOUR PEANUT GALLERY OF SORTS.
SHIK-TUKTHHCH
YO, RIDDLE ME THIS, BATMAN. WHEN IS A RIDDLE NOT A RIDDLE?
YOU DIDN'T HAVE TO COME HERE, IDIOT. IT IS OUR PLAYGROUND.
WHEN IT'S A JOKE ON YOU, BAT BRAIN!
"NUT" GALLERY... THIS CAN'T BE HAPPENING.
IT'S LIKE OLD HOME WEEK, ISN'T IT?
TEA FOR TWO, BATMAN.
TIME TO PAY THE PIPER, DARLING. AND I'M GETTING MUCH, MUCH BETTER, THANKS FOR ASKING.
YOU WERE RIGHT. CLOWNS.
PRIORITIES, BATS. BRIGHT GUY LIKE YOU NEEDS PRIORITIES.

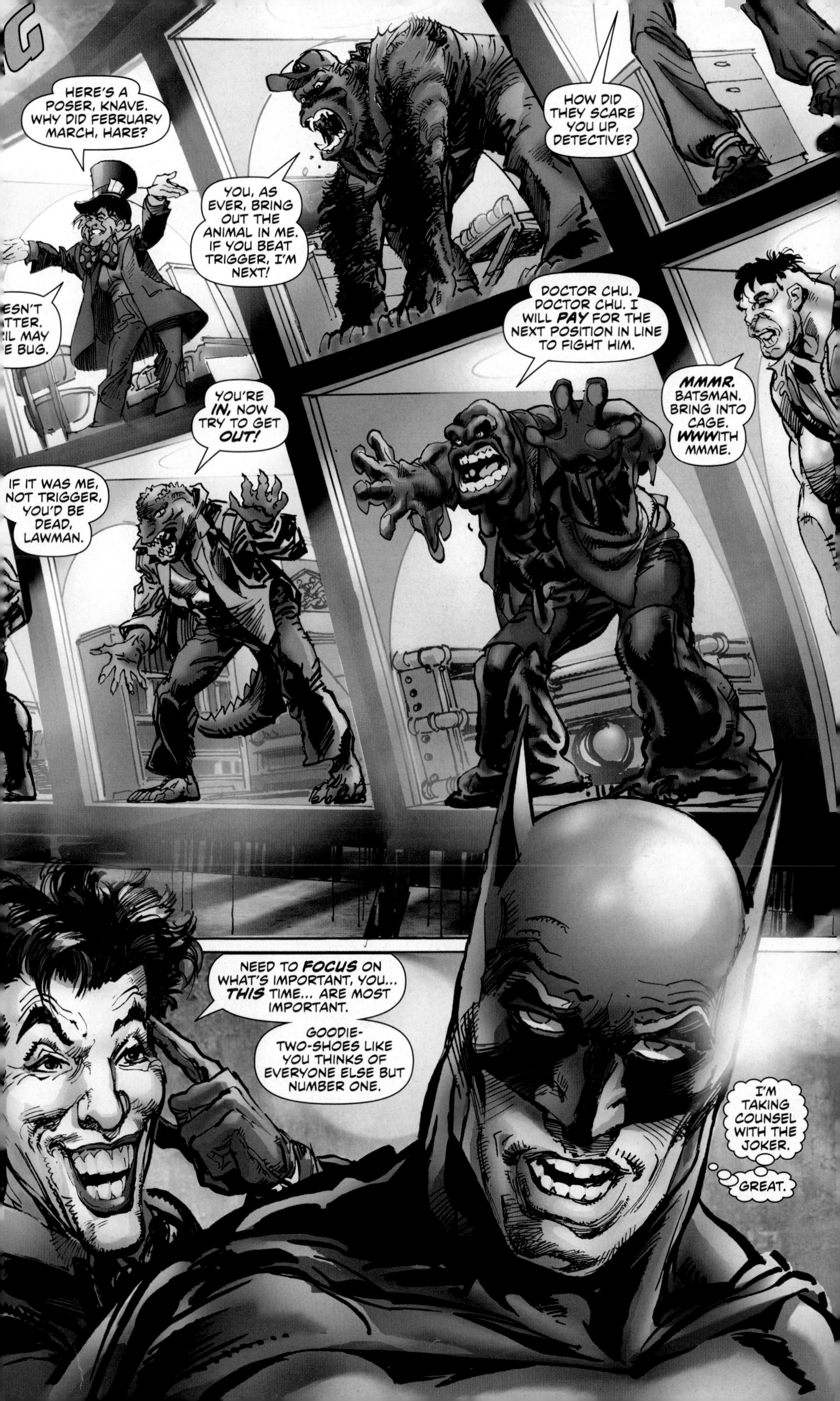

HERE'S A POSER, KNAVE. WHY DID FEBRUARY MARCH, HARE?
YOU, AS EVER, BRING OUT THE ANIMAL IN ME. IF YOU BEAT TRIGGER, I'M NEXT!
HOW DID THEY SCARE YOU UP, DETECTIVE?
ESN'T
TTER.
IL MAY
E BUG.
DOCTOR CHU. DOCTOR CHU. I WILL PAY FOR THE NEXT POSITION IN LINE TO FIGHT HIM.
MMMR. BATSMAN. BRING INTO CAGE. WWWITH MMME.
YOU'RE IN, NOW TRY TO GET OUT!
IF IT WAS ME, NOT TRIGGER, YOU'D BE DEAD, LAWMAN.
NEED TO FOCUS ON WHAT'S IMPORTANT, YOU... THIS TIME... ARE MOST IMPORTANT.
GOODIE-TWO-SHOES LIKE YOU THINKS OF EVERYONE ELSE BUT NUMBER ONE.
I'M TAKING COUNSEL WITH THE JOKER.
GREAT.

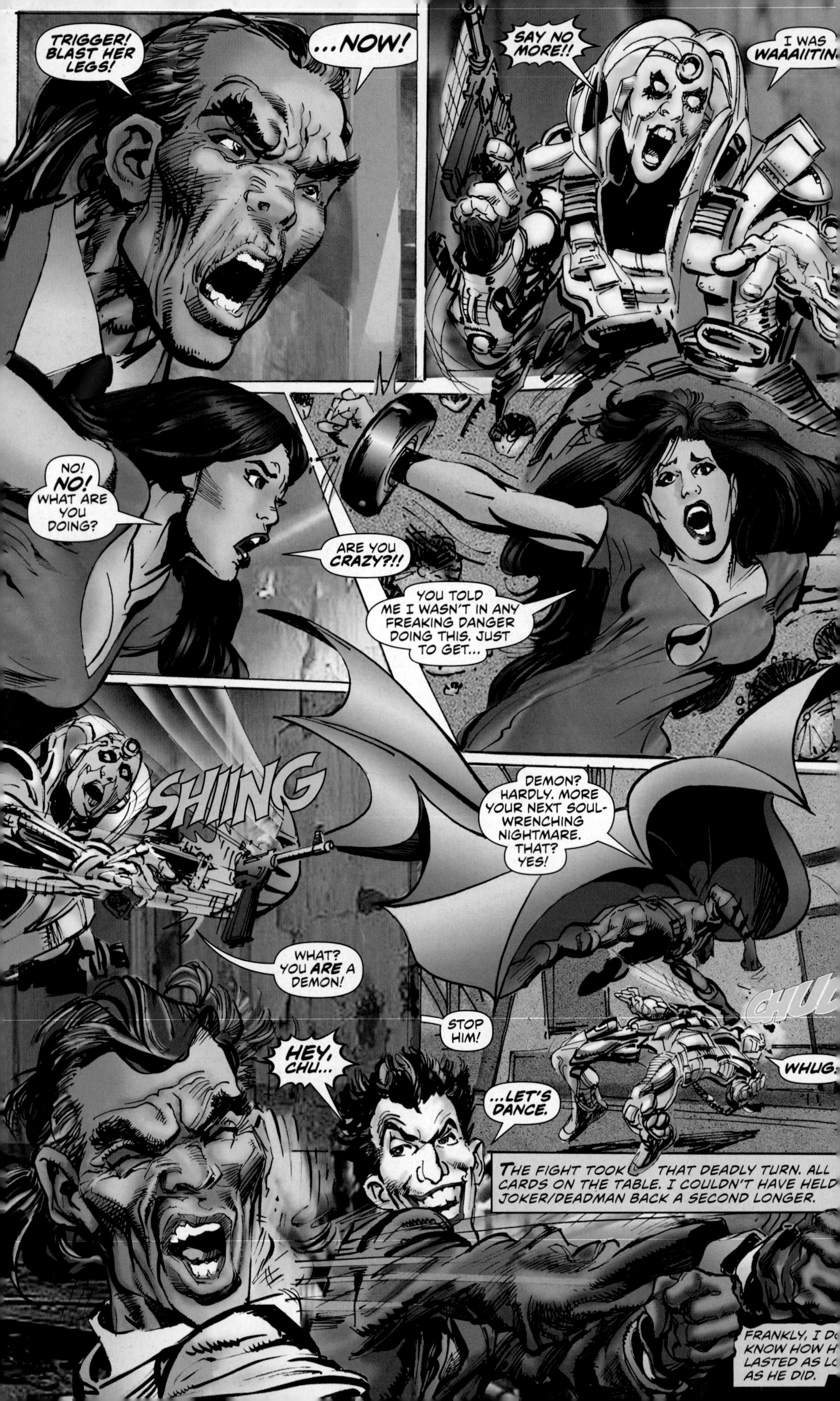

TRIGGER! BLAST HER LEGS!
...NOW!
SAY NO MORE!!
I WAS WAAAIITIN
NO! NO! WHAT ARE YOU DOING?
ARE YOU CRAZY?!!
YOU TOLD ME I WASN'T IN ANY FREAKING DANGER DOING THIS. JUST TO GET...
SHING
DEMON? HARDLY. MORE YOUR NEXT SOUL-WRENCHING NIGHTMARE. THAT? YES!
WHAT? YOU ARE A DEMON!
STOP HIM!
HEY, CHU...
...LET'S DANCE.
WHUG
THE FIGHT TOOK THAT DEADLY TURN. ALL CARDS ON THE TABLE. I COULDN'T HAVE HELD JOKER/DEADMAN BACK A SECOND LONGER.
FRANKLY, I D KNOW HOW H LASTED AS L AS HE DID.

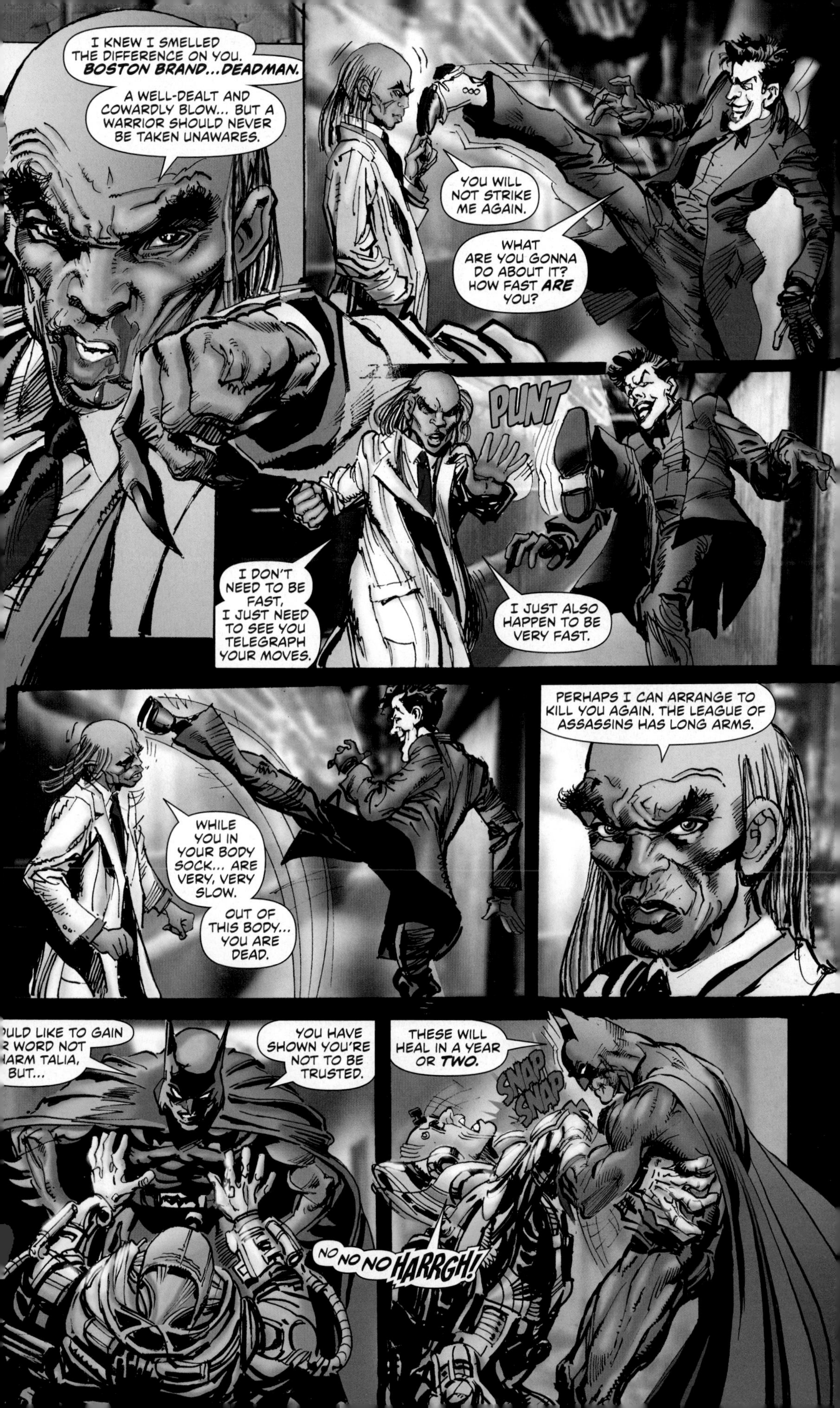

I KNEW I SMELLED THE DIFFERENCE ON YOU. BOSTON BRAND...DEADMAN.
A WELL-DEALT AND COWARDLY BLOW... BUT A WARRIOR SHOULD NEVER BE TAKEN UNAWARES.
YOU WILL NOT STRIKE ME AGAIN.
WHAT ARE YOU GONNA DO ABOUT IT? HOW FAST ARE YOU?
PUNT
I DON'T NEED TO BE FAST, I JUST NEED TO SEE YOU TELEGRAPH YOUR MOVES.
I JUST ALSO HAPPEN TO BE VERY FAST.
WHILE YOU IN YOUR BODY SOCK... ARE VERY, VERY SLOW.
OUT OF THIS BODY... YOU ARE DEAD.
PERHAPS I CAN ARRANGE TO KILL YOU AGAIN. THE LEAGUE OF ASSASSINS HAS LONG ARMS.
OULD LIKE TO GAIN R WORD NOT HARM TALIA, BUT...
YOU HAVE SHOWN YOU'RE NOT TO BE TRUSTED.
THESE WILL HEAL IN A YEAR OR TWO.
SNAP SNAP
NO NO NO HARRGH!

I'M COMING, TALIA.

OH...OH...OH MY ELBOWS... I'M BROKEN.

BOSTON, DON'T WORRY, THAT'S NOT TALIA. JUST GOOD MAKE-UP. IT'S NOT HER VOICE.

GOOD... HEY, SENSEI... I'VE BEEN TRAINING.

NOT ENOUGH!

OO

CASE IN POINT. A WEAPON CONSTRAINS THE HANDS FROM WARRIOR'S WORK.

HAH, MISSED!

DID I?

C'MON, DOC, KNOCK THAT WANNA-BE FOR A LOOP. WIPE THAT GRIN OFFA HIS STUPID PUSS.

LET ME AT HIM, DOC.

JOKER, ≡WAAK≡ WE BELIEVE IN YOU. YOU'RE THE MAN. JACK THAT SHRIMP UP.

COME ON!

HE PASSED ME BY FOR TEMPORARY RELEASE.

FINIS HIM, PAST FAC FOO

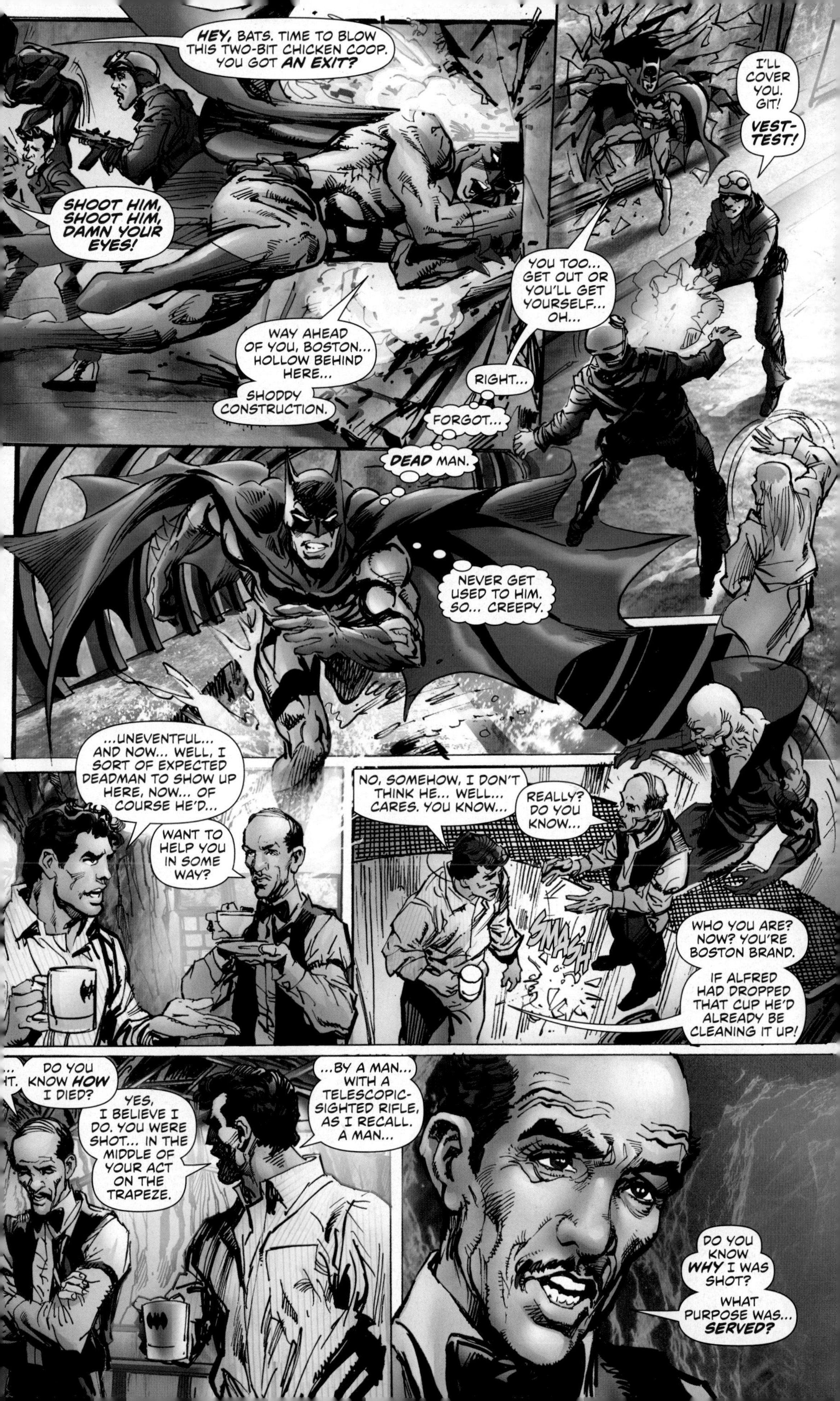

HEY, BATS. TIME TO BLOW THIS TWO-BIT CHICKEN COOP. YOU GOT AN EXIT?
SHOOT HIM, SHOOT HIM, DAMN YOUR EYES!
WAY AHEAD OF YOU, BOSTON... HOLLOW BEHIND HERE...
SHODDY CONSTRUCTION.
I'LL COVER YOU. GIT!
VEST-TEST!
YOU TOO... GET OUT OR YOU'LL GET YOURSELF... OH...
RIGHT...
FORGOT...
DEAD MAN.
NEVER GET USED TO HIM. SO... CREEPY.
...UNEVENTFUL... AND NOW... WELL, I SORT OF EXPECTED DEADMAN TO SHOW UP HERE, NOW... OF COURSE HE'D...
WANT TO HELP YOU IN SOME WAY?
NO, SOMEHOW, I DON'T THINK HE... WELL... CARES. YOU KNOW...
REALLY? DO YOU KNOW...
SMASH
WHO YOU ARE? NOW? YOU'RE BOSTON BRAND.
IF ALFRED HAD DROPPED THAT CUP HE'D ALREADY BE CLEANING IT UP!
DO YOU KNOW HOW I DIED?
YES, I BELIEVE I DO. YOU WERE SHOT... IN THE MIDDLE OF YOUR ACT ON THE TRAPEZE.
...BY A MAN... WITH A TELESCOPIC-SIGHTED RIFLE, AS I RECALL. A MAN...
DO YOU KNOW WHY I WAS SHOT?
WHAT PURPOSE WAS... SERVED?

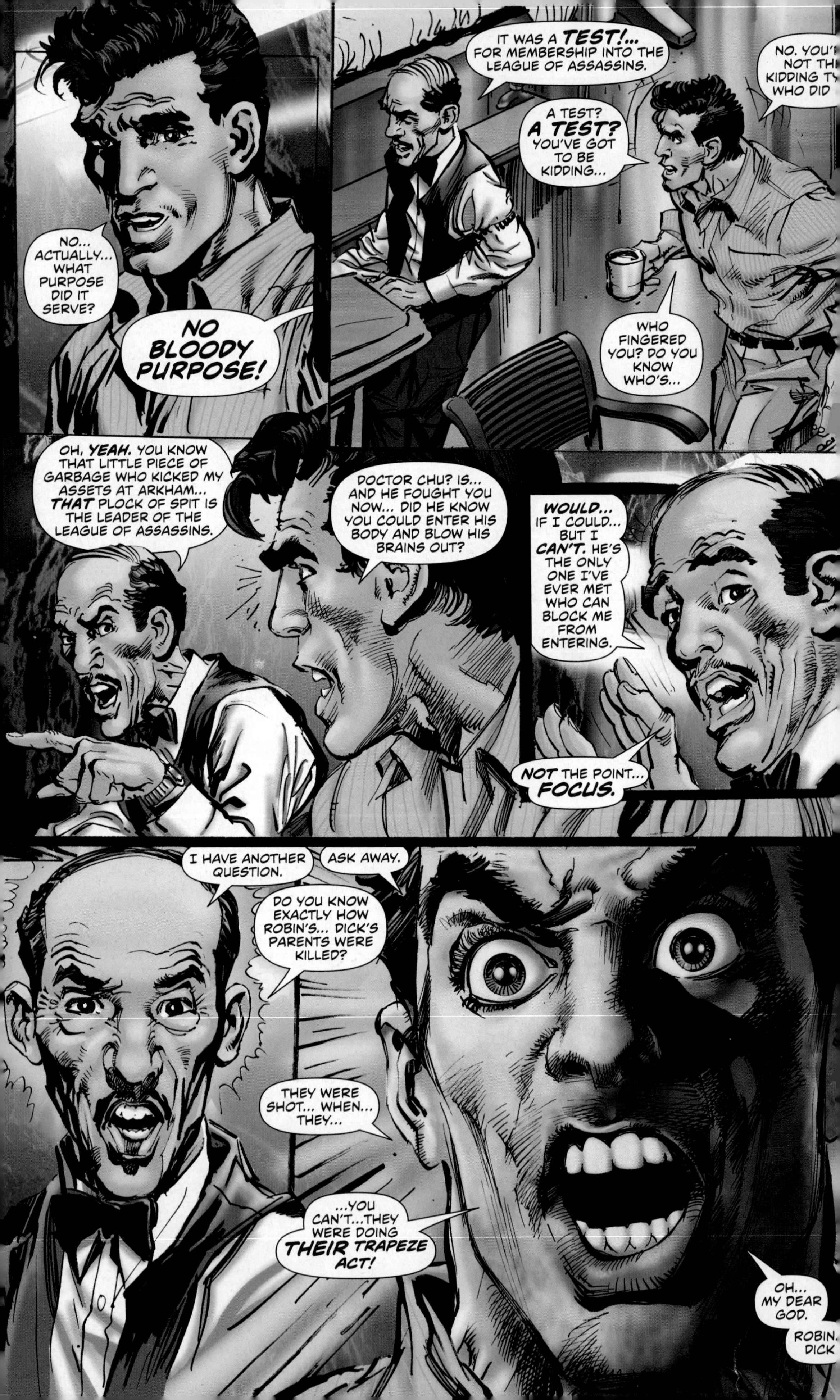

NO... ACTUALLY... WHAT PURPOSE DID IT SERVE?
NO BLOODY PURPOSE!
IT WAS A TEST!... FOR MEMBERSHIP INTO THE LEAGUE OF ASSASSINS.
A TEST? A TEST? YOU'VE GOT TO BE KIDDING...
NO. YOU'
NOT TH
KIDDING TY
WHO DID
WHO FINGERED YOU? DO YOU KNOW WHO'S...
OH, YEAH. YOU KNOW THAT LITTLE PIECE OF GARBAGE WHO KICKED MY ASSETS AT ARKHAM... THAT PLOCK OF SPIT IS THE LEADER OF THE LEAGUE OF ASSASSINS.
DOCTOR CHU? IS... AND HE FOUGHT YOU NOW... DID HE KNOW YOU COULD ENTER HIS BODY AND BLOW HIS BRAINS OUT?
WOULD... IF I COULD... BUT I CAN'T. HE'S THE ONLY ONE I'VE EVER MET WHO CAN BLOCK ME FROM ENTERING.
NOT THE POINT... FOCUS.
I HAVE ANOTHER QUESTION.
ASK AWAY.
DO YOU KNOW EXACTLY HOW ROBIN'S... DICK'S PARENTS WERE KILLED?
THEY WERE SHOT... WHEN... THEY...
...YOU CAN'T...THEY WERE DOING THEIR TRAPEZE ACT!
OH... MY DEAR GOD.
ROBIN
DICK

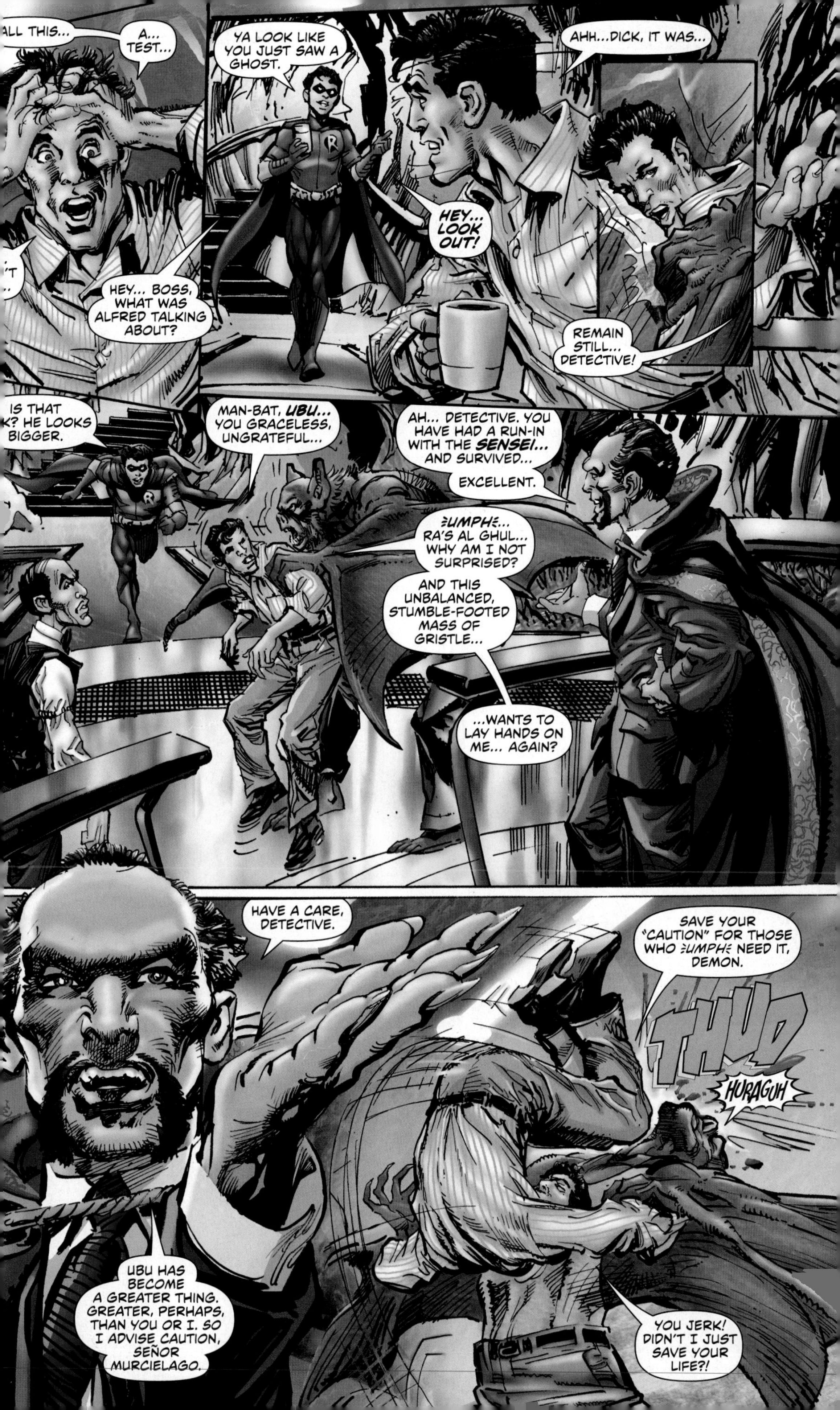
ALL THIS...
A... TEST...
HEY... BOSS, WHAT WAS ALFRED TALKING ABOUT?
YA LOOK LIKE YOU JUST SAW A GHOST.
HEY... LOOK OUT!
AHH...DICK, IT WAS...
REMAIN STILL... DETECTIVE!
IS THAT K? HE LOOKS BIGGER.
MAN-BAT, UBU... YOU GRACELESS, UNGRATEFUL...
AH... DETECTIVE. YOU HAVE HAD A RUN-IN WITH THE SENSEI... AND SURVIVED...
EXCELLENT.
UMPH... RA'S AL GHUL... WHY AM I NOT SURPRISED?
AND THIS UNBALANCED, STUMBLE-FOOTED MASS OF GRISTLE...
...WANTS TO LAY HANDS ON ME... AGAIN?
HAVE A CARE, DETECTIVE.
SAVE YOUR "CAUTION" FOR THOSE WHO UMPH NEED IT, DEMON.
THUD
HURAGUH
UBU HAS BECOME A GREATER THING. GREATER, PERHAPS, THAN YOU OR I. SO I ADVISE CAUTION, SEÑOR MURCIELAGO.
YOU JERK! DIDN'T I JUST SAVE YOUR LIFE?!

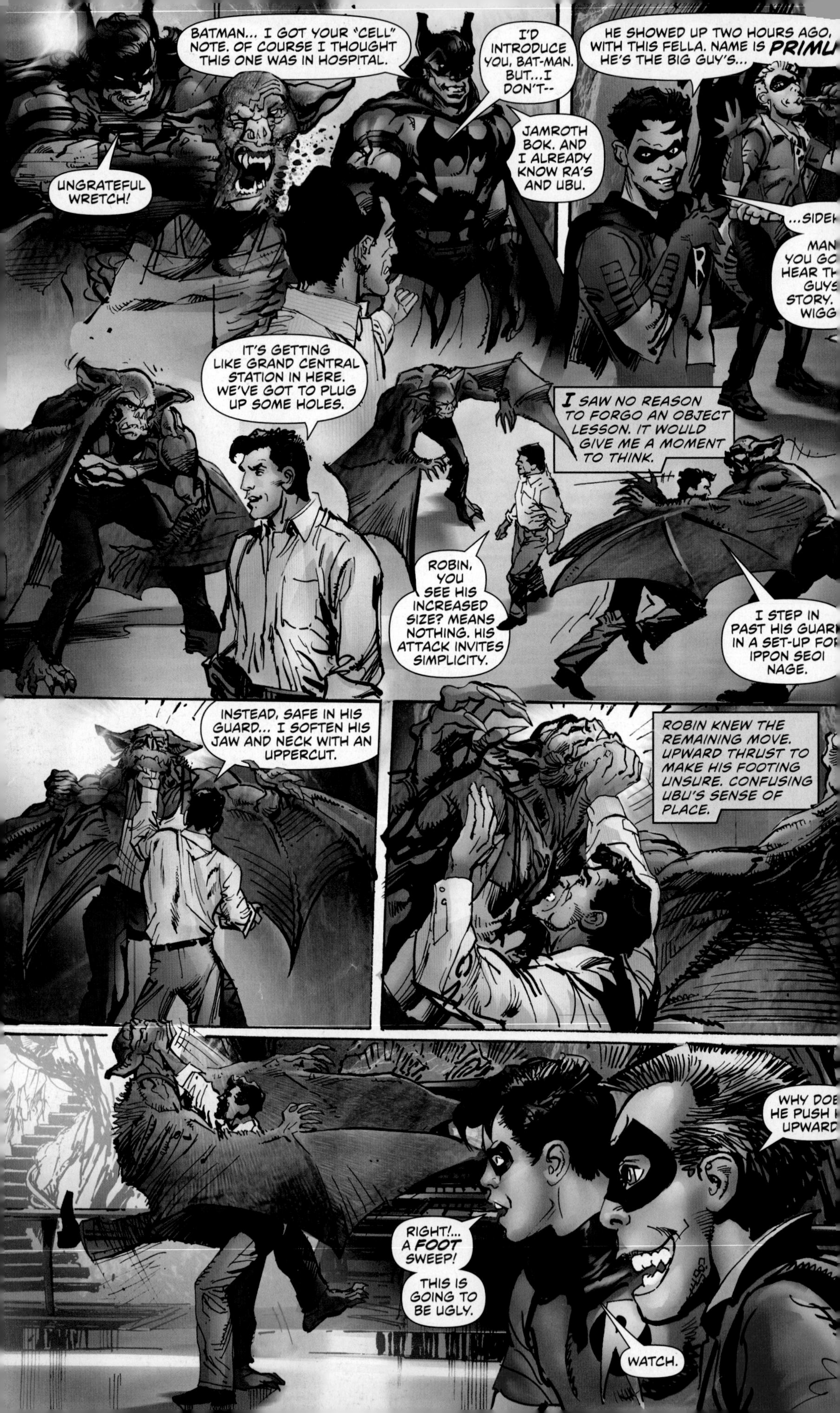
BATMAN... I GOT YOUR "CELL" NOTE. OF COURSE I THOUGHT THIS ONE WAS IN HOSPITAL.
UNGRATEFUL WRETCH!
I'D INTRODUCE YOU, BAT-MAN. BUT...I DON'T--
JAMROTH BOK. AND I ALREADY KNOW RA'S AND UBU.
HE SHOWED UP TWO HOURS AGO, WITH THIS FELLA. NAME IS PRIMU
HE'S THE BIG GUY'S...
...SIDEK
MAN YOU GO HEAR TH GUYS STORY. WIGG
IT'S GETTING LIKE GRAND CENTRAL STATION IN HERE. WE'VE GOT TO PLUG UP SOME HOLES.
I SAW NO REASON TO FORGO AN OBJECT LESSON. IT WOULD GIVE ME A MOMENT TO THINK.
ROBIN, YOU SEE HIS INCREASED SIZE? MEANS NOTHING. HIS ATTACK INVITES SIMPLICITY.
I STEP IN PAST HIS GUAR IN A SET-UP FO IPPON SEOI NAGE.
INSTEAD, SAFE IN HIS GUARD... I SOFTEN HIS JAW AND NECK WITH AN UPPERCUT.
ROBIN KNEW THE REMAINING MOVE. UPWARD THRUST TO MAKE HIS FOOTING UNSURE. CONFUSING UBU'S SENSE OF PLACE.
WHY DOE HE PUSH UPWARD
RIGHT!... A FOOT SWEEP!
THIS IS GOING TO BE UGLY.
WATCH.

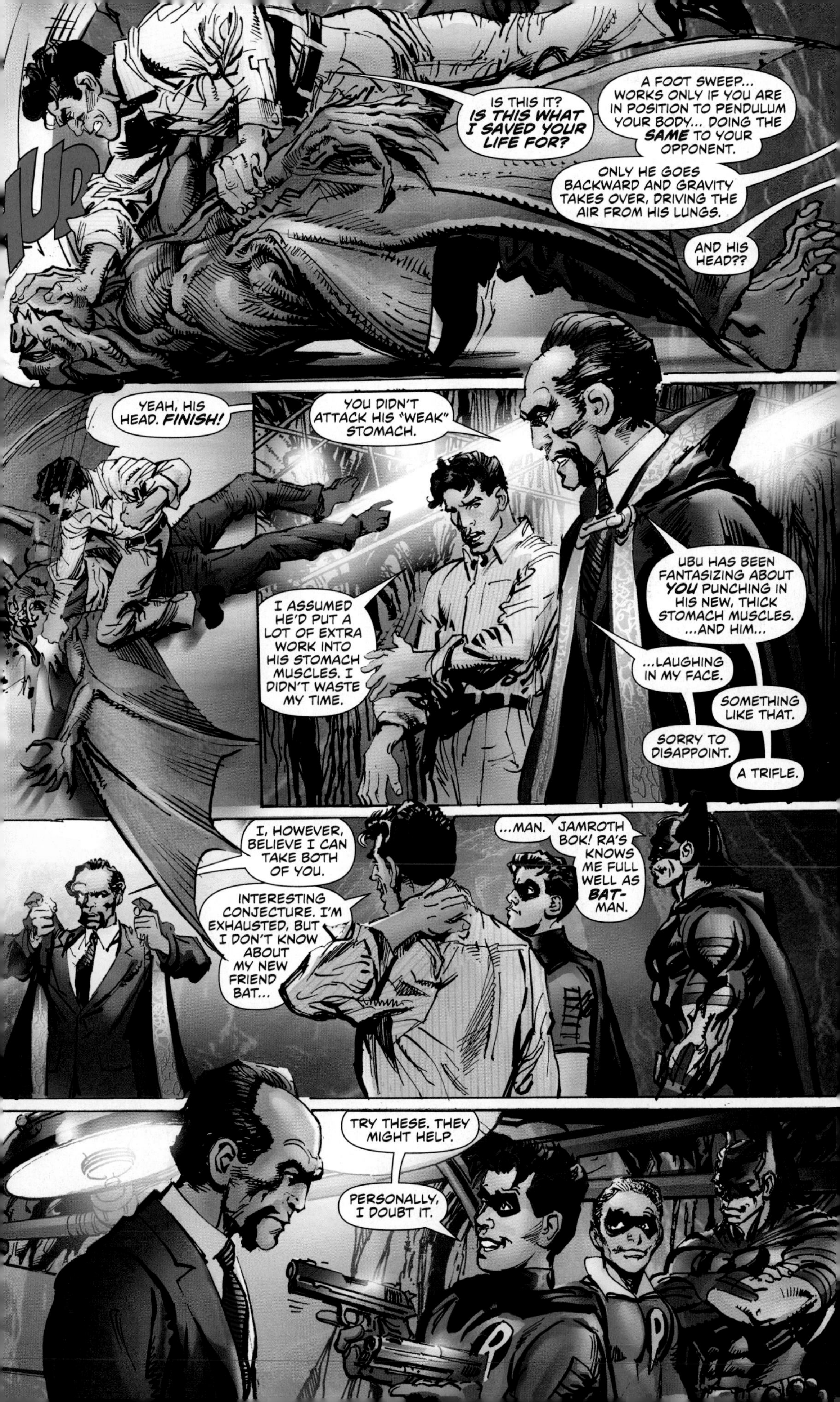
HUD
IS THIS IT? IS THIS WHAT I SAVED YOUR LIFE FOR?
A FOOT SWEEP... WORKS ONLY IF YOU ARE IN POSITION TO PENDULUM YOUR BODY... DOING THE SAME TO YOUR OPPONENT.
ONLY HE GOES BACKWARD AND GRAVITY TAKES OVER, DRIVING THE AIR FROM HIS LUNGS.
AND HIS HEAD??
YEAH, HIS HEAD. FINISH!
YOU DIDN'T ATTACK HIS "WEAK" STOMACH.
I ASSUMED HE'D PUT A LOT OF EXTRA WORK INTO HIS STOMACH MUSCLES. I DIDN'T WASTE MY TIME.
UBU HAS BEEN FANTASIZING ABOUT YOU PUNCHING IN HIS NEW, THICK STOMACH MUSCLES. ...AND HIM...
...LAUGHING IN MY FACE.
SOMETHING LIKE THAT.
SORRY TO DISAPPOINT.
A TRIFLE.
I, HOWEVER, BELIEVE I CAN TAKE BOTH OF YOU.
INTERESTING CONJECTURE. I'M EXHAUSTED, BUT I DON'T KNOW ABOUT MY NEW FRIEND BAT...
...MAN.
JAMROTH BOK! RA'S KNOWS ME FULL WELL AS BAT-MAN.
TRY THESE. THEY MIGHT HELP.
PERSONALLY, I DOUBT IT.

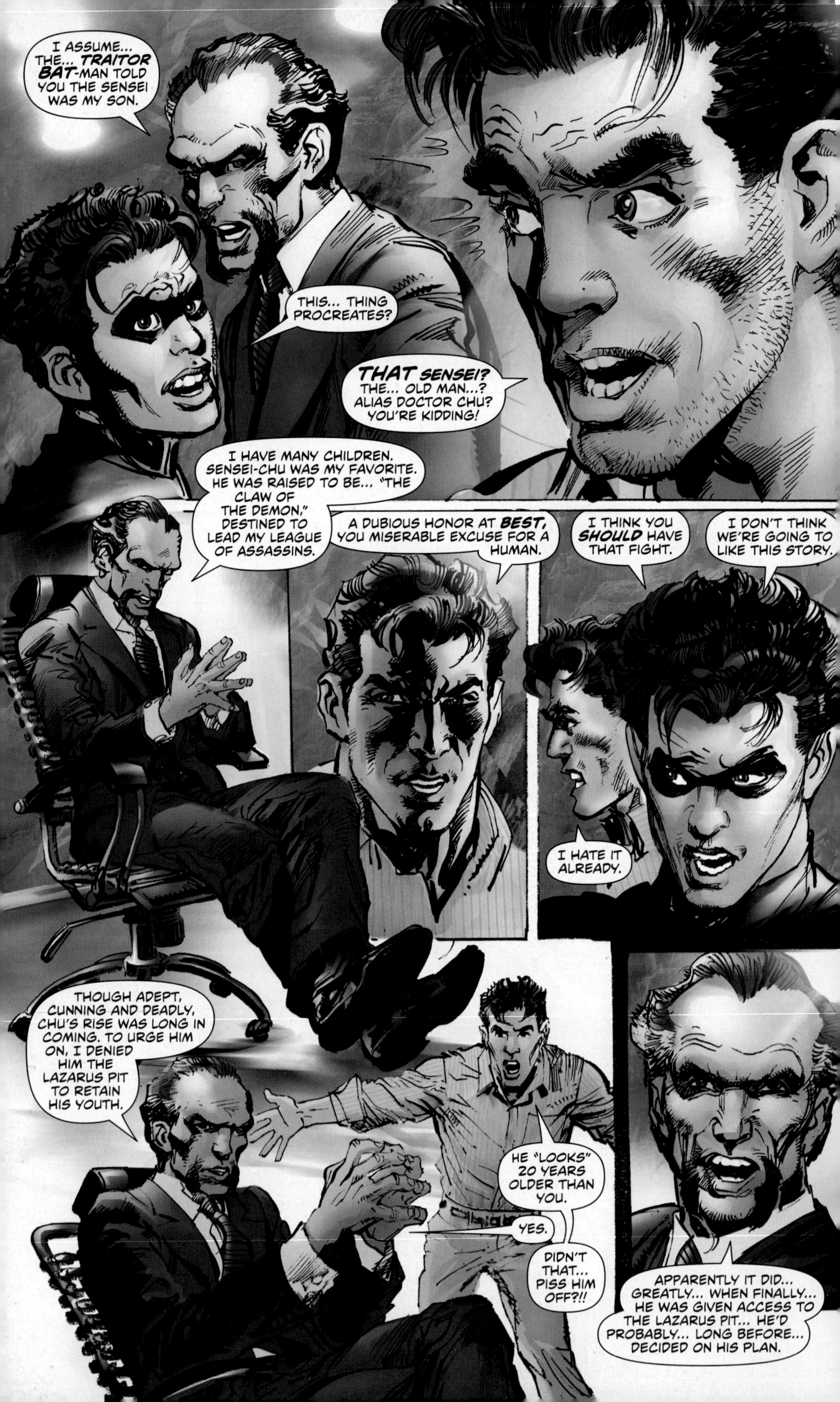

I ASSUME... THE... TRAITOR BAT-MAN TOLD YOU THE SENSEI WAS MY SON.
THIS... THING PROCREATES?
THAT SENSEI? THE... OLD MAN...? ALIAS DOCTOR CHU? YOU'RE KIDDING!
I HAVE MANY CHILDREN. SENSEI-CHU WAS MY FAVORITE. HE WAS RAISED TO BE... "THE CLAW OF THE DEMON," DESTINED TO LEAD MY LEAGUE OF ASSASSINS.
A DUBIOUS HONOR AT BEST, YOU MISERABLE EXCUSE FOR A HUMAN.
I THINK YOU SHOULD HAVE THAT FIGHT.
I DON'T THINK WE'RE GOING TO LIKE THIS STORY.
I HATE IT ALREADY.
THOUGH ADEPT, CUNNING AND DEADLY, CHU'S RISE WAS LONG IN COMING. TO URGE HIM ON, I DENIED HIM THE LAZARUS PIT TO RETAIN HIS YOUTH.
HE "LOOKS" 20 YEARS OLDER THAN YOU.
YES.
DIDN'T THAT... PISS HIM OFF?!!
APPARENTLY IT DID... GREATLY... WHEN FINALLY... HE WAS GIVEN ACCESS TO THE LAZARUS PIT... HE'D PROBABLY... LONG BEFORE... DECIDED ON HIS PLAN.

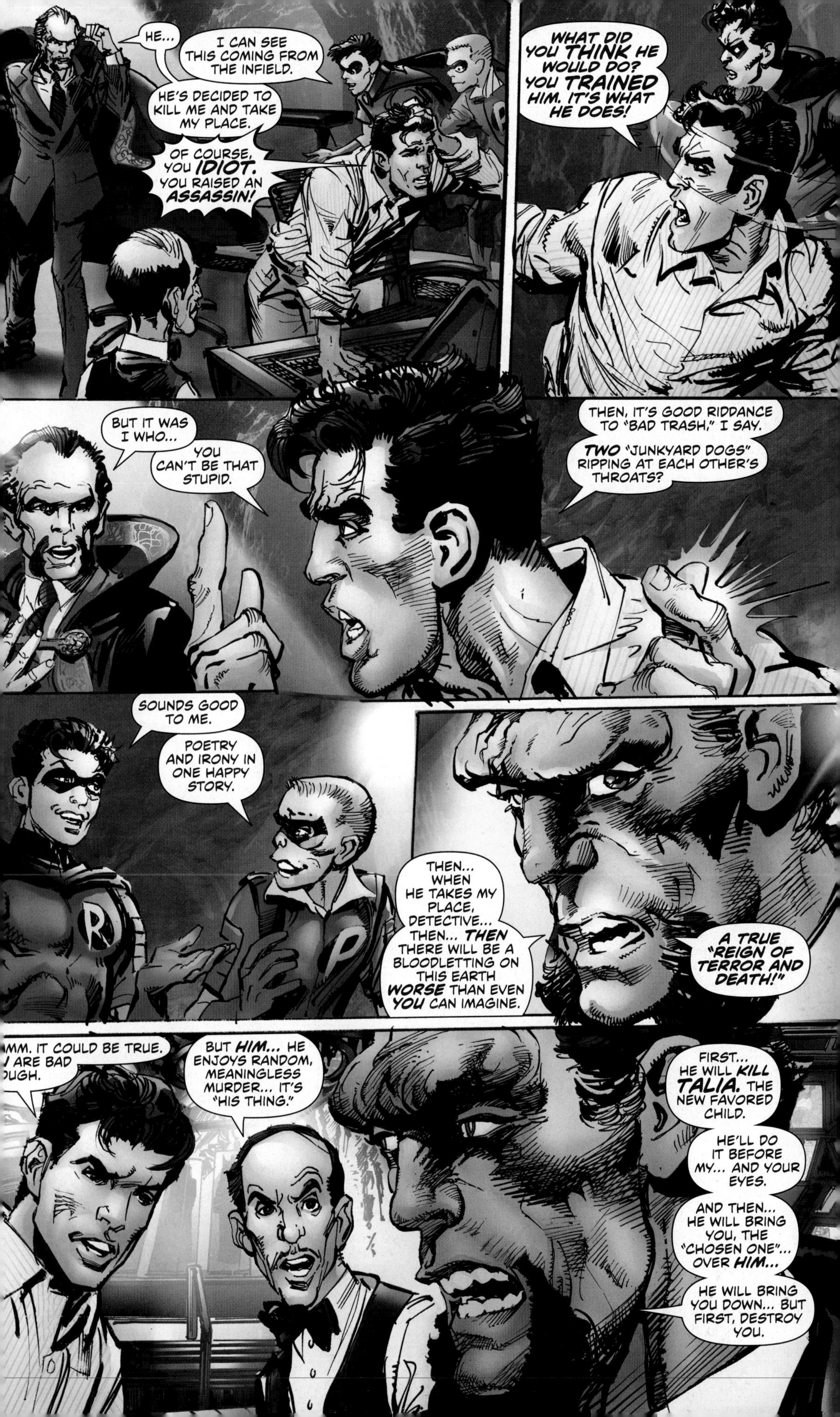
HE...
I CAN SEE THIS COMING FROM THE INFIELD.
HE'S DECIDED TO KILL ME AND TAKE MY PLACE.
OF COURSE, YOU IDIOT. YOU RAISED AN ASSASSIN!
WHAT DID YOU THINK HE WOULD DO? YOU TRAINED HIM. IT'S WHAT HE DOES!
BUT IT WAS I WHO...
YOU CAN'T BE THAT STUPID.
THEN, IT'S GOOD RIDDANCE TO "BAD TRASH," I SAY.
TWO "JUNKYARD DOGS" RIPPING AT EACH OTHER'S THROATS?
SOUNDS GOOD TO ME.
POETRY AND IRONY IN ONE HAPPY STORY.
THEN... WHEN HE TAKES MY PLACE, DETECTIVE... THEN... THEN THERE WILL BE A BLOODLETTING ON THIS EARTH WORSE THAN EVEN YOU CAN IMAGINE.
A TRUE "REIGN OF TERROR AND DEATH!"
MM. IT COULD BE TRUE. ARE BAD UGH.
BUT HIM... HE ENJOYS RANDOM, MEANINGLESS MURDER... IT'S "HIS THING."
FIRST... HE WILL KILL TALIA. THE NEW FAVORED CHILD.
HE'LL DO IT BEFORE MY... AND YOUR EYES.
AND THEN... HE WILL BRING YOU, THE "CHOSEN ONE"... OVER HIM...
HE WILL BRING YOU DOWN... BUT FIRST, DESTROY YOU.

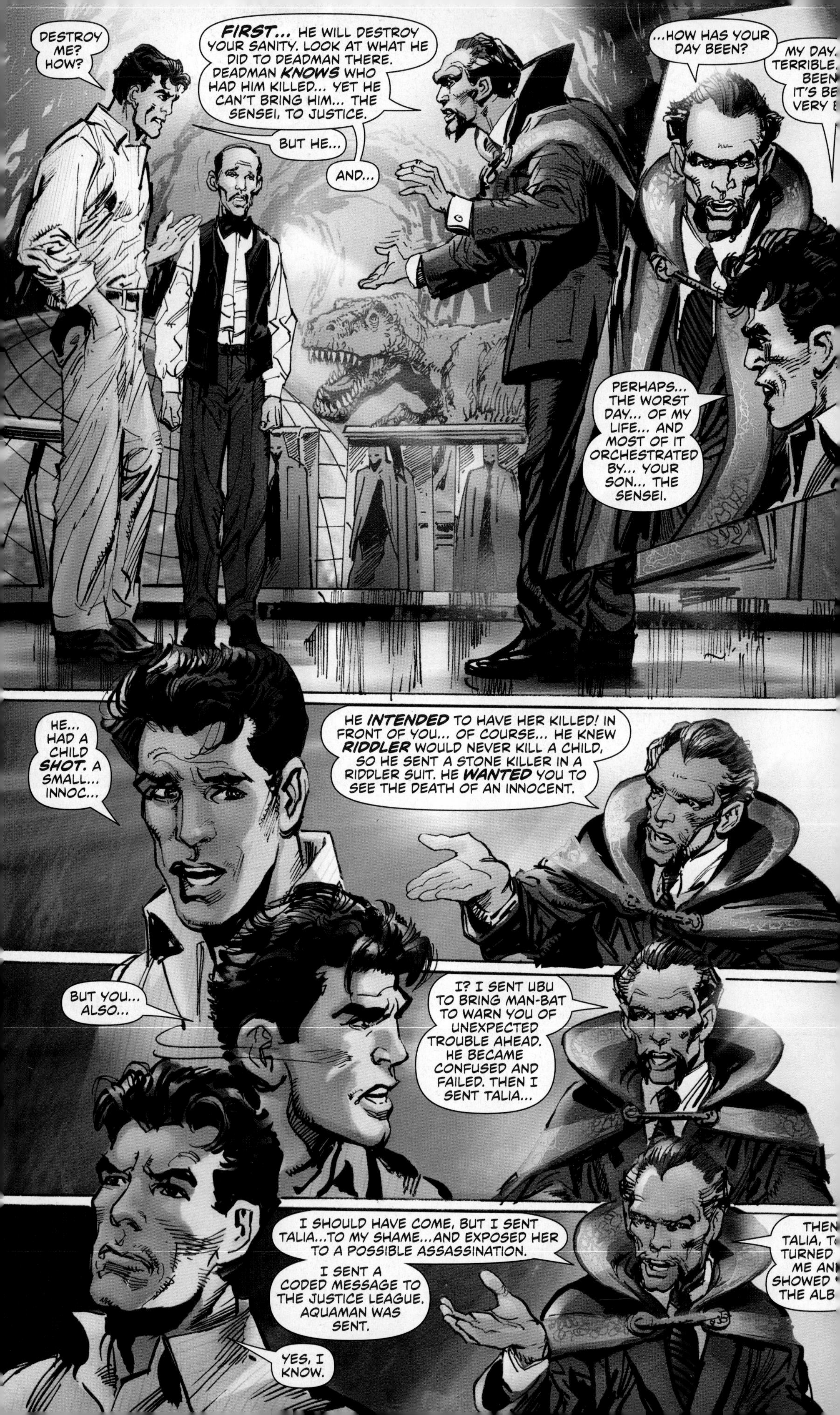
DESTROY ME? HOW?
FIRST... HE WILL DESTROY YOUR SANITY. LOOK AT WHAT HE DID TO DEADMAN THERE. DEADMAN KNOWS WHO HAD HIM KILLED... YET HE CAN'T BRING HIM... THE SENSEI, TO JUSTICE.
BUT HE...
AND...
...HOW HAS YOUR DAY BEEN?
MY DAY. TERRIBLE. BEEN IT'S BE VERY
PERHAPS... THE WORST DAY... OF MY LIFE... AND MOST OF IT ORCHESTRATED BY... YOUR SON... THE SENSEI.
HE... HAD A CHILD SHOT. A SMALL... INNOC...
HE INTENDED TO HAVE HER KILLED! IN FRONT OF YOU... OF COURSE... HE KNEW RIDDLER WOULD NEVER KILL A CHILD, SO HE SENT A STONE KILLER IN A RIDDLER SUIT. HE WANTED YOU TO SEE THE DEATH OF AN INNOCENT.
BUT YOU... ALSO...
I? I SENT UBU TO BRING MAN-BAT TO WARN YOU OF UNEXPECTED TROUBLE AHEAD. HE BECAME CONFUSED AND FAILED. THEN I SENT TALIA...
I SHOULD HAVE COME, BUT I SENT TALIA...TO MY SHAME...AND EXPOSED HER TO A POSSIBLE ASSASSINATION.
I SENT A CODED MESSAGE TO THE JUSTICE LEAGUE. AQUAMAN WAS SENT.
THEN TALIA, T TURNED ME AN SHOWED THE ALB
YES, I KNOW.

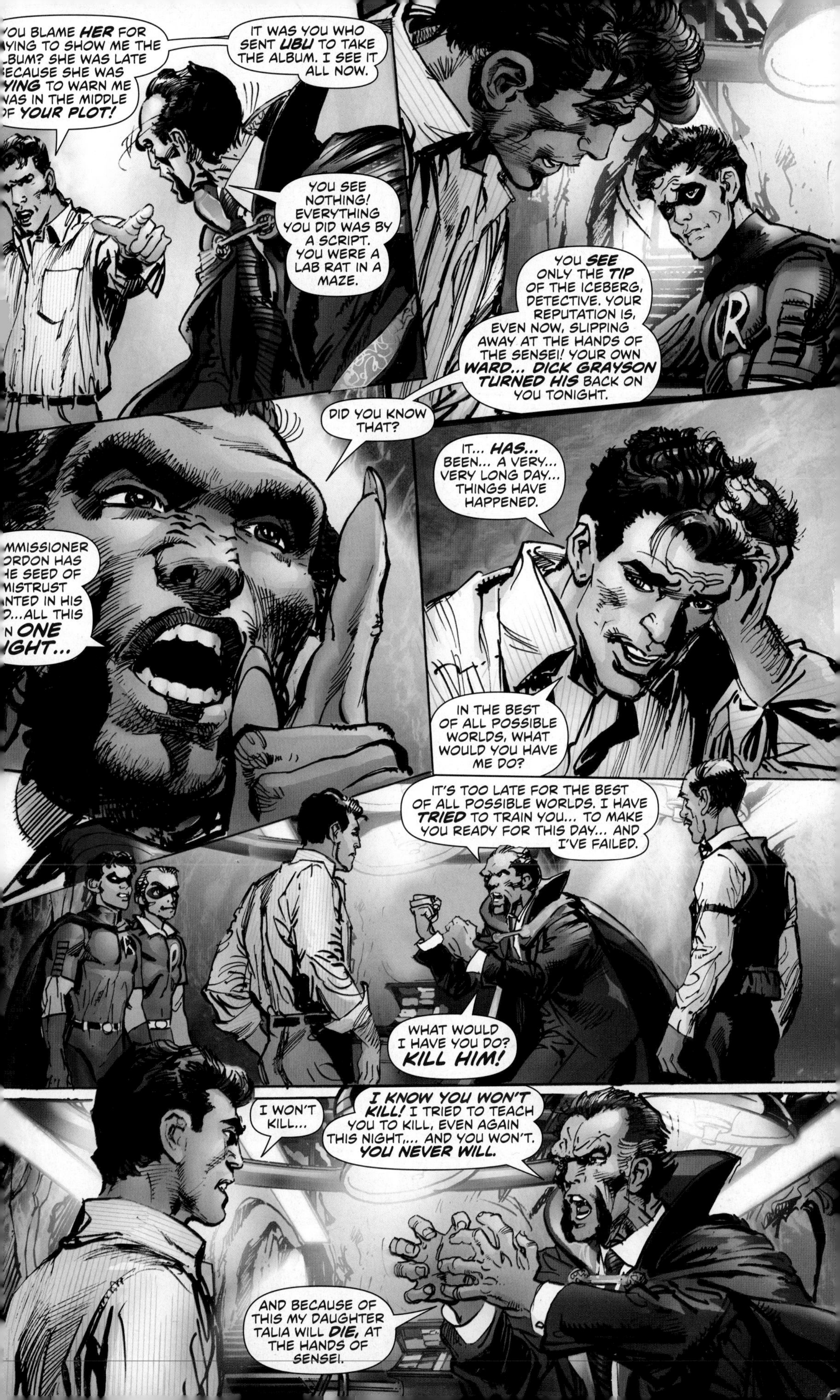

YOU BLAME HER FOR YING TO SHOW ME THE LBUM? SHE WAS LATE ECAUSE SHE WAS YING TO WARN ME VAS IN THE MIDDLE OF YOUR PLOT!
IT WAS YOU WHO SENT UBU TO TAKE THE ALBUM. I SEE IT ALL NOW.
YOU SEE NOTHING! EVERYTHING YOU DID WAS BY A SCRIPT. YOU WERE A LAB RAT IN A MAZE.
YOU SEE ONLY THE TIP OF THE ICEBERG, DETECTIVE. YOUR REPUTATION IS, EVEN NOW, SLIPPING AWAY AT THE HANDS OF THE SENSEI! YOUR OWN WARD... DICK GRAYSON TURNED HIS BACK ON YOU TONIGHT.
DID YOU KNOW THAT?
MMISSIONER ORDON HAS HE SEED OF MISTRUST NTED IN HIS D...ALL THIS N ONE IGHT...
IT... HAS... BEEN... A VERY... VERY LONG DAY... THINGS HAVE HAPPENED.
IN THE BEST OF ALL POSSIBLE WORLDS, WHAT WOULD YOU HAVE ME DO?
IT'S TOO LATE FOR THE BEST OF ALL POSSIBLE WORLDS. I HAVE TRIED TO TRAIN YOU... TO MAKE YOU READY FOR THIS DAY... AND I'VE FAILED.
WHAT WOULD I HAVE YOU DO? KILL HIM!
I WON'T KILL...
I KNOW YOU WON'T KILL! I TRIED TO TEACH YOU TO KILL, EVEN AGAIN THIS NIGHT.... AND YOU WON'T. YOU NEVER WILL.
AND BECAUSE OF THIS MY DAUGHTER TALIA WILL DIE, AT THE HANDS OF SENSEI.

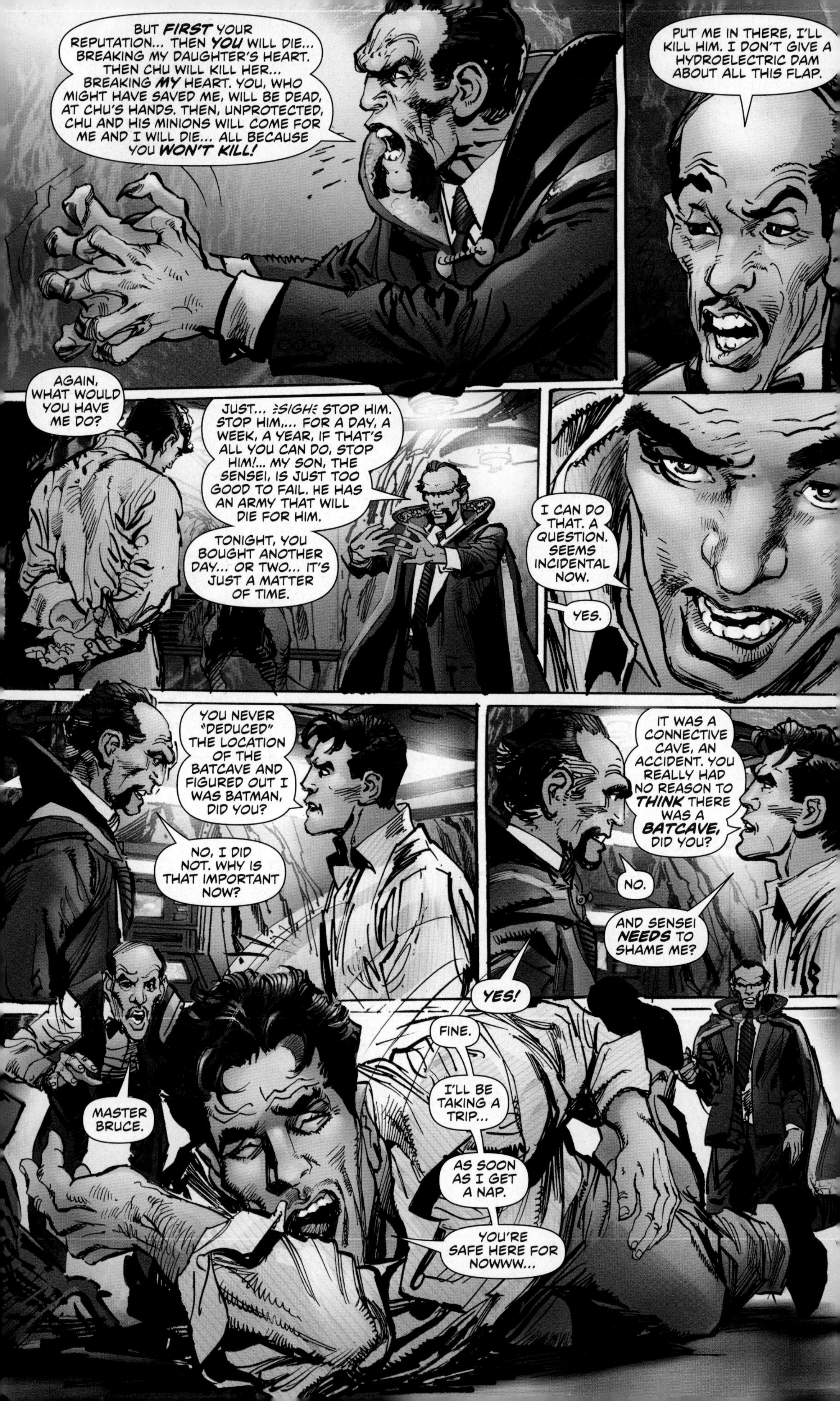
BUT FIRST YOUR REPUTATION... THEN YOU WILL DIE... BREAKING MY DAUGHTER'S HEART. THEN CHU WILL KILL HER... BREAKING MY HEART. YOU, WHO MIGHT HAVE SAVED ME, WILL BE DEAD, AT CHU'S HANDS. THEN, UNPROTECTED, CHU AND HIS MINIONS WILL COME FOR ME AND I WILL DIE... ALL BECAUSE YOU WON'T KILL!
PUT ME IN THERE, I'LL KILL HIM. I DON'T GIVE A HYDROELECTRIC DAM ABOUT ALL THIS FLAP.
AGAIN, WHAT WOULD YOU HAVE ME DO?
JUST... SIGH STOP HIM. STOP HIM,... FOR A DAY, A WEEK, A YEAR, IF THAT'S ALL YOU CAN DO, STOP HIM!... MY SON, THE SENSEI, IS JUST TOO GOOD TO FAIL. HE HAS AN ARMY THAT WILL DIE FOR HIM.
TONIGHT, YOU BOUGHT ANOTHER DAY... OR TWO... IT'S JUST A MATTER OF TIME.
I CAN DO THAT. A QUESTION. SEEMS INCIDENTAL NOW.
YES.
YOU NEVER "DEDUCED" THE LOCATION OF THE BATCAVE AND FIGURED OUT I WAS BATMAN, DID YOU?
NO, I DID NOT. WHY IS THAT IMPORTANT NOW?
IT WAS A CONNECTIVE CAVE, AN ACCIDENT. YOU REALLY HAD NO REASON TO THINK THERE WAS A BATCAVE, DID YOU?
NO.
AND SENSEI NEEDS TO SHAME ME?
YES!
MASTER BRUCE.
FINE.
I'LL BE TAKING A TRIP...
AS SOON AS I GET A NAP.
YOU'RE SAFE HERE FOR NOWWW...

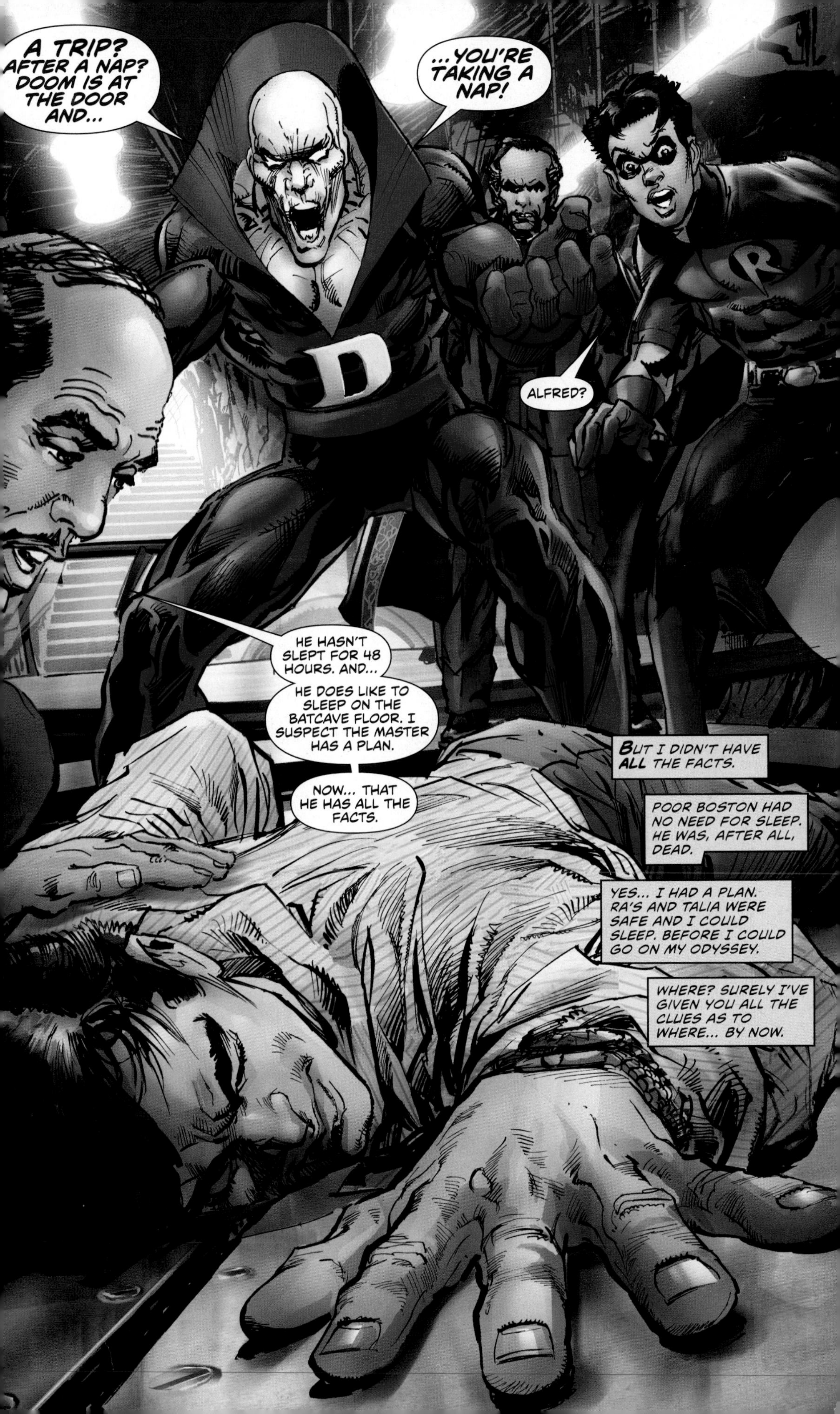
A TRIP? AFTER A NAP? DOOM IS AT THE DOOR AND...
...YOU'RE TAKING A NAP!
ALFRED?
HE HASN'T SLEPT FOR 48 HOURS. AND...
HE DOES LIKE TO SLEEP ON THE BATCAVE FLOOR. I SUSPECT THE MASTER HAS A PLAN.
NOW... THAT HE HAS ALL THE FACTS.
BUT I DIDN'T HAVE ALL THE FACTS.
POOR BOSTON HAD NO NEED FOR SLEEP. HE WAS, AFTER ALL, DEAD.
YES... I HAD A PLAN. RA'S AND TALIA WERE SAFE AND I COULD SLEEP. BEFORE I COULD GO ON MY ODYSSEY.
WHERE? SURELY I'VE GIVEN YOU ALL THE CLUES AS TO WHERE... BY NOW.

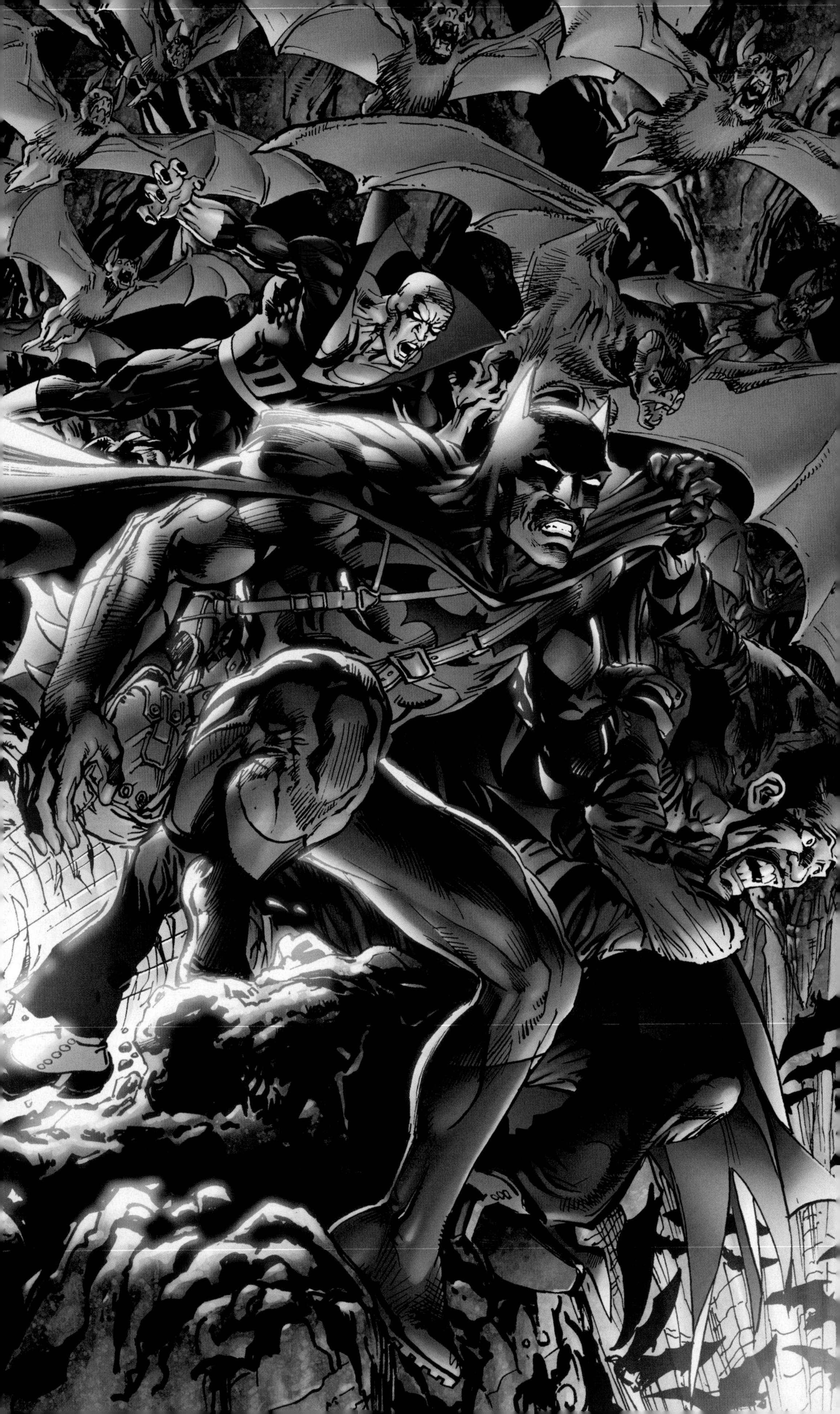

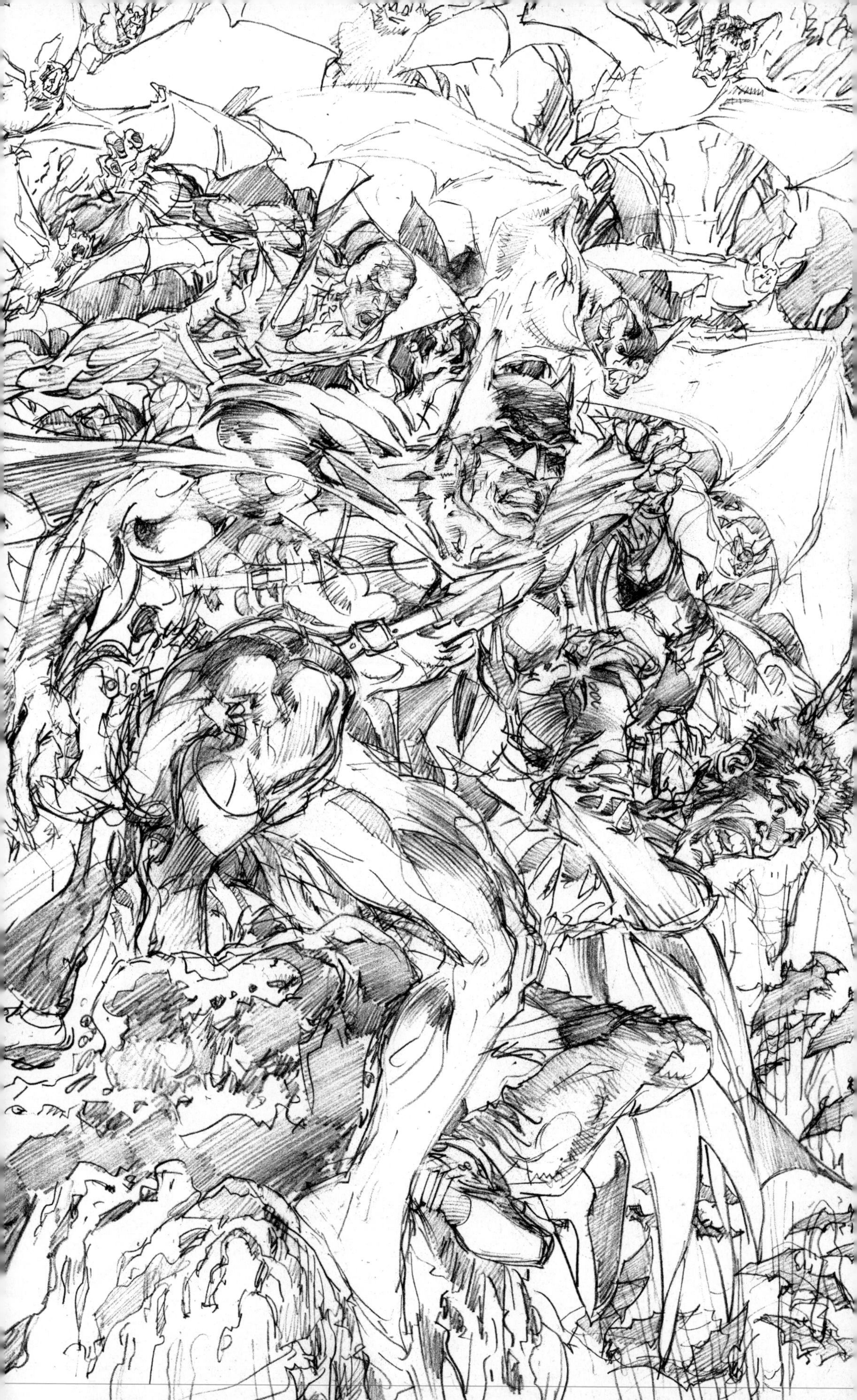

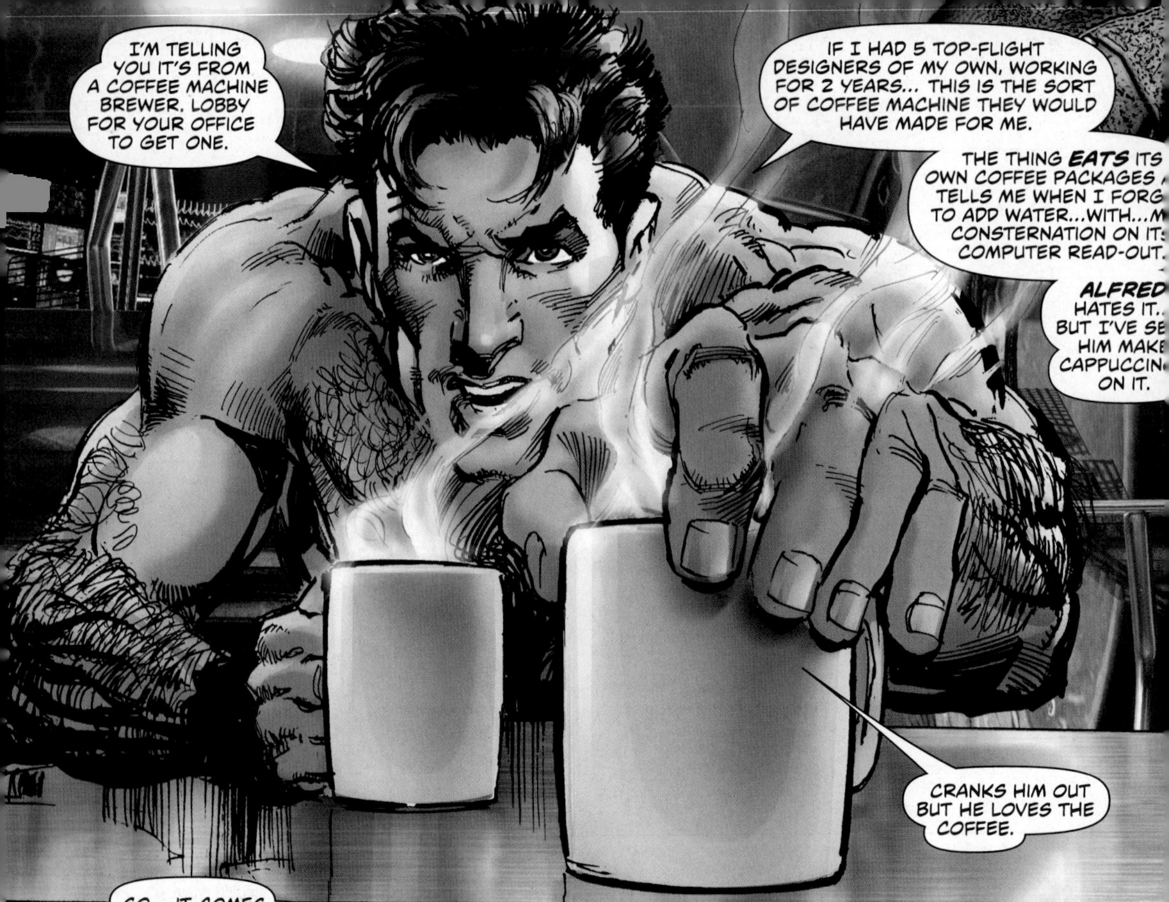
I'M TELLING YOU IT'S FROM A COFFEE MACHINE BREWER. LOBBY FOR YOUR OFFICE TO GET ONE.
IF I HAD 5 TOP-FLIGHT DESIGNERS OF MY OWN, WORKING FOR 2 YEARS... THIS IS THE SORT OF COFFEE MACHINE THEY WOULD HAVE MADE FOR ME.
THE THING EATS ITS OWN COFFEE PACKAGES, TELLS ME WHEN I FORG TO ADD WATER...WITH...M CONSTERNATION ON ITS COMPUTER READ-OUT.
ALFRED HATES IT... BUT I'VE SE HIM MAKE CAPPUCCIN ON IT.
CRANKS HIM OUT BUT HE LOVES THE COFFEE.

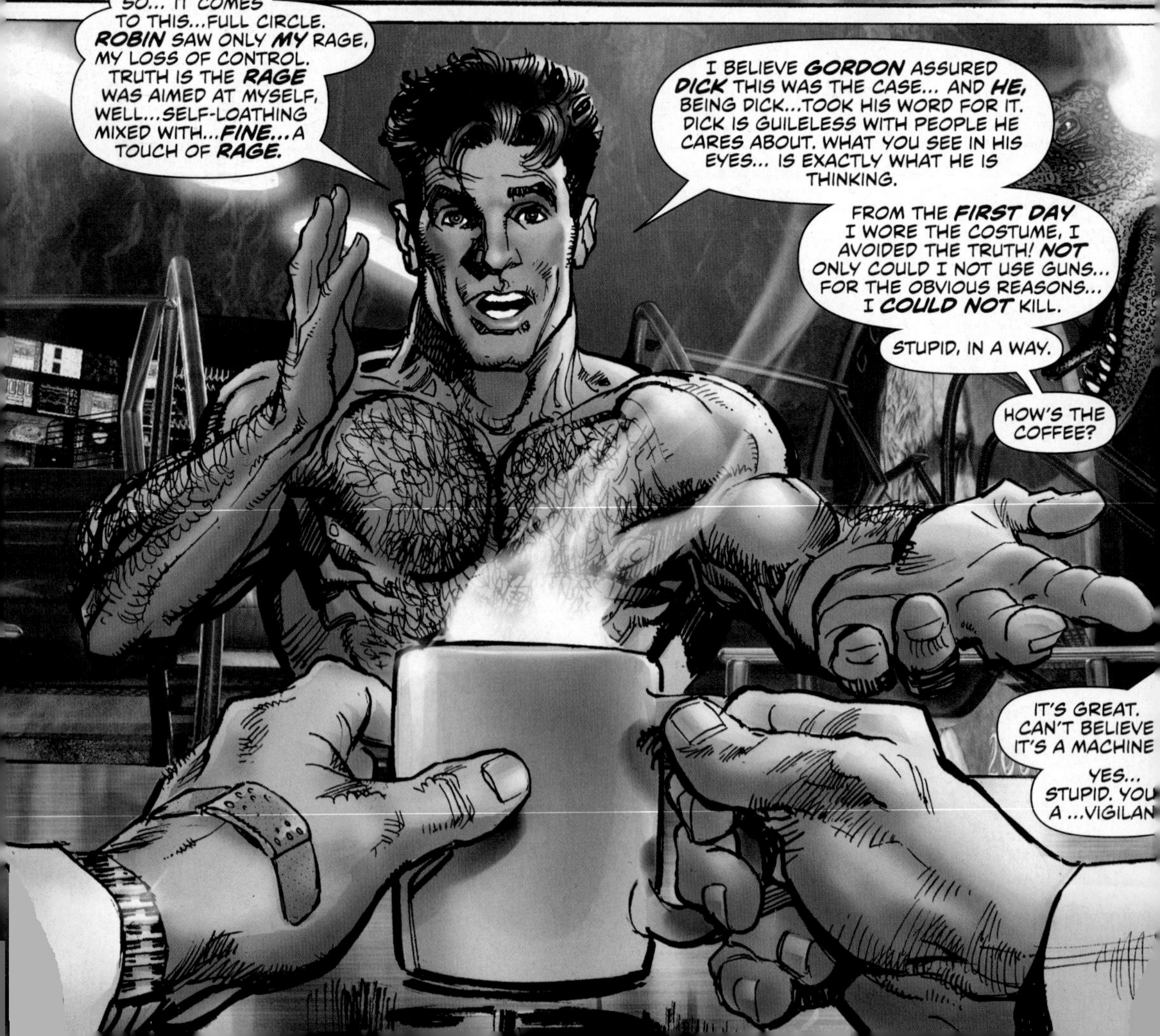
SO... IT COMES TO THIS...FULL CIRCLE. ROBIN SAW ONLY MY RAGE, MY LOSS OF CONTROL. TRUTH IS THE RAGE WAS AIMED AT MYSELF, WELL...SELF-LOATHING MIXED WITH...FINE...A TOUCH OF RAGE.
I BELIEVE GORDON ASSURED DICK THIS WAS THE CASE... AND HE, BEING DICK...TOOK HIS WORD FOR IT. DICK IS GUILELESS WITH PEOPLE HE CARES ABOUT. WHAT YOU SEE IN HIS EYES... IS EXACTLY WHAT HE IS THINKING.
FROM THE FIRST DAY I WORE THE COSTUME, I AVOIDED THE TRUTH! NOT ONLY COULD I NOT USE GUNS... FOR THE OBVIOUS REASONS... I COULD NOT KILL.
STUPID, IN A WAY.
HOW'S THE COFFEE?
IT'S GREAT. CAN'T BELIEVE IT'S A MACHINE
YES... STUPID. YOU A ...VIGILAN

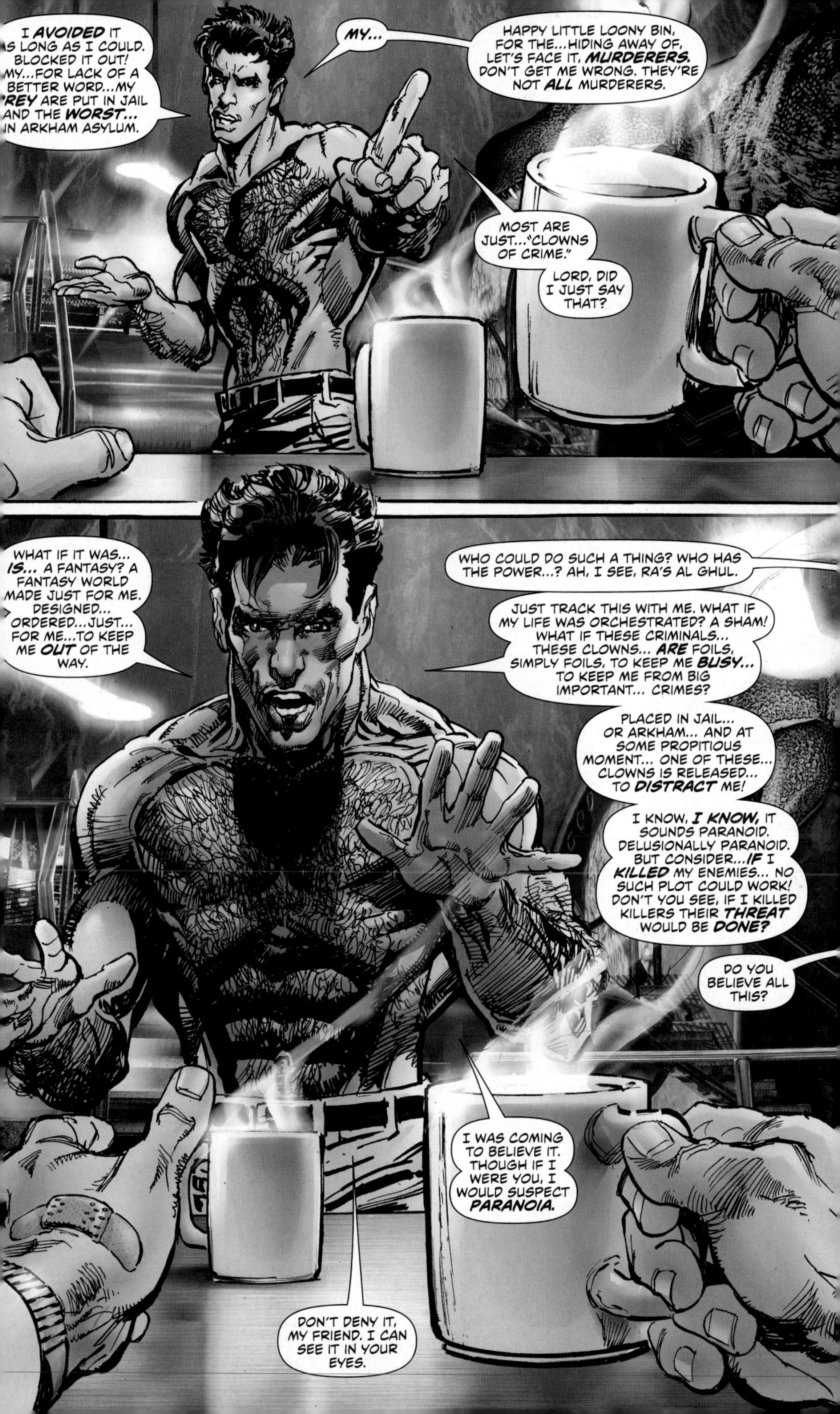
I AVOIDED IT AS LONG AS I COULD. BLOCKED IT OUT! MY...FOR LACK OF A BETTER WORD...MY PREY ARE PUT IN JAIL AND THE WORST... IN ARKHAM ASYLUM.
MY...
HAPPY LITTLE LOONY BIN, FOR THE...HIDING AWAY OF, LET'S FACE IT, MURDERERS. DON'T GET ME WRONG. THEY'RE NOT ALL MURDERERS.
MOST ARE JUST..."CLOWNS OF CRIME."
LORD, DID I JUST SAY THAT?
WHAT IF IT WAS... IS... A FANTASY? A FANTASY WORLD MADE JUST FOR ME. DESIGNED... ORDERED...JUST... FOR ME...TO KEEP ME OUT OF THE WAY.
WHO COULD DO SUCH A THING? WHO HAS THE POWER...? AH, I SEE, RA'S AL GHUL.
JUST TRACK THIS WITH ME. WHAT IF MY LIFE WAS ORCHESTRATED? A SHAM! WHAT IF THESE CRIMINALS... THESE CLOWNS... ARE FOILS, SIMPLY FOILS, TO KEEP ME BUSY... TO KEEP ME FROM BIG IMPORTANT... CRIMES?
PLACED IN JAIL... OR ARKHAM... AND AT SOME PROPITIOUS MOMENT... ONE OF THESE... CLOWNS IS RELEASED... TO DISTRACT ME!
I KNOW, I KNOW, IT SOUNDS PARANOID. DELUSIONALLY PARANOID. BUT CONSIDER...IF I KILLED MY ENEMIES... NO SUCH PLOT COULD WORK! DON'T YOU SEE, IF I KILLED KILLERS THEIR THREAT WOULD BE DONE?
DO YOU BELIEVE ALL THIS?
I WAS COMING TO BELIEVE IT. THOUGH IF I WERE YOU, I WOULD SUSPECT PARANOIA.
DON'T DENY IT, MY FRIEND. I CAN SEE IT IN YOUR EYES.

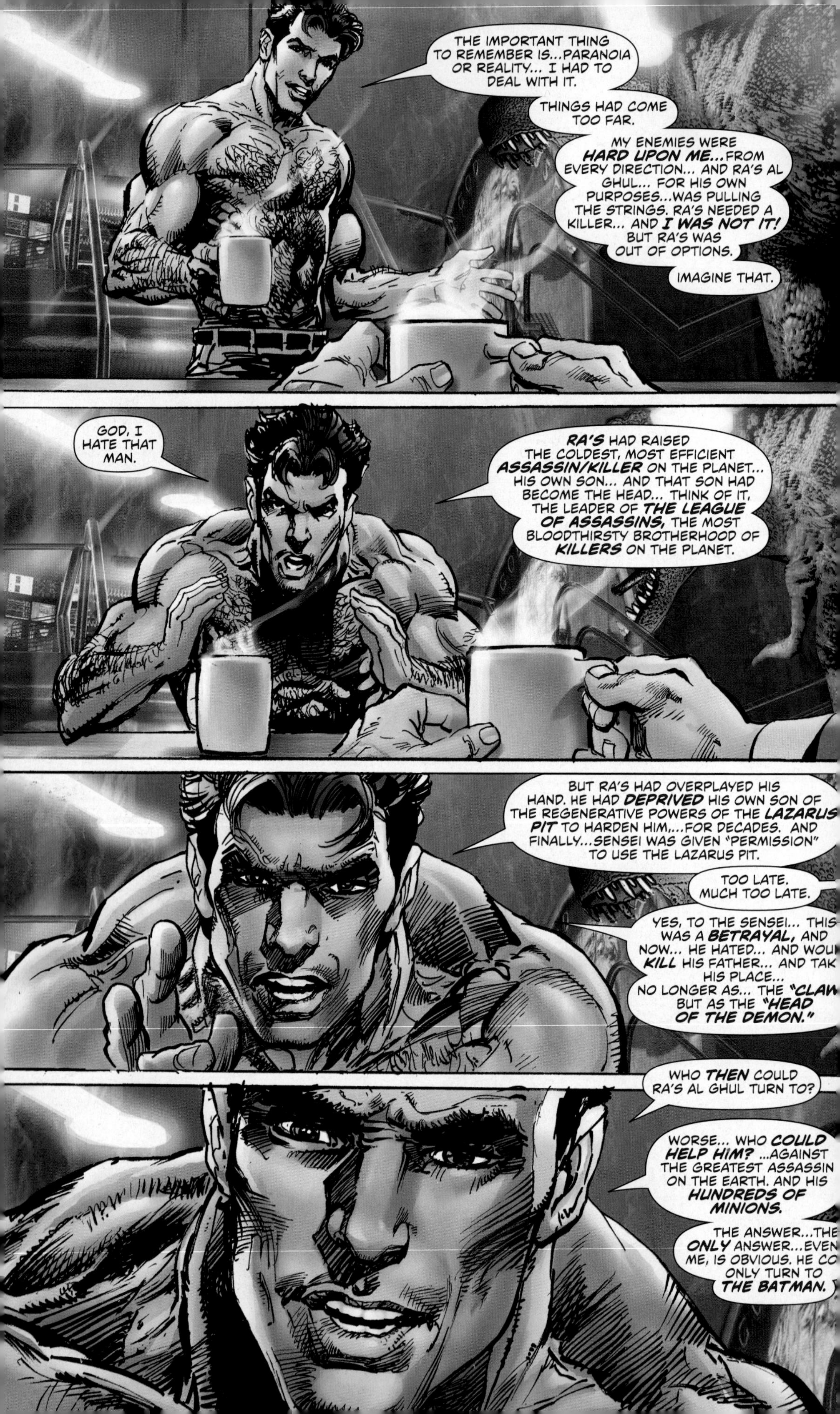
THE IMPORTANT THING TO REMEMBER IS...PARANOIA OR REALITY... I HAD TO DEAL WITH IT.
THINGS HAD COME TOO FAR.
MY ENEMIES WERE HARD UPON ME...FROM EVERY DIRECTION... AND RA'S AL GHUL... FOR HIS OWN PURPOSES...WAS PULLING THE STRINGS. RA'S NEEDED A KILLER... AND I WAS NOT IT! BUT RA'S WAS OUT OF OPTIONS.
IMAGINE THAT.
GOD, I HATE THAT MAN.
RA'S HAD RAISED THE COLDEST, MOST EFFICIENT ASSASSIN/KILLER ON THE PLANET... HIS OWN SON... AND THAT SON HAD BECOME THE HEAD... THINK OF IT, THE LEADER OF THE LEAGUE OF ASSASSINS, THE MOST BLOODTHIRSTY BROTHERHOOD OF KILLERS ON THE PLANET.
BUT RA'S HAD OVERPLAYED HIS HAND. HE HAD DEPRIVED HIS OWN SON OF THE REGENERATIVE POWERS OF THE LAZARUS PIT TO HARDEN HIM,...FOR DECADES. AND FINALLY...SENSEI WAS GIVEN "PERMISSION" TO USE THE LAZARUS PIT.
TOO LATE. MUCH TOO LATE.
YES, TO THE SENSEI... THIS WAS A BETRAYAL, AND NOW... HE HATED... AND WOU KILL HIS FATHER... AND TAK HIS PLACE... NO LONGER AS... THE "CLAW BUT AS THE "HEAD OF THE DEMON."
WHO THEN COULD RA'S AL GHUL TURN TO?
WORSE... WHO COULD HELP HIM? ...AGAINST THE GREATEST ASSASSIN ON THE EARTH. AND HIS HUNDREDS OF MINIONS.
THE ANSWER...THE ONLY ANSWER...EVEN ME, IS OBVIOUS. HE CO ONLY TURN TO THE BATMAN.

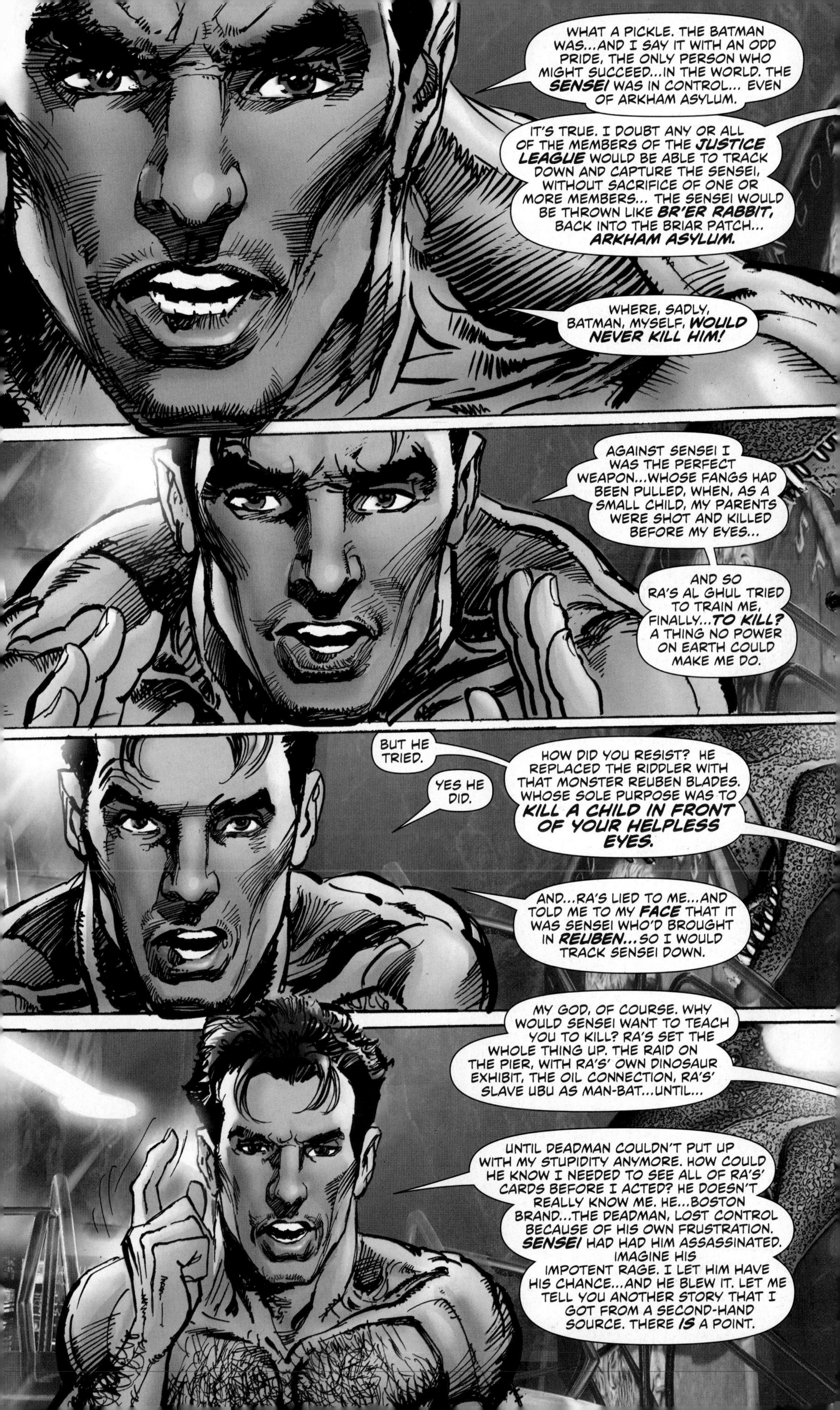
WHAT A PICKLE. THE BATMAN WAS...AND I SAY IT WITH AN ODD PRIDE, THE ONLY PERSON WHO MIGHT SUCCEED...IN THE WORLD. THE SENSEI WAS IN CONTROL... EVEN OF ARKHAM ASYLUM.
IT'S TRUE. I DOUBT ANY OR ALL OF THE MEMBERS OF THE JUSTICE LEAGUE WOULD BE ABLE TO TRACK DOWN AND CAPTURE THE SENSEI, WITHOUT SACRIFICE OF ONE OR MORE MEMBERS... THE SENSEI WOULD BE THROWN LIKE BR'ER RABBIT, BACK INTO THE BRIAR PATCH... ARKHAM ASYLUM.
WHERE, SADLY, BATMAN, MYSELF, WOULD NEVER KILL HIM!
AGAINST SENSEI I WAS THE PERFECT WEAPON...WHOSE FANGS HAD BEEN PULLED, WHEN, AS A SMALL CHILD, MY PARENTS WERE SHOT AND KILLED BEFORE MY EYES...
AND SO RA'S AL GHUL TRIED TO TRAIN ME, FINALLY...TO KILL? A THING NO POWER ON EARTH COULD MAKE ME DO.
BUT HE TRIED.
YES HE DID.
HOW DID YOU RESIST? HE REPLACED THE RIDDLER WITH THAT MONSTER REUBEN BLADES. WHOSE SOLE PURPOSE WAS TO KILL A CHILD IN FRONT OF YOUR HELPLESS EYES.
AND...RA'S LIED TO ME...AND TOLD ME TO MY FACE THAT IT WAS SENSEI WHO'D BROUGHT IN REUBEN...SO I WOULD TRACK SENSEI DOWN.
MY GOD, OF COURSE. WHY WOULD SENSEI WANT TO TEACH YOU TO KILL? RA'S SET THE WHOLE THING UP. THE RAID ON THE PIER, WITH RA'S' OWN DINOSAUR EXHIBIT, THE OIL CONNECTION, RA'S' SLAVE UBU AS MAN-BAT...UNTIL...
UNTIL DEADMAN COULDN'T PUT UP WITH MY STUPIDITY ANYMORE. HOW COULD HE KNOW I NEEDED TO SEE ALL OF RA'S' CARDS BEFORE I ACTED? HE DOESN'T REALLY KNOW ME. HE...BOSTON BRAND...THE DEADMAN, LOST CONTROL BECAUSE OF HIS OWN FRUSTRATION. SENSEI HAD HAD HIM ASSASSINATED. IMAGINE HIS IMPOTENT RAGE. I LET HIM HAVE HIS CHANCE...AND HE BLEW IT. LET ME TELL YOU ANOTHER STORY THAT I GOT FROM A SECOND-HAND SOURCE. THERE IS A POINT.

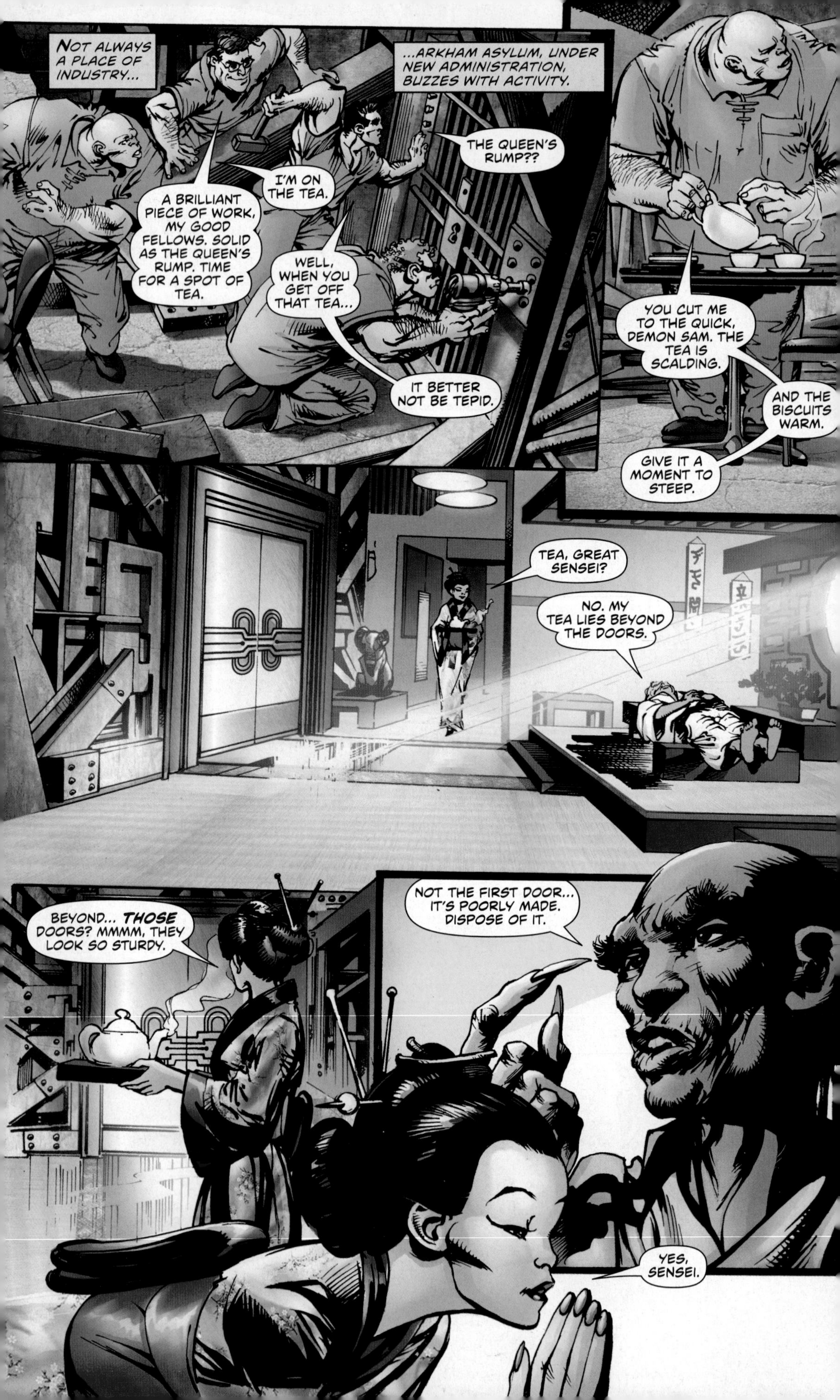
NOT ALWAYS A PLACE OF INDUSTRY...
...ARKHAM ASYLUM, UNDER NEW ADMINISTRATION, BUZZES WITH ACTIVITY.
A BRILLIANT PIECE OF WORK, MY GOOD FELLOWS. SOLID AS THE QUEEN'S RUMP. TIME FOR A SPOT OF TEA.
I'M ON THE TEA.
THE QUEEN'S RUMP??
WELL, WHEN YOU GET OFF THAT TEA...
IT BETTER NOT BE TEPID.
YOU CUT ME TO THE QUICK, DEMON SAM. THE TEA IS SCALDING.
AND THE BISCUITS WARM.
GIVE IT A MOMENT TO STEEP.
TEA, GREAT SENSEI?
NO. MY TEA LIES BEYOND THE DOORS.
BEYOND... THOSE DOORS? MMMM, THEY LOOK SO STURDY.
NOT THE FIRST DOOR... IT'S POORLY MADE. DISPOSE OF IT.
YES, SENSEI.

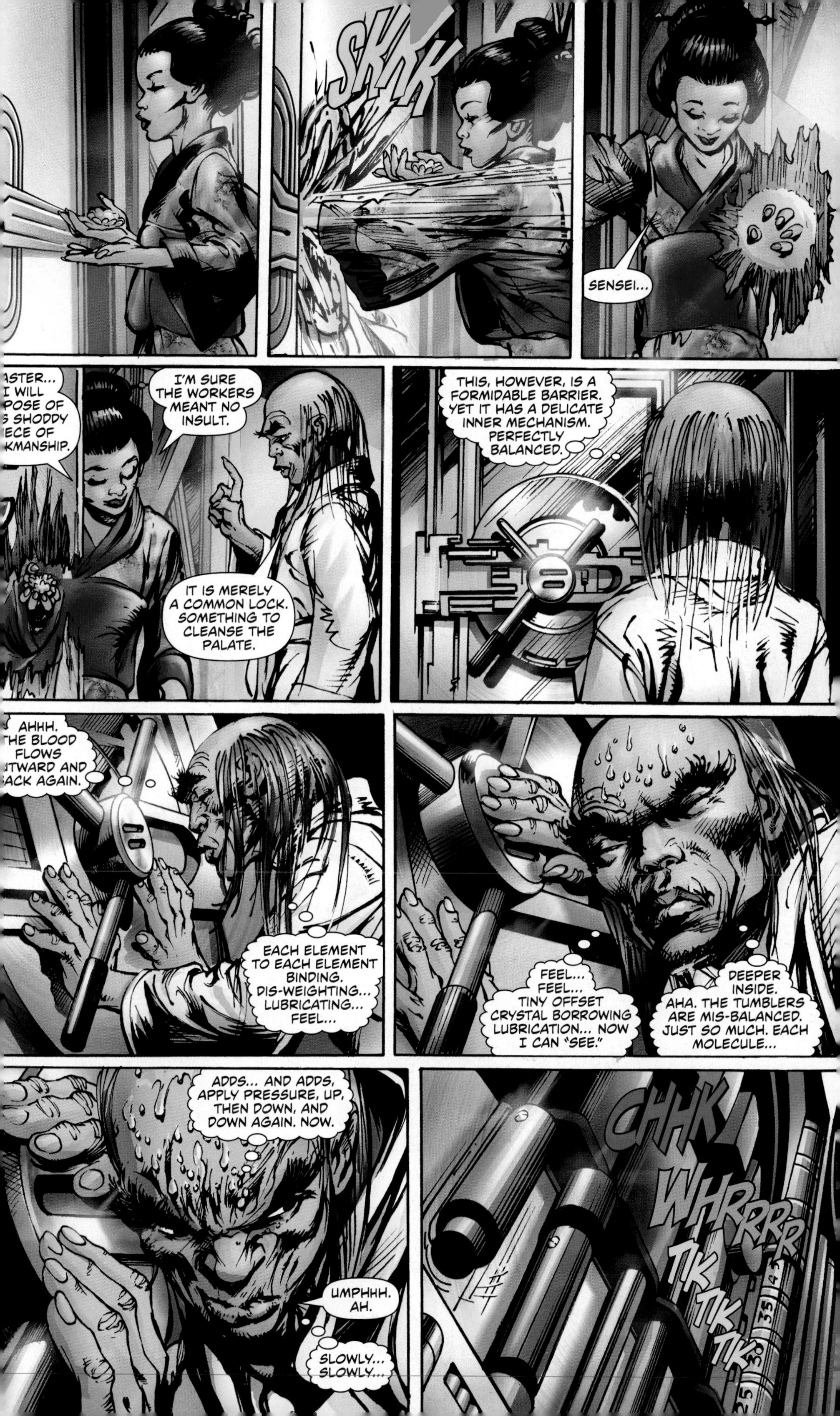
SKKK
SENSEI...
...ASTER... I WILL ...POSE OF ...S SHODDY ...ECE OF ...KMANSHIP.
I'M SURE THE WORKERS MEANT NO INSULT.
IT IS MERELY A COMMON LOCK. SOMETHING TO CLEANSE THE PALATE.
THIS, HOWEVER, IS A FORMIDABLE BARRIER. YET IT HAS A DELICATE INNER MECHANISM. PERFECTLY BALANCED.
AHHH. THE BLOOD FLOWS ...UTWARD AND ...ACK AGAIN.
EACH ELEMENT TO EACH ELEMENT BINDING. DIS-WEIGHTING... LUBRICATING... FEEL...
FEEL... FEEL... TINY OFFSET CRYSTAL BORROWING LUBRICATION... NOW I CAN "SEE."
DEEPER INSIDE. AHA. THE TUMBLERS ARE MIS-BALANCED. JUST SO MUCH. EACH MOLECULE...
ADDS... AND ADDS, APPLY PRESSURE, UP, THEN DOWN, AND DOWN AGAIN. NOW.
UMPHHH. AH.
SLOWLY... SLOWLY...
CHHK
WHRRRR
TIK TIK TIK TIK

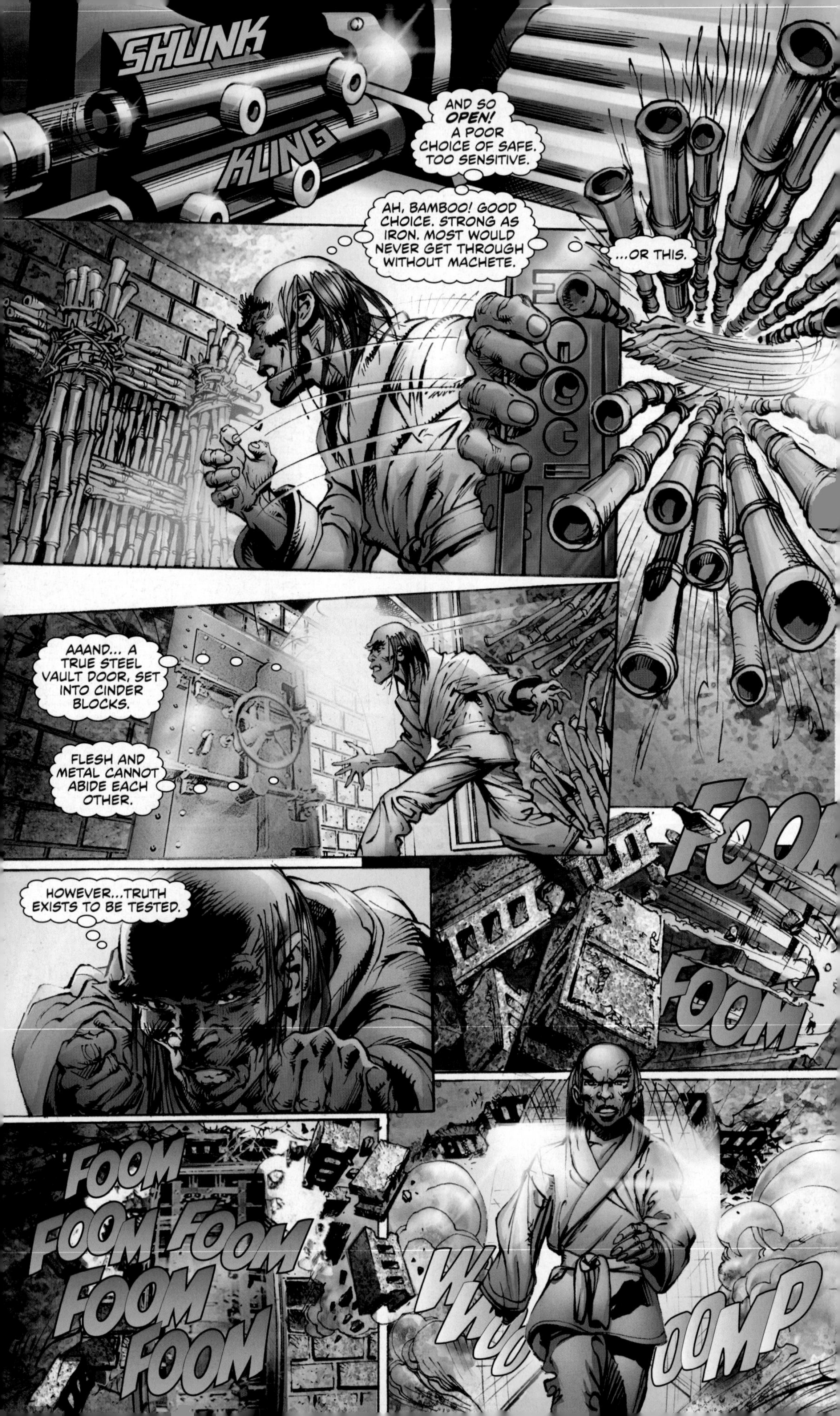
SHUNK
KLING
AND SO OPEN! A POOR CHOICE OF SAFE. TOO SENSITIVE.
AH, BAMBOO! GOOD CHOICE. STRONG AS IRON. MOST WOULD NEVER GET THROUGH WITHOUT MACHETE.
...OR THIS.
AAAND... A TRUE STEEL VAULT DOOR, SET INTO CINDER BLOCKS.
FLESH AND METAL CANNOT ABIDE EACH OTHER.
HOWEVER...TRUTH EXISTS TO BE TESTED.
FOOM
FOOM
FOOM
FOOM FOOM
FOOM
FOOM

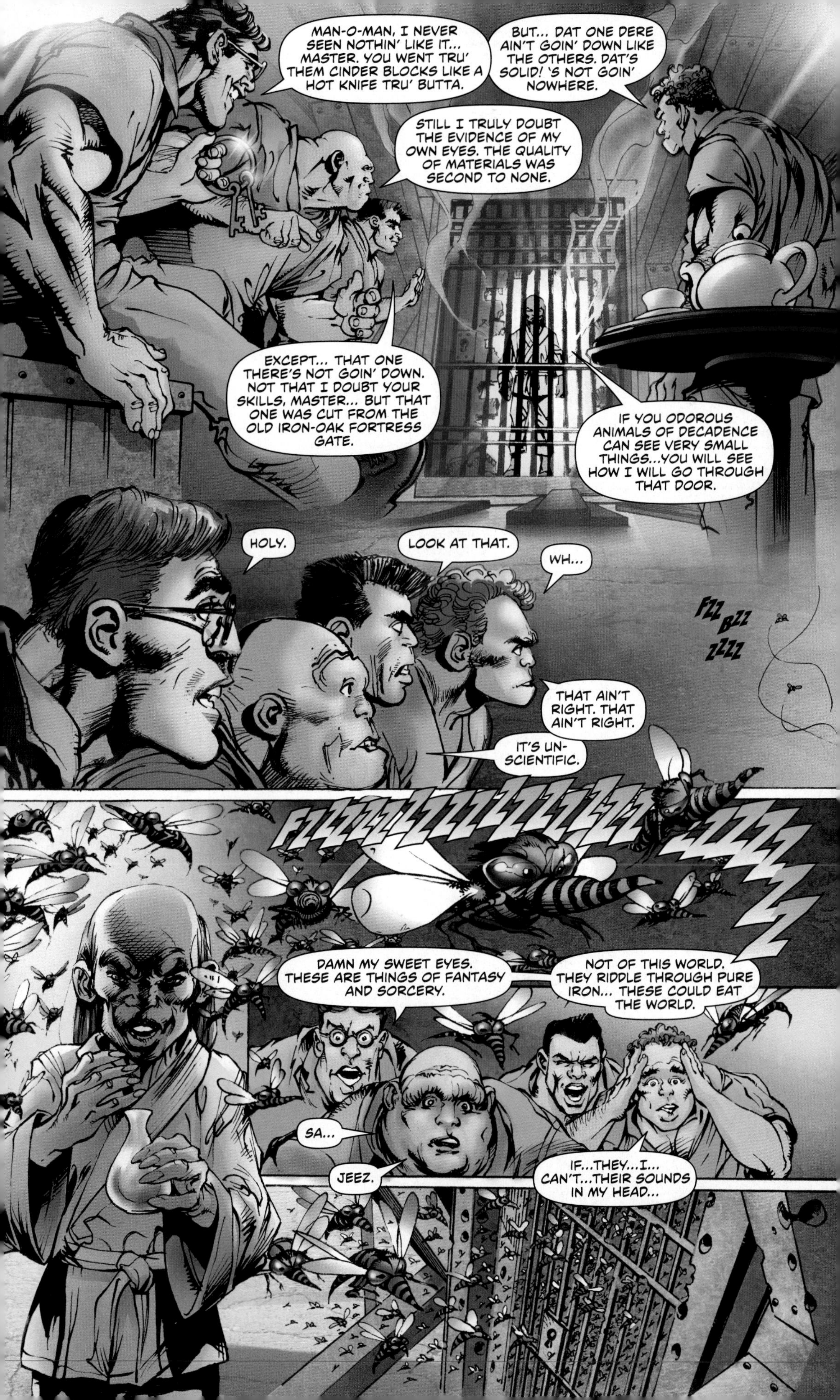
MAN-O-MAN, I NEVER SEEN NOTHIN' LIKE IT... MASTER. YOU WENT TRU' THEM CINDER BLOCKS LIKE A HOT KNIFE TRU' BUTTA.
BUT... DAT ONE DERE AIN'T GOIN' DOWN LIKE THE OTHERS. DAT'S SOLID! 'S NOT GOIN' NOWHERE.
STILL I TRULY DOUBT THE EVIDENCE OF MY OWN EYES. THE QUALITY OF MATERIALS WAS SECOND TO NONE.
EXCEPT... THAT ONE THERE'S NOT GOIN' DOWN. NOT THAT I DOUBT YOUR SKILLS, MASTER... BUT THAT ONE WAS CUT FROM THE OLD IRON-OAK FORTRESS GATE.
IF YOU ODOROUS ANIMALS OF DECADENCE CAN SEE VERY SMALL THINGS...YOU WILL SEE HOW I WILL GO THROUGH THAT DOOR.
HOLY.
LOOK AT THAT.
WH...
FZZ BZZ ZZZZ
THAT AIN'T RIGHT. THAT AIN'T RIGHT.
IT'S UN-SCIENTIFIC.
FZZZZZZZZZZZZZZZZZZZZZZ
DAMN MY SWEET EYES. THESE ARE THINGS OF FANTASY AND SORCERY.
NOT OF THIS WORLD. THEY RIDDLE THROUGH PURE IRON... THESE COULD EAT THE WORLD.
SA...
JEEZ.
IF...THEY...I... CAN'T...THEIR SOUNDS IN MY HEAD...

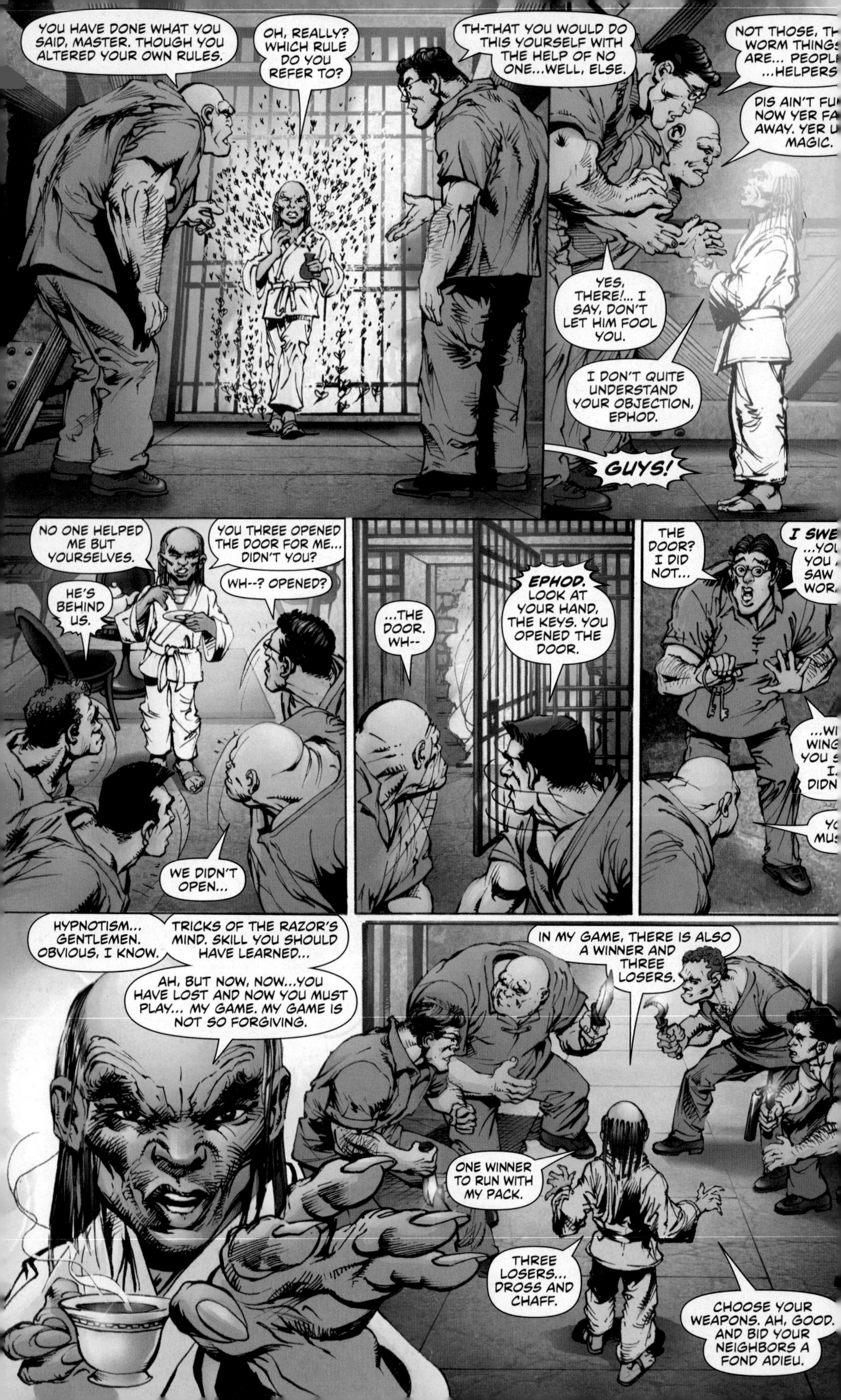
YOU HAVE DONE WHAT YOU SAID, MASTER. THOUGH YOU ALTERED YOUR OWN RULES.
OH, REALLY? WHICH RULE DO YOU REFER TO?
TH-THAT YOU WOULD DO THIS YOURSELF WITH THE HELP OF NO ONE...WELL, ELSE.
NOT THOSE, TH WORM THINGS ARE... PEOPL ...HELPERS
DIS AIN'T FU NOW YER FA AWAY. YER U MAGIC.
YES, THERE!... I SAY, DON'T LET HIM FOOL YOU.
I DON'T QUITE UNDERSTAND YOUR OBJECTION, EPHOD.
GUYS!
NO ONE HELPED ME BUT YOURSELVES.
YOU THREE OPENED THE DOOR FOR ME... DIDN'T YOU?
HE'S BEHIND US.
WH--? OPENED?
WE DIDN'T OPEN...
...THE DOOR. WH--
EPHOD. LOOK AT YOUR HAND, THE KEYS. YOU OPENED THE DOOR.
THE DOOR? I DID NOT...
I SWE ...YOU YOU SAW WOR
...WI WING YOU S I. DIDN
YO MUS
HYPNOTISM... GENTLEMEN. OBVIOUS, I KNOW.
TRICKS OF THE RAZOR'S MIND. SKILL YOU SHOULD HAVE LEARNED...
AH, BUT NOW, NOW...YOU HAVE LOST AND NOW YOU MUST PLAY... MY GAME. MY GAME IS NOT SO FORGIVING.
IN MY GAME, THERE IS ALSO A WINNER AND THREE LOSERS.
ONE WINNER TO RUN WITH MY PACK.
THREE LOSERS... DROSS AND CHAFF.
CHOOSE YOUR WEAPONS. AH, GOOD. AND BID YOUR NEIGHBORS A FOND ADIEU.

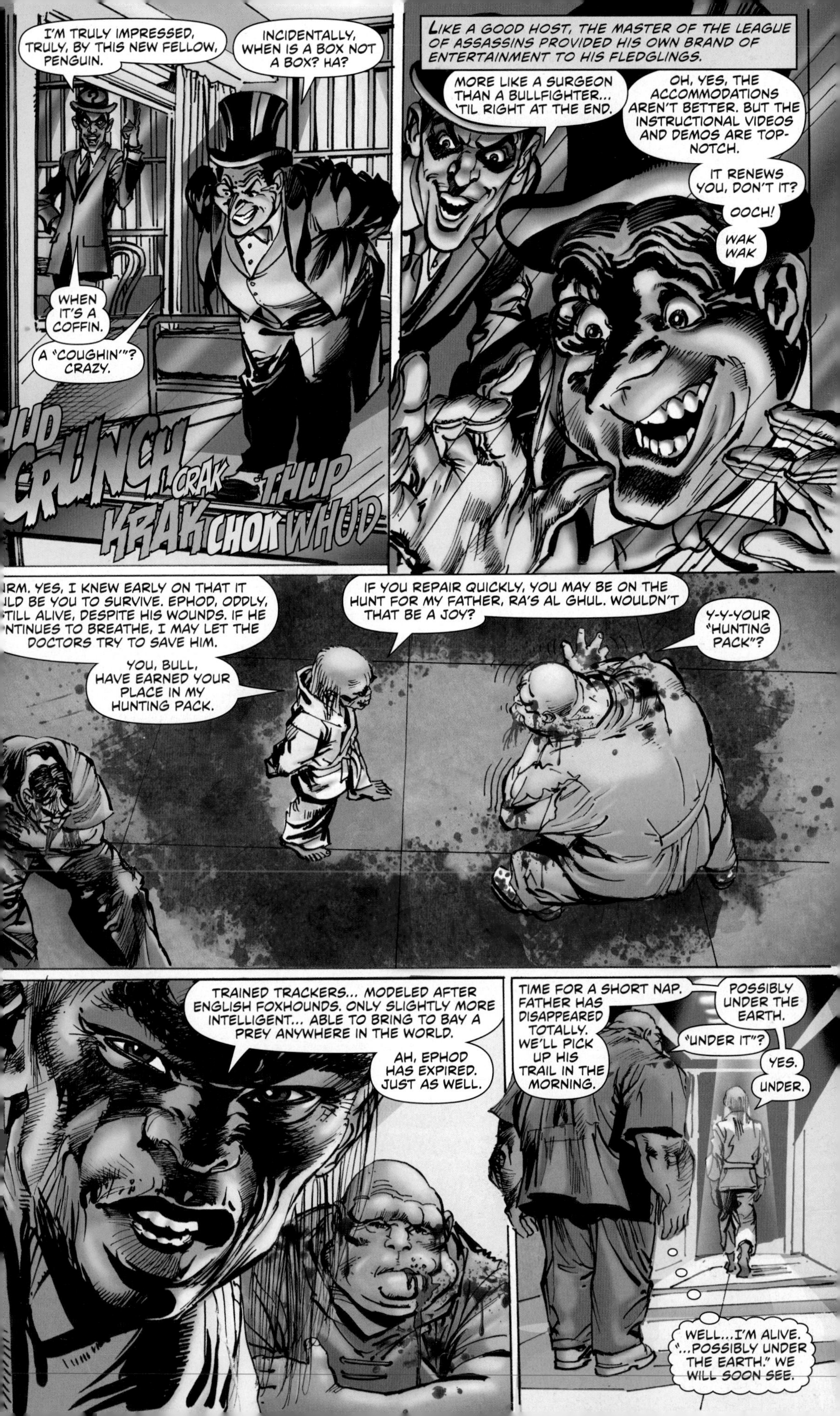
I'M TRULY IMPRESSED, TRULY, BY THIS NEW FELLOW, PENGUIN.
INCIDENTALLY, WHEN IS A BOX NOT A BOX? HA?
WHEN IT'S A COFFIN.
A "COUGHIN'"? CRAZY.
HUD CRUNCH CRAK THUP KRAK CHOK WHUD
LIKE A GOOD HOST, THE MASTER OF THE LEAGUE OF ASSASSINS PROVIDED HIS OWN BRAND OF ENTERTAINMENT TO HIS FLEDGLINGS.
MORE LIKE A SURGEON THAN A BULLFIGHTER... 'TIL RIGHT AT THE END.
OH, YES, THE ACCOMMODATIONS AREN'T BETTER. BUT THE INSTRUCTIONAL VIDEOS AND DEMOS ARE TOP-NOTCH.
IT RENEWS YOU, DON'T IT?
OOCH!
WAK WAK
RM. YES, I KNEW EARLY ON THAT IT
LD BE YOU TO SURVIVE. EPHOD, ODDLY,
TILL ALIVE, DESPITE HIS WOUNDS. IF HE
NTINUES TO BREATHE, I MAY LET THE DOCTORS TRY TO SAVE HIM.
YOU, BULL, HAVE EARNED YOUR PLACE IN MY HUNTING PACK.
IF YOU REPAIR QUICKLY, YOU MAY BE ON THE HUNT FOR MY FATHER, RA'S AL GHUL. WOULDN'T THAT BE A JOY?
Y-Y-YOUR "HUNTING PACK"?
TRAINED TRACKERS... MODELED AFTER ENGLISH FOXHOUNDS. ONLY SLIGHTLY MORE INTELLIGENT... ABLE TO BRING TO BAY A PREY ANYWHERE IN THE WORLD.
AH, EPHOD HAS EXPIRED. JUST AS WELL.
TIME FOR A SHORT NAP. FATHER HAS DISAPPEARED TOTALLY. WE'LL PICK UP HIS TRAIL IN THE MORNING.
POSSIBLY UNDER THE EARTH.
"UNDER IT"?
YES. UNDER.
WELL...I'M ALIVE. "...POSSIBLY UNDER THE EARTH." WE WILL SOON SEE.

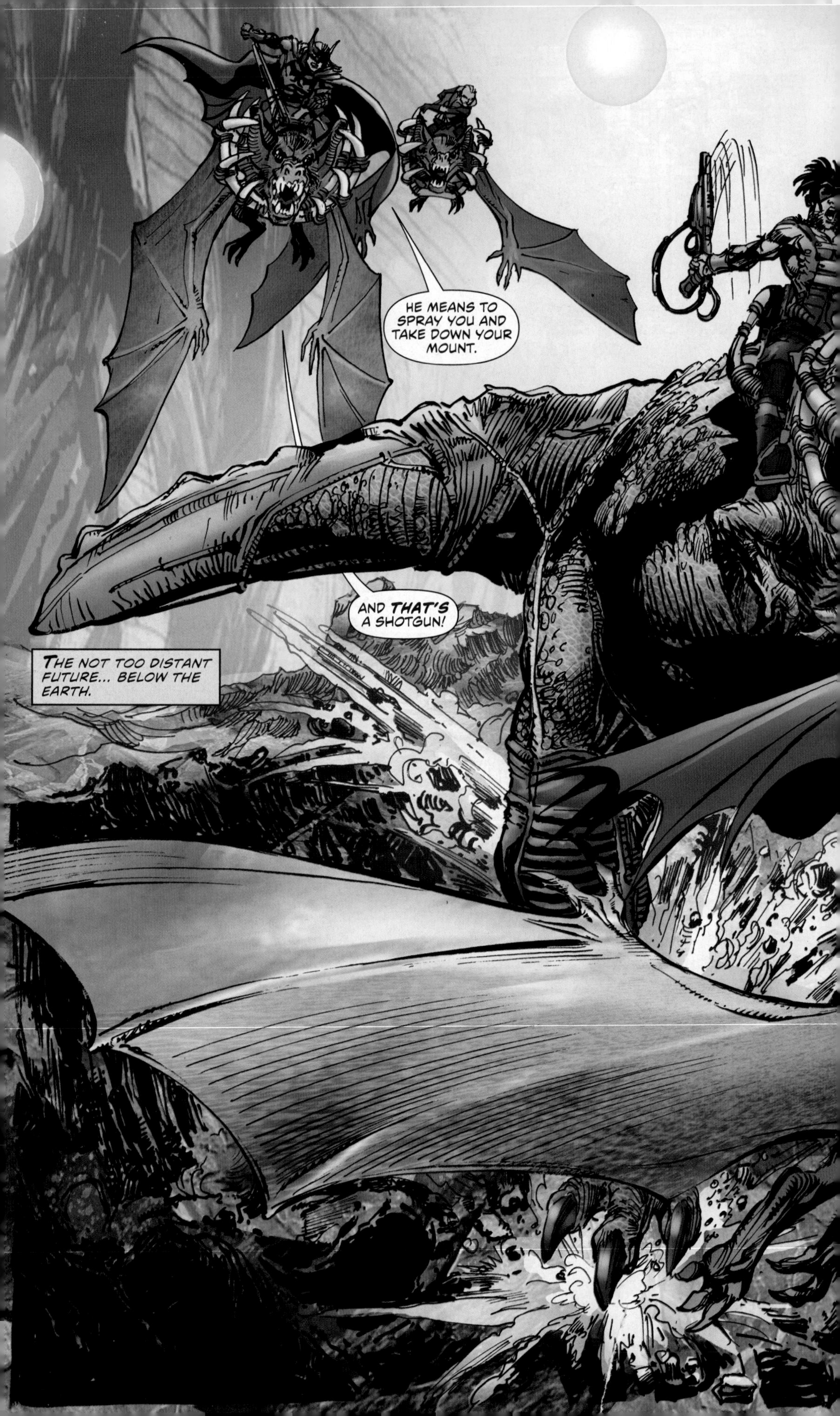
THE NOT TOO DISTANT FUTURE... BELOW THE EARTH.
HE MEANS TO SPRAY YOU AND TAKE DOWN YOUR MOUNT.
AND THAT'S A SHOTGUN!

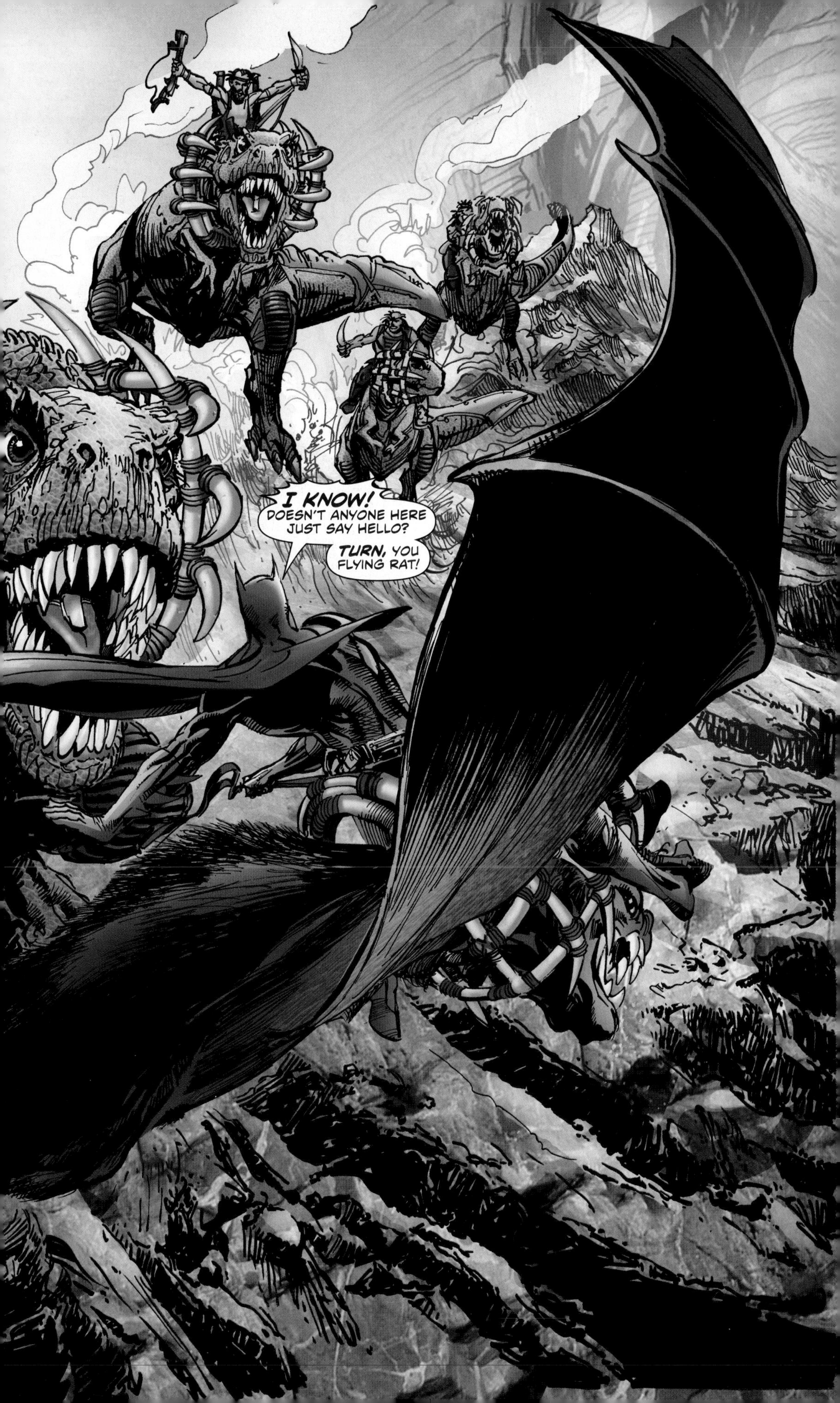
I KNOW!
DOESN'T ANYONE HERE JUST SAY HELLO?
TURN, YOU FLYING RAT!

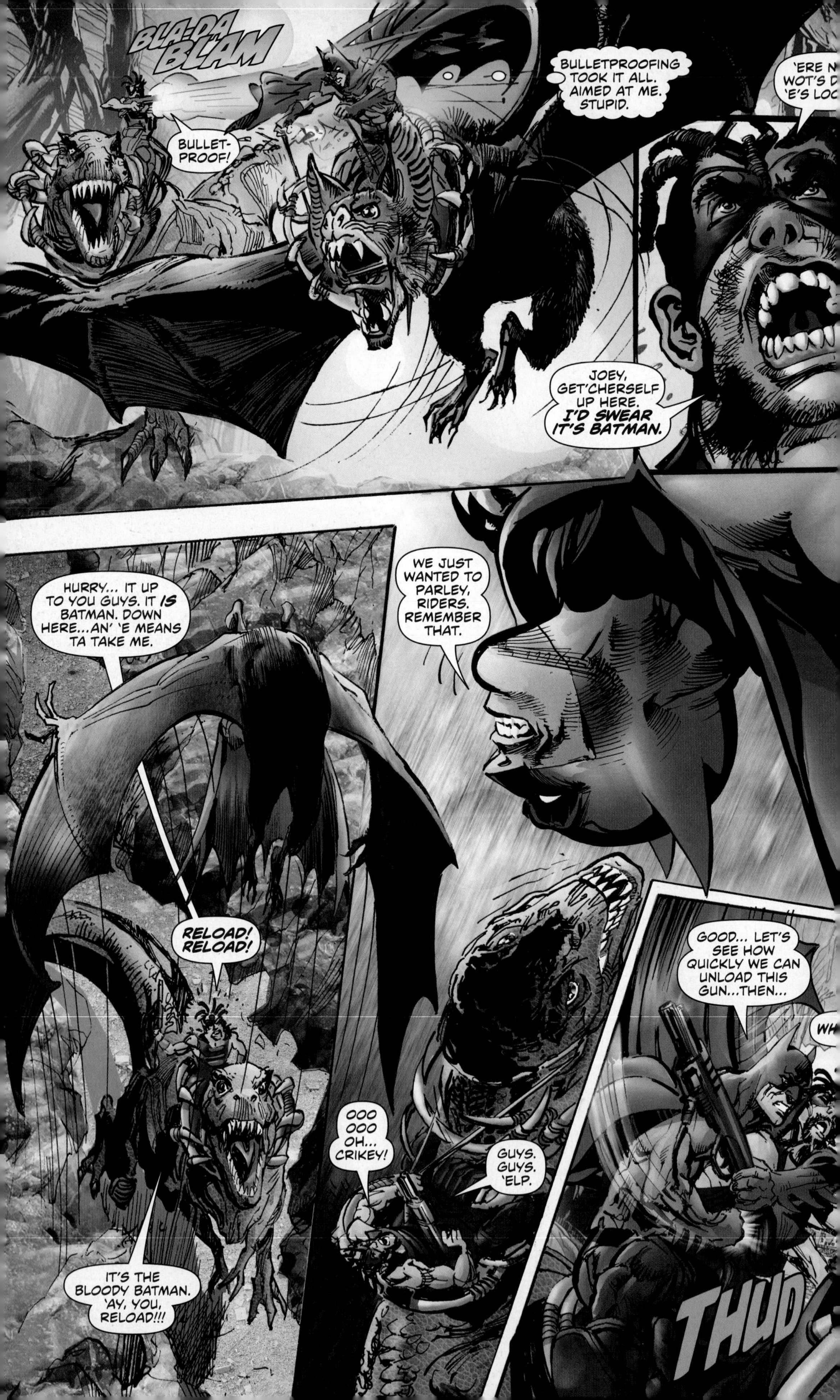
BLA-DA BLAM
BULLET-PROOF!
BULLETPROOFING TOOK IT ALL. AIMED AT ME. STUPID.
JOEY, GET'CHERSELF UP HERE. I'D SWEAR IT'S BATMAN.
HURRY... IT UP TO YOU GUYS. IT IS BATMAN. DOWN HERE...AN' 'E MEANS TA TAKE ME.
WE JUST WANTED TO PARLEY, RIDERS. REMEMBER THAT.
RELOAD! RELOAD!
IT'S THE BLOODY BATMAN. 'AY, YOU, RELOAD!!!
OOO OOO OH... CRIKEY!
GUYS. GUYS. 'ELP.
GOOD... LET'S SEE HOW QUICKLY WE CAN UNLOAD THIS GUN...THEN...
THUD

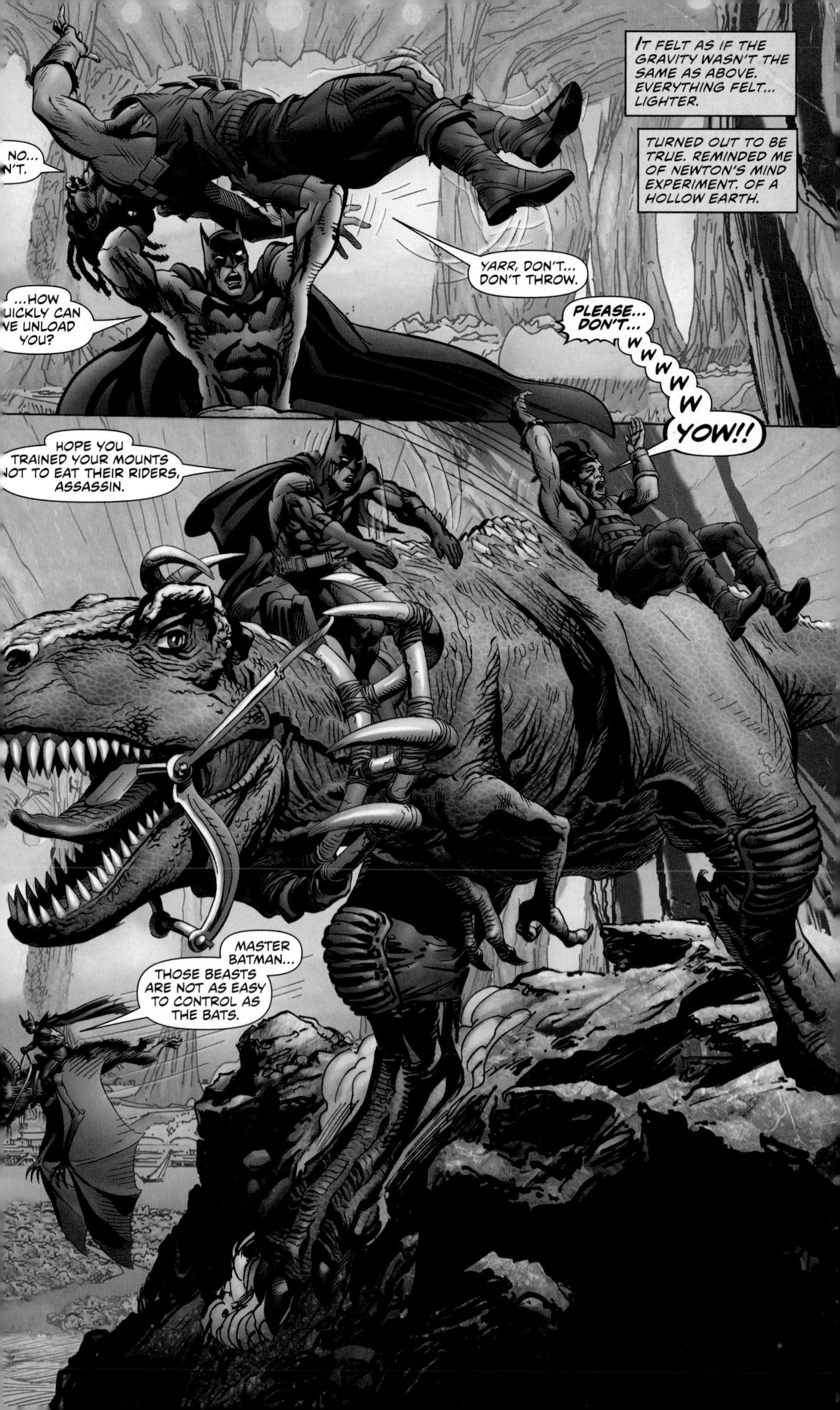

IT FELT AS IF THE GRAVITY WASN'T THE SAME AS ABOVE. EVERYTHING FELT... LIGHTER.
TURNED OUT TO BE TRUE. REMINDED ME OF NEWTON'S MIND EXPERIMENT. OF A HOLLOW EARTH.
NO... N'T.
...HOW UICKLY CAN VE UNLOAD YOU?
YARR, DON'T... DON'T THROW.
PLEASE... DON'T... WWWWW YOW!!
HOPE YOU TRAINED YOUR MOUNTS NOT TO EAT THEIR RIDERS, ASSASSIN.
MASTER BATMAN... THOSE BEASTS ARE NOT AS EASY TO CONTROL AS THE BATS.

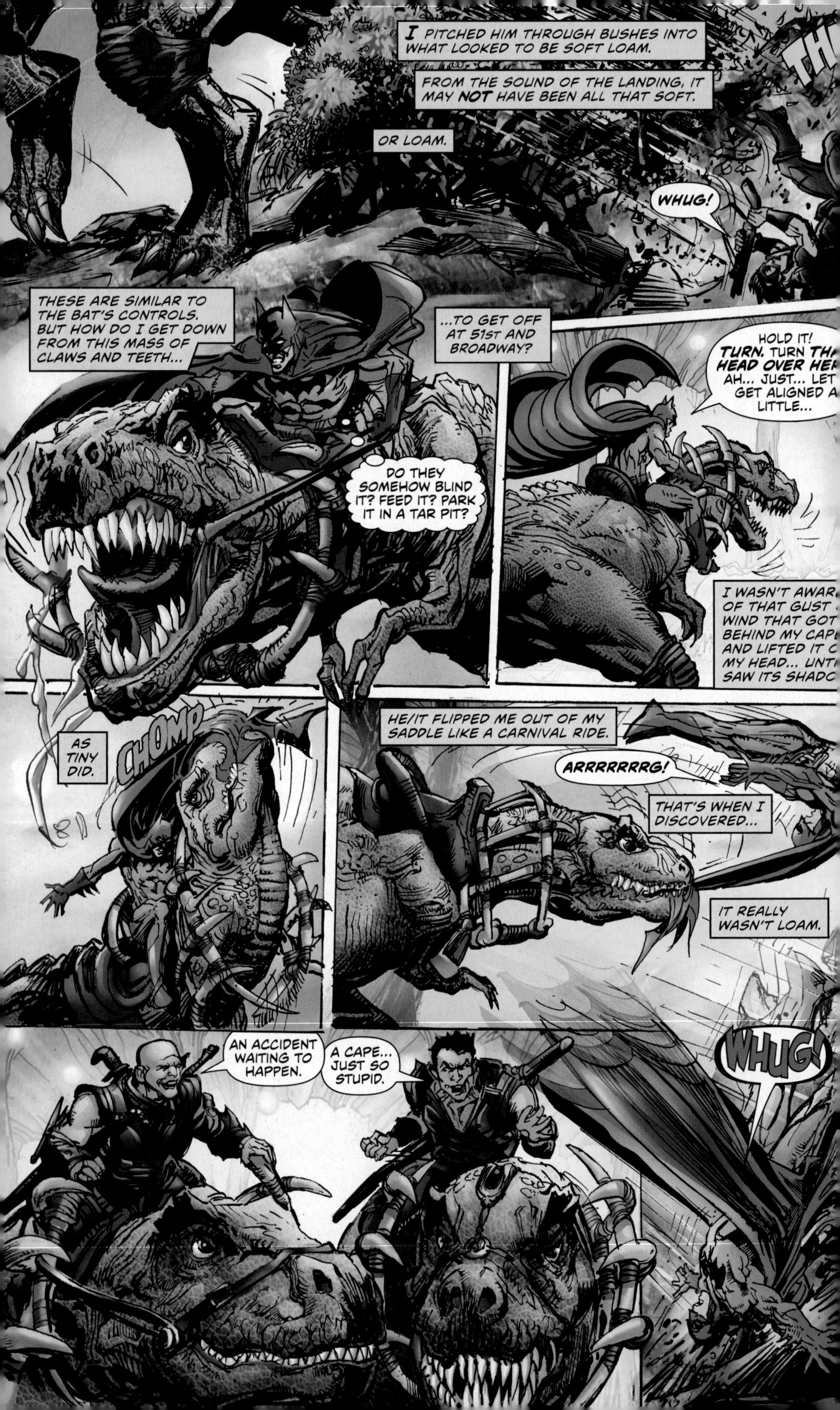

I PITCHED HIM THROUGH BUSHES INTO WHAT LOOKED TO BE SOFT LOAM.
FROM THE SOUND OF THE LANDING, IT MAY NOT HAVE BEEN ALL THAT SOFT.
OR LOAM.
WHUG!
THESE ARE SIMILAR TO THE BAT'S CONTROLS. BUT HOW DO I GET DOWN FROM THIS MASS OF CLAWS AND TEETH...
...TO GET OFF AT 51ST AND BROADWAY?
DO THEY SOMEHOW BLIND IT? FEED IT? PARK IT IN A TAR PIT?
HOLD IT! TURN. TURN
AH... JUST... LET
GET ALIGNED A
LITTLE...
AS TINY DID.
CHOMP
HE/IT FLIPPED ME OUT OF MY SADDLE LIKE A CARNIVAL RIDE.
ARRRRRRRG!
THAT'S WHEN I DISCOVERED...
IT REALLY WASN'T LOAM.
AN ACCIDENT WAITING TO HAPPEN.
A CAPE... JUST SO STUPID.
WHUG!

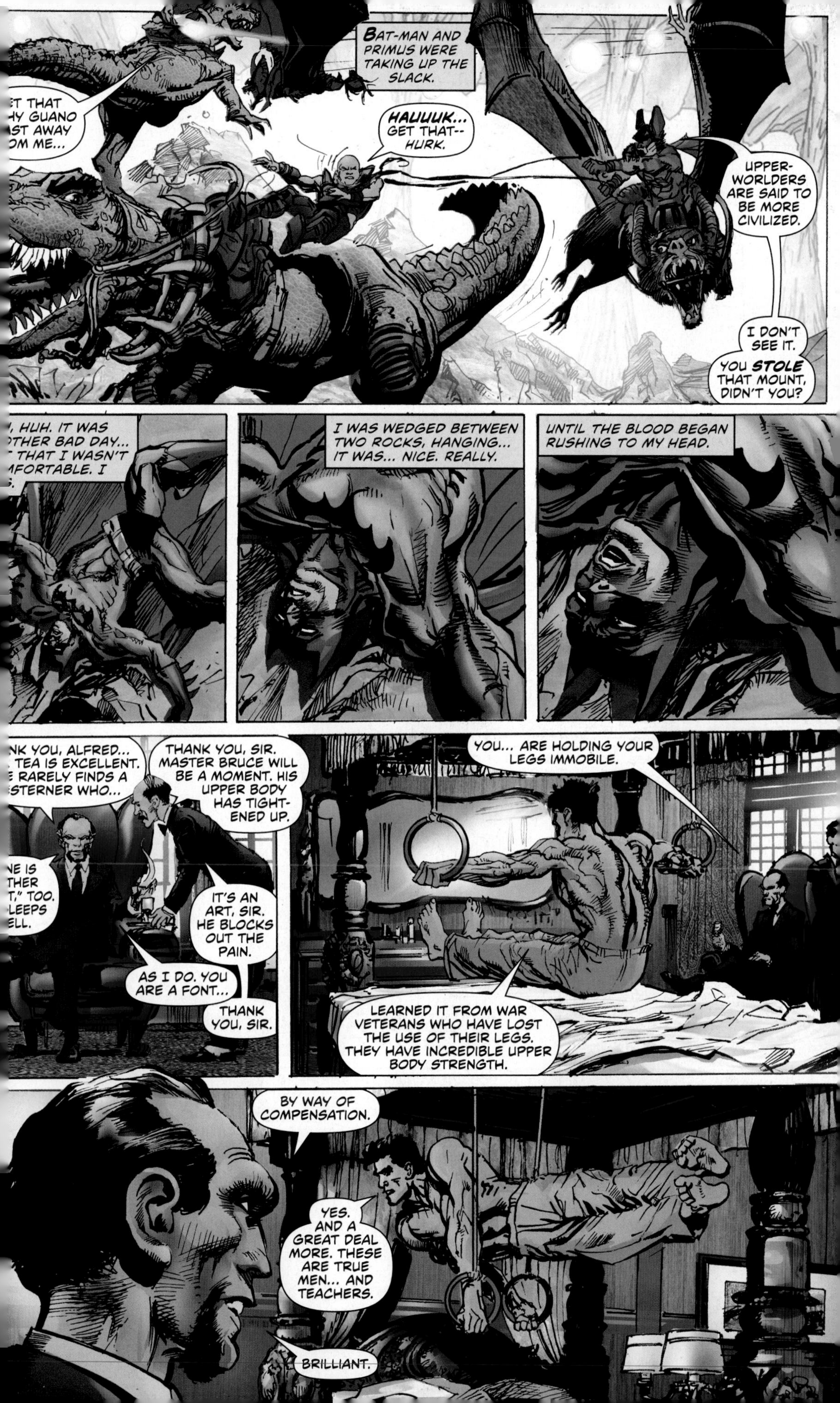

BAT-MAN AND PRIMUS WERE TAKING UP THE SLACK.
ET THAT HY GUANO AST AWAY OM ME...
HAUUUK... GET THAT-- HURK.
UPPER-WORLDERS ARE SAID TO BE MORE CIVILIZED.
I DON'T SEE IT.
YOU STOLE THAT MOUNT, DIDN'T YOU?
, HUH. IT WAS OTHER BAD DAY... T THAT I WASN'T MFORTABLE. I
I WAS WEDGED BETWEEN TWO ROCKS, HANGING... IT WAS... NICE. REALLY.
UNTIL THE BLOOD BEGAN RUSHING TO MY HEAD.
NK YOU, ALFRED... TEA IS EXCELLENT. E RARELY FINDS A ESTERNER WHO...
THANK YOU, SIR. MASTER BRUCE WILL BE A MOMENT. HIS UPPER BODY HAS TIGHTENED UP.
NE IS THER T," TOO. LEEPS ELL.
IT'S AN ART, SIR. HE BLOCKS OUT THE PAIN.
AS I DO. YOU ARE A FONT...
THANK YOU, SIR.
YOU... ARE HOLDING YOUR LEGS IMMOBILE.
LEARNED IT FROM WAR VETERANS WHO HAVE LOST THE USE OF THEIR LEGS. THEY HAVE INCREDIBLE UPPER BODY STRENGTH.
BY WAY OF COMPENSATION.
YES. AND A GREAT DEAL MORE. THESE ARE TRUE MEN... AND TEACHERS.
BRILLIANT.

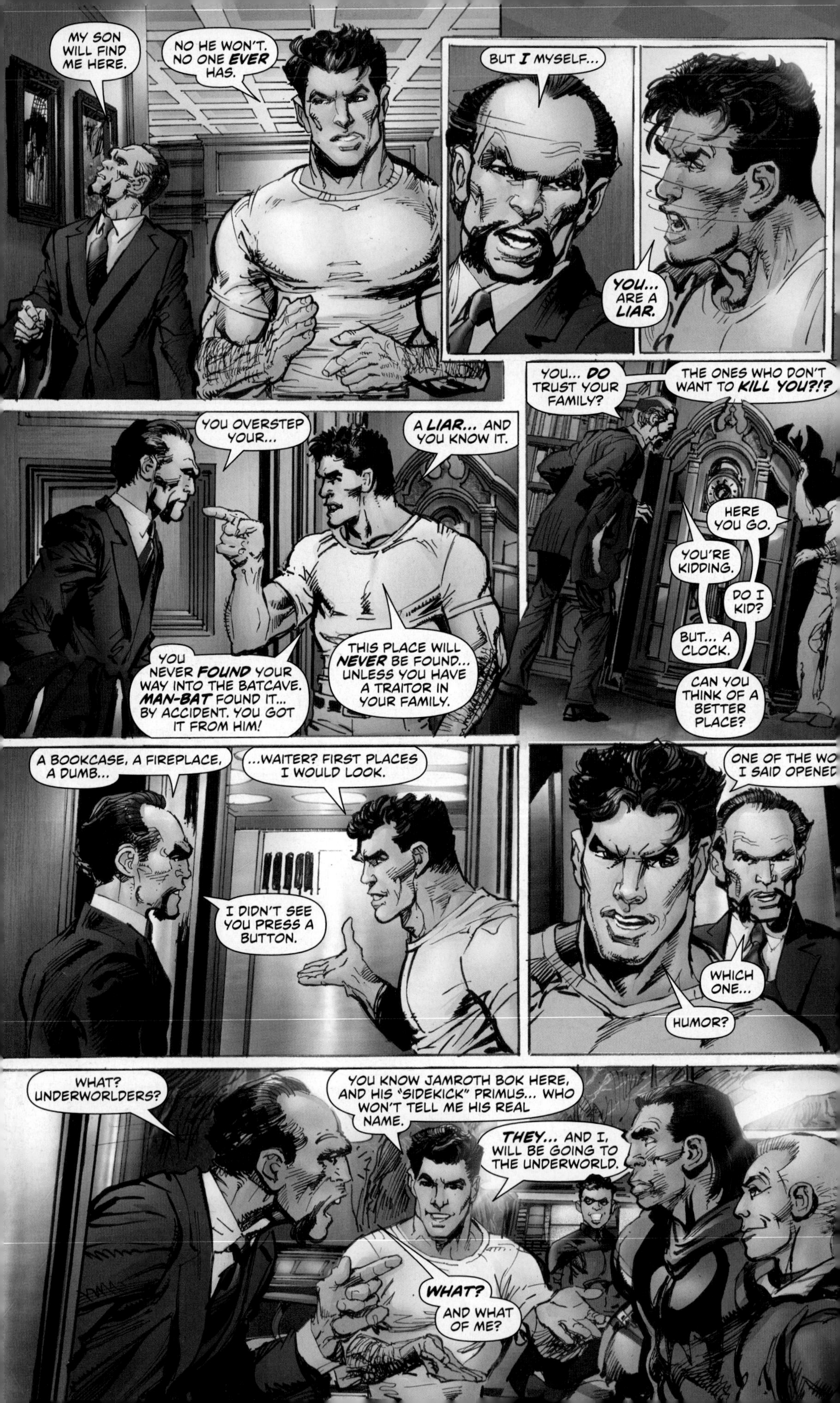

MY SON WILL FIND ME HERE.
NO HE WON'T. NO ONE EVER HAS.
BUT I MYSELF...
YOU... ARE A LIAR.
YOU OVERSTEP YOUR...
A LIAR... AND YOU KNOW IT.
YOU NEVER FOUND YOUR WAY INTO THE BATCAVE. MAN-BAT FOUND IT... BY ACCIDENT. YOU GOT IT FROM HIM!
THIS PLACE WILL NEVER BE FOUND... UNLESS YOU HAVE A TRAITOR IN YOUR FAMILY.
YOU... DO TRUST YOUR FAMILY?
THE ONES WHO DON'T WANT TO KILL YOU?!?
HERE YOU GO.
YOU'RE KIDDING.
DO I KID?
BUT... A CLOCK.
CAN YOU THINK OF A BETTER PLACE?
A BOOKCASE, A FIREPLACE, A DUMB...
...WAITER? FIRST PLACES I WOULD LOOK.
I DIDN'T SEE YOU PRESS A BUTTON.
ONE OF THE WO
I SAID OPENED
WHICH ONE...
HUMOR?
WHAT? UNDERWORLDERS?
YOU KNOW JAMROTH BOK HERE, AND HIS "SIDEKICK" PRIMUS... WHO WON'T TELL ME HIS REAL NAME.
THEY... AND I, WILL BE GOING TO THE UNDERWORLD.
WHAT? AND WHAT OF ME?

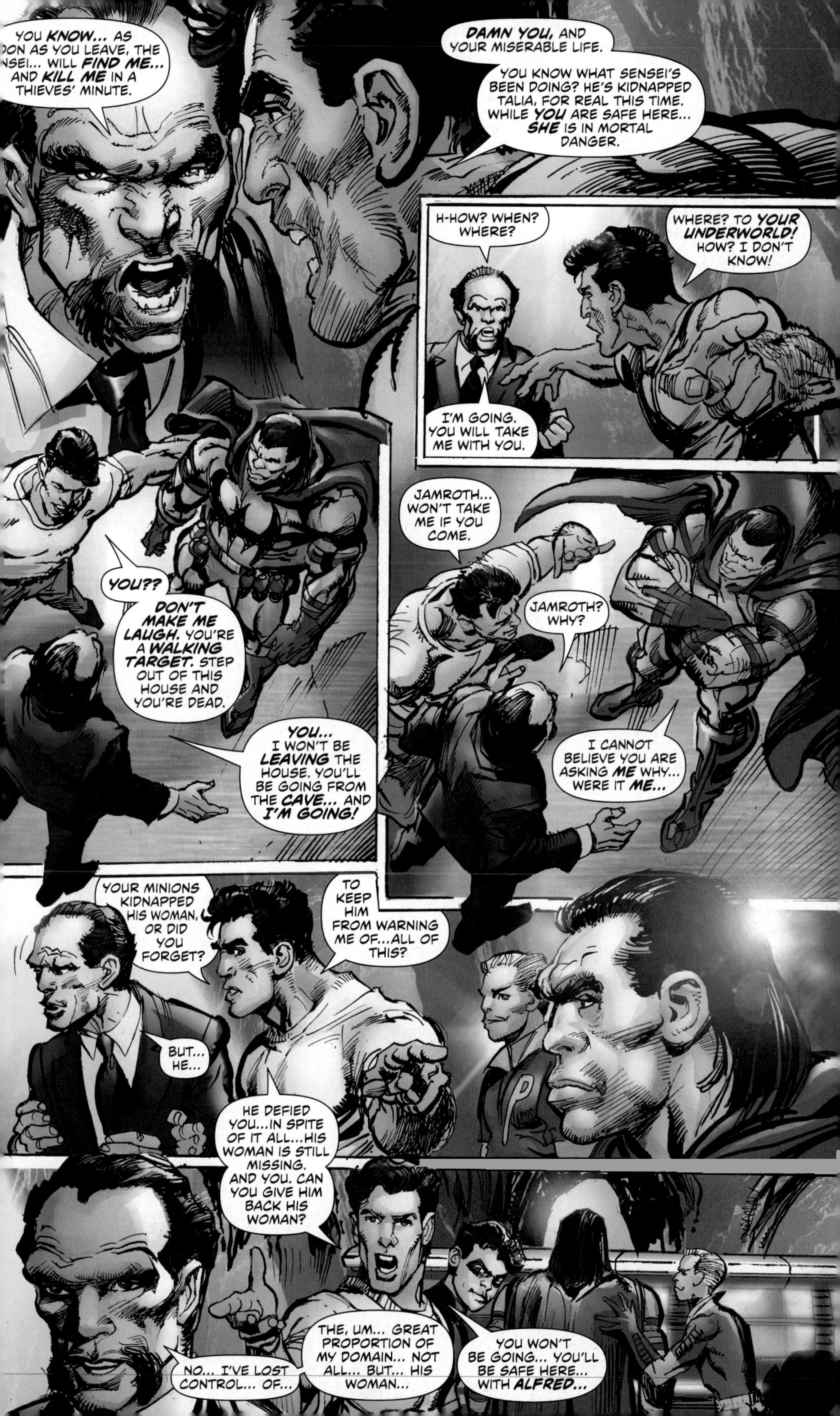
YOU KNOW... AS
OON AS YOU LEAVE, THE
NSEI... WILL FIND ME...
AND KILL ME IN A
THIEVES' MINUTE.
DAMN YOU, AND YOUR MISERABLE LIFE.
YOU KNOW WHAT SENSEI'S BEEN DOING? HE'S KIDNAPPED TALIA, FOR REAL THIS TIME. WHILE YOU ARE SAFE HERE... SHE IS IN MORTAL DANGER.
H-HOW? WHEN? WHERE?
WHERE? TO YOUR UNDERWORLD! HOW? I DON'T KNOW!
I'M GOING. YOU WILL TAKE ME WITH YOU.
YOU?? DON'T MAKE ME LAUGH. YOU'RE A WALKING TARGET. STEP OUT OF THIS HOUSE AND YOU'RE DEAD.
YOU... I WON'T BE LEAVING THE HOUSE. YOU'LL BE GOING FROM THE CAVE... AND I'M GOING!
JAMROTH... WON'T TAKE ME IF YOU COME.
JAMROTH? WHY?
I CANNOT BELIEVE YOU ARE ASKING ME WHY... WERE IT ME...
YOUR MINIONS KIDNAPPED HIS WOMAN, OR DID YOU FORGET?
TO KEEP HIM FROM WARNING ME OF...ALL OF THIS?
BUT... HE...
HE DEFIED YOU...IN SPITE OF IT ALL...HIS WOMAN IS STILL MISSING. AND YOU. CAN YOU GIVE HIM BACK HIS WOMAN?
NO... I'VE LOST CONTROL... OF...
THE, UM... GREAT PROPORTION OF MY DOMAIN... NOT ALL... BUT... HIS WOMAN...
YOU WON'T BE GOING... YOU'LL BE SAFE HERE... WITH ALFRED...

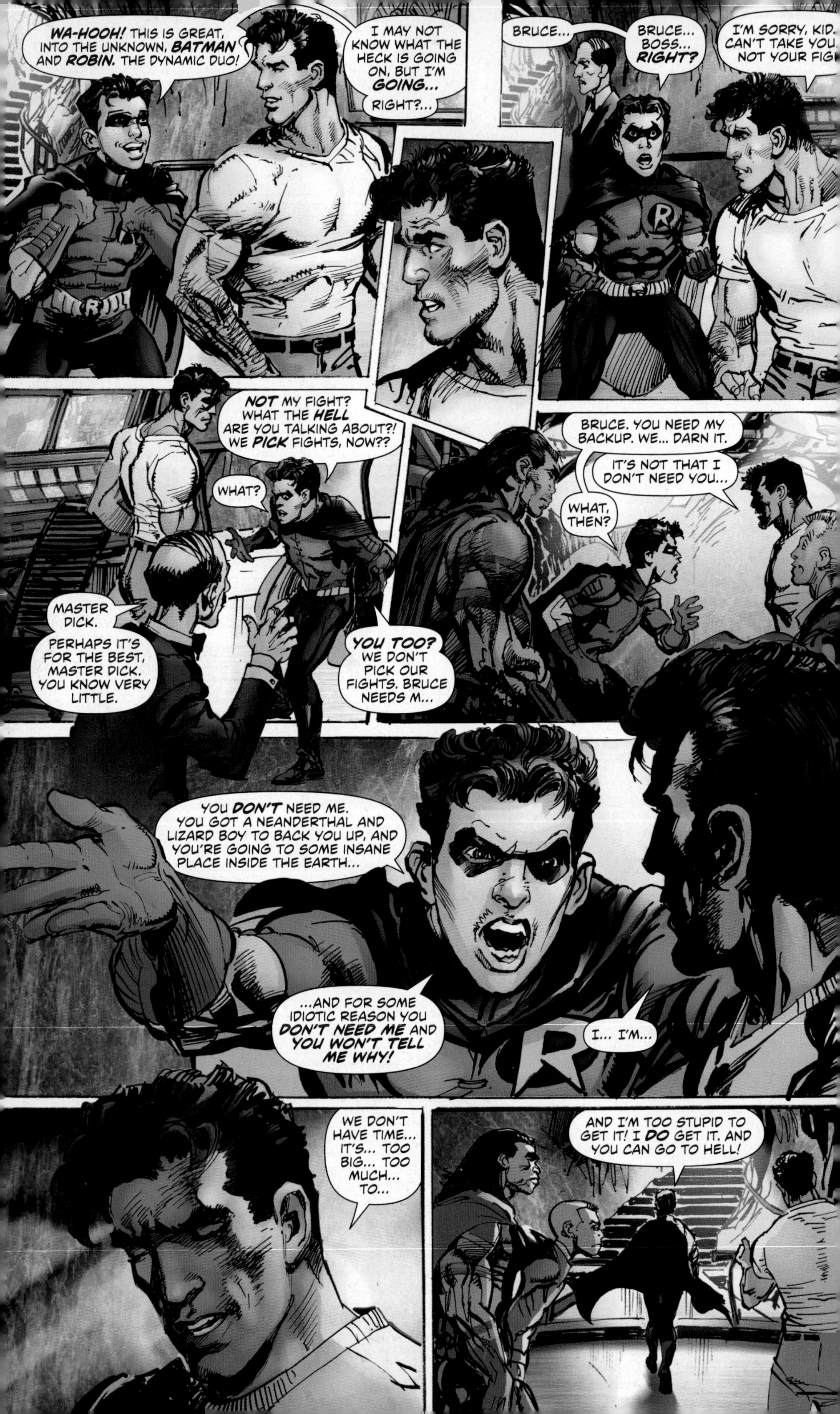
WA-HOOH! THIS IS GREAT, INTO THE UNKNOWN, BATMAN AND ROBIN. THE DYNAMIC DUO!
I MAY NOT KNOW WHAT THE HECK IS GOING ON, BUT I'M GOING...
RIGHT?...
BRUCE...
BRUCE... BOSS... RIGHT?
I'M SORRY, KID. CAN'T TAKE YOU. NOT YOUR FIG
NOT MY FIGHT? WHAT THE HELL ARE YOU TALKING ABOUT?! WE PICK FIGHTS, NOW??
WHAT?
MASTER DICK.
PERHAPS IT'S FOR THE BEST, MASTER DICK. YOU KNOW VERY LITTLE.
YOU TOO? WE DON'T PICK OUR FIGHTS. BRUCE NEEDS M...
BRUCE. YOU NEED MY BACKUP. WE... DARN IT.
IT'S NOT THAT I DON'T NEED YOU...
WHAT, THEN?
YOU DON'T NEED ME. YOU GOT A NEANDERTHAL AND LIZARD BOY TO BACK YOU UP, AND YOU'RE GOING TO SOME INSANE PLACE INSIDE THE EARTH...
...AND FOR SOME IDIOTIC REASON YOU DON'T NEED ME AND YOU WON'T TELL ME WHY!
I... I'M...
WE DON'T HAVE TIME... IT'S... TOO BIG... TOO MUCH... TO...
AND I'M TOO STUPID TO GET IT! I DO GET IT. AND YOU CAN GO TO HELL!

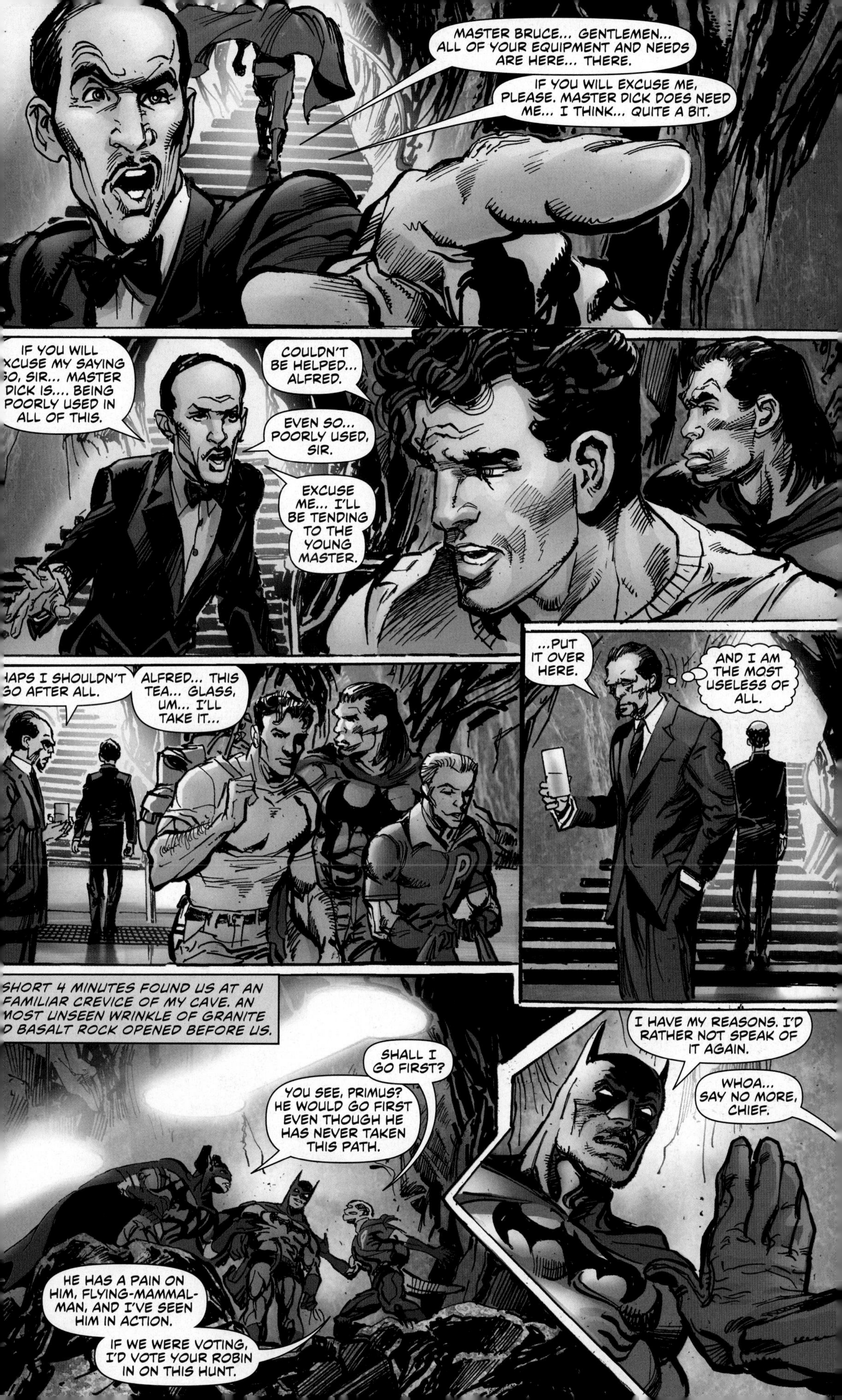
MASTER BRUCE... GENTLEMEN... ALL OF YOUR EQUIPMENT AND NEEDS ARE HERE... THERE.
IF YOU WILL EXCUSE ME, PLEASE. MASTER DICK DOES NEED ME... I THINK... QUITE A BIT.
IF YOU WILL XCUSE MY SAYING SO, SIR... MASTER DICK IS.... BEING POORLY USED IN ALL OF THIS.
COULDN'T BE HELPED... ALFRED.
EVEN SO... POORLY USED, SIR.
EXCUSE ME... I'LL BE TENDING TO THE YOUNG MASTER.
HAPS I SHOULDN'T GO AFTER ALL.
ALFRED... THIS TEA... GLASS, UM... I'LL TAKE IT...
...PUT IT OVER HERE.
AND I AM THE MOST USELESS OF ALL.
SHORT 4 MINUTES FOUND US AT AN FAMILIAR CREVICE OF MY CAVE. AN MOST UNSEEN WRINKLE OF GRANITE D BASALT ROCK OPENED BEFORE US.
SHALL I GO FIRST?
YOU SEE, PRIMUS? HE WOULD GO FIRST EVEN THOUGH HE HAS NEVER TAKEN THIS PATH.
HE HAS A PAIN ON HIM, FLYING-MAMMAL-MAN, AND I'VE SEEN HIM IN ACTION.
IF WE WERE VOTING, I'D VOTE YOUR ROBIN IN ON THIS HUNT.
I HAVE MY REASONS. I'D RATHER NOT SPEAK OF IT AGAIN.
WHOA... SAY NO MORE, CHIEF.

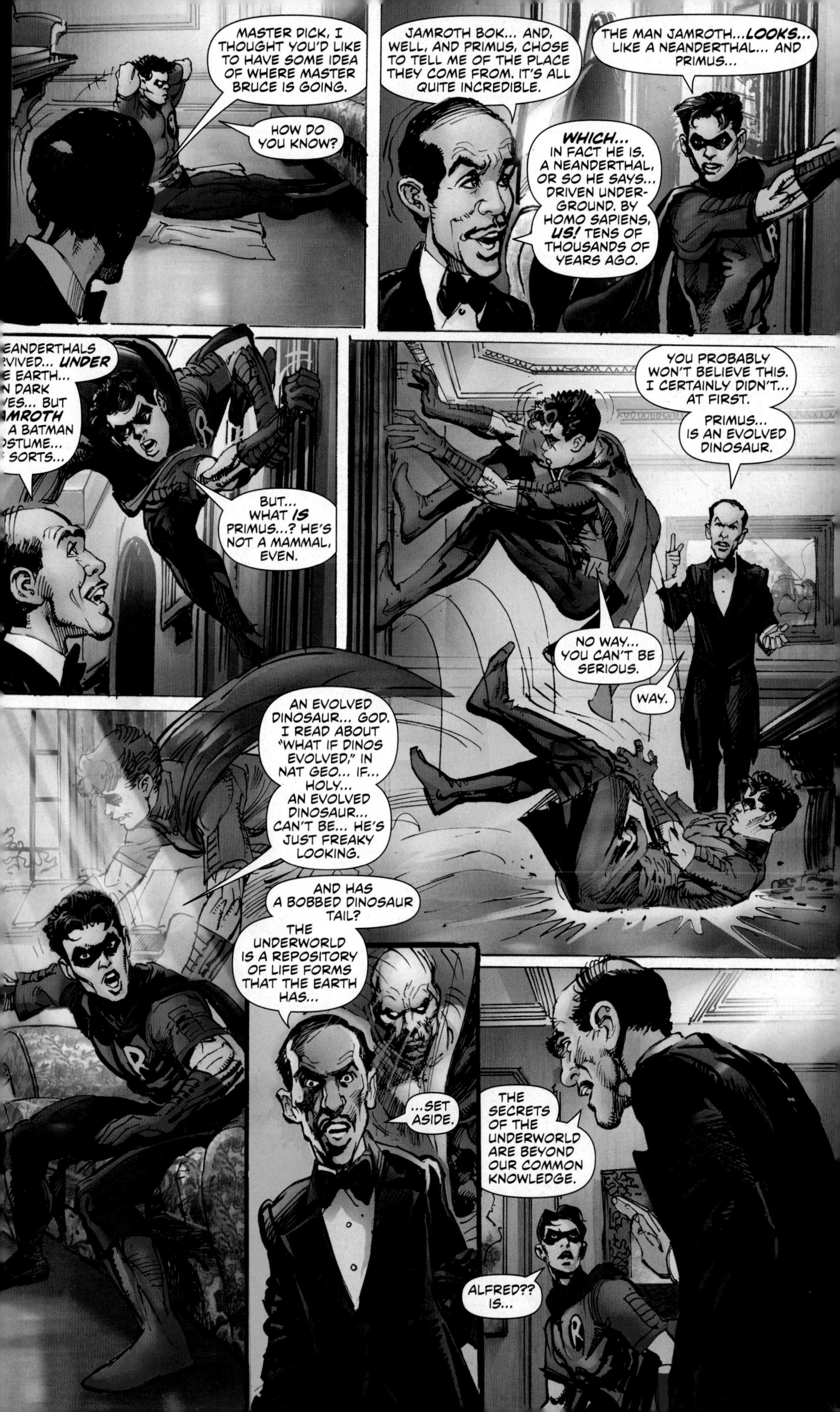
MASTER DICK, I THOUGHT YOU'D LIKE TO HAVE SOME IDEA OF WHERE MASTER BRUCE IS GOING.
HOW DO YOU KNOW?
JAMROTH BOK... AND, WELL, AND PRIMUS, CHOSE TO TELL ME OF THE PLACE THEY COME FROM. IT'S ALL QUITE INCREDIBLE.
THE MAN JAMROTH...LOOKS... LIKE A NEANDERTHAL... AND PRIMUS...
WHICH... IN FACT HE IS. A NEANDERTHAL, OR SO HE SAYS... DRIVEN UNDERGROUND. BY HOMO SAPIENS, US! TENS OF THOUSANDS OF YEARS AGO.
EANDERTHALS RVIVED... UNDER E EARTH... N DARK VES... BUT AMROTH A BATMAN OSTUME... SORTS...
BUT... WHAT IS PRIMUS...? HE'S NOT A MAMMAL, EVEN.
YOU PROBABLY WON'T BELIEVE THIS. I CERTAINLY DIDN'T... AT FIRST.
PRIMUS... IS AN EVOLVED DINOSAUR.
NO WAY... YOU CAN'T BE SERIOUS.
WAY.
AN EVOLVED DINOSAUR... GOD. I READ ABOUT "WHAT IF DINOS EVOLVED," IN NAT GEO... IF... HOLY... AN EVOLVED DINOSAUR... CAN'T BE... HE'S JUST FREAKY LOOKING.
AND HAS A BOBBED DINOSAUR TAIL?
THE UNDERWORLD IS A REPOSITORY OF LIFE FORMS THAT THE EARTH HAS...
...SET ASIDE.
THE SECRETS OF THE UNDERWORLD ARE BEYOND OUR COMMON KNOWLEDGE.
ALFRED?? IS...

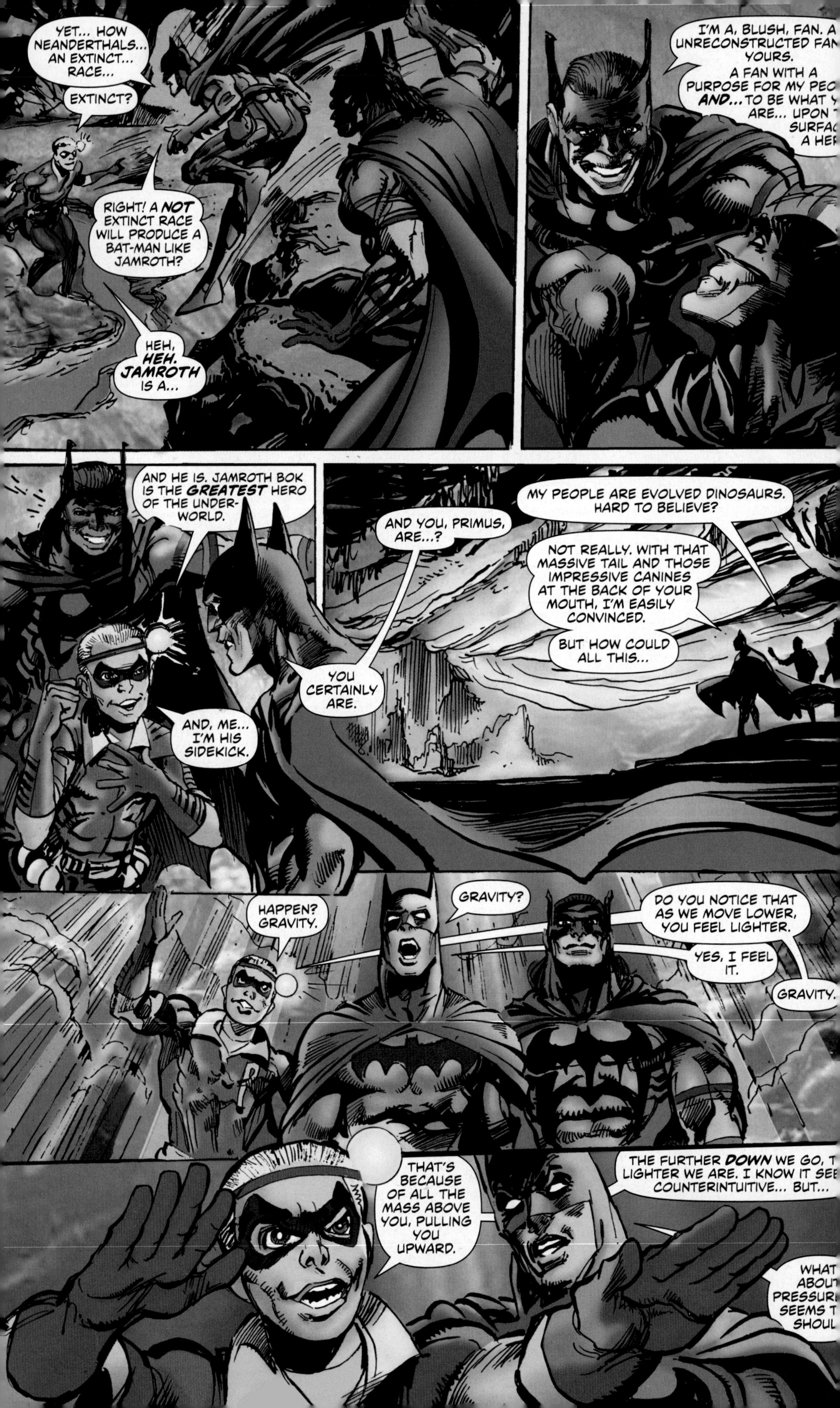

YET... HOW NEANDERTHALS... AN EXTINCT... RACE...
EXTINCT?
RIGHT! A NOT EXTINCT RACE WILL PRODUCE A BAT-MAN LIKE JAMROTH?
HEH, HEH. JAMROTH IS A...
I'M A, BLUSH, FAN. A UNRECONSTRUCTED FAN YOURS.
A FAN WITH A PURPOSE FOR MY PEO AND... TO BE WHAT Y ARE... UPON T SURFAC A HER
AND HE IS. JAMROTH BOK IS THE GREATEST HERO OF THE UNDER-WORLD.
AND YOU, PRIMUS, ARE...?
YOU CERTAINLY ARE.
AND, ME... I'M HIS SIDEKICK.
MY PEOPLE ARE EVOLVED DINOSAURS. HARD TO BELIEVE?
NOT REALLY. WITH THAT MASSIVE TAIL AND THOSE IMPRESSIVE CANINES AT THE BACK OF YOUR MOUTH, I'M EASILY CONVINCED.
BUT HOW COULD ALL THIS...
HAPPEN? GRAVITY.
GRAVITY?
DO YOU NOTICE THAT AS WE MOVE LOWER, YOU FEEL LIGHTER.
YES, I FEEL IT.
GRAVITY.
THAT'S BECAUSE OF ALL THE MASS ABOVE YOU, PULLING YOU UPWARD.
THE FURTHER DOWN WE GO, T LIGHTER WE ARE. I KNOW IT SEE COUNTERINTUITIVE... BUT...
WHAT ABOUT PRESSUR SEEMS T SHOUL

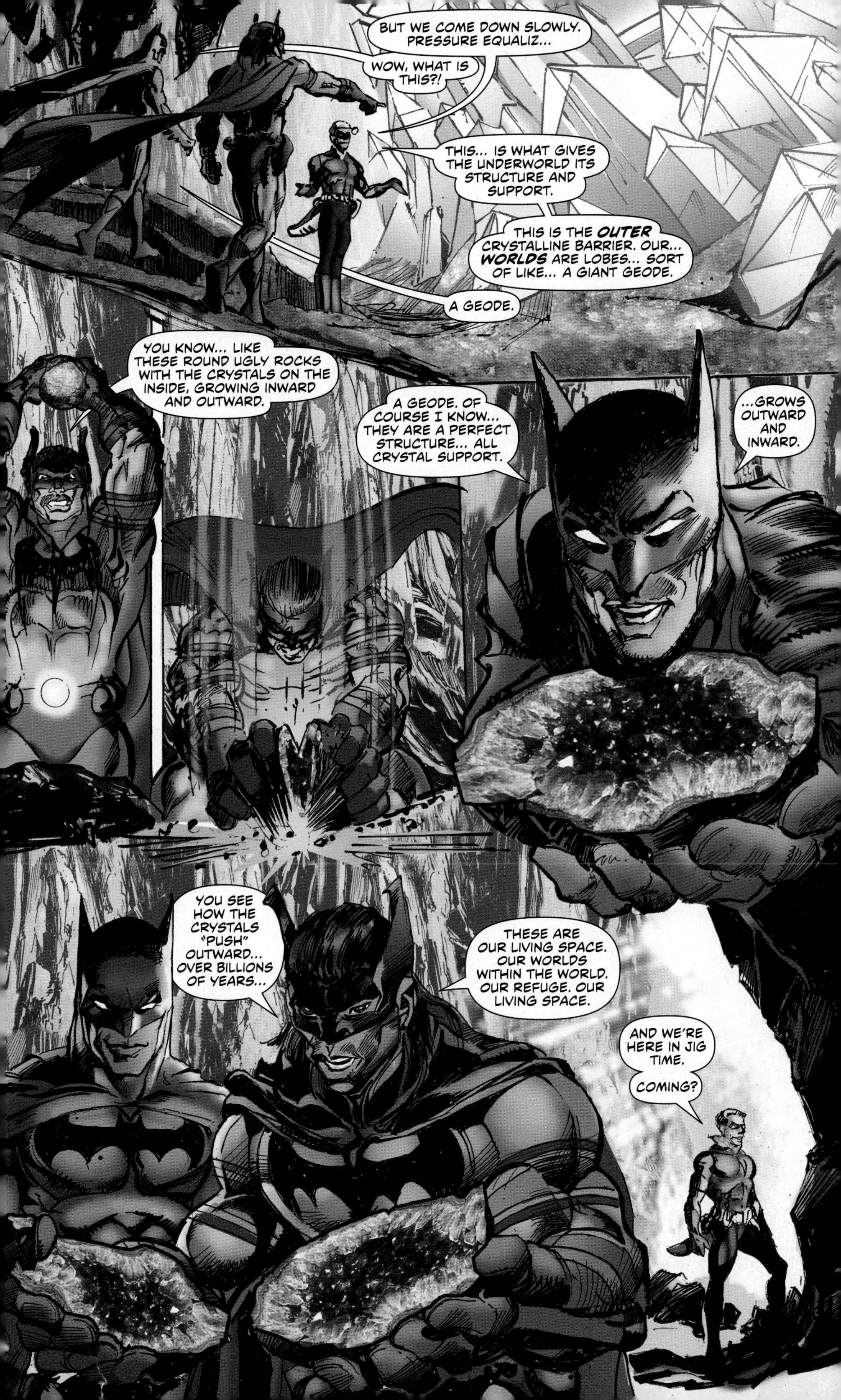
BUT WE COME DOWN SLOWLY. PRESSURE EQUALIZ...
WOW, WHAT IS THIS?!
THIS... IS WHAT GIVES THE UNDERWORLD ITS STRUCTURE AND SUPPORT.
THIS IS THE ***OUTER*** CRYSTALLINE BARRIER. OUR... ***WORLDS*** ARE LOBES... SORT OF LIKE... A GIANT GEODE.
A GEODE.
YOU KNOW... LIKE THESE ROUND UGLY ROCKS WITH THE CRYSTALS ON THE INSIDE, GROWING INWARD AND OUTWARD.
A GEODE. OF COURSE I KNOW... THEY ARE A PERFECT STRUCTURE... ALL CRYSTAL SUPPORT.
...GROWS OUTWARD AND INWARD.
YOU SEE HOW THE CRYSTALS "PUSH" OUTWARD... OVER BILLIONS OF YEARS...
THESE ARE OUR LIVING SPACE. OUR WORLDS WITHIN THE WORLD. OUR REFUGE. OUR LIVING SPACE.
AND WE'RE HERE IN JIG TIME.
COMING?

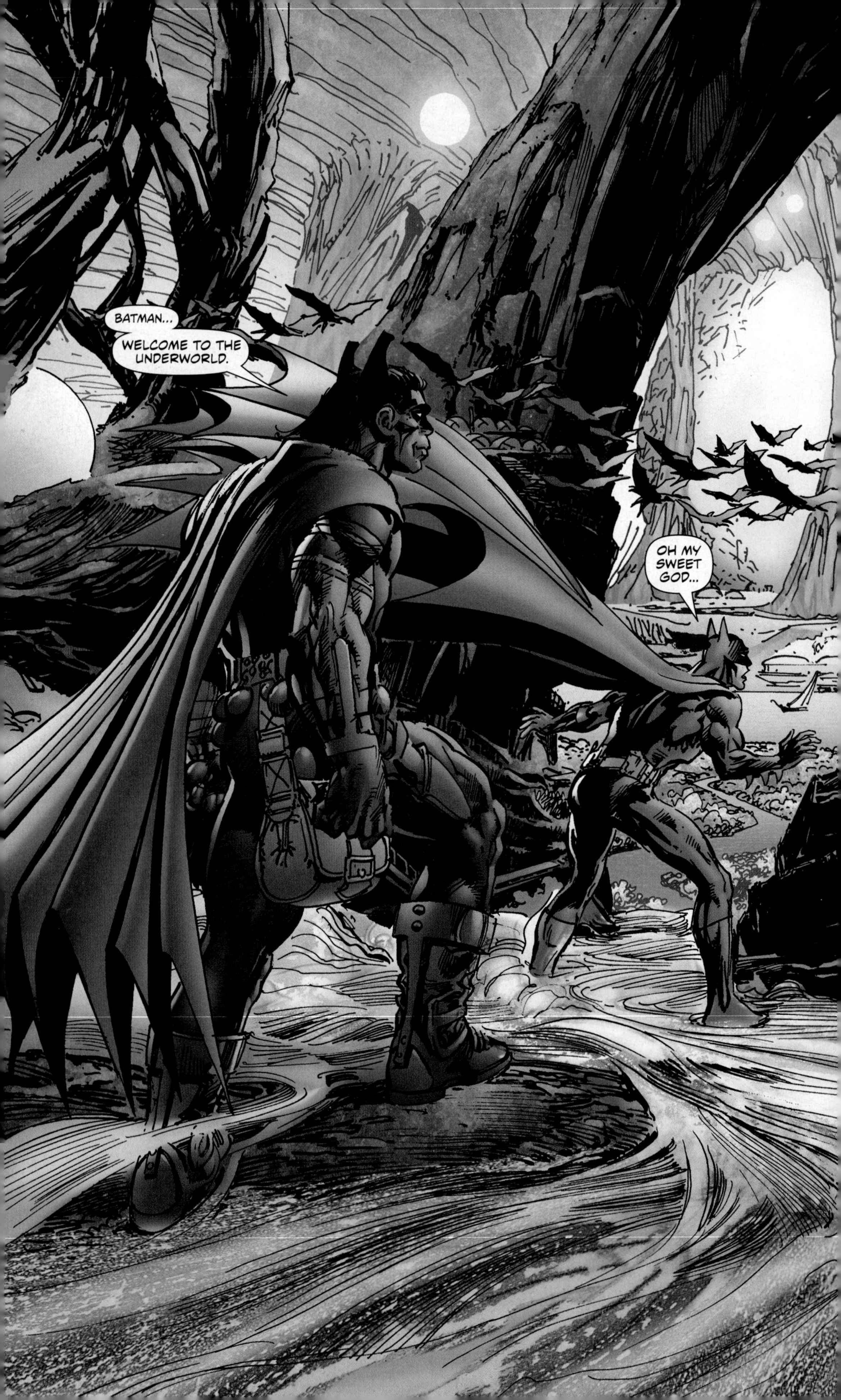
BATMAN...
WELCOME TO THE UNDERWORLD.
OH MY SWEET GOD...

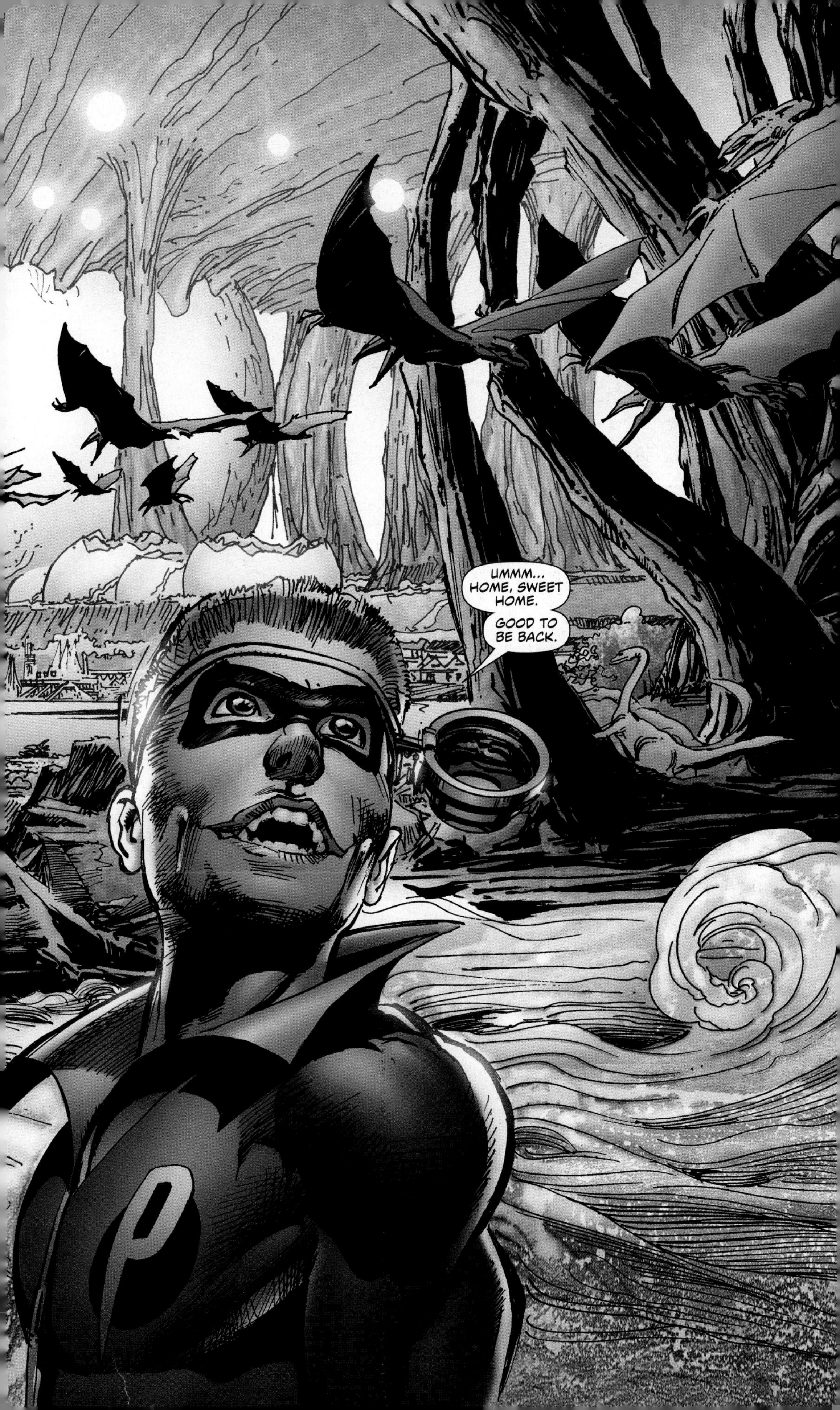
UMMM... HOME, SWEET HOME.
GOOD TO BE BACK.

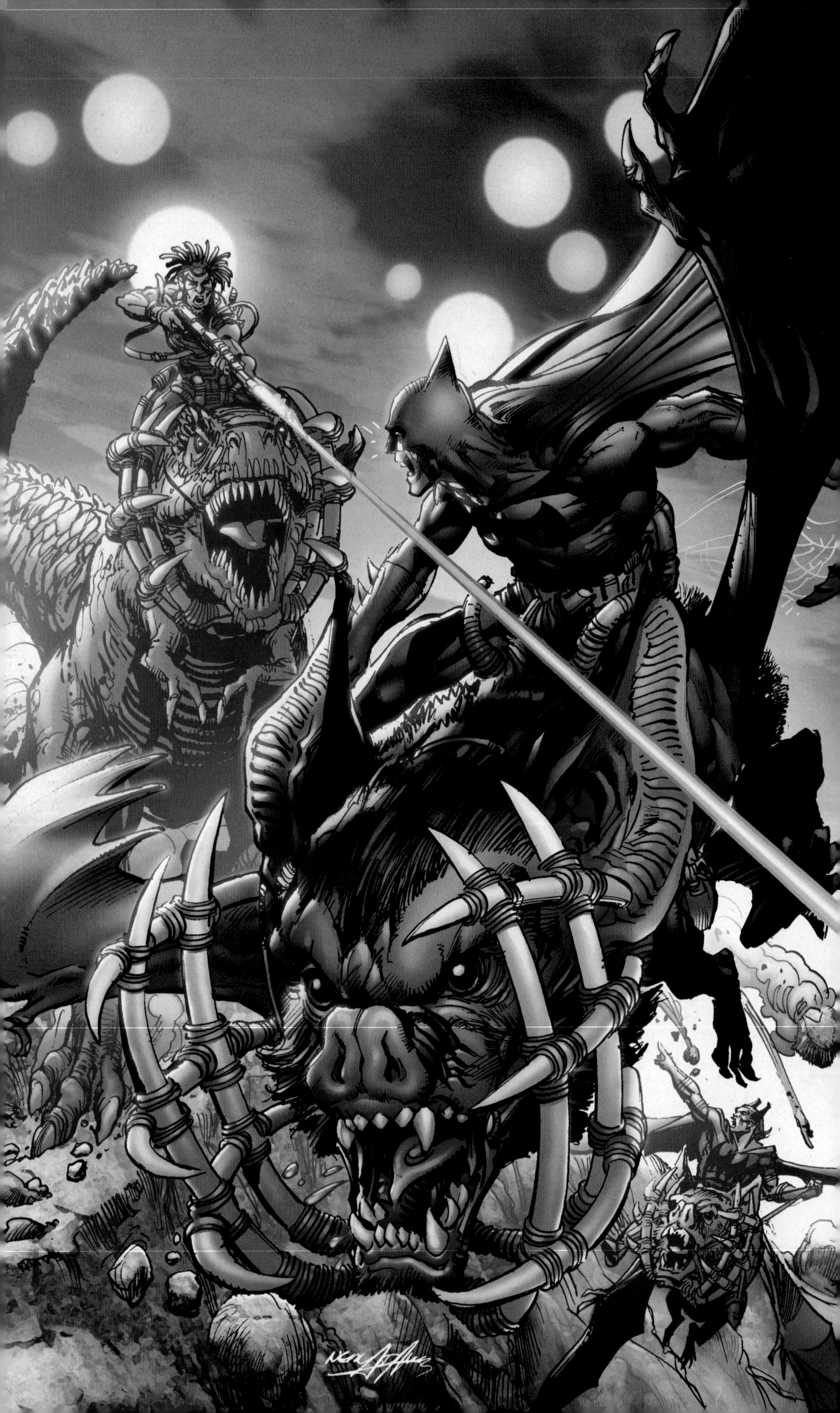

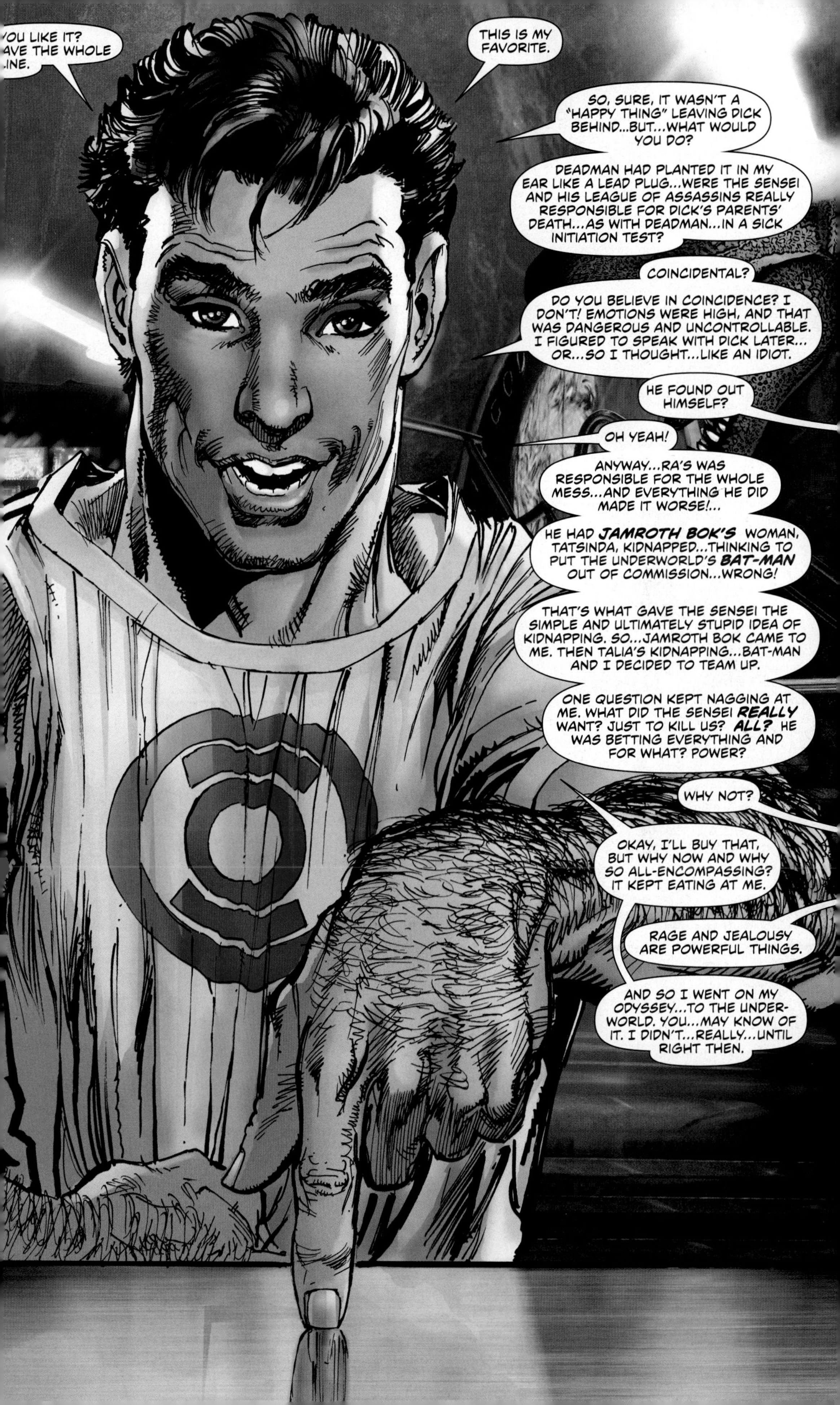
YOU LIKE IT? HAVE THE WHOLE LINE.
THIS IS MY FAVORITE.
SO, SURE, IT WASN'T A "HAPPY THING" LEAVING DICK BEHIND...BUT...WHAT WOULD YOU DO?
DEADMAN HAD PLANTED IT IN MY EAR LIKE A LEAD PLUG...WERE THE SENSEI AND HIS LEAGUE OF ASSASSINS REALLY RESPONSIBLE FOR DICK'S PARENTS' DEATH...AS WITH DEADMAN...IN A SICK INITIATION TEST?
COINCIDENTAL?
DO YOU BELIEVE IN COINCIDENCE? I DON'T! EMOTIONS WERE HIGH, AND THAT WAS DANGEROUS AND UNCONTROLLABLE. I FIGURED TO SPEAK WITH DICK LATER... OR...SO I THOUGHT...LIKE AN IDIOT.
HE FOUND OUT HIMSELF?
OH YEAH!
ANYWAY...RA'S WAS RESPONSIBLE FOR THE WHOLE MESS...AND EVERYTHING HE DID MADE IT WORSE!...
HE HAD ***JAMROTH BOK'S*** WOMAN, TATSINDA, KIDNAPPED...THINKING TO PUT THE UNDERWORLD'S ***BAT-MAN*** OUT OF COMMISSION...WRONG!
THAT'S WHAT GAVE THE SENSEI THE SIMPLE AND ULTIMATELY STUPID IDEA OF KIDNAPPING. SO...JAMROTH BOK CAME TO ME. THEN TALIA'S KIDNAPPING...BAT-MAN AND I DECIDED TO TEAM UP.
ONE QUESTION KEPT NAGGING AT ME. WHAT DID THE SENSEI ***REALLY*** WANT? JUST TO KILL US? ***ALL?*** HE WAS BETTING EVERYTHING AND FOR WHAT? POWER?
WHY NOT?
OKAY, I'LL BUY THAT, BUT WHY NOW AND WHY SO ALL-ENCOMPASSING? IT KEPT EATING AT ME.
RAGE AND JEALOUSY ARE POWERFUL THINGS.
AND SO I WENT ON MY ODYSSEY...TO THE UNDER-WORLD. YOU...MAY KNOW OF IT. I DIDN'T...REALLY...UNTIL RIGHT THEN.

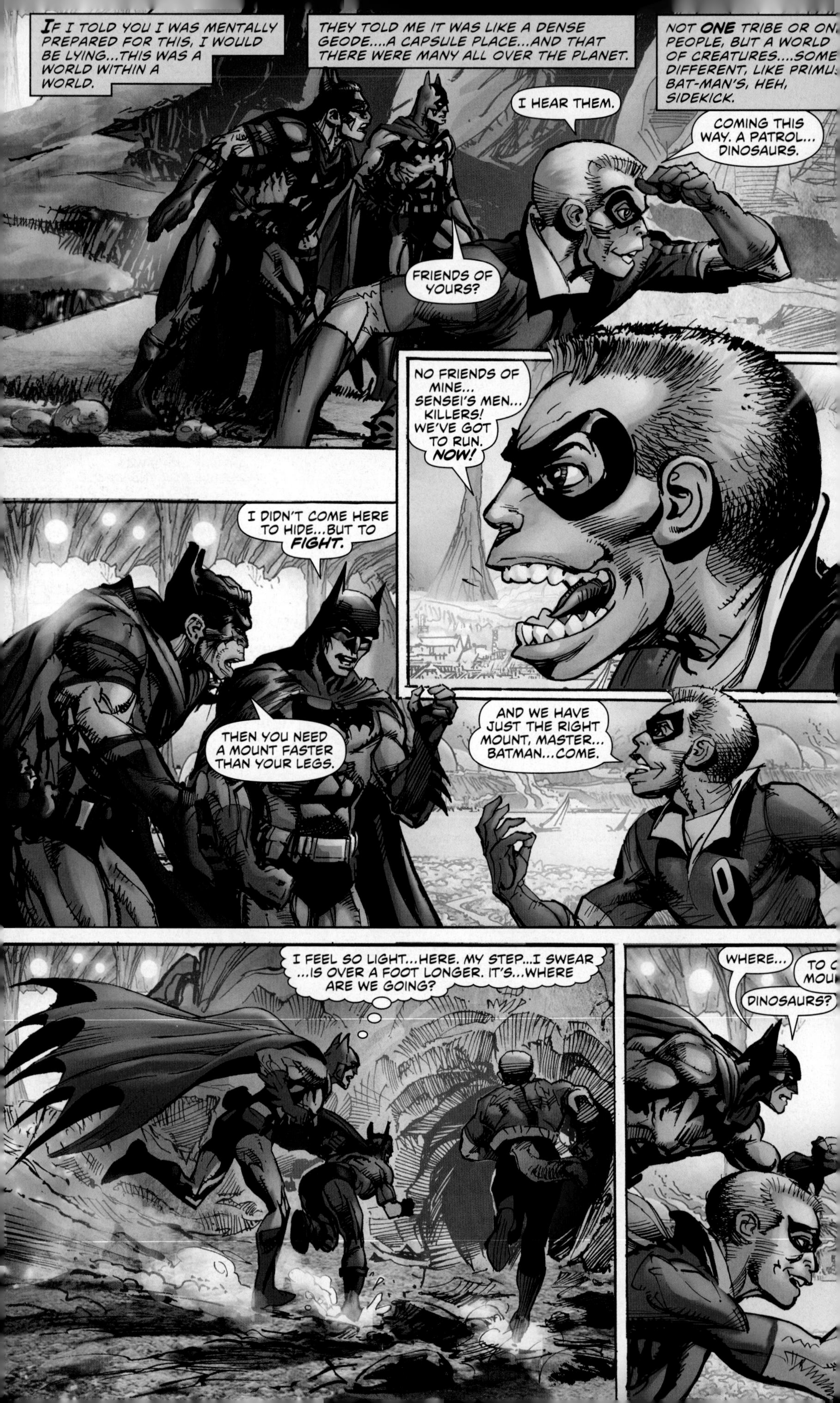
IF I TOLD YOU I WAS MENTALLY PREPARED FOR THIS, I WOULD BE LYING...THIS WAS A WORLD WITHIN A WORLD.
THEY TOLD ME IT WAS LIKE A DENSE GEODE....A CAPSULE PLACE...AND THAT THERE WERE MANY ALL OVER THE PLANET.
NOT ONE TRIBE OR ON PEOPLE, BUT A WORLD OF CREATURES....SOME DIFFERENT, LIKE PRIMU BAT-MAN'S, HEH, SIDEKICK.
I HEAR THEM.
COMING THIS WAY. A PATROL... DINOSAURS.
FRIENDS OF YOURS?
NO FRIENDS OF MINE... SENSEI'S MEN... KILLERS! WE'VE GOT TO RUN. NOW!
I DIDN'T COME HERE TO HIDE...BUT TO FIGHT.
THEN YOU NEED A MOUNT FASTER THAN YOUR LEGS.
AND WE HAVE JUST THE RIGHT MOUNT, MASTER... BATMAN...COME.
I FEEL SO LIGHT...HERE. MY STEP...I SWEAR ...IS OVER A FOOT LONGER. IT'S...WHERE ARE WE GOING?
WHERE...
DINOSAURS?

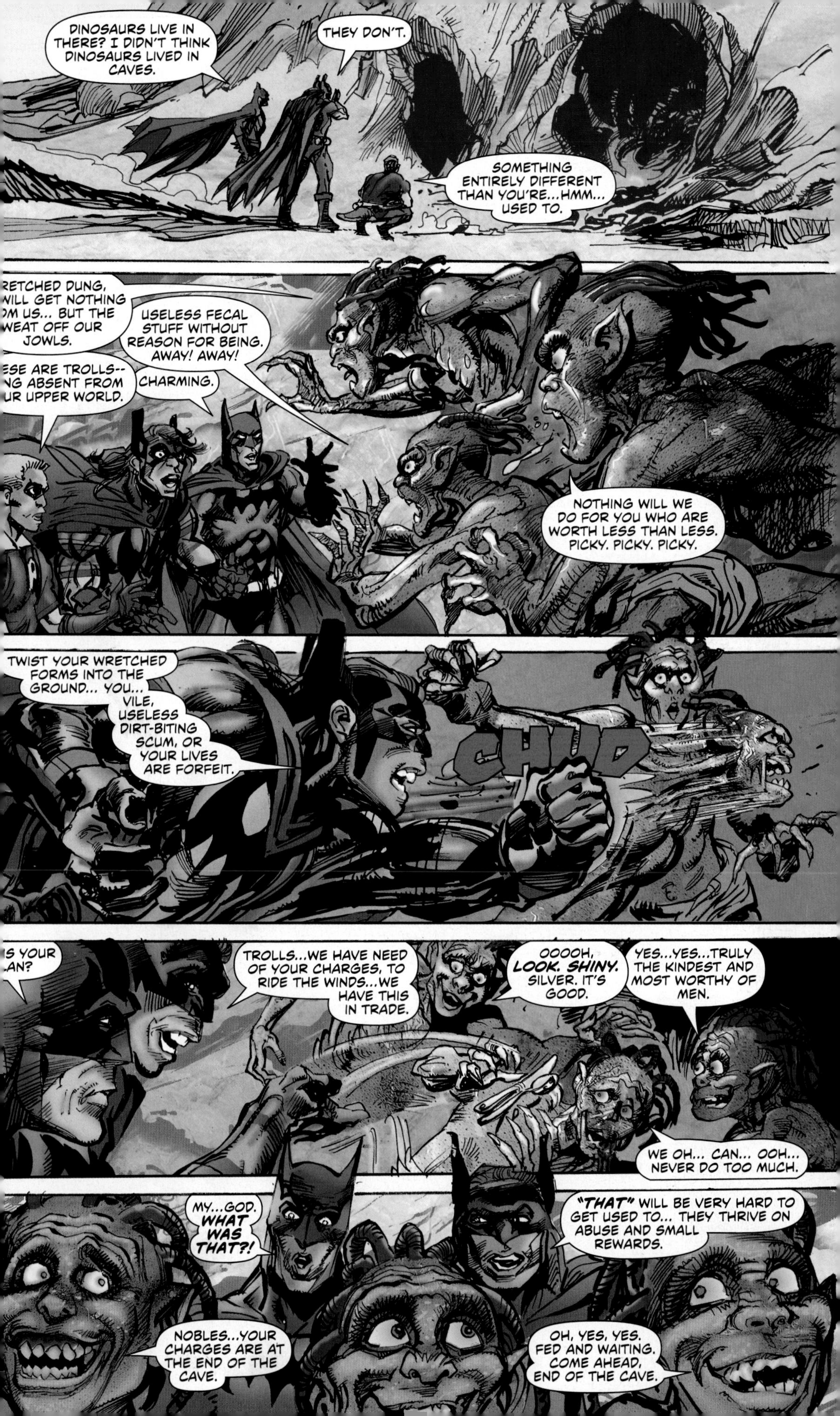
DINOSAURS LIVE IN THERE? I DIDN'T THINK DINOSAURS LIVED IN CAVES.
THEY DON'T.
SOMETHING ENTIRELY DIFFERENT THAN YOU'RE...HMM... USED TO.
RETCHED DUNG, WILL GET NOTHING OM US... BUT THE WEAT OFF OUR JOWLS.
USELESS FECAL STUFF WITHOUT REASON FOR BEING. AWAY! AWAY!
ESE ARE TROLLS-- NG ABSENT FROM UR UPPER WORLD.
CHARMING.
NOTHING WILL WE DO FOR YOU WHO ARE WORTH LESS THAN LESS. PICKY. PICKY. PICKY.
TWIST YOUR WRETCHED FORMS INTO THE GROUND... YOU... VILE, USELESS DIRT-BITING SCUM, OR YOUR LIVES ARE FORFEIT.
CHUD
S YOUR AN?
TROLLS...WE HAVE NEED OF YOUR CHARGES, TO RIDE THE WINDS...WE HAVE THIS IN TRADE.
OOOOH, **LOOK. SHINY.** SILVER. IT'S GOOD.
YES...YES...TRULY THE KINDEST AND MOST WORTHY OF MEN.
WE OH... CAN... OOH... NEVER DO TOO MUCH.
MY...GOD. ***WHAT WAS THAT?!***
"THAT" WILL BE VERY HARD TO GET USED TO... THEY THRIVE ON ABUSE AND SMALL REWARDS.
NOBLES...YOUR CHARGES ARE AT THE END OF THE CAVE.
OH, YES, YES. FED AND WAITING. COME AHEAD, END OF THE CAVE.

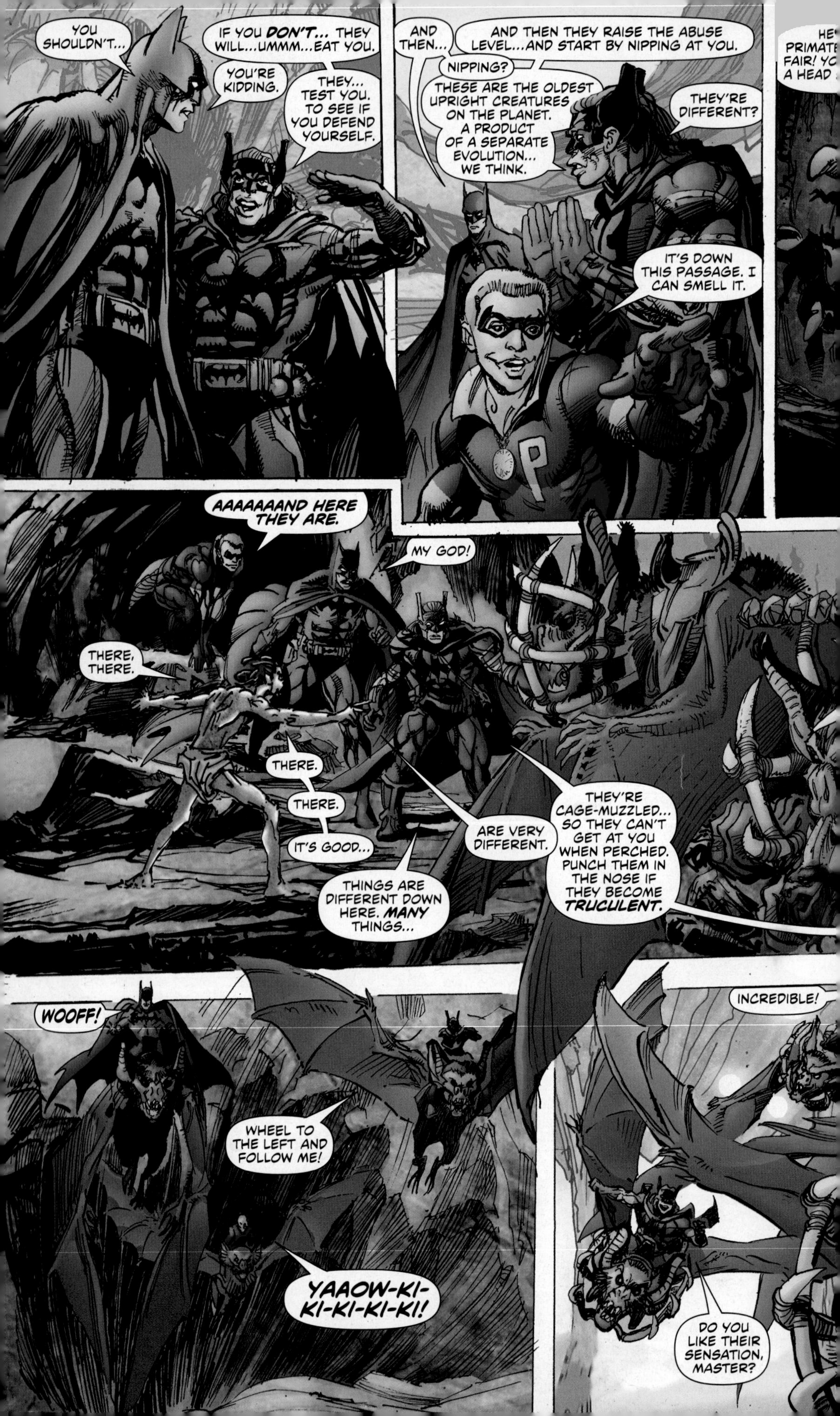
YOU SHOULDN'T...
IF YOU ***DON'T...*** THEY WILL...UMMM...EAT YOU.
YOU'RE KIDDING.
THEY... TEST YOU. TO SEE IF YOU DEFEND YOURSELF.
AND THEN...
AND THEN THEY RAISE THE ABUSE LEVEL...AND START BY NIPPING AT YOU.
NIPPING?
THESE ARE THE OLDEST UPRIGHT CREATURES ON THE PLANET. A PRODUCT OF A SEPARATE EVOLUTION... WE THINK.
THEY'RE DIFFERENT?
IT'S DOWN THIS PASSAGE. I CAN SMELL IT.
AAAAAAAND HERE THEY ARE.
MY GOD!
THERE, THERE.
THERE.
THERE.
IT'S GOOD...
THINGS ARE DIFFERENT DOWN HERE. ***MANY*** THINGS...
ARE VERY DIFFERENT.
THEY'RE CAGE-MUZZLED... SO THEY CAN'T GET AT YOU WHEN PERCHED. PUNCH THEM IN THE NOSE IF THEY BECOME ***TRUCULENT.***
WOOFF!
WHEEL TO THE LEFT AND FOLLOW ME!
YAAOW-KI-KI-KI-KI-KI!
INCREDIBLE!
DO YOU LIKE THEIR SENSATION, MASTER?

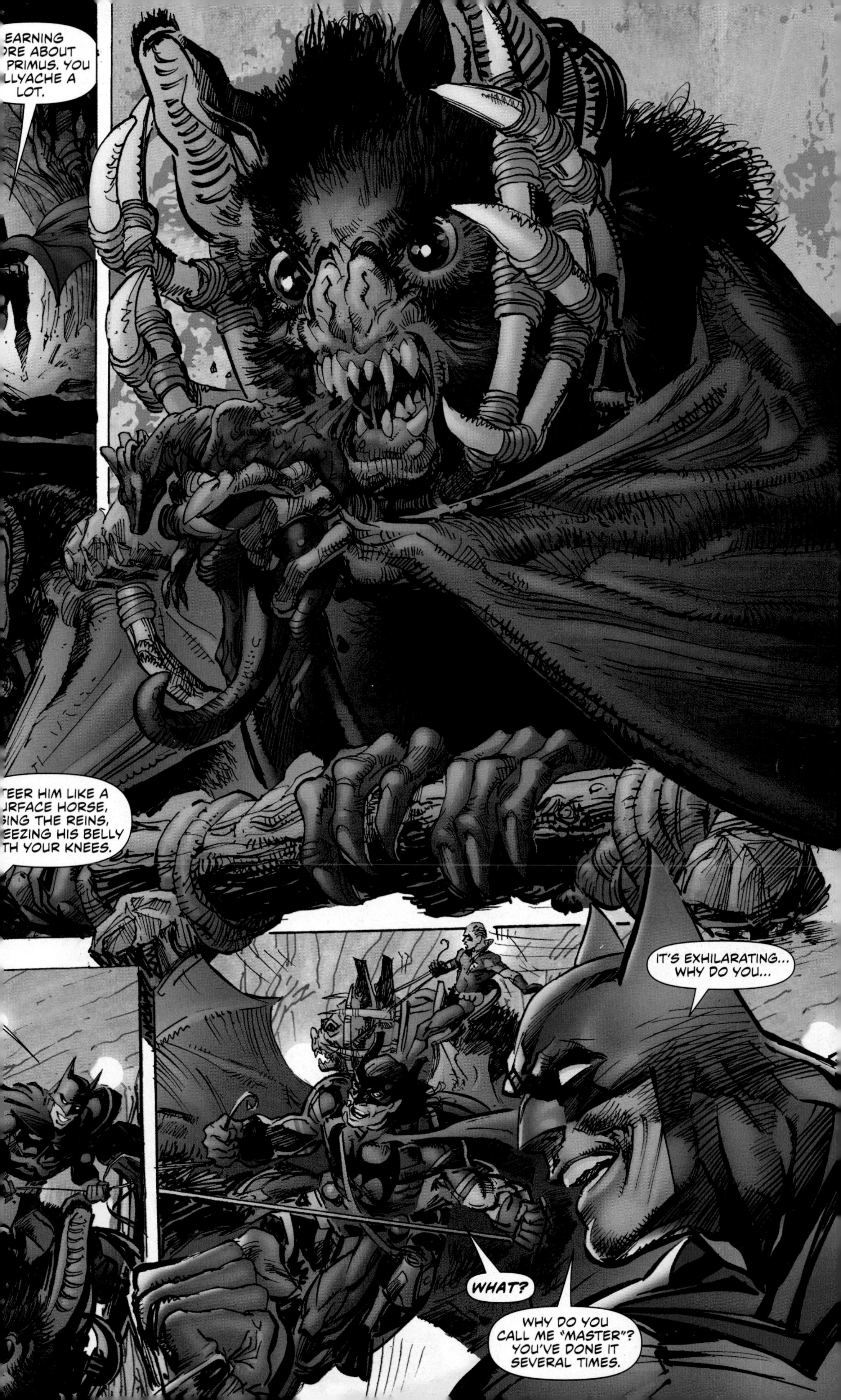
EARNING
ORE ABOUT
PRIMUS. YOU
LLYACHE A
LOT.
TEER HIM LIKE A
URFACE HORSE,
GING THE REINS,
EEZING HIS BELLY
TH YOUR KNEES.
IT'S EXHILARATING...
WHY DO YOU...
WHAT?
WHY DO YOU
CALL ME "MASTER"?
YOU'VE DONE IT
SEVERAL TIMES.

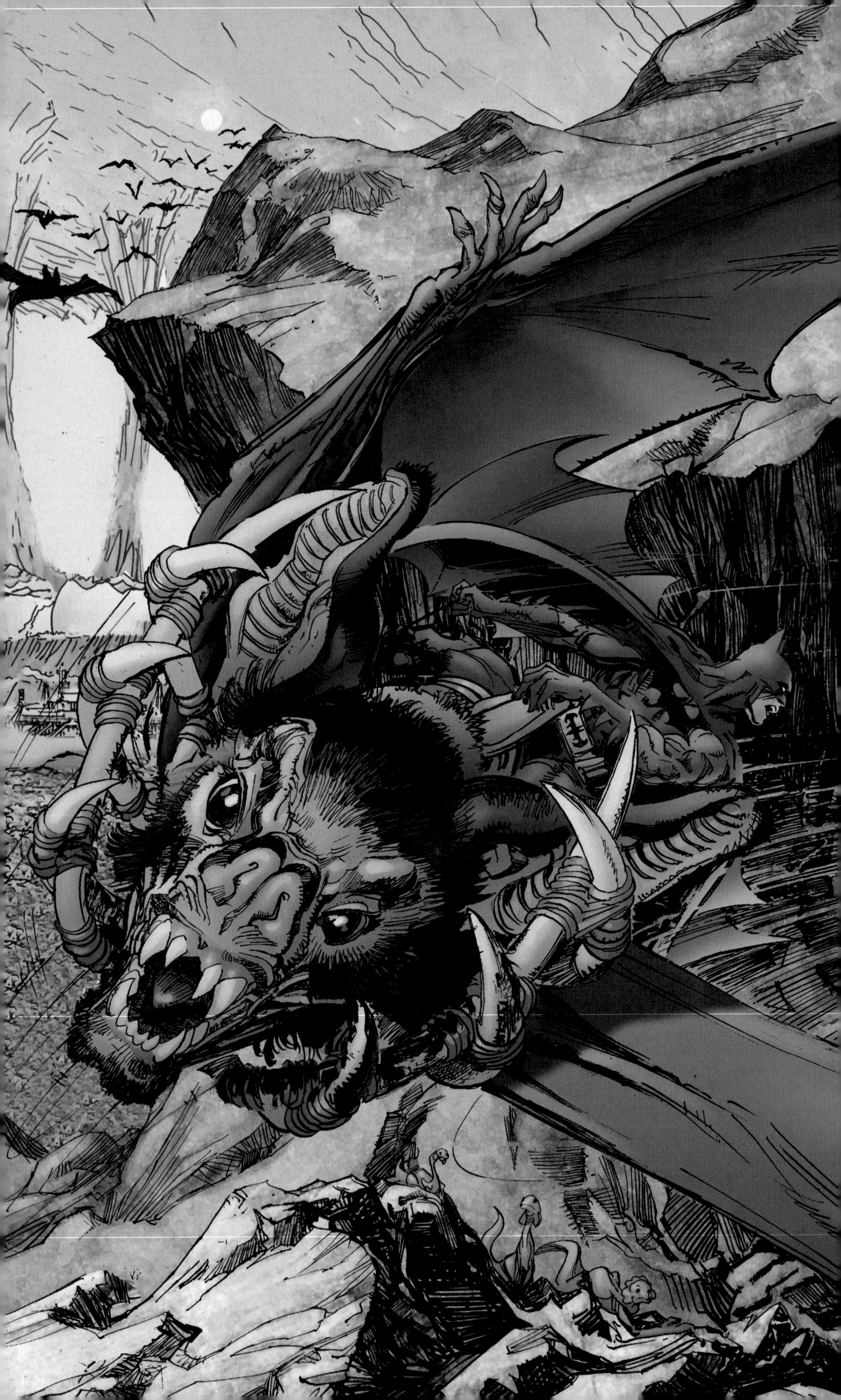

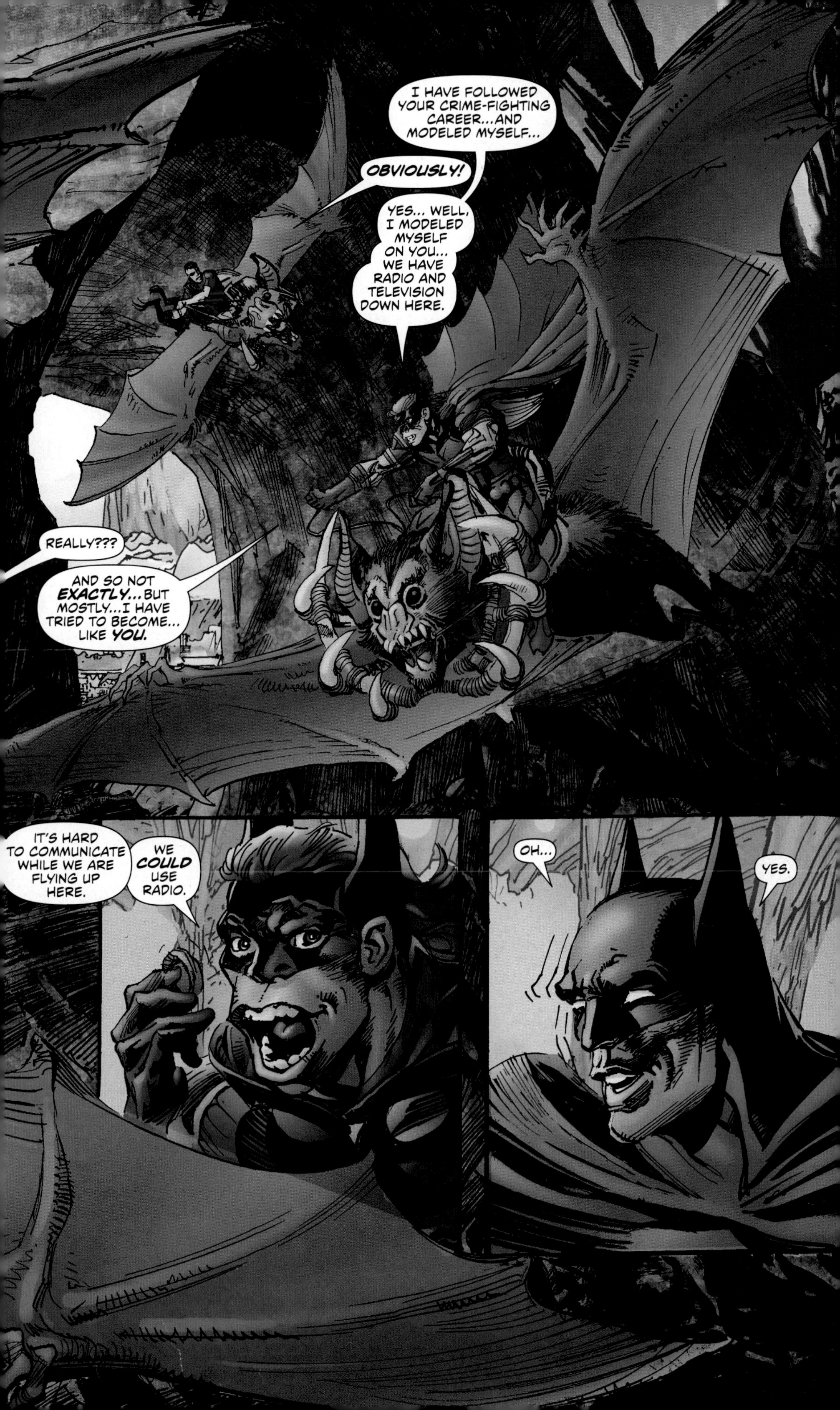
I HAVE FOLLOWED YOUR CRIME-FIGHTING CAREER...AND MODELED MYSELF...
OBVIOUSLY!
YES... WELL, I MODELED MYSELF ON YOU... WE HAVE RADIO AND TELEVISION DOWN HERE.
REALLY???
AND SO NOT EXACTLY...BUT MOSTLY...I HAVE TRIED TO BECOME... LIKE YOU.
IT'S HARD TO COMMUNICATE WHILE WE ARE FLYING UP HERE.
WE COULD USE RADIO.
OH...
YES.

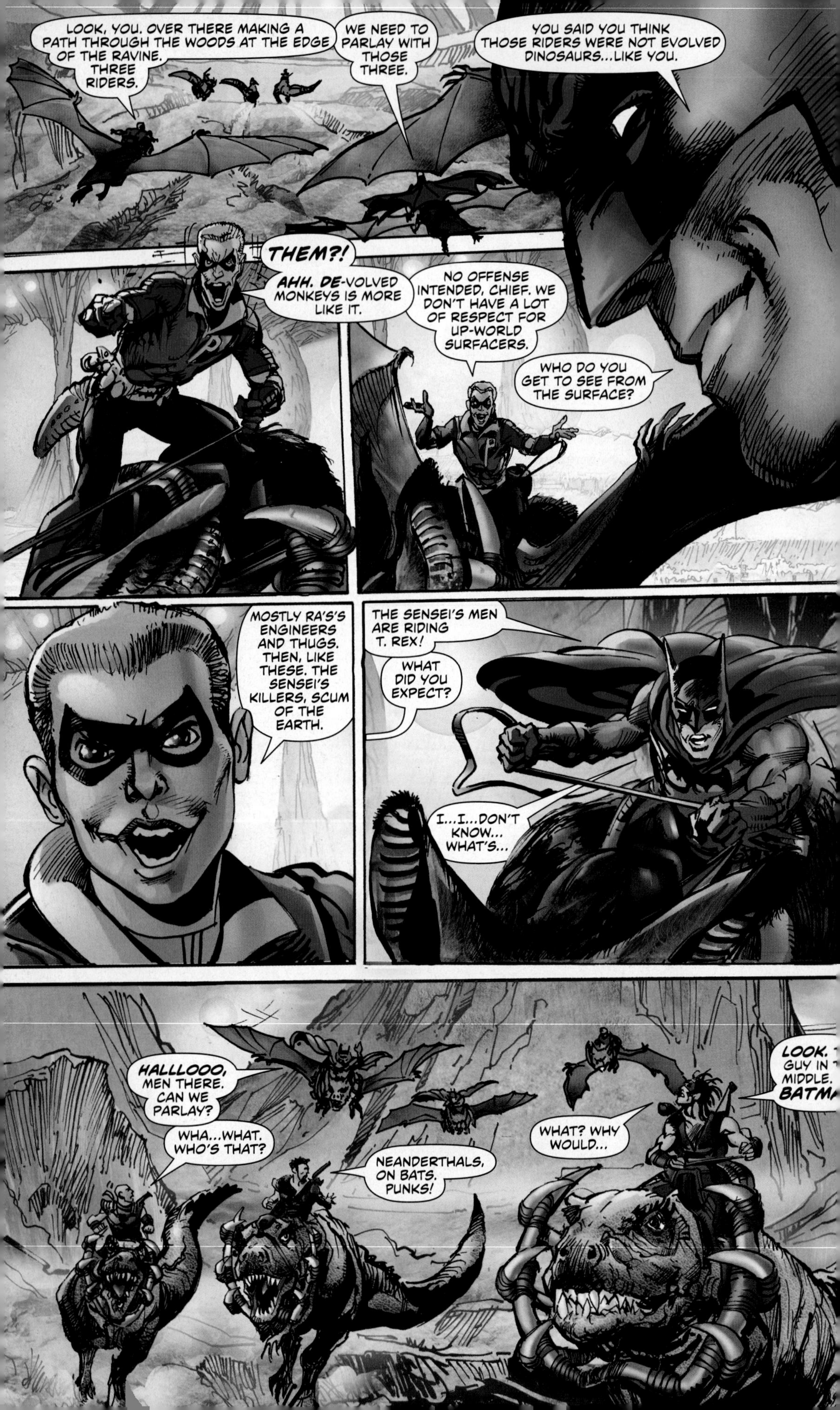
LOOK, YOU. OVER THERE MAKING A PATH THROUGH THE WOODS AT THE EDGE OF THE RAVINE. THREE RIDERS.
WE NEED TO PARLAY WITH THOSE THREE.
YOU SAID YOU THINK THOSE RIDERS WERE NOT EVOLVED DINOSAURS...LIKE YOU.
THEM?!
AHH. DE-VOLVED MONKEYS IS MORE LIKE IT.
NO OFFENSE INTENDED, CHIEF. WE DON'T HAVE A LOT OF RESPECT FOR UP-WORLD SURFACERS.
WHO DO YOU GET TO SEE FROM THE SURFACE?
MOSTLY RA'S'S ENGINEERS AND THUGS. THEN, LIKE THESE. THE SENSEI'S KILLERS, SCUM OF THE EARTH.
THE SENSEI'S MEN ARE RIDING T. REX!
WHAT DID YOU EXPECT?
I...I...DON'T KNOW... WHAT'S...
HALLLOOO, MEN THERE. CAN WE PARLAY?
WHA...WHAT. WHO'S THAT?
NEANDERTHALS, ON BATS. PUNKS!
WHAT? WHY WOULD...
LOOK.
MIDDLE.

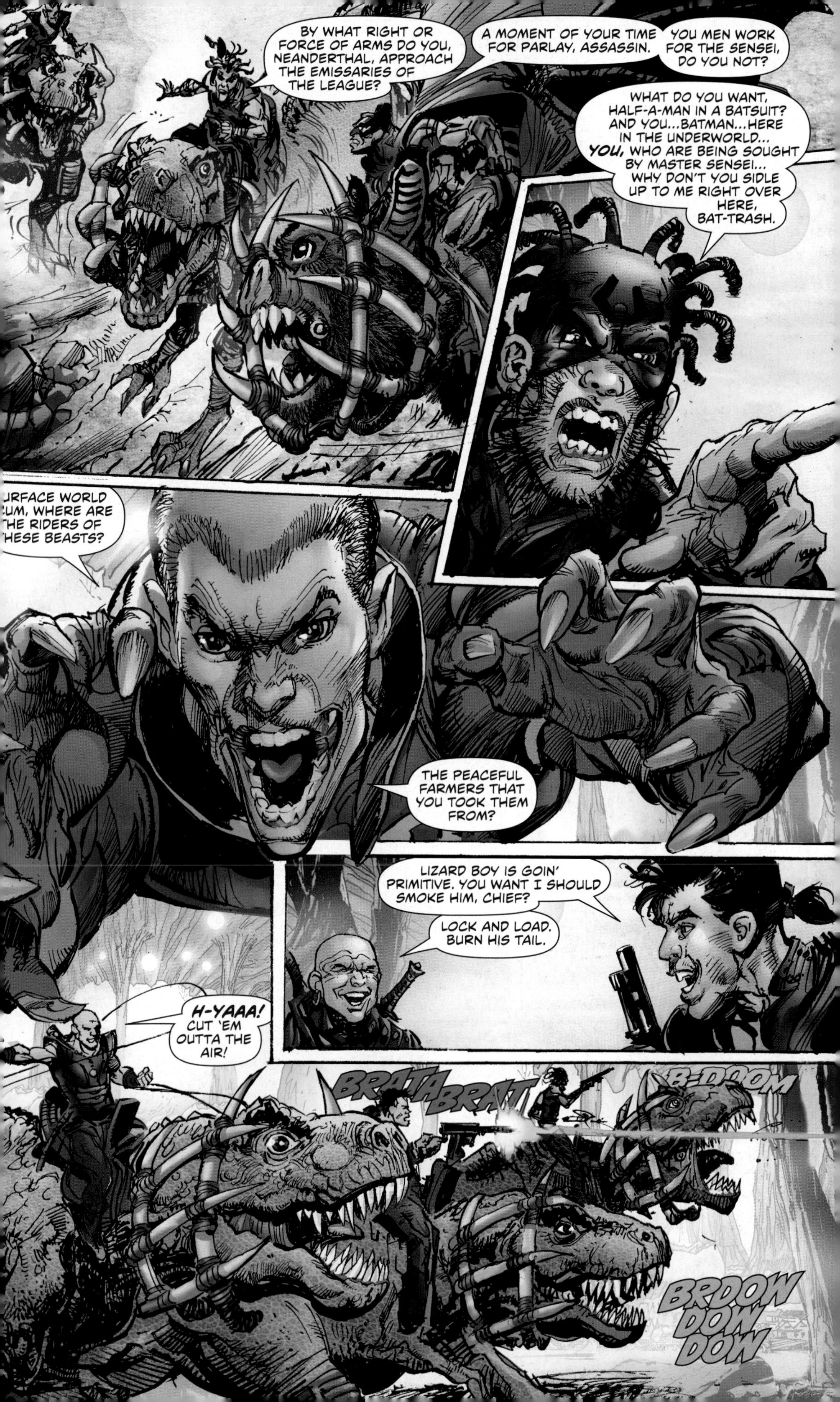
BY WHAT RIGHT OR FORCE OF ARMS DO YOU, NEANDERTHAL, APPROACH THE EMISSARIES OF THE LEAGUE?
A MOMENT OF YOUR TIME FOR PARLAY, ASSASSIN.
YOU MEN WORK FOR THE SENSEI, DO YOU NOT?
WHAT DO YOU WANT, HALF-A-MAN IN A BATSUIT? AND YOU...BATMAN...HERE IN THE UNDERWORLD... YOU, WHO ARE BEING SOUGHT BY MASTER SENSEI... WHY DON'T YOU SIDLE UP TO ME RIGHT OVER HERE, BAT-TRASH.
URFACE WORLD CUM, WHERE ARE THE RIDERS OF THESE BEASTS?
THE PEACEFUL FARMERS THAT YOU TOOK THEM FROM?
LIZARD BOY IS GOIN' PRIMITIVE. YOU WANT I SHOULD SMOKE HIM, CHIEF?
LOCK AND LOAD. BURN HIS TAIL.
H-YAAA! CUT 'EM OUTTA THE AIR!
BRATA BRAT
B-DOOM
BRDOW DOW DOW

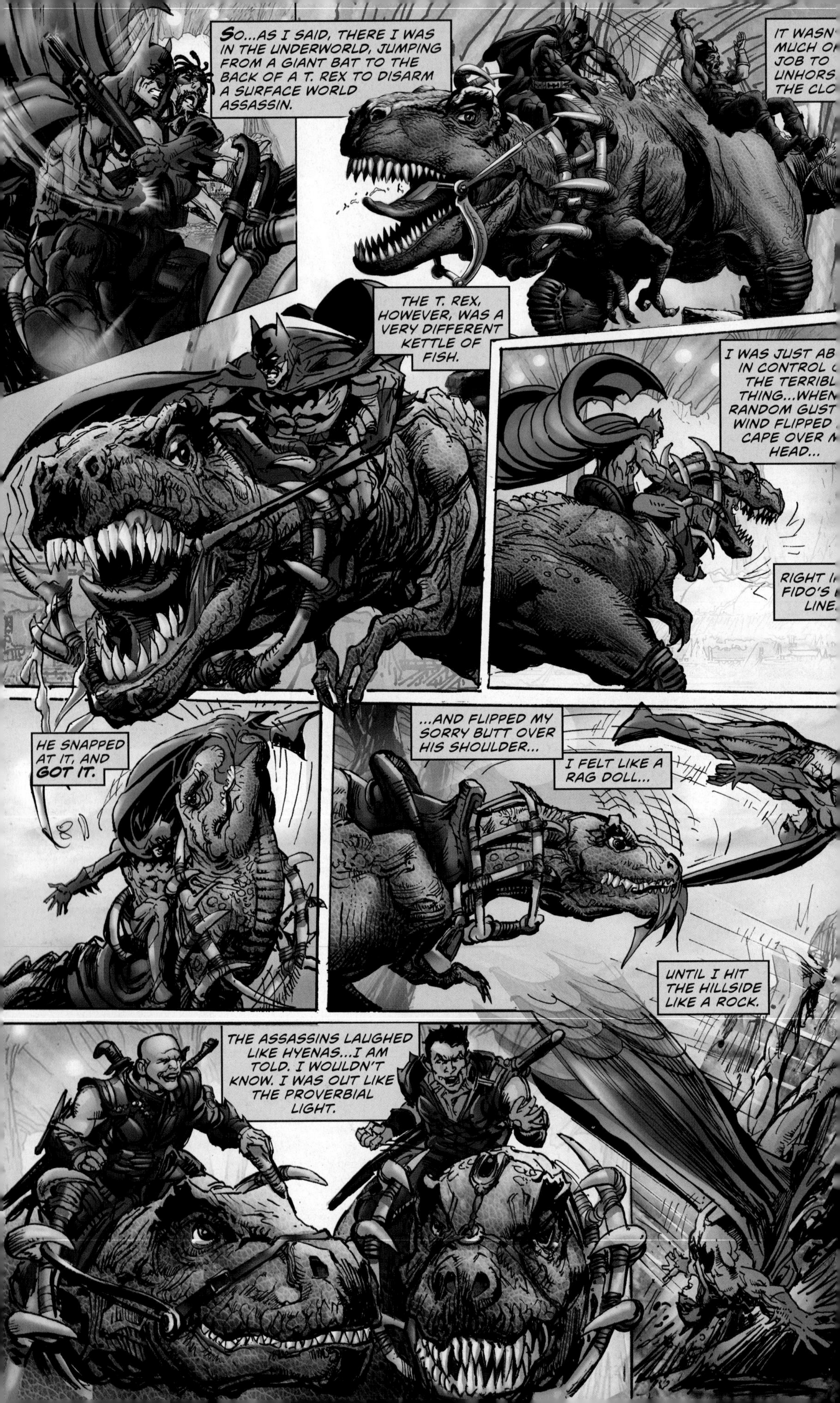
SO...AS I SAID, THERE I WAS IN THE UNDERWORLD, JUMPING FROM A GIANT BAT TO THE BACK OF A T. REX TO DISARM A SURFACE WORLD ASSASSIN.
IT WASN MUCH OF JOB TO UNHORS THE CLO
THE T. REX, HOWEVER, WAS A VERY DIFFERENT KETTLE OF FISH.
I WAS JUST AB IN CONTROL THE TERRIBL THING...WHEN RANDOM GUST WIND FLIPPED CAPE OVER M HEAD...
RIGHT I FIDO'S LINE.
HE SNAPPED AT IT, AND GOT IT.
...AND FLIPPED MY SORRY BUTT OVER HIS SHOULDER...
I FELT LIKE A RAG DOLL...
UNTIL I HIT THE HILLSIDE LIKE A ROCK.
THE ASSASSINS LAUGHED LIKE HYENAS...I AM TOLD. I WOULDN'T KNOW. I WAS OUT LIKE THE PROVERBIAL LIGHT.

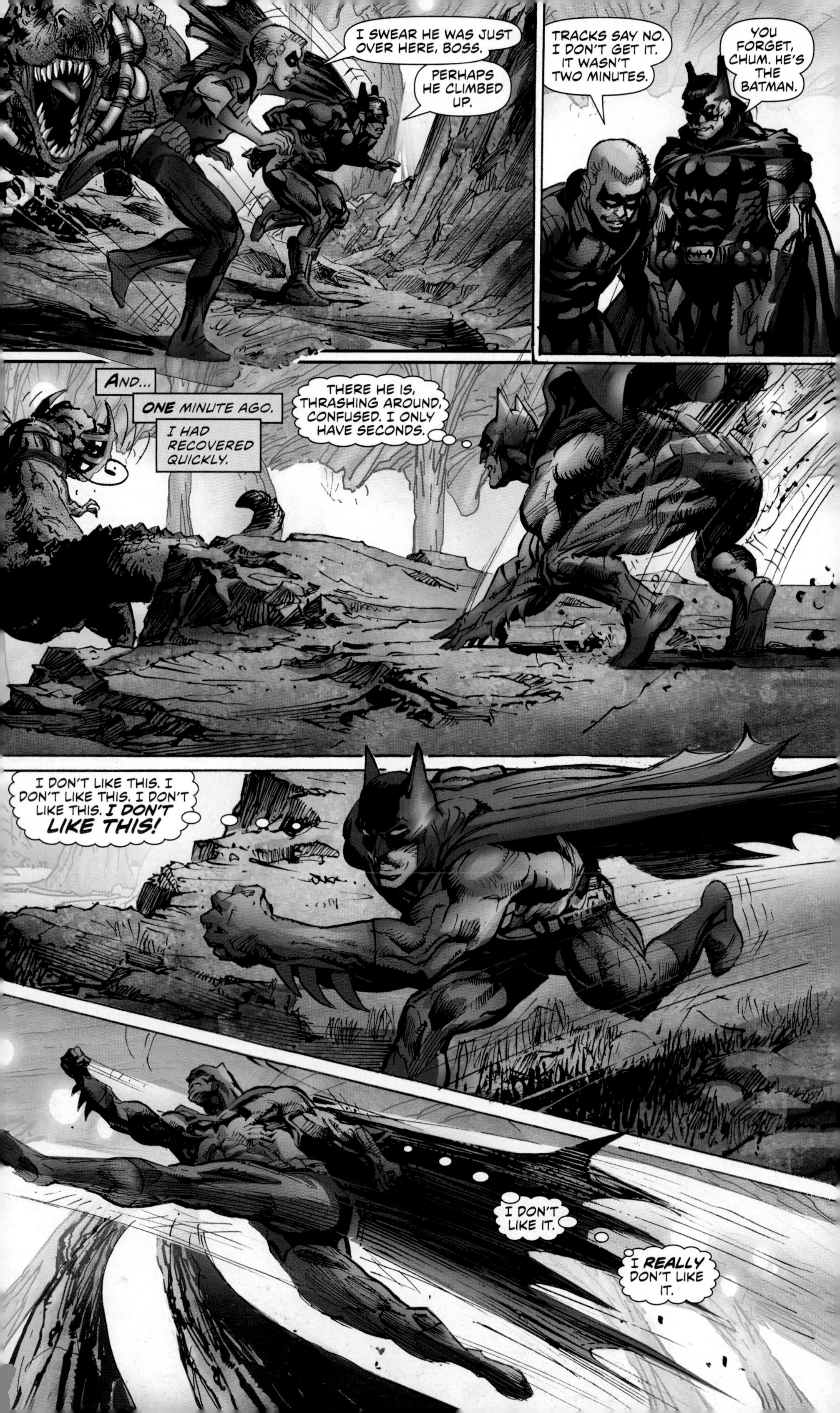
I SWEAR HE WAS JUST OVER HERE, BOSS.
PERHAPS HE CLIMBED UP.
TRACKS SAY NO. I DON'T GET IT. IT WASN'T TWO MINUTES.
YOU FORGET, CHUM. HE'S THE BATMAN.
AND...
ONE MINUTE AGO.
I HAD RECOVERED QUICKLY.
THERE HE IS, THRASHING AROUND, CONFUSED. I ONLY HAVE SECONDS.
I DON'T LIKE THIS. I DON'T LIKE THIS. I DON'T LIKE THIS. I DON'T LIKE THIS!
I DON'T LIKE IT.
I REALLY DON'T LIKE IT.

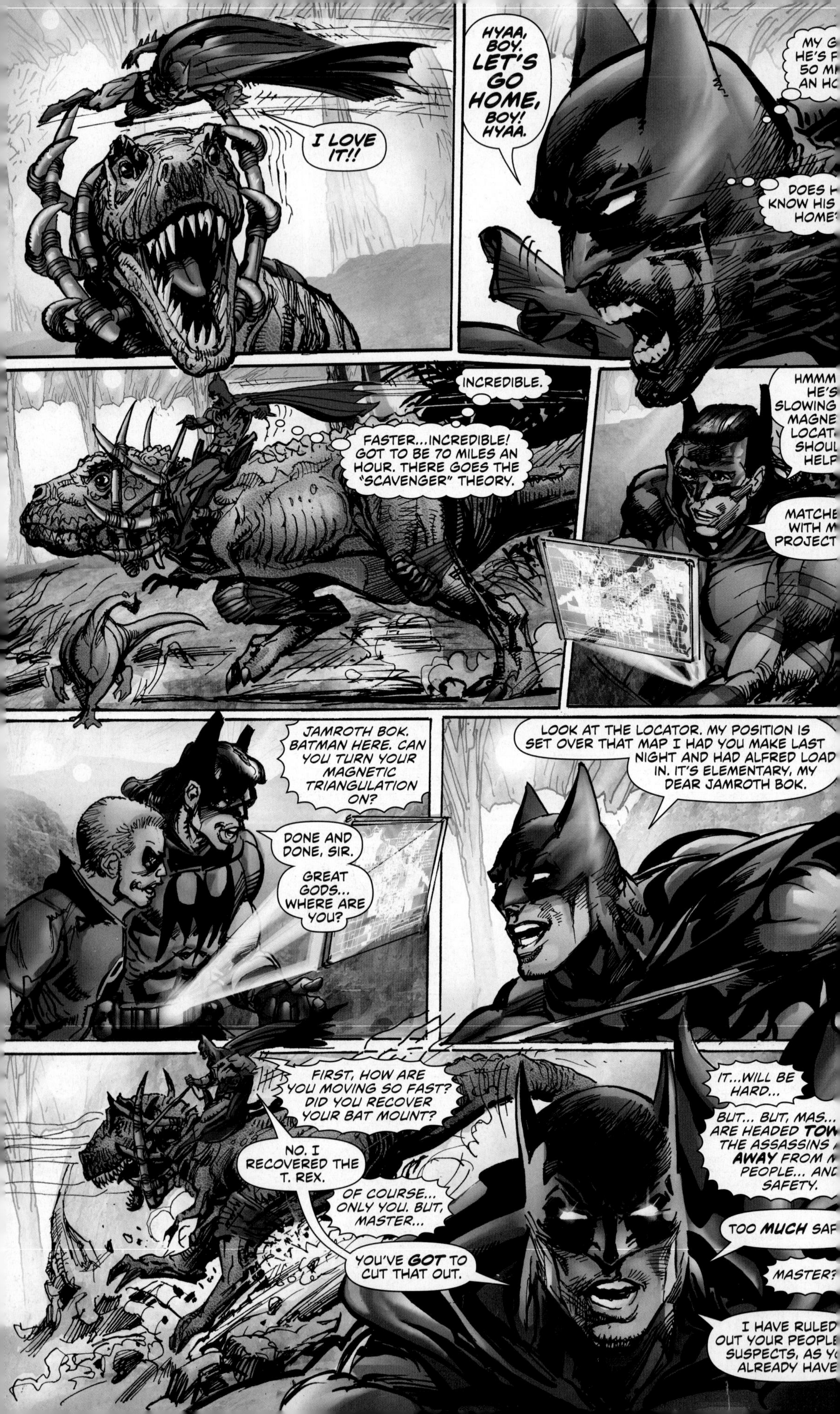
I LOVE IT!!
HYAA, BOY. LET'S GO HOME, BOY! HYAA.
MY G HE'S F 50 MI AN HO
DOES H KNOW HIS HOME?
INCREDIBLE.
FASTER...INCREDIBLE! GOT TO BE 70 MILES AN HOUR. THERE GOES THE "SCAVENGER" THEORY.
HMMM HE'S SLOWING MAGNE LOCAT SHOUL HELP
MATCHE WITH M PROJECT
JAMROTH BOK. BATMAN HERE. CAN YOU TURN YOUR MAGNETIC TRIANGULATION ON?
DONE AND DONE, SIR.
GREAT GODS... WHERE ARE YOU?
LOOK AT THE LOCATOR. MY POSITION IS SET OVER THAT MAP I HAD YOU MAKE LAST NIGHT AND HAD ALFRED LOAD IN. IT'S ELEMENTARY, MY DEAR JAMROTH BOK.
FIRST, HOW ARE YOU MOVING SO FAST? DID YOU RECOVER YOUR BAT MOUNT?
NO. I RECOVERED THE T. REX.
OF COURSE... ONLY YOU. BUT, MASTER...
YOU'VE GOT TO CUT THAT OUT.
IT...WILL BE HARD...
BUT... BUT, MAS... ARE HEADED TOW THE ASSASSINS AWAY FROM M PEOPLE... AND SAFETY.
TOO MUCH SAF
MASTER?
I HAVE RULED OUT YOUR PEOPLE SUSPECTS, AS YO ALREADY HAVE

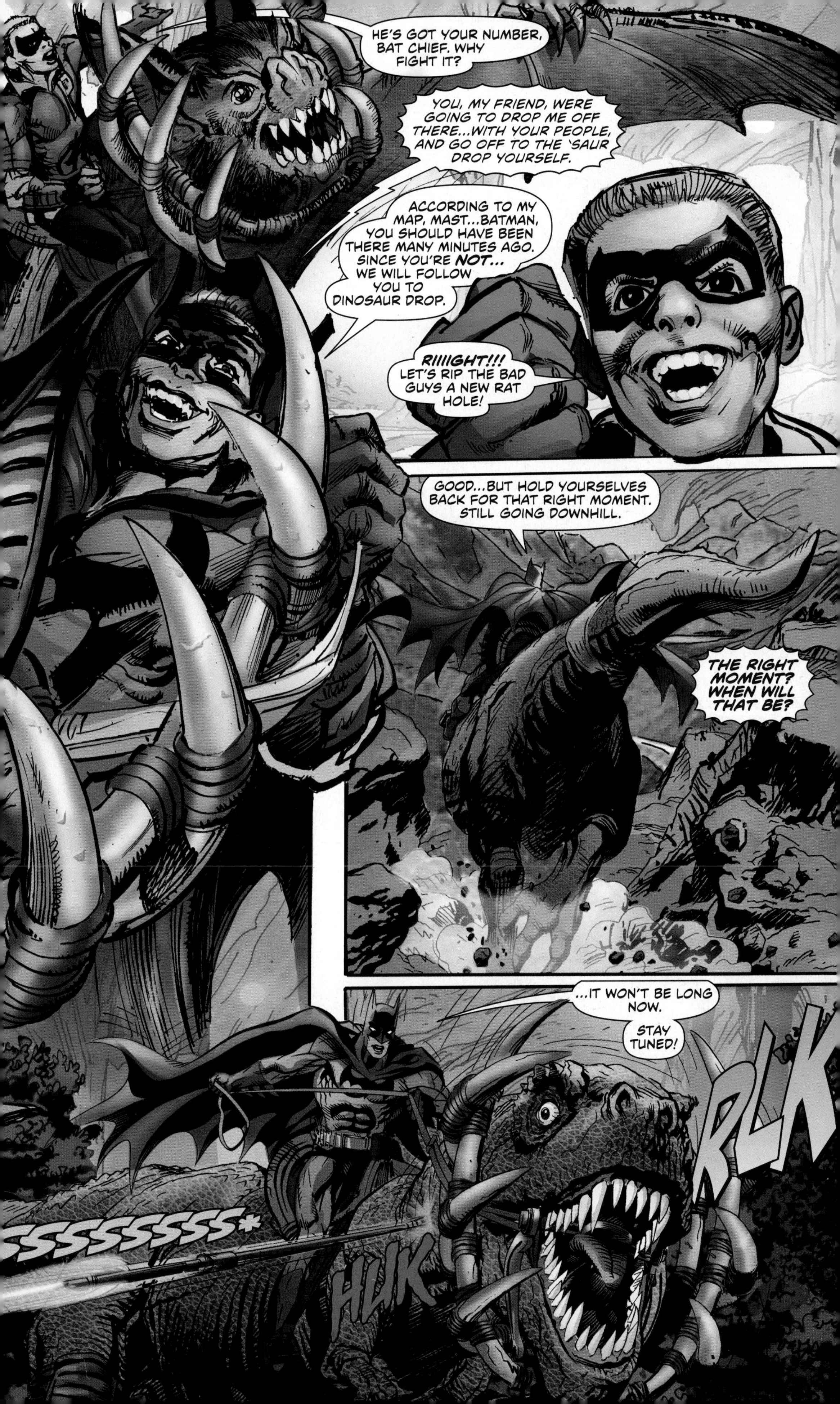
HE'S GOT YOUR NUMBER, BAT CHIEF. WHY FIGHT IT?
YOU, MY FRIEND, WERE GOING TO DROP ME OFF THERE...WITH YOUR PEOPLE, AND GO OFF TO THE 'SAUR DROP YOURSELF.
ACCORDING TO MY MAP, MAST...BATMAN, YOU SHOULD HAVE BEEN THERE MANY MINUTES AGO. SINCE YOU'RE NOT... WE WILL FOLLOW YOU TO DINOSAUR DROP.
RIIIIGHT!!! LET'S RIP THE BAD GUYS A NEW RAT HOLE!
GOOD...BUT HOLD YOURSELVES BACK FOR THAT RIGHT MOMENT. STILL GOING DOWNHILL.
THE RIGHT MOMENT? WHEN WILL THAT BE?
...IT WON'T BE LONG NOW.
STAY TUNED!
RLK
SSSSSSSS*
HUK

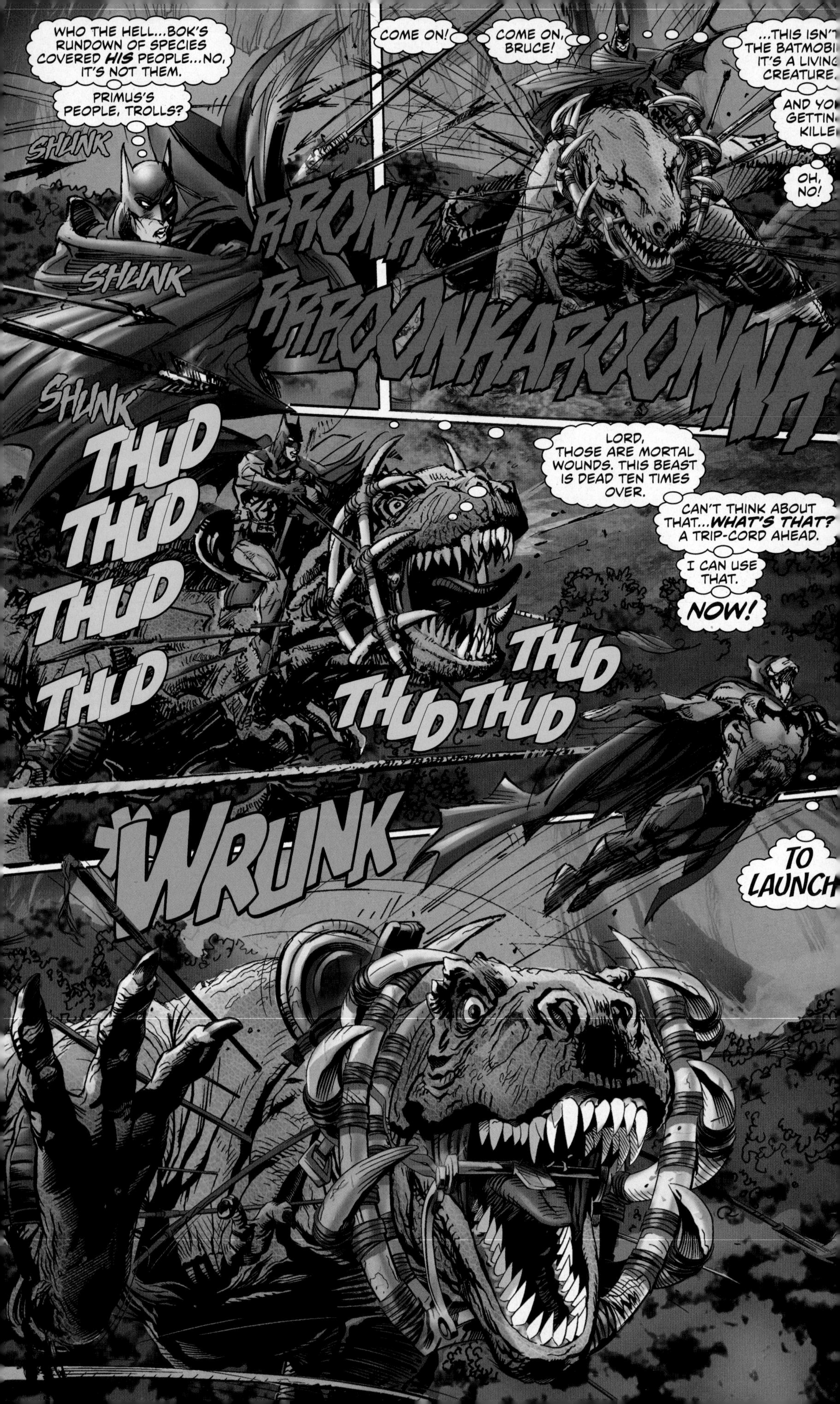
WHO THE HELL...BOK'S RUNDOWN OF SPECIES COVERED HIS PEOPLE...NO, IT'S NOT THEM.
PRIMUS'S PEOPLE, TROLLS?
SHUNK
SHUNK
COME ON!
COME ON, BRUCE!
...THIS ISN'T THE BATMOBI IT'S A LIVING CREATURE.
AND YO GETTIN KILLE
OH, NO!
RRONK
RRROONKAROONNK
SHUNK
THUD THUD THUD THUD
LORD, THOSE ARE MORTAL WOUNDS. THIS BEAST IS DEAD TEN TIMES OVER.
CAN'T THINK ABOUT THAT...WHAT'S THAT? A TRIP-CORD AHEAD.
I CAN USE THAT.
NOW!
THUD THUD THUD
WRUNK
TO LAUNCH

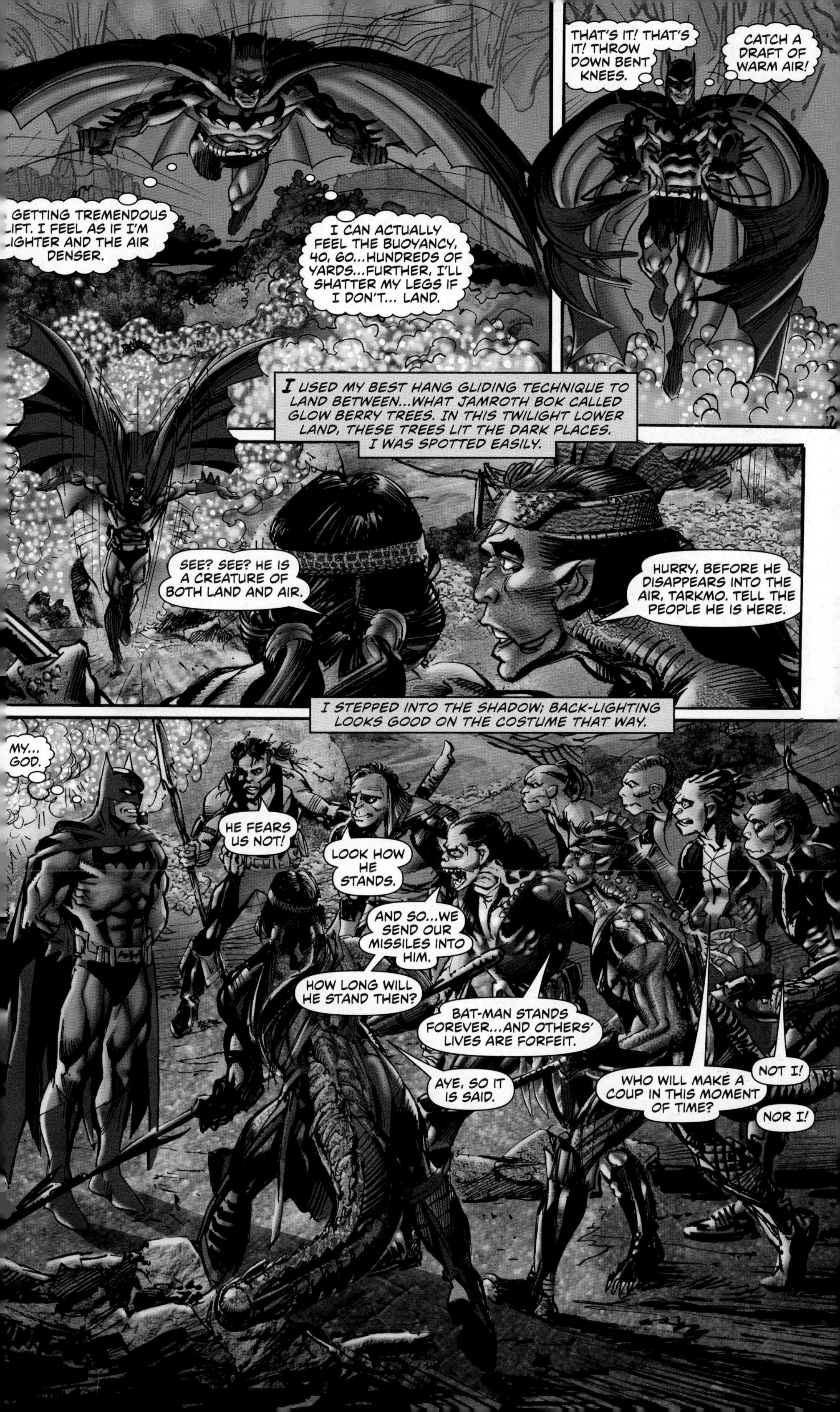
GETTING TREMENDOUS LIFT. I FEEL AS IF I'M LIGHTER AND THE AIR DENSER.
I CAN ACTUALLY FEEL THE BUOYANCY, 40, 60...HUNDREDS OF YARDS...FURTHER, I'LL SHATTER MY LEGS IF I DON'T... LAND.
THAT'S IT! THAT'S IT! THROW DOWN BENT KNEES.
CATCH A DRAFT OF WARM AIR!
I USED MY BEST HANG GLIDING TECHNIQUE TO LAND BETWEEN...WHAT JAMROTH BOK CALLED GLOW BERRY TREES. IN THIS TWILIGHT LOWER LAND, THESE TREES LIT THE DARK PLACES. I WAS SPOTTED EASILY.
SEE? SEE? HE IS A CREATURE OF BOTH LAND AND AIR.
HURRY, BEFORE HE DISAPPEARS INTO THE AIR, TARKMO. TELL THE PEOPLE HE IS HERE.
I STEPPED INTO THE SHADOW; BACK-LIGHTING LOOKS GOOD ON THE COSTUME THAT WAY.
MY... GOD.
HE FEARS US NOT!
LOOK HOW HE STANDS.
AND SO...WE SEND OUR MISSILES INTO HIM.
HOW LONG WILL HE STAND THEN?
BAT-MAN STANDS FOREVER...AND OTHERS' LIVES ARE FORFEIT.
AYE, SO IT IS SAID.
WHO WILL MAKE A COUP IN THIS MOMENT OF TIME?
NOT I!
NOR I!

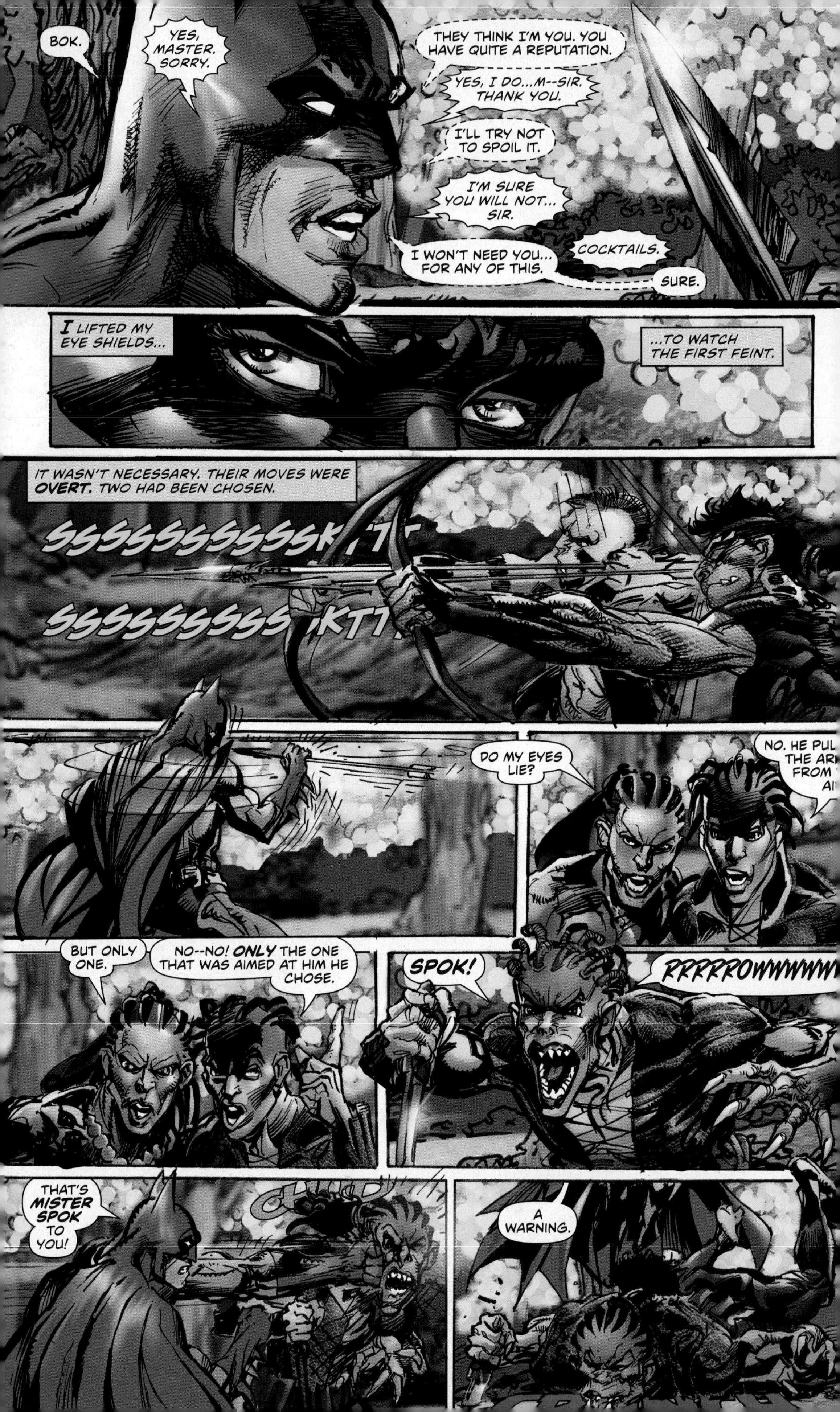
BOK.
YES, MASTER. SORRY.
THEY THINK I'M YOU. YOU HAVE QUITE A REPUTATION.
YES, I DO...M--SIR. THANK YOU.
I'LL TRY NOT TO SPOIL IT.
I'M SURE YOU WILL NOT... SIR.
I WON'T NEED YOU... FOR ANY OF THIS.
COCKTAILS.
SURE.
I LIFTED MY EYE SHIELDS...
...TO WATCH THE FIRST FEINT.
IT WASN'T NECESSARY. THEIR MOVES WERE OVERT. TWO HAD BEEN CHOSEN.
DO MY EYES LIE?
BUT ONLY ONE.
NO--NO! ONLY THE ONE THAT WAS AIMED AT HIM HE CHOSE.
SPOK!
THAT'S MISTER SPOK TO YOU!
A WARNING.

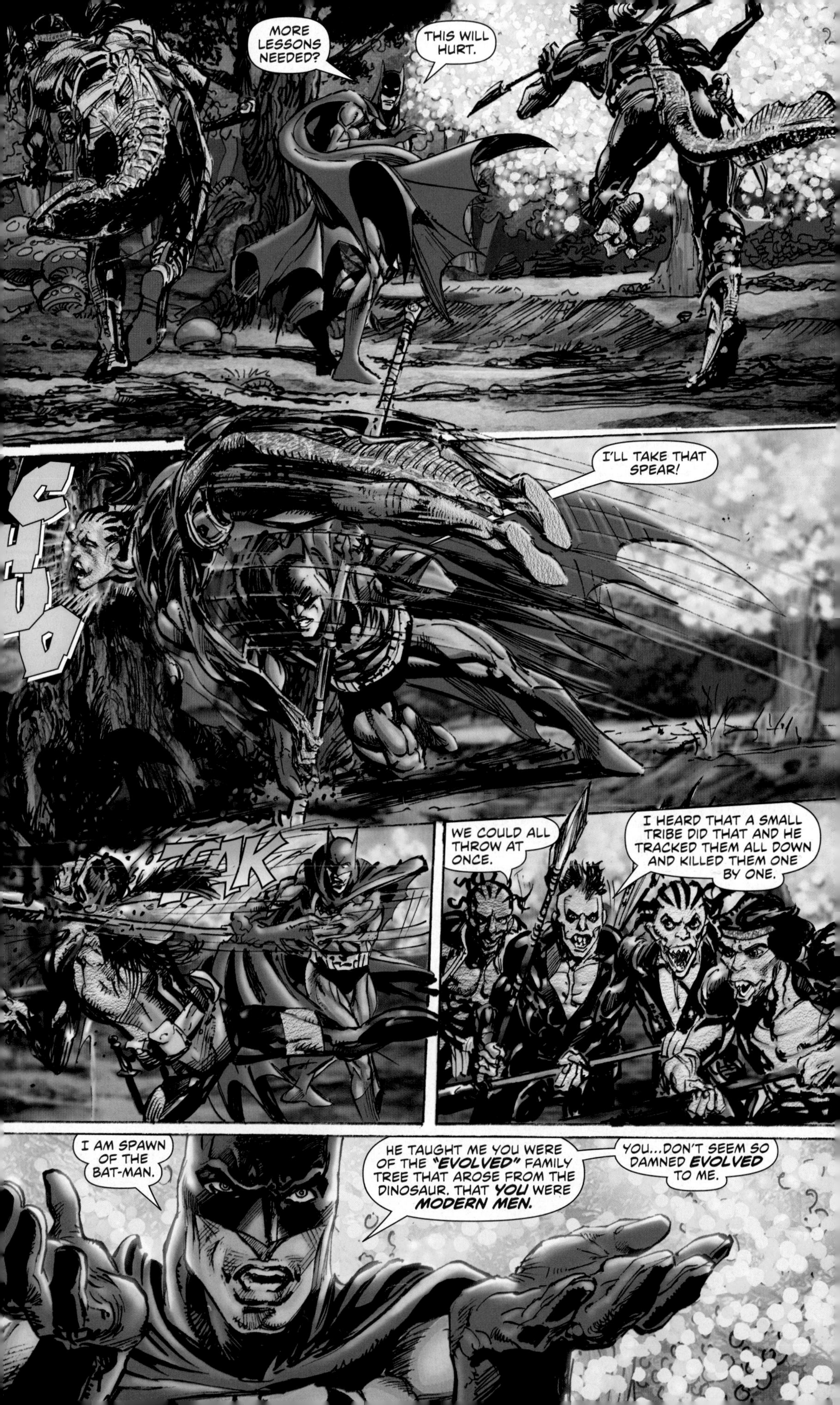
MORE LESSONS NEEDED?
THIS WILL HURT.
I'LL TAKE THAT SPEAR!
CHUD
WE COULD ALL THROW AT ONCE.
I HEARD THAT A SMALL TRIBE DID THAT AND HE TRACKED THEM ALL DOWN AND KILLED THEM ONE BY ONE.
I AM SPAWN OF THE BAT-MAN.
HE TAUGHT ME YOU WERE OF THE "EVOLVED" FAMILY TREE THAT AROSE FROM THE DINOSAUR. THAT YOU WERE MODERN MEN.
YOU...DON'T SEEM SO DAMNED EVOLVED TO ME.

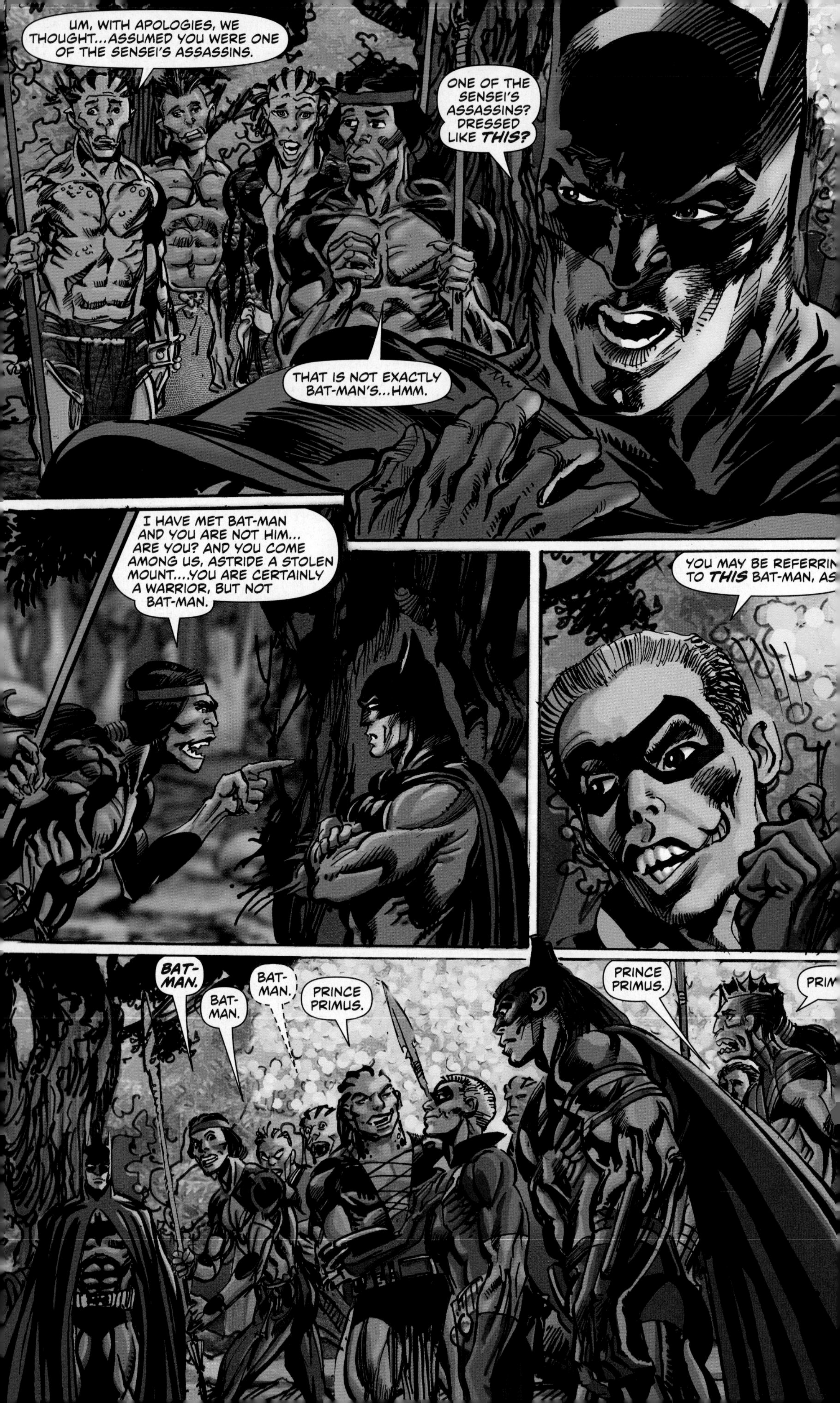
UM, WITH APOLOGIES, WE THOUGHT...ASSUMED YOU WERE ONE OF THE SENSEI'S ASSASSINS.
ONE OF THE SENSEI'S ASSASSINS? DRESSED LIKE THIS?
THAT IS NOT EXACTLY BAT-MAN'S...HMM.
I HAVE MET BAT-MAN AND YOU ARE NOT HIM... ARE YOU? AND YOU COME AMONG US, ASTRIDE A STOLEN MOUNT....YOU ARE CERTAINLY A WARRIOR, BUT NOT BAT-MAN.
YOU MAY BE REFERRIN
TO THIS BAT-MAN, AS
BAT-MAN.
BAT-MAN.
BAT-MAN.
PRINCE PRIMUS.
PRINCE PRIMUS.
PRIM

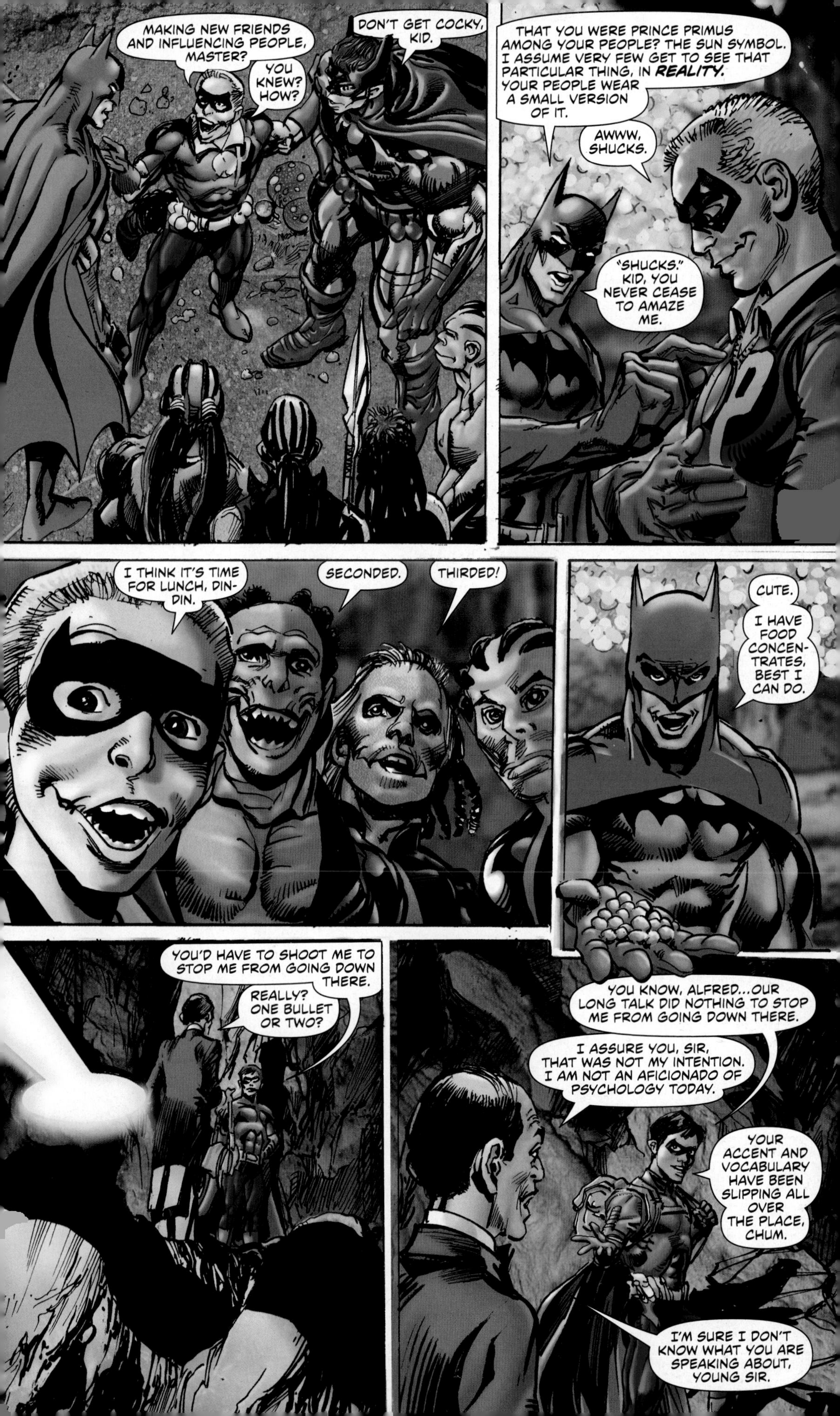
MAKING NEW FRIENDS AND INFLUENCING PEOPLE, MASTER?
DON'T GET COCKY, KID.
YOU KNEW? HOW?
THAT YOU WERE PRINCE PRIMUS AMONG YOUR PEOPLE? THE SUN SYMBOL. I ASSUME VERY FEW GET TO SEE THAT PARTICULAR THING, IN **REALITY.** YOUR PEOPLE WEAR A SMALL VERSION OF IT.
AWWW, SHUCKS.
"SHUCKS." KID, YOU NEVER CEASE TO AMAZE ME.
I THINK IT'S TIME FOR LUNCH, DIN-DIN.
SECONDED.
THIRDED!
CUTE.
I HAVE FOOD CONCEN-TRATES, BEST I CAN DO.
YOU'D HAVE TO SHOOT ME TO STOP ME FROM GOING DOWN THERE.
REALLY? ONE BULLET OR TWO?
YOU KNOW, ALFRED...OUR LONG TALK DID NOTHING TO STOP ME FROM GOING DOWN THERE.
I ASSURE YOU, SIR, THAT WAS NOT MY INTENTION. I AM NOT AN AFICIONADO OF PSYCHOLOGY TODAY.
YOUR ACCENT AND VOCABULARY HAVE BEEN SLIPPING ALL OVER THE PLACE, CHUM.
I'M SURE I DON'T KNOW WHAT YOU ARE SPEAKING ABOUT, YOUNG SIR.

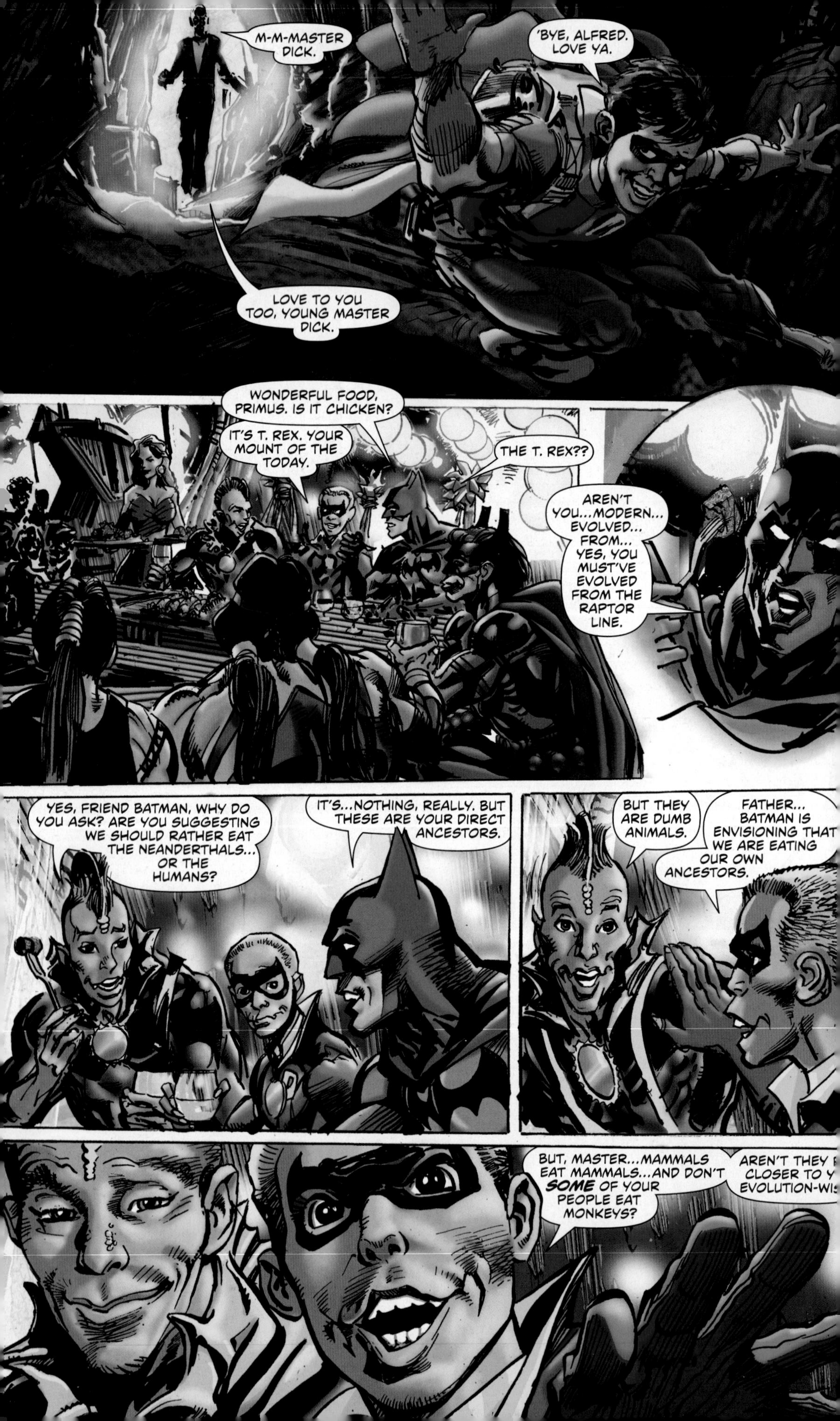
M-M-MASTER DICK.
'BYE, ALFRED. LOVE YA.
LOVE TO YOU TOO, YOUNG MASTER DICK.
WONDERFUL FOOD, PRIMUS. IS IT CHICKEN?
IT'S T. REX. YOUR MOUNT OF THE TODAY.
THE T. REX??
AREN'T YOU...MODERN... EVOLVED... FROM... YES, YOU MUST'VE EVOLVED FROM THE RAPTOR LINE.
YES, FRIEND BATMAN, WHY DO YOU ASK? ARE YOU SUGGESTING WE SHOULD RATHER EAT THE NEANDERTHALS... OR THE HUMANS?
IT'S...NOTHING, REALLY. BUT THESE ARE YOUR DIRECT ANCESTORS.
BUT THEY ARE DUMB ANIMALS.
FATHER... BATMAN IS ENVISIONING THAT WE ARE EATING OUR OWN ANCESTORS.
BUT, MASTER...MAMMALS EAT MAMMALS...AND DON'T ***SOME*** OF YOUR PEOPLE EAT MONKEYS?

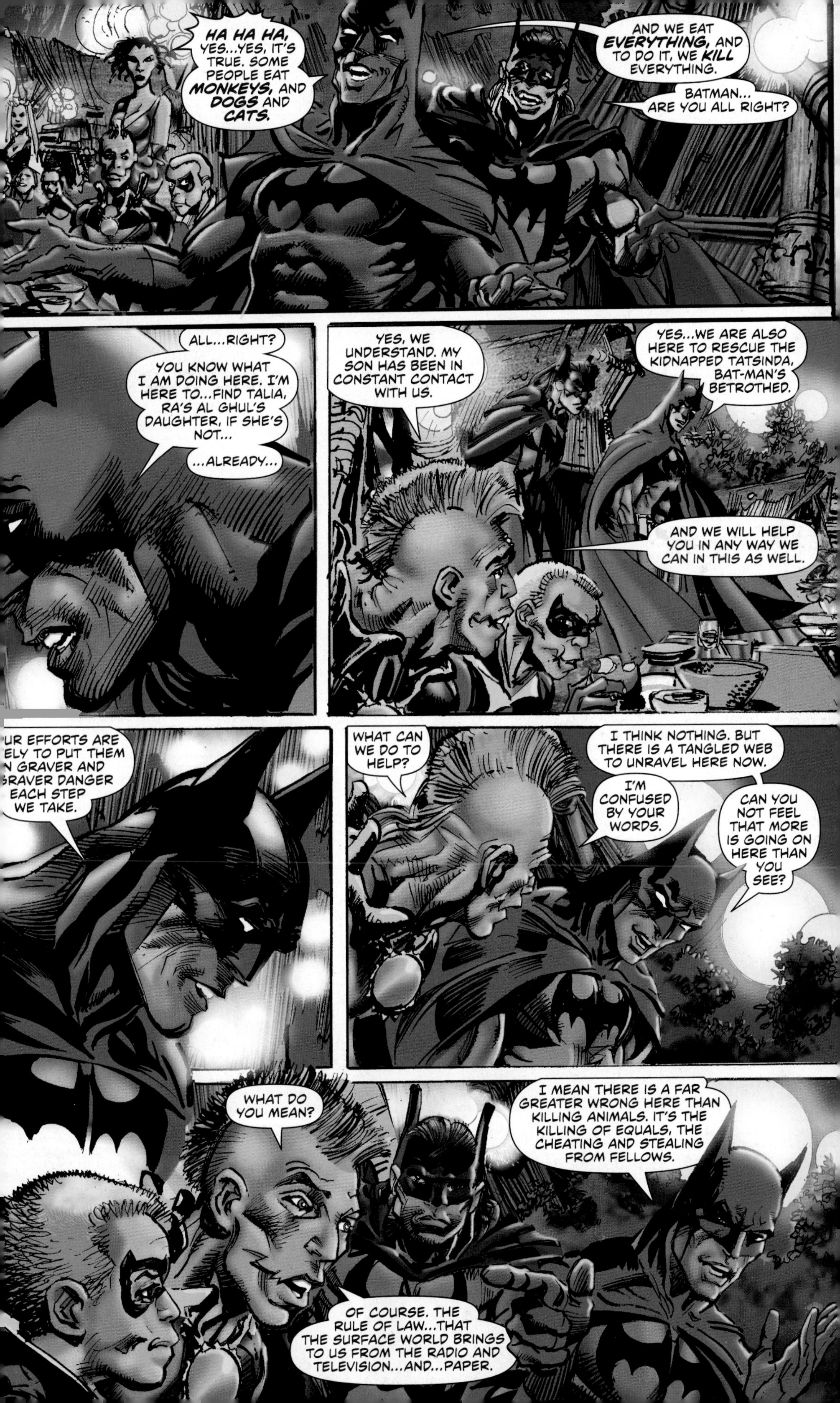
HA HA HA, YES...YES, IT'S TRUE. SOME PEOPLE EAT MONKEYS, AND DOGS AND CATS.
AND WE EAT EVERYTHING, AND TO DO IT, WE KILL EVERYTHING.
BATMAN... ARE YOU ALL RIGHT?
ALL...RIGHT?
YOU KNOW WHAT I AM DOING HERE. I'M HERE TO...FIND TALIA, RA'S AL GHUL'S DAUGHTER, IF SHE'S NOT...
...ALREADY...
YES, WE UNDERSTAND. MY SON HAS BEEN IN CONSTANT CONTACT WITH US.
YES...WE ARE ALSO HERE TO RESCUE THE KIDNAPPED TATSINDA, BAT-MAN'S BETROTHED.
AND WE WILL HELP YOU IN ANY WAY WE CAN IN THIS AS WELL.
UR EFFORTS ARE ELY TO PUT THEM N GRAVER AND GRAVER DANGER EACH STEP WE TAKE.
WHAT CAN WE DO TO HELP?
I THINK NOTHING. BUT THERE IS A TANGLED WEB TO UNRAVEL HERE NOW.
I'M CONFUSED BY YOUR WORDS.
CAN YOU NOT FEEL THAT MORE IS GOING ON HERE THAN YOU SEE?
WHAT DO YOU MEAN?
I MEAN THERE IS A FAR GREATER WRONG HERE THAN KILLING ANIMALS. IT'S THE KILLING OF EQUALS, THE CHEATING AND STEALING FROM FELLOWS.
OF COURSE. THE RULE OF LAW...THAT THE SURFACE WORLD BRINGS TO US FROM THE RADIO AND TELEVISION...AND...PAPER.

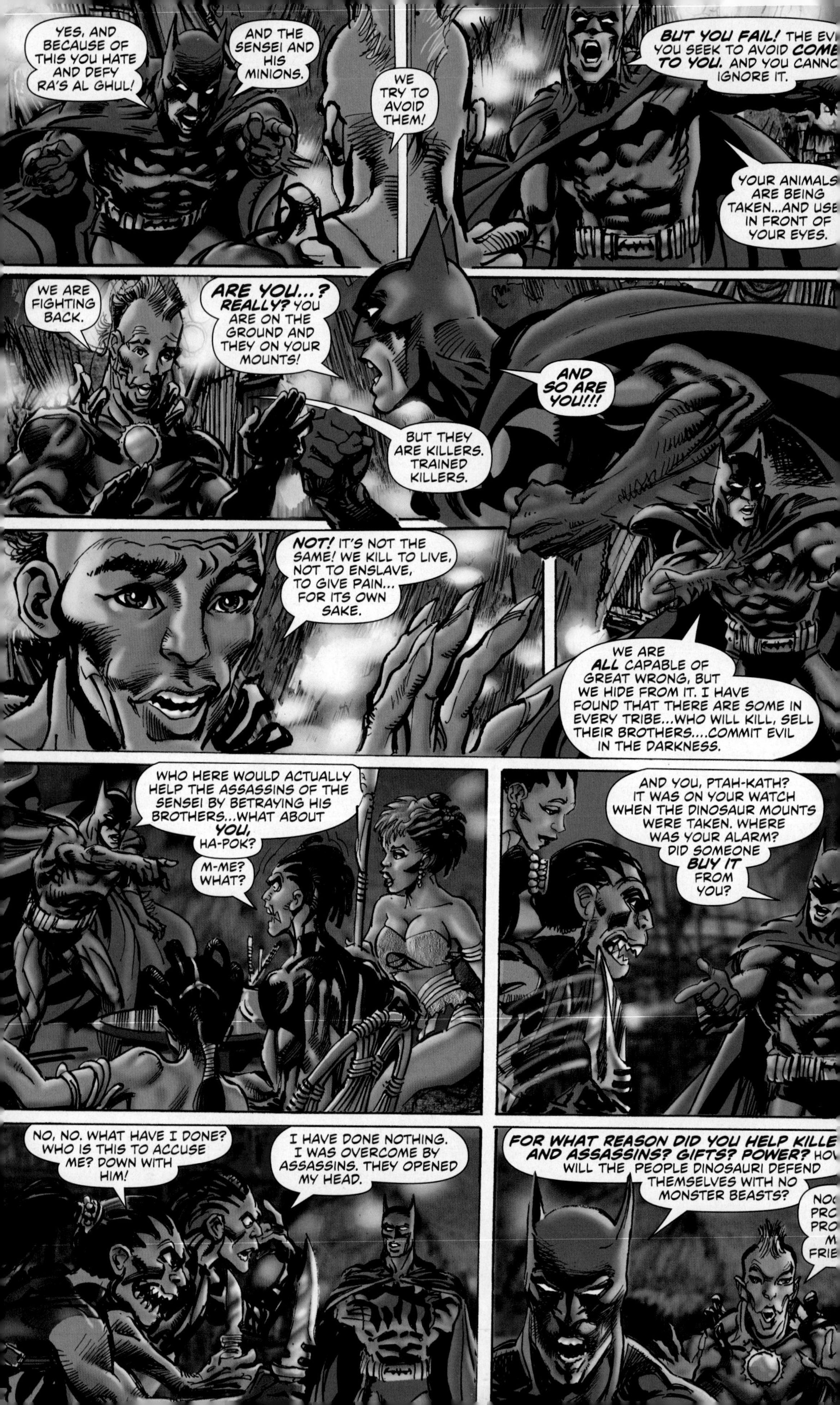

YES, AND BECAUSE OF THIS YOU HATE AND DEFY RA'S AL GHUL!
AND THE SENSEI AND HIS MINIONS.
WE TRY TO AVOID THEM!
BUT YOU FAIL! THE EVI YOU SEEK TO AVOID COME TO YOU. AND YOU CANNO IGNORE IT.
YOUR ANIMALS ARE BEING TAKEN...AND USE IN FRONT OF YOUR EYES.
WE ARE FIGHTING BACK.
ARE YOU...? REALLY? YOU ARE ON THE GROUND AND THEY ON YOUR MOUNTS!
AND SO ARE YOU!!!
BUT THEY ARE KILLERS. TRAINED KILLERS.
NOT! IT'S NOT THE SAME! WE KILL TO LIVE, NOT TO ENSLAVE, TO GIVE PAIN... FOR ITS OWN SAKE.
WE ARE ALL CAPABLE OF GREAT WRONG, BUT WE HIDE FROM IT. I HAVE FOUND THAT THERE ARE SOME IN EVERY TRIBE...WHO WILL KILL, SELL THEIR BROTHERS....COMMIT EVIL IN THE DARKNESS.
WHO HERE WOULD ACTUALLY HELP THE ASSASSINS OF THE SENSEI BY BETRAYING HIS BROTHERS...WHAT ABOUT YOU, HA-POK?
M-ME? WHAT?
AND YOU, PTAH-KATH? IT WAS ON YOUR WATCH WHEN THE DINOSAUR MOUNTS WERE TAKEN. WHERE WAS YOUR ALARM? DID SOMEONE BUY IT FROM YOU?
NO, NO. WHAT HAVE I DONE? WHO IS THIS TO ACCUSE ME? DOWN WITH HIM!
I HAVE DONE NOTHING. I WAS OVERCOME BY ASSASSINS. THEY OPENED MY HEAD.
FOR WHAT REASON DID YOU HELP KILLE AND ASSASSINS? GIFTS? POWER? HOW WILL THE PEOPLE DINOSAURI DEFEND THEMSELVES WITH NO MONSTER BEASTS?
NO PRO PRO M FRIE

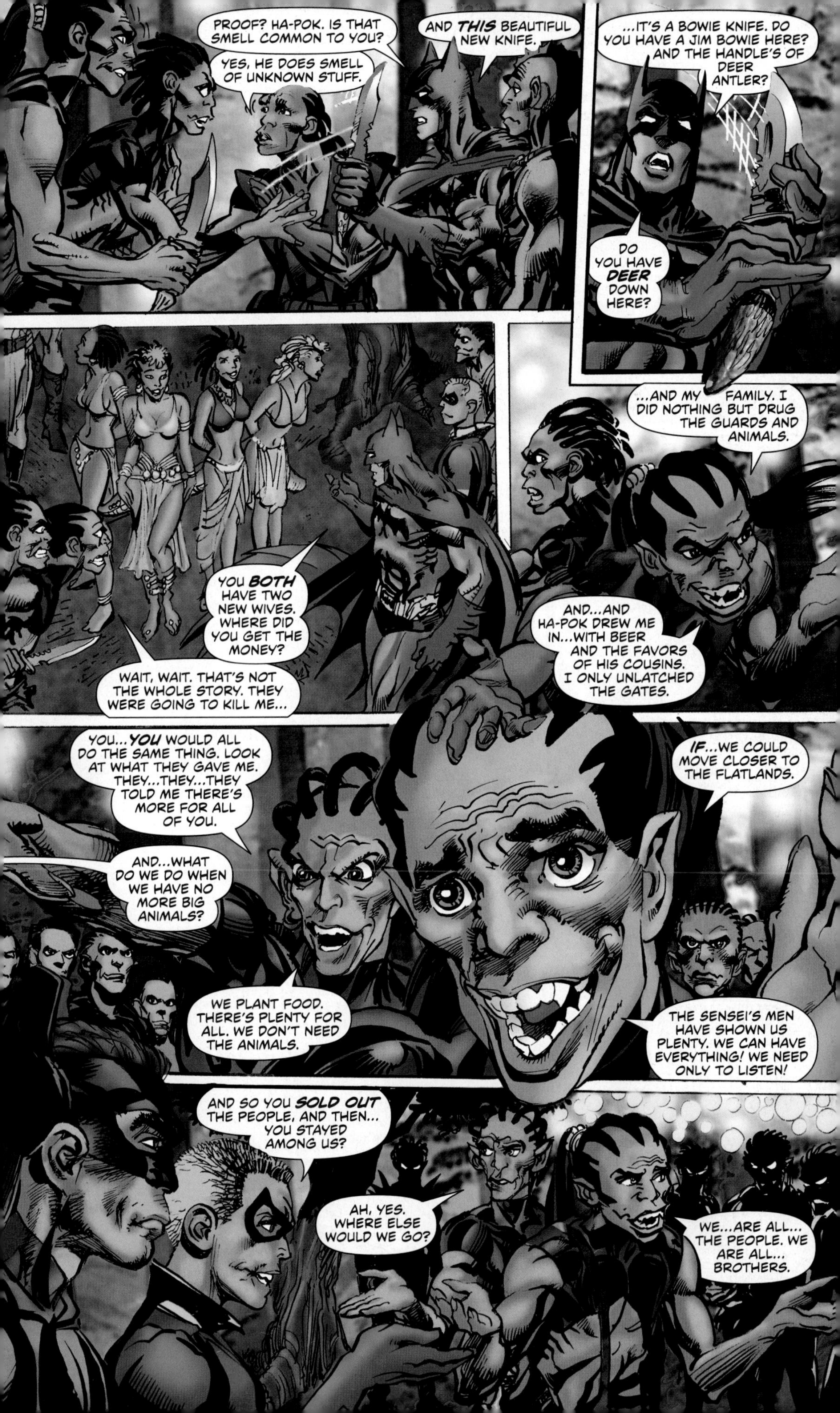
PROOF? HA-POK. IS THAT SMELL COMMON TO YOU?
YES, HE DOES SMELL OF UNKNOWN STUFF.
AND THIS BEAUTIFUL NEW KNIFE.
...IT'S A BOWIE KNIFE. DO YOU HAVE A JIM BOWIE HERE? AND THE HANDLE'S OF DEER ANTLER?
DO YOU HAVE DEER DOWN HERE?
YOU BOTH HAVE TWO NEW WIVES. WHERE DID YOU GET THE MONEY?
WAIT, WAIT. THAT'S NOT THE WHOLE STORY. THEY WERE GOING TO KILL ME...
...AND MY FAMILY. I DID NOTHING BUT DRUG THE GUARDS AND ANIMALS.
AND...AND HA-POK DREW ME IN...WITH BEER AND THE FAVORS OF HIS COUSINS. I ONLY UNLATCHED THE GATES.
YOU...YOU WOULD ALL DO THE SAME THING. LOOK AT WHAT THEY GAVE ME. THEY...THEY...THEY TOLD ME THERE'S MORE FOR ALL OF YOU.
IF...WE COULD MOVE CLOSER TO THE FLATLANDS.
AND...WHAT DO WE DO WHEN WE HAVE NO MORE BIG ANIMALS?
WE PLANT FOOD. THERE'S PLENTY FOR ALL. WE DON'T NEED THE ANIMALS.
THE SENSEI'S MEN HAVE SHOWN US PLENTY. WE CAN HAVE EVERYTHING! WE NEED ONLY TO LISTEN!
AND SO YOU SOLD OUT THE PEOPLE, AND THEN... YOU STAYED AMONG US?
AH, YES. WHERE ELSE WOULD WE GO?
WE...ARE ALL... THE PEOPLE. WE ARE ALL... BROTHERS.

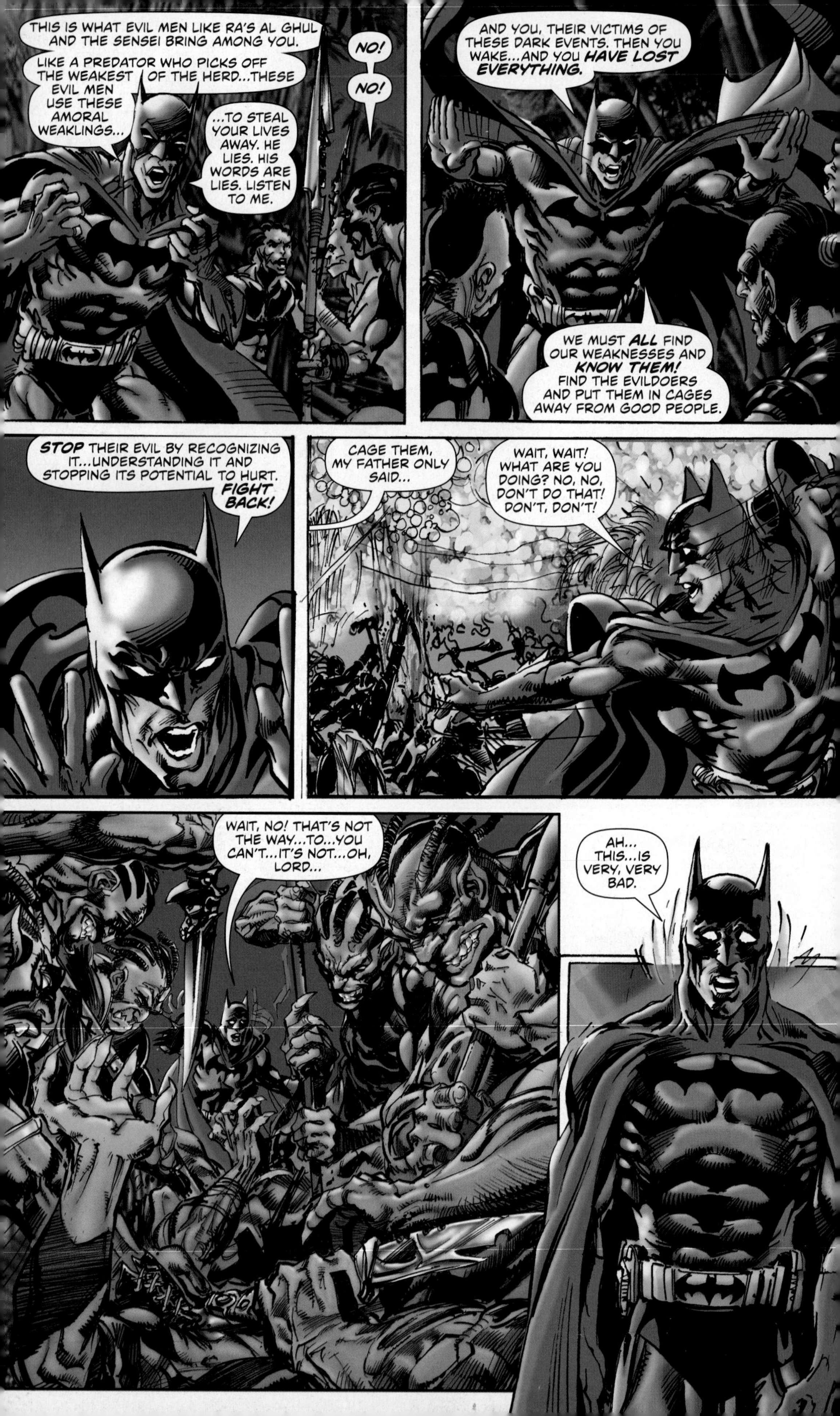

THIS IS WHAT EVIL MEN LIKE RA'S AL GHUL AND THE SENSEI BRING AMONG YOU.
LIKE A PREDATOR WHO PICKS OFF THE WEAKEST OF THE HERD...THESE EVIL MEN USE THESE AMORAL WEAKLINGS...
...TO STEAL YOUR LIVES AWAY. HE LIES. HIS WORDS ARE LIES. LISTEN TO ME.
NO!
NO!
AND YOU, THEIR VICTIMS OF THESE DARK EVENTS. THEN YOU WAKE...AND YOU HAVE LOST EVERYTHING.
WE MUST ALL FIND OUR WEAKNESSES AND KNOW THEM! FIND THE EVILDOERS AND PUT THEM IN CAGES AWAY FROM GOOD PEOPLE.
STOP THEIR EVIL BY RECOGNIZING IT...UNDERSTANDING IT AND STOPPING ITS POTENTIAL TO HURT. FIGHT BACK!
CAGE THEM, MY FATHER ONLY SAID...
WAIT, WAIT! WHAT ARE YOU DOING? NO, NO, DON'T DO THAT! DON'T, DON'T!
WAIT, NO! THAT'S NOT THE WAY...TO...YOU CAN'T...IT'S NOT...OH, LORD...
AH... THIS...IS VERY, VERY BAD.

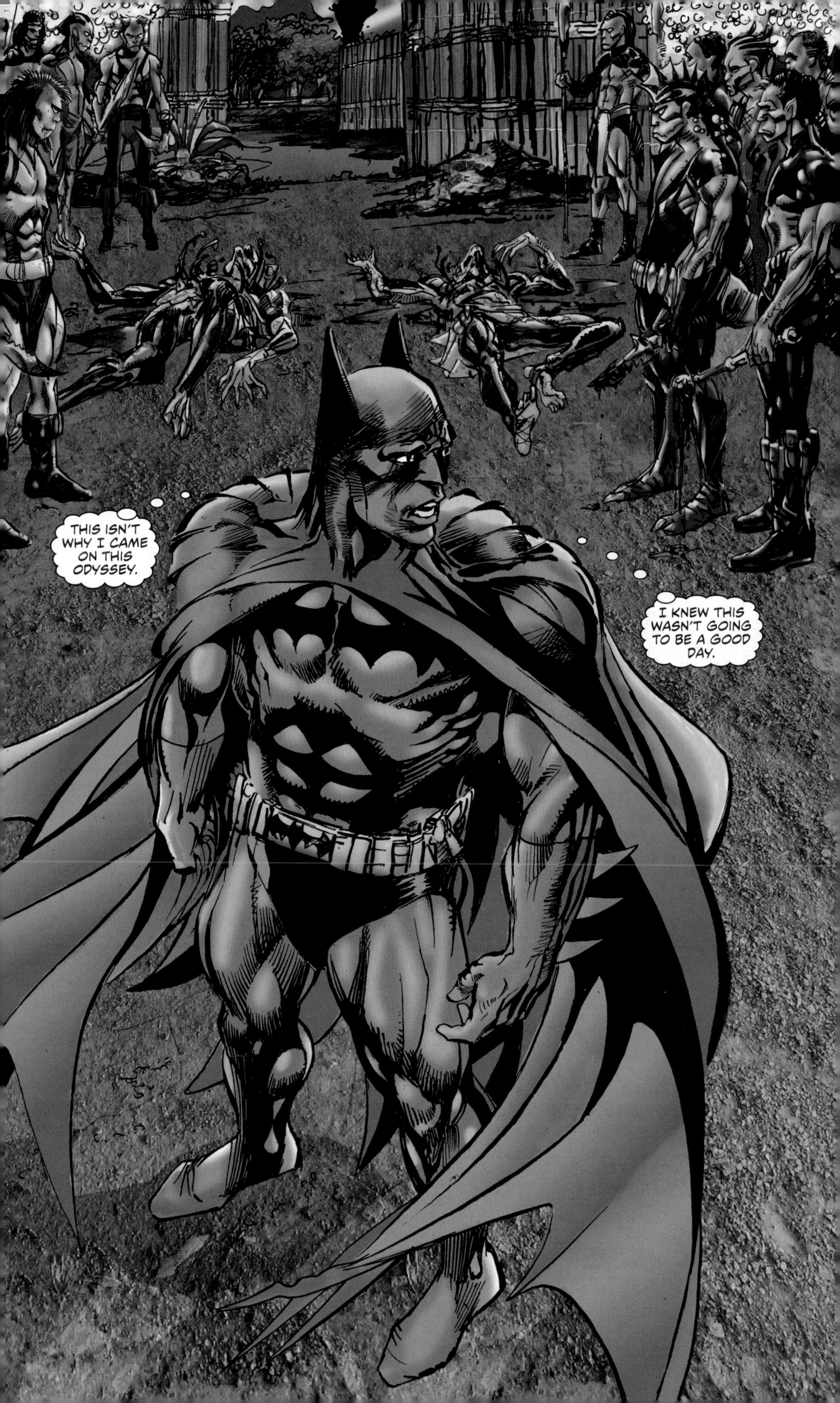
THIS ISN'T WHY I CAME ON THIS ODYSSEY.
I KNEW THIS WASN'T GOING TO BE A GOOD DAY.

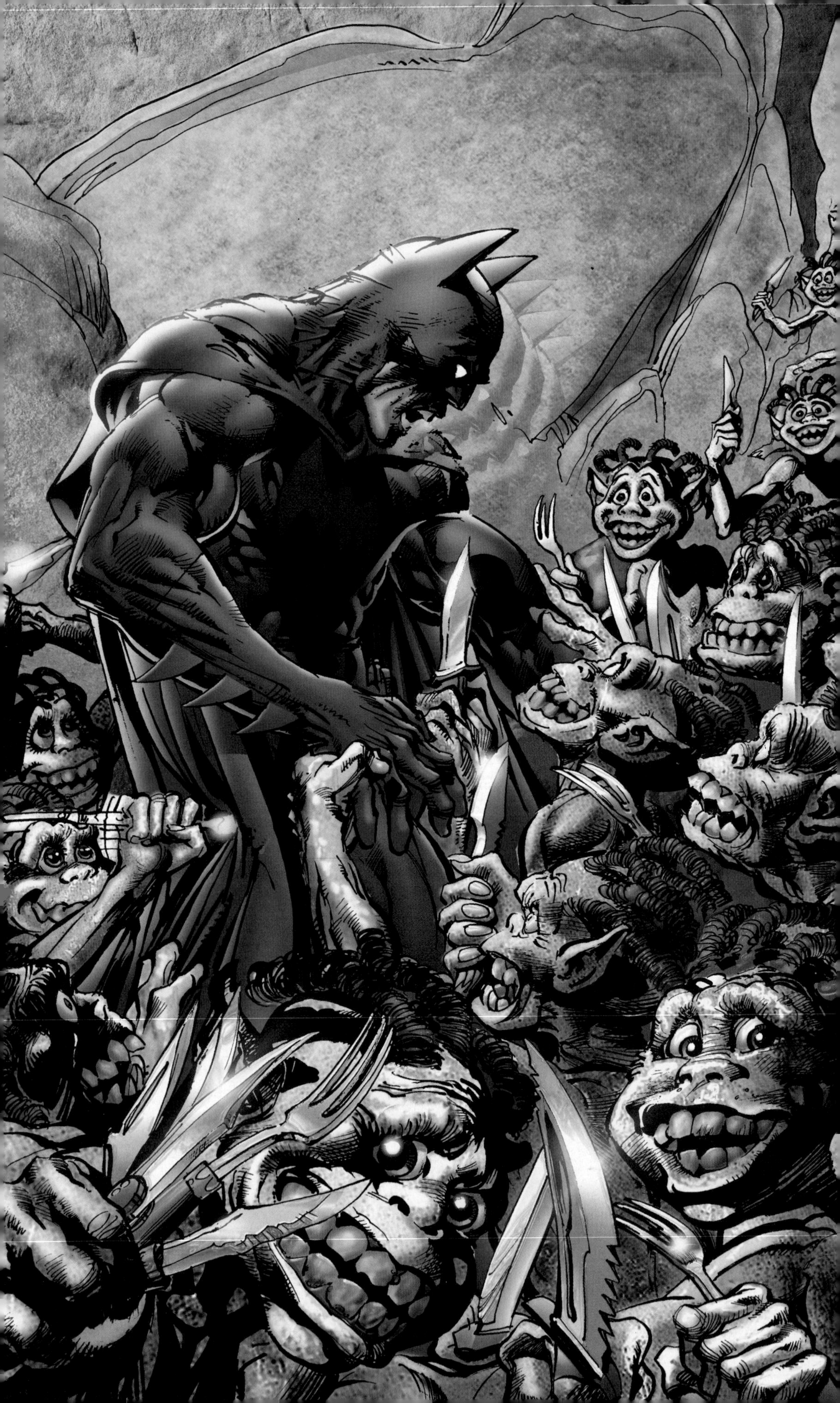

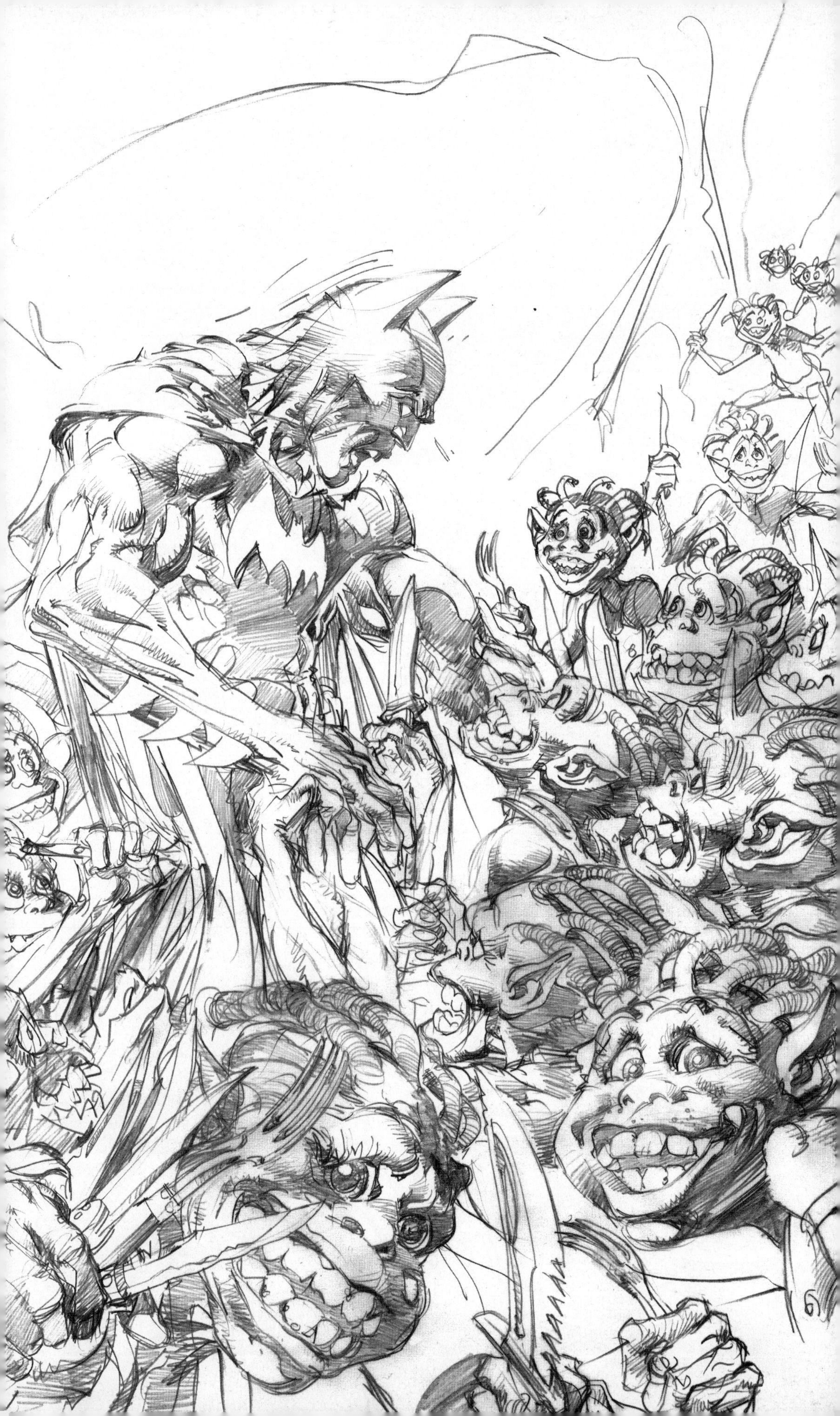

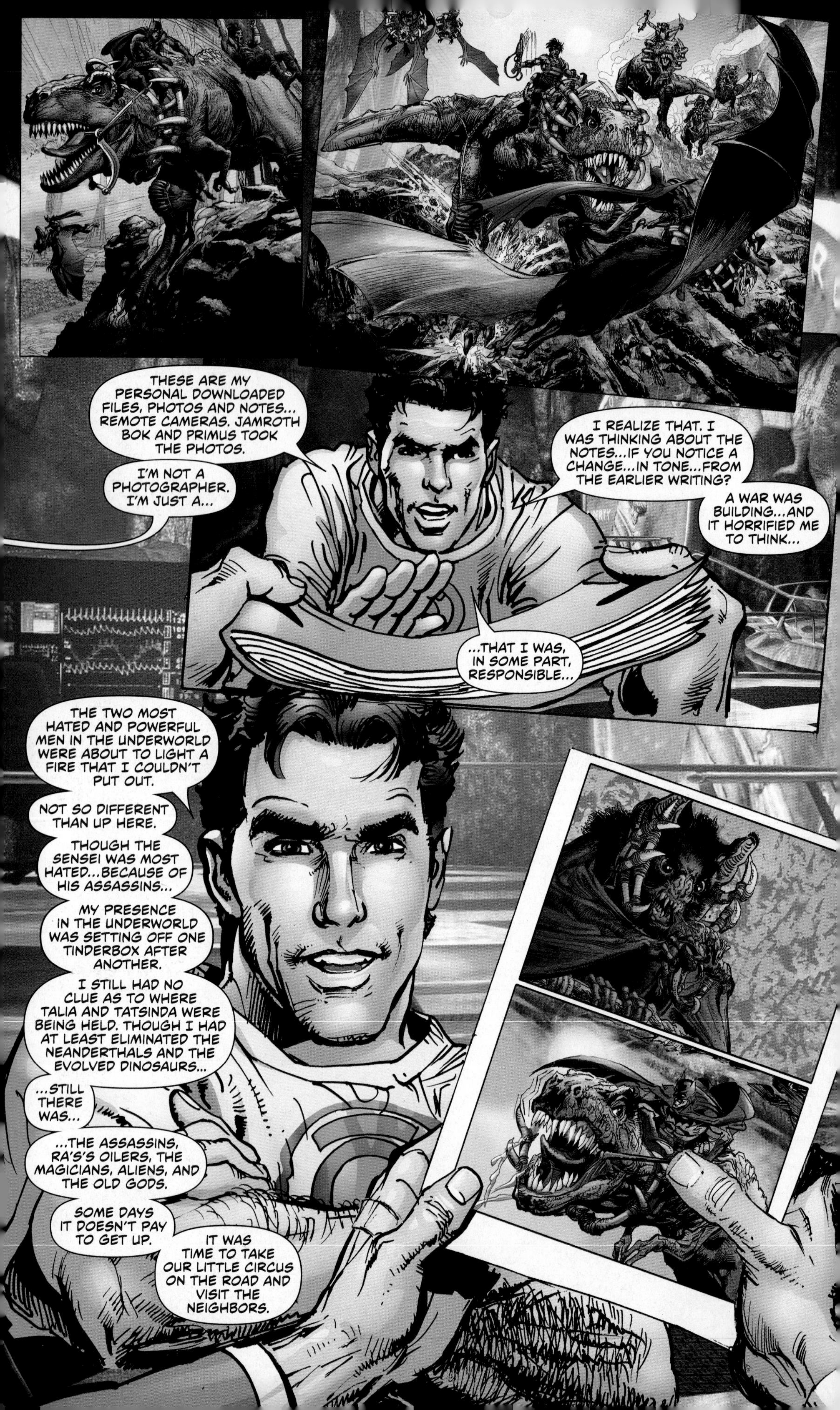
THESE ARE MY PERSONAL DOWNLOADED FILES, PHOTOS AND NOTES... REMOTE CAMERAS. JAMROTH BOK AND PRIMUS TOOK THE PHOTOS.
I'M NOT A PHOTOGRAPHER. I'M JUST A...
I REALIZE THAT. I WAS THINKING ABOUT THE NOTES...IF YOU NOTICE A CHANGE...IN TONE...FROM THE EARLIER WRITING?
A WAR WAS BUILDING...AND IT HORRIFIED ME TO THINK...
...THAT I WAS, IN SOME PART, RESPONSIBLE...
THE TWO MOST HATED AND POWERFUL MEN IN THE UNDERWORLD WERE ABOUT TO LIGHT A FIRE THAT I COULDN'T PUT OUT.
NOT SO DIFFERENT THAN UP HERE.
THOUGH THE SENSEI WAS MOST HATED...BECAUSE OF HIS ASSASSINS...
MY PRESENCE IN THE UNDERWORLD WAS SETTING OFF ONE TINDERBOX AFTER ANOTHER.
I STILL HAD NO CLUE AS TO WHERE TALIA AND TATSINDA WERE BEING HELD. THOUGH I HAD AT LEAST ELIMINATED THE NEANDERTHALS AND THE EVOLVED DINOSAURS...
...STILL THERE WAS...
...THE ASSASSINS, RA'S'S OILERS, THE MAGICIANS, ALIENS, AND THE OLD GODS.
SOME DAYS IT DOESN'T PAY TO GET UP.
IT WAS TIME TO TAKE OUR LITTLE CIRCUS ON THE ROAD AND VISIT THE NEIGHBORS.

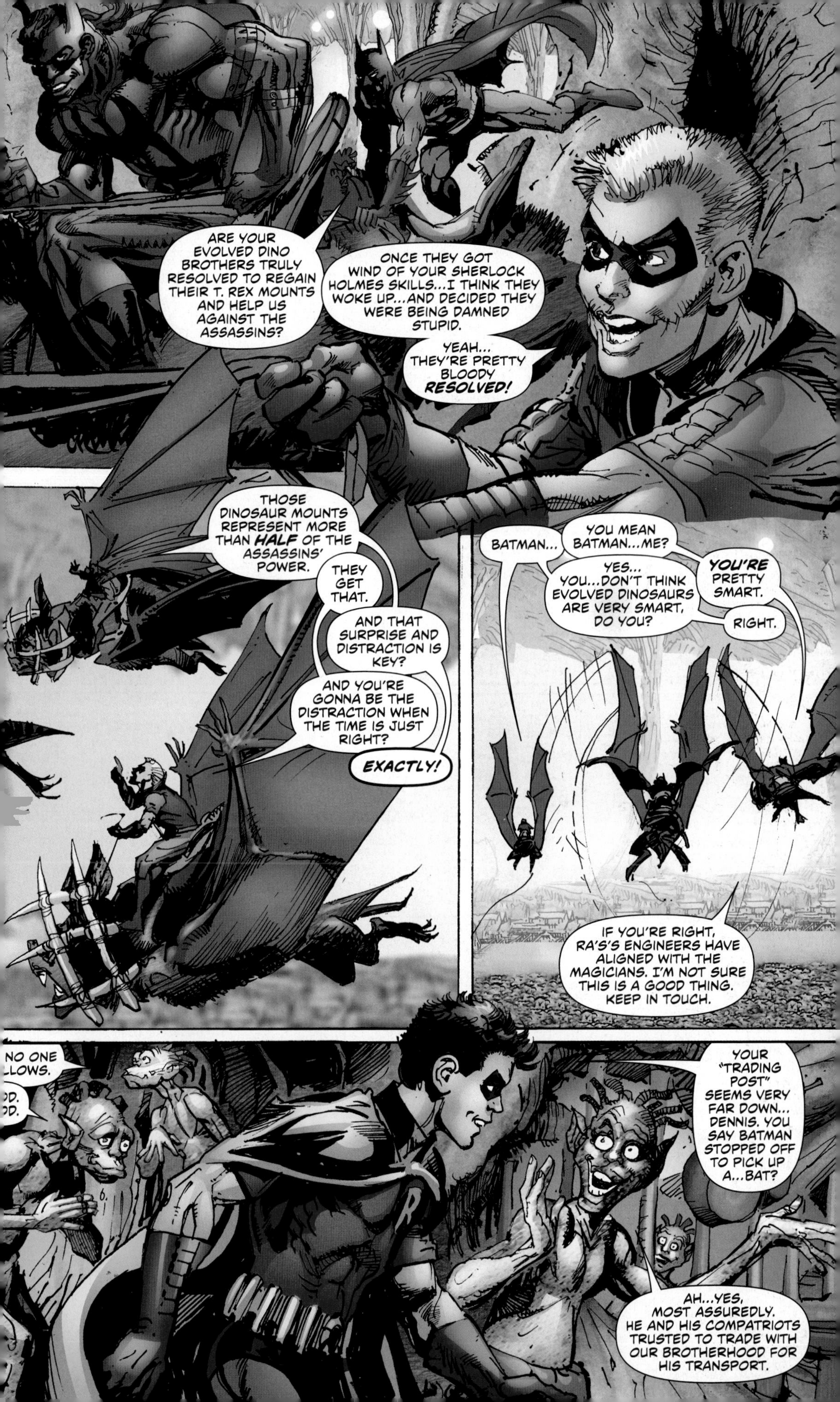

ARE YOUR EVOLVED DINO BROTHERS TRULY RESOLVED TO REGAIN THEIR T. REX MOUNTS AND HELP US AGAINST THE ASSASSINS?
ONCE THEY GOT WIND OF YOUR SHERLOCK HOLMES SKILLS...I THINK THEY WOKE UP...AND DECIDED THEY WERE BEING DAMNED STUPID.
YEAH... THEY'RE PRETTY BLOODY **RESOLVED!**
THOSE DINOSAUR MOUNTS REPRESENT MORE THAN **HALF** OF THE ASSASSINS' POWER.
THEY GET THAT.
AND THAT SURPRISE AND DISTRACTION IS KEY?
AND YOU'RE GONNA BE THE DISTRACTION WHEN THE TIME IS JUST RIGHT?
EXACTLY!
BATMAN...
YOU MEAN BATMAN...ME?
YES... YOU...DON'T THINK EVOLVED DINOSAURS ARE VERY SMART, DO YOU?
YOU'RE PRETTY SMART.
RIGHT.
IF YOU'RE RIGHT, RA'S'S ENGINEERS HAVE ALIGNED WITH THE MAGICIANS. I'M NOT SURE THIS IS A GOOD THING. KEEP IN TOUCH.
NO ONE
YOUR "TRADING POST" SEEMS VERY FAR DOWN... DENNIS. YOU SAY BATMAN STOPPED OFF TO PICK UP A...BAT?
AH...YES, MOST ASSUREDLY. HE AND HIS COMPATRIOTS TRUSTED TO TRADE WITH OUR BROTHERHOOD FOR HIS TRANSPORT.

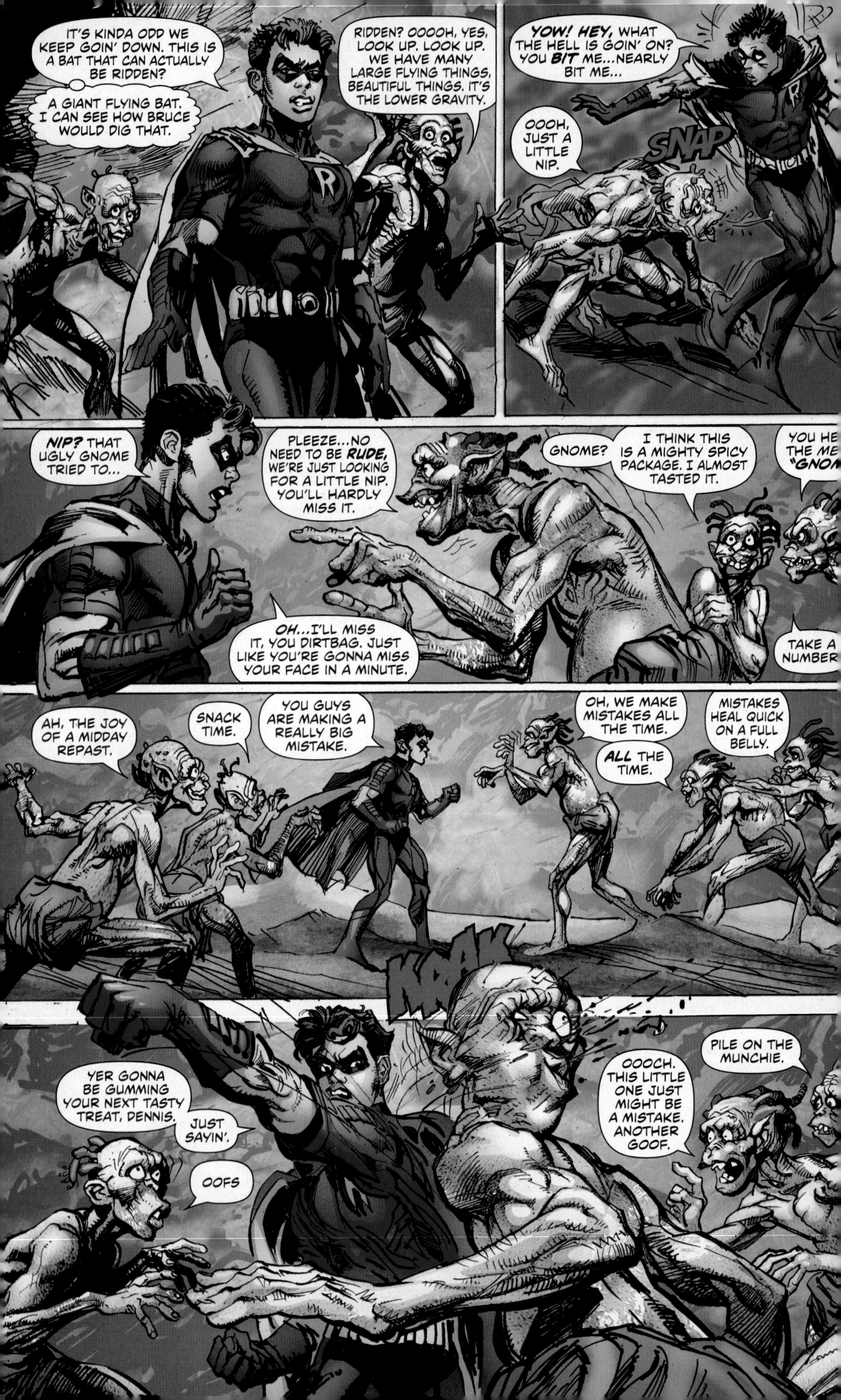

IT'S KINDA ODD WE KEEP GOIN' DOWN. THIS IS A BAT THAT CAN ACTUALLY BE RIDDEN?
A GIANT FLYING BAT. I CAN SEE HOW BRUCE WOULD DIG THAT.
RIDDEN? OOOOH, YES, LOOK UP. LOOK UP. WE HAVE MANY LARGE FLYING THINGS, BEAUTIFUL THINGS. IT'S THE LOWER GRAVITY.
YOW! HEY, WHAT THE HELL IS GOIN' ON? YOU BIT ME...NEARLY BIT ME...
OOOH, JUST A LITTLE NIP.
SNAP
NIP? THAT UGLY GNOME TRIED TO...
PLEEZE...NO NEED TO BE RUDE, WE'RE JUST LOOKING FOR A LITTLE NIP. YOU'LL HARDLY MISS IT.
GNOME?
I THINK THIS IS A MIGHTY SPICY PACKAGE. I ALMOST TASTED IT.
OH...I'LL MISS IT, YOU DIRTBAG. JUST LIKE YOU'RE GONNA MISS YOUR FACE IN A MINUTE.
TAKE A NUMBER
AH, THE JOY OF A MIDDAY REPAST.
SNACK TIME.
YOU GUYS ARE MAKING A REALLY BIG MISTAKE.
OH, WE MAKE MISTAKES ALL THE TIME.
ALL THE TIME.
MISTAKES HEAL QUICK ON A FULL BELLY.
KRAK
YER GONNA BE GUMMING YOUR NEXT TASTY TREAT, DENNIS.
JUST SAYIN'.
OOFS
OOOCH. THIS LITTLE ONE JUST MIGHT BE A MISTAKE. ANOTHER GOOF.
PILE ON THE MUNCHIE.

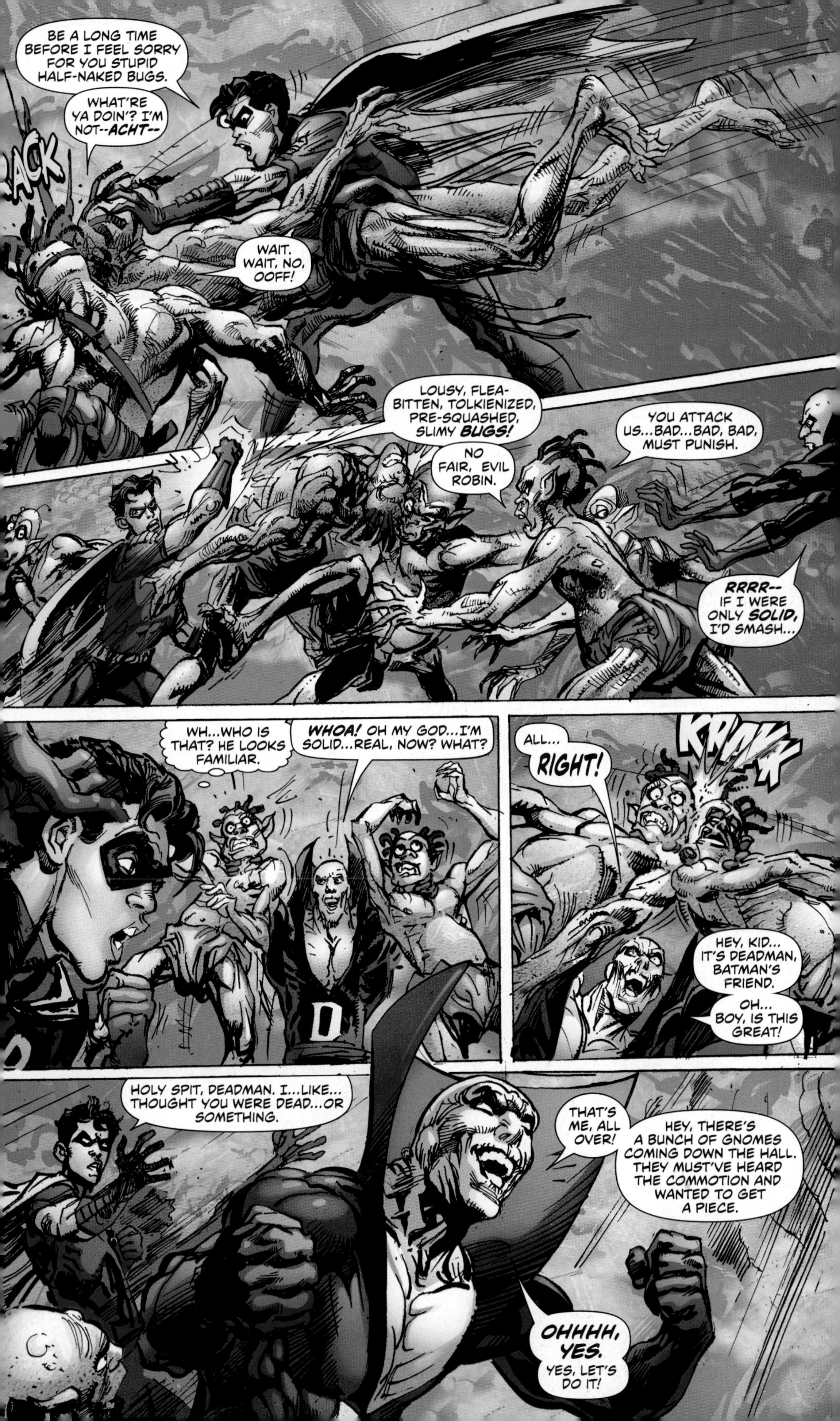

ACK
BE A LONG TIME BEFORE I FEEL SORRY FOR YOU STUPID HALF-NAKED BUGS.
WHAT'RE YA DOIN'? I'M NOT--ACHT--
WAIT. WAIT, NO, OOFF!
LOUSY, FLEA-BITTEN, TOLKIENIZED, PRE-SQUASHED, SLIMY BUGS!
NO FAIR, EVIL ROBIN.
YOU ATTACK US...BAD...BAD, BAD, MUST PUNISH.
RRRR-- IF I WERE ONLY SOLID, I'D SMASH...
WH...WHO IS THAT? HE LOOKS FAMILIAR.
WHOA! OH MY GOD...I'M SOLID...REAL, NOW? WHAT?
ALL... RIGHT!
KRAAK
HEY, KID... IT'S DEADMAN, BATMAN'S FRIEND.
OH... BOY, IS THIS GREAT!
HOLY SPIT, DEADMAN. I...LIKE... THOUGHT YOU WERE DEAD...OR SOMETHING.
THAT'S ME, ALL OVER!
HEY, THERE'S A BUNCH OF GNOMES COMING DOWN THE HALL. THEY MUST'VE HEARD THE COMMOTION AND WANTED TO GET A PIECE.
OHHHH, YES. YES, LET'S DO IT!

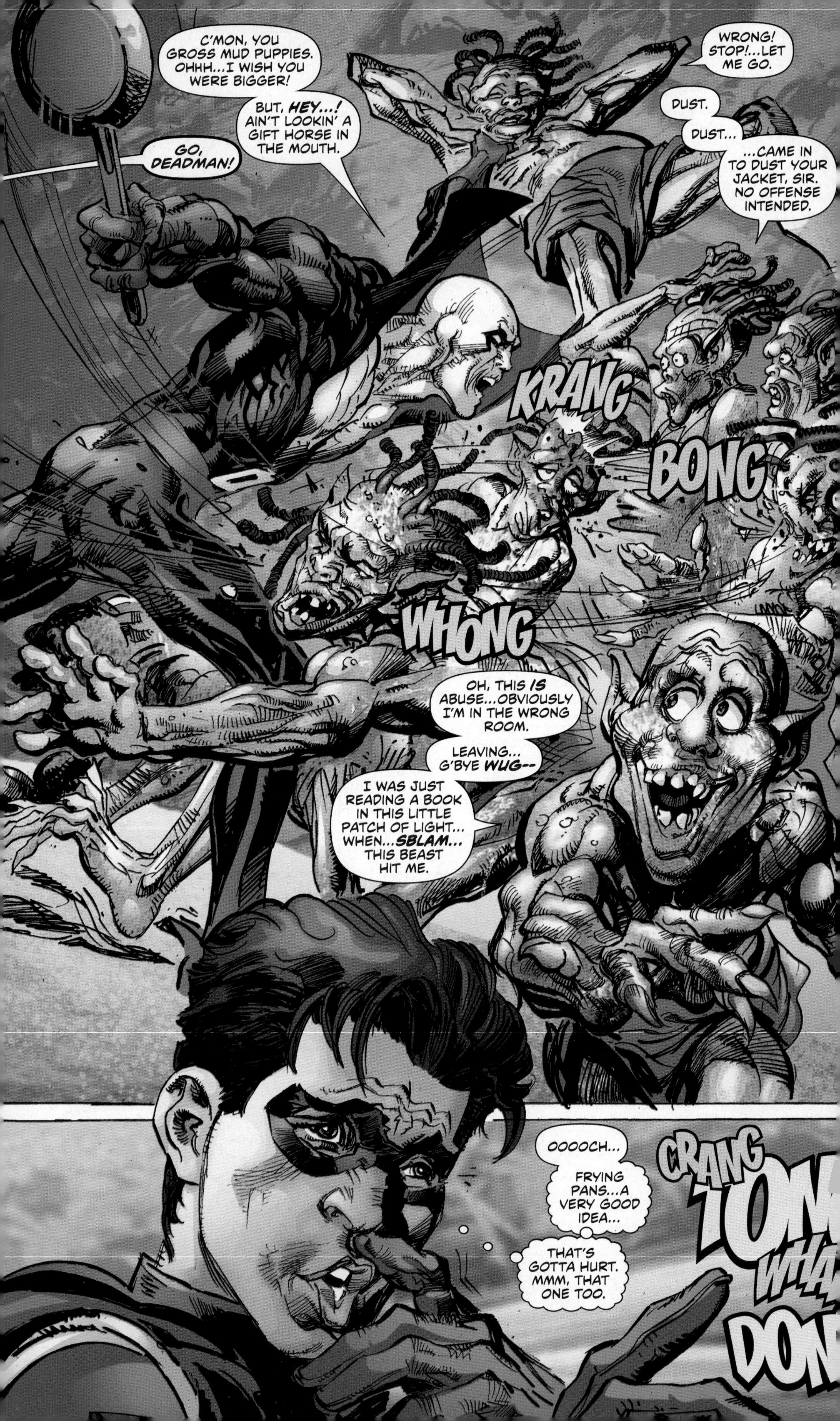
C'MON, YOU GROSS MUD PUPPIES. OHHH...I WISH YOU WERE BIGGER!
BUT, HEY...! AIN'T LOOKIN' A GIFT HORSE IN THE MOUTH.
GO, DEADMAN!
WRONG! STOP!...LET ME GO.
DUST.
DUST...
...CAME IN TO DUST YOUR JACKET, SIR. NO OFFENSE INTENDED.
KRANG
BONG
WHONG
OH, THIS IS ABUSE...OBVIOUSLY I'M IN THE WRONG ROOM.
LEAVING... G'BYE WUG--
I WAS JUST READING A BOOK IN THIS LITTLE PATCH OF LIGHT... WHEN...SBLAM... THIS BEAST HIT ME.
OOOOCH...
FRYING PANS...A VERY GOOD IDEA...
THAT'S GOTTA HURT. MMM, THAT ONE TOO.
CRANG

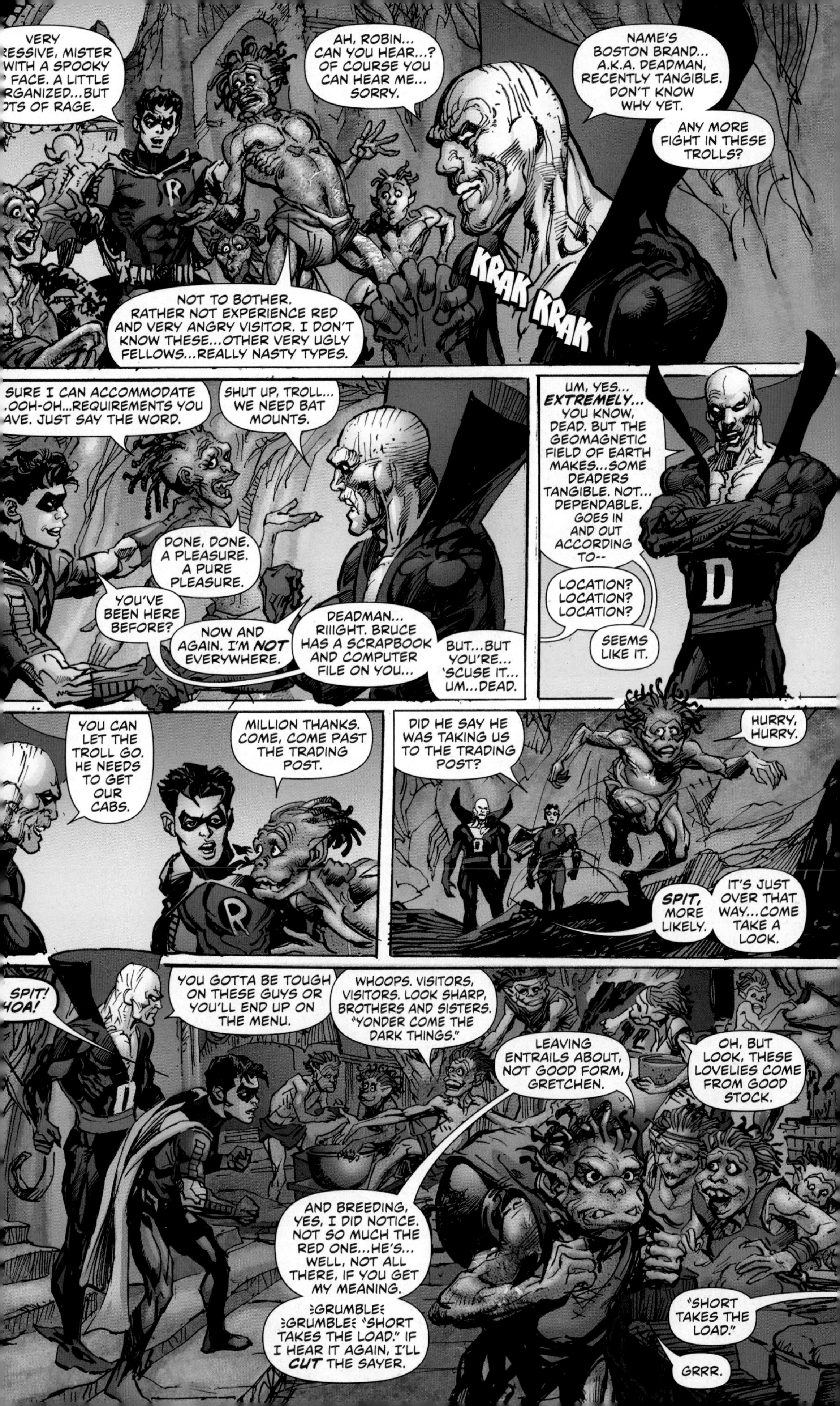
VERY
RESSIVE, MISTER
WITH A SPOOKY
FACE. A LITTLE
RGANIZED...BUT
OTS OF RAGE.
AH, ROBIN... CAN YOU HEAR...? OF COURSE YOU CAN HEAR ME... SORRY.
NAME'S BOSTON BRAND... A.K.A. DEADMAN, RECENTLY TANGIBLE. DON'T KNOW WHY YET.
ANY MORE FIGHT IN THESE TROLLS?
KRAK KRAK
NOT TO BOTHER. RATHER NOT EXPERIENCE RED AND VERY ANGRY VISITOR. I DON'T KNOW THESE...OTHER VERY UGLY FELLOWS...REALLY NASTY TYPES.
SURE I CAN ACCOMMODATE
.OOH-OH...REQUIREMENTS YOU
AVE. JUST SAY THE WORD.
SHUT UP, TROLL... WE NEED BAT MOUNTS.
DONE, DONE. A PLEASURE. A PURE PLEASURE.
YOU'VE BEEN HERE BEFORE?
NOW AND AGAIN. I'M *NOT* EVERYWHERE.
DEADMAN... RIIIGHT. BRUCE HAS A SCRAPBOOK AND COMPUTER FILE ON YOU...
BUT...BUT YOU'RE... 'SCUSE IT... UM...DEAD.
UM, YES... ***EXTREMELY...*** YOU KNOW, DEAD. BUT THE GEOMAGNETIC FIELD OF EARTH MAKES...SOME DEADERS TANGIBLE. NOT... DEPENDABLE. GOES IN AND OUT ACCORDING TO--
LOCATION? LOCATION? LOCATION?
SEEMS LIKE IT.
YOU CAN LET THE TROLL GO. HE NEEDS TO GET OUR CABS.
MILLION THANKS. COME, COME PAST THE TRADING POST.
DID HE SAY HE WAS TAKING US TO THE TRADING POST?
HURRY, HURRY.
SPIT, MORE LIKELY.
IT'S JUST OVER THAT WAY...COME TAKE A LOOK.
SPIT!
HOA!
YOU GOTTA BE TOUGH ON THESE GUYS OR YOU'LL END UP ON THE MENU.
WHOOPS. VISITORS, VISITORS. LOOK SHARP, BROTHERS AND SISTERS. "YONDER COME THE DARK THINGS."
LEAVING ENTRAILS ABOUT, NOT GOOD FORM, GRETCHEN.
OH, BUT LOOK, THESE LOVELIES COME FROM GOOD STOCK.
AND BREEDING, YES, I DID NOTICE. NOT SO MUCH THE RED ONE...HE'S... WELL, NOT ALL THERE, IF YOU GET MY MEANING.
GRUMBLE GRUMBLE "SHORT TAKES THE LOAD." IF I HEAR IT AGAIN, I'LL ***CUT*** THE SAYER.
"SHORT TAKES THE LOAD."
GRRR.

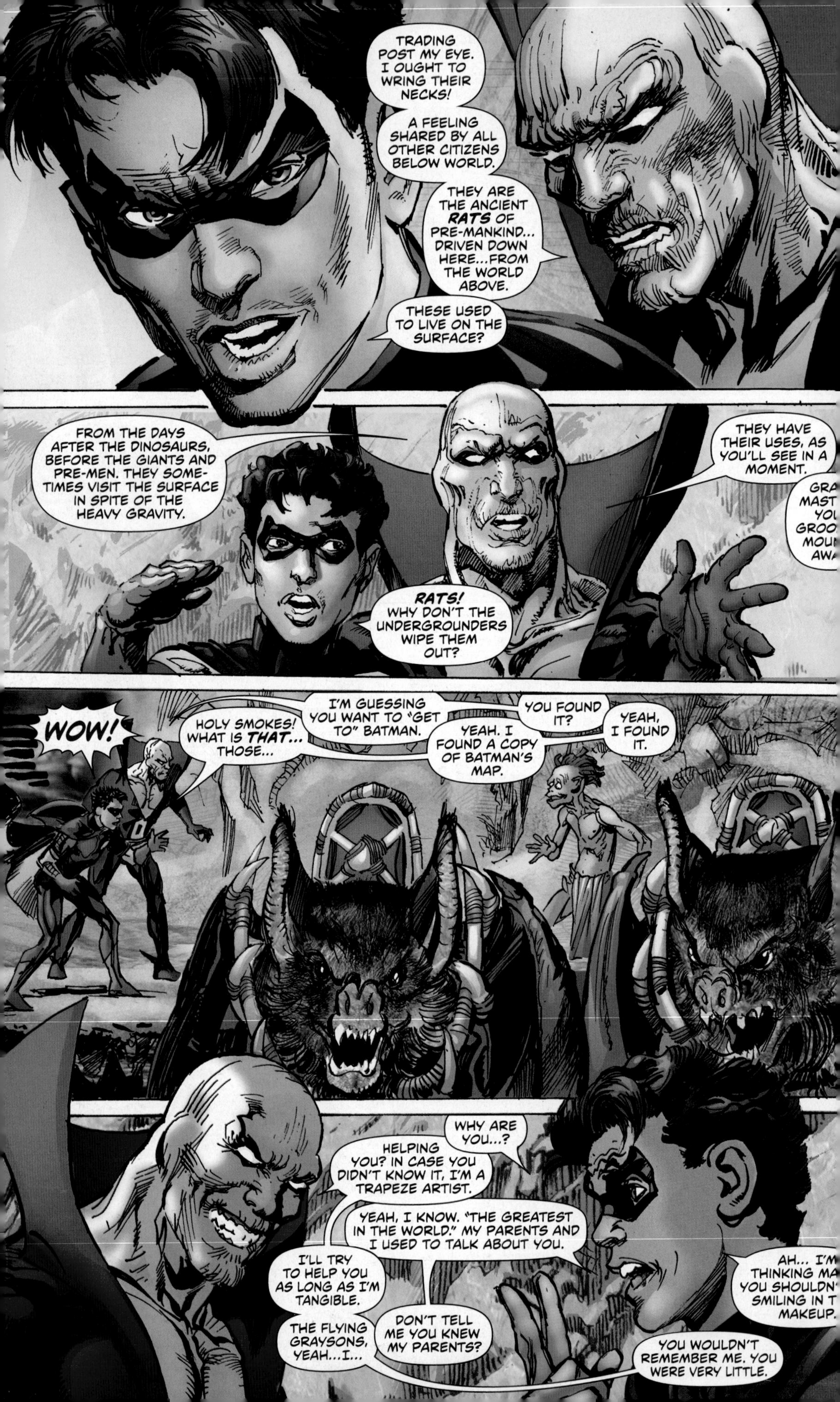

TRADING POST MY EYE. I OUGHT TO WRING THEIR NECKS!
A FEELING SHARED BY ALL OTHER CITIZENS BELOW WORLD.
THEY ARE THE ANCIENT RATS OF PRE-MANKIND... DRIVEN DOWN HERE...FROM THE WORLD ABOVE.
THESE USED TO LIVE ON THE SURFACE?
FROM THE DAYS AFTER THE DINOSAURS, BEFORE THE GIANTS AND PRE-MEN. THEY SOMETIMES VISIT THE SURFACE IN SPITE OF THE HEAVY GRAVITY.
RATS! WHY DON'T THE UNDERGROUNDERS WIPE THEM OUT?
THEY HAVE THEIR USES, AS YOU'LL SEE IN A MOMENT.
WOW!
HOLY SMOKES! WHAT IS THAT... THOSE...
I'M GUESSING YOU WANT TO "GET TO" BATMAN.
YEAH. I FOUND A COPY OF BATMAN'S MAP.
YOU FOUND IT?
YEAH, I FOUND IT.
WHY ARE YOU...?
HELPING YOU? IN CASE YOU DIDN'T KNOW IT, I'M A TRAPEZE ARTIST.
YEAH, I KNOW. "THE GREATEST IN THE WORLD." MY PARENTS AND I USED TO TALK ABOUT YOU.
I'LL TRY TO HELP YOU AS LONG AS I'M TANGIBLE.
THE FLYING GRAYSONS, YEAH...I...
DON'T TELL ME YOU KNEW MY PARENTS?
YOU WOULDN'T REMEMBER ME. YOU WERE VERY LITTLE.

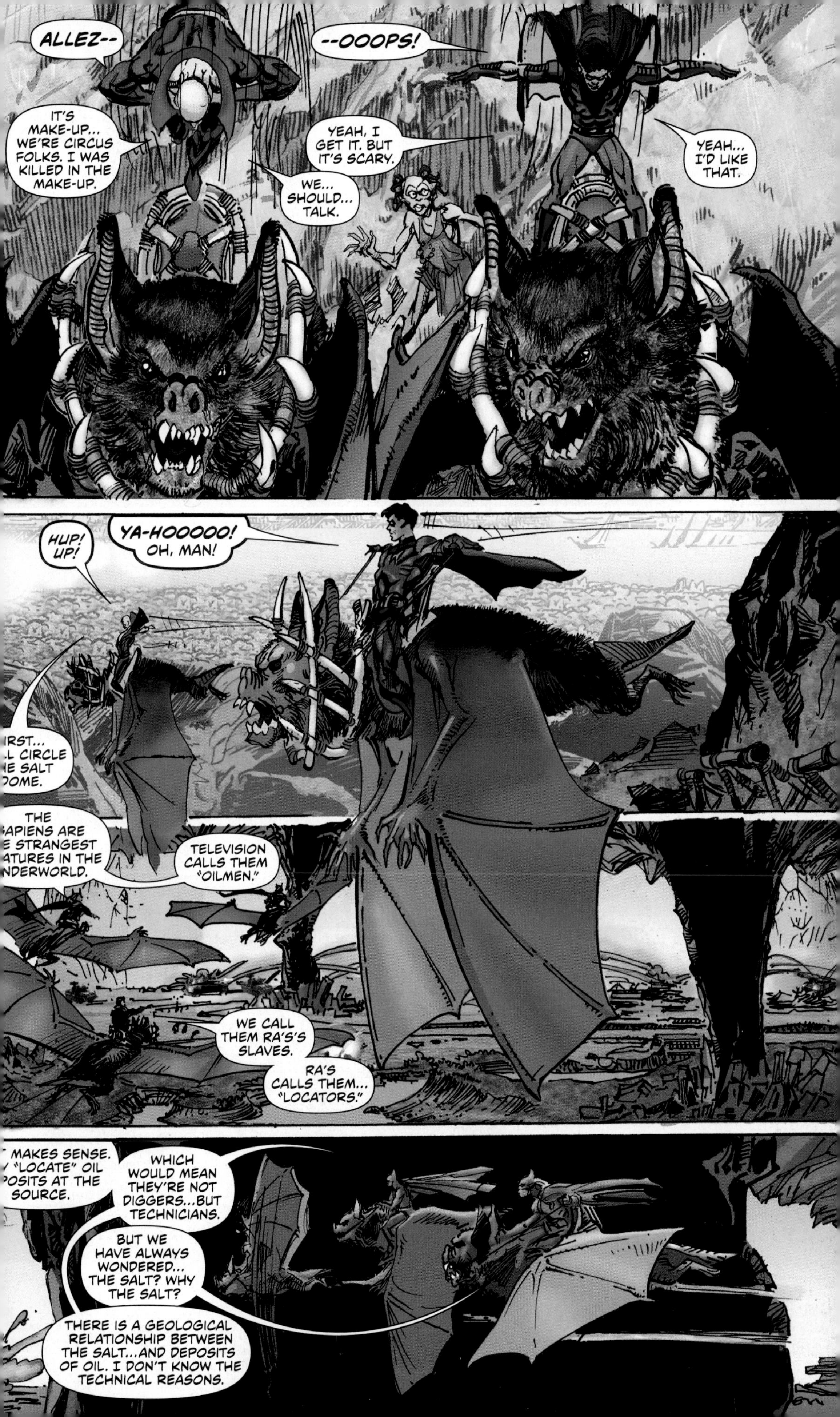
ALLEZ--
--OOOPS!
IT'S MAKE-UP... WE'RE CIRCUS FOLKS. I WAS KILLED IN THE MAKE-UP.
YEAH, I GET IT. BUT IT'S SCARY.
WE... SHOULD... TALK.
YEAH... I'D LIKE THAT.
HUP! UP!
YA-HOOOOO! OH, MAN!
IRST... L CIRCLE IE SALT DOME.
THE SAPIENS ARE E STRANGEST ATURES IN THE NDERWORLD.
TELEVISION CALLS THEM "OILMEN."
WE CALL THEM RA'S'S SLAVES.
RA'S CALLS THEM... "LOCATORS."
T MAKES SENSE. "LOCATE" OIL POSITS AT THE SOURCE.
WHICH WOULD MEAN THEY'RE NOT DIGGERS...BUT TECHNICIANS.
BUT WE HAVE ALWAYS WONDERED... THE SALT? WHY THE SALT?
THERE IS A GEOLOGICAL RELATIONSHIP BETWEEN THE SALT...AND DEPOSITS OF OIL. I DON'T KNOW THE TECHNICAL REASONS.

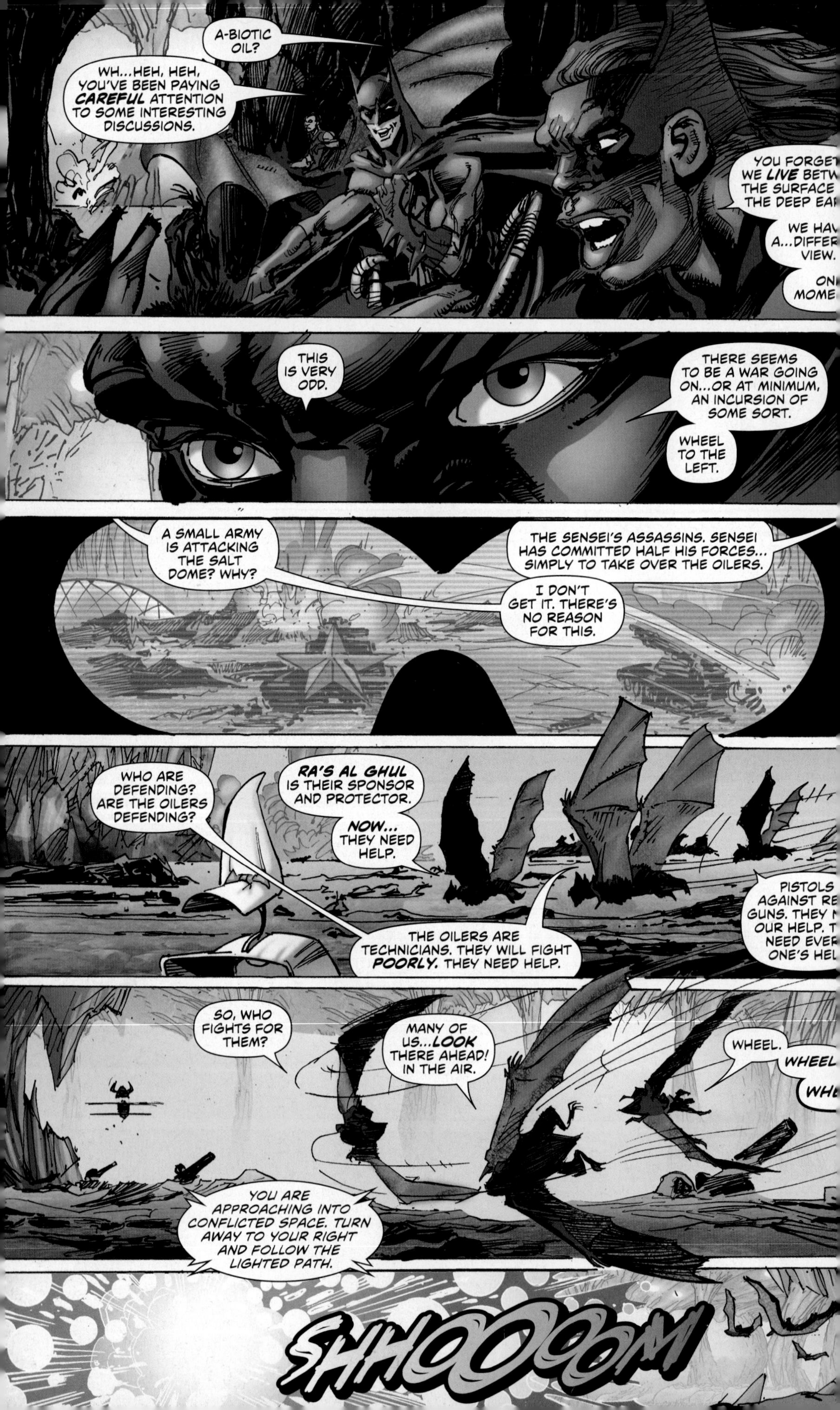

A-BIOTIC OIL?
WH...HEH, HEH, YOU'VE BEEN PAYING CAREFUL ATTENTION TO SOME INTERESTING DISCUSSIONS.
YOU FORGET WE LIVE BETW THE SURFACE THE DEEP EA
WE HAV A...DIFFER VIEW.
ON MOME
THIS IS VERY ODD.
THERE SEEMS TO BE A WAR GOING ON...OR AT MINIMUM, AN INCURSION OF SOME SORT.
WHEEL TO THE LEFT.
A SMALL ARMY IS ATTACKING THE SALT DOME? WHY?
THE SENSEI'S ASSASSINS. SENSEI HAS COMMITTED HALF HIS FORCES... SIMPLY TO TAKE OVER THE OILERS.
I DON'T GET IT. THERE'S NO REASON FOR THIS.
WHO ARE DEFENDING? ARE THE OILERS DEFENDING?
RA'S AL GHUL IS THEIR SPONSOR AND PROTECTOR.
NOW... THEY NEED HELP.
THE OILERS ARE TECHNICIANS. THEY WILL FIGHT POORLY. THEY NEED HELP.
PISTOLS AGAINST RE GUNS. THEY OUR HELP. T NEED EVER ONE'S HEL
SO, WHO FIGHTS FOR THEM?
MANY OF US...LOOK THERE AHEAD! IN THE AIR.
WHEEL.
WHEEL
WH
YOU ARE APPROACHING INTO CONFLICTED SPACE. TURN AWAY TO YOUR RIGHT AND FOLLOW THE LIGHTED PATH.
SHHOOOOOM

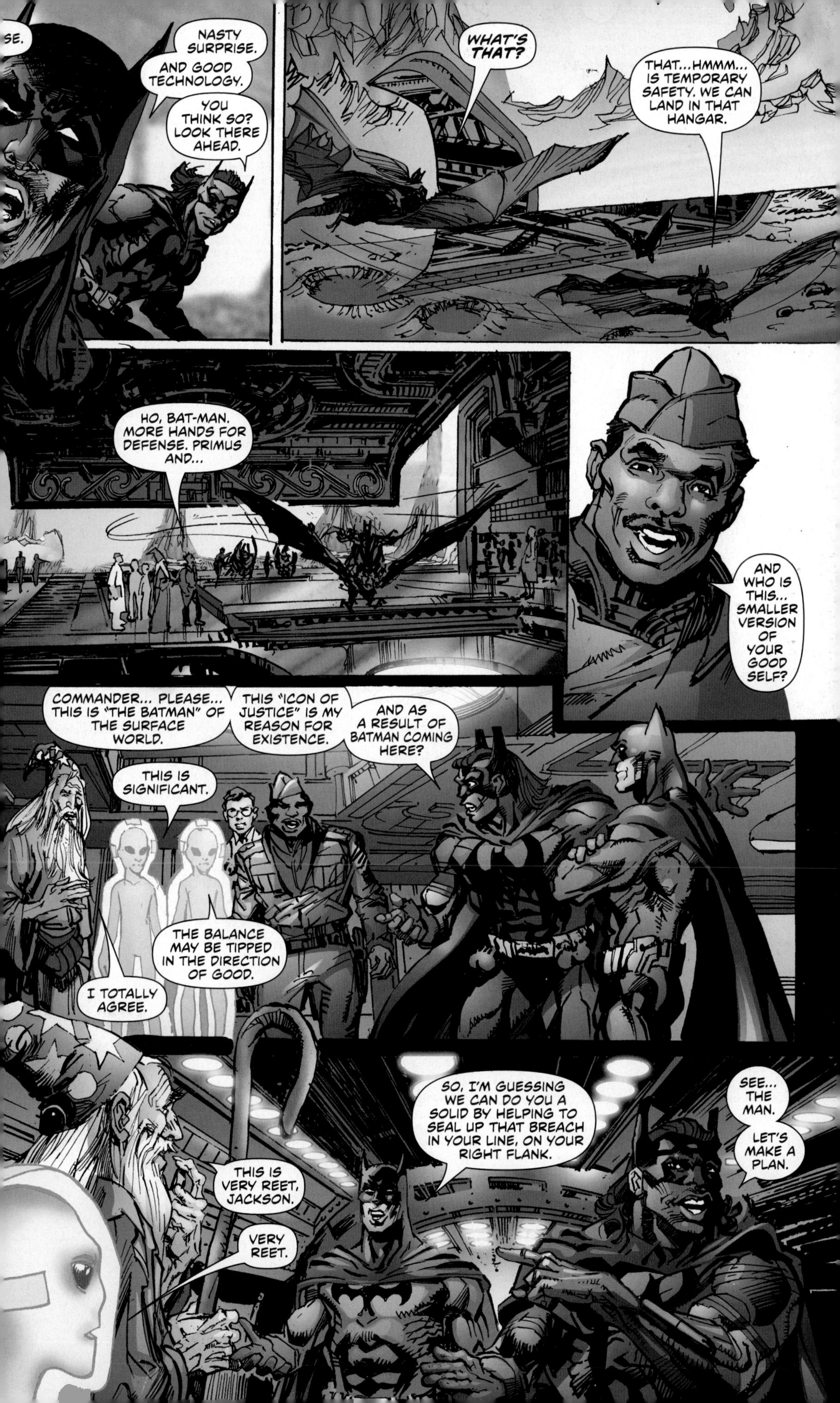
SE.
NASTY SURPRISE.
AND GOOD TECHNOLOGY.
YOU THINK SO? LOOK THERE AHEAD.
WHAT'S THAT?
THAT...HMMM... IS TEMPORARY SAFETY. WE CAN LAND IN THAT HANGAR.
HO, BAT-MAN. MORE HANDS FOR DEFENSE. PRIMUS AND...
AND WHO IS THIS... SMALLER VERSION OF YOUR GOOD SELF?
COMMANDER... PLEASE... THIS IS "THE BATMAN" OF THE SURFACE WORLD.
THIS "ICON OF JUSTICE" IS MY REASON FOR EXISTENCE.
AND AS A RESULT OF BATMAN COMING HERE?
THIS IS SIGNIFICANT.
THE BALANCE MAY BE TIPPED IN THE DIRECTION OF GOOD.
I TOTALLY AGREE.
SO, I'M GUESSING WE CAN DO YOU A SOLID BY HELPING TO SEAL UP THAT BREACH IN YOUR LINE, ON YOUR RIGHT FLANK.
SEE... THE MAN.
LET'S MAKE A PLAN.
THIS IS VERY REET, JACKSON.
VERY REET.

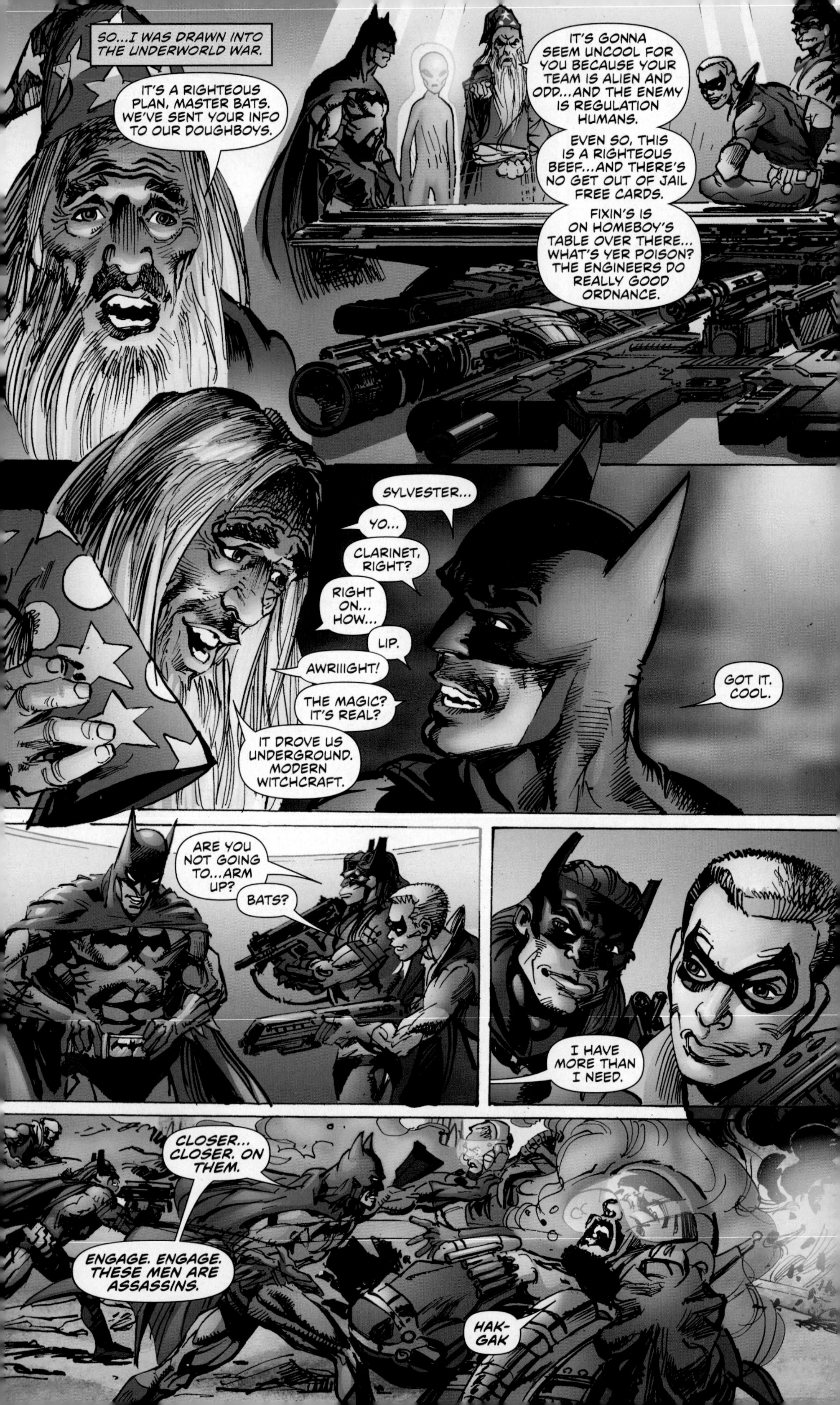
SO...I WAS DRAWN INTO THE UNDERWORLD WAR.
IT'S A RIGHTEOUS PLAN, MASTER BATS. WE'VE SENT YOUR INFO TO OUR DOUGHBOYS.
IT'S GONNA SEEM UNCOOL FOR YOU BECAUSE YOUR TEAM IS ALIEN AND ODD...AND THE ENEMY IS REGULATION HUMANS.
EVEN SO, THIS IS A RIGHTEOUS BEEF...AND THERE'S NO GET OUT OF JAIL FREE CARDS.
FIXIN'S IS ON HOMEBOY'S TABLE OVER THERE... WHAT'S YER POISON? THE ENGINEERS DO REALLY GOOD ORDNANCE.
SYLVESTER...
YO...
CLARINET, RIGHT?
RIGHT ON... HOW...
LIP.
AWRIIIGHT!
THE MAGIC? IT'S REAL?
IT DROVE US UNDERGROUND. MODERN WITCHCRAFT.
GOT IT. COOL.
ARE YOU NOT GOING TO...ARM UP?
BATS?
I HAVE MORE THAN I NEED.
CLOSER... CLOSER. ON THEM.
ENGAGE. ENGAGE. THESE MEN ARE ASSASSINS.
HAK-GAK

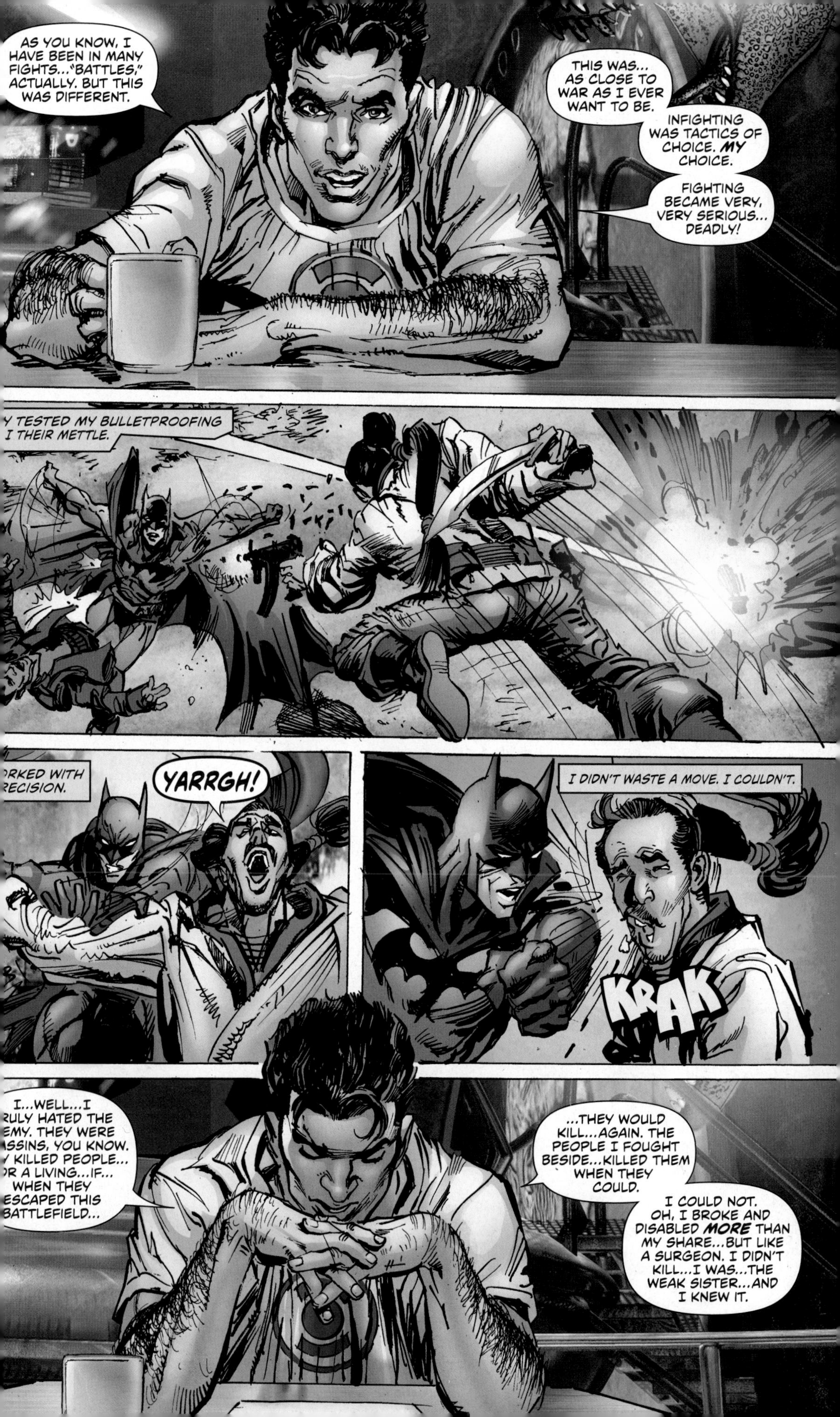

AS YOU KNOW, I HAVE BEEN IN MANY FIGHTS..."BATTLES," ACTUALLY. BUT THIS WAS DIFFERENT.
THIS WAS... AS CLOSE TO WAR AS I EVER WANT TO BE.
INFIGHTING WAS TACTICS OF CHOICE. MY CHOICE.
FIGHTING BECAME VERY, VERY SERIOUS... DEADLY!
Y TESTED MY BULLETPROOFING I THEIR METTLE.
ORKED WITH RECISION.
YARRGH!
I DIDN'T WASTE A MOVE. I COULDN'T.
KRAK
I...WELL...I RULY HATED THE EMY. THEY WERE ASSINS, YOU KNOW. Y KILLED PEOPLE... OR A LIVING...IF... WHEN THEY ESCAPED THIS BATTLEFIELD...
...THEY WOULD KILL...AGAIN. THE PEOPLE I FOUGHT BESIDE...KILLED THEM WHEN THEY COULD.
I COULD NOT. OH, I BROKE AND DISABLED MORE THAN MY SHARE...BUT LIKE A SURGEON. I DIDN'T KILL...I WAS...THE WEAK SISTER...AND I KNEW IT.

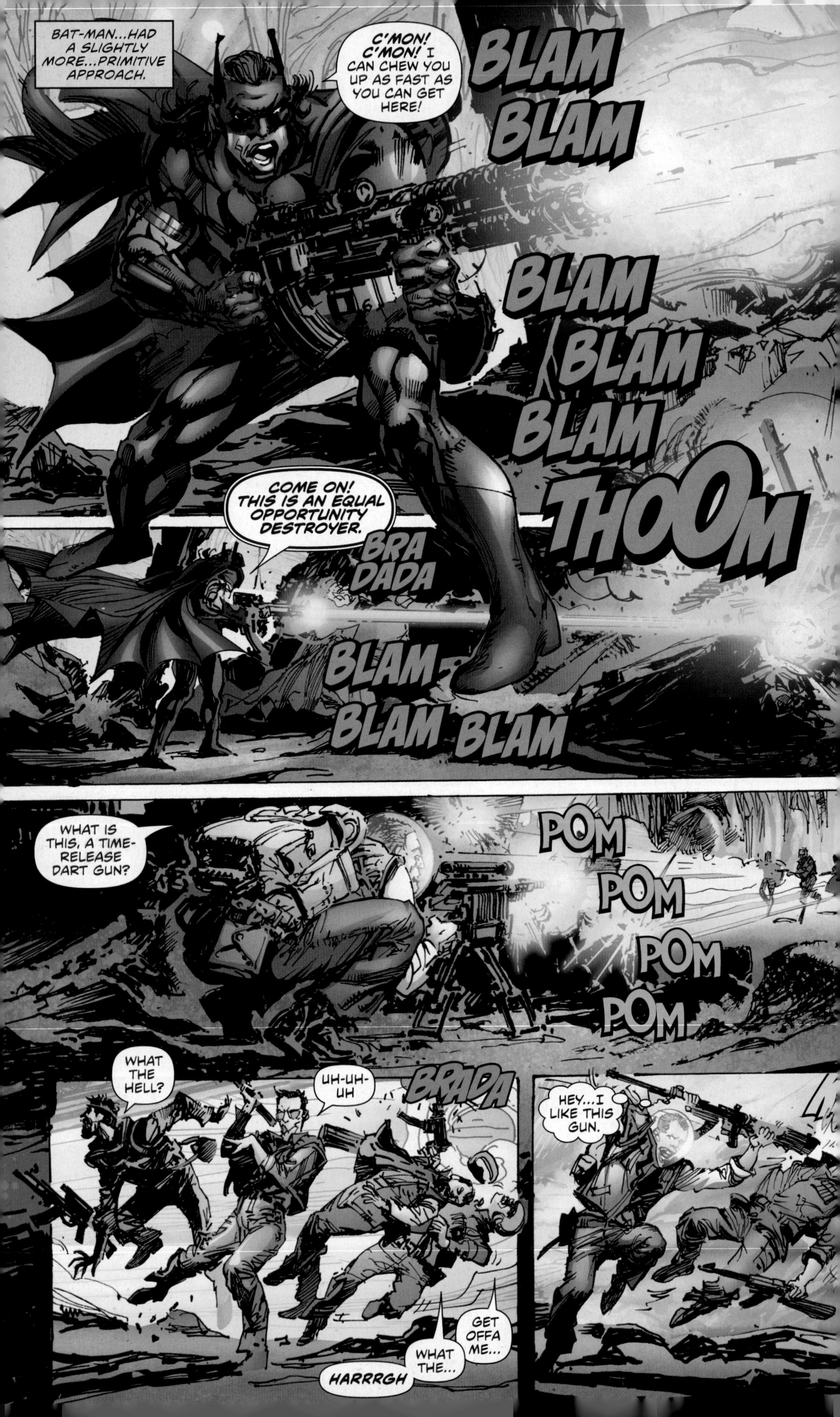
BAT-MAN...HAD A SLIGHTLY MORE...PRIMITIVE APPROACH.
C'MON! C'MON! I CAN CHEW YOU UP AS FAST AS YOU CAN GET HERE!
BLAM BLAM
BLAM BLAM BLAM
THOOM
COME ON! THIS IS AN EQUAL OPPORTUNITY DESTROYER.
BRA DADA
BLAM BLAM BLAM
WHAT IS THIS, A TIME-RELEASE DART GUN?
POM POM POM POM
WHAT THE HELL?
UH-UH-UH
BRADA
GET OFFA ME...
WHAT THE...
HARRRGH
HEY...I LIKE THIS GUN.

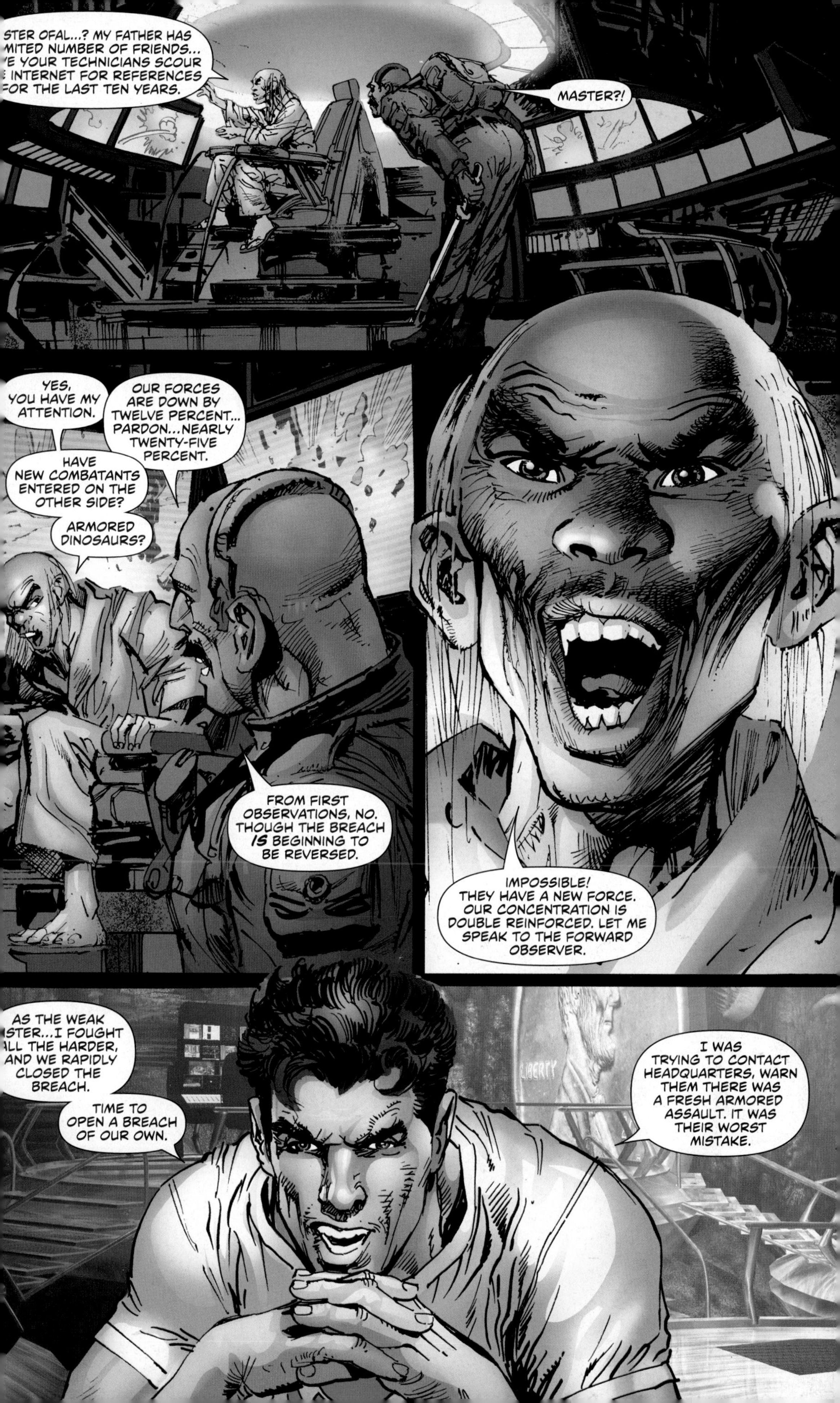
STER OFAL...? MY FATHER HAS
MITED NUMBER OF FRIENDS...
'E YOUR TECHNICIANS SCOUR
INTERNET FOR REFERENCES
FOR THE LAST TEN YEARS.
MASTER?!
YES, YOU HAVE MY ATTENTION.
OUR FORCES ARE DOWN BY TWELVE PERCENT... PARDON...NEARLY TWENTY-FIVE PERCENT.
HAVE NEW COMBATANTS ENTERED ON THE OTHER SIDE?
ARMORED DINOSAURS?
FROM FIRST OBSERVATIONS, NO. THOUGH THE BREACH *IS* BEGINNING TO BE REVERSED.
IMPOSSIBLE! THEY HAVE A NEW FORCE. OUR CONCENTRATION IS DOUBLE REINFORCED. LET ME SPEAK TO THE FORWARD OBSERVER.
AS THE WEAK
STER...I FOUGHT
LL THE HARDER,
AND WE RAPIDLY
CLOSED THE
BREACH.
TIME TO OPEN A BREACH OF OUR OWN.
I WAS TRYING TO CONTACT HEADQUARTERS, WARN THEM THERE WAS A FRESH ARMORED ASSAULT. IT WAS THEIR WORST MISTAKE.
LIBERTY

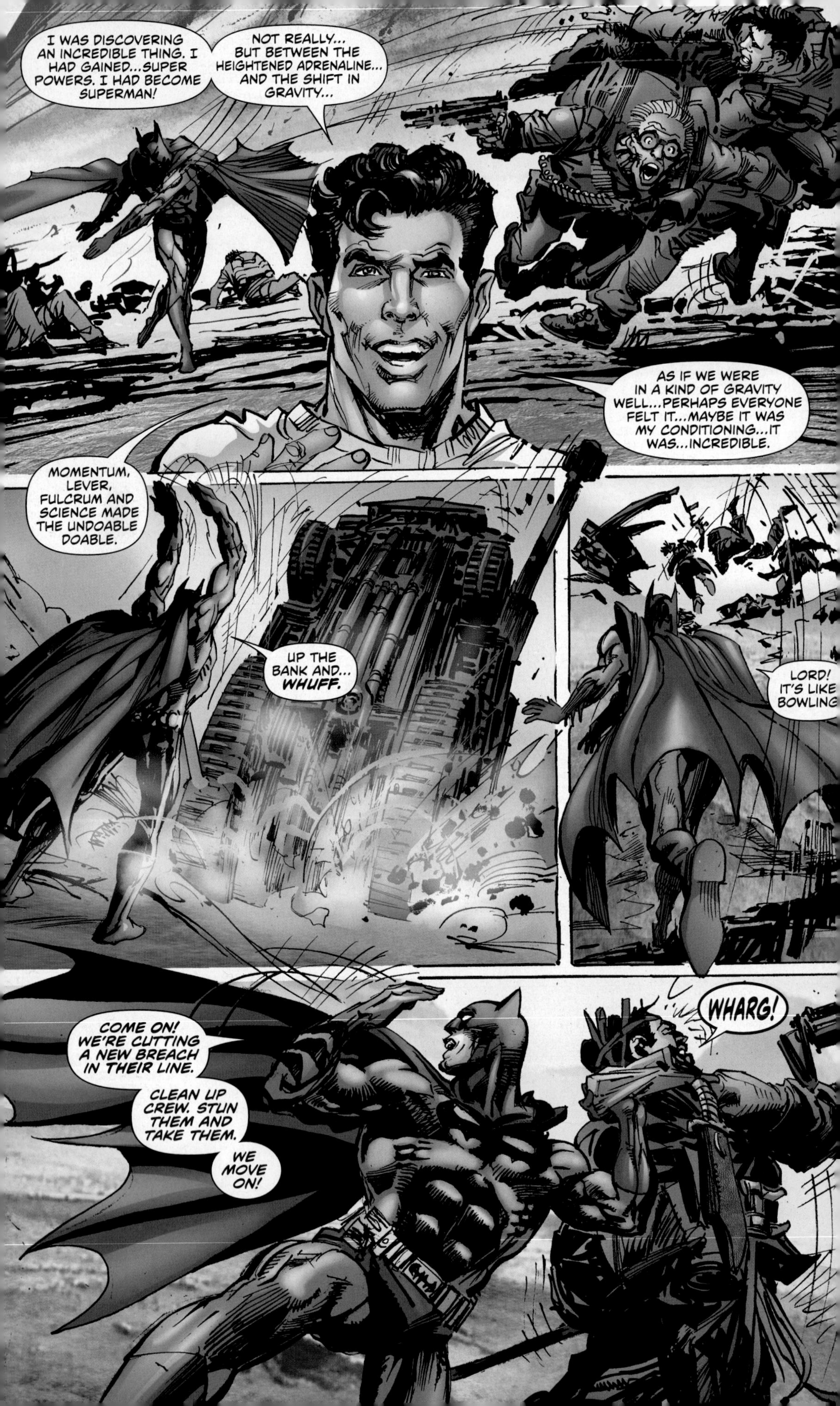
I WAS DISCOVERING AN INCREDIBLE THING. I HAD GAINED...SUPER POWERS. I HAD BECOME SUPERMAN!
NOT REALLY... BUT BETWEEN THE HEIGHTENED ADRENALINE... AND THE SHIFT IN GRAVITY...
AS IF WE WERE IN A KIND OF GRAVITY WELL...PERHAPS EVERYONE FELT IT...MAYBE IT WAS MY CONDITIONING...IT WAS...INCREDIBLE.
MOMENTUM, LEVER, FULCRUM AND SCIENCE MADE THE UNDOABLE DOABLE.
UP THE BANK AND... WHUFF.
LORD! IT'S LIKE BOWLING
COME ON! WE'RE CUTTING A NEW BREACH IN THEIR LINE.
CLEAN UP CREW. STUN THEM AND TAKE THEM.
WE MOVE ON!
WHARG!

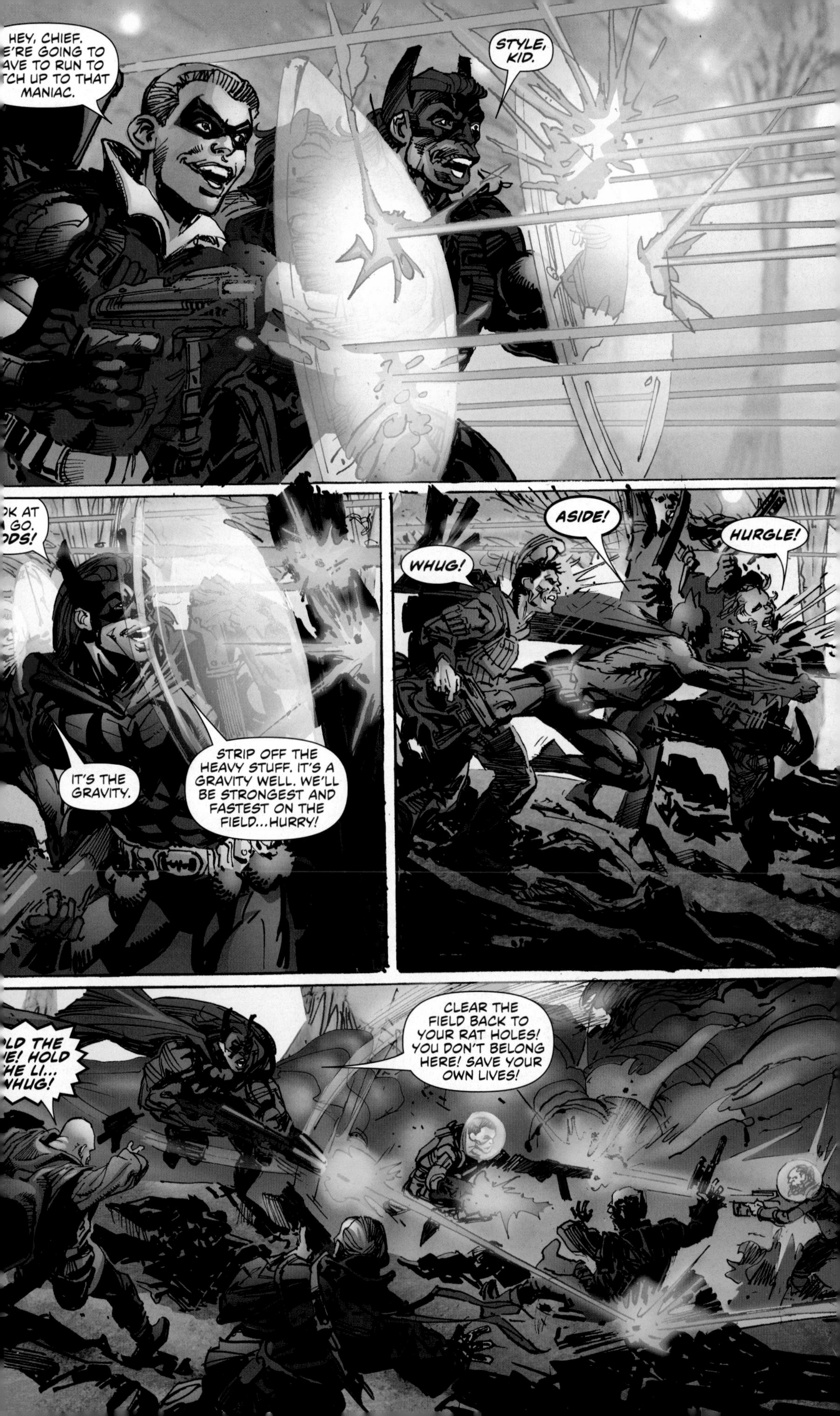
HEY, CHIEF. E'RE GOING TO AVE TO RUN TO TCH UP TO THAT MANIAC.
STYLE, KID.
OK AT A GO. ODS!
IT'S THE GRAVITY.
STRIP OFF THE HEAVY STUFF. IT'S A GRAVITY WELL. WE'LL BE STRONGEST AND FASTEST ON THE FIELD...HURRY!
ASIDE!
WHUG!
HURGLE!
OLD THE E! HOLD THE LI... WHUG!
CLEAR THE FIELD BACK TO YOUR RAT HOLES! YOU DON'T BELONG HERE! SAVE YOUR OWN LIVES!

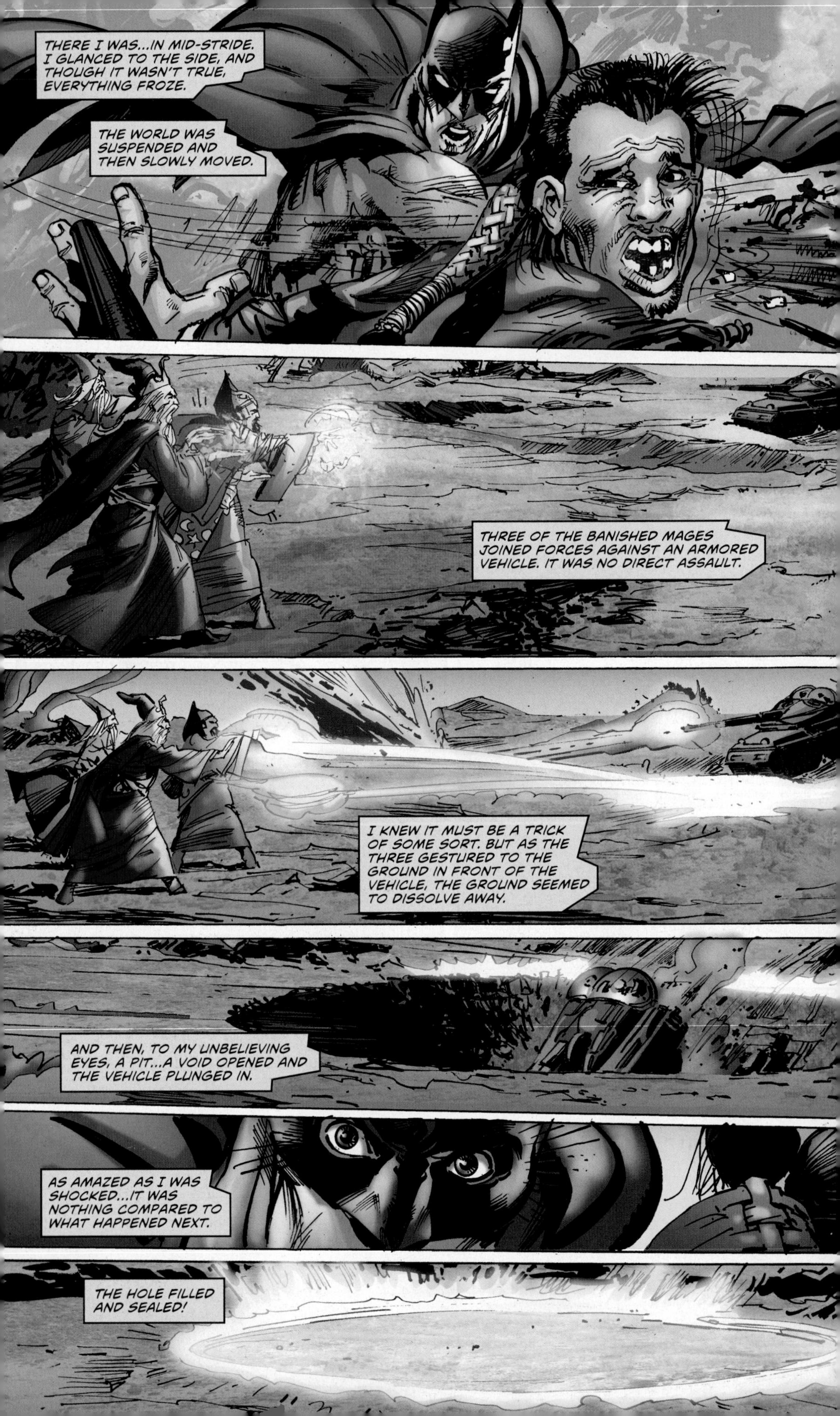
THERE I WAS...IN MID-STRIDE. I GLANCED TO THE SIDE, AND THOUGH IT WASN'T TRUE, EVERYTHING FROZE.
THE WORLD WAS SUSPENDED AND THEN SLOWLY MOVED.
THREE OF THE BANISHED MAGES JOINED FORCES AGAINST AN ARMORED VEHICLE. IT WAS NO DIRECT ASSAULT.
I KNEW IT MUST BE A TRICK OF SOME SORT. BUT AS THE THREE GESTURED TO THE GROUND IN FRONT OF THE VEHICLE, THE GROUND SEEMED TO DISSOLVE AWAY.
AND THEN, TO MY UNBELIEVING EYES, A PIT...A VOID OPENED AND THE VEHICLE PLUNGED IN.
AS AMAZED AS I WAS SHOCKED...IT WAS NOTHING COMPARED TO WHAT HAPPENED NEXT.
THE HOLE FILLED AND SEALED!

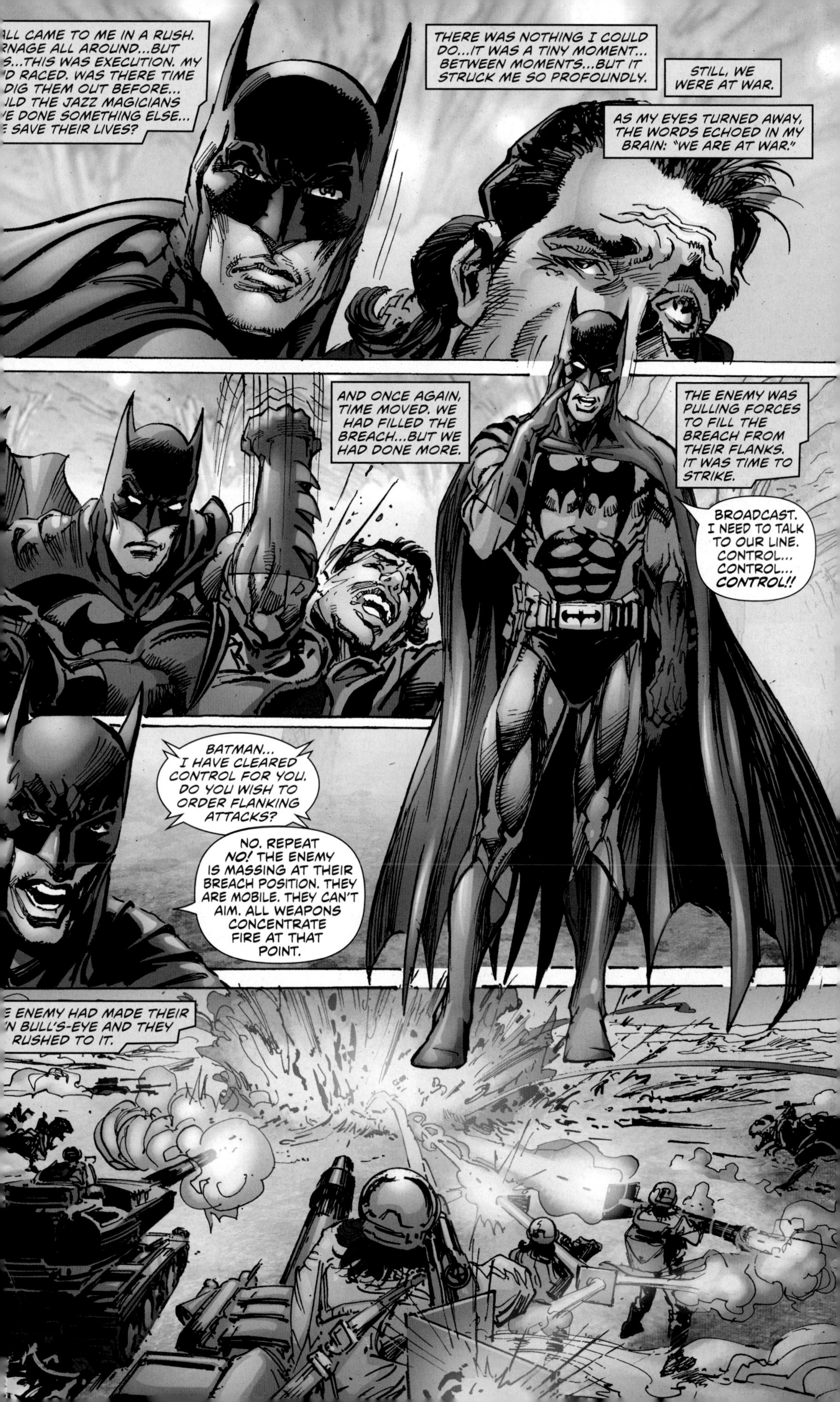
ALL CAME TO ME IN A RUSH. RNAGE ALL AROUND...BUT S...THIS WAS EXECUTION. MY D RACED. WAS THERE TIME DIG THEM OUT BEFORE... ULD THE JAZZ MAGICIANS VE DONE SOMETHING ELSE... E SAVE THEIR LIVES?
THERE WAS NOTHING I COULD DO...IT WAS A TINY MOMENT... BETWEEN MOMENTS...BUT IT STRUCK ME SO PROFOUNDLY.
STILL, WE WERE AT WAR.
AS MY EYES TURNED AWAY, THE WORDS ECHOED IN MY BRAIN: "WE ARE AT WAR."
AND ONCE AGAIN, TIME MOVED. WE HAD FILLED THE BREACH...BUT WE HAD DONE MORE.
THE ENEMY WAS PULLING FORCES TO FILL THE BREACH FROM THEIR FLANKS. IT WAS TIME TO STRIKE.
BROADCAST. I NEED TO TALK TO OUR LINE. CONTROL... CONTROL... CONTROL!!
BATMAN... I HAVE CLEARED CONTROL FOR YOU. DO YOU WISH TO ORDER FLANKING ATTACKS?
NO. REPEAT NO! THE ENEMY IS MASSING AT THEIR BREACH POSITION. THEY ARE MOBILE. THEY CAN'T AIM. ALL WEAPONS CONCENTRATE FIRE AT THAT POINT.
E ENEMY HAD MADE THEIR N BULL'S-EYE AND THEY RUSHED TO IT.

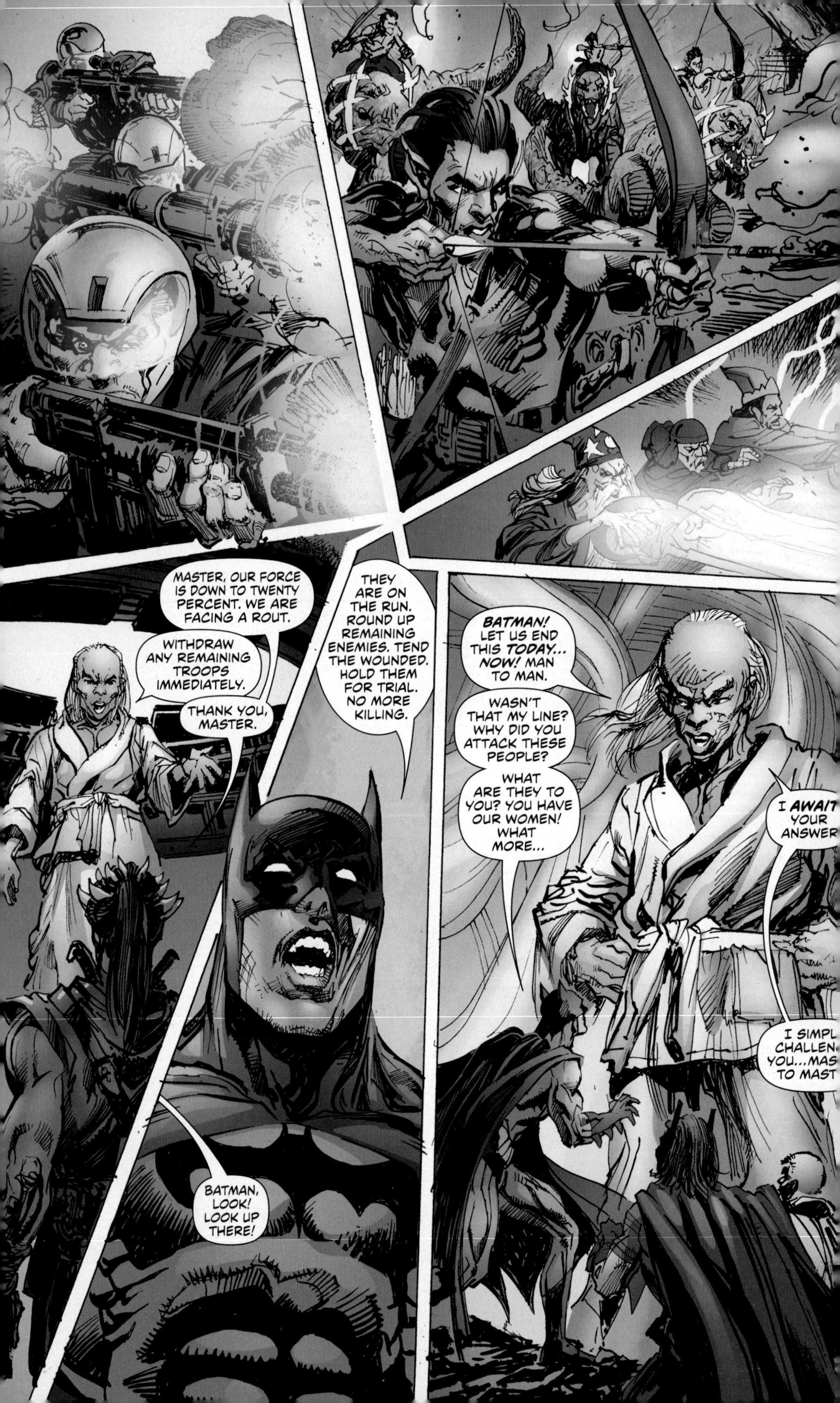
MASTER, OUR FORCE IS DOWN TO TWENTY PERCENT. WE ARE FACING A ROUT.
WITHDRAW ANY REMAINING TROOPS IMMEDIATELY.
THANK YOU, MASTER.
THEY ARE ON THE RUN. ROUND UP REMAINING ENEMIES. TEND THE WOUNDED. HOLD THEM FOR TRIAL. NO MORE KILLING.
BATMAN, LOOK! LOOK UP THERE!
BATMAN! LET US END THIS TODAY... NOW! MAN TO MAN.
WASN'T THAT MY LINE? WHY DID YOU ATTACK THESE PEOPLE?
WHAT ARE THEY TO YOU? YOU HAVE OUR WOMEN! WHAT MORE...
I AWAIT YOUR ANSWER
I SIMPL CHALLEN YOU...MAS TO MAST

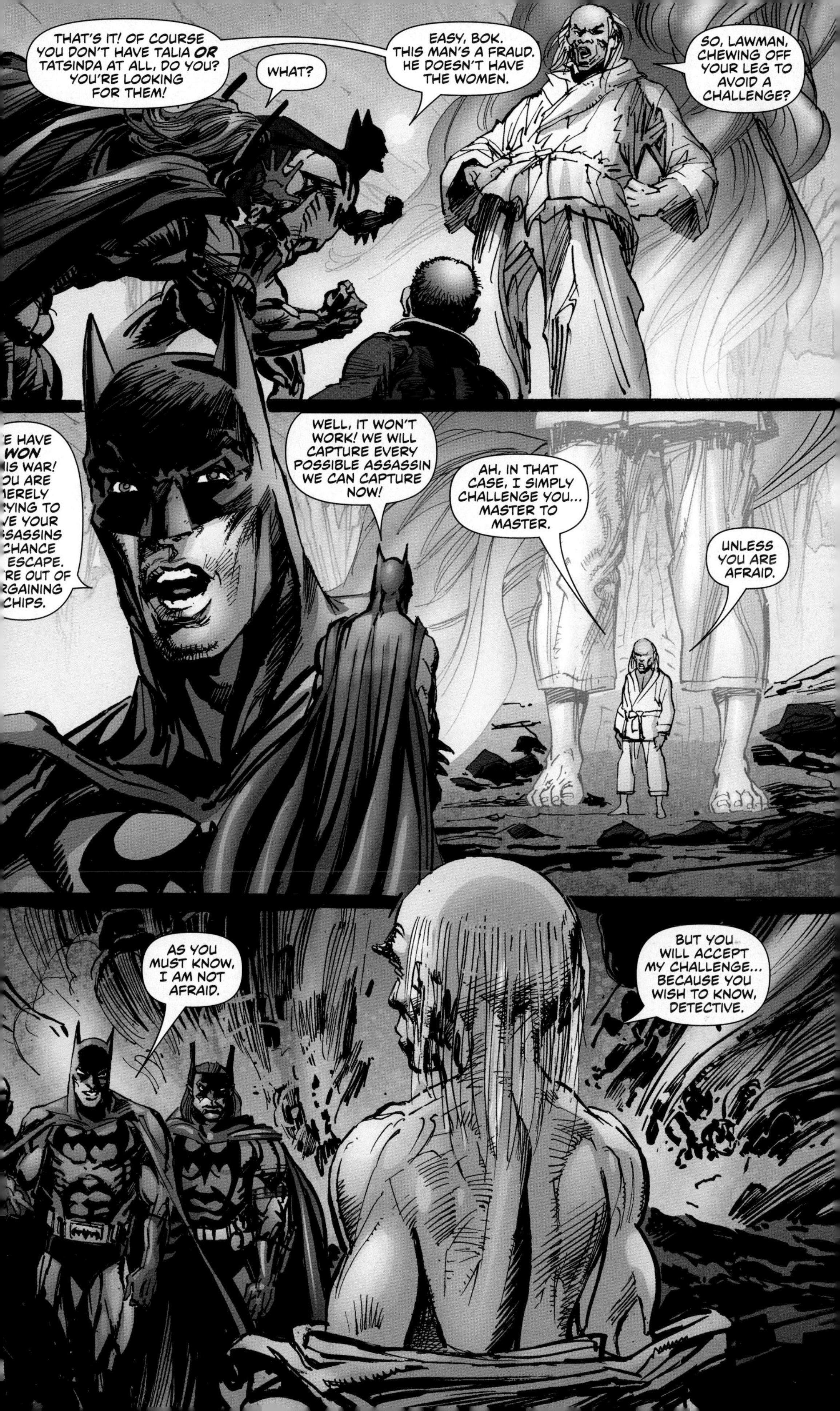
THAT'S IT! OF COURSE YOU DON'T HAVE TALIA OR TATSINDA AT ALL, DO YOU? YOU'RE LOOKING FOR THEM!
WHAT?
EASY, BOK. THIS MAN'S A FRAUD. HE DOESN'T HAVE THE WOMEN.
SO, LAWMAN, CHEWING OFF YOUR LEG TO AVOID A CHALLENGE?
E HAVE WON IS WAR! OU ARE IERELY YING TO VE YOUR SSASSINS CHANCE ESCAPE. RE OUT OF RGAINING CHIPS.
WELL, IT WON'T WORK! WE WILL CAPTURE EVERY POSSIBLE ASSASSIN WE CAN CAPTURE NOW!
AH, IN THAT CASE, I SIMPLY CHALLENGE YOU... MASTER TO MASTER.
UNLESS YOU ARE AFRAID.
AS YOU MUST KNOW, I AM NOT AFRAID.
BUT YOU WILL ACCEPT MY CHALLENGE... BECAUSE YOU WISH TO KNOW, DETECTIVE.

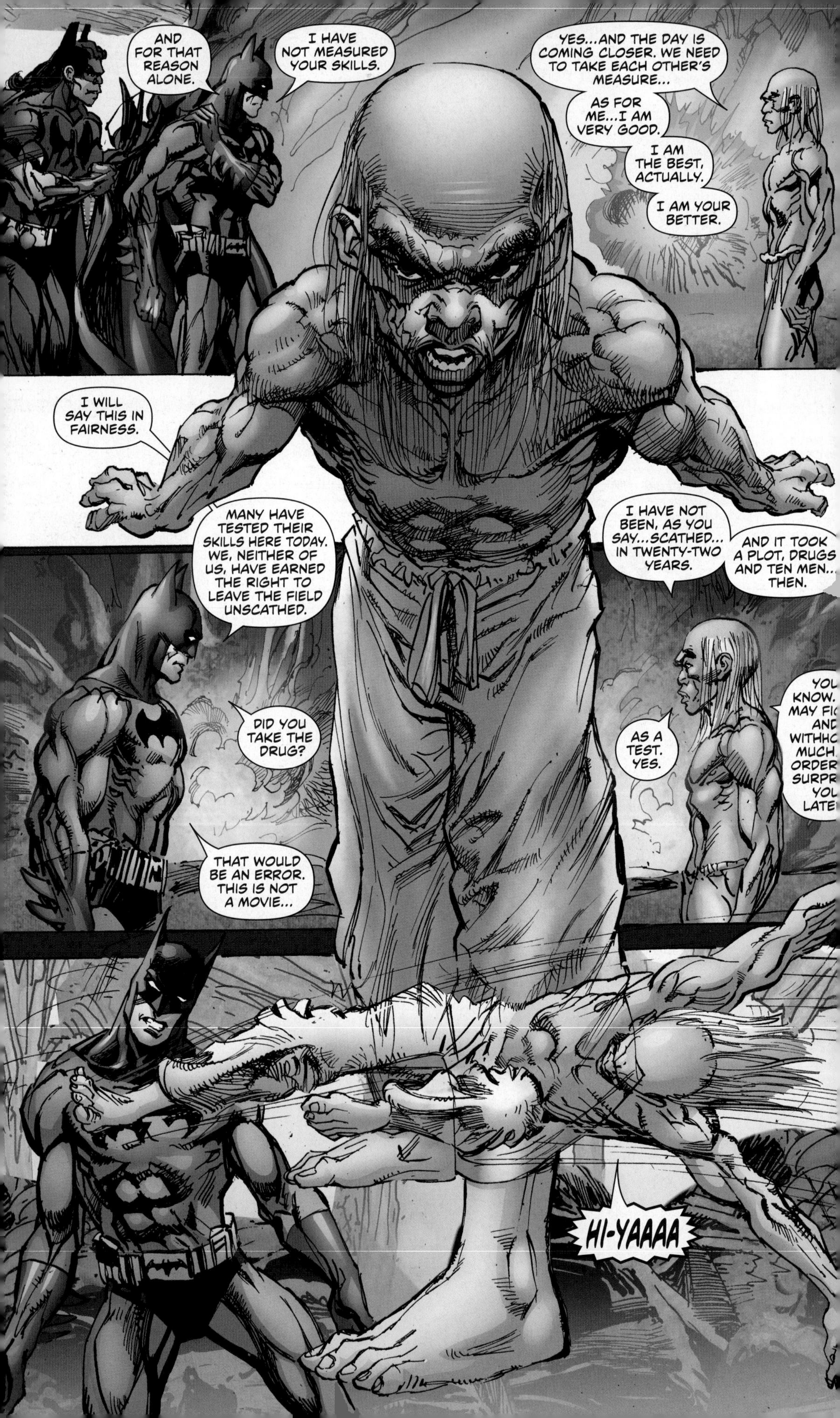
AND FOR THAT REASON ALONE.
I HAVE NOT MEASURED YOUR SKILLS.
YES...AND THE DAY IS COMING CLOSER. WE NEED TO TAKE EACH OTHER'S MEASURE...
AS FOR ME...I AM VERY GOOD.
I AM THE BEST, ACTUALLY.
I AM YOUR BETTER.
I WILL SAY THIS IN FAIRNESS.
MANY HAVE TESTED THEIR SKILLS HERE TODAY. WE, NEITHER OF US, HAVE EARNED THE RIGHT TO LEAVE THE FIELD UNSCATHED.
I HAVE NOT BEEN, AS YOU SAY...SCATHED... IN TWENTY-TWO YEARS.
AND IT TOOK A PLOT, DRUGS AND TEN MEN... THEN.
DID YOU TAKE THE DRUG?
AS A TEST. YES.
THAT WOULD BE AN ERROR. THIS IS NOT A MOVIE...
HI-YAAAA

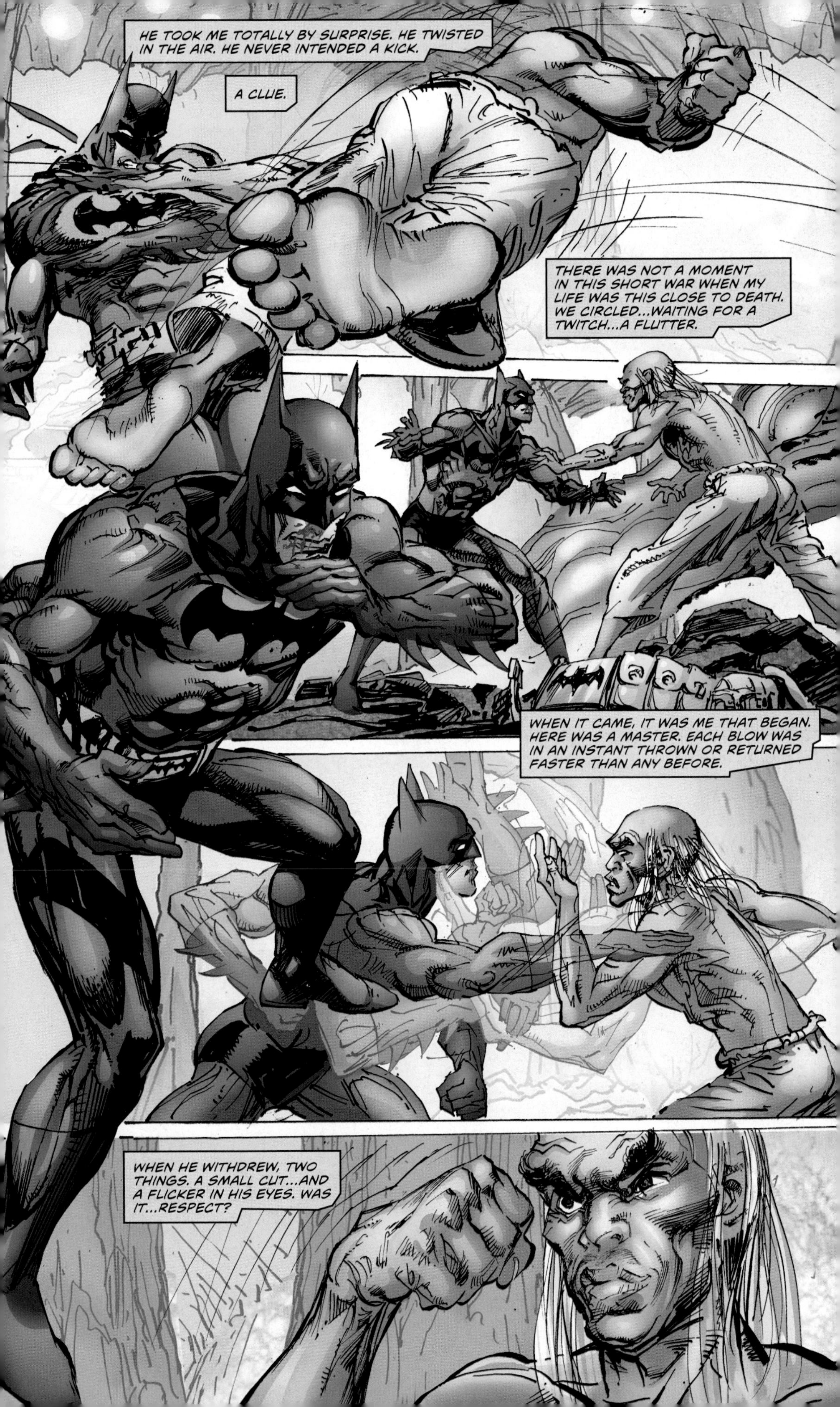
HE TOOK ME TOTALLY BY SURPRISE. HE TWISTED IN THE AIR. HE NEVER INTENDED A KICK.
A CLUE.
THERE WAS NOT A MOMENT IN THIS SHORT WAR WHEN MY LIFE WAS THIS CLOSE TO DEATH. WE CIRCLED...WAITING FOR A TWITCH...A FLUTTER.
WHEN IT CAME, IT WAS ME THAT BEGAN. HERE WAS A MASTER. EACH BLOW WAS IN AN INSTANT THROWN OR RETURNED FASTER THAN ANY BEFORE.
WHEN HE WITHDREW, TWO THINGS. A SMALL CUT...AND A FLICKER IN HIS EYES. WAS IT...RESPECT?

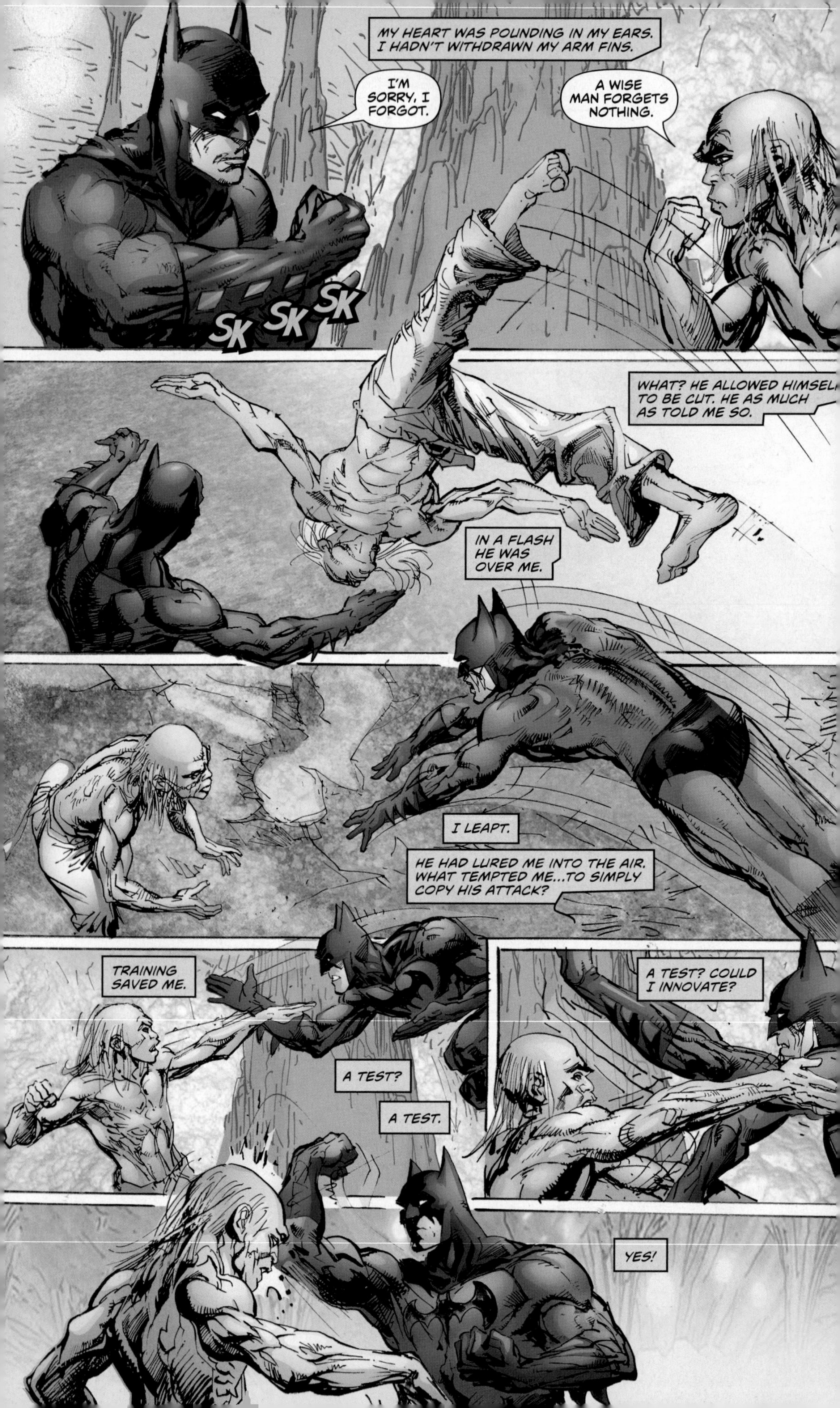
MY HEART WAS POUNDING IN MY EARS. I HADN'T WITHDRAWN MY ARM FINS.
I'M SORRY, I FORGOT.
A WISE MAN FORGETS NOTHING.
SK SK SK
WHAT? HE ALLOWED HIMSEL TO BE CUT. HE AS MUCH AS TOLD ME SO.
IN A FLASH HE WAS OVER ME.
I LEAPT.
HE HAD LURED ME INTO THE AIR. WHAT TEMPTED ME...TO SIMPLY COPY HIS ATTACK?
TRAINING SAVED ME.
A TEST? COULD I INNOVATE?
A TEST?
A TEST.
YES!

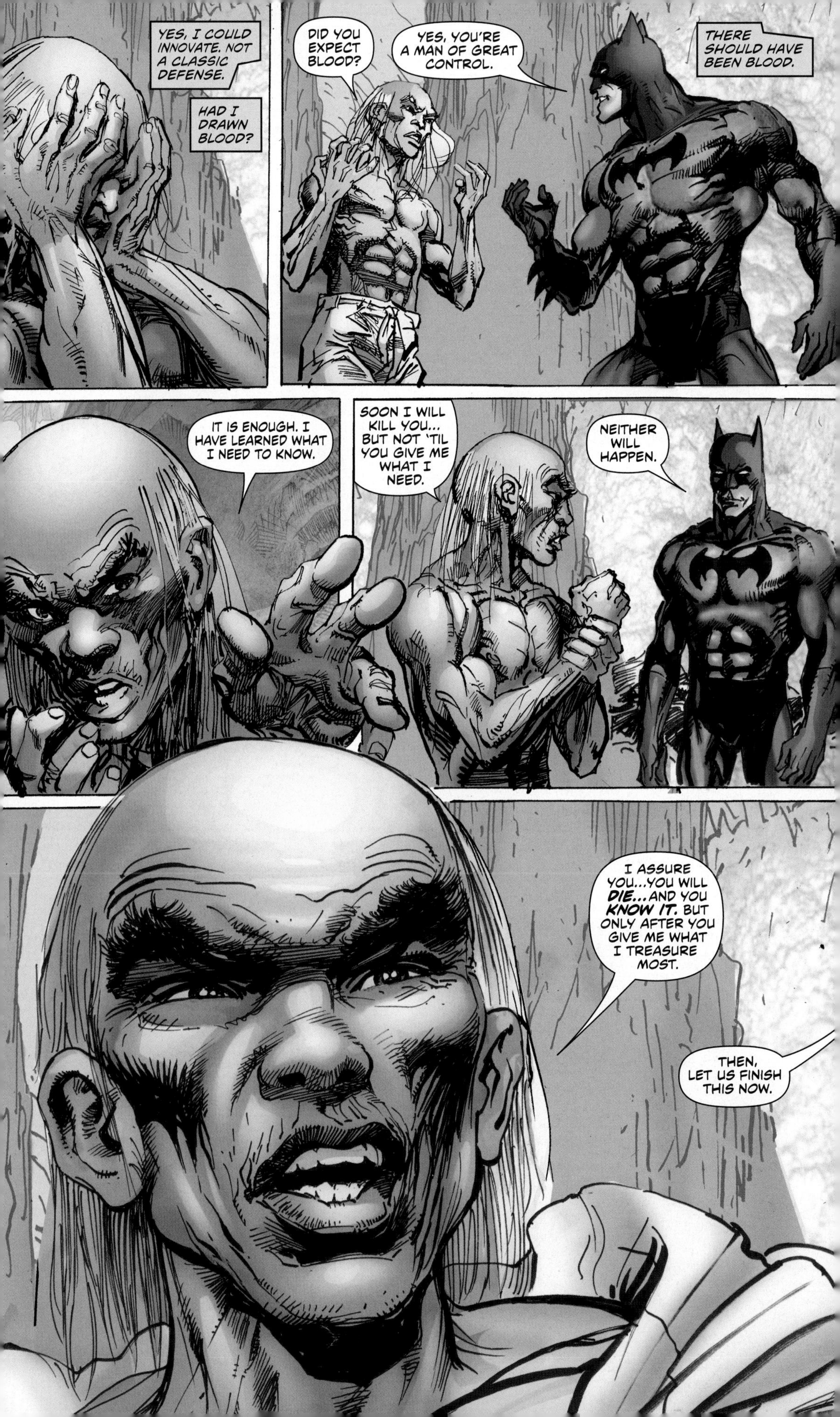
YES, I COULD INNOVATE. NOT A CLASSIC DEFENSE.
HAD I DRAWN BLOOD?
DID YOU EXPECT BLOOD?
YES, YOU'RE A MAN OF GREAT CONTROL.
THERE SHOULD HAVE BEEN BLOOD.
IT IS ENOUGH. I HAVE LEARNED WHAT I NEED TO KNOW.
SOON I WILL KILL YOU... BUT NOT 'TIL YOU GIVE ME WHAT I NEED.
NEITHER WILL HAPPEN.
I ASSURE YOU...YOU WILL DIE...AND YOU KNOW IT. BUT ONLY AFTER YOU GIVE ME WHAT I TREASURE MOST.
THEN, LET US FINISH THIS NOW.

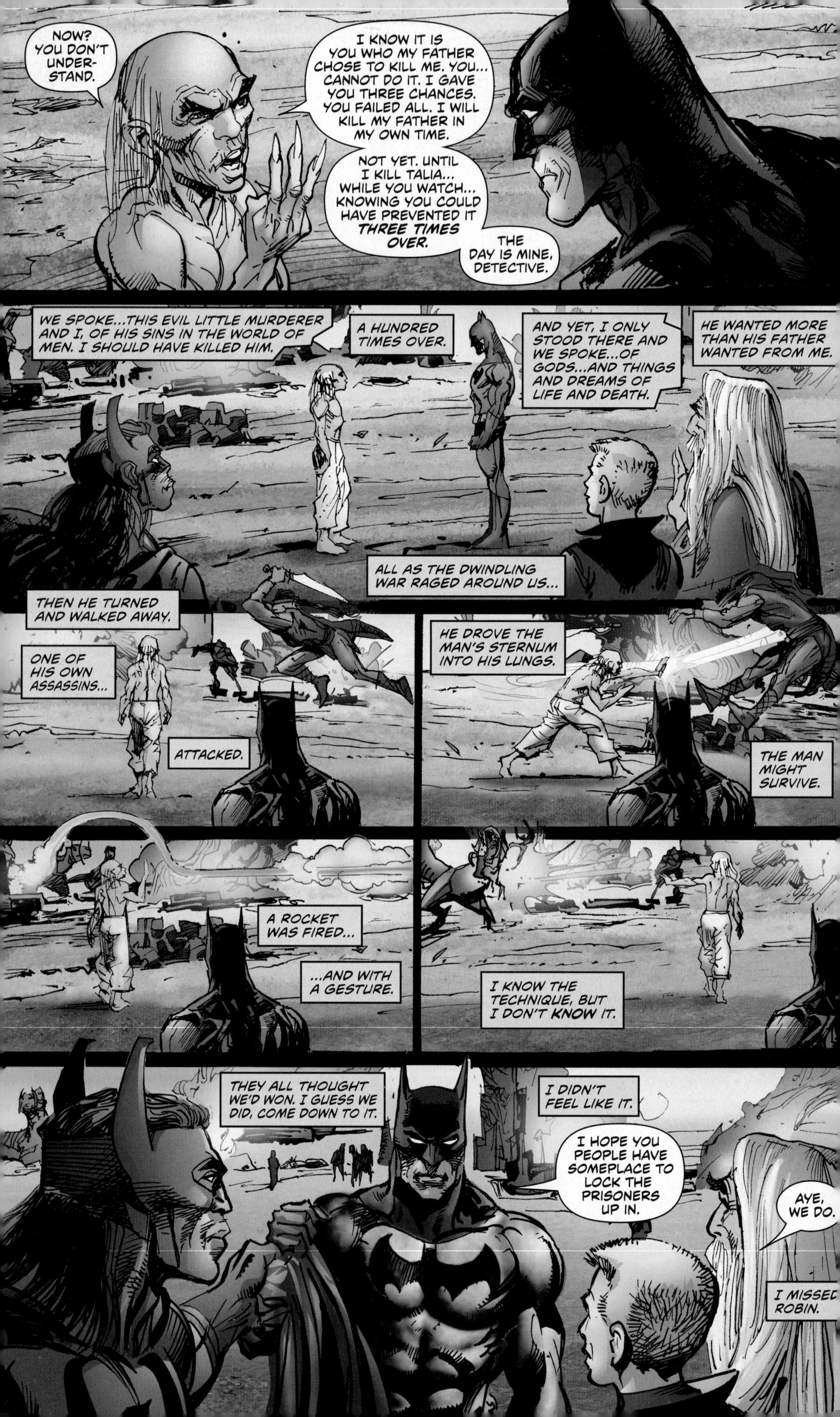
NOW? YOU DON'T UNDER-STAND.
I KNOW IT IS YOU WHO MY FATHER CHOSE TO KILL ME. YOU... CANNOT DO IT. I GAVE YOU THREE CHANCES. YOU FAILED ALL. I WILL KILL MY FATHER IN MY OWN TIME.
NOT YET. UNTIL I KILL TALIA... WHILE YOU WATCH... KNOWING YOU COULD HAVE PREVENTED IT THREE TIMES OVER.
THE DAY IS MINE, DETECTIVE.
WE SPOKE...THIS EVIL LITTLE MURDERER AND I, OF HIS SINS IN THE WORLD OF MEN. I SHOULD HAVE KILLED HIM.
A HUNDRED TIMES OVER.
AND YET, I ONLY STOOD THERE AND WE SPOKE...OF GODS...AND THINGS AND DREAMS OF LIFE AND DEATH.
HE WANTED MORE THAN HIS FATHER WANTED FROM ME.
ALL AS THE DWINDLING WAR RAGED AROUND US...
THEN HE TURNED AND WALKED AWAY.
ONE OF HIS OWN ASSASSINS...
ATTACKED.
HE DROVE THE MAN'S STERNUM INTO HIS LUNGS.
THE MAN MIGHT SURVIVE.
A ROCKET WAS FIRED...
...AND WITH A GESTURE.
I KNOW THE TECHNIQUE, BUT I DON'T KNOW IT.
THEY ALL THOUGHT WE'D WON. I GUESS WE DID, COME DOWN TO IT.
I DIDN'T FEEL LIKE IT.
I HOPE YOU PEOPLE HAVE SOMEPLACE TO LOCK THE PRISONERS UP IN.
AYE, WE DO.
I MISSED ROBIN.

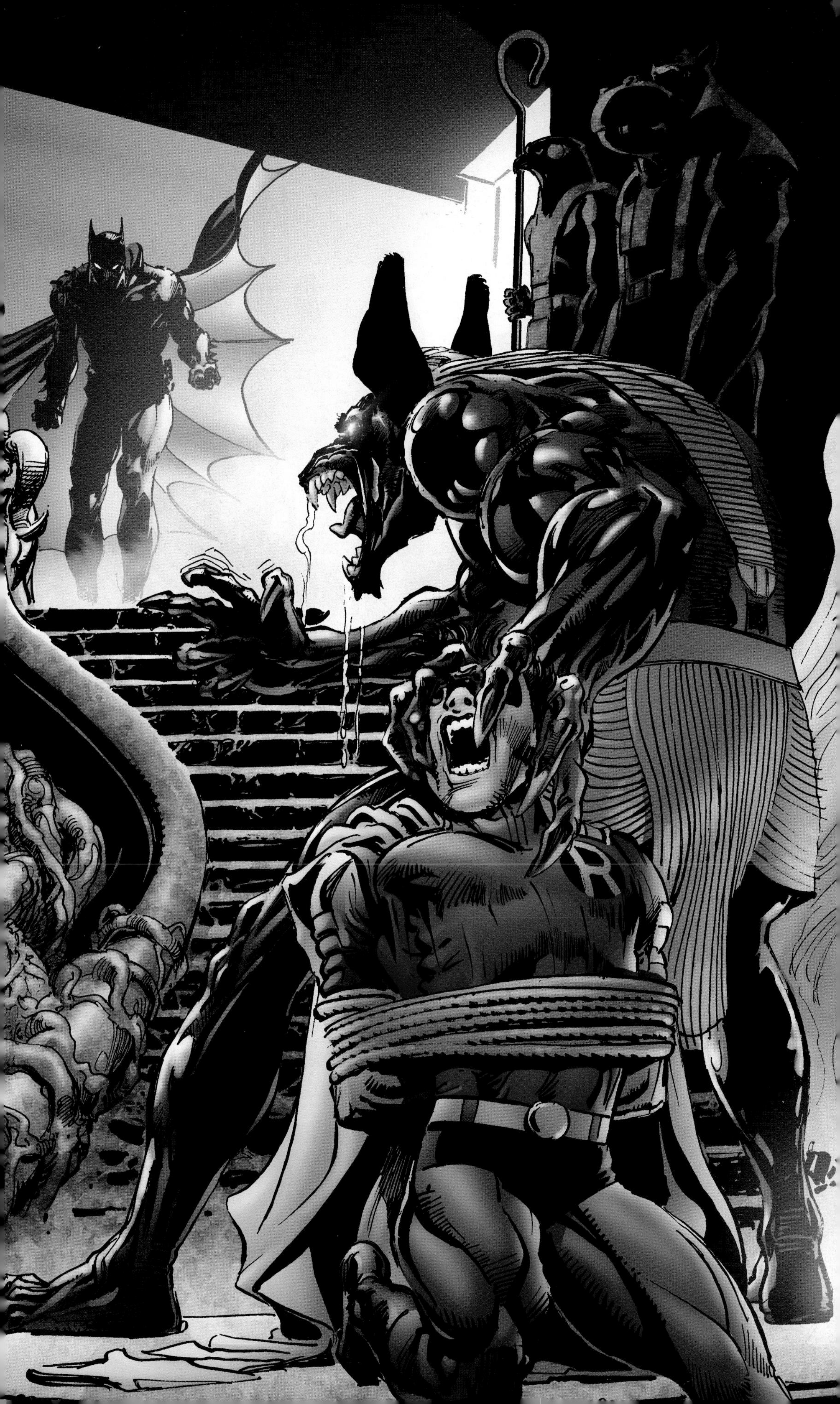

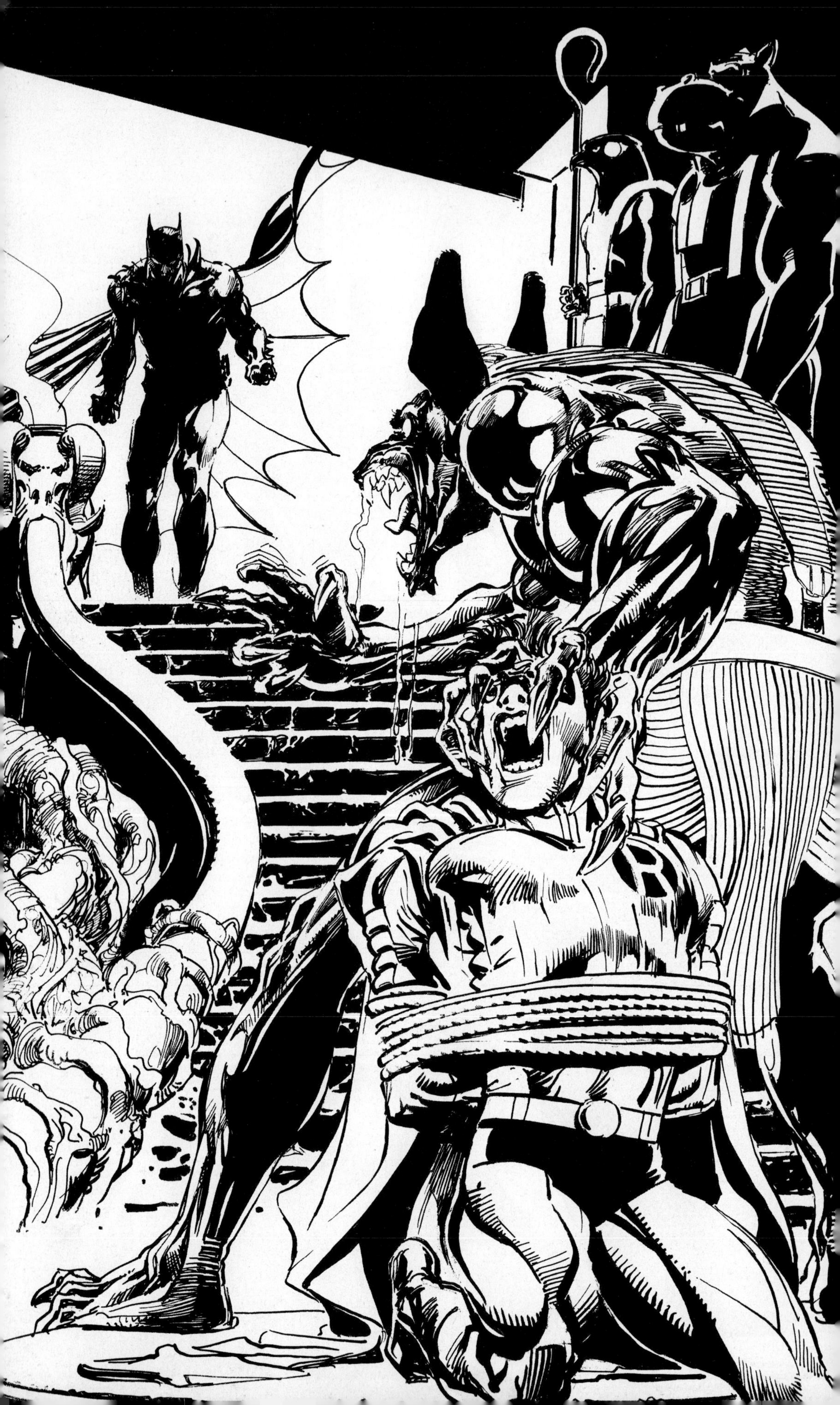

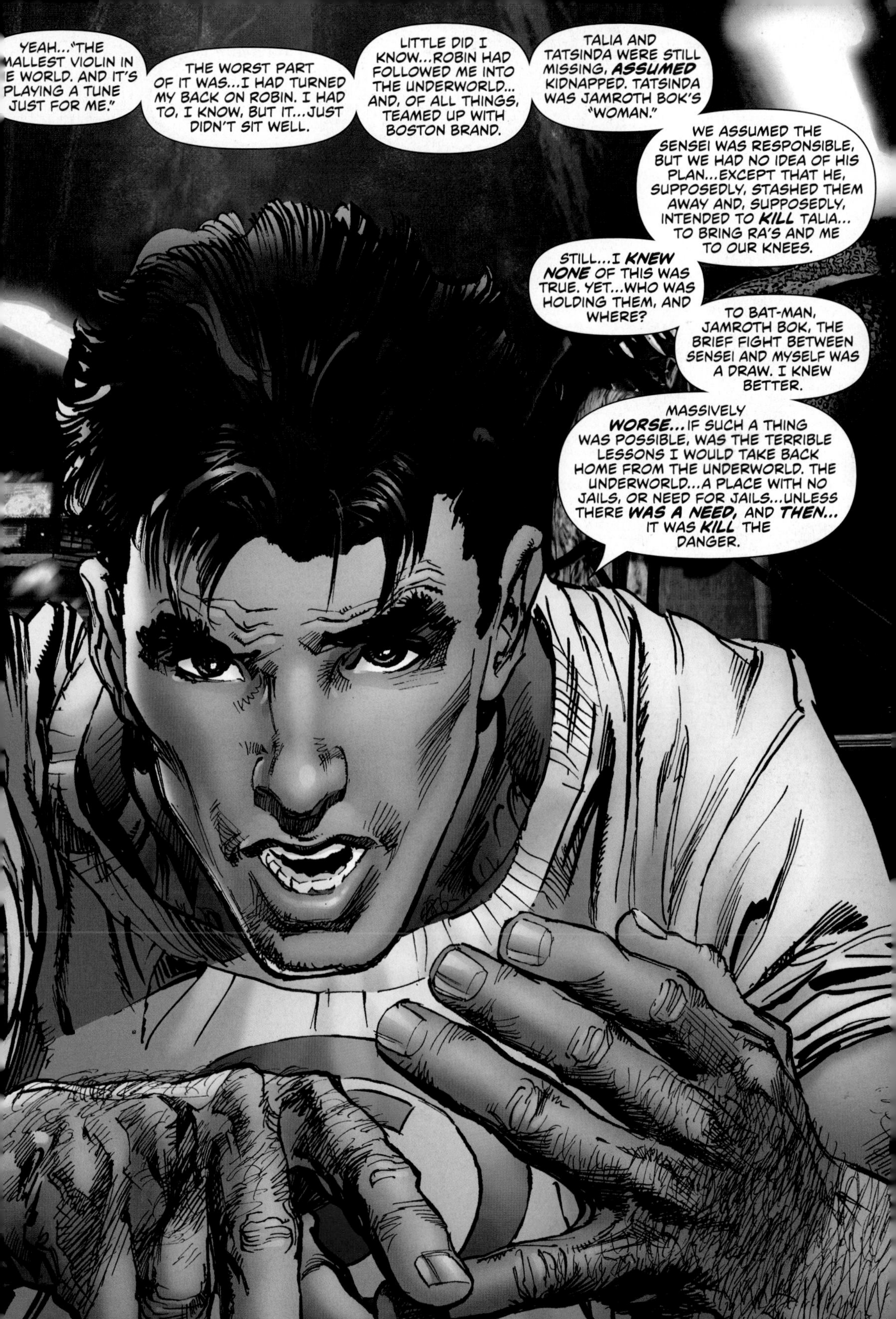
YEAH..."THE MALLEST VIOLIN IN E WORLD. AND IT'S PLAYING A TUNE JUST FOR ME."
THE WORST PART OF IT WAS...I HAD TURNED MY BACK ON ROBIN. I HAD TO, I KNOW, BUT IT...JUST DIDN'T SIT WELL.
LITTLE DID I KNOW...ROBIN HAD FOLLOWED ME INTO THE UNDERWORLD... AND, OF ALL THINGS, TEAMED UP WITH BOSTON BRAND.
TALIA AND TATSINDA WERE STILL MISSING, ASSUMED KIDNAPPED. TATSINDA WAS JAMROTH BOK'S "WOMAN."
WE ASSUMED THE SENSEI WAS RESPONSIBLE, BUT WE HAD NO IDEA OF HIS PLAN...EXCEPT THAT HE, SUPPOSEDLY, STASHED THEM AWAY AND, SUPPOSEDLY, INTENDED TO KILL TALIA... TO BRING RA'S AND ME TO OUR KNEES.
STILL...I KNEW NONE OF THIS WAS TRUE. YET...WHO WAS HOLDING THEM, AND WHERE?
TO BAT-MAN, JAMROTH BOK, THE BRIEF FIGHT BETWEEN SENSEI AND MYSELF WAS A DRAW. I KNEW BETTER.
MASSIVELY WORSE... IF SUCH A THING WAS POSSIBLE, WAS THE TERRIBLE LESSONS I WOULD TAKE BACK HOME FROM THE UNDERWORLD. THE UNDERWORLD...A PLACE WITH NO JAILS, OR NEED FOR JAILS...UNLESS THERE WAS A NEED, AND THEN... IT WAS KILL THE DANGER.

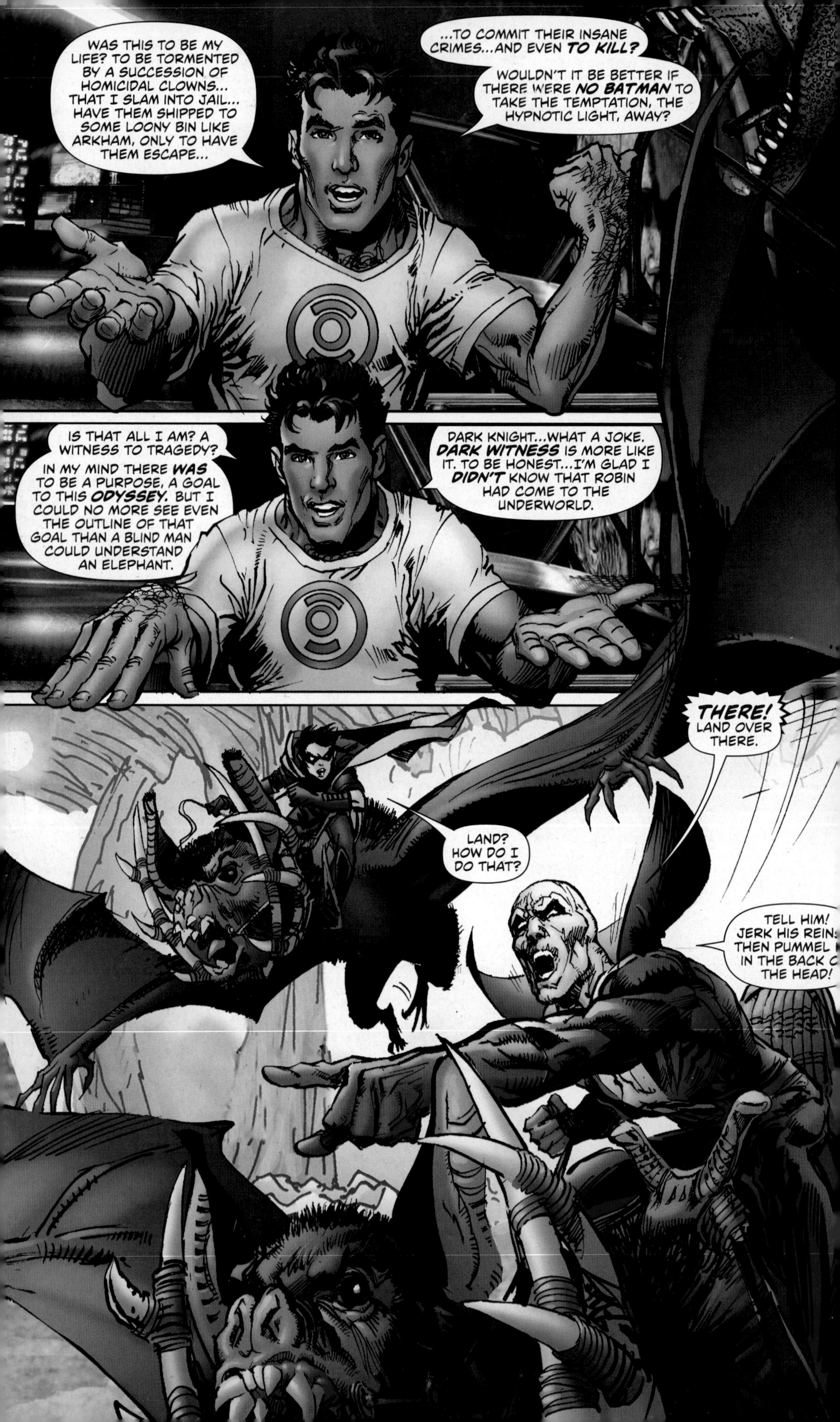
WAS THIS TO BE MY LIFE? TO BE TORMENTED BY A SUCCESSION OF HOMICIDAL CLOWNS... THAT I SLAM INTO JAIL... HAVE THEM SHIPPED TO SOME LOONY BIN LIKE ARKHAM, ONLY TO HAVE THEM ESCAPE...
...TO COMMIT THEIR INSANE CRIMES...AND EVEN TO KILL?
WOULDN'T IT BE BETTER IF THERE WERE NO BATMAN TO TAKE THE TEMPTATION, THE HYPNOTIC LIGHT, AWAY?
IS THAT ALL I AM? A WITNESS TO TRAGEDY?
IN MY MIND THERE WAS TO BE A PURPOSE, A GOAL TO THIS ODYSSEY. BUT I COULD NO MORE SEE EVEN THE OUTLINE OF THAT GOAL THAN A BLIND MAN COULD UNDERSTAND AN ELEPHANT.
DARK KNIGHT...WHAT A JOKE. DARK WITNESS IS MORE LIKE IT. TO BE HONEST...I'M GLAD I DIDN'T KNOW THAT ROBIN HAD COME TO THE UNDERWORLD.
THERE! LAND OVER THERE.
LAND? HOW DO I DO THAT?
TELL HIM! JERK HIS REINS THEN PUMMEL IN THE BACK C THE HEAD!

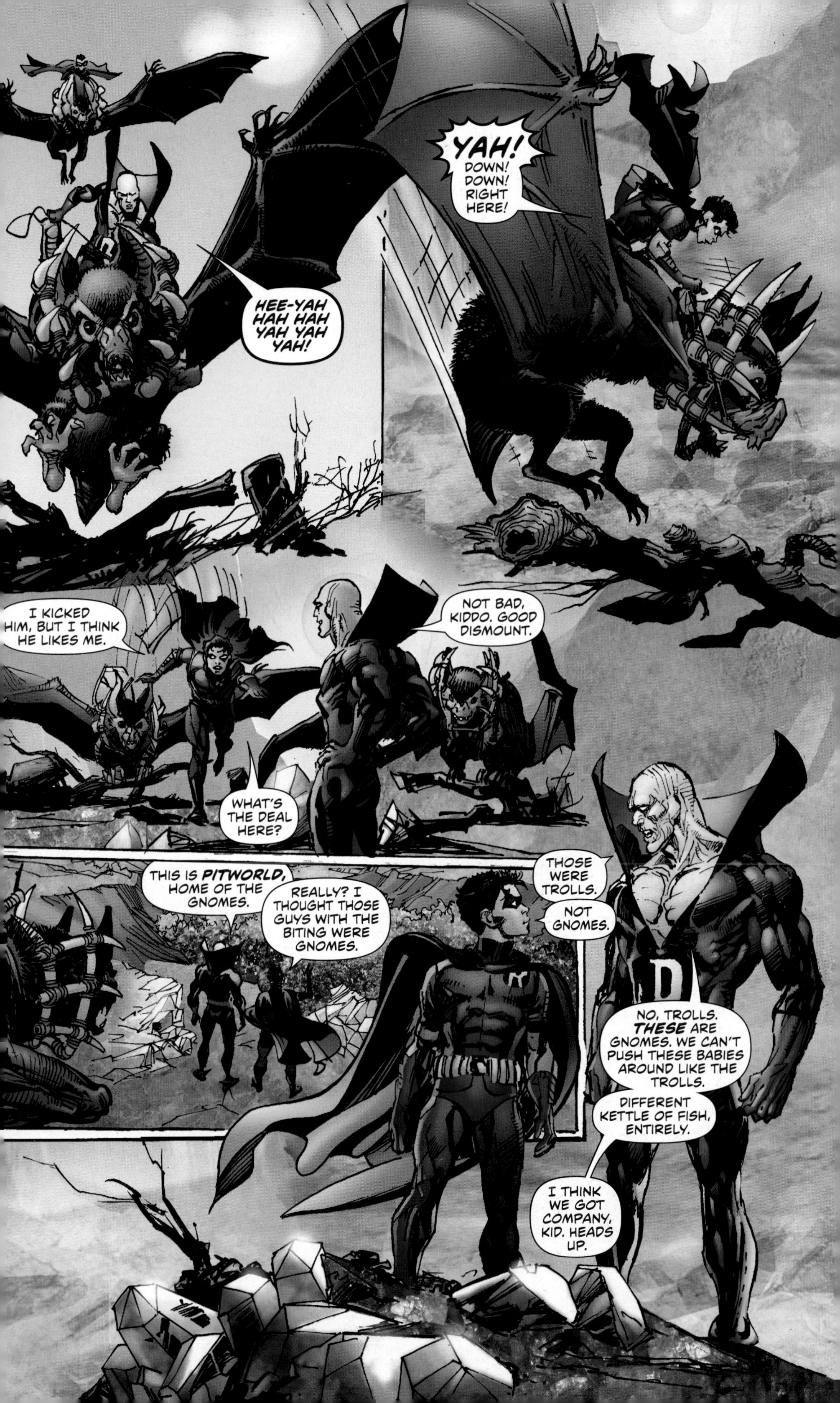
HEE-YAH HAH HAH YAH YAH YAH!
YAH! DOWN! DOWN! RIGHT HERE!
I KICKED HIM, BUT I THINK HE LIKES ME.
NOT BAD, KIDDO. GOOD DISMOUNT.
WHAT'S THE DEAL HERE?
THIS IS PITWORLD, HOME OF THE GNOMES.
REALLY? I THOUGHT THOSE GUYS WITH THE BITING WERE GNOMES.
THOSE WERE TROLLS.
NOT GNOMES.
NO, TROLLS. THESE ARE GNOMES. WE CAN'T PUSH THESE BABIES AROUND LIKE THE TROLLS.
DIFFERENT KETTLE OF FISH, ENTIRELY.
I THINK WE GOT COMPANY, KID. HEADS UP.

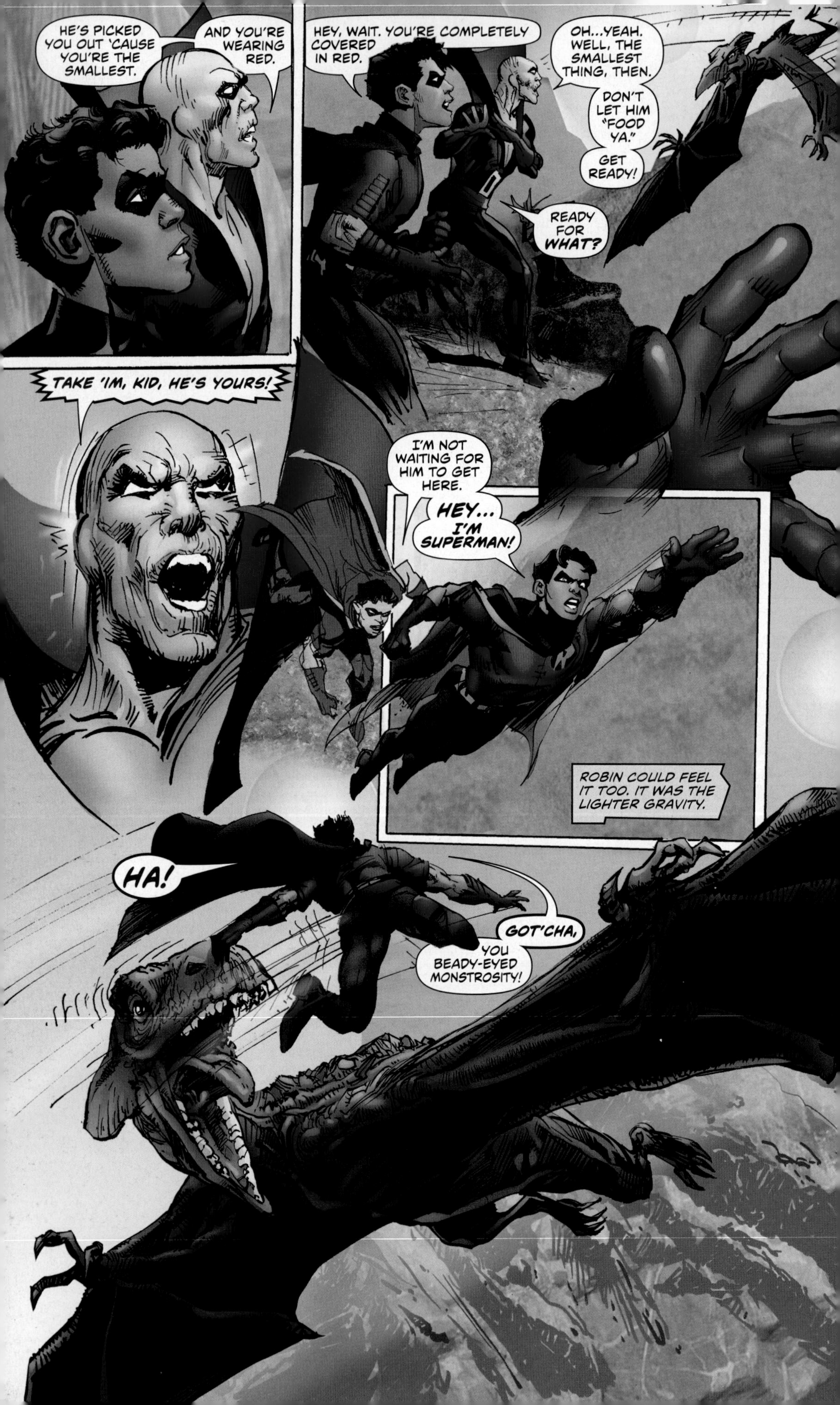

HE'S PICKED YOU OUT 'CAUSE YOU'RE THE SMALLEST.
AND YOU'RE WEARING RED.
HEY, WAIT. YOU'RE COMPLETELY COVERED IN RED.
OH...YEAH. WELL, THE SMALLEST THING, THEN.
DON'T LET HIM "FOOD YA."
GET READY!
READY FOR WHAT?
TAKE 'IM, KID, HE'S YOURS!
I'M NOT WAITING FOR HIM TO GET HERE.
HEY... I'M SUPERMAN!
ROBIN COULD FEEL IT TOO. IT WAS THE LIGHTER GRAVITY.
HA!
GOT'CHA,
YOU BEADY-EYED MONSTROSITY!

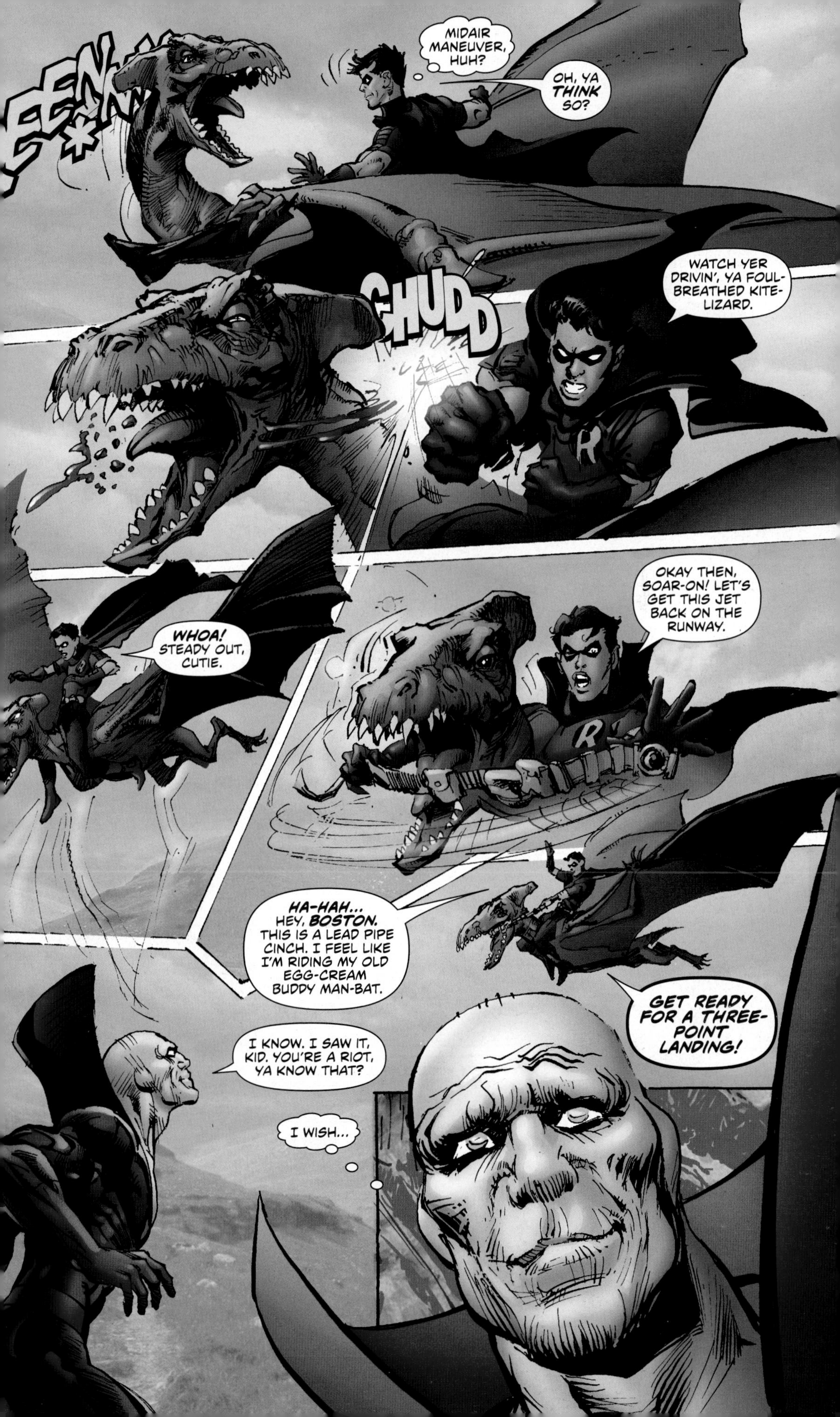

FEEN*
MIDAIR MANEUVER, HUH?
OH, YA THINK SO?
CHUDD
WATCH YER DRIVIN', YA FOUL-BREATHED KITE-LIZARD.
WHOA! STEADY OUT, CUTIE.
OKAY THEN, SOAR-ON! LET'S GET THIS JET BACK ON THE RUNWAY.
HA-HAH... HEY, BOSTON. THIS IS A LEAD PIPE CINCH. I FEEL LIKE I'M RIDING MY OLD EGG-CREAM BUDDY MAN-BAT.
GET READY FOR A THREE-POINT LANDING!
I KNOW. I SAW IT, KID. YOU'RE A RIOT, YA KNOW THAT?
I WISH...

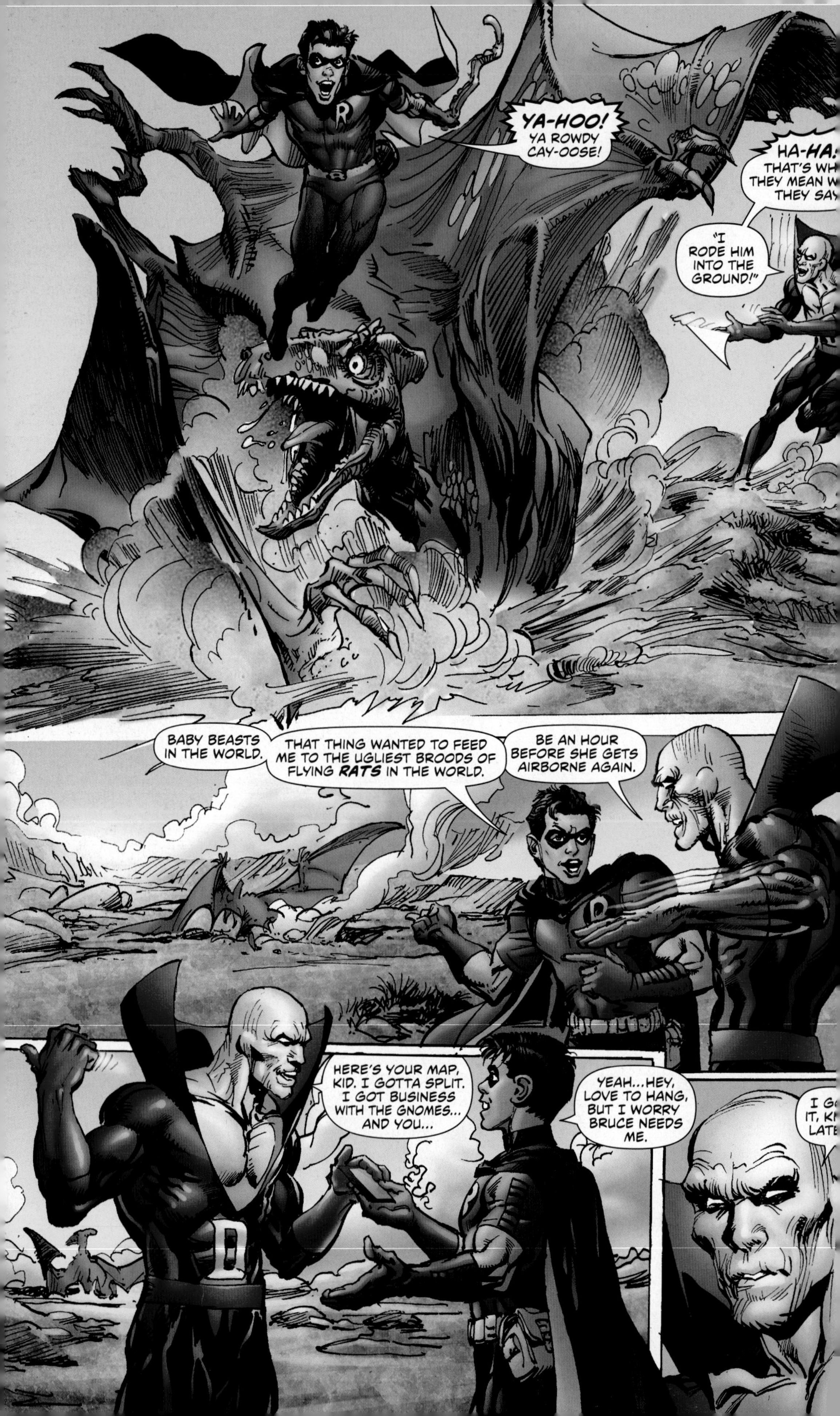
YA-HOO! YA ROWDY CAY-OOSE!
HA-HA! THAT'S WH THEY MEAN W THEY SAY
"I RODE HIM INTO THE GROUND!"
BABY BEASTS IN THE WORLD.
THAT THING WANTED TO FEED ME TO THE UGLIEST BROODS OF FLYING RATS IN THE WORLD.
BE AN HOUR BEFORE SHE GETS AIRBORNE AGAIN.
HERE'S YOUR MAP, KID. I GOTTA SPLIT. I GOT BUSINESS WITH THE GNOMES... AND YOU...
YEAH...HEY, LOVE TO HANG, BUT I WORRY BRUCE NEEDS ME.
I G IT, K LATE

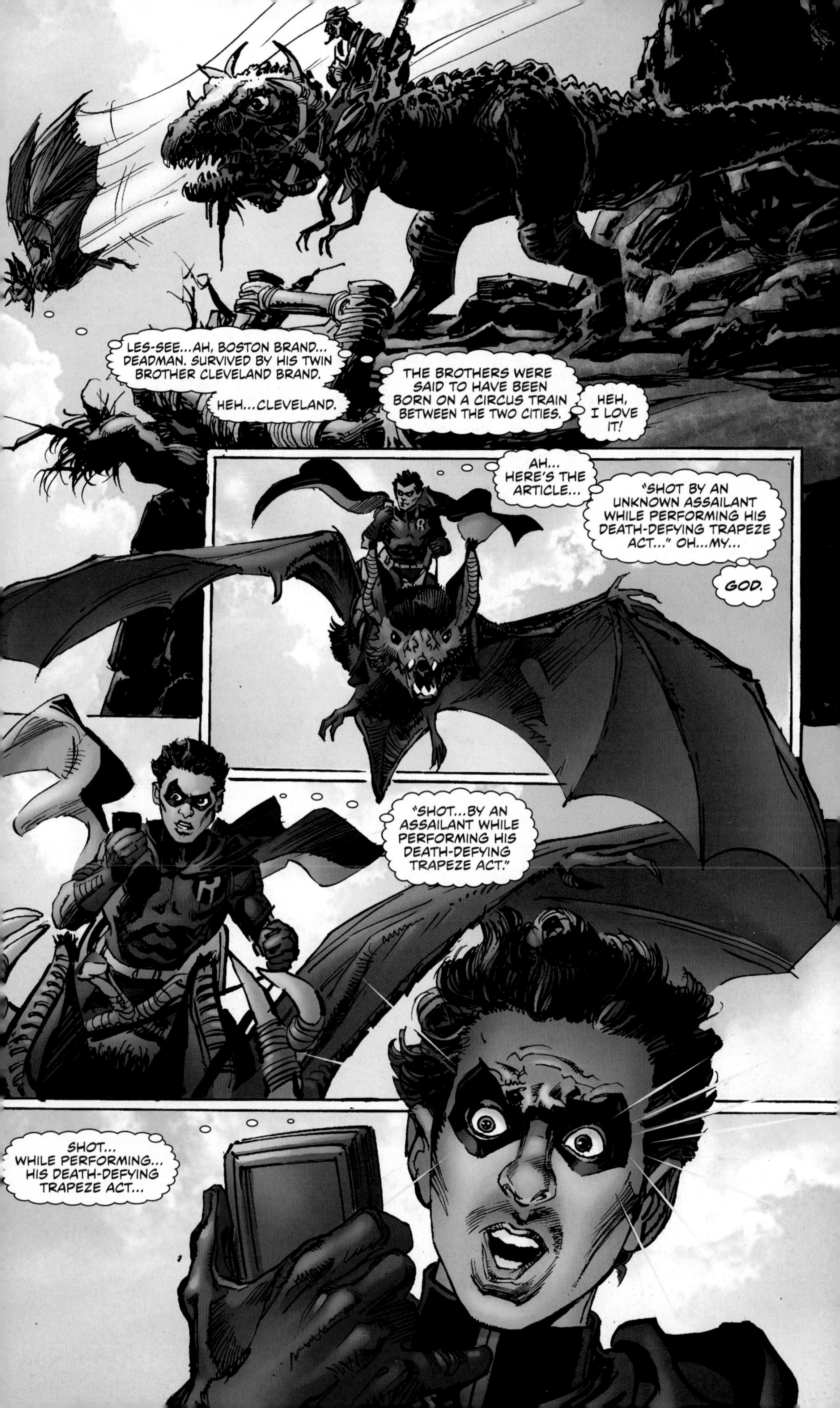
LES-SEE...AH, BOSTON BRAND... DEADMAN. SURVIVED BY HIS TWIN BROTHER CLEVELAND BRAND.
HEH...CLEVELAND.
THE BROTHERS WERE SAID TO HAVE BEEN BORN ON A CIRCUS TRAIN BETWEEN THE TWO CITIES.
HEH, I LOVE IT!
AH... HERE'S THE ARTICLE...
"SHOT BY AN UNKNOWN ASSAILANT WHILE PERFORMING HIS DEATH-DEFYING TRAPEZE ACT..." OH...MY...
GOD.
"SHOT...BY AN ASSAILANT WHILE PERFORMING HIS DEATH-DEFYING TRAPEZE ACT."
SHOT... WHILE PERFORMING... HIS DEATH-DEFYING TRAPEZE ACT...

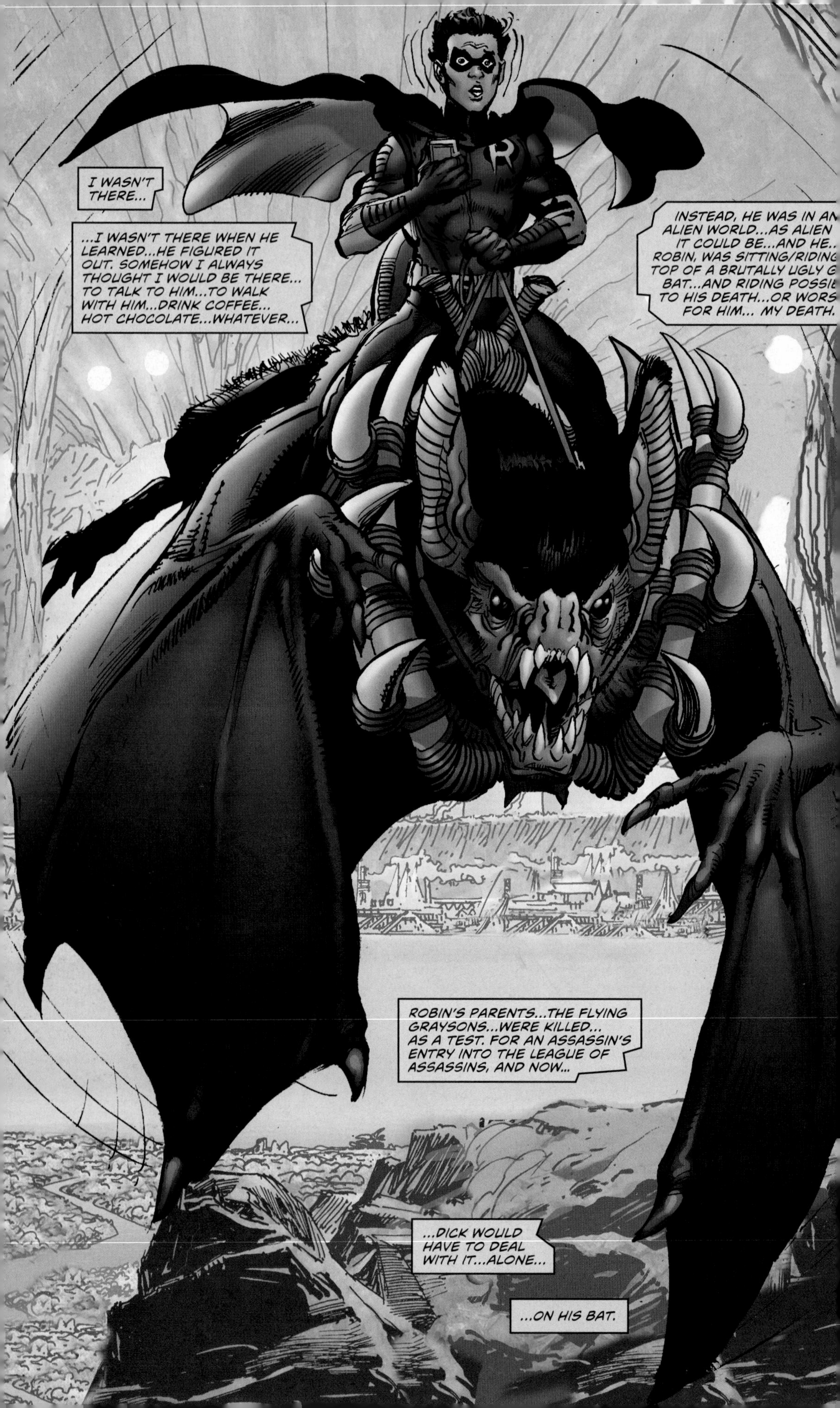

I WASN'T THERE...
...I WASN'T THERE WHEN HE LEARNED...HE FIGURED IT OUT. SOMEHOW I ALWAYS THOUGHT I WOULD BE THERE... TO TALK TO HIM...TO WALK WITH HIM...DRINK COFFEE... HOT CHOCOLATE...WHATEVER...
INSTEAD, HE WAS IN AN ALIEN WORLD...AS ALIEN IT COULD BE...AND HE... ROBIN, WAS SITTING/RIDING TOP OF A BRUTALLY UGLY G BAT...AND RIDING POSSI TO HIS DEATH...OR WORS FOR HIM... MY DEATH.
ROBIN'S PARENTS...THE FLYING GRAYSONS...WERE KILLED... AS A TEST. FOR AN ASSASSIN'S ENTRY INTO THE LEAGUE OF ASSASSINS, AND NOW...
...DICK WOULD HAVE TO DEAL WITH IT...ALONE...
...ON HIS BAT.

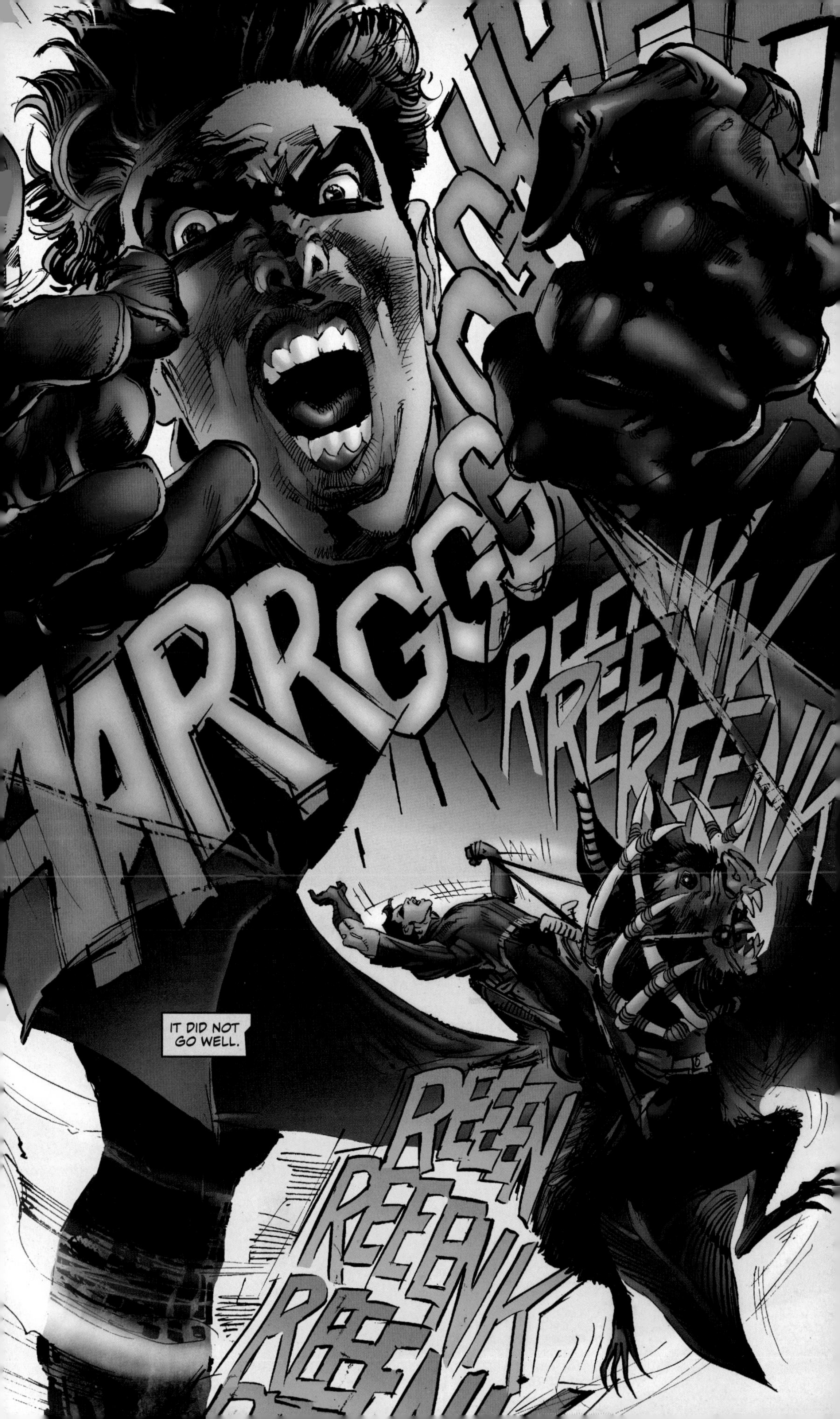

ARRGG
REEENK REEENK REEENK
IT DID NOT GO WELL.
REEEN REEENK

HERE, BY TREATY, WE MAY ALL PRACTICE OUR MAGICS AND VARIOUS SCIENCES.

TREATY? WITH RA'S?

IT'S **NOT** A TREATY **WE** WERE PART OF. ASHAMED, A VERY OLD TREATY...TO PRESERVE THE UNDERWORLD.

I SEE MORE THAN JUST ALIENS, GREYS AND MAGICIANS...

I SEE MEMBERS OF ANCIENT CIVILIZATIONS. EGYPTIANS, ANIMEN. PEOPLE WHO...

AND THIS... MUCH OF THE LIBRARY AT ALEXANDRIA IS HERE...

...THE WARP AND WOOF OF OTHER...

MY GOD! **THE LIBRARY AT ALEXANDRIA!**

I'M GUESSING THIS HAS SOME SIGNIFICANCE TO YOU, MASTER.

I...I... I DON'T KNOW WHAT TO...SAY...

HEY, YO CAN GLO TOME A TIME YOU THE NE

IT'S NOT LIKE YOU GUYS **AREN'T** THE HEROES OF THE WHOLE ROCKIN' UNDERWORLD.

SEE THOSE GUYS OVER THERE? THEY'RE WRITING HISTORIES OF WHAT HAPPENED HERE TODAY.

PLEASE, GUYS, FOR THE SUMER NETWORK, TEN MINUTES ANYTIME.

FOR TELEVISION?

FOR THE **INTRA**NET. WE DON'T BROADCAST FOR THE ABOVE WORLD. YOU CAN IMAGINE WHY NOT.

YES. YES.

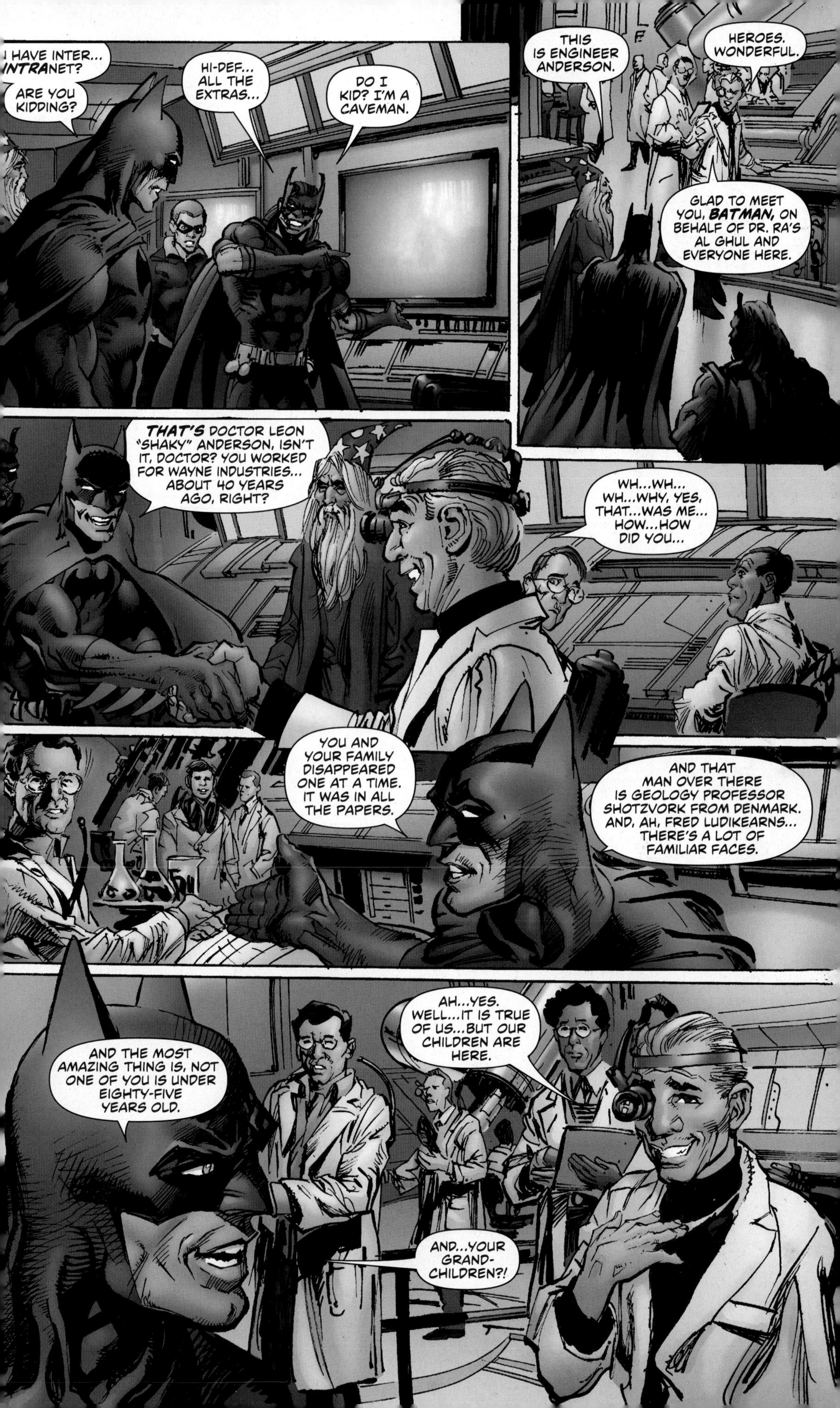

HAVE INTER... INTRANET?
ARE YOU KIDDING?
HI-DEF... ALL THE EXTRAS...
DO I KID? I'M A CAVEMAN.
THIS IS ENGINEER ANDERSON.
HEROES. WONDERFUL.
GLAD TO MEET YOU, BATMAN, ON BEHALF OF DR. RA'S AL GHUL AND EVERYONE HERE.
THAT'S DOCTOR LEON "SHAKY" ANDERSON, ISN'T IT, DOCTOR? YOU WORKED FOR WAYNE INDUSTRIES... ABOUT 40 YEARS AGO, RIGHT?
WH...WH... WH...WHY, YES, THAT...WAS ME... HOW...HOW DID YOU...
YOU AND YOUR FAMILY DISAPPEARED ONE AT A TIME. IT WAS IN ALL THE PAPERS.
AND THAT MAN OVER THERE IS GEOLOGY PROFESSOR SHOTZVORK FROM DENMARK. AND, AH, FRED LUDIKEARNS... THERE'S A LOT OF FAMILIAR FACES.
AND THE MOST AMAZING THING IS, NOT ONE OF YOU IS UNDER EIGHTY-FIVE YEARS OLD.
AH...YES. WELL...IT IS TRUE OF US...BUT OUR CHILDREN ARE HERE.
AND...YOUR GRAND-CHILDREN?!

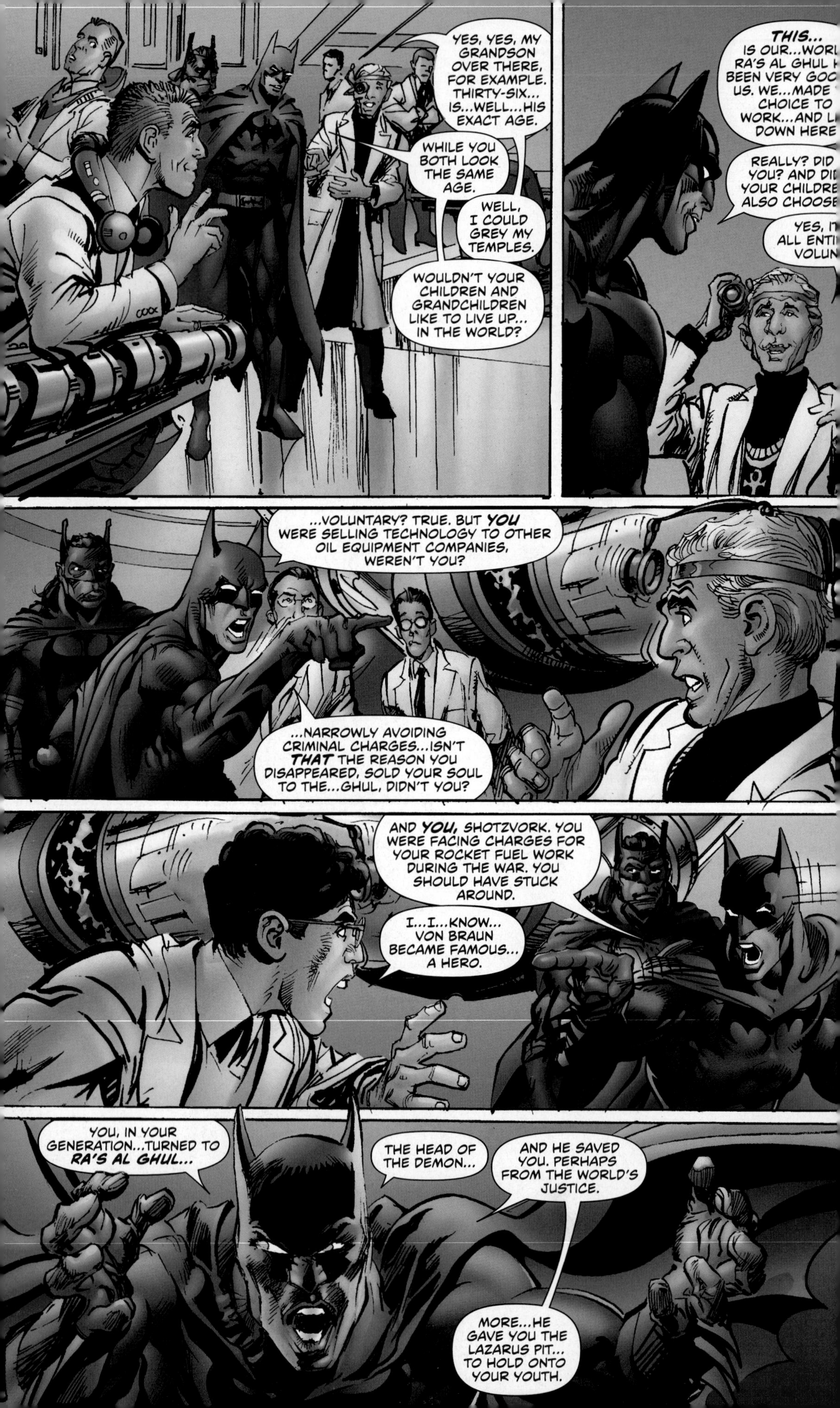

YES, YES, MY GRANDSON OVER THERE, FOR EXAMPLE. THIRTY-SIX... IS...WELL...HIS EXACT AGE.
WHILE YOU BOTH LOOK THE SAME AGE.
WELL, I COULD GREY MY TEMPLES.
WOULDN'T YOUR CHILDREN AND GRANDCHILDREN LIKE TO LIVE UP... IN THE WORLD?
THIS... IS OUR...WORL RA'S AL GHUL H BEEN VERY GOO US. WE...MADE CHOICE TO WORK...AND L DOWN HERE
REALLY? DID YOU? AND DID YOUR CHILDRE ALSO CHOOSE
YES, I ALL ENTI VOLUN
...VOLUNTARY? TRUE. BUT YOU WERE SELLING TECHNOLOGY TO OTHER OIL EQUIPMENT COMPANIES, WEREN'T YOU?
...NARROWLY AVOIDING CRIMINAL CHARGES...ISN'T THAT THE REASON YOU DISAPPEARED, SOLD YOUR SOUL TO THE...GHUL, DIDN'T YOU?
AND YOU, SHOTZVORK. YOU WERE FACING CHARGES FOR YOUR ROCKET FUEL WORK DURING THE WAR. YOU SHOULD HAVE STUCK AROUND.
I...I...KNOW... VON BRAUN BECAME FAMOUS... A HERO.
YOU, IN YOUR GENERATION...TURNED TO RA'S AL GHUL...
THE HEAD OF THE DEMON...
AND HE SAVED YOU. PERHAPS FROM THE WORLD'S JUSTICE.
MORE...HE GAVE YOU THE LAZARUS PIT... TO HOLD ONTO YOUR YOUTH.

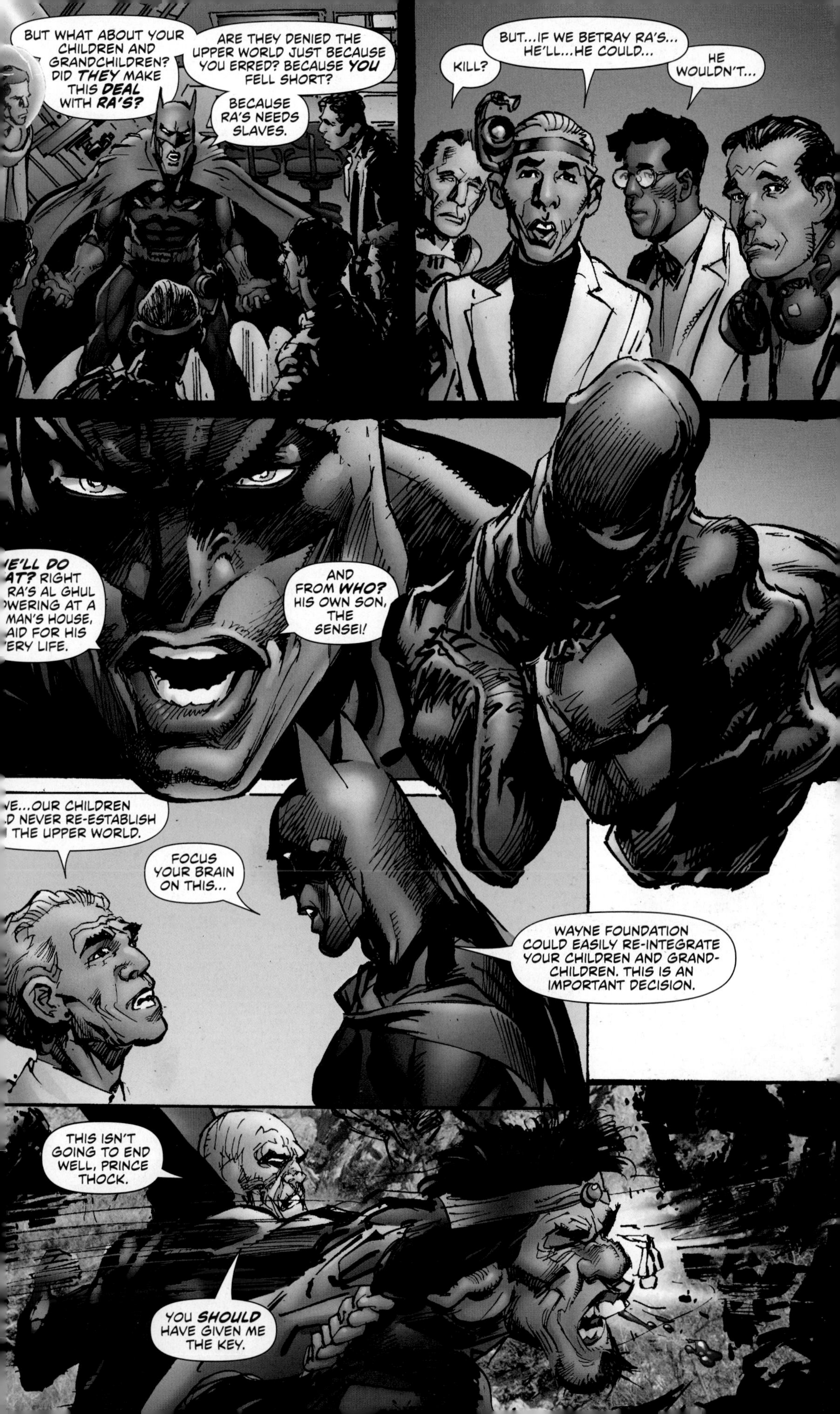

BUT WHAT ABOUT YOUR CHILDREN AND GRANDCHILDREN? DID THEY MAKE THIS DEAL WITH RA'S?
ARE THEY DENIED THE UPPER WORLD JUST BECAUSE YOU ERRED? BECAUSE YOU FELL SHORT?
BECAUSE RA'S NEEDS SLAVES.
KILL?
BUT...IF WE BETRAY RA'S... HE'LL...HE COULD...
HE WOULDN'T...
'E'LL DO AT? RIGHT RA'S AL GHUL OWERING AT A MAN'S HOUSE, AID FOR HIS ERY LIFE.
AND FROM WHO? HIS OWN SON, THE SENSEI!
VE...OUR CHILDREN D NEVER RE-ESTABLISH THE UPPER WORLD.
FOCUS YOUR BRAIN ON THIS...
WAYNE FOUNDATION COULD EASILY RE-INTEGRATE YOUR CHILDREN AND GRAND-CHILDREN. THIS IS AN IMPORTANT DECISION.
THIS ISN'T GOING TO END WELL, PRINCE THOCK.
YOU SHOULD HAVE GIVEN ME THE KEY.

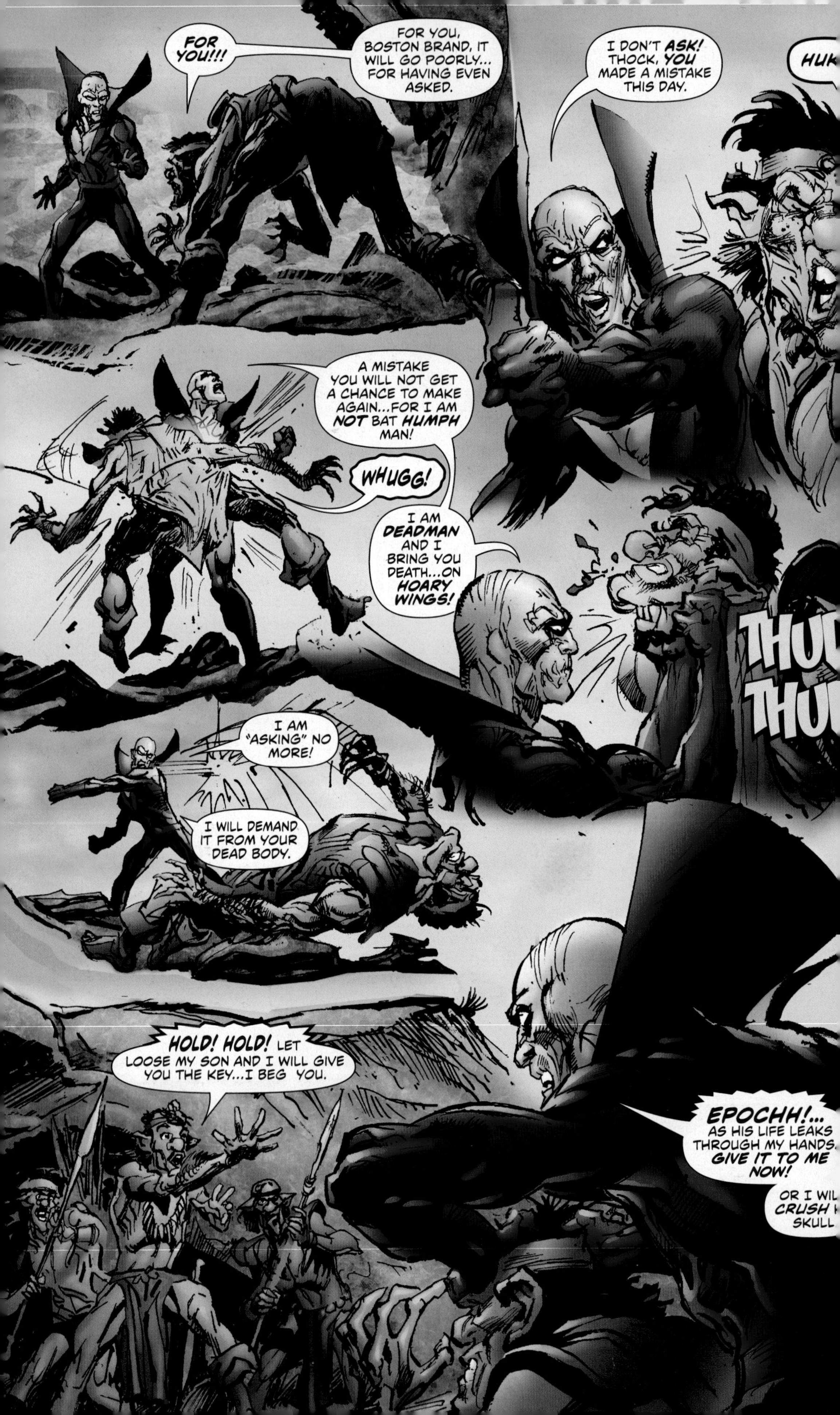

FOR YOU!!!
FOR YOU, BOSTON BRAND, IT WILL GO POORLY... FOR HAVING EVEN ASKED.
I DON'T ASK! THOCK, YOU MADE A MISTAKE THIS DAY.
A MISTAKE YOU WILL NOT GET A CHANCE TO MAKE AGAIN...FOR I AM NOT BAT HUMPH MAN!
WHUGG!
I AM DEADMAN AND I BRING YOU DEATH...ON HOARY WINGS!
I AM "ASKING" NO MORE!
I WILL DEMAND IT FROM YOUR DEAD BODY.
HOLD! HOLD! LET LOOSE MY SON AND I WILL GIVE YOU THE KEY...I BEG YOU.
EPOCHH!... AS HIS LIFE LEAKS THROUGH MY HANDS, GIVE IT TO ME NOW!

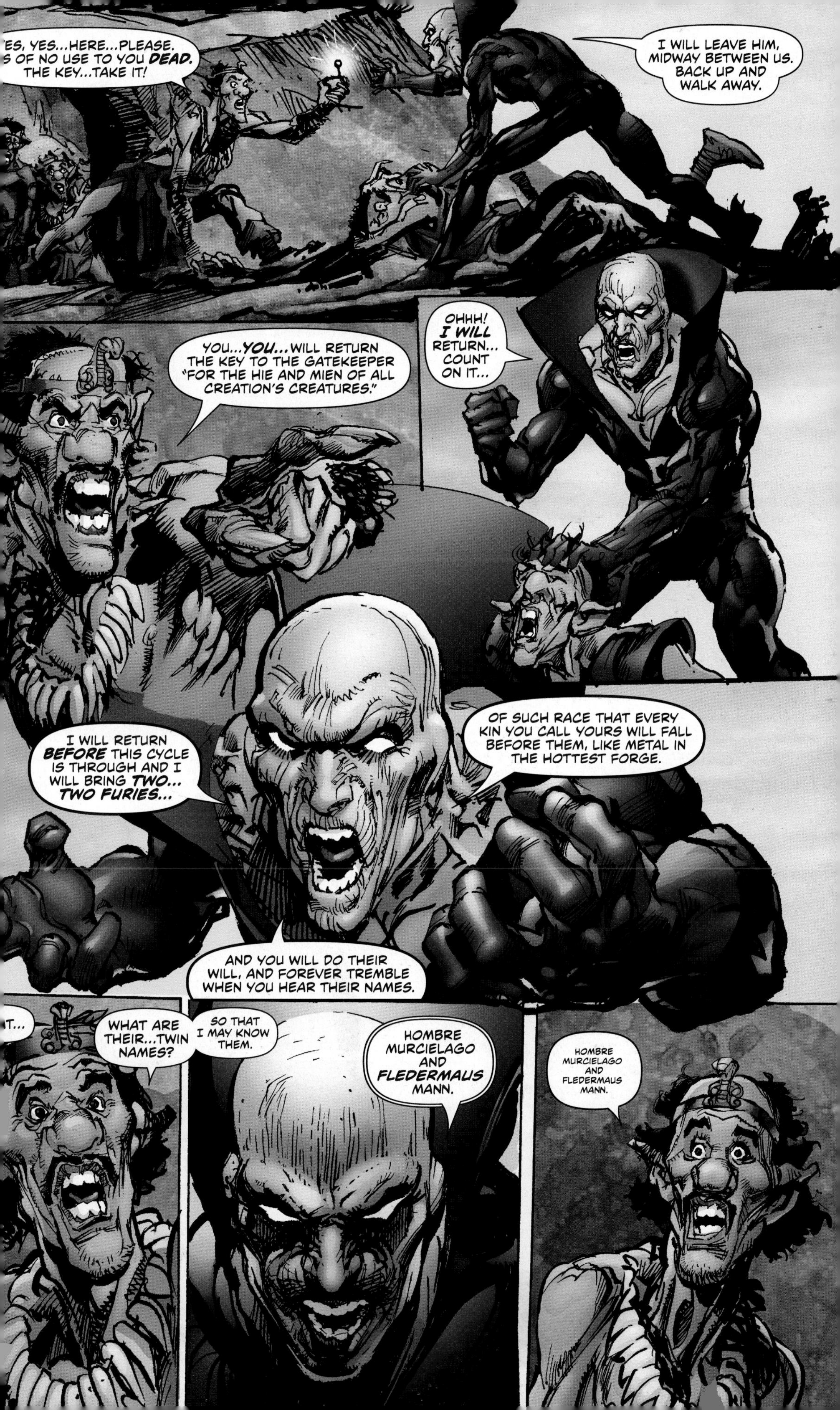

'ES, YES...HERE...PLEASE. 'S OF NO USE TO YOU DEAD. THE KEY...TAKE IT!
I WILL LEAVE HIM, MIDWAY BETWEEN US. BACK UP AND WALK AWAY.
YOU...YOU...WILL RETURN THE KEY TO THE GATEKEEPER "FOR THE HIE AND MIEN OF ALL CREATION'S CREATURES."
OHHH! I WILL RETURN... COUNT ON IT...
I WILL RETURN BEFORE THIS CYCLE IS THROUGH AND I WILL BRING TWO... TWO FURIES...
OF SUCH RACE THAT EVERY KIN YOU CALL YOURS WILL FALL BEFORE THEM, LIKE METAL IN THE HOTTEST FORGE.
AND YOU WILL DO THEIR WILL, AND FOREVER TREMBLE WHEN YOU HEAR THEIR NAMES.
T...
WHAT ARE THEIR...TWIN NAMES?
SO THAT I MAY KNOW THEM.
HOMBRE MURCIELAGO AND FLEDERMAUS MANN.
HOMBRE MURCIELAGO AND FLEDERMAUS MANN.

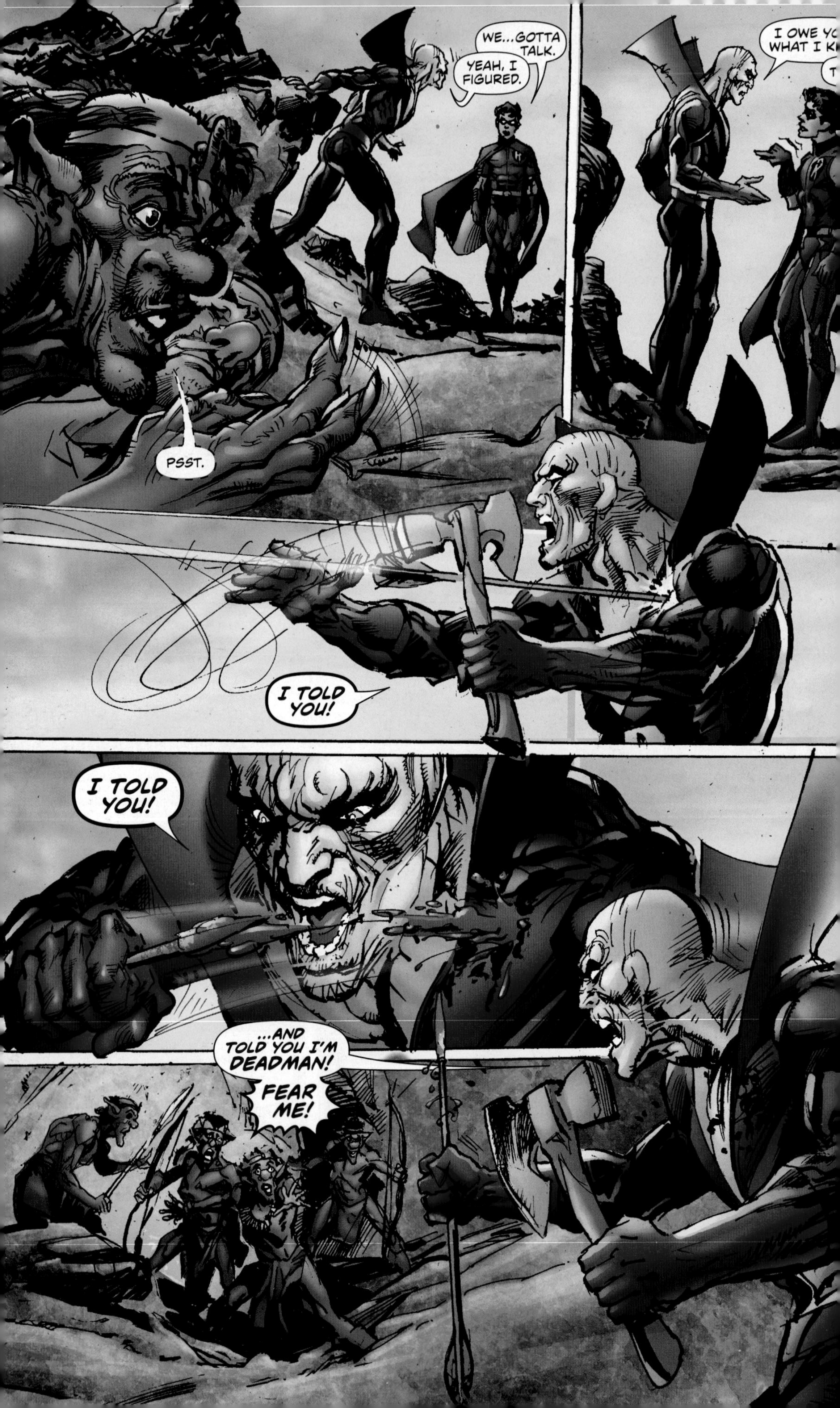
WE...GOTTA TALK.
YEAH, I FIGURED.
I OWE YO
WHAT I K
PSST.
I TOLD YOU!
I TOLD YOU!
...AND TOLD YOU I'M DEADMAN!
FEAR ME!

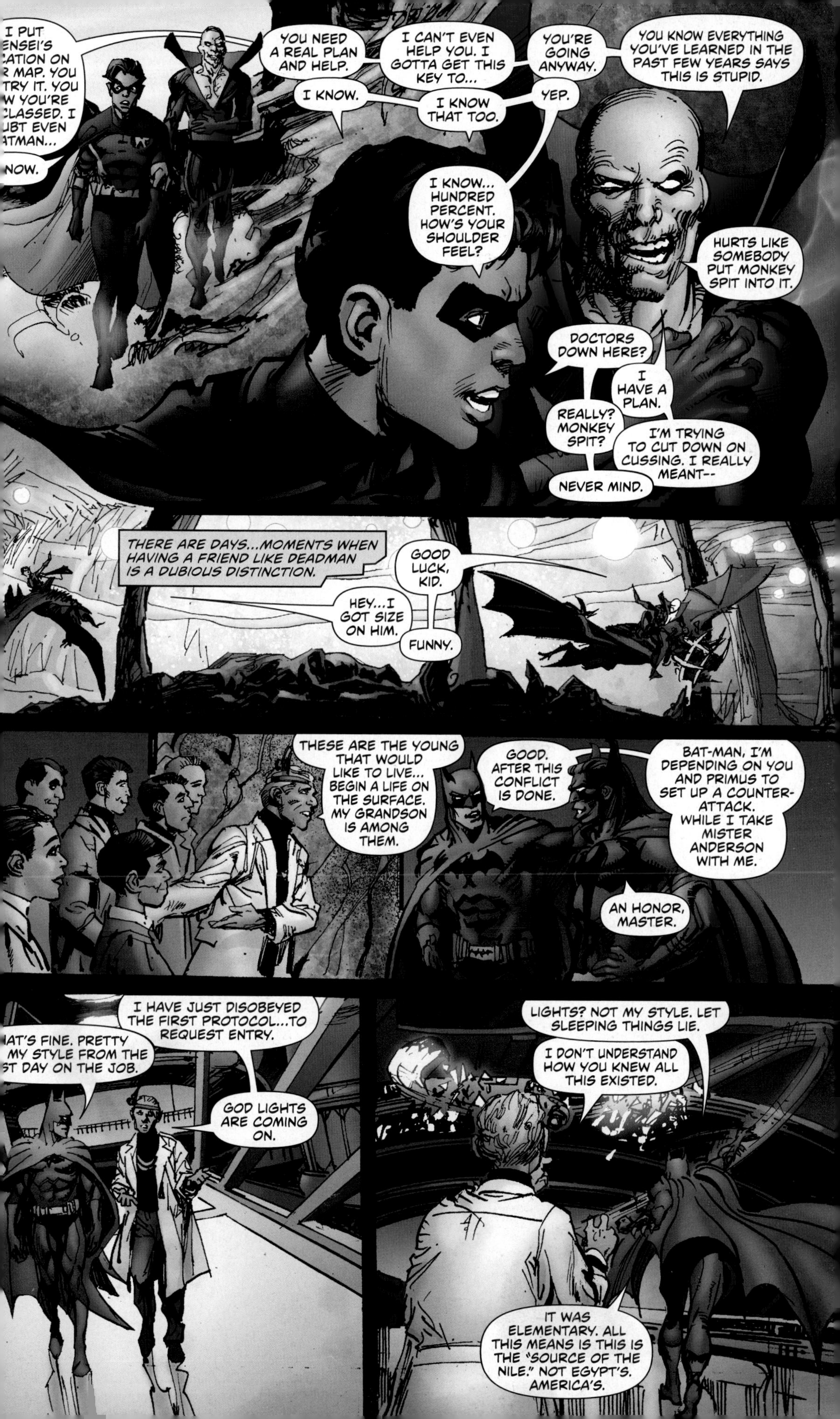
I PUT
ENSEI'S
CATION ON
R MAP. YOU
TRY IT. YOU
W YOU'RE
CLASSED. I
UBT EVEN
ATMAN...
NOW.
YOU NEED A REAL PLAN AND HELP.
I KNOW.
I CAN'T EVEN HELP YOU. I GOTTA GET THIS KEY TO...
I KNOW THAT TOO.
YOU'RE GOING ANYWAY.
YEP.
YOU KNOW EVERYTHING YOU'VE LEARNED IN THE PAST FEW YEARS SAYS THIS IS STUPID.
I KNOW... HUNDRED PERCENT. HOW'S YOUR SHOULDER FEEL?
HURTS LIKE SOMEBODY PUT MONKEY SPIT INTO IT.
DOCTORS DOWN HERE?
I HAVE A PLAN.
REALLY? MONKEY SPIT?
I'M TRYING TO CUT DOWN ON CUSSING. I REALLY MEANT--
NEVER MIND.
THERE ARE DAYS...MOMENTS WHEN HAVING A FRIEND LIKE DEADMAN IS A DUBIOUS DISTINCTION.
GOOD LUCK, KID.
HEY...I GOT SIZE ON HIM.
FUNNY.
THESE ARE THE YOUNG THAT WOULD LIKE TO LIVE... BEGIN A LIFE ON THE SURFACE. MY GRANDSON IS AMONG THEM.
GOOD. AFTER THIS CONFLICT IS DONE.
BAT-MAN, I'M DEPENDING ON YOU AND PRIMUS TO SET UP A COUNTER-ATTACK. WHILE I TAKE MISTER ANDERSON WITH ME.
AN HONOR, MASTER.
I HAVE JUST DISOBEYED THE FIRST PROTOCOL...TO REQUEST ENTRY.
AT'S FINE. PRETTY MY STYLE FROM THE ST DAY ON THE JOB.
GOD LIGHTS ARE COMING ON.
LIGHTS? NOT MY STYLE. LET SLEEPING THINGS LIE.
I DON'T UNDERSTAND HOW YOU KNEW ALL THIS EXISTED.
IT WAS ELEMENTARY. ALL THIS MEANS IS THIS IS THE "SOURCE OF THE NILE." NOT EGYPT'S. AMERICA'S.

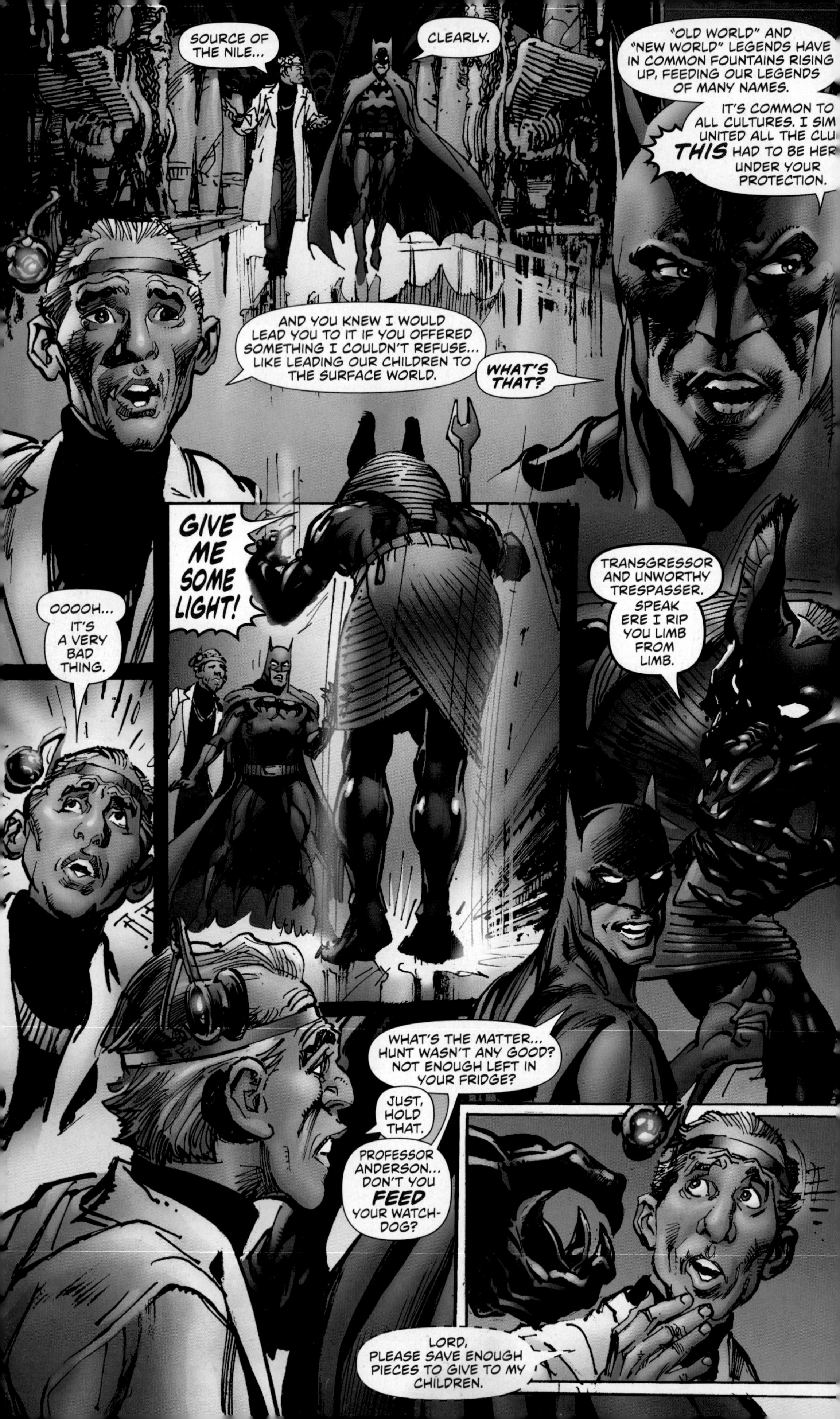
SOURCE OF THE NILE...
CLEARLY.
"OLD WORLD" AND "NEW WORLD" LEGENDS HAVE IN COMMON FOUNTAINS RISING UP, FEEDING OUR LEGENDS OF MANY NAMES.
IT'S COMMON TO ALL CULTURES. I SIM UNITED ALL THE CLU THIS HAD TO BE HER UNDER YOUR PROTECTION.
AND YOU KNEW I WOULD LEAD YOU TO IT IF YOU OFFERED SOMETHING I COULDN'T REFUSE... LIKE LEADING OUR CHILDREN TO THE SURFACE WORLD.
WHAT'S THAT?
GIVE ME SOME LIGHT!
OOOOH... IT'S A VERY BAD THING.
TRANSGRESSOR AND UNWORTHY TRESPASSER. SPEAK ERE I RIP YOU LIMB FROM LIMB.
WHAT'S THE MATTER... HUNT WASN'T ANY GOOD? NOT ENOUGH LEFT IN YOUR FRIDGE?
JUST, HOLD THAT.
PROFESSOR ANDERSON... DON'T YOU FEED YOUR WATCH-DOG?
LORD, PLEASE SAVE ENOUGH PIECES TO GIVE TO MY CHILDREN.

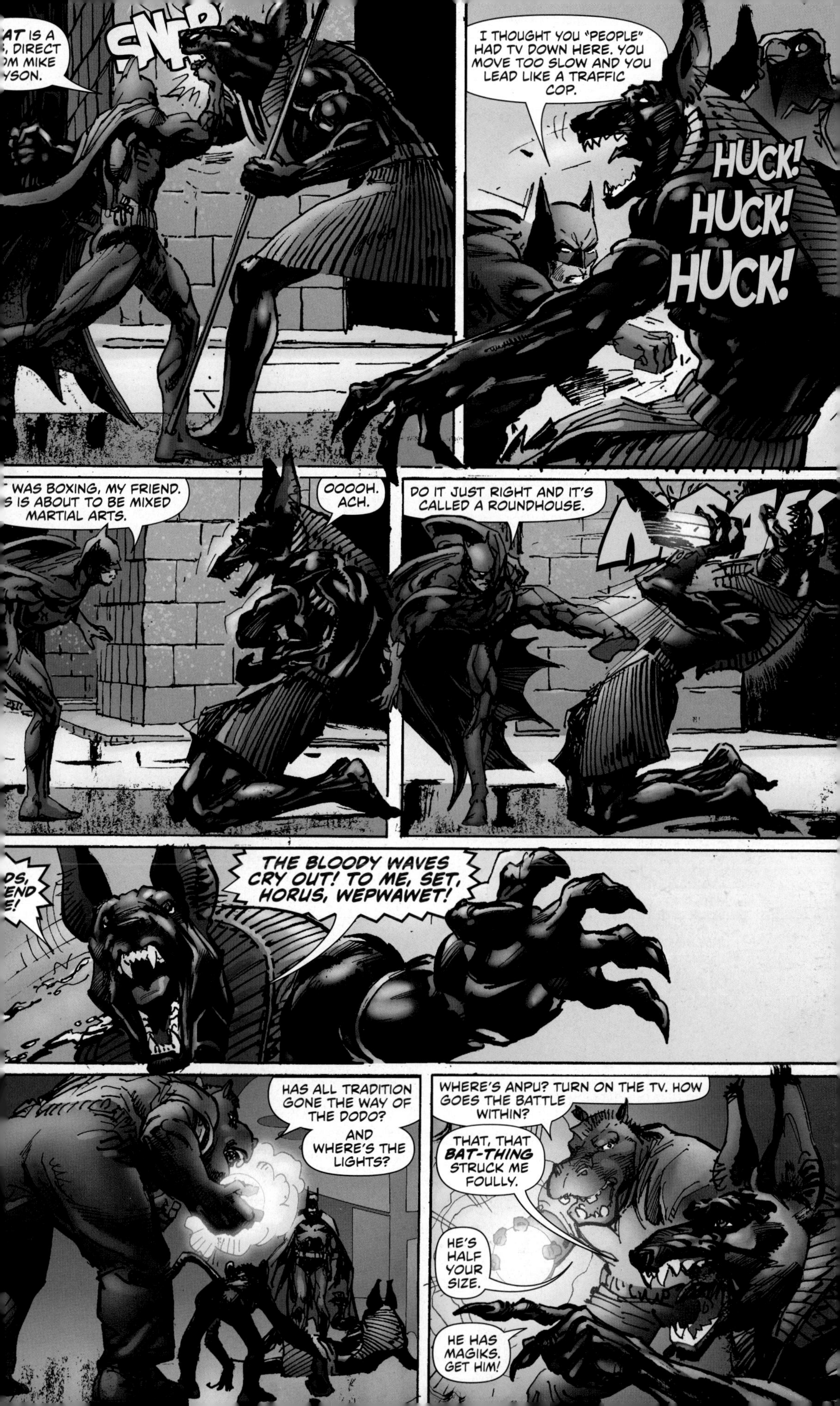

AT IS A , DIRECT OM MIKE YSON.
I THOUGHT YOU "PEOPLE" HAD TV DOWN HERE. YOU MOVE TOO SLOW AND YOU LEAD LIKE A TRAFFIC COP.
HUCK! HUCK! HUCK!
WAS BOXING, MY FRIEND. S IS ABOUT TO BE MIXED MARTIAL ARTS.
OOOOH. ACH.
DO IT JUST RIGHT AND IT'S CALLED A ROUNDHOUSE.
THE BLOODY WAVES CRY OUT! TO ME, SET, HORUS, WEPWAWET!
HAS ALL TRADITION GONE THE WAY OF THE DODO?
AND WHERE'S THE LIGHTS?
WHERE'S ANPU? TURN ON THE TV. HOW GOES THE BATTLE WITHIN?
THAT, THAT BAT-THING STRUCK ME FOULLY.
HE'S HALF YOUR SIZE.
HE HAS MAGIKS. GET HIM!

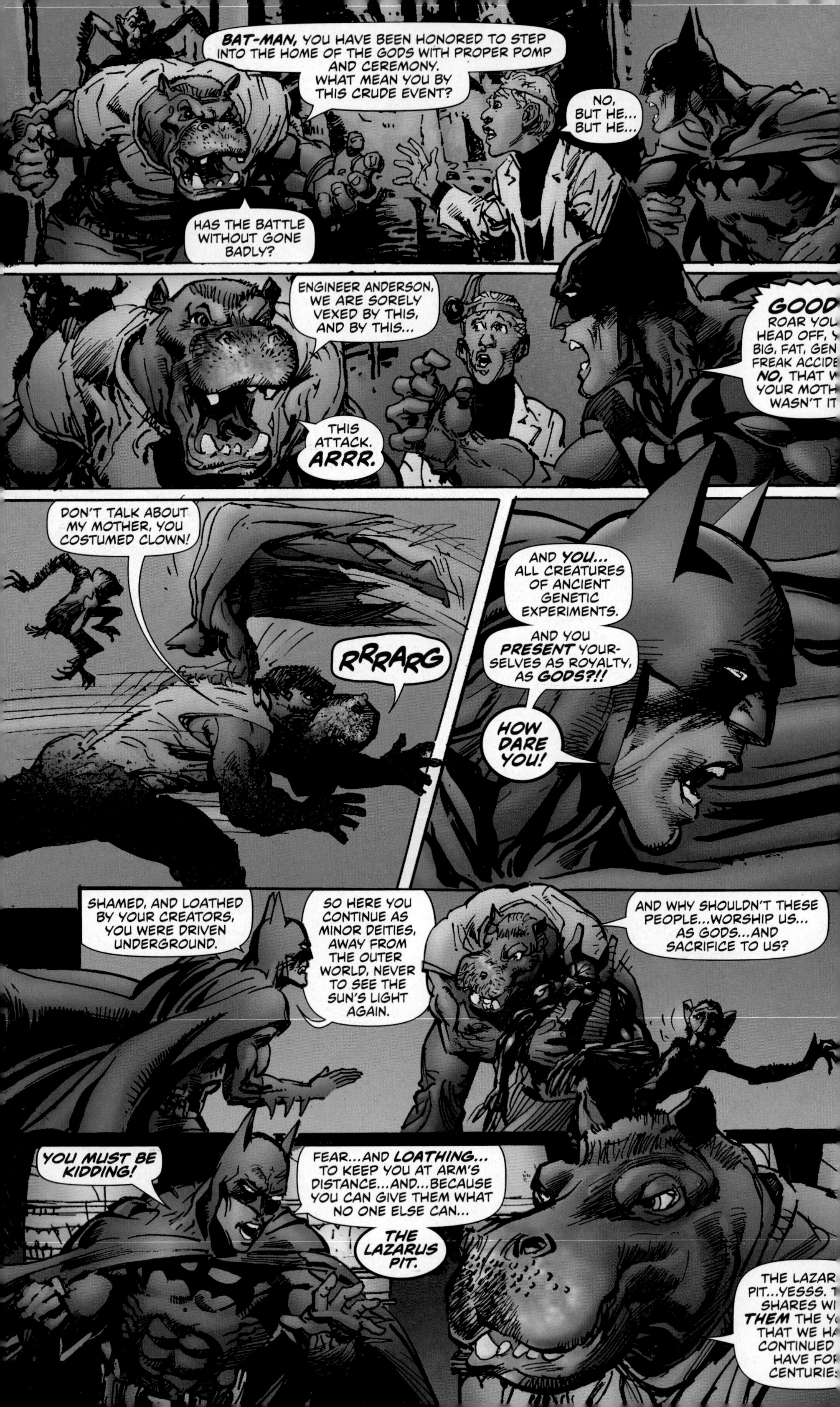

BAT-MAN, YOU HAVE BEEN HONORED TO STEP INTO THE HOME OF THE GODS WITH PROPER POMP AND CEREMONY. WHAT MEAN YOU BY THIS CRUDE EVENT?
HAS THE BATTLE WITHOUT GONE BADLY?
NO, BUT HE... BUT HE...
ENGINEER ANDERSON, WE ARE SORELY VEXED BY THIS, AND BY THIS...
THIS ATTACK. ARRR.
GOOD ROAR YOU HEAD OFF, Y BIG, FAT, GEN FREAK ACCIDE NO, THAT W YOUR MOTH WASN'T IT
DON'T TALK ABOUT MY MOTHER, YOU COSTUMED CLOWN!
RRRARG
AND YOU... ALL CREATURES OF ANCIENT GENETIC EXPERIMENTS.
AND YOU PRESENT YOUR-SELVES AS ROYALTY, AS GODS?!!
HOW DARE YOU!
SHAMED, AND LOATHED BY YOUR CREATORS, YOU WERE DRIVEN UNDERGROUND.
SO HERE YOU CONTINUE AS MINOR DEITIES, AWAY FROM THE OUTER WORLD, NEVER TO SEE THE SUN'S LIGHT AGAIN.
AND WHY SHOULDN'T THESE PEOPLE...WORSHIP US... AS GODS...AND SACRIFICE TO US?
YOU MUST BE KIDDING!
FEAR...AND LOATHING... TO KEEP YOU AT ARM'S DISTANCE...AND...BECAUSE YOU CAN GIVE THEM WHAT NO ONE ELSE CAN...
THE LAZARUS PIT.
THE LAZAR PIT...YESSS. T SHARES WI THEM THE Y THAT WE HA CONTINUED HAVE FOR CENTURIES

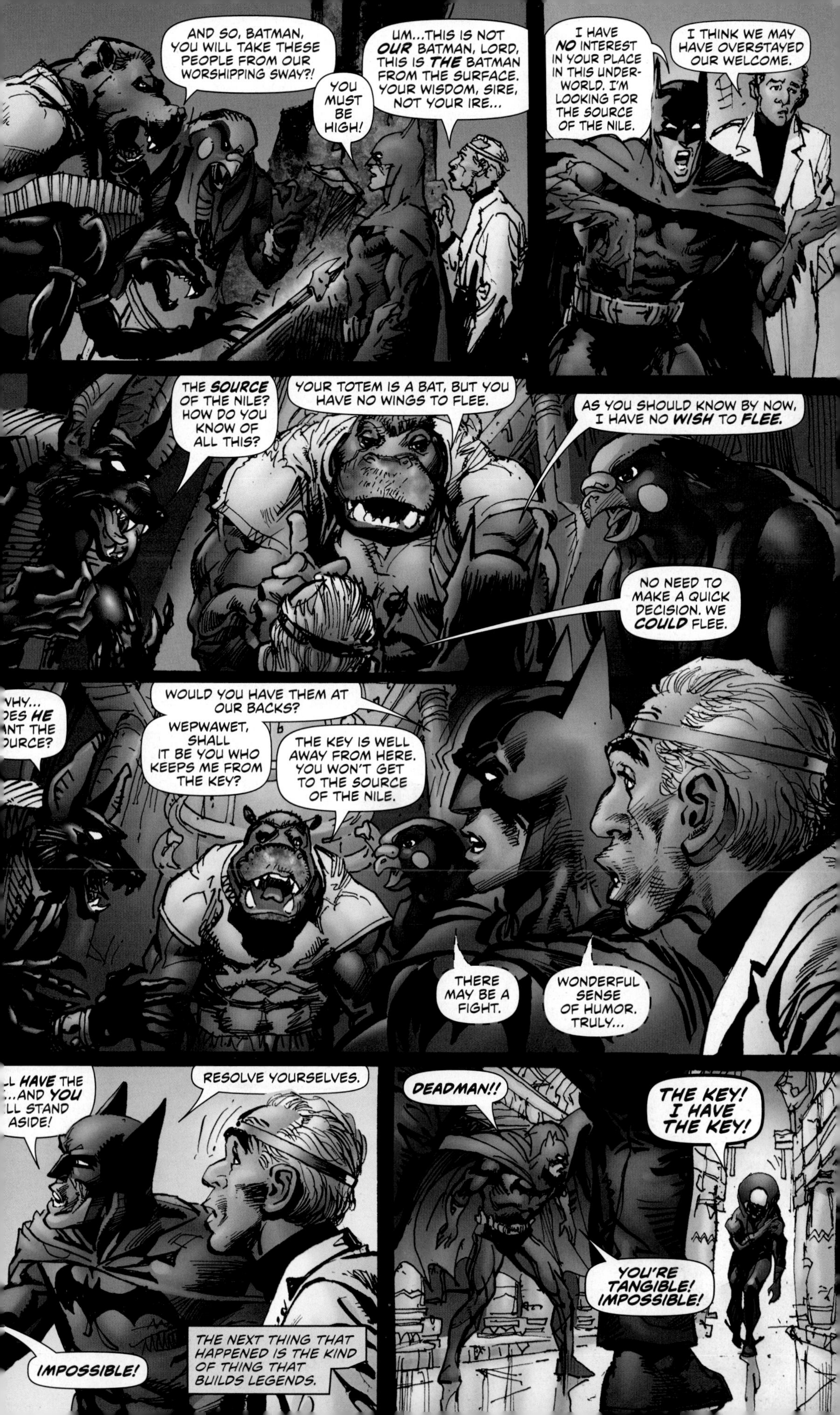

AND SO, BATMAN, YOU WILL TAKE THESE PEOPLE FROM OUR WORSHIPPING SWAY?!
YOU MUST BE HIGH!
UM...THIS IS NOT OUR BATMAN, LORD, THIS IS THE BATMAN FROM THE SURFACE. YOUR WISDOM, SIRE, NOT YOUR IRE...
I HAVE NO INTEREST IN YOUR PLACE IN THIS UNDERWORLD. I'M LOOKING FOR THE SOURCE OF THE NILE.
I THINK WE MAY HAVE OVERSTAYED OUR WELCOME.
THE SOURCE OF THE NILE? HOW DO YOU KNOW OF ALL THIS?
YOUR TOTEM IS A BAT, BUT YOU HAVE NO WINGS TO FLEE.
AS YOU SHOULD KNOW BY NOW, I HAVE NO WISH TO FLEE.
NO NEED TO MAKE A QUICK DECISION. WE COULD FLEE.
VHY... DES HE ANT THE OURCE?
WOULD YOU HAVE THEM AT OUR BACKS?
WEPWAWET, SHALL IT BE YOU WHO KEEPS ME FROM THE KEY?
THE KEY IS WELL AWAY FROM HERE. YOU WON'T GET TO THE SOURCE OF THE NILE.
THERE MAY BE A FIGHT.
WONDERFUL SENSE OF HUMOR. TRULY...
L HAVE THE ...AND YOU LL STAND ASIDE!
RESOLVE YOURSELVES.
IMPOSSIBLE!
THE NEXT THING THAT HAPPENED IS THE KIND OF THING THAT BUILDS LEGENDS.
DEADMAN!!
THE KEY! I HAVE THE KEY!
YOU'RE TANGIBLE! IMPOSSIBLE!

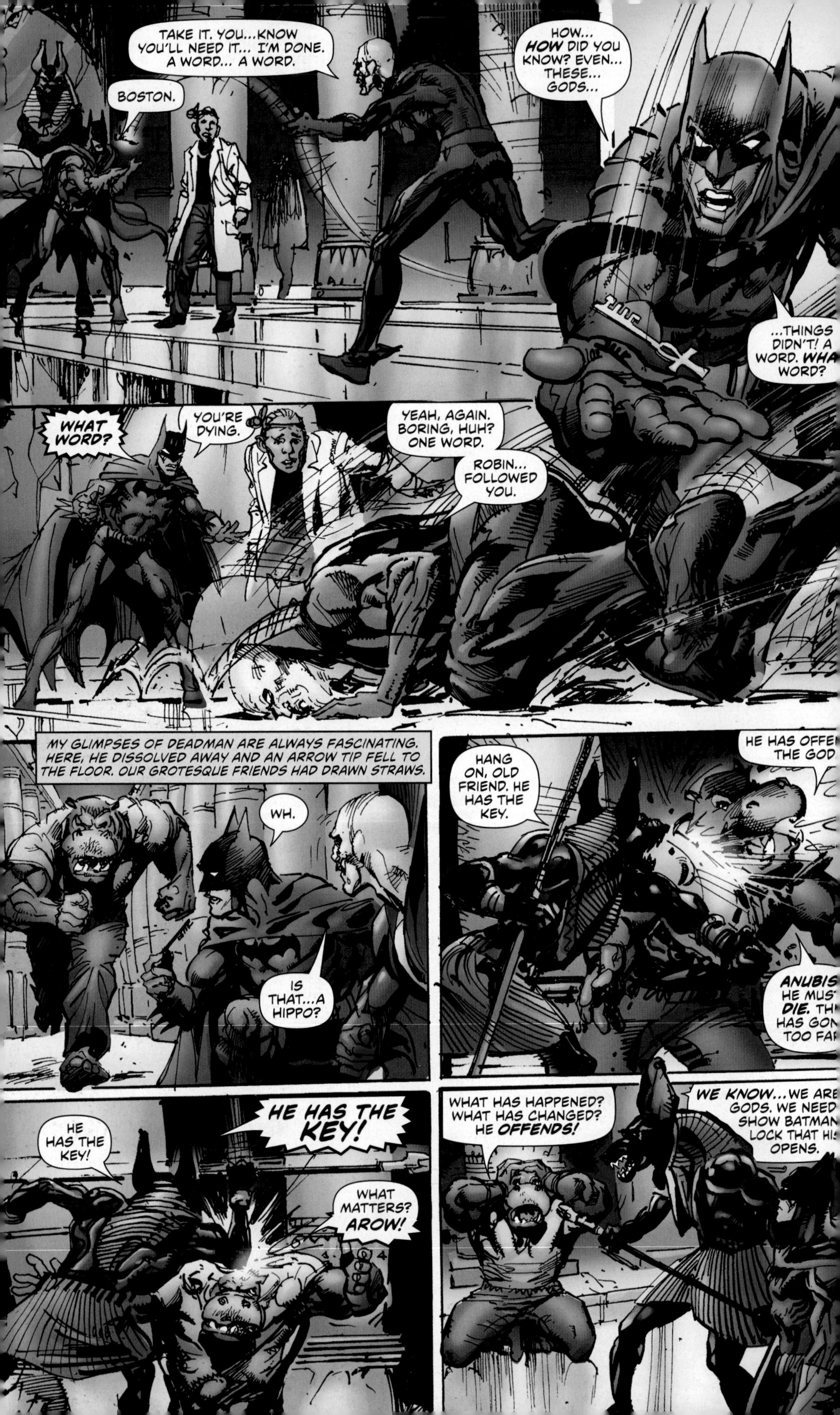

TAKE IT. YOU...KNOW YOU'LL NEED IT... I'M DONE. A WORD... A WORD.
BOSTON.
HOW... HOW DID YOU KNOW? EVEN... THESE... GODS...
...THINGS DIDN'T! A WORD. WHA WORD?
WHAT WORD?
YOU'RE DYING.
YEAH, AGAIN. BORING, HUH? ONE WORD.
ROBIN... FOLLOWED YOU.
MY GLIMPSES OF DEADMAN ARE ALWAYS FASCINATING. HERE, HE DISSOLVED AWAY AND AN ARROW TIP FELL TO THE FLOOR. OUR GROTESQUE FRIENDS HAD DRAWN STRAWS.
WH.
IS THAT...A HIPPO?
HANG ON, OLD FRIEND. HE HAS THE KEY.
HE HAS OFFE THE GOD
ANUBIS HE MUST DIE. TH HAS GON TOO FA
HE HAS THE KEY!
HE HAS THE KEY!
WHAT MATTERS? AROW!
WHAT HAS HAPPENED? WHAT HAS CHANGED? HE OFFENDS!
WE KNOW...WE ARE GODS. WE NEED SHOW BATMAN LOCK THAT HI OPENS.

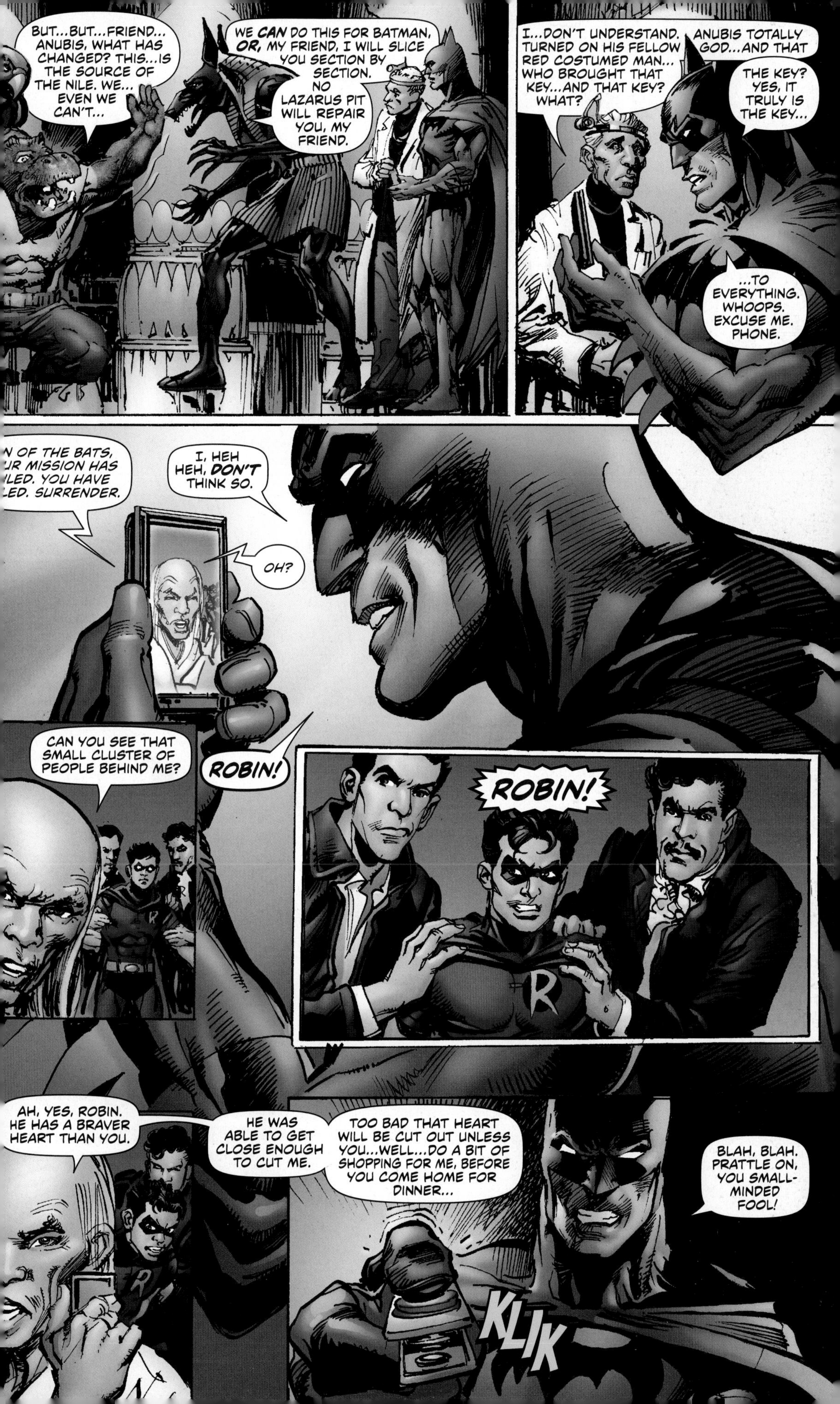

BUT...BUT...FRIEND... ANUBIS, WHAT HAS CHANGED? THIS...IS THE SOURCE OF THE NILE. WE... EVEN WE CAN'T...
WE CAN DO THIS FOR BATMAN, OR, MY FRIEND, I WILL SLICE YOU SECTION BY SECTION. NO LAZARUS PIT WILL REPAIR YOU, MY FRIEND.
I...DON'T UNDERSTAND. ANUBIS TOTALLY TURNED ON HIS FELLOW GOD...AND THAT RED COSTUMED MAN... WHO BROUGHT THAT KEY...AND THAT KEY? WHAT?
THE KEY? YES, IT TRULY IS THE KEY...
...TO EVERYTHING. WHOOPS. EXCUSE ME. PHONE.
N OF THE BATS, UR MISSION HAS ILED. YOU HAVE LED. SURRENDER.
I, HEH HEH, DON'T THINK SO.
OH?
CAN YOU SEE THAT SMALL CLUSTER OF PEOPLE BEHIND ME?
ROBIN!
ROBIN!
AH, YES, ROBIN. HE HAS A BRAVER HEART THAN YOU.
HE WAS ABLE TO GET CLOSE ENOUGH TO CUT ME.
TOO BAD THAT HEART WILL BE CUT OUT UNLESS YOU...WELL...DO A BIT OF SHOPPING FOR ME, BEFORE YOU COME HOME FOR DINNER...
BLAH, BLAH. PRATTLE ON, YOU SMALL-MINDED FOOL!
KLIK

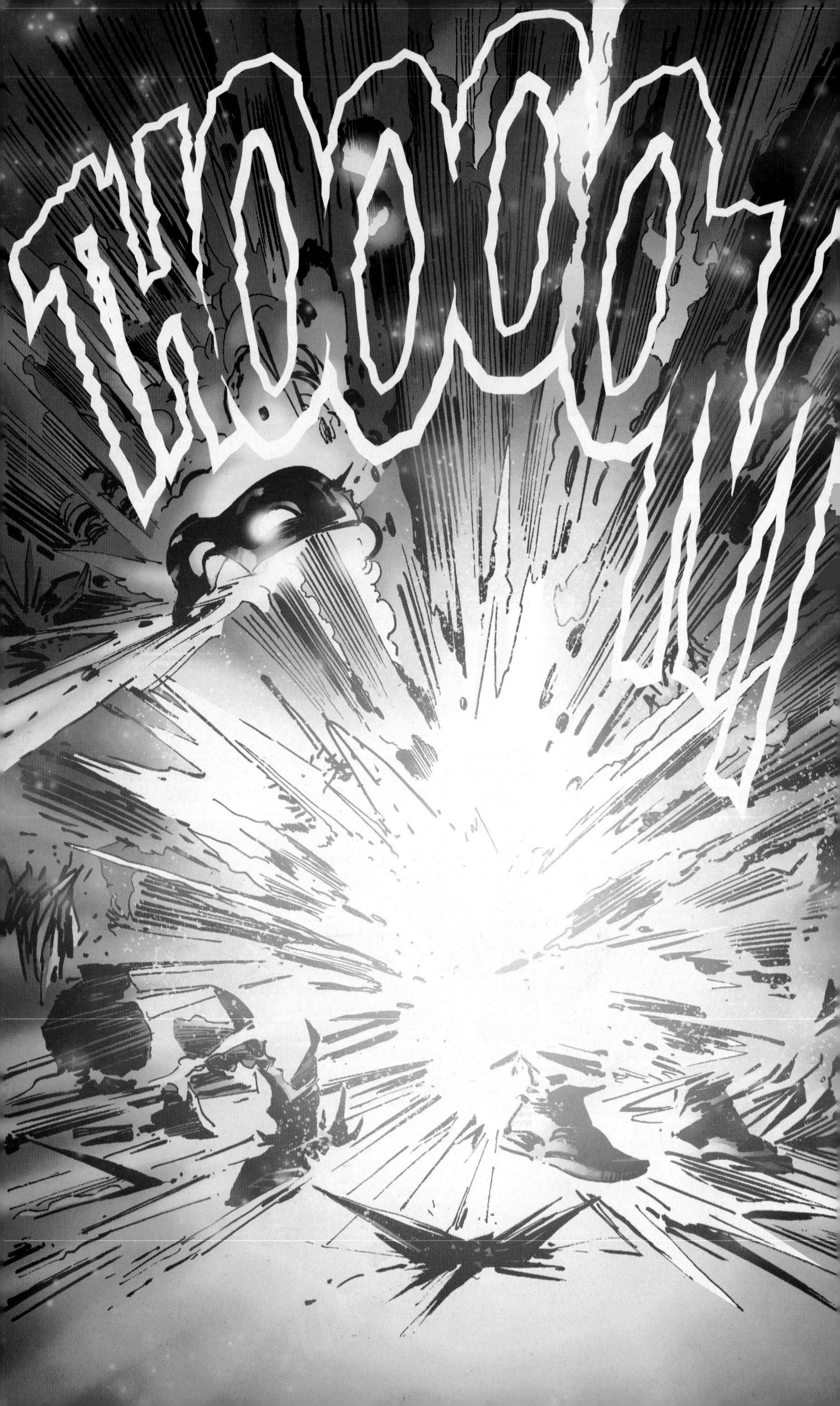
THOOOOM

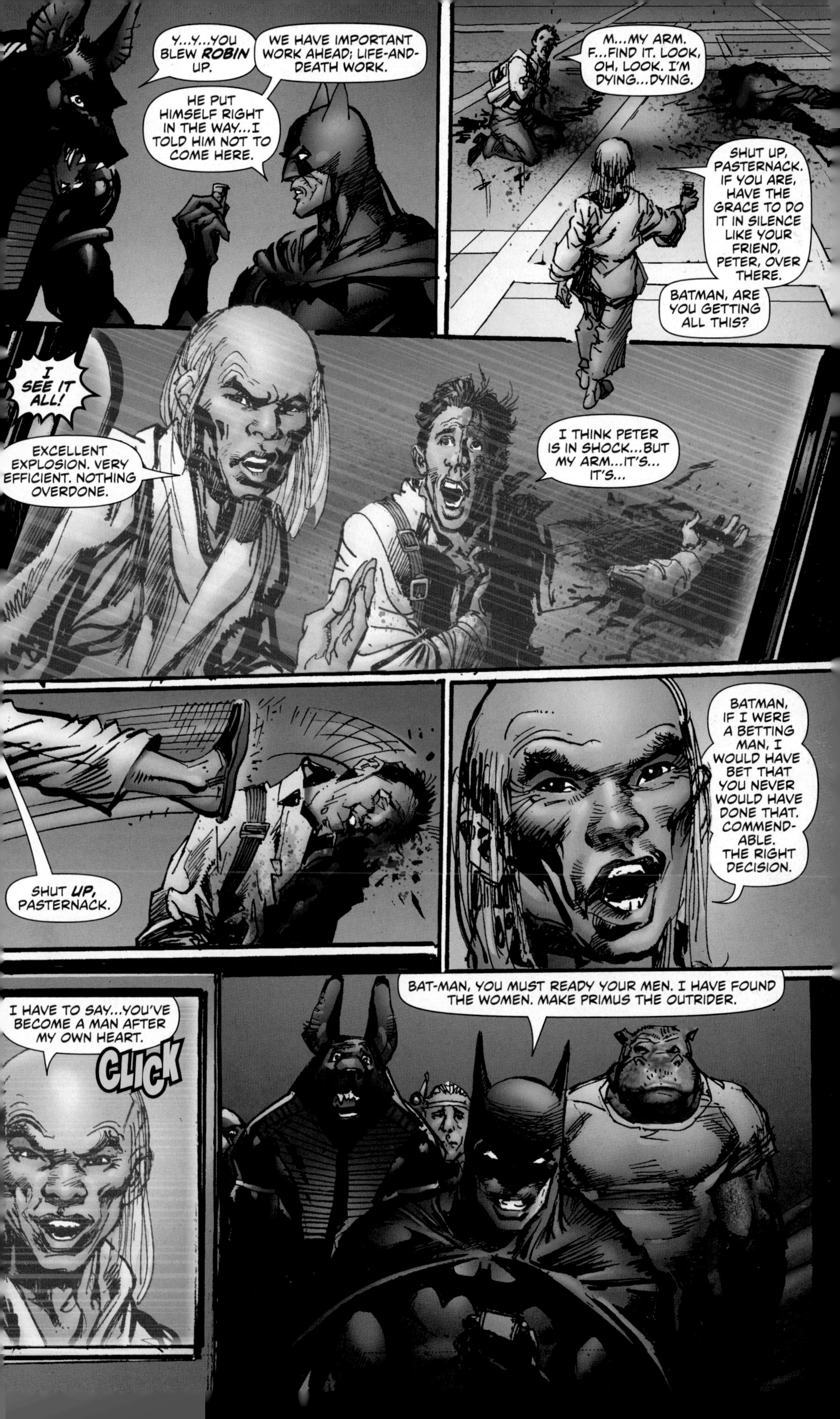
Y...Y...YOU BLEW ROBIN UP.
WE HAVE IMPORTANT WORK AHEAD; LIFE-AND-DEATH WORK.
HE PUT HIMSELF RIGHT IN THE WAY...I TOLD HIM NOT TO COME HERE.
M...MY ARM. F...FIND IT. LOOK, OH, LOOK. I'M DYING...DYING.
SHUT UP, PASTERNACK. IF YOU ARE, HAVE THE GRACE TO DO IT IN SILENCE LIKE YOUR FRIEND, PETER, OVER THERE.
BATMAN, ARE YOU GETTING ALL THIS?
I SEE IT ALL!
EXCELLENT EXPLOSION. VERY EFFICIENT. NOTHING OVERDONE.
I THINK PETER IS IN SHOCK...BUT MY ARM...IT'S... IT'S...
SHUT UP, PASTERNACK.
BATMAN, IF I WERE A BETTING MAN, I WOULD HAVE BET THAT YOU NEVER WOULD HAVE DONE THAT. COMMEND-ABLE. THE RIGHT DECISION.
I HAVE TO SAY...YOU'VE BECOME A MAN AFTER MY OWN HEART.
CLICK
BAT-MAN, YOU MUST READY YOUR MEN. I HAVE FOUND THE WOMEN. MAKE PRIMUS THE OUTRIDER.

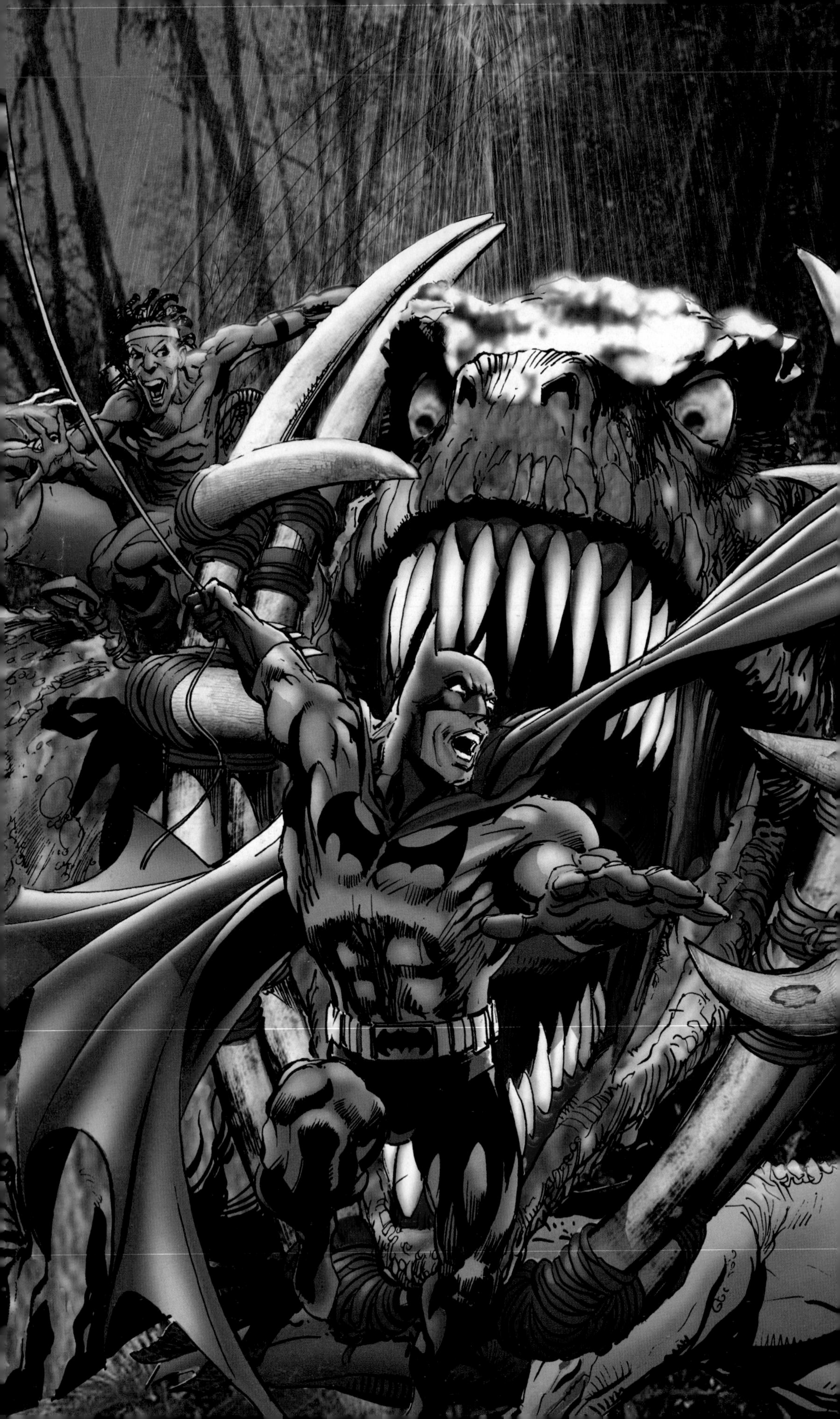

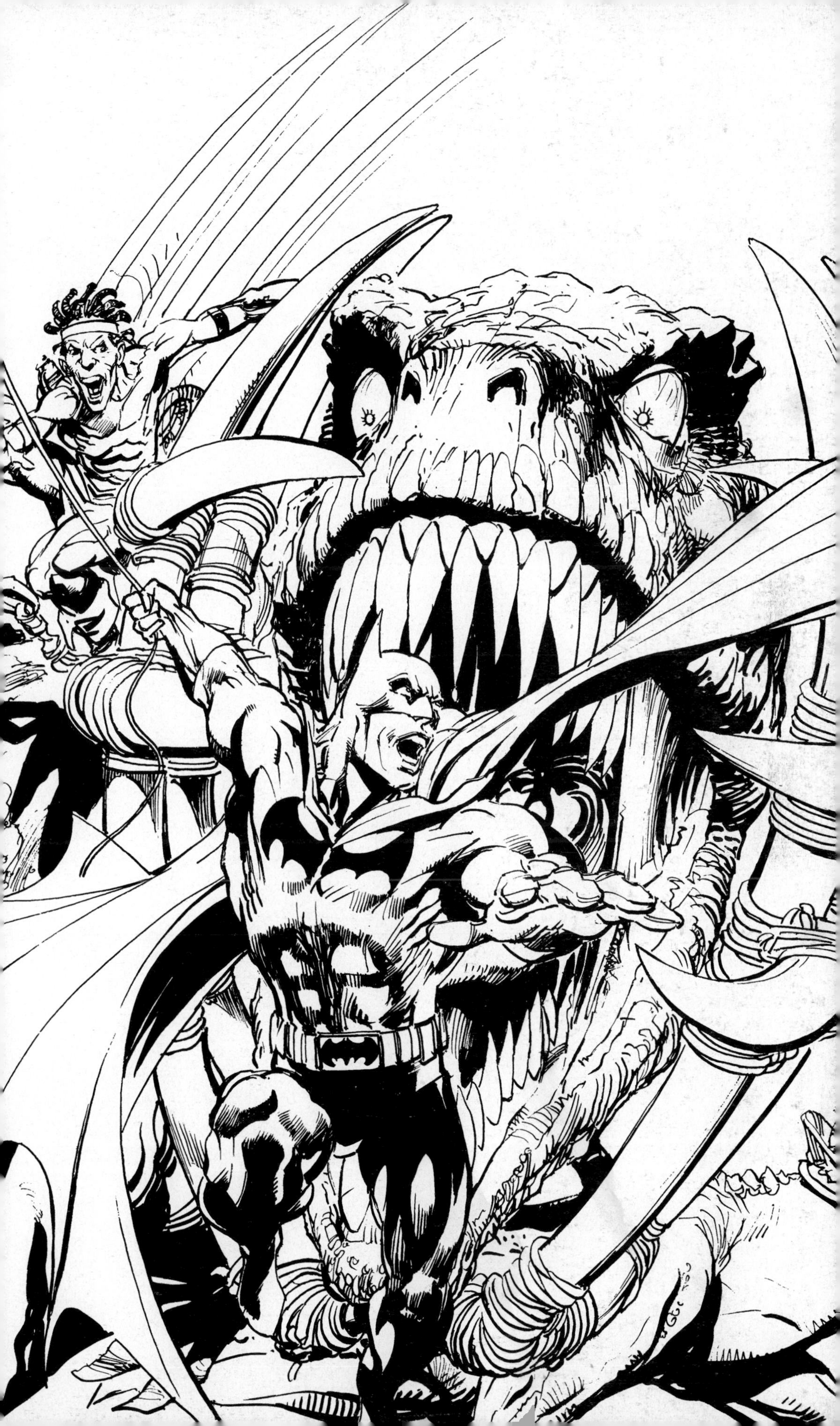

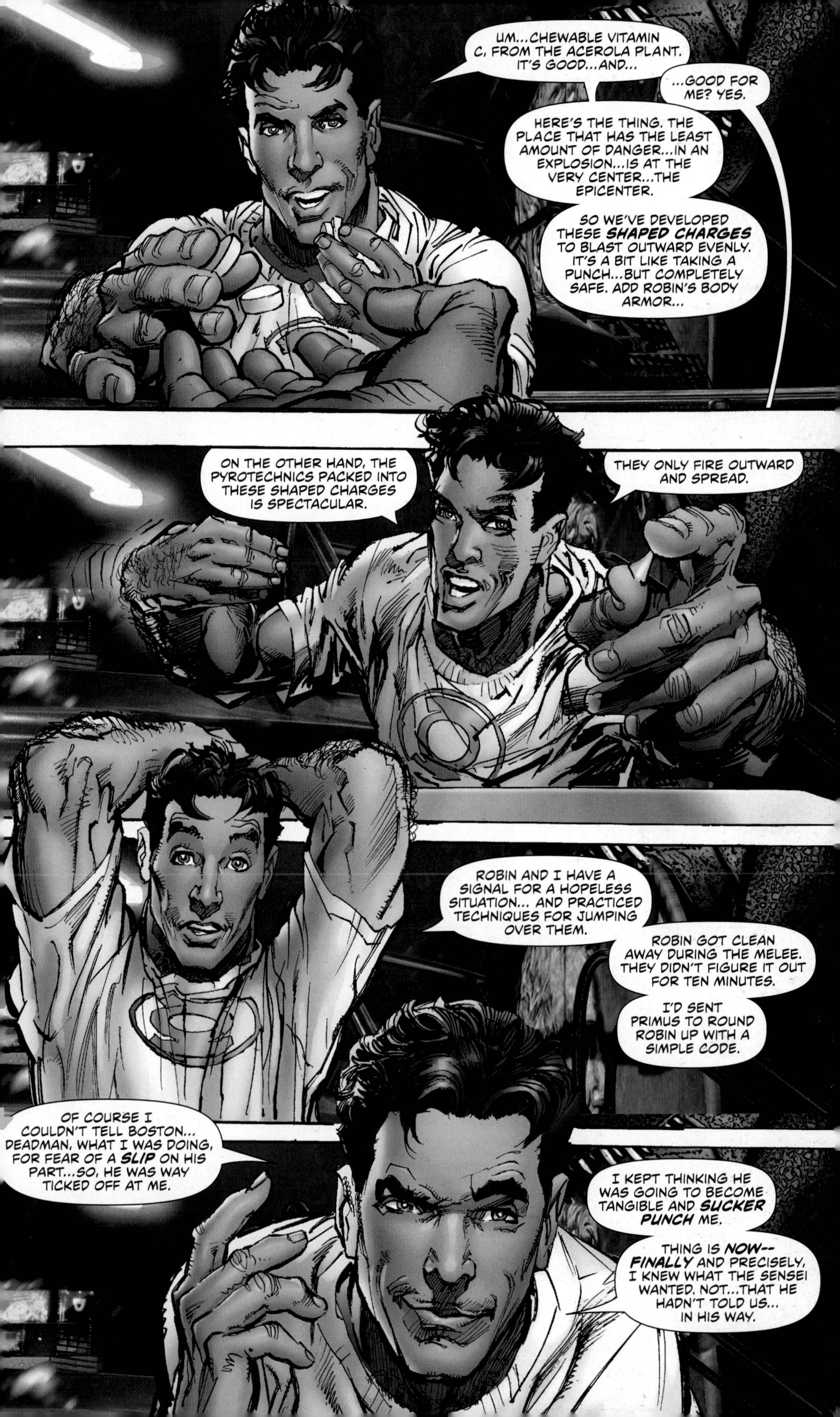
UM...CHEWABLE VITAMIN C, FROM THE ACEROLA PLANT. IT'S GOOD...AND...
...GOOD FOR ME? YES.
HERE'S THE THING. THE PLACE THAT HAS THE LEAST AMOUNT OF DANGER...IN AN EXPLOSION...IS AT THE VERY CENTER...THE EPICENTER.
SO WE'VE DEVELOPED THESE **SHAPED CHARGES** TO BLAST OUTWARD EVENLY. IT'S A BIT LIKE TAKING A PUNCH...BUT COMPLETELY SAFE. ADD ROBIN'S BODY ARMOR...
ON THE OTHER HAND, THE PYROTECHNICS PACKED INTO THESE SHAPED CHARGES IS SPECTACULAR.
THEY ONLY FIRE OUTWARD AND SPREAD.
ROBIN AND I HAVE A SIGNAL FOR A HOPELESS SITUATION... AND PRACTICED TECHNIQUES FOR JUMPING OVER THEM.
ROBIN GOT CLEAN AWAY DURING THE MELEE. THEY DIDN'T FIGURE IT OUT FOR TEN MINUTES.
I'D SENT PRIMUS TO ROUND ROBIN UP WITH A SIMPLE CODE.
OF COURSE I COULDN'T TELL BOSTON... DEADMAN, WHAT I WAS DOING, FOR FEAR OF A **SLIP** ON HIS PART...SO, HE WAS WAY TICKED OFF AT ME.
I KEPT THINKING HE WAS GOING TO BECOME TANGIBLE AND **SUCKER PUNCH** ME.
THING IS **NOW-- FINALLY** AND PRECISELY, I KNEW WHAT THE SENSEI WANTED. NOT...THAT HE HADN'T TOLD US... IN HIS WAY.

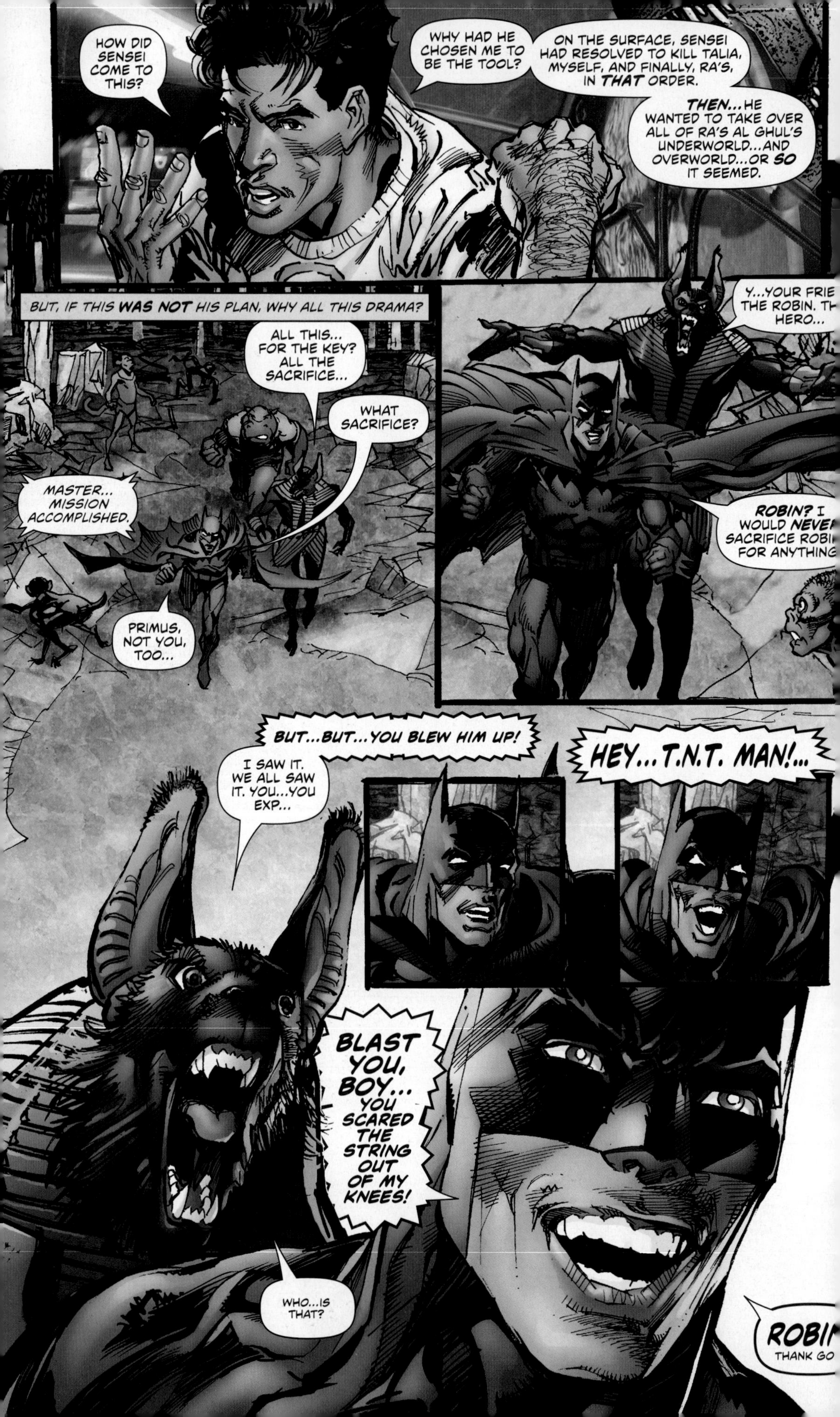
HOW DID SENSEI COME TO THIS?
WHY HAD HE CHOSEN ME TO BE THE TOOL?
ON THE SURFACE, SENSEI HAD RESOLVED TO KILL TALIA, MYSELF, AND FINALLY, RA'S, IN THAT ORDER.
THEN...HE WANTED TO TAKE OVER ALL OF RA'S AL GHUL'S UNDERWORLD...AND OVERWORLD...OR SO IT SEEMED.
BUT, IF THIS WAS NOT HIS PLAN, WHY ALL THIS DRAMA?
ALL THIS... FOR THE KEY? ALL THE SACRIFICE...
WHAT SACRIFICE?
MASTER... MISSION ACCOMPLISHED.
PRIMUS, NOT YOU, TOO...
Y...YOUR FRIE THE ROBIN. TH HERO...
ROBIN? I WOULD NEVE SACRIFICE ROBI FOR ANYTHING
BUT...BUT...YOU BLEW HIM UP!
I SAW IT. WE ALL SAW IT. YOU...YOU EXP...
HEY...T.N.T. MAN!...
BLAST YOU, BOY... YOU SCARED THE STRING OUT OF MY KNEES!
WHO...IS THAT?
ROBI THANK GO

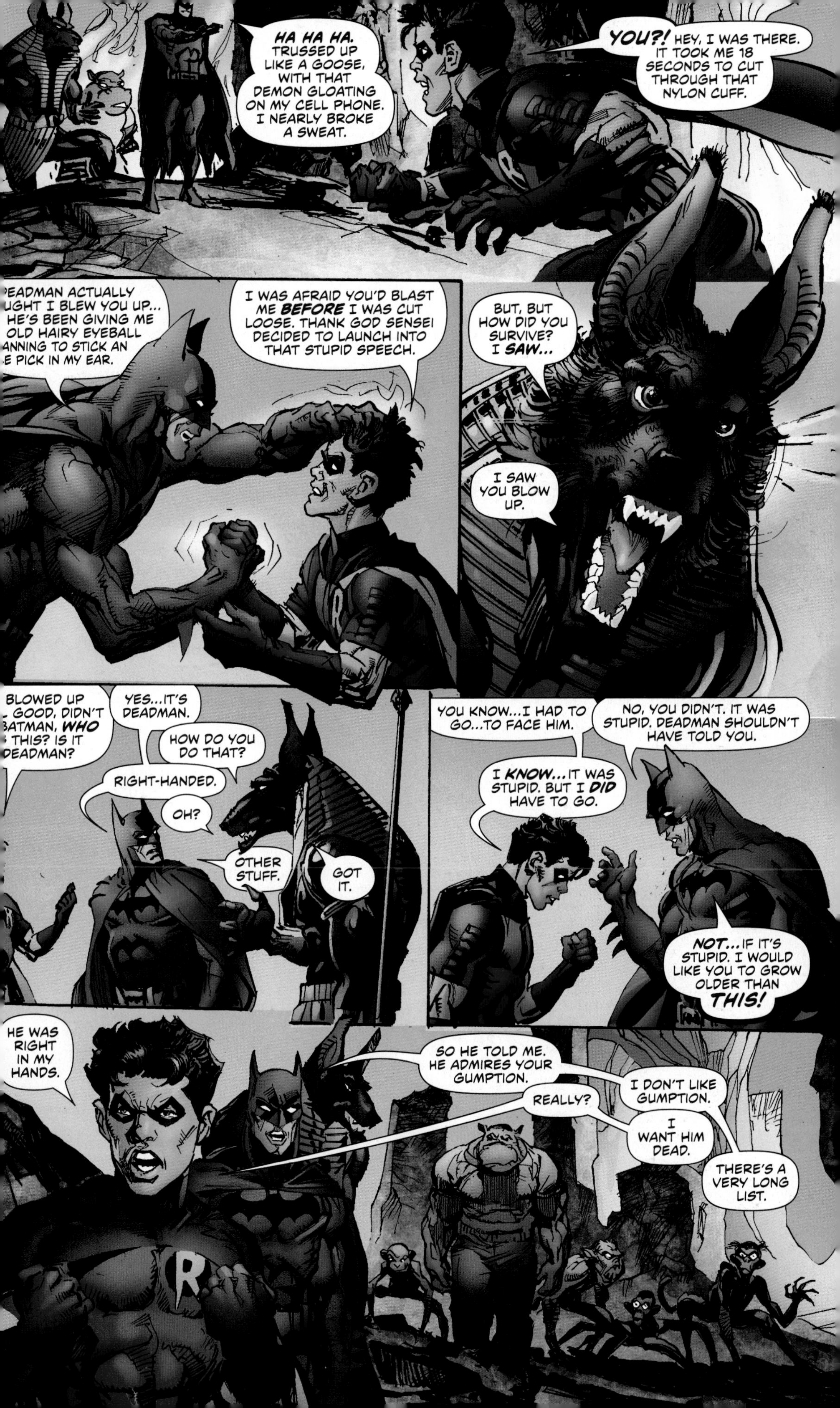

HA HA HA. TRUSSED UP LIKE A GOOSE, WITH THAT DEMON GLOATING ON MY CELL PHONE. I NEARLY BROKE A SWEAT.
YOU?! HEY, I WAS THERE. IT TOOK ME 18 SECONDS TO CUT THROUGH THAT NYLON CUFF.
EADMAN ACTUALLY UGHT I BLEW YOU UP... HE'S BEEN GIVING ME OLD HAIRY EYEBALL ANNING TO STICK AN E PICK IN MY EAR.
I WAS AFRAID YOU'D BLAST ME BEFORE I WAS CUT LOOSE. THANK GOD SENSEI DECIDED TO LAUNCH INTO THAT STUPID SPEECH.
BUT, BUT HOW DID YOU SURVIVE? I SAW...
I SAW YOU BLOW UP.
BLOWED UP GOOD, DIDN'T ATMAN, WHO THIS? IS IT DEADMAN?
YES...IT'S DEADMAN.
HOW DO YOU DO THAT?
RIGHT-HANDED.
OH?
OTHER STUFF.
GOT IT.
YOU KNOW...I HAD TO GO...TO FACE HIM.
NO, YOU DIDN'T. IT WAS STUPID. DEADMAN SHOULDN'T HAVE TOLD YOU.
I KNOW...IT WAS STUPID. BUT I DID HAVE TO GO.
NOT...IF IT'S STUPID. I WOULD LIKE YOU TO GROW OLDER THAN THIS!
HE WAS RIGHT IN MY HANDS.
SO HE TOLD ME. HE ADMIRES YOUR GUMPTION.
I DON'T LIKE GUMPTION.
REALLY?
I WANT HIM DEAD.
THERE'S A VERY LONG LIST.

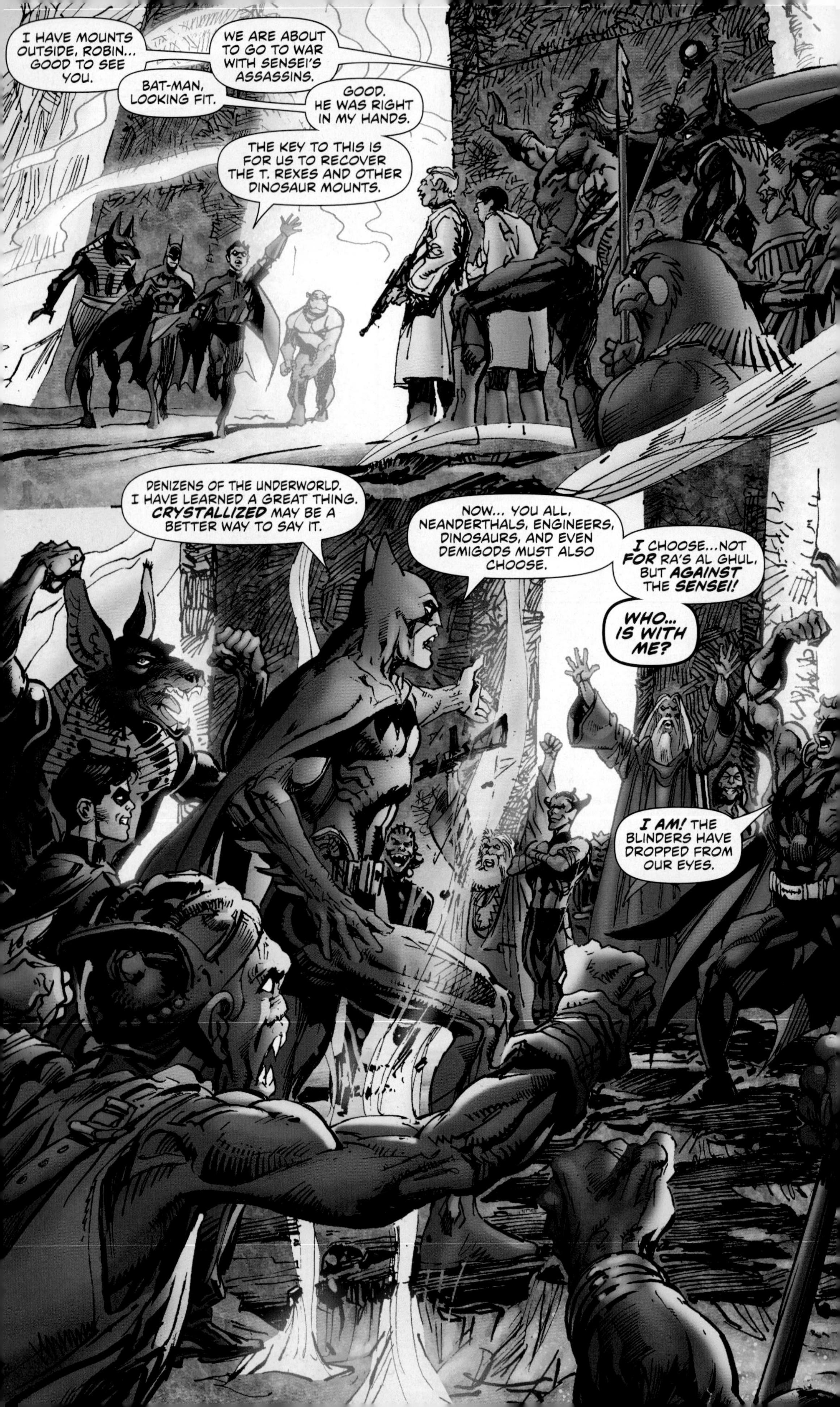
I HAVE MOUNTS OUTSIDE, ROBIN... GOOD TO SEE YOU.
WE ARE ABOUT TO GO TO WAR WITH SENSEI'S ASSASSINS.
BAT-MAN, LOOKING FIT.
GOOD. HE WAS RIGHT IN MY HANDS.
THE KEY TO THIS IS FOR US TO RECOVER THE T. REXES AND OTHER DINOSAUR MOUNTS.
DENIZENS OF THE UNDERWORLD. I HAVE LEARNED A GREAT THING. CRYSTALLIZED MAY BE A BETTER WAY TO SAY IT.
NOW... YOU ALL, NEANDERTHALS, ENGINEERS, DINOSAURS, AND EVEN DEMIGODS MUST ALSO CHOOSE.
I CHOOSE...NOT FOR RA'S AL GHUL, BUT AGAINST THE SENSEI!
WHO... IS WITH ME?
I AM! THE BLINDERS HAVE DROPPED FROM OUR EYES.

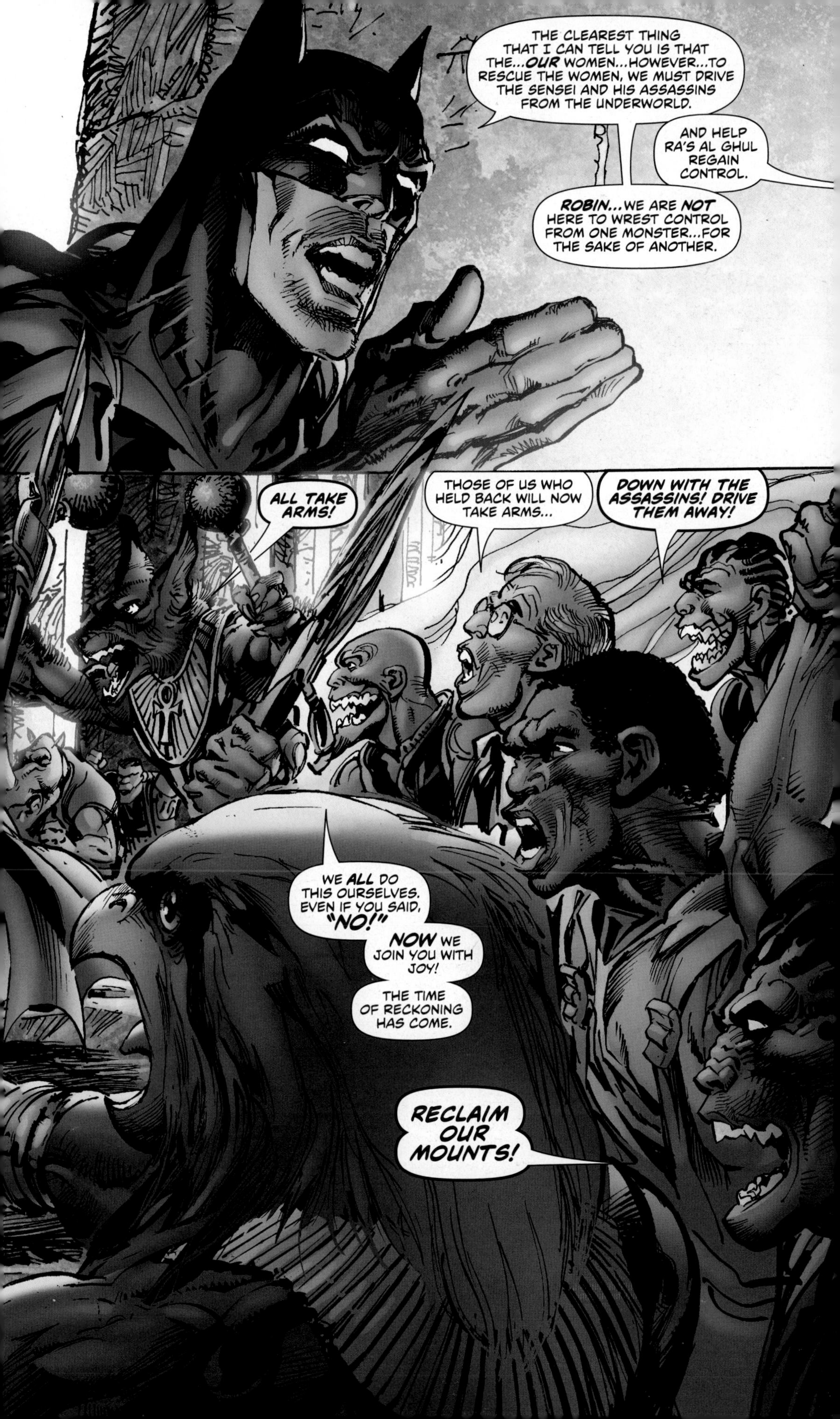
THE CLEAREST THING THAT I CAN TELL YOU IS THAT THE...OUR WOMEN...HOWEVER...TO RESCUE THE WOMEN, WE MUST DRIVE THE SENSEI AND HIS ASSASSINS FROM THE UNDERWORLD.
AND HELP RA'S AL GHUL REGAIN CONTROL.
ROBIN...WE ARE NOT HERE TO WREST CONTROL FROM ONE MONSTER...FOR THE SAKE OF ANOTHER.
ALL TAKE ARMS!
THOSE OF US WHO HELD BACK WILL NOW TAKE ARMS...
DOWN WITH THE ASSASSINS! DRIVE THEM AWAY!
WE ALL DO THIS OURSELVES. EVEN IF YOU SAID, "NO!"
NOW WE JOIN YOU WITH JOY!
THE TIME OF RECKONING HAS COME.
RECLAIM OUR MOUNTS!

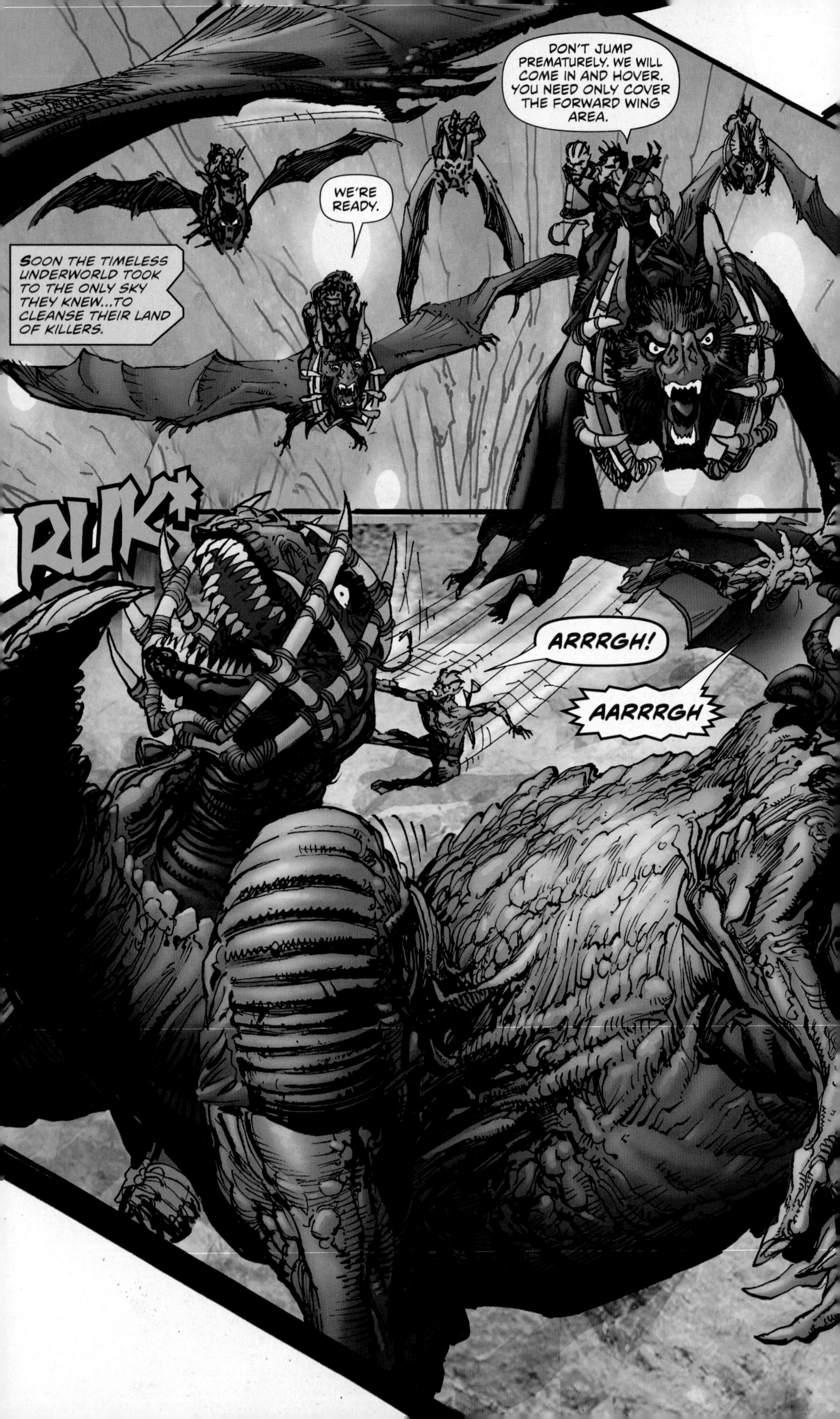
DON'T JUMP PREMATURELY. WE WILL COME IN AND HOVER. YOU NEED ONLY COVER THE FORWARD WING AREA.
WE'RE READY.
SOON THE TIMELESS UNDERWORLD TOOK TO THE ONLY SKY THEY KNEW...TO CLEANSE THEIR LAND OF KILLERS.
RUK*
ARRRGH!
AARRRGH

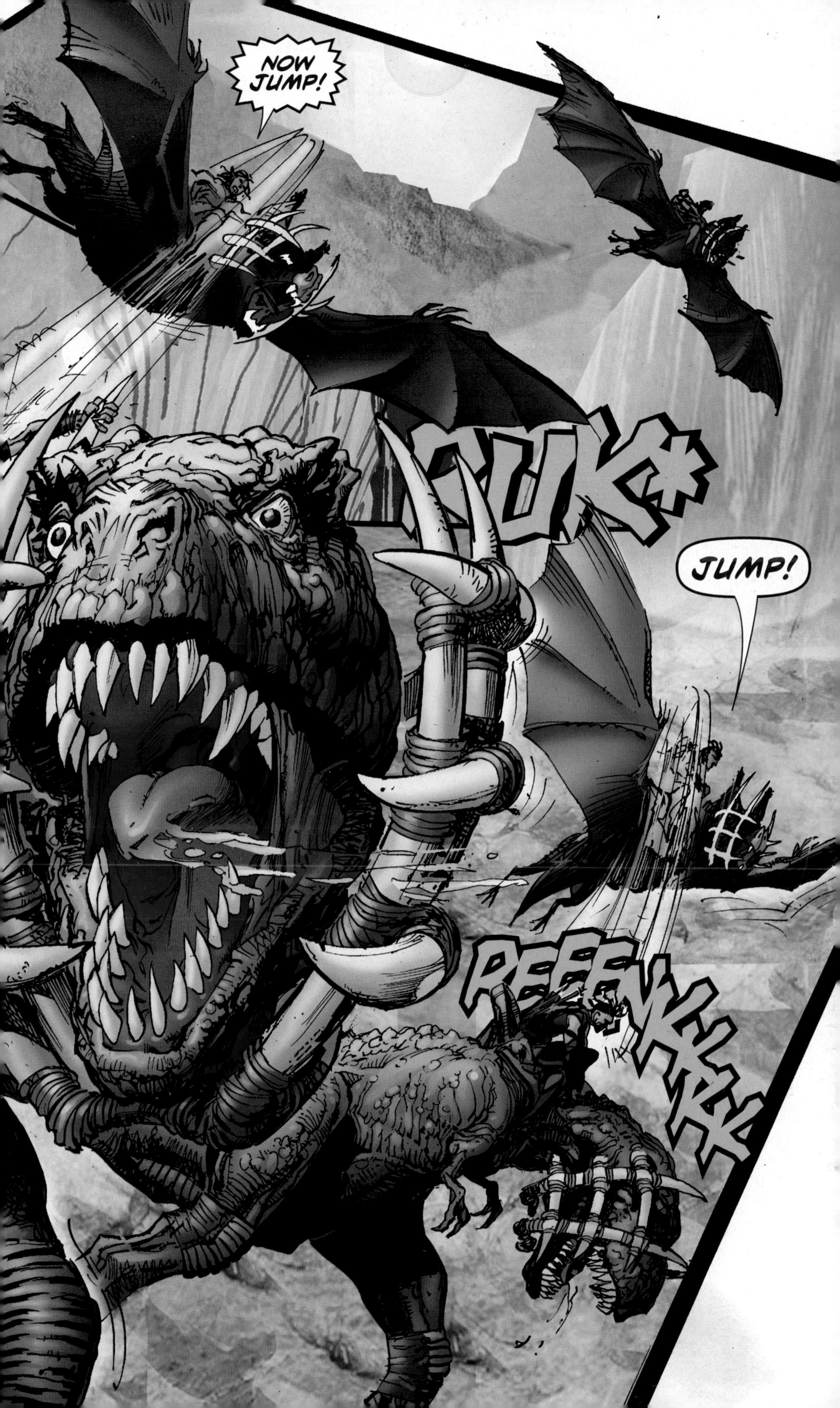
NOW JUMP!
JUMP!

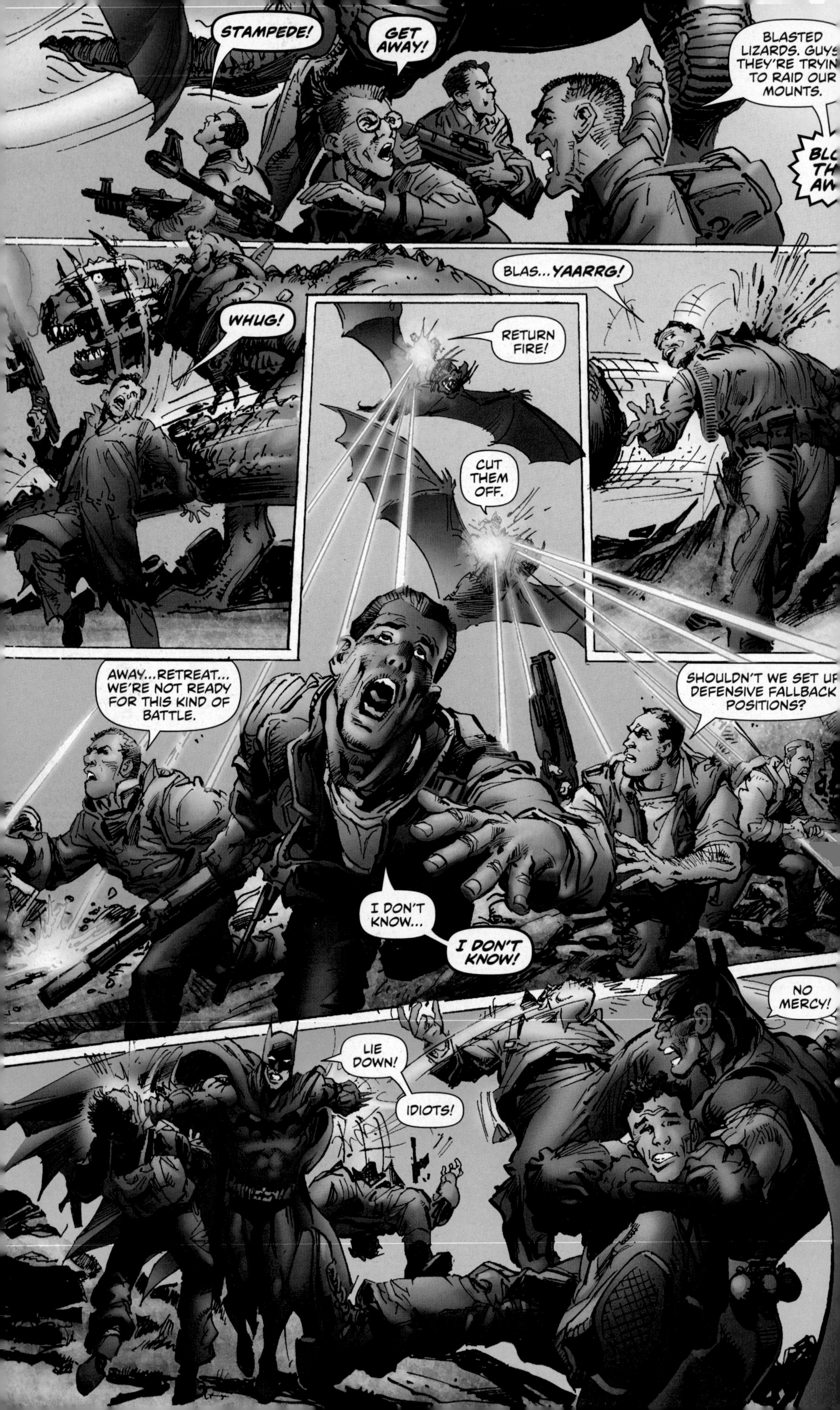
STAMPEDE!
GET AWAY!
BLASTED LIZARDS. GUYS THEY'RE TRYIN TO RAID OUR MOUNTS.
BLAS...YAARRG!
WHUG!
RETURN FIRE!
CUT THEM OFF.
AWAY...RETREAT... WE'RE NOT READY FOR THIS KIND OF BATTLE.
SHOULDN'T WE SET UP DEFENSIVE FALLBACK POSITIONS?
I DON'T KNOW...
I DON'T KNOW!
NO MERCY!
LIE DOWN!
IDIOTS!

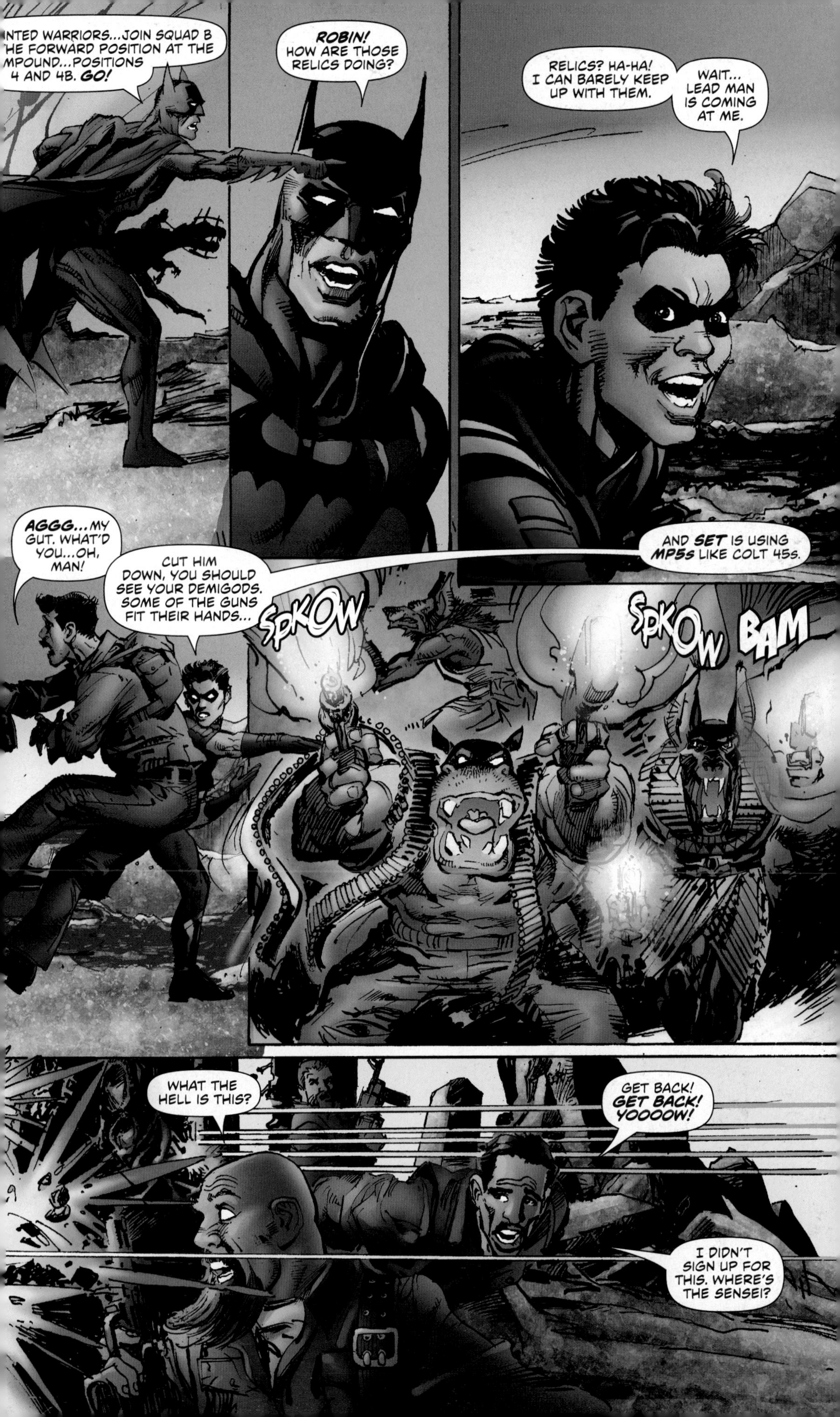
NTED WARRIORS...JOIN SQUAD B
HE FORWARD POSITION AT THE
MPOUND...POSITIONS
4 AND 4B. GO!
ROBIN! HOW ARE THOSE RELICS DOING?
RELICS? HA-HA! I CAN BARELY KEEP UP WITH THEM.
WAIT... LEAD MAN IS COMING AT ME.
AND SET IS USING MP5s LIKE COLT 45s.
AGGG...MY GUT. WHAT'D YOU...OH, MAN!
CUT HIM DOWN, YOU SHOULD SEE YOUR DEMIGODS. SOME OF THE GUNS FIT THEIR HANDS...
SPKOW
SPKOW
BAM
WHAT THE HELL IS THIS?
GET BACK! GET BACK! YOOOOW!
I DIDN'T SIGN UP FOR THIS. WHERE'S THE SENSEI?

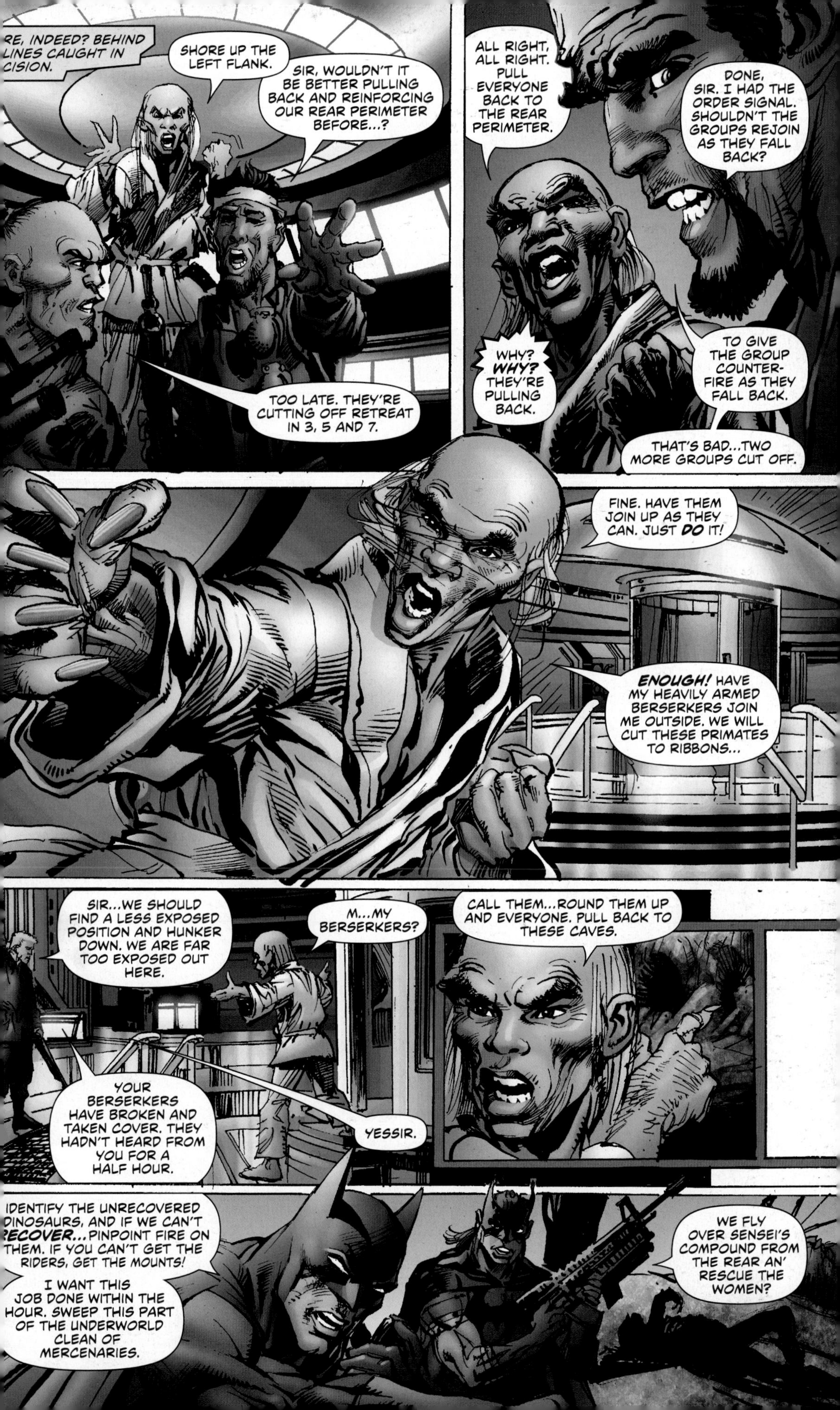

RE, INDEED? BEHIND
LINES CAUGHT IN
CISION.
SHORE UP THE LEFT FLANK.
SIR, WOULDN'T IT BE BETTER PULLING BACK AND REINFORCING OUR REAR PERIMETER BEFORE...?
TOO LATE. THEY'RE CUTTING OFF RETREAT IN 3, 5 AND 7.
ALL RIGHT, ALL RIGHT. PULL EVERYONE BACK TO THE REAR PERIMETER.
DONE, SIR. I HAD THE ORDER SIGNAL. SHOULDN'T THE GROUPS REJOIN AS THEY FALL BACK?
WHY? ***WHY?*** THEY'RE PULLING BACK.
TO GIVE THE GROUP COUNTER-FIRE AS THEY FALL BACK.
THAT'S BAD...TWO MORE GROUPS CUT OFF.
FINE. HAVE THEM JOIN UP AS THEY CAN. JUST ***DO*** IT!
ENOUGH! HAVE MY HEAVILY ARMED BERSERKERS JOIN ME OUTSIDE. WE WILL CUT THESE PRIMATES TO RIBBONS...
SIR...WE SHOULD FIND A LESS EXPOSED POSITION AND HUNKER DOWN. WE ARE FAR TOO EXPOSED OUT HERE.
M...MY BERSERKERS?
YOUR BERSERKERS HAVE BROKEN AND TAKEN COVER. THEY HADN'T HEARD FROM YOU FOR A HALF HOUR.
CALL THEM...ROUND THEM UP AND EVERYONE. PULL BACK TO THESE CAVES.
YESSIR.
IDENTIFY THE UNRECOVERED DINOSAURS, AND IF WE CAN'T ***RECOVER...*** PINPOINT FIRE ON THEM. IF YOU CAN'T GET THE RIDERS, GET THE MOUNTS!
I WANT THIS JOB DONE WITHIN THE HOUR. SWEEP THIS PART OF THE UNDERWORLD CLEAN OF MERCENARIES.
WE FLY OVER SENSEI'S COMPOUND FROM THE REAR AN' RESCUE THE WOMEN?

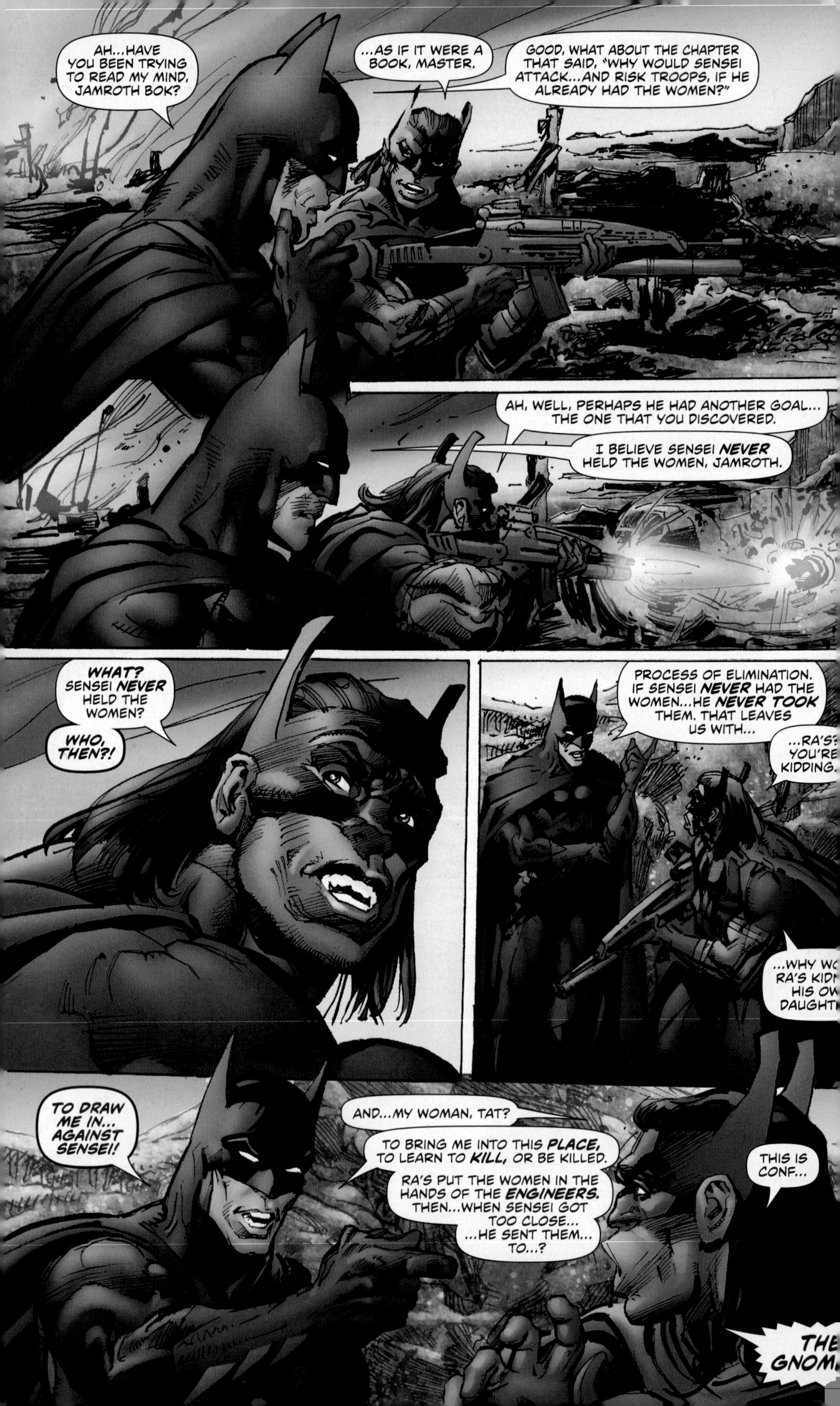

AH...HAVE YOU BEEN TRYING TO READ MY MIND, JAMROTH BOK?
...AS IF IT WERE A BOOK, MASTER.
GOOD, WHAT ABOUT THE CHAPTER THAT SAID, "WHY WOULD SENSEI ATTACK...AND RISK TROOPS, IF HE ALREADY HAD THE WOMEN?"
AH, WELL, PERHAPS HE HAD ANOTHER GOAL... THE ONE THAT YOU DISCOVERED.
I BELIEVE SENSEI NEVER HELD THE WOMEN, JAMROTH.
WHAT? SENSEI NEVER HELD THE WOMEN?
WHO, THEN?!
PROCESS OF ELIMINATION. IF SENSEI NEVER HAD THE WOMEN...HE NEVER TOOK THEM. THAT LEAVES US WITH...
TO DRAW ME IN... AGAINST SENSEI!
AND...MY WOMAN, TAT?
TO BRING ME INTO THIS PLACE, TO LEARN TO KILL, OR BE KILLED.
RA'S PUT THE WOMEN IN THE HANDS OF THE ENGINEERS. THEN...WHEN SENSEI GOT TOO CLOSE... ...HE SENT THEM... TO...?
THIS IS CONF...

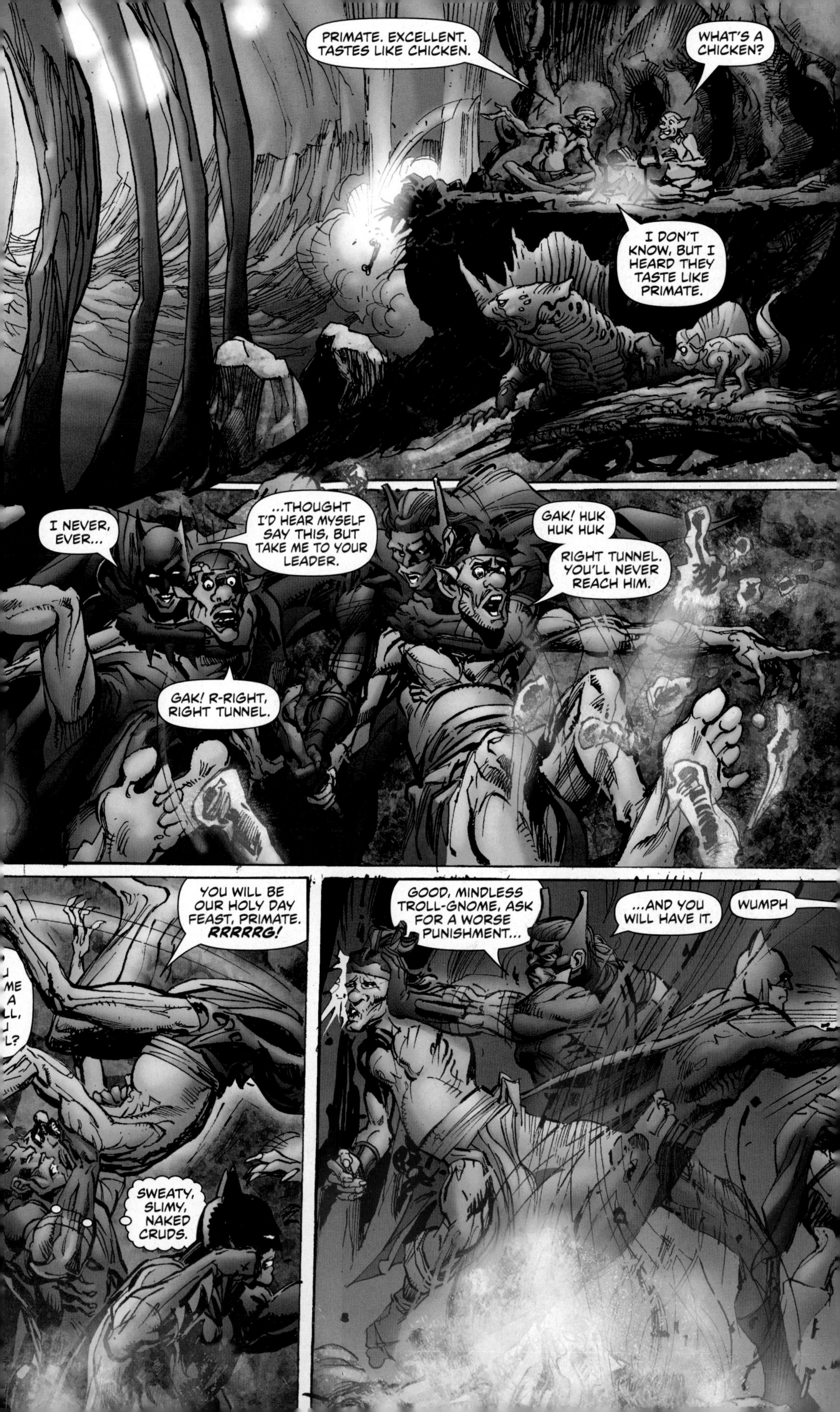
PRIMATE. EXCELLENT. TASTES LIKE CHICKEN.
WHAT'S A CHICKEN?
I DON'T KNOW, BUT I HEARD THEY TASTE LIKE PRIMATE.
I NEVER, EVER...
...THOUGHT I'D HEAR MYSELF SAY THIS, BUT TAKE ME TO YOUR LEADER.
GAK! R-RIGHT, RIGHT TUNNEL.
GAK! HUK HUK HUK
RIGHT TUNNEL. YOU'LL NEVER REACH HIM.
YOU WILL BE OUR HOLY DAY FEAST, PRIMATE. ***RRRRRG!***
SWEATY, SLIMY, NAKED CRUDS.
GOOD, MINDLESS TROLL-GNOME, ASK FOR A WORSE PUNISHMENT...
...AND YOU WILL HAVE IT.
WUMPH

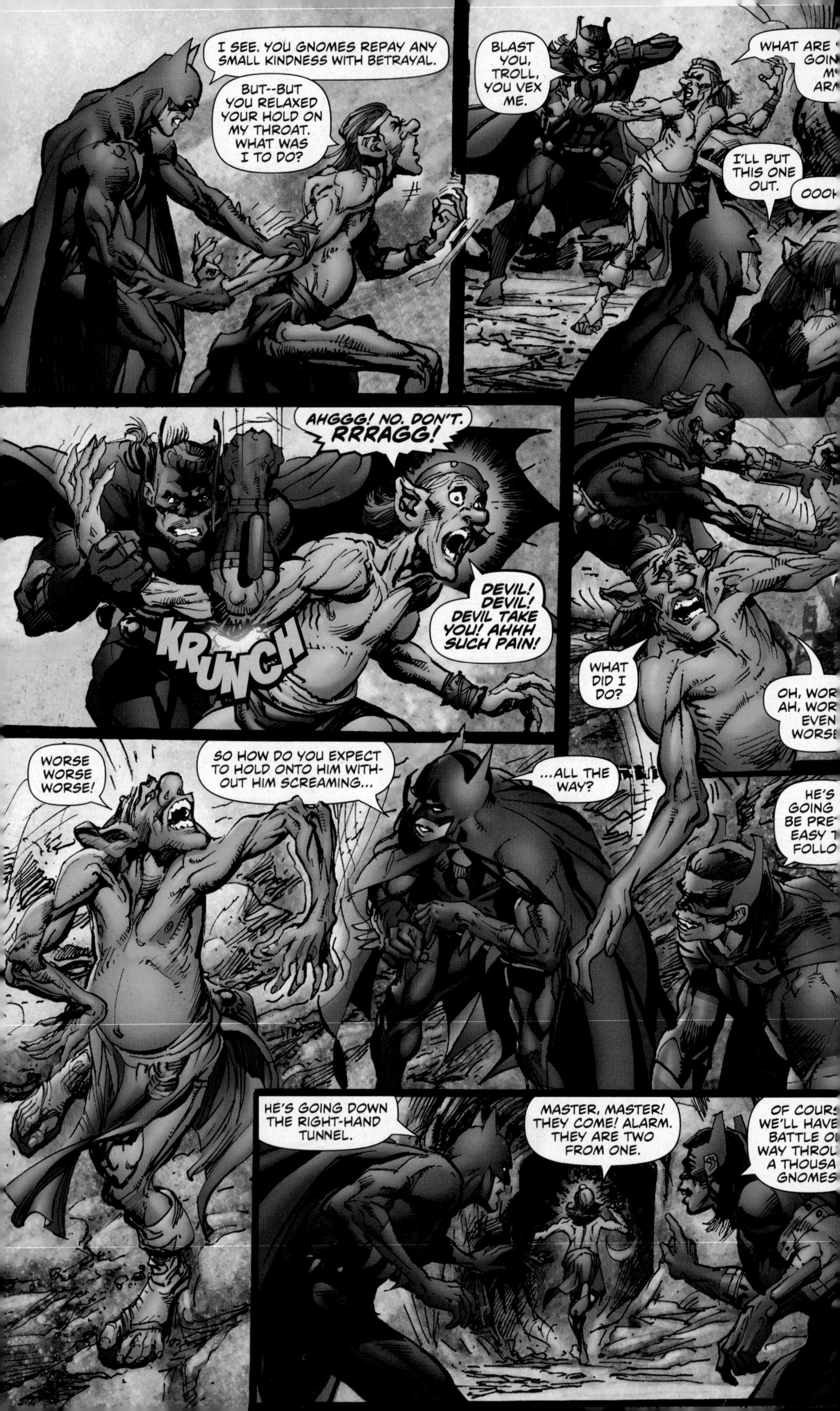

I SEE. YOU GNOMES REPAY ANY SMALL KINDNESS WITH BETRAYAL.
BUT--BUT YOU RELAXED YOUR HOLD ON MY THROAT. WHAT WAS I TO DO?
BLAST YOU, TROLL, YOU VEX ME.
I'LL PUT THIS ONE OUT.
AHGGG! NO. DON'T. RRRAGG!
KRUNCH
DEVIL! DEVIL! DEVIL TAKE YOU! AHHH SUCH PAIN!
WHAT DID I DO?
WORSE WORSE WORSE!
SO HOW DO YOU EXPECT TO HOLD ONTO HIM WITHOUT HIM SCREAMING...
...ALL THE WAY?
HE'S GOING DOWN THE RIGHT-HAND TUNNEL.
MASTER, MASTER! THEY COME! ALARM. THEY ARE TWO FROM ONE.

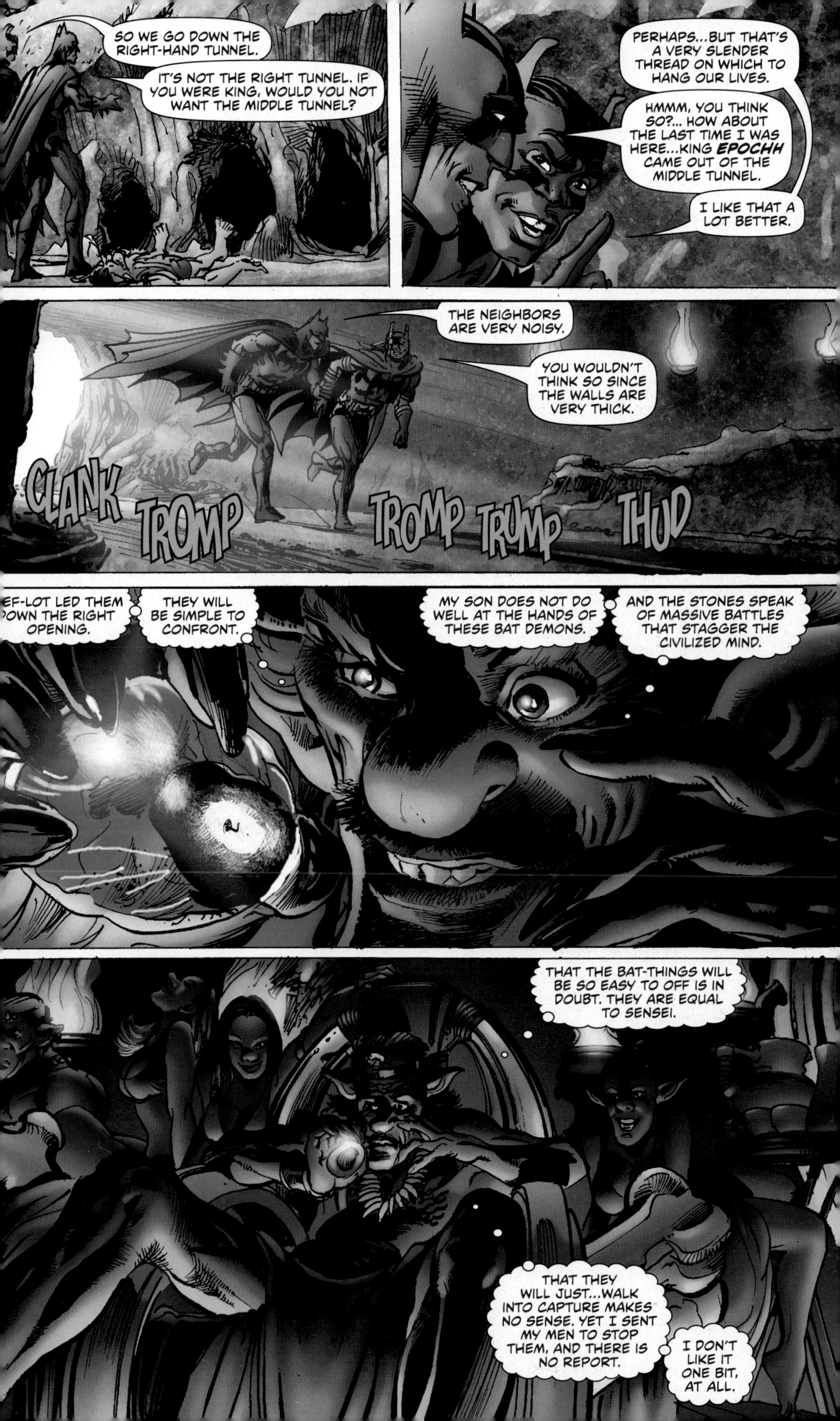
SO WE GO DOWN THE RIGHT-HAND TUNNEL.
IT'S NOT THE RIGHT TUNNEL. IF YOU WERE KING, WOULD YOU NOT WANT THE MIDDLE TUNNEL?
PERHAPS...BUT THAT'S A VERY SLENDER THREAD ON WHICH TO HANG OUR LIVES.
HMMM, YOU THINK SO?... HOW ABOUT THE LAST TIME I WAS HERE...KING **EPOCHH** CAME OUT OF THE MIDDLE TUNNEL.
I LIKE THAT A LOT BETTER.
THE NEIGHBORS ARE VERY NOISY.
YOU WOULDN'T THINK SO SINCE THE WALLS ARE VERY THICK.
CLANK
TROMP
TROMP
TRUMP
THUD
EF-LOT LED THEM DOWN THE RIGHT OPENING.
THEY WILL BE SIMPLE TO CONFRONT.
MY SON DOES NOT DO WELL AT THE HANDS OF THESE BAT DEMONS.
AND THE STONES SPEAK OF MASSIVE BATTLES THAT STAGGER THE CIVILIZED MIND.
THAT THE BAT-THINGS WILL BE SO EASY TO OFF IS IN DOUBT. THEY ARE EQUAL TO SENSEI.
THAT THEY WILL JUST...WALK INTO CAPTURE MAKES NO SENSE. YET I SENT MY MEN TO STOP THEM, AND THERE IS NO REPORT.
I DON'T LIKE IT ONE BIT, AT ALL.

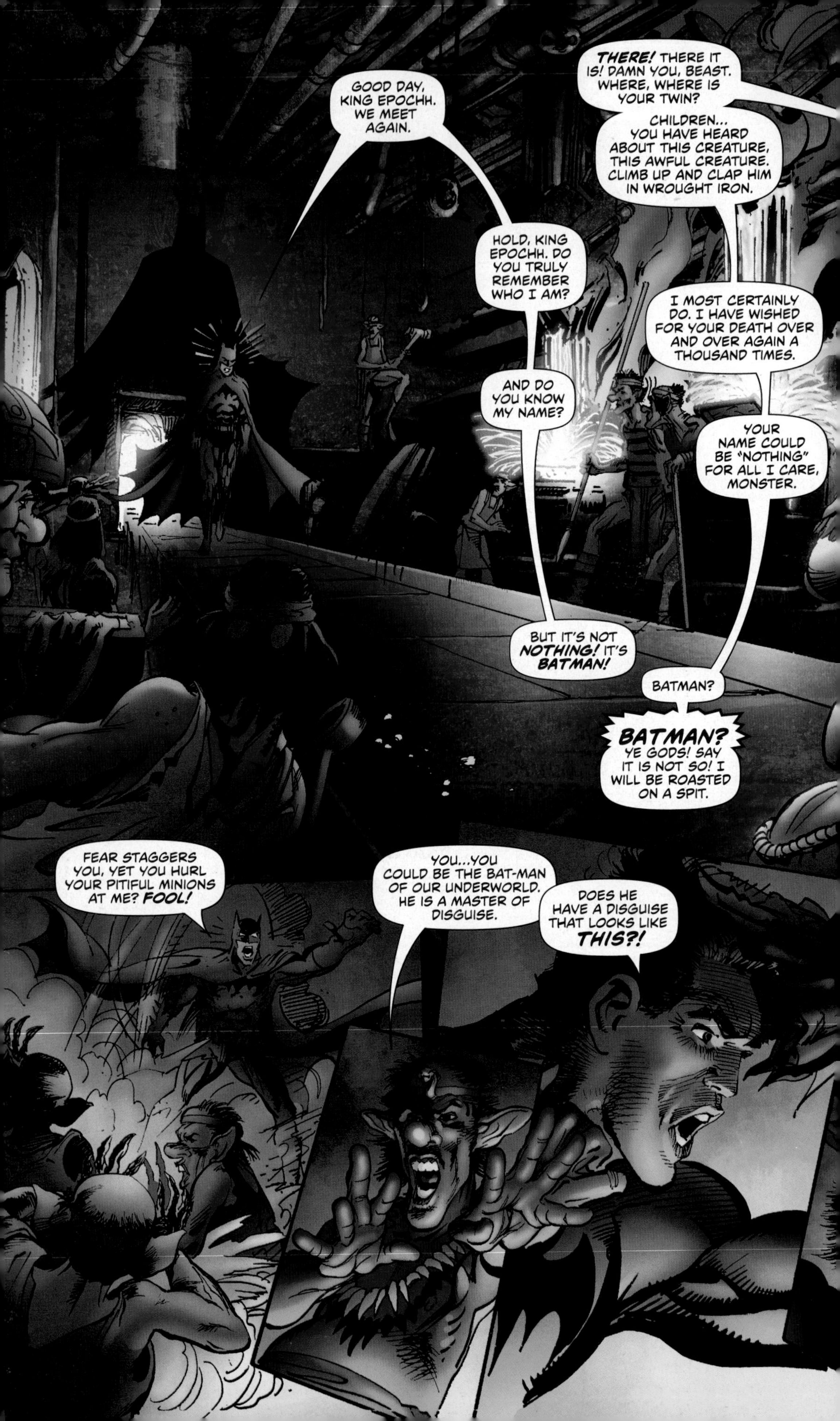
GOOD DAY, KING EPOCHH. WE MEET AGAIN.
THERE! THERE IT IS! DAMN YOU, BEAST. WHERE, WHERE IS YOUR TWIN?
CHILDREN... YOU HAVE HEARD ABOUT THIS CREATURE, THIS AWFUL CREATURE. CLIMB UP AND CLAP HIM IN WROUGHT IRON.
HOLD, KING EPOCHH. DO YOU TRULY REMEMBER WHO I AM?
I MOST CERTAINLY DO. I HAVE WISHED FOR YOUR DEATH OVER AND OVER AGAIN A THOUSAND TIMES.
AND DO YOU KNOW MY NAME?
YOUR NAME COULD BE "NOTHING" FOR ALL I CARE, MONSTER.
BUT IT'S NOT NOTHING! IT'S BATMAN!
BATMAN?
BATMAN? YE GODS! SAY IT IS NOT SO! I WILL BE ROASTED ON A SPIT.
FEAR STAGGERS YOU, YET YOU HURL YOUR PITIFUL MINIONS AT ME? FOOL!
YOU...YOU COULD BE THE BAT-MAN OF OUR UNDERWORLD. HE IS A MASTER OF DISGUISE.
DOES HE HAVE A DISGUISE THAT LOOKS LIKE THIS?!

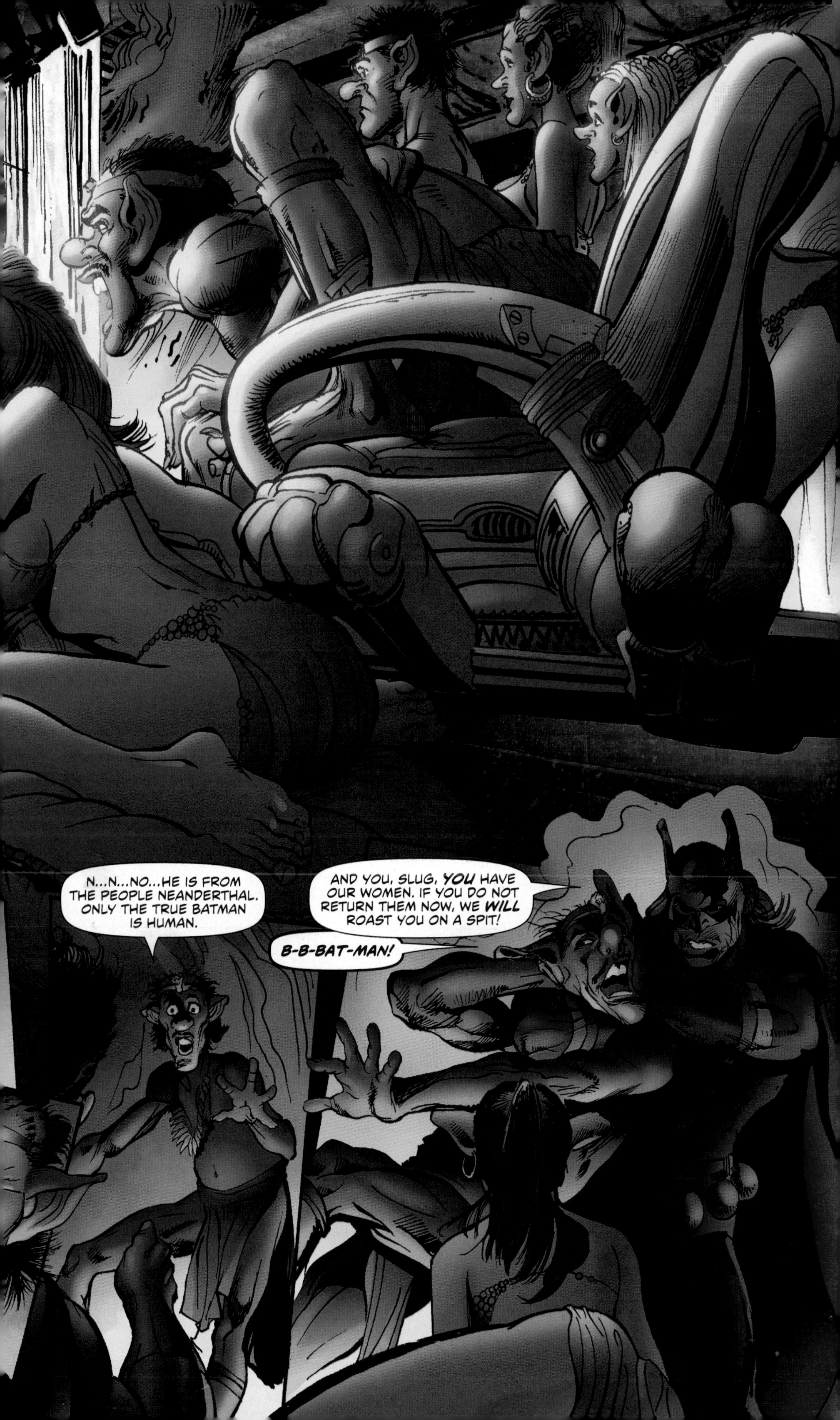
N...N...NO...HE IS FROM THE PEOPLE NEANDERTHAL. ONLY THE TRUE BATMAN IS HUMAN.
AND YOU, SLUG, YOU HAVE OUR WOMEN. IF YOU DO NOT RETURN THEM NOW, WE WILL ROAST YOU ON A SPIT!
B-B-BAT-MAN!

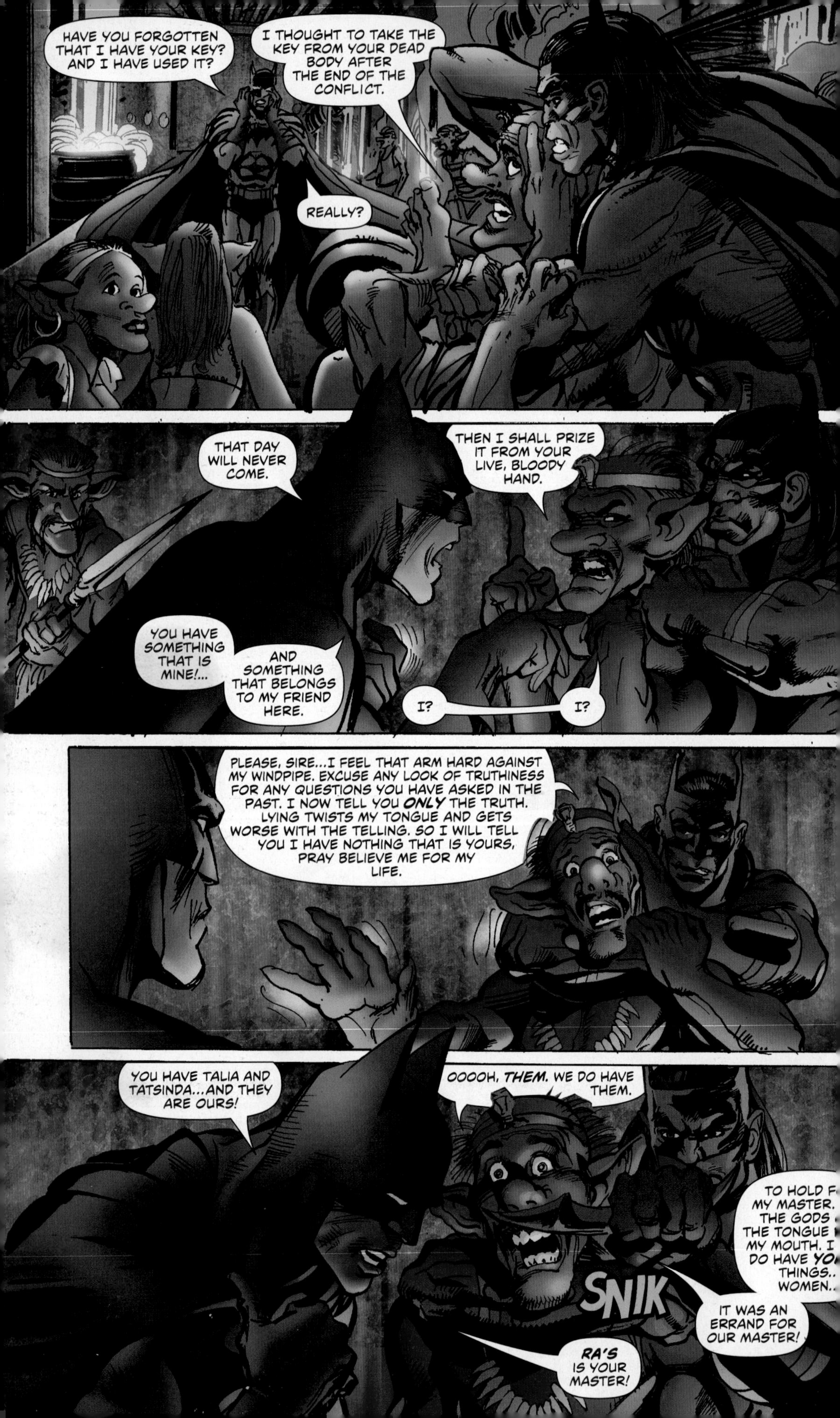
HAVE YOU FORGOTTEN THAT I HAVE YOUR KEY? AND I HAVE USED IT?
I THOUGHT TO TAKE THE KEY FROM YOUR DEAD BODY AFTER THE END OF THE CONFLICT.
REALLY?
THAT DAY WILL NEVER COME.
THEN I SHALL PRIZE IT FROM YOUR LIVE, BLOODY HAND.
YOU HAVE SOMETHING THAT IS MINE!...
AND SOMETHING THAT BELONGS TO MY FRIEND HERE.
I?
I?
PLEASE, SIRE...I FEEL THAT ARM HARD AGAINST MY WINDPIPE. EXCUSE ANY LOOK OF TRUTHINESS FOR ANY QUESTIONS YOU HAVE ASKED IN THE PAST. I NOW TELL YOU ONLY THE TRUTH. LYING TWISTS MY TONGUE AND GETS WORSE WITH THE TELLING. SO I WILL TELL YOU I HAVE NOTHING THAT IS YOURS, PRAY BELIEVE ME FOR MY LIFE.
YOU HAVE TALIA AND TATSINDA...AND THEY ARE OURS!
OOOOH, THEM. WE DO HAVE THEM.
SNIK
IT WAS AN ERRAND FOR OUR MASTER!
RA'S IS YOUR MASTER!

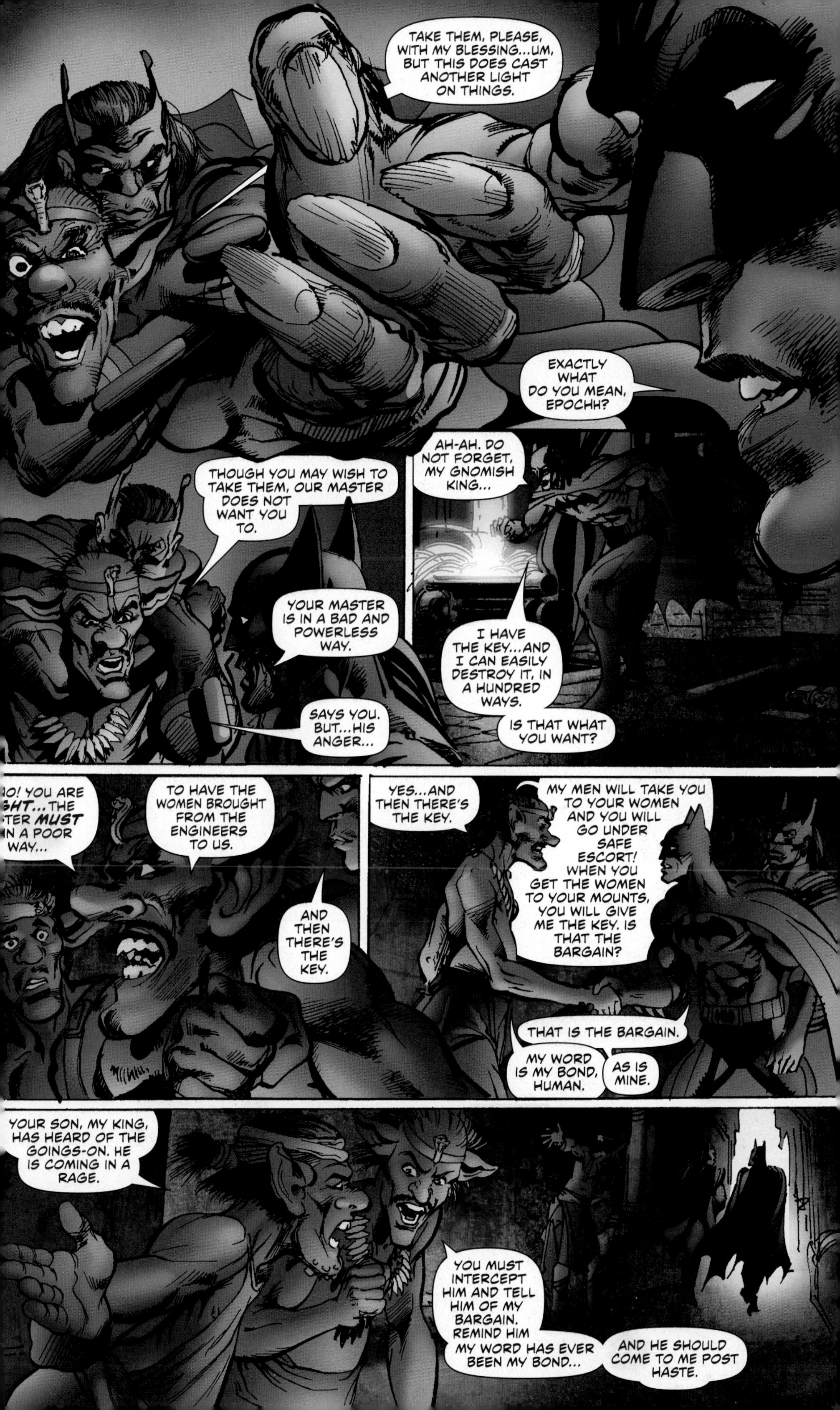

TAKE THEM, PLEASE, WITH MY BLESSING...UM, BUT THIS DOES CAST ANOTHER LIGHT ON THINGS.
EXACTLY WHAT DO YOU MEAN, EPOCHH?
THOUGH YOU MAY WISH TO TAKE THEM, OUR MASTER DOES NOT WANT YOU TO.
YOUR MASTER IS IN A BAD AND POWERLESS WAY.
SAYS YOU. BUT...HIS ANGER...
AH-AH. DO NOT FORGET, MY GNOMISH KING...
I HAVE THE KEY...AND I CAN EASILY DESTROY IT, IN A HUNDRED WAYS.
IS THAT WHAT YOU WANT?
TO HAVE THE WOMEN BROUGHT FROM THE ENGINEERS TO US.
AND THEN THERE'S THE KEY.
YES...AND THEN THERE'S THE KEY.
MY MEN WILL TAKE YOU TO YOUR WOMEN AND YOU WILL GO UNDER SAFE ESCORT! WHEN YOU GET THE WOMEN TO YOUR MOUNTS, YOU WILL GIVE ME THE KEY. IS THAT THE BARGAIN?
THAT IS THE BARGAIN.
MY WORD IS MY BOND, HUMAN.
AS IS MINE.
YOUR SON, MY KING, HAS HEARD OF THE GOINGS-ON. HE IS COMING IN A RAGE.
YOU MUST INTERCEPT HIM AND TELL HIM OF MY BARGAIN. REMIND HIM MY WORD HAS EVER BEEN MY BOND...
AND HE SHOULD COME TO ME POST HASTE.

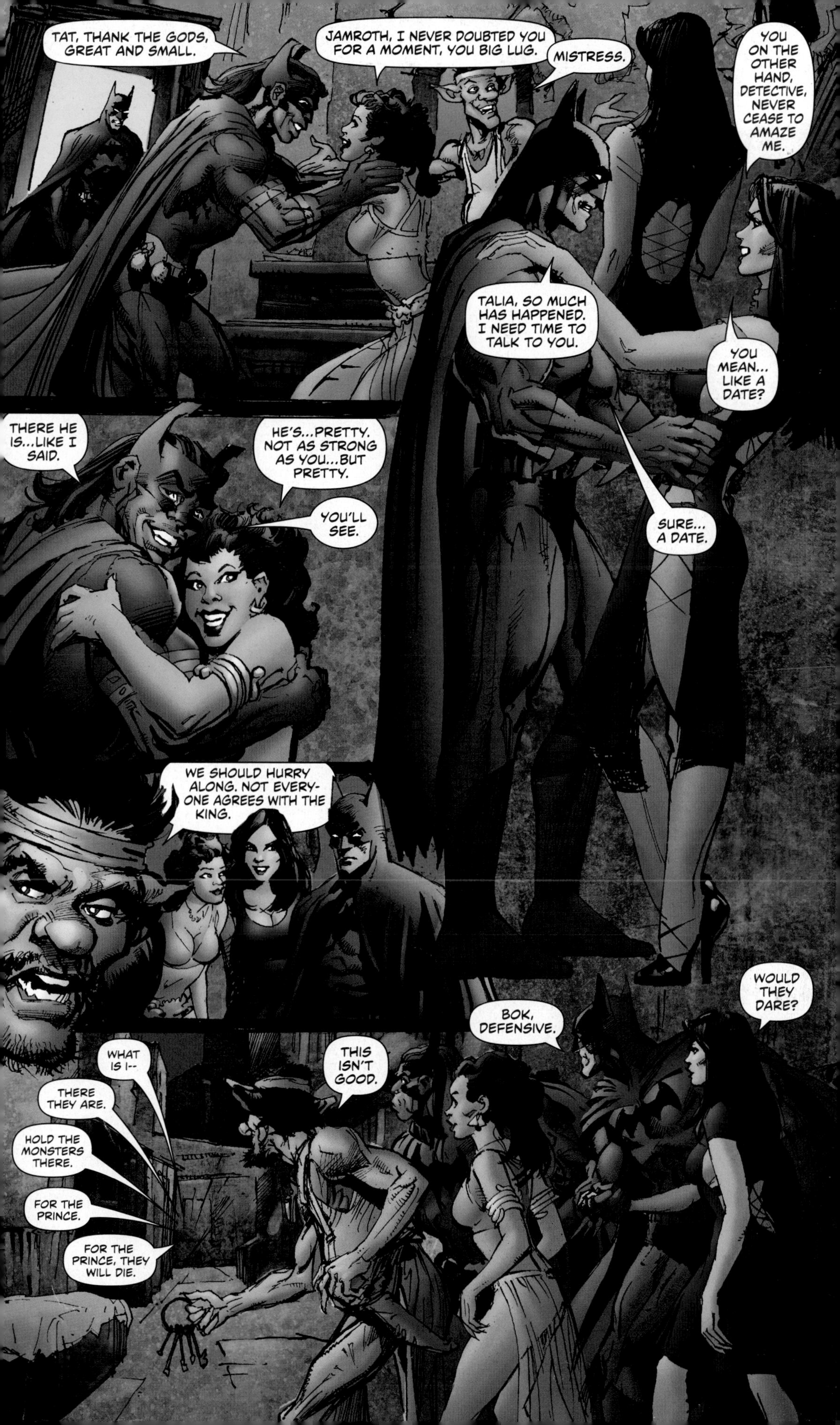
TAT, THANK THE GODS, GREAT AND SMALL.
JAMROTH, I NEVER DOUBTED YOU FOR A MOMENT, YOU BIG LUG.
MISTRESS.
YOU ON THE OTHER HAND, DETECTIVE, NEVER CEASE TO AMAZE ME.
TALIA, SO MUCH HAS HAPPENED. I NEED TIME TO TALK TO YOU.
YOU MEAN... LIKE A DATE?
SURE... A DATE.
THERE HE IS...LIKE I SAID.
HE'S...PRETTY. NOT AS STRONG AS YOU...BUT PRETTY.
YOU'LL SEE.
WE SHOULD HURRY ALONG. NOT EVERY-ONE AGREES WITH THE KING.
WHAT IS I--
THERE THEY ARE.
HOLD THE MONSTERS THERE.
FOR THE PRINCE.
FOR THE PRINCE, THEY WILL DIE.
THIS ISN'T GOOD.
BOK, DEFENSIVE.
WOULD THEY DARE?

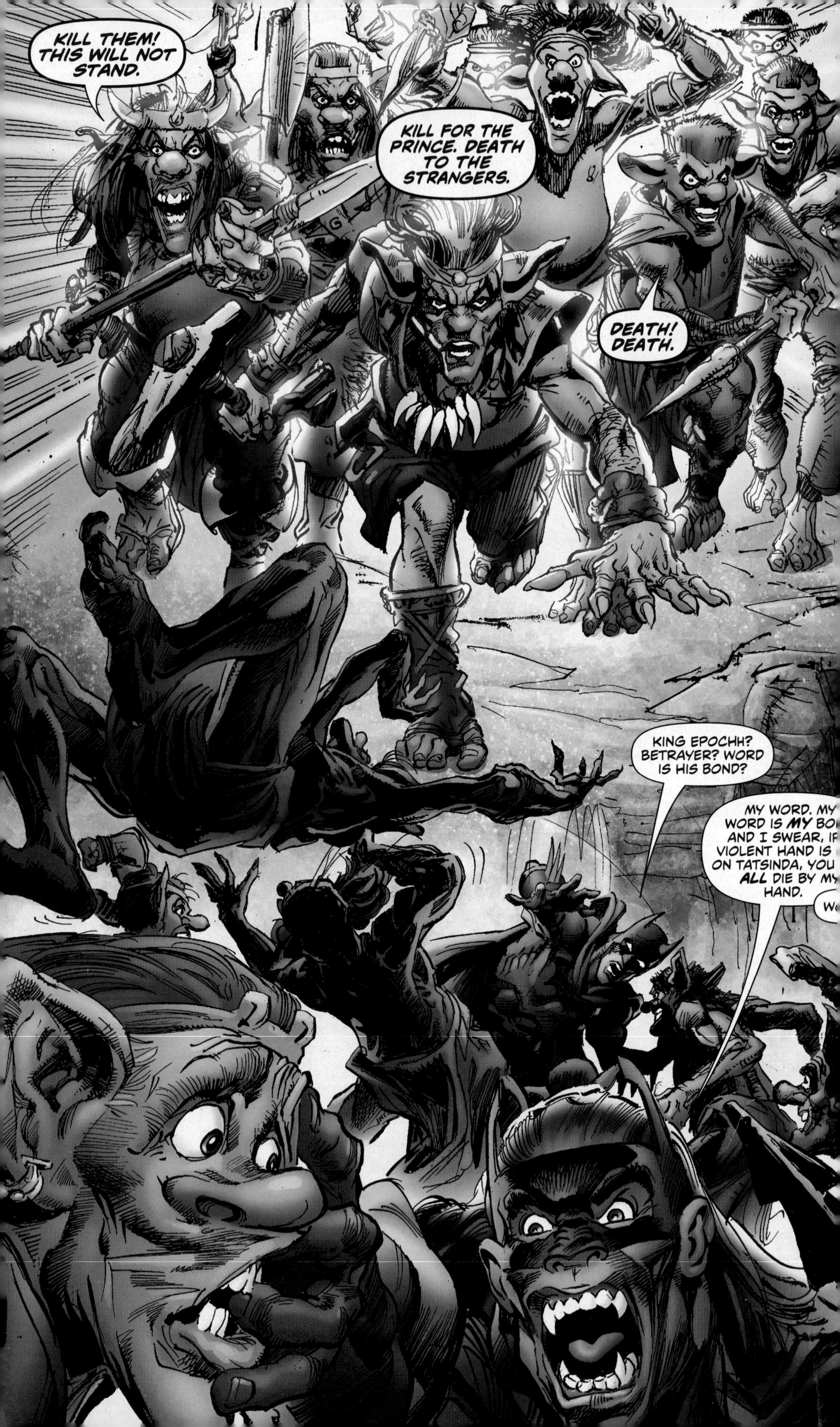
KILL THEM! THIS WILL NOT STAND.
KILL FOR THE PRINCE. DEATH TO THE STRANGERS.
DEATH! DEATH.
KING EPOCHH? BETRAYER? WORD IS HIS BOND?
MY WORD. MY WORD IS MY BO AND I SWEAR, IF VIOLENT HAND IS ON TATSINDA, YOU ALL DIE BY MY HAND.

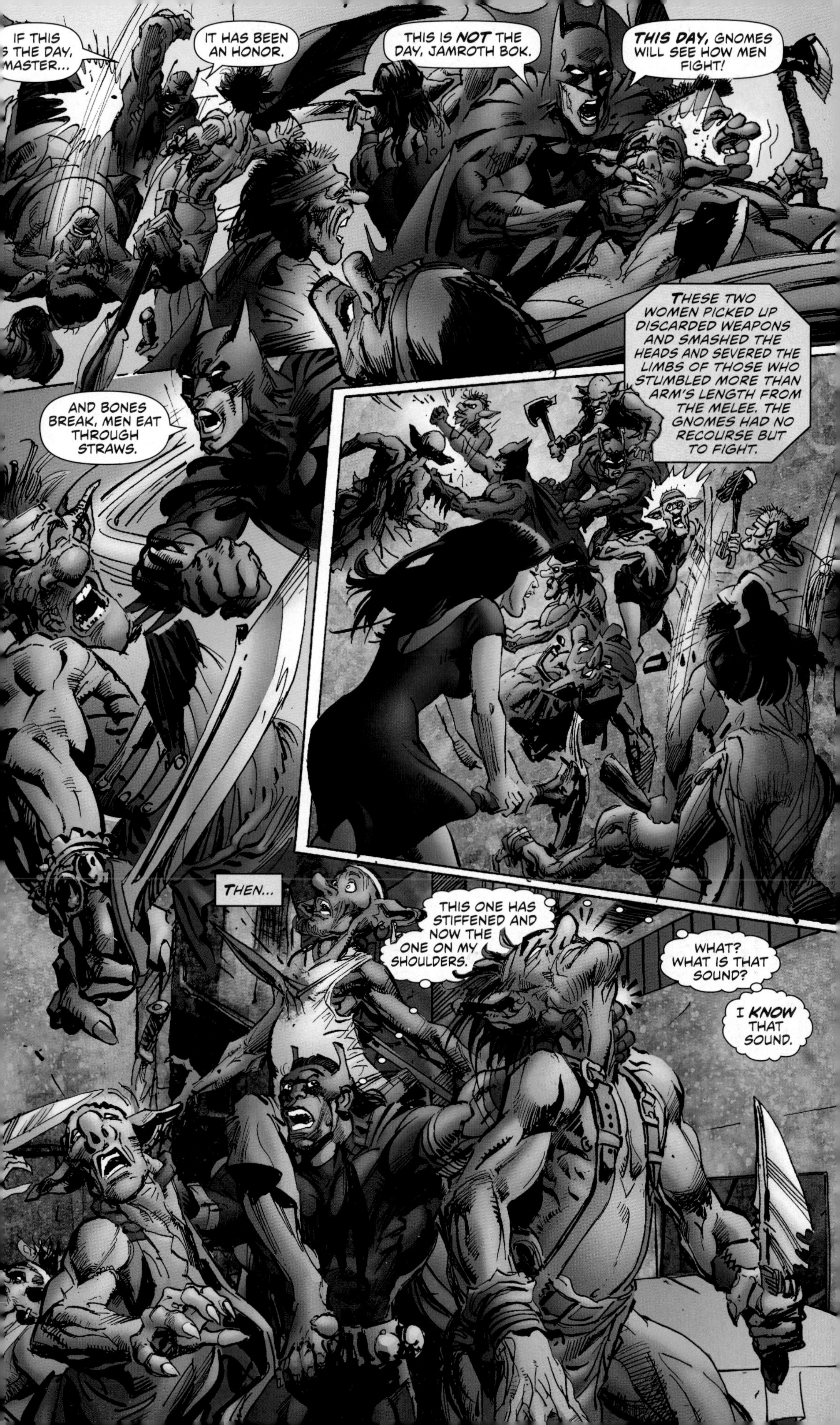

IF THIS IS THE DAY, MASTER...
IT HAS BEEN AN HONOR.
THIS IS NOT THE DAY, JAMROTH BOK.
THIS DAY, GNOMES WILL SEE HOW MEN FIGHT!
AND BONES BREAK, MEN EAT THROUGH STRAWS.
THESE TWO WOMEN PICKED UP DISCARDED WEAPONS AND SMASHED THE HEADS AND SEVERED THE LIMBS OF THOSE WHO STUMBLED MORE THAN ARM'S LENGTH FROM THE MELEE. THE GNOMES HAD NO RECOURSE BUT TO FIGHT.
THEN...
THIS ONE HAS STIFFENED AND NOW THE ONE ON MY SHOULDERS.
WHAT? WHAT IS THAT SOUND?
I KNOW THAT SOUND.

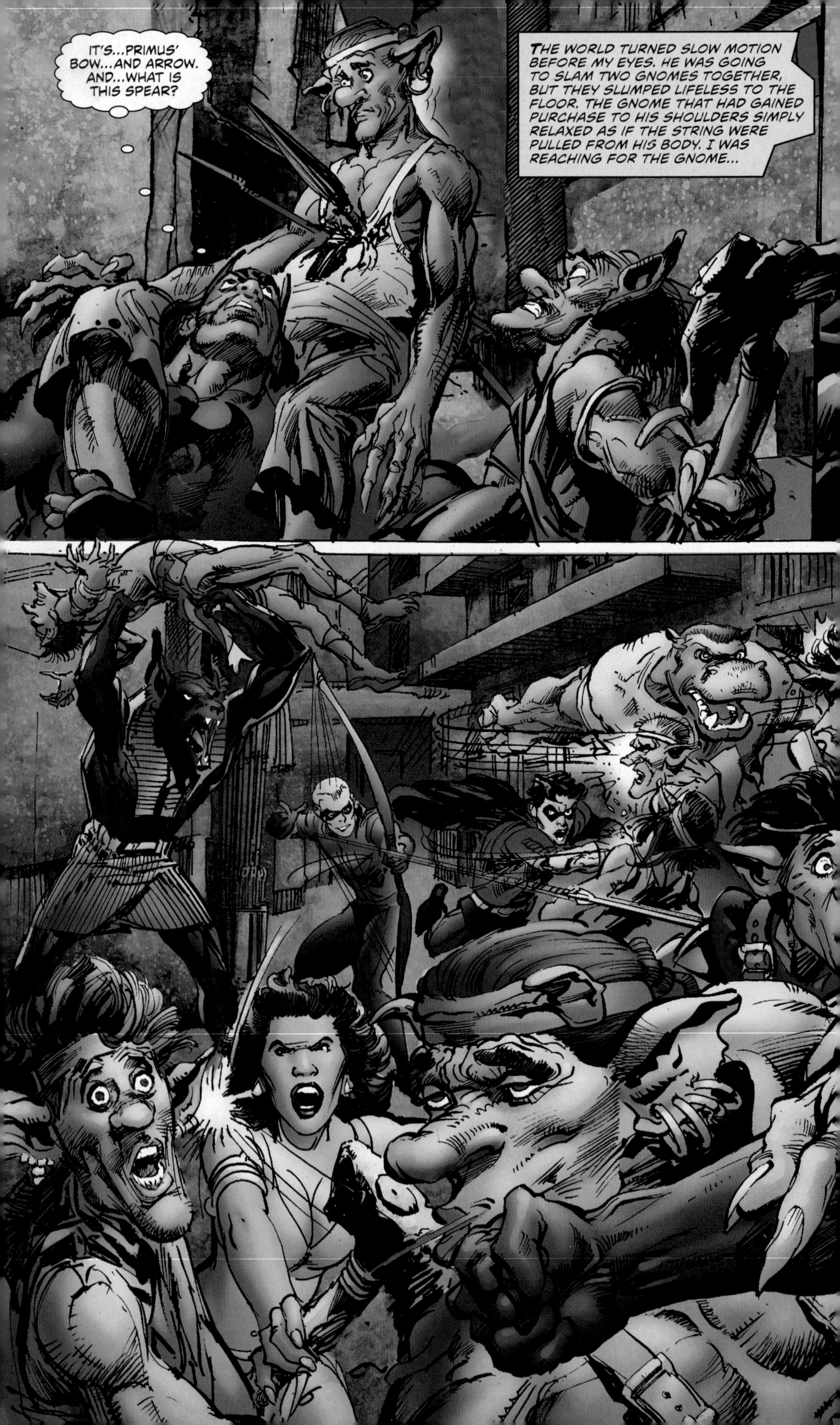
IT'S...PRIMUS' BOW...AND ARROW. AND...WHAT IS THIS SPEAR?
THE WORLD TURNED SLOW MOTION BEFORE MY EYES. HE WAS GOING TO SLAM TWO GNOMES TOGETHER, BUT THEY SLUMPED LIFELESS TO THE FLOOR. THE GNOME THAT HAD GAINED PURCHASE TO HIS SHOULDERS SIMPLY RELAXED AS IF THE STRING WERE PULLED FROM HIS BODY. I WAS REACHING FOR THE GNOME...

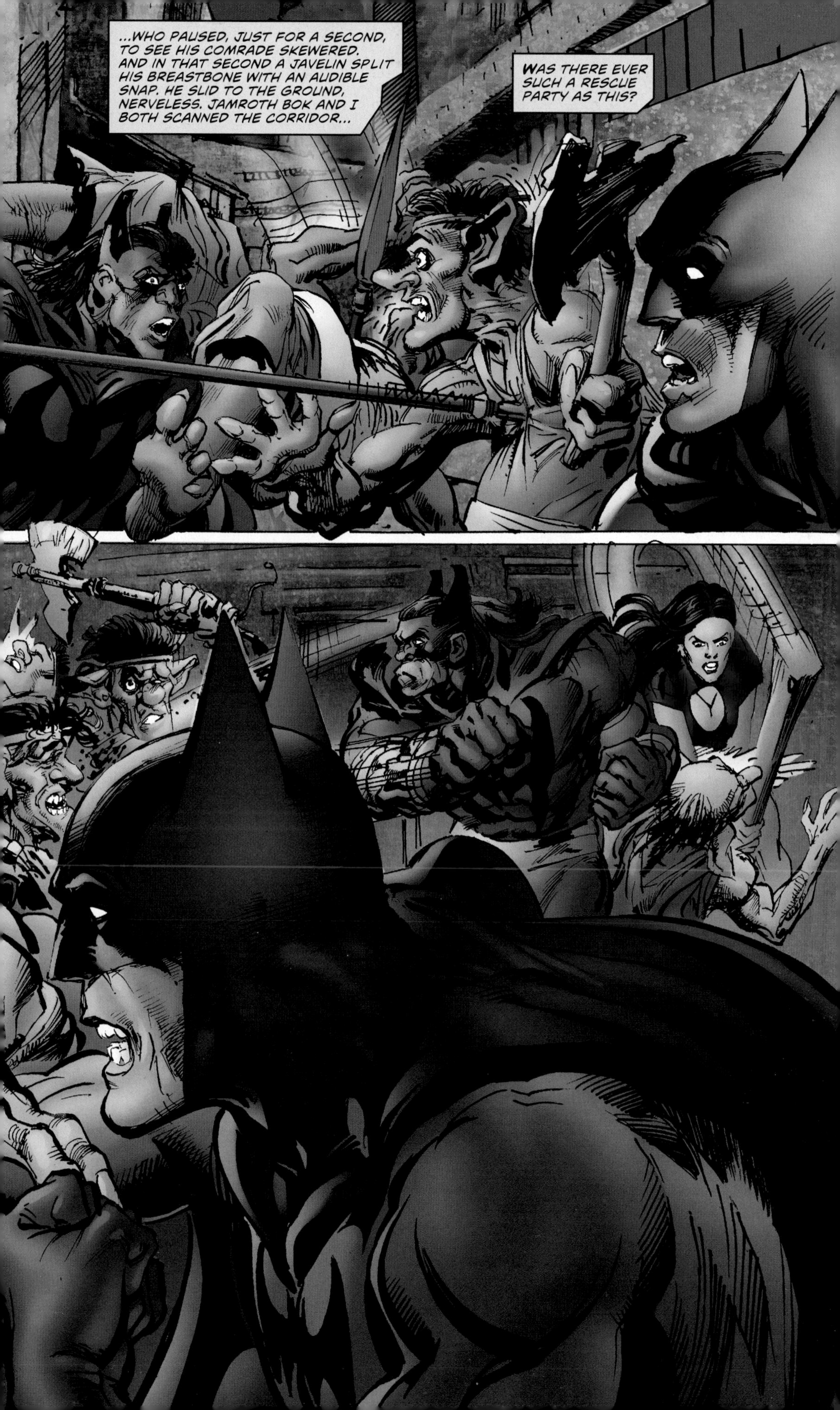
...WHO PAUSED, JUST FOR A SECOND, TO SEE HIS COMRADE SKEWERED. AND IN THAT SECOND A JAVELIN SPLIT HIS BREASTBONE WITH AN AUDIBLE SNAP. HE SLID TO THE GROUND, NERVELESS. JAMROTH BOK AND I BOTH SCANNED THE CORRIDOR...
WAS THERE EVER SUCH A RESCUE PARTY AS THIS?

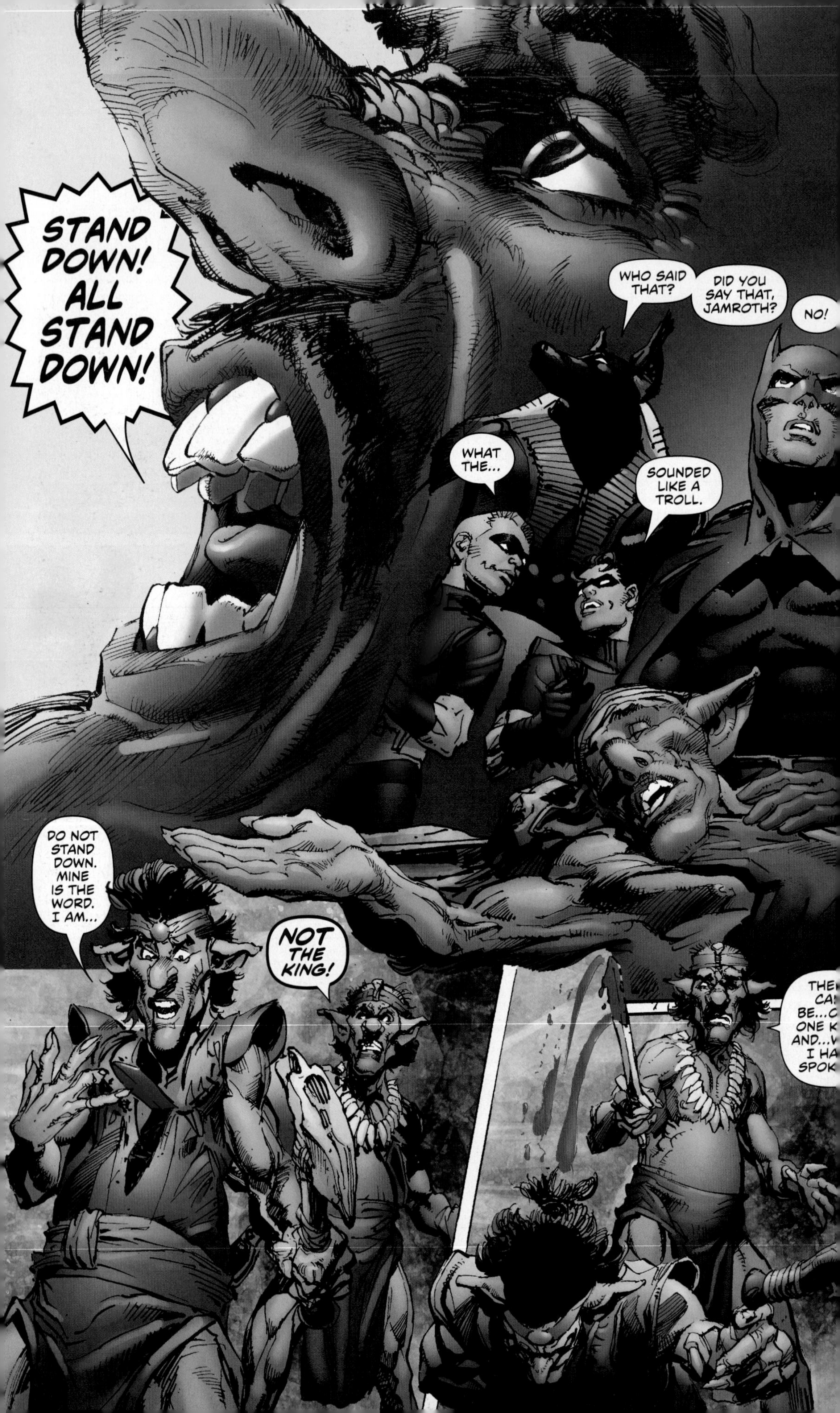
STAND DOWN! ALL STAND DOWN!
WHO SAID THAT?
DID YOU SAY THAT, JAMROTH?
NO!
WHAT THE...
SOUNDED LIKE A TROLL.
DO NOT STAND DOWN. MINE IS THE WORD. I AM...
NOT THE KING!

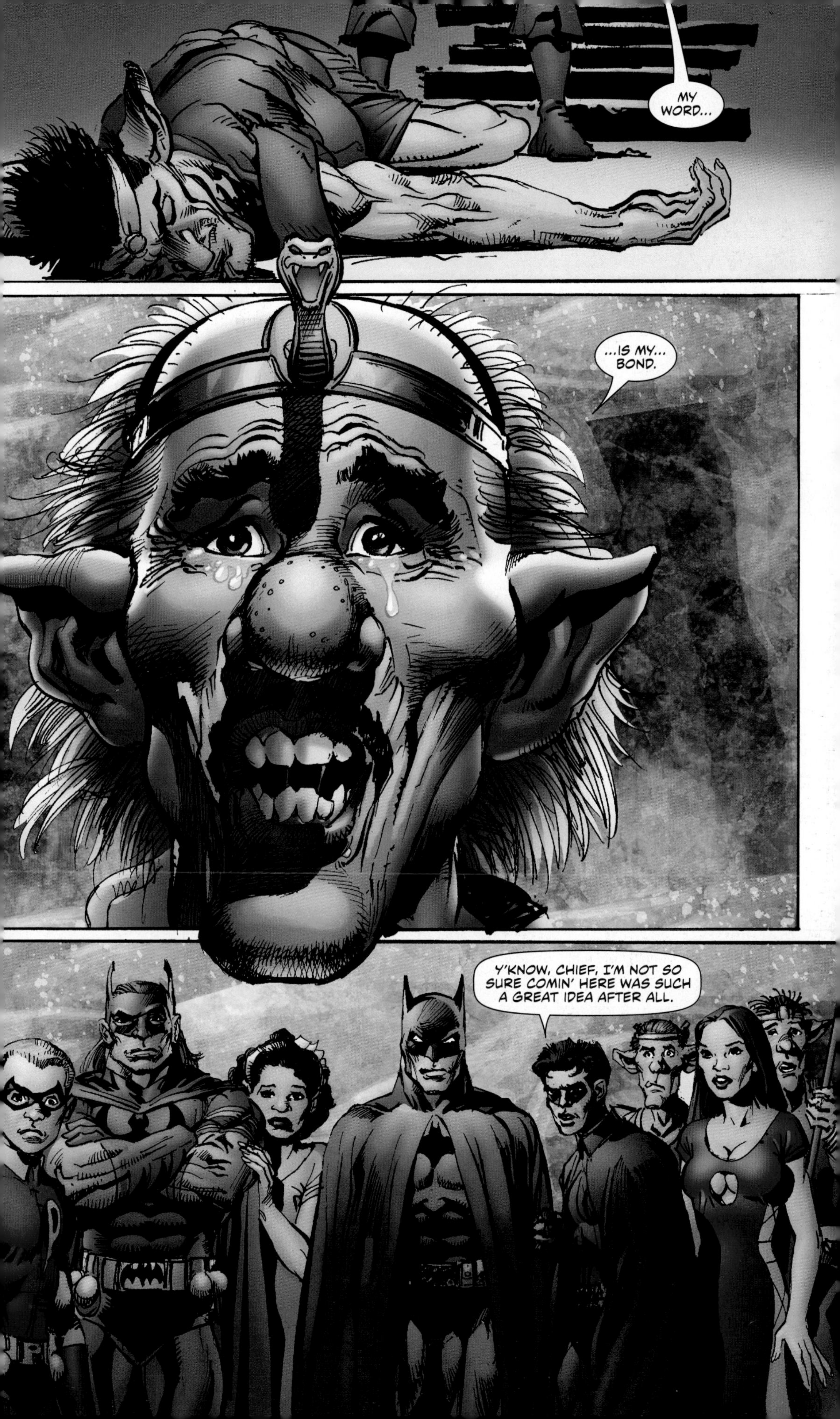
MY WORD...
...IS MY... BOND.
Y'KNOW, CHIEF, I'M NOT SO SURE COMIN' HERE WAS SUCH A GREAT IDEA AFTER ALL.

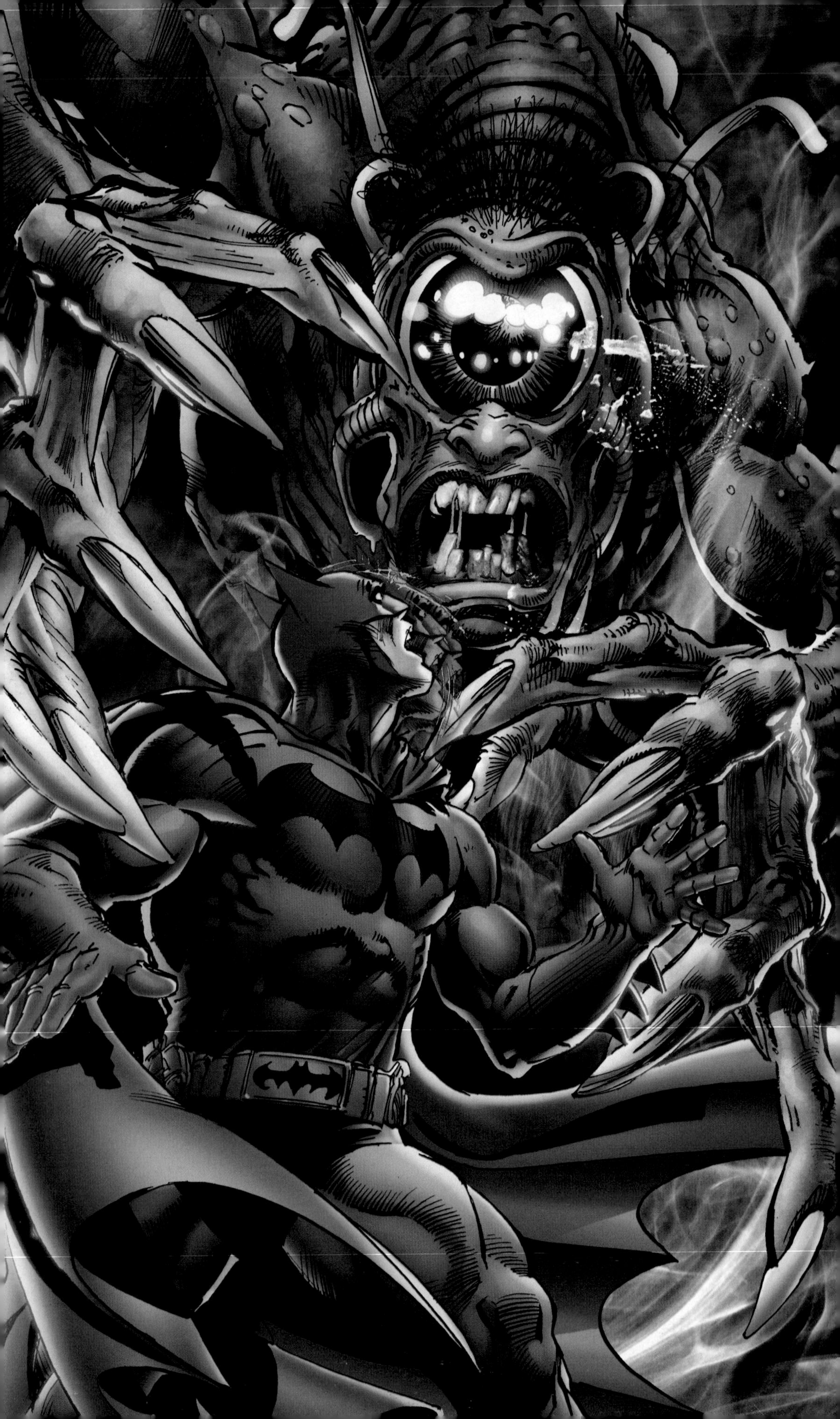

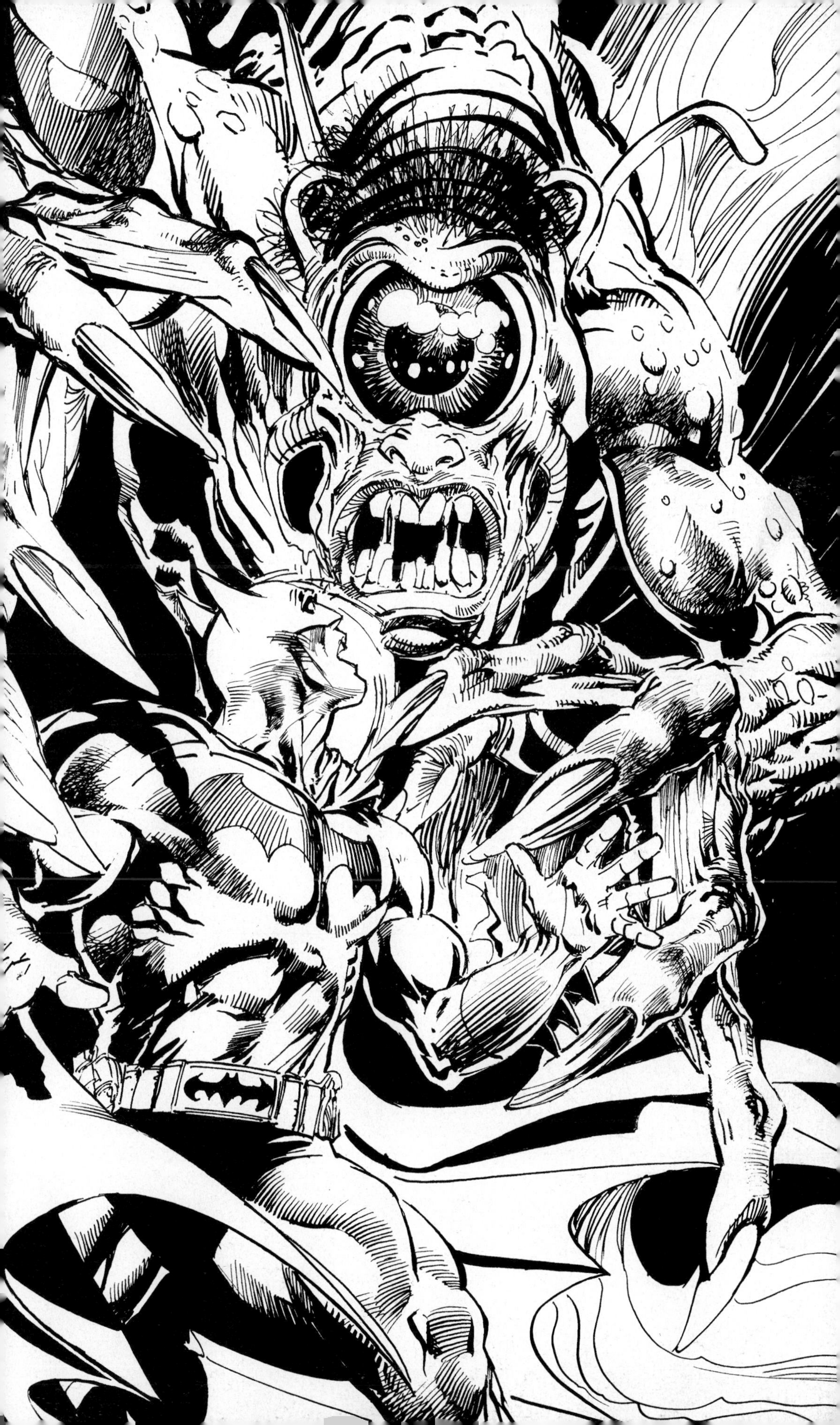

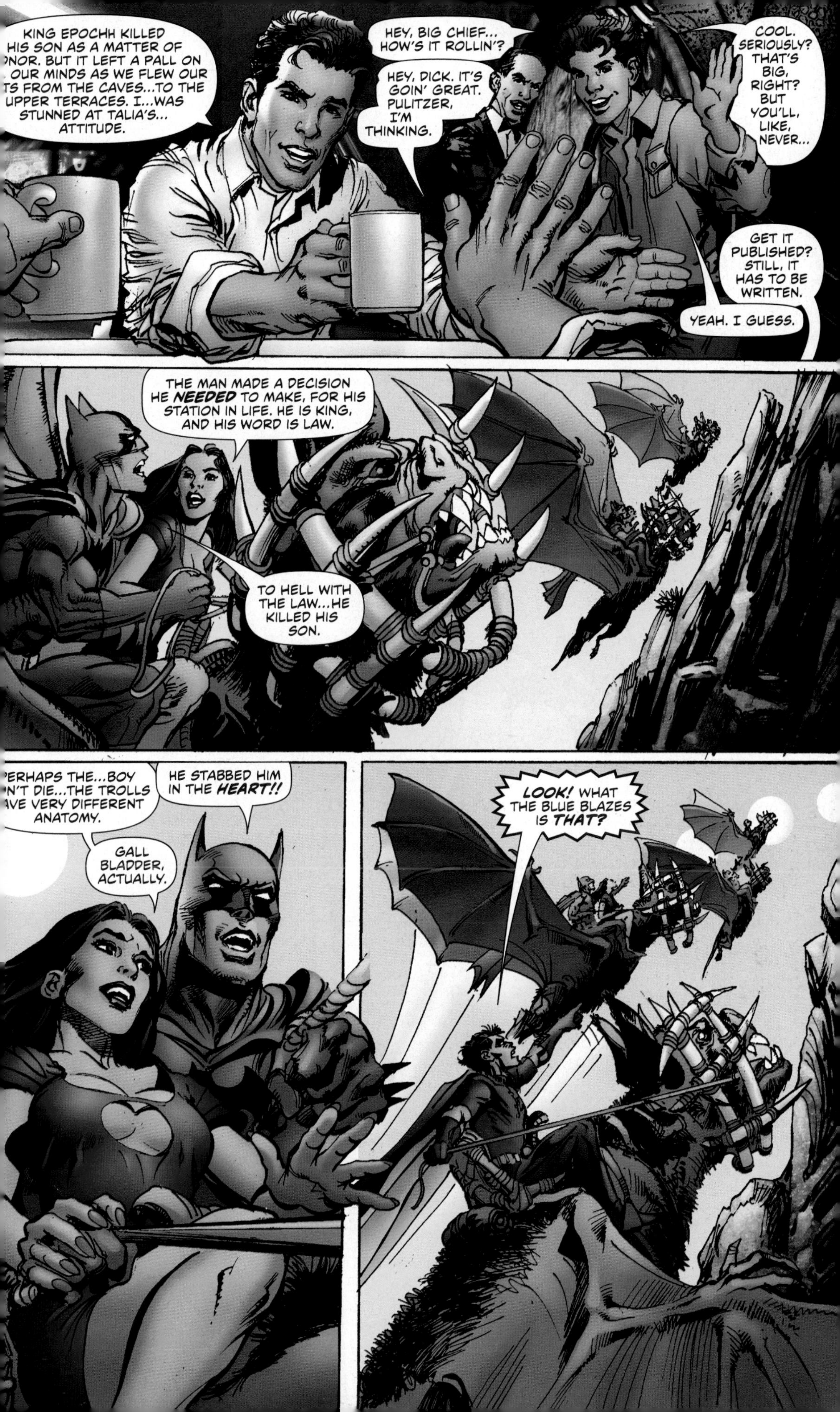
KING EPOCHH KILLED HIS SON AS A MATTER OF ONOR. BUT IT LEFT A PALL ON OUR MINDS AS WE FLEW OUR TS FROM THE CAVES...TO THE UPPER TERRACES. I...WAS STUNNED AT TALIA'S... ATTITUDE.
HEY, BIG CHIEF... HOW'S IT ROLLIN'?
HEY, DICK. IT'S GOIN' GREAT. PULITZER, I'M THINKING.
COOL. SERIOUSLY? THAT'S BIG, RIGHT? BUT YOU'LL, LIKE, NEVER...
GET IT PUBLISHED? STILL, IT HAS TO BE WRITTEN.
YEAH. I GUESS.
THE MAN MADE A DECISION HE NEEDED TO MAKE, FOR HIS STATION IN LIFE. HE IS KING, AND HIS WORD IS LAW.
TO HELL WITH THE LAW...HE KILLED HIS SON.
PERHAPS THE...BOY N'T DIE...THE TROLLS AVE VERY DIFFERENT ANATOMY.
HE STABBED HIM IN THE HEART!!
GALL BLADDER, ACTUALLY.
LOOK! WHAT THE BLUE BLAZES IS THAT?

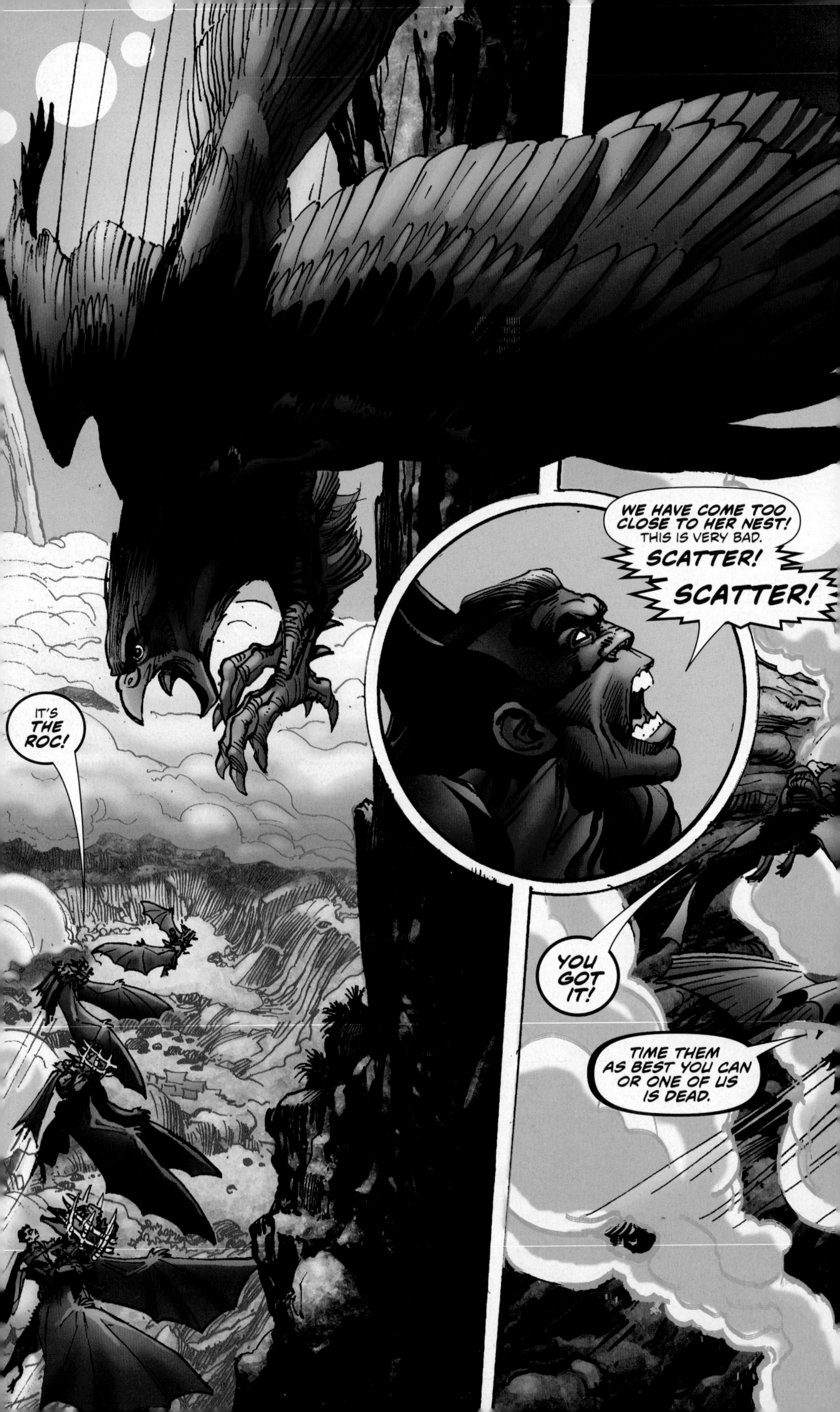
WE HAVE COME TOO CLOSE TO HER NEST! THIS IS VERY BAD.
SCATTER!
SCATTER!
IT'S THE ROC!
YOU GOT IT!
TIME THEM AS BEST YOU CAN OR ONE OF US IS DEAD.

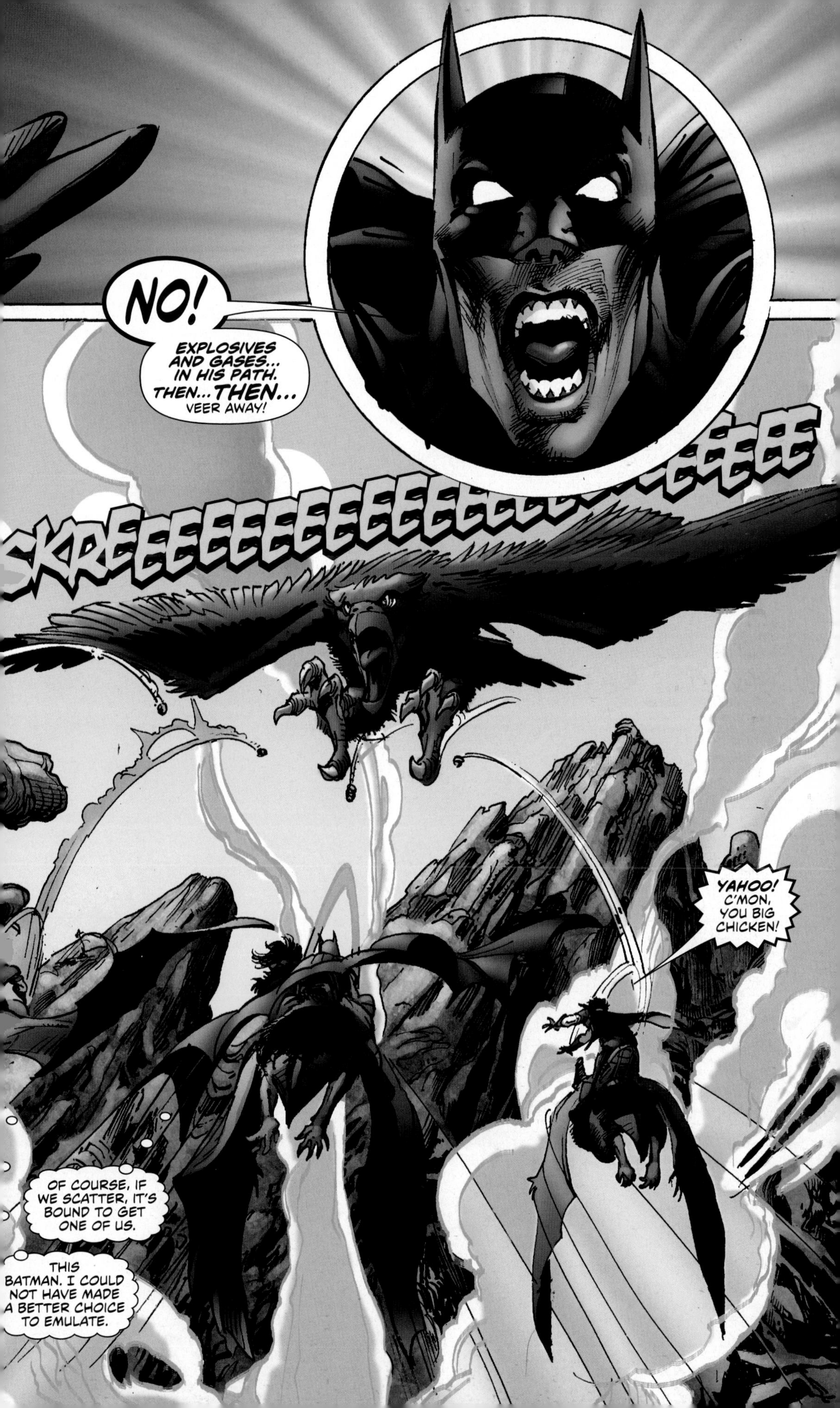
NO!
EXPLOSIVES AND GASES... IN HIS PATH. THEN... THEN... VEER AWAY!
SKREEEEEEEEEEEEEEEEEEEEEEEEE
YAHOO! C'MON, YOU BIG CHICKEN!
OF COURSE, IF WE SCATTER, IT'S BOUND TO GET ONE OF US.
THIS BATMAN. I COULD NOT HAVE MADE A BETTER CHOICE TO EMULATE.

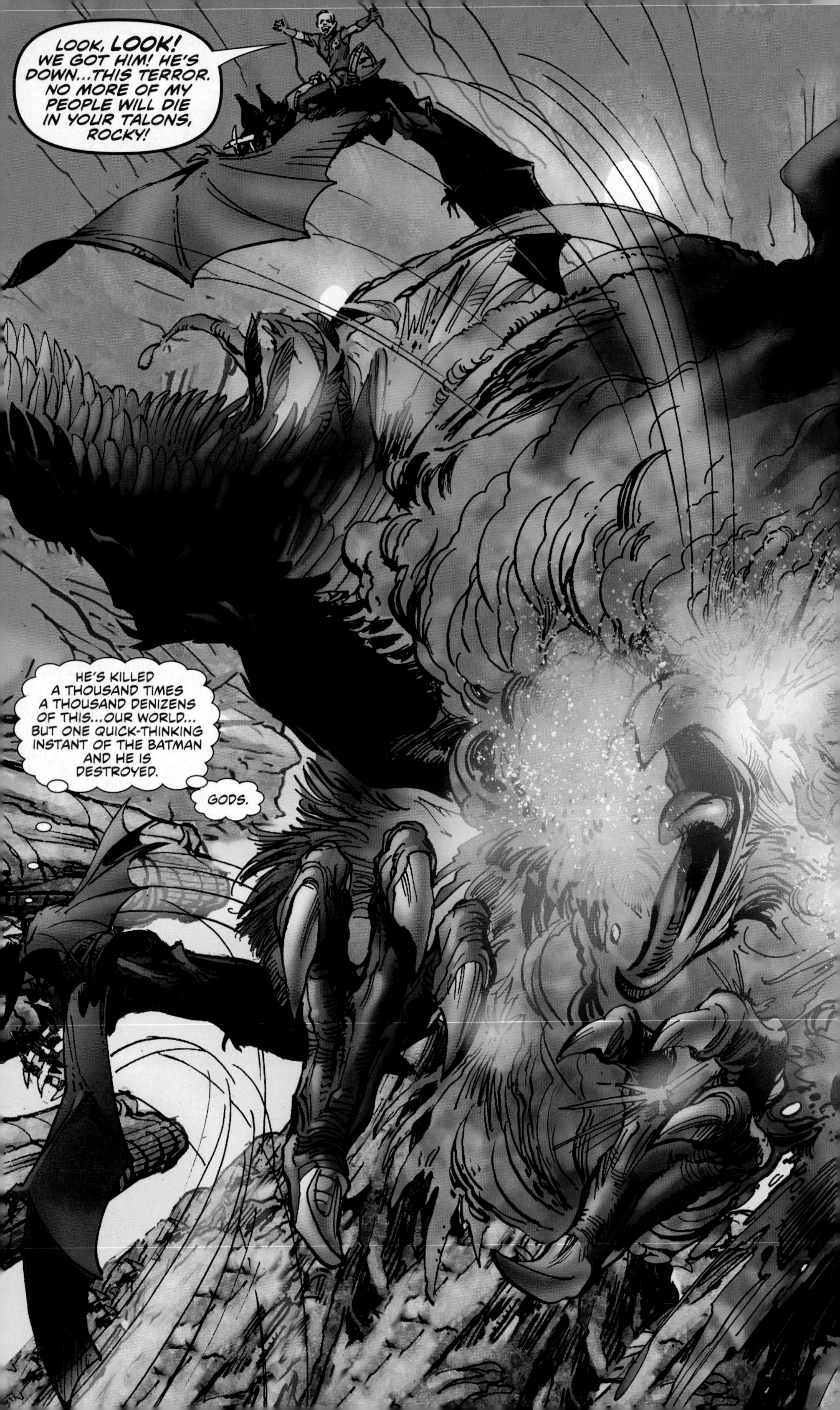
LOOK, LOOK! WE GOT HIM! HE'S DOWN...THIS TERROR. NO MORE OF MY PEOPLE WILL DIE IN YOUR TALONS, ROCKY!
HE'S KILLED A THOUSAND TIMES A THOUSAND DENIZENS OF THIS...OUR WORLD... BUT ONE QUICK-THINKING INSTANT OF THE BATMAN AND HE IS DESTROYED.
GODS.

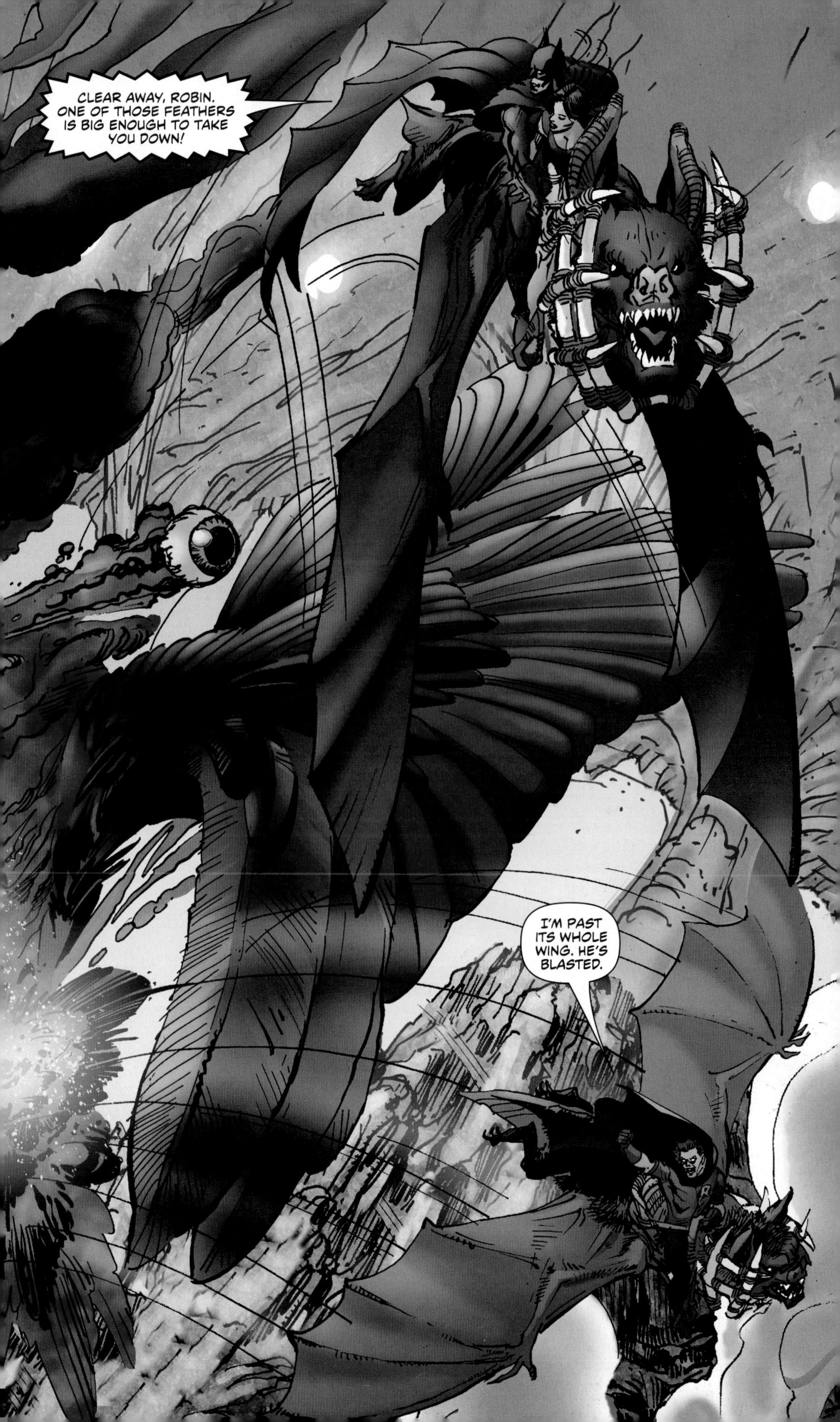
CLEAR AWAY, ROBIN. ONE OF THOSE FEATHERS IS BIG ENOUGH TO TAKE YOU DOWN!
I'M PAST ITS WHOLE WING. HE'S BLASTED.

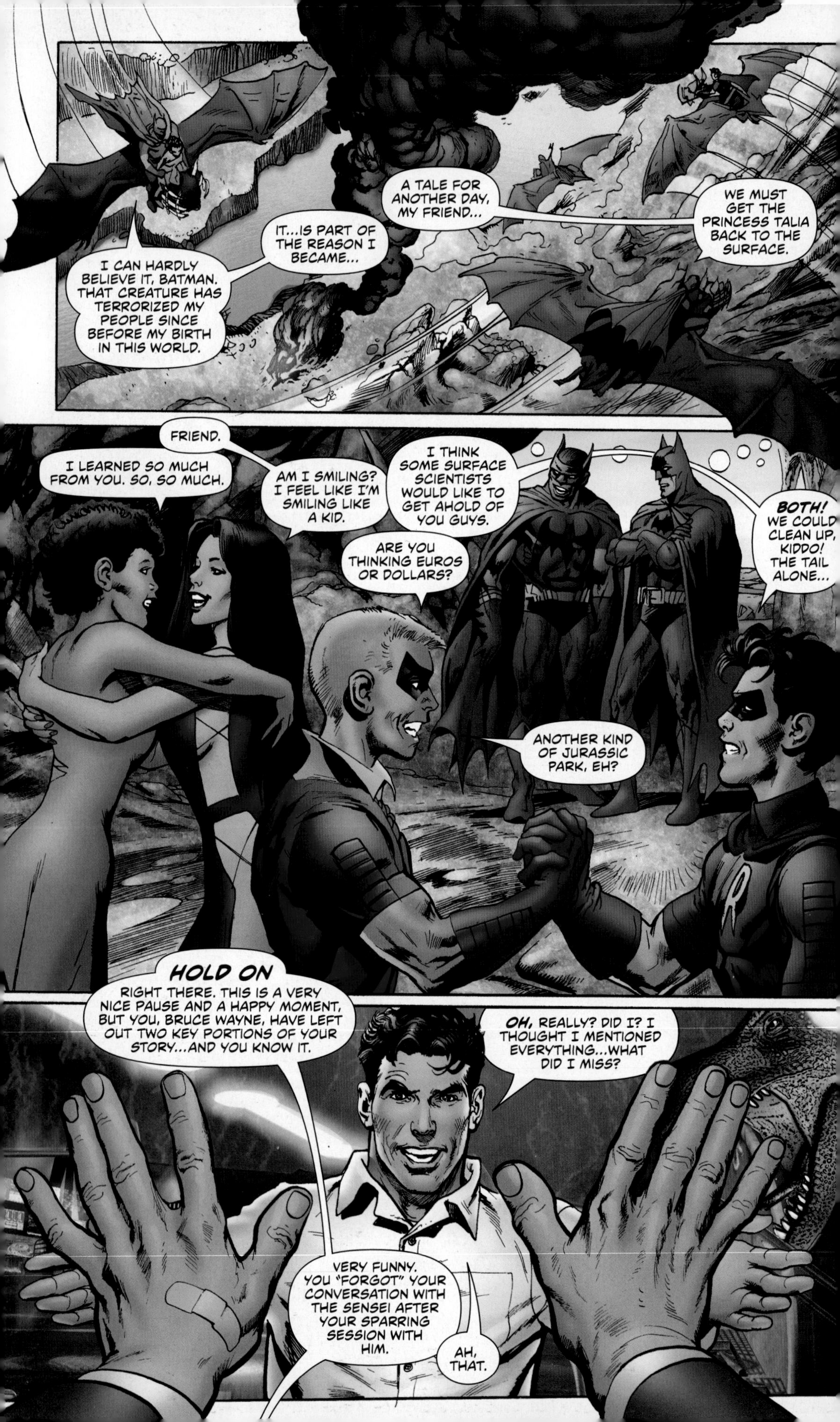
I CAN HARDLY BELIEVE IT, BATMAN. THAT CREATURE HAS TERRORIZED MY PEOPLE SINCE BEFORE MY BIRTH IN THIS WORLD.
IT...IS PART OF THE REASON I BECAME...
A TALE FOR ANOTHER DAY, MY FRIEND...
WE MUST GET THE PRINCESS TALIA BACK TO THE SURFACE.
I LEARNED SO MUCH FROM YOU. SO, SO MUCH.
FRIEND.
AM I SMILING? I FEEL LIKE I'M SMILING LIKE A KID.
I THINK SOME SURFACE SCIENTISTS WOULD LIKE TO GET AHOLD OF YOU GUYS.
ARE YOU THINKING EUROS OR DOLLARS?
BOTH! WE COULD CLEAN UP, KIDDO! THE TAIL ALONE...
ANOTHER KIND OF JURASSIC PARK, EH?
HOLD ON RIGHT THERE. THIS IS A VERY NICE PAUSE AND A HAPPY MOMENT, BUT YOU, BRUCE WAYNE, HAVE LEFT OUT TWO KEY PORTIONS OF YOUR STORY...AND YOU KNOW IT.
OH, REALLY? DID I? I THOUGHT I MENTIONED EVERYTHING...WHAT DID I MISS?
VERY FUNNY. YOU "FORGOT" YOUR CONVERSATION WITH THE SENSEI AFTER YOUR SPARRING SESSION WITH HIM.
AH, THAT.

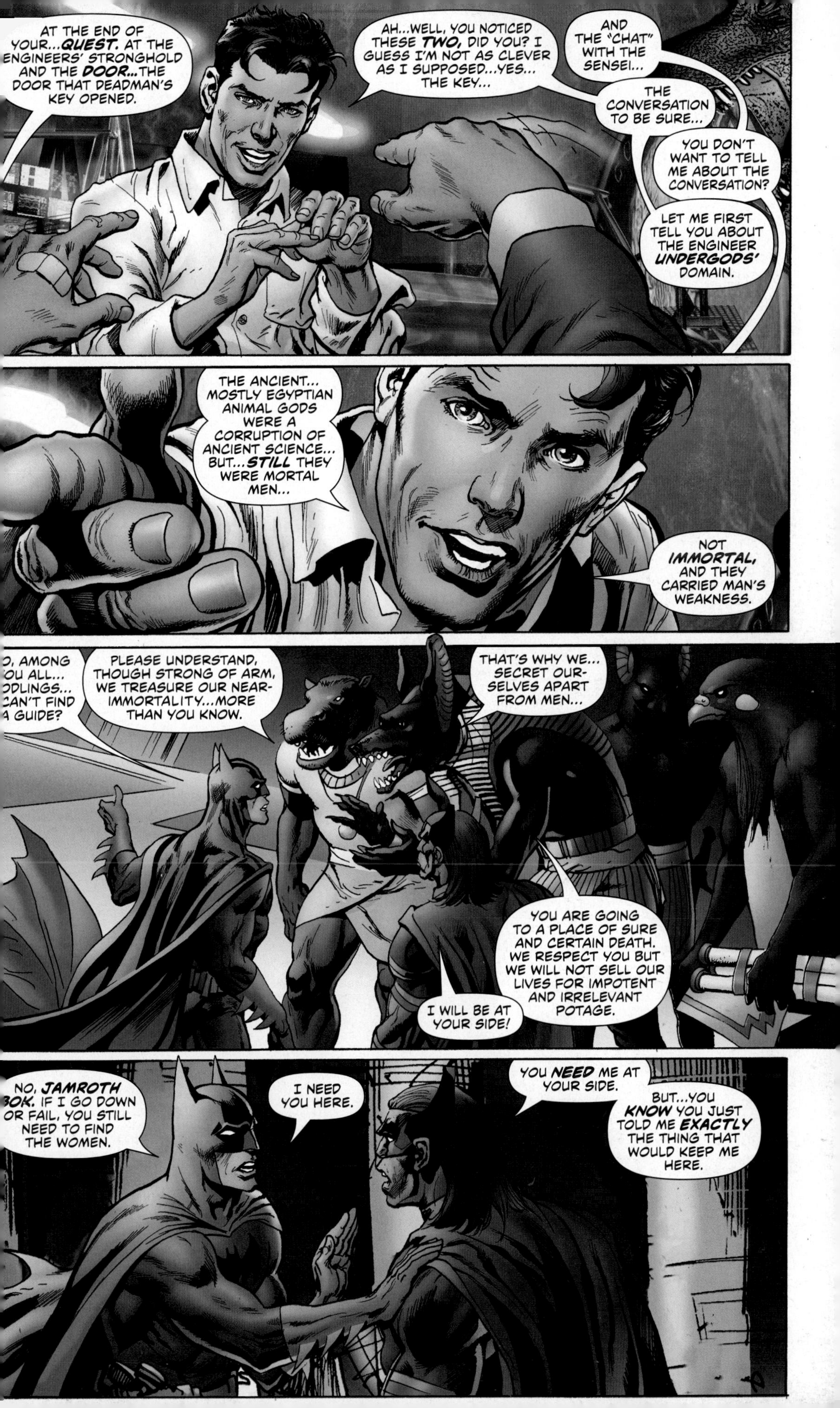

AT THE END OF YOUR...QUEST. AT THE ENGINEERS' STRONGHOLD AND THE DOOR...THE DOOR THAT DEADMAN'S KEY OPENED.
AH...WELL, YOU NOTICED THESE TWO, DID YOU? I GUESS I'M NOT AS CLEVER AS I SUPPOSED...YES... THE KEY...
AND THE "CHAT" WITH THE SENSEI...
THE CONVERSATION TO BE SURE...
YOU DON'T WANT TO TELL ME ABOUT THE CONVERSATION?
LET ME FIRST TELL YOU ABOUT THE ENGINEER UNDERGODS' DOMAIN.
THE ANCIENT... MOSTLY EGYPTIAN ANIMAL GODS WERE A CORRUPTION OF ANCIENT SCIENCE... BUT...STILL THEY WERE MORTAL MEN...
NOT IMMORTAL, AND THEY CARRIED MAN'S WEAKNESS.
O, AMONG OU ALL... ODLINGS... CAN'T FIND A GUIDE?
PLEASE UNDERSTAND, THOUGH STRONG OF ARM, WE TREASURE OUR NEAR-IMMORTALITY...MORE THAN YOU KNOW.
THAT'S WHY WE... SECRET OUR-SELVES APART FROM MEN...
YOU ARE GOING TO A PLACE OF SURE AND CERTAIN DEATH. WE RESPECT YOU BUT WE WILL NOT SELL OUR LIVES FOR IMPOTENT AND IRRELEVANT POTAGE.
I WILL BE AT YOUR SIDE!
NO, JAMROTH BOK. IF I GO DOWN OR FAIL, YOU STILL NEED TO FIND THE WOMEN.
I NEED YOU HERE.
YOU NEED ME AT YOUR SIDE.
BUT...YOU KNOW YOU JUST TOLD ME EXACTLY THE THING THAT WOULD KEEP ME HERE.

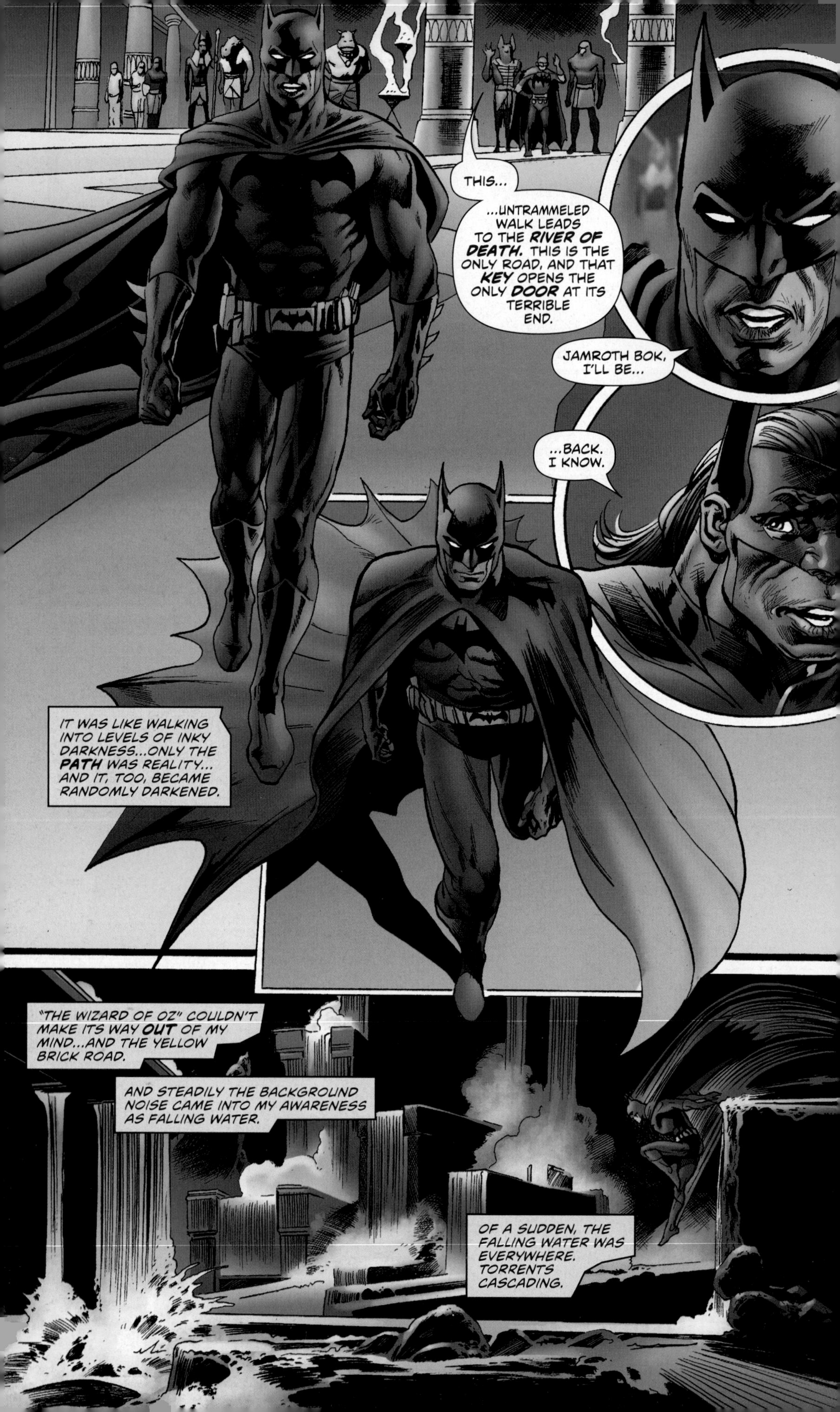
THIS...
...UNTRAMMELED WALK LEADS TO THE RIVER OF DEATH. THIS IS THE ONLY ROAD, AND THAT KEY OPENS THE ONLY DOOR AT ITS TERRIBLE END.
JAMROTH BOK, I'LL BE...
...BACK. I KNOW.
IT WAS LIKE WALKING INTO LEVELS OF INKY DARKNESS...ONLY THE PATH WAS REALITY... AND IT, TOO, BECAME RANDOMLY DARKENED.
"THE WIZARD OF OZ" COULDN'T MAKE ITS WAY OUT OF MY MIND...AND THE YELLOW BRICK ROAD.
AND STEADILY THE BACKGROUND NOISE CAME INTO MY AWARENESS AS FALLING WATER.
OF A SUDDEN, THE FALLING WATER WAS EVERYWHERE. TORRENTS CASCADING.

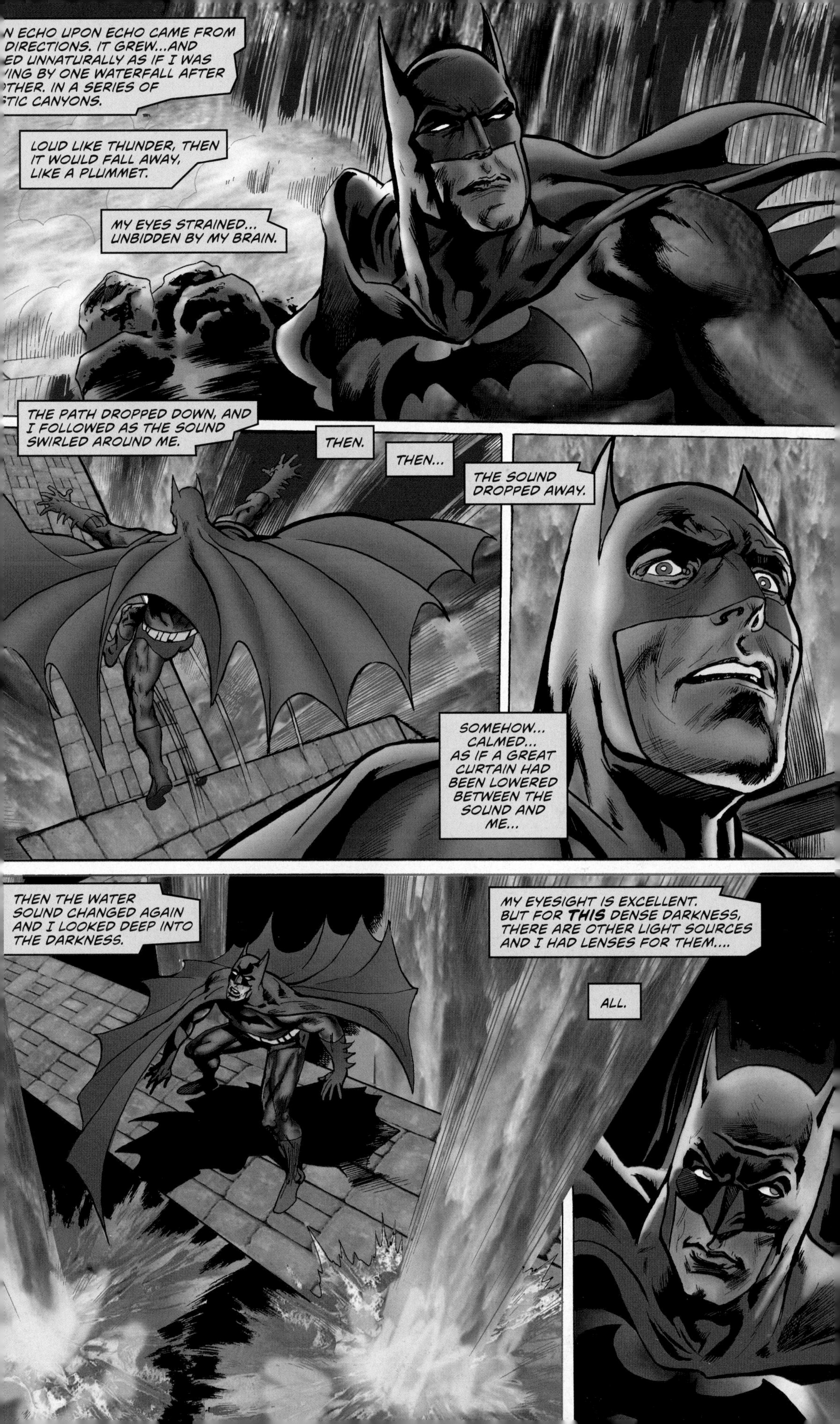
N ECHO UPON ECHO CAME FROM DIRECTIONS. IT GREW...AND ED UNNATURALLY AS IF I WAS VING BY ONE WATERFALL AFTER OTHER. IN A SERIES OF STIC CANYONS.
LOUD LIKE THUNDER, THEN IT WOULD FALL AWAY, LIKE A PLUMMET.
MY EYES STRAINED... UNBIDDEN BY MY BRAIN.
THE PATH DROPPED DOWN, AND I FOLLOWED AS THE SOUND SWIRLED AROUND ME.
THEN.
THEN...
THE SOUND DROPPED AWAY.
SOMEHOW... CALMED... AS IF A GREAT CURTAIN HAD BEEN LOWERED BETWEEN THE SOUND AND ME...
THEN THE WATER SOUND CHANGED AGAIN AND I LOOKED DEEP INTO THE DARKNESS.
MY EYESIGHT IS EXCELLENT. BUT FOR THIS DENSE DARKNESS, THERE ARE OTHER LIGHT SOURCES AND I HAD LENSES FOR THEM....
ALL.

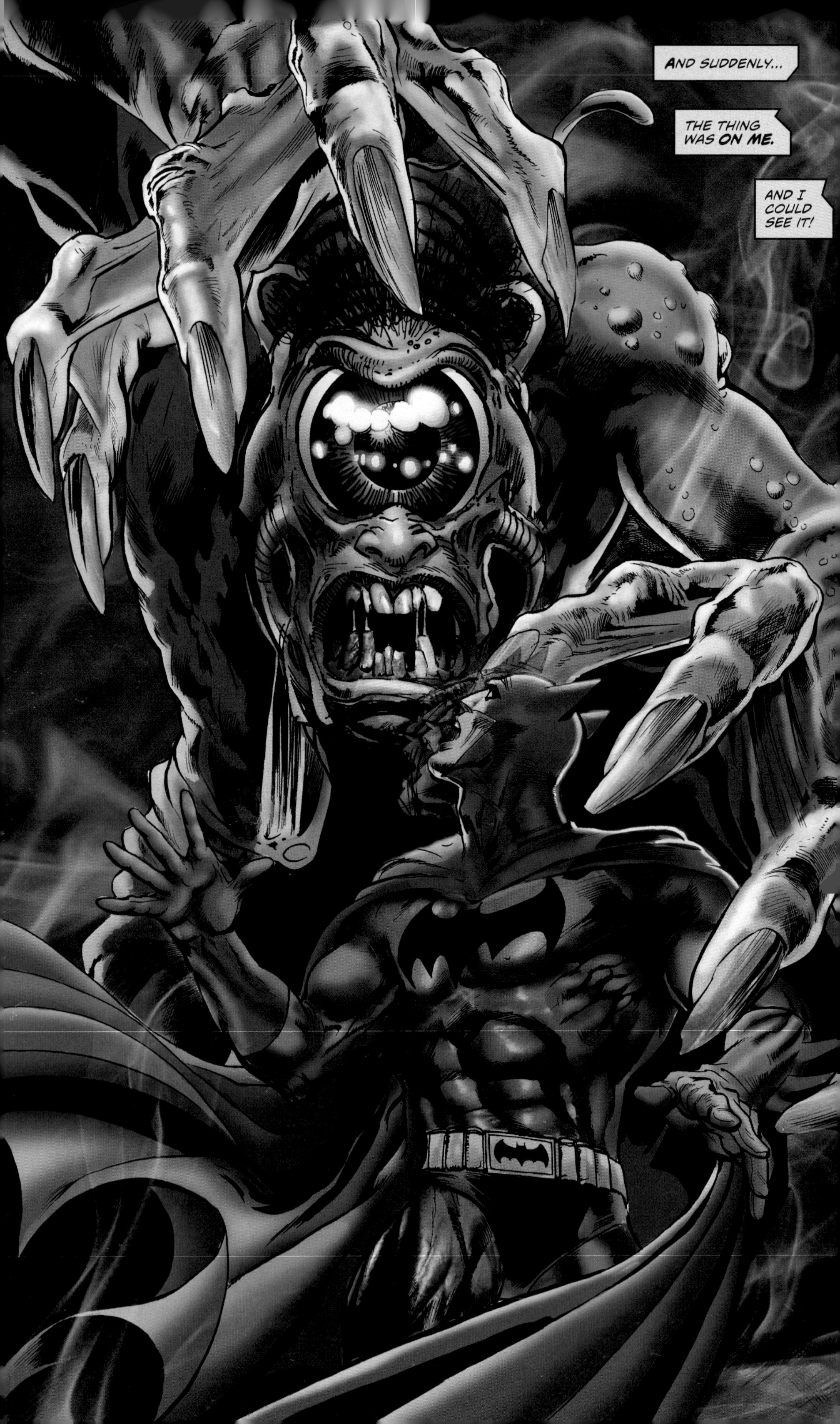
AND SUDDENLY...
THE THING WAS ON ME.
AND I COULD SEE IT!

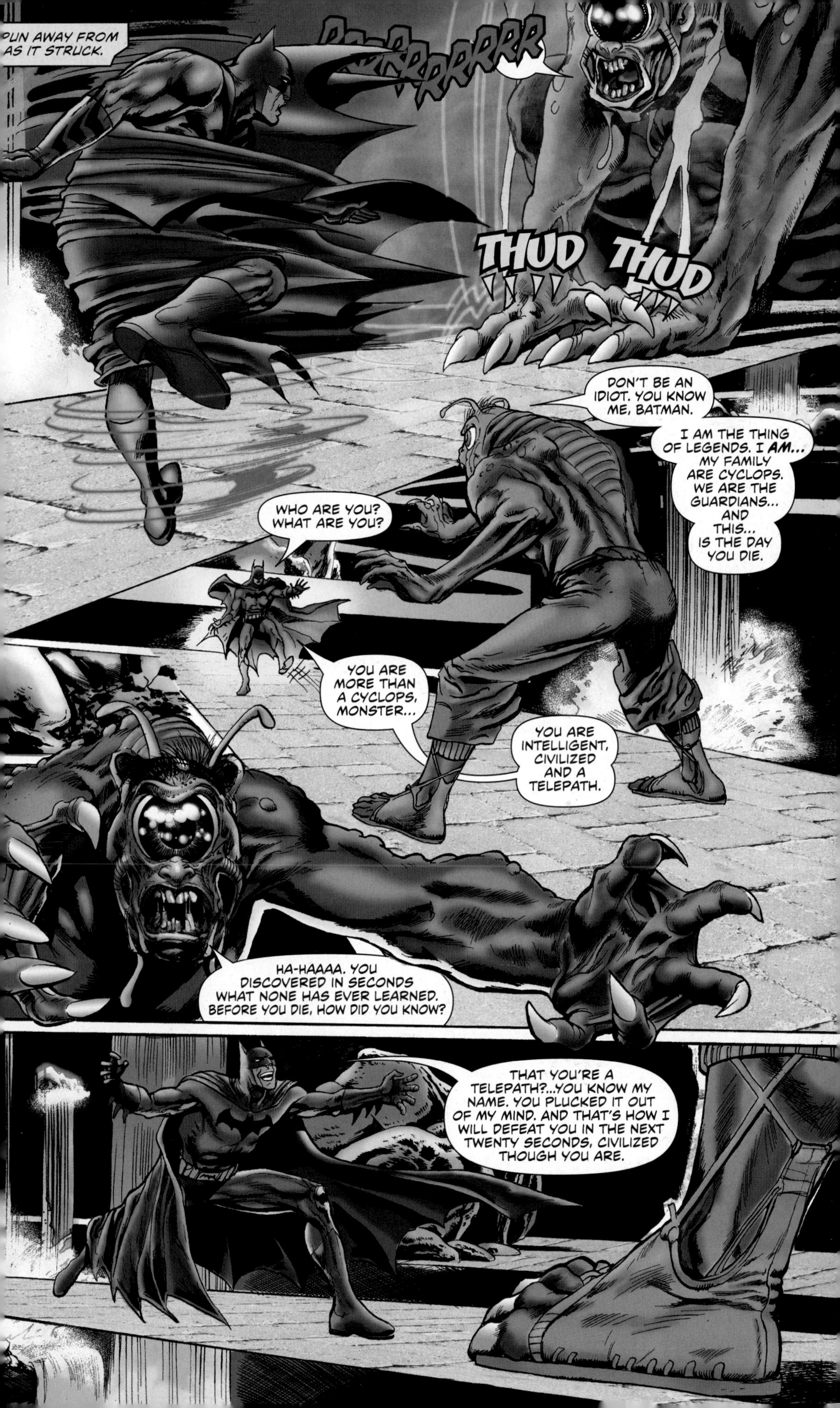

PUN AWAY FROM
AS IT STRUCK.
RRRRRRRRRR
THUD THUD
DON'T BE AN IDIOT. YOU KNOW ME, BATMAN.
I AM THE THING OF LEGENDS. I AM... MY FAMILY ARE CYCLOPS. WE ARE THE GUARDIANS... AND THIS... IS THE DAY YOU DIE.
WHO ARE YOU? WHAT ARE YOU?
YOU ARE MORE THAN A CYCLOPS, MONSTER...
YOU ARE INTELLIGENT, CIVILIZED AND A TELEPATH.
HA-HAAAA. YOU DISCOVERED IN SECONDS WHAT NONE HAS EVER LEARNED. BEFORE YOU DIE, HOW DID YOU KNOW?
THAT YOU'RE A TELEPATH?...YOU KNOW MY NAME. YOU PLUCKED IT OUT OF MY MIND. AND THAT'S HOW I WILL DEFEAT YOU IN THE NEXT TWENTY SECONDS, CIVILIZED THOUGH YOU ARE.

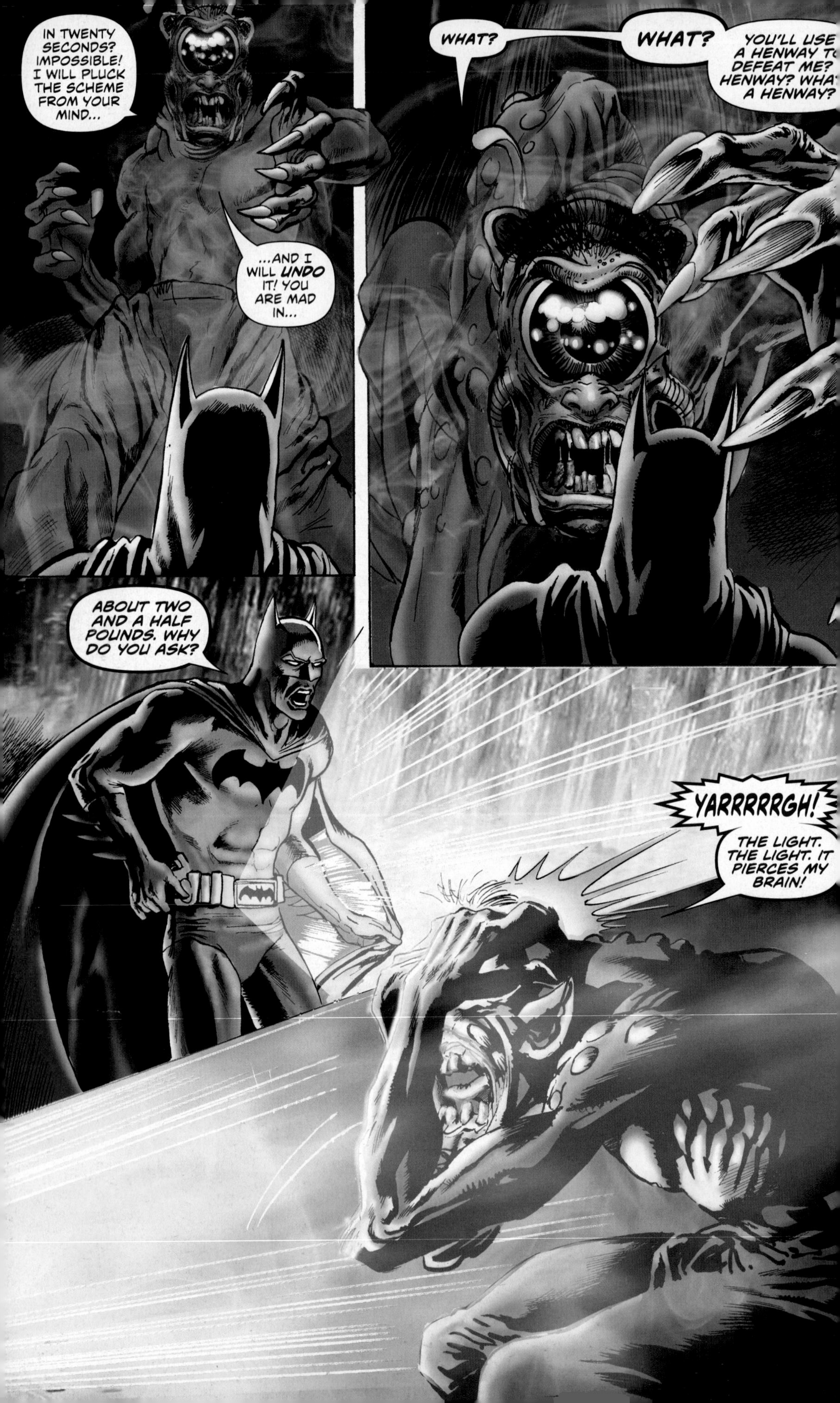
IN TWENTY SECONDS? IMPOSSIBLE! I WILL PLUCK THE SCHEME FROM YOUR MIND...
...AND I WILL UNDO IT! YOU ARE MAD IN...
WHAT?
WHAT?
YOU'LL USE A HENWAY TO DEFEAT ME? HENWAY? WHAT'S A HENWAY?
ABOUT TWO AND A HALF POUNDS. WHY DO YOU ASK?
YARRRRRGH!
THE LIGHT. THE LIGHT. IT PIERCES MY BRAIN!

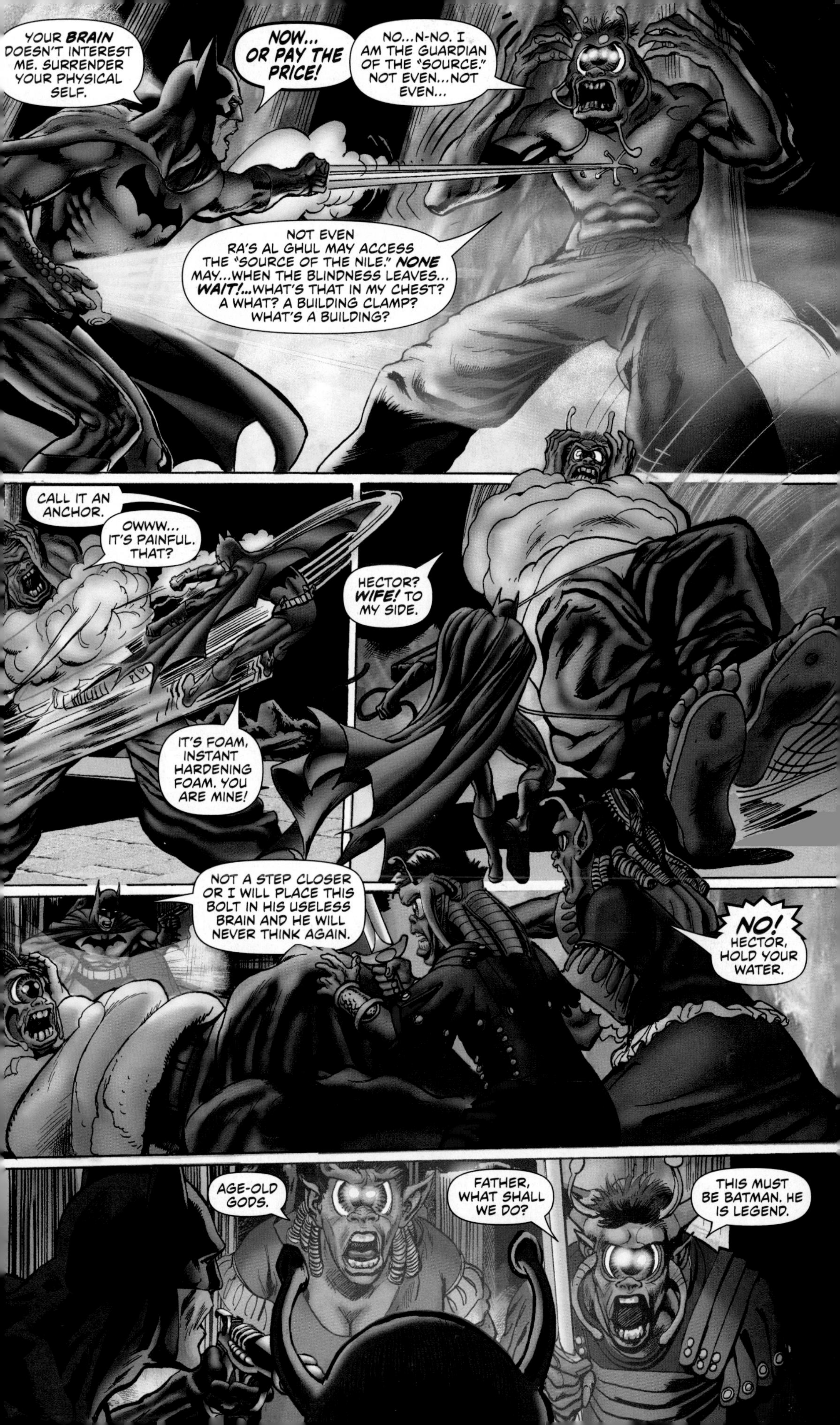
YOUR BRAIN DOESN'T INTEREST ME. SURRENDER YOUR PHYSICAL SELF.
NOW... OR PAY THE PRICE!
NO...N-NO. I AM THE GUARDIAN OF THE "SOURCE." NOT EVEN...NOT EVEN...
NOT EVEN RA'S AL GHUL MAY ACCESS THE "SOURCE OF THE NILE." NONE MAY...WHEN THE BLINDNESS LEAVES... WAIT!...WHAT'S THAT IN MY CHEST? A WHAT? A BUILDING CLAMP? WHAT'S A BUILDING?
CALL IT AN ANCHOR.
OWWW... IT'S PAINFUL. THAT?
HECTOR? WIFE! TO MY SIDE.
IT'S FOAM, INSTANT HARDENING FOAM. YOU ARE MINE!
NOT A STEP CLOSER OR I WILL PLACE THIS BOLT IN HIS USELESS BRAIN AND HE WILL NEVER THINK AGAIN.
NO! HECTOR, HOLD YOUR WATER.
AGE-OLD GODS.
FATHER, WHAT SHALL WE DO?
THIS MUST BE BATMAN. HE IS LEGEND.

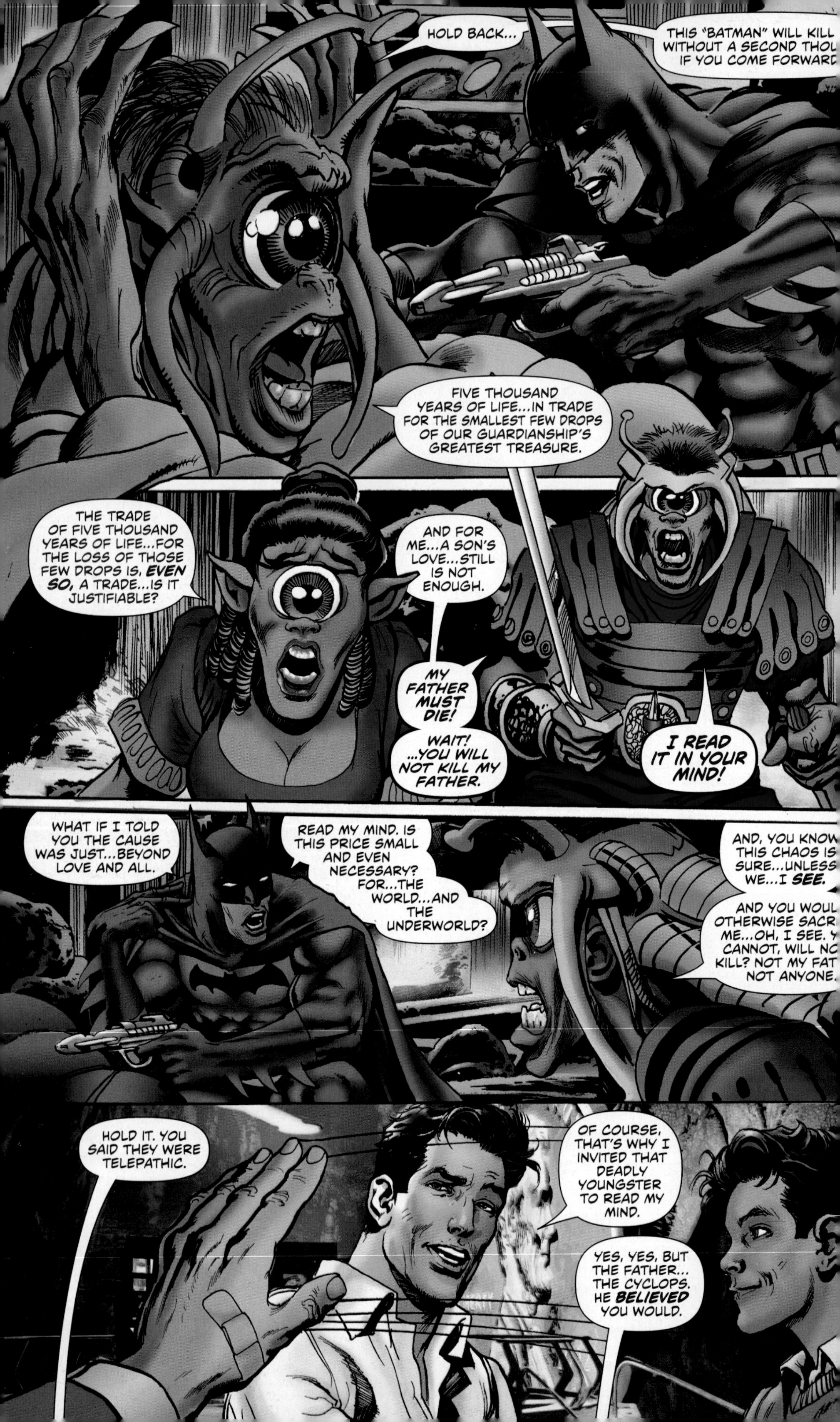
HOLD BACK...
THIS "BATMAN" WILL KILL WITHOUT A SECOND THOU IF YOU COME FORWARD
FIVE THOUSAND YEARS OF LIFE...IN TRADE FOR THE SMALLEST FEW DROPS OF OUR GUARDIANSHIP'S GREATEST TREASURE.
THE TRADE OF FIVE THOUSAND YEARS OF LIFE...FOR THE LOSS OF THOSE FEW DROPS IS, EVEN SO, A TRADE...IS IT JUSTIFIABLE?
AND FOR ME...A SON'S LOVE...STILL IS NOT ENOUGH.
MY FATHER MUST DIE!
WAIT! ...YOU WILL NOT KILL MY FATHER.
I READ IT IN YOUR MIND!
WHAT IF I TOLD YOU THE CAUSE WAS JUST...BEYOND LOVE AND ALL.
READ MY MIND. IS THIS PRICE SMALL AND EVEN NECESSARY? FOR...THE WORLD...AND THE UNDERWORLD?
AND, YOU KNOW THIS CHAOS IS SURE...UNLESS WE...I SEE.
AND YOU WOUL OTHERWISE SACR ME...OH, I SEE. Y CANNOT, WILL NO KILL? NOT MY FAT NOT ANYONE.
HOLD IT. YOU SAID THEY WERE TELEPATHIC.
OF COURSE, THAT'S WHY I INVITED THAT DEADLY YOUNGSTER TO READ MY MIND.
YES, YES, BUT THE FATHER... THE CYCLOPS. HE BELIEVED YOU WOULD.

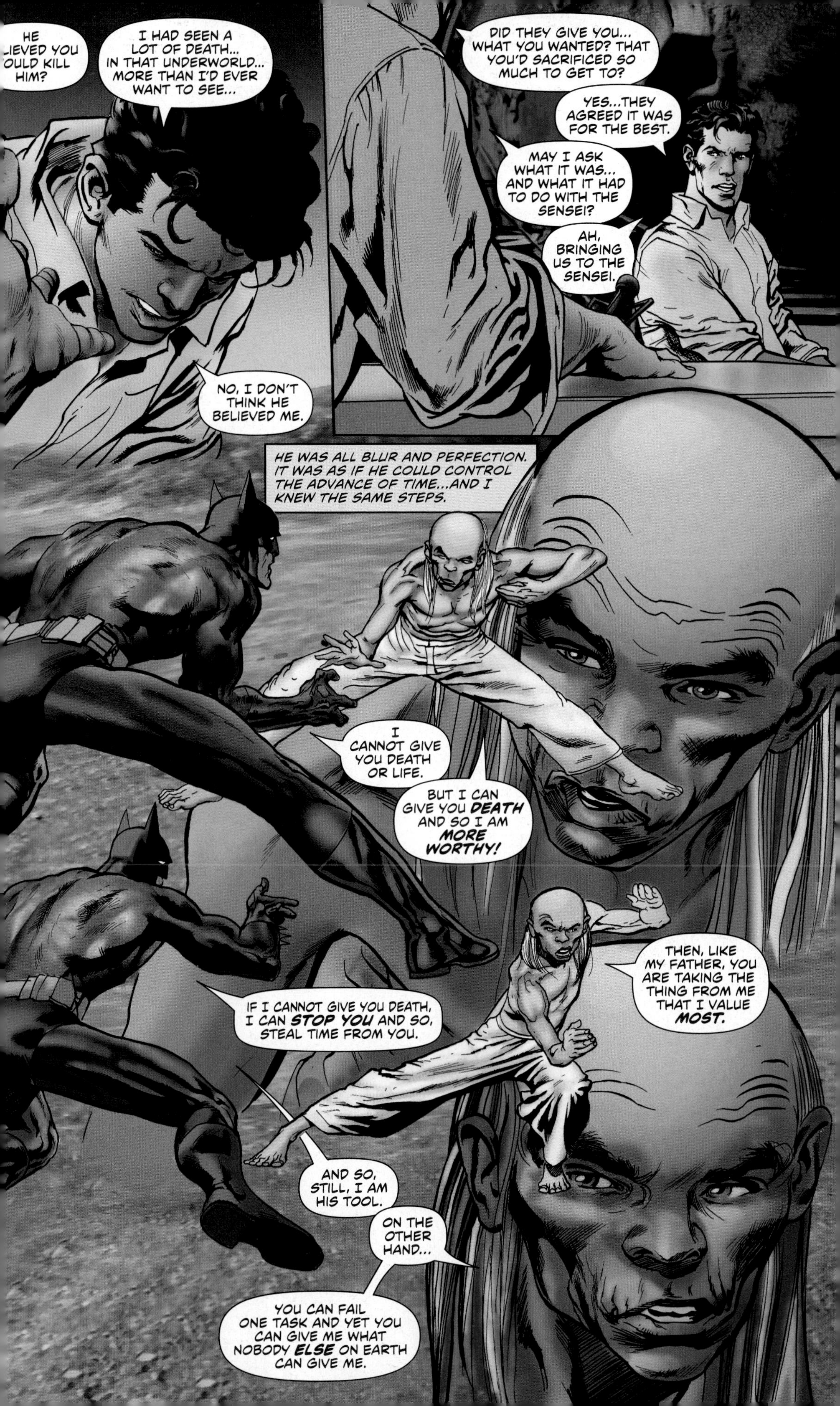

HE
LIEVED YOU
OULD KILL
HIM?
I HAD SEEN A LOT OF DEATH... IN THAT UNDERWORLD... MORE THAN I'D EVER WANT TO SEE...
NO, I DON'T THINK HE BELIEVED ME.
DID THEY GIVE YOU... WHAT YOU WANTED? THAT YOU'D SACRIFICED SO MUCH TO GET TO?
YES...THEY AGREED IT WAS FOR THE BEST.
MAY I ASK WHAT IT WAS... AND WHAT IT HAD TO DO WITH THE SENSEI?
AH, BRINGING US TO THE SENSEI.
HE WAS ALL BLUR AND PERFECTION. IT WAS AS IF HE COULD CONTROL THE ADVANCE OF TIME...AND I KNEW THE SAME STEPS.
I CANNOT GIVE YOU DEATH OR LIFE.
BUT I CAN GIVE YOU DEATH AND SO I AM MORE WORTHY!
IF I CANNOT GIVE YOU DEATH, I CAN STOP YOU AND SO, STEAL TIME FROM YOU.
THEN, LIKE MY FATHER, YOU ARE TAKING THE THING FROM ME THAT I VALUE MOST.
AND SO, STILL, I AM HIS TOOL.
ON THE OTHER HAND...
YOU CAN FAIL ONE TASK AND YET YOU CAN GIVE ME WHAT NOBODY ELSE ON EARTH CAN GIVE ME.

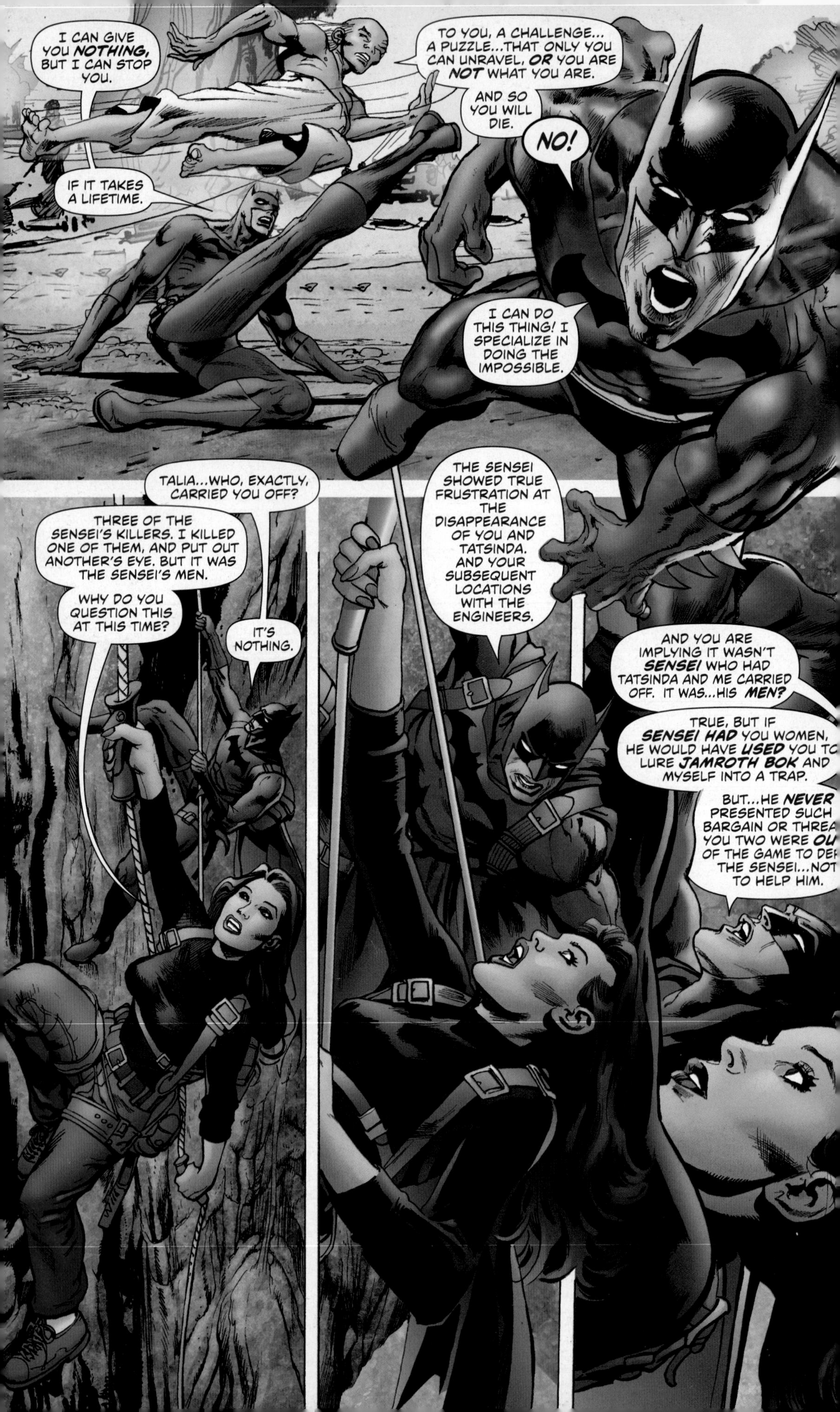
I CAN GIVE YOU NOTHING, BUT I CAN STOP YOU.
TO YOU, A CHALLENGE... A PUZZLE...THAT ONLY YOU CAN UNRAVEL, OR YOU ARE NOT WHAT YOU ARE.
AND SO YOU WILL DIE.
NO!
IF IT TAKES A LIFETIME.
I CAN DO THIS THING! I SPECIALIZE IN DOING THE IMPOSSIBLE.
TALIA...WHO, EXACTLY, CARRIED YOU OFF?
THREE OF THE SENSEI'S KILLERS. I KILLED ONE OF THEM, AND PUT OUT ANOTHER'S EYE. BUT IT WAS THE SENSEI'S MEN.
WHY DO YOU QUESTION THIS AT THIS TIME?
IT'S NOTHING.
THE SENSEI SHOWED TRUE FRUSTRATION AT THE DISAPPEARANCE OF YOU AND TATSINDA. AND YOUR SUBSEQUENT LOCATIONS WITH THE ENGINEERS.
AND YOU ARE IMPLYING IT WASN'T SENSEI WHO HAD TATSINDA AND ME CARRIED OFF. IT WAS...HIS MEN?
TRUE, BUT IF SENSEI HAD YOU WOMEN, HE WOULD HAVE USED YOU TO LURE JAMROTH BOK AND MYSELF INTO A TRAP.
BUT...HE NEVER PRESENTED SUCH BARGAIN OR THREA YOU TWO WERE OU OF THE GAME TO DEF THE SENSEI...NOT TO HELP HIM.

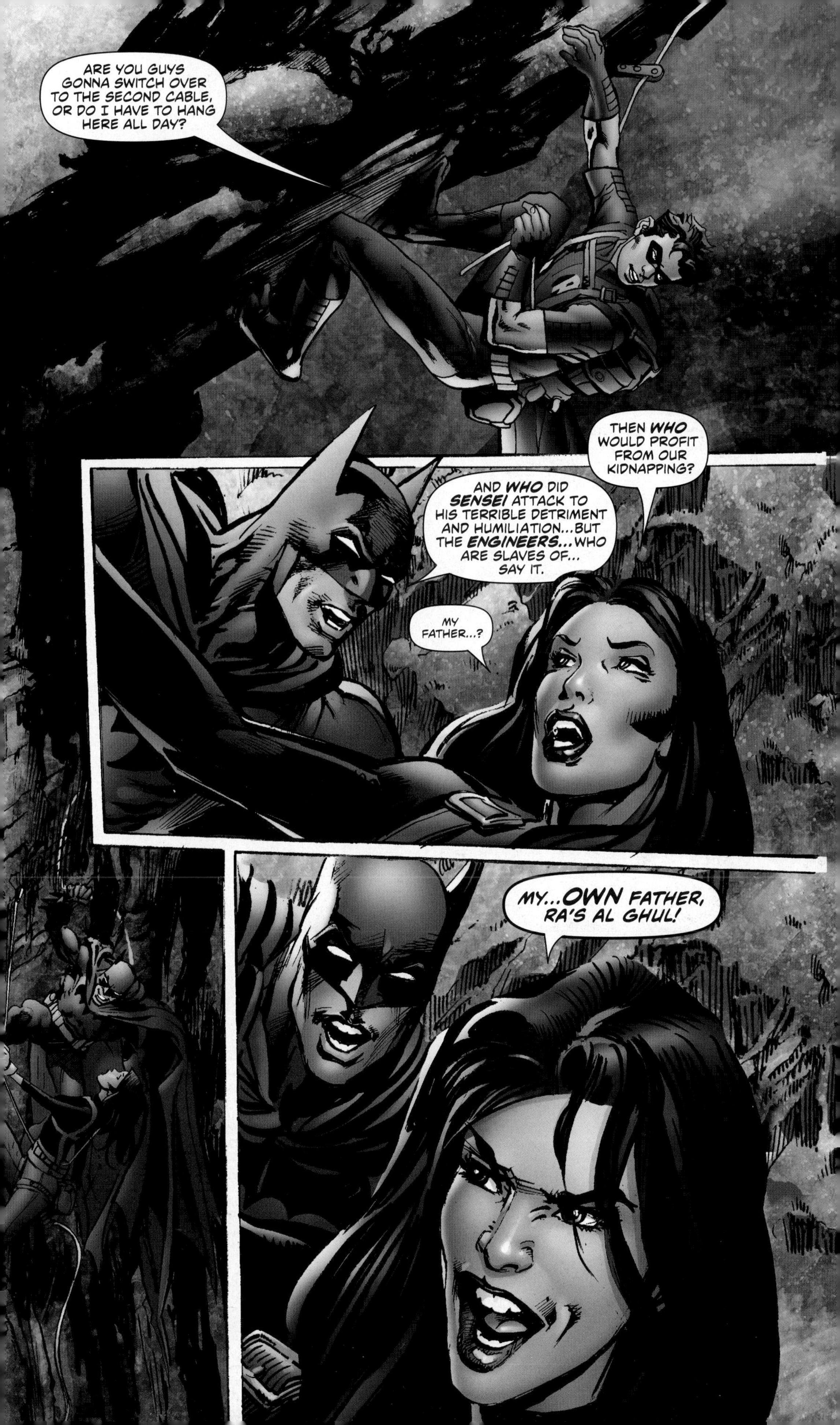
ARE YOU GUYS GONNA SWITCH OVER TO THE SECOND CABLE, OR DO I HAVE TO HANG HERE ALL DAY?
THEN WHO WOULD PROFIT FROM OUR KIDNAPPING?
AND WHO DID SENSEI ATTACK TO HIS TERRIBLE DETRIMENT AND HUMILIATION...BUT THE ENGINEERS...WHO ARE SLAVES OF... SAY IT.
MY FATHER...?
MY...OWN FATHER, RA'S AL GHUL!

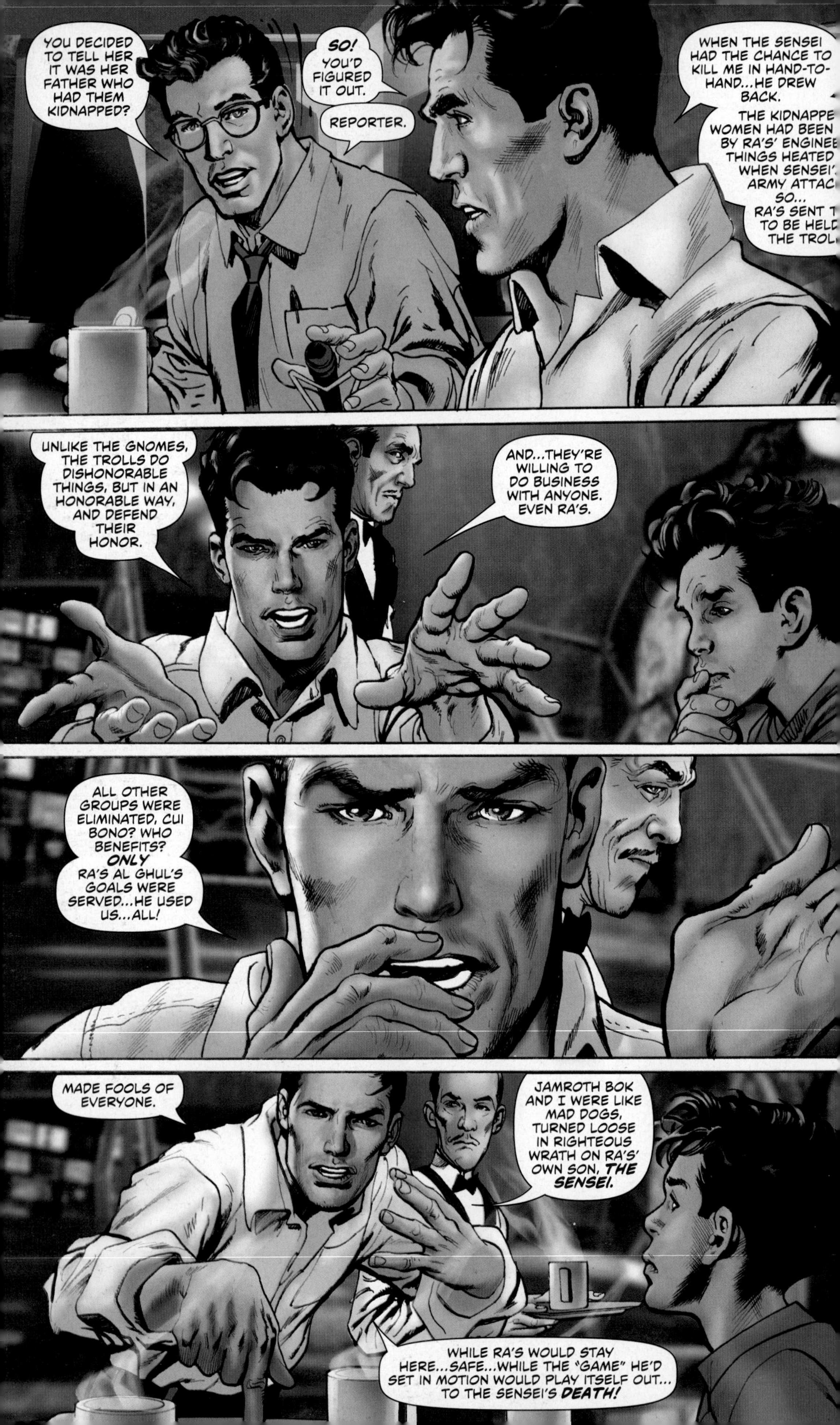
YOU DECIDED TO TELL HER IT WAS HER FATHER WHO HAD THEM KIDNAPPED?
SO! YOU'D FIGURED IT OUT.
REPORTER.
WHEN THE SENSEI HAD THE CHANCE TO KILL ME IN HAND-TO-HAND...HE DREW BACK.
THE KIDNAPPE WOMEN HAD BEEN BY RA'S' ENGINEE THINGS HEATED WHEN SENSEI' ARMY ATTAC SO... RA'S SENT T TO BE HELD THE TROL
UNLIKE THE GNOMES, THE TROLLS DO DISHONORABLE THINGS, BUT IN AN HONORABLE WAY, AND DEFEND THEIR HONOR.
AND...THEY'RE WILLING TO DO BUSINESS WITH ANYONE. EVEN RA'S.
ALL OTHER GROUPS WERE ELIMINATED, CUI BONO? WHO BENEFITS? ONLY RA'S AL GHUL'S GOALS WERE SERVED...HE USED US...ALL!
MADE FOOLS OF EVERYONE.
JAMROTH BOK AND I WERE LIKE MAD DOGS, TURNED LOOSE IN RIGHTEOUS WRATH ON RA'S' OWN SON, THE SENSEI.
WHILE RA'S WOULD STAY HERE...SAFE...WHILE THE "GAME" HE'D SET IN MOTION WOULD PLAY ITSELF OUT... TO THE SENSEI'S DEATH!

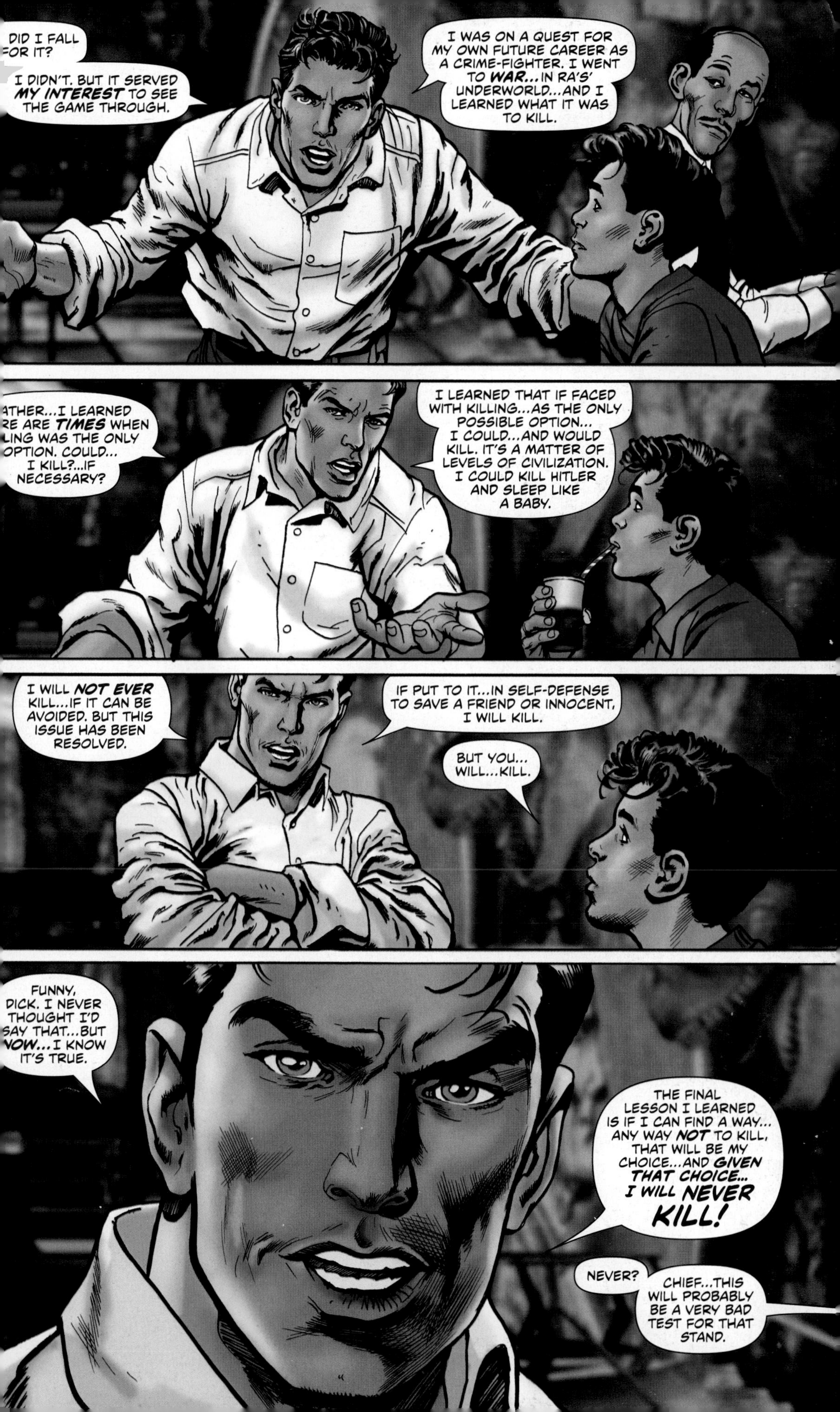

DID I FALL
FOR IT?
I DIDN'T. BUT IT SERVED MY INTEREST TO SEE THE GAME THROUGH.
I WAS ON A QUEST FOR MY OWN FUTURE CAREER AS A CRIME-FIGHTER. I WENT TO WAR... IN RA'S' UNDERWORLD...AND I LEARNED WHAT IT WAS TO KILL.
ATHER...I LEARNED RE ARE TIMES WHEN LING WAS THE ONLY OPTION. COULD... I KILL?...IF NECESSARY?
I LEARNED THAT IF FACED WITH KILLING...AS THE ONLY POSSIBLE OPTION... I COULD...AND WOULD KILL. IT'S A MATTER OF LEVELS OF CIVILIZATION. I COULD KILL HITLER AND SLEEP LIKE A BABY.
I WILL NOT EVER KILL...IF IT CAN BE AVOIDED. BUT THIS ISSUE HAS BEEN RESOLVED.
IF PUT TO IT...IN SELF-DEFENSE TO SAVE A FRIEND OR INNOCENT, I WILL KILL.
BUT YOU... WILL...KILL.
FUNNY, DICK. I NEVER THOUGHT I'D SAY THAT...BUT NOW...I KNOW IT'S TRUE.
THE FINAL LESSON I LEARNED IS IF I CAN FIND A WAY... ANY WAY NOT TO KILL, THAT WILL BE MY CHOICE...AND GIVEN THAT CHOICE... I WILL NEVER KILL!
NEVER?
CHIEF...THIS WILL PROBABLY BE A VERY BAD TEST FOR THAT STAND.

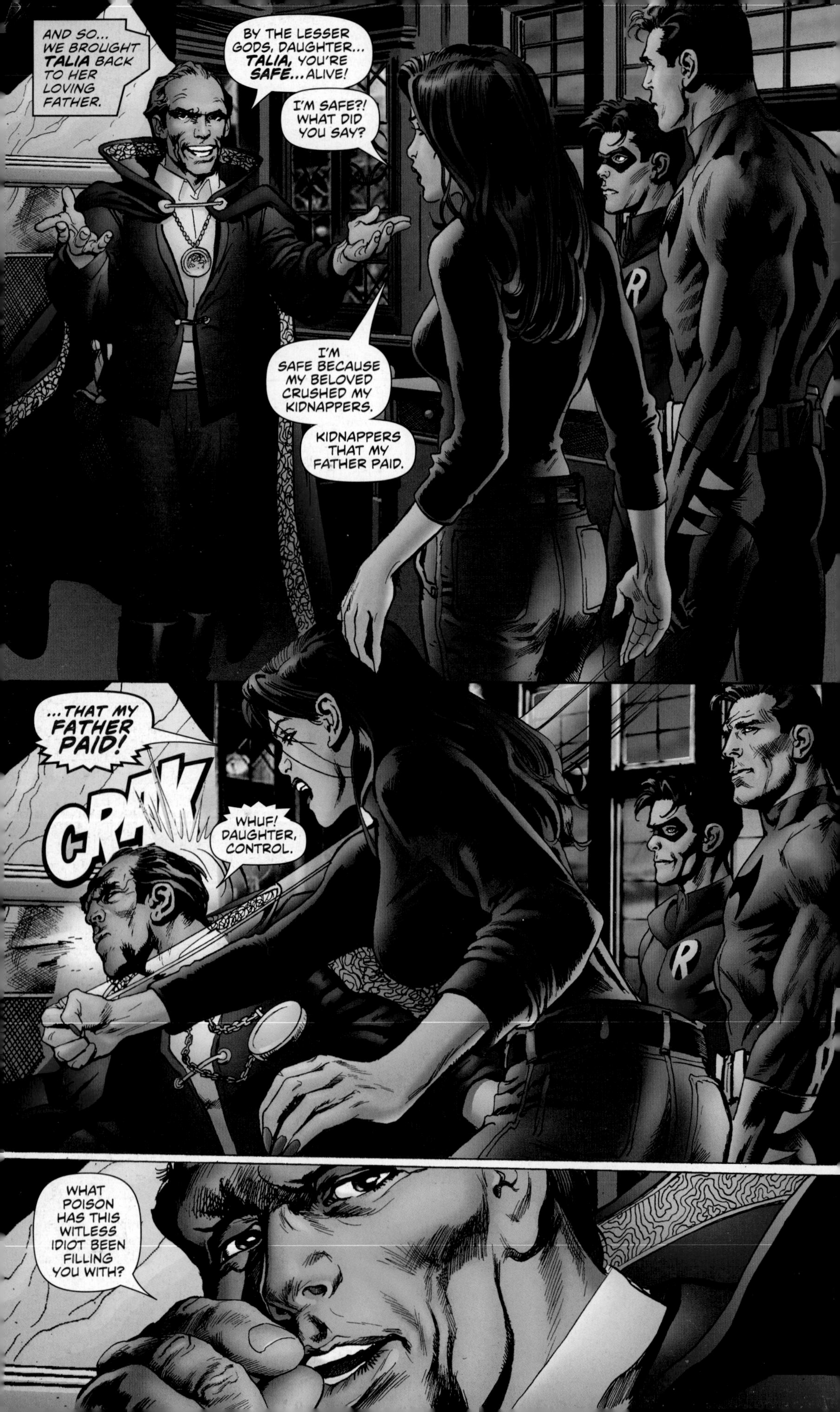
AND SO... WE BROUGHT TALIA BACK TO HER LOVING FATHER.
BY THE LESSER GODS, DAUGHTER... TALIA, YOU'RE SAFE... ALIVE!
I'M SAFE?! WHAT DID YOU SAY?
I'M SAFE BECAUSE MY BELOVED CRUSHED MY KIDNAPPERS.
KIDNAPPERS THAT MY FATHER PAID.
...THAT MY FATHER PAID!
CRAK
WHUF! DAUGHTER, CONTROL.
WHAT POISON HAS THIS WITLESS IDIOT BEEN FILLING YOU WITH?

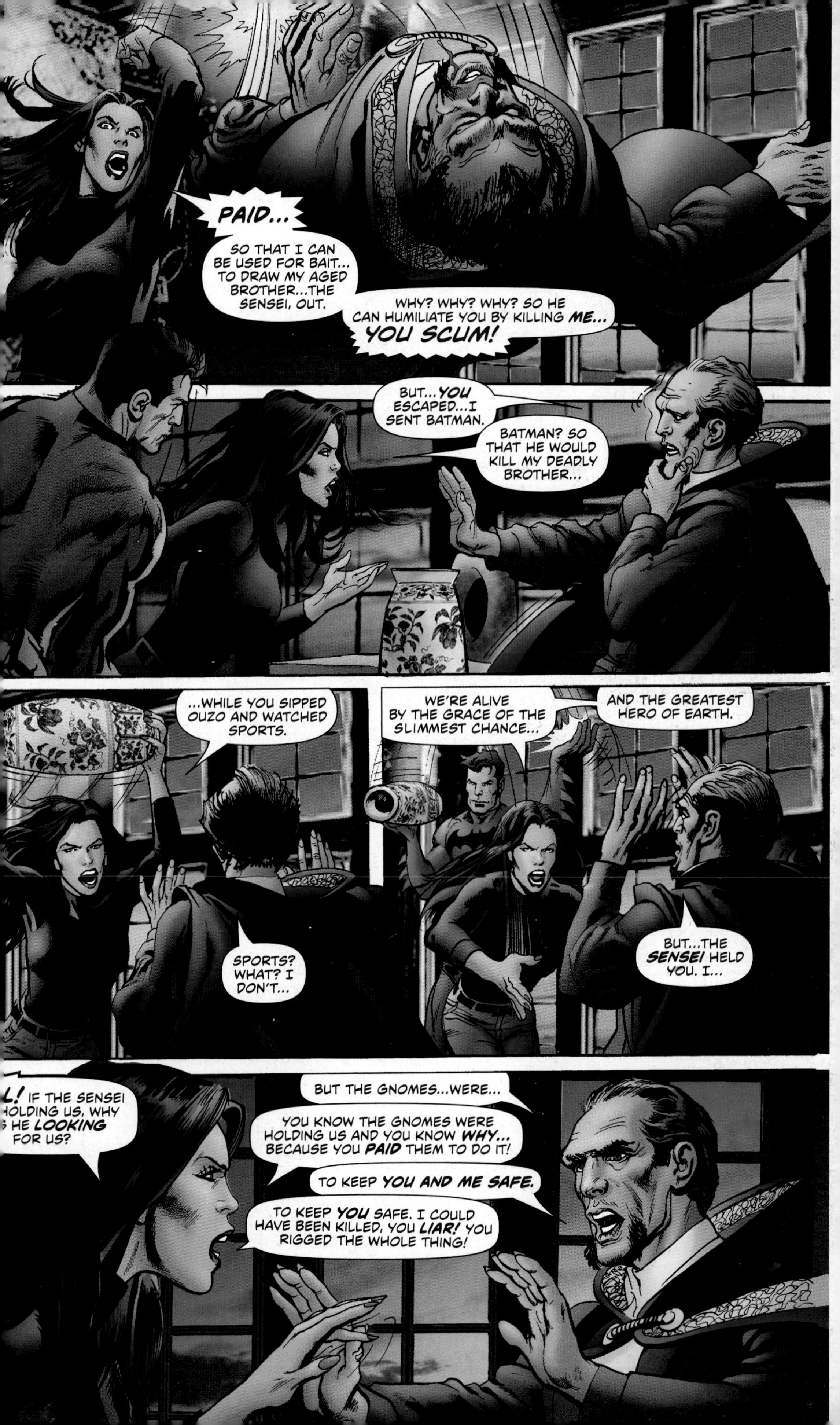
PAID...
SO THAT I CAN BE USED FOR BAIT... TO DRAW MY AGED BROTHER...THE SENSEI, OUT.
WHY? WHY? WHY? SO HE CAN HUMILIATE YOU BY KILLING ME...
YOU SCUM!
BUT...YOU ESCAPED...I SENT BATMAN.
BATMAN? SO THAT HE WOULD KILL MY DEADLY BROTHER...
...WHILE YOU SIPPED OUZO AND WATCHED SPORTS.
SPORTS? WHAT? I DON'T...
WE'RE ALIVE BY THE GRACE OF THE SLIMMEST CHANCE...
AND THE GREATEST HERO OF EARTH.
BUT...THE SENSEI HELD YOU. I...
IF THE SENSEI HOLDING US, WHY HE LOOKING FOR US?
BUT THE GNOMES...WERE...
YOU KNOW THE GNOMES WERE HOLDING US AND YOU KNOW WHY... BECAUSE YOU PAID THEM TO DO IT!
TO KEEP YOU AND ME SAFE.
TO KEEP YOU SAFE. I COULD HAVE BEEN KILLED, YOU LIAR! YOU RIGGED THE WHOLE THING!

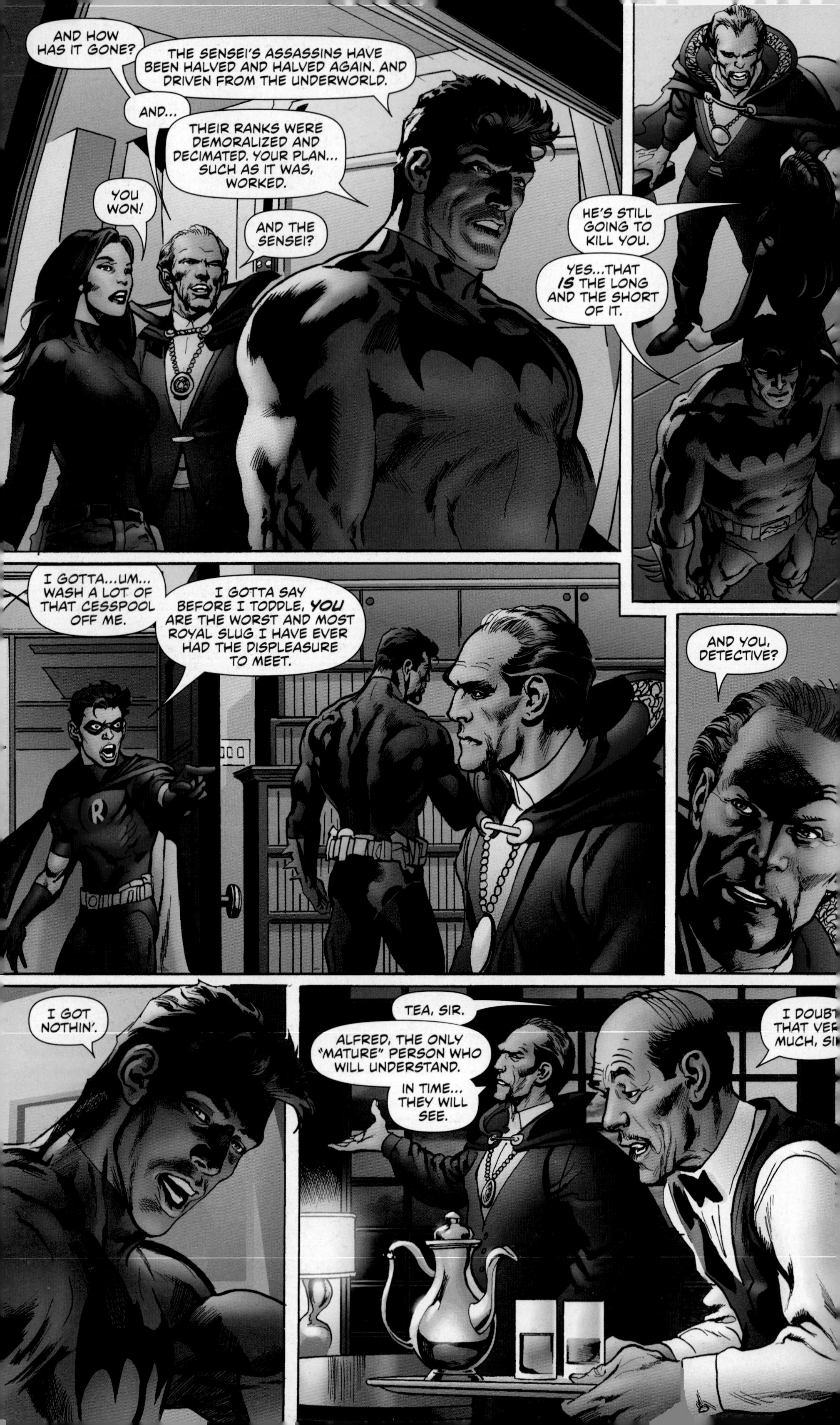

AND HOW HAS IT GONE?
THE SENSEI'S ASSASSINS HAVE BEEN HALVED AND HALVED AGAIN. AND DRIVEN FROM THE UNDERWORLD.
AND...
THEIR RANKS WERE DEMORALIZED AND DECIMATED. YOUR PLAN... SUCH AS IT WAS, WORKED.
YOU WON!
AND THE SENSEI?
HE'S STILL GOING TO KILL YOU.
YES...THAT *IS* THE LONG AND THE SHORT OF IT.
I GOTTA...UM... WASH A LOT OF THAT CESSPOOL OFF ME.
I GOTTA SAY BEFORE I TODDLE, *YOU* ARE THE WORST AND MOST ROYAL SLUG I HAVE EVER HAD THE DISPLEASURE TO MEET.
AND YOU, DETECTIVE?
I GOT NOTHIN'.
TEA, SIR.
ALFRED, THE ONLY "MATURE" PERSON WHO WILL UNDERSTAND.
IN TIME... THEY WILL SEE.

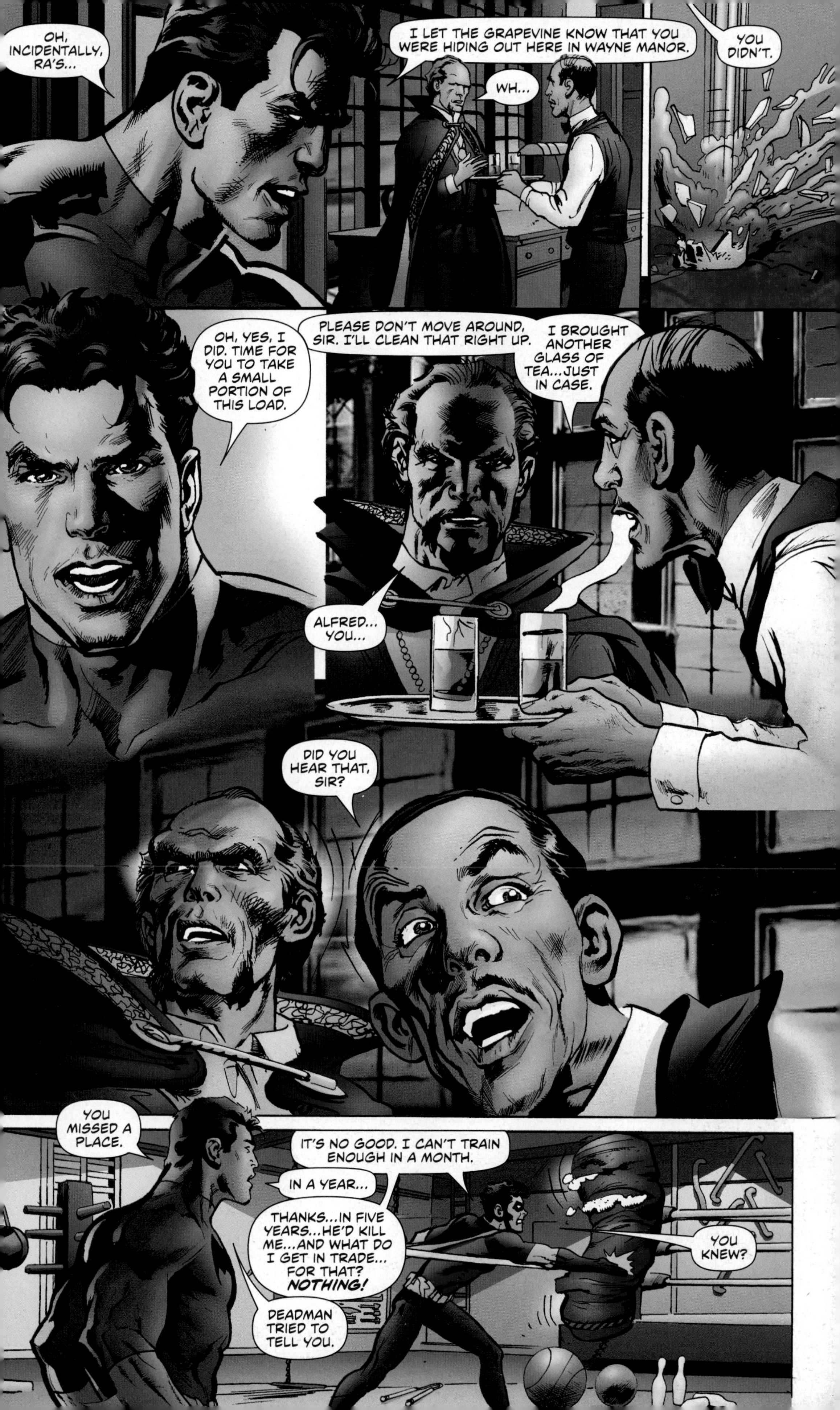

OH, INCIDENTALLY, RA'S...
I LET THE GRAPEVINE KNOW THAT YOU WERE HIDING OUT HERE IN WAYNE MANOR.
WH...
YOU DIDN'T.
OH, YES, I DID. TIME FOR YOU TO TAKE A SMALL PORTION OF THIS LOAD.
PLEASE DON'T MOVE AROUND, SIR. I'LL CLEAN THAT RIGHT UP.
I BROUGHT ANOTHER GLASS OF TEA...JUST IN CASE.
ALFRED... YOU...
DID YOU HEAR THAT, SIR?
YOU MISSED A PLACE.
IT'S NO GOOD. I CAN'T TRAIN ENOUGH IN A MONTH.
IN A YEAR...
THANKS...IN FIVE YEARS...HE'D KILL ME...AND WHAT DO I GET IN TRADE... FOR THAT? ***NOTHING!***
YOU KNEW?
DEADMAN TRIED TO TELL YOU.

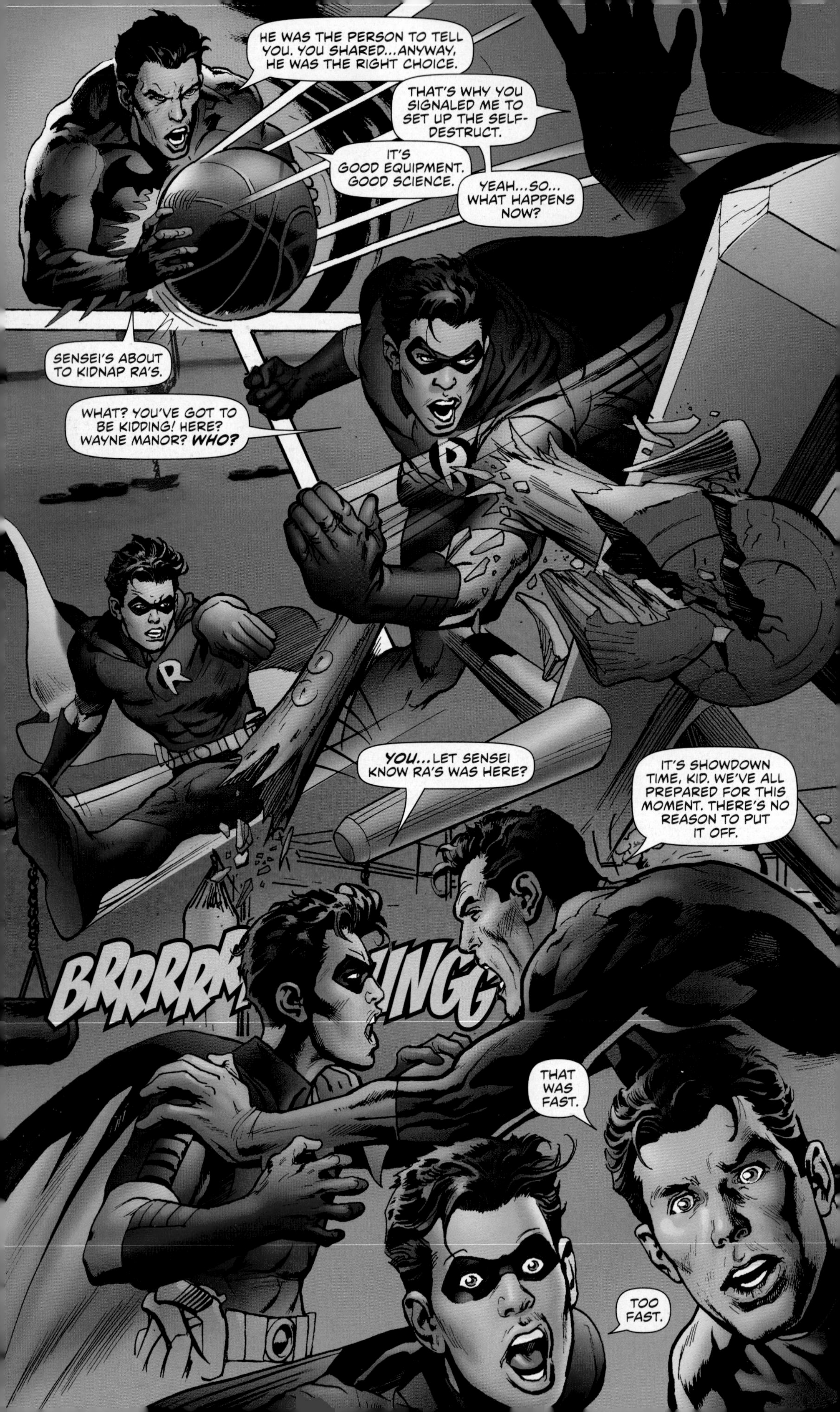
HE WAS THE PERSON TO TELL YOU. YOU SHARED...ANYWAY, HE WAS THE RIGHT CHOICE.
THAT'S WHY YOU SIGNALED ME TO SET UP THE SELF-DESTRUCT.
IT'S GOOD EQUIPMENT. GOOD SCIENCE.
YEAH...SO... WHAT HAPPENS NOW?
SENSEI'S ABOUT TO KIDNAP RA'S.
WHAT? YOU'VE GOT TO BE KIDDING! HERE? WAYNE MANOR? WHO?
YOU...LET SENSEI KNOW RA'S WAS HERE?
IT'S SHOWDOWN TIME, KID. WE'VE ALL PREPARED FOR THIS MOMENT. THERE'S NO REASON TO PUT IT OFF.
BRRRR
INGG
THAT WAS FAST.
TOO FAST.

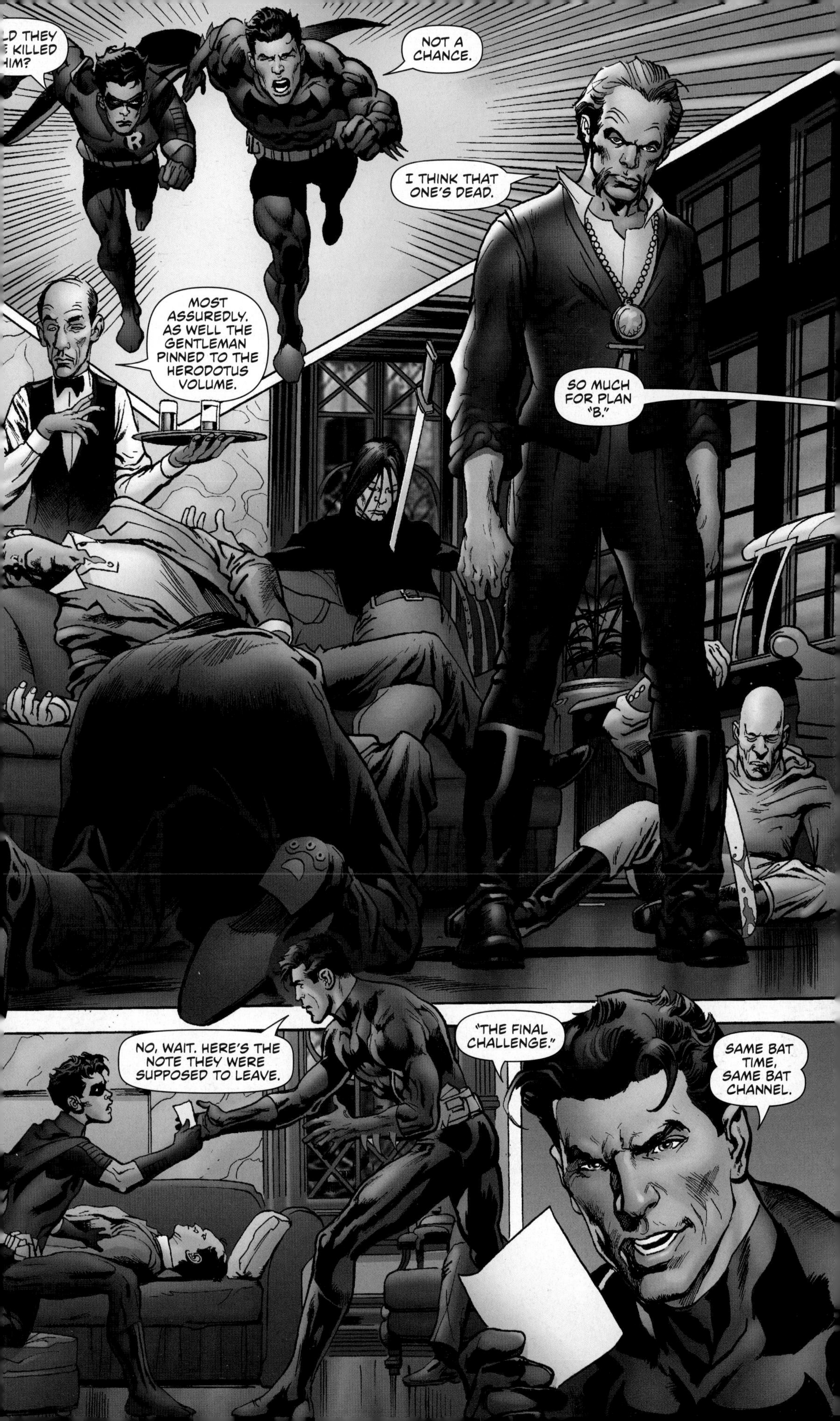
LD THEY
E KILLED
HIM?
NOT A CHANCE.
I THINK THAT ONE'S DEAD.
MOST ASSUREDLY. AS WELL THE GENTLEMAN PINNED TO THE HERODOTUS VOLUME.
SO MUCH FOR PLAN "B."
NO, WAIT. HERE'S THE NOTE THEY WERE SUPPOSED TO LEAVE.
"THE FINAL CHALLENGE."
SAME BAT TIME, SAME BAT CHANNEL.

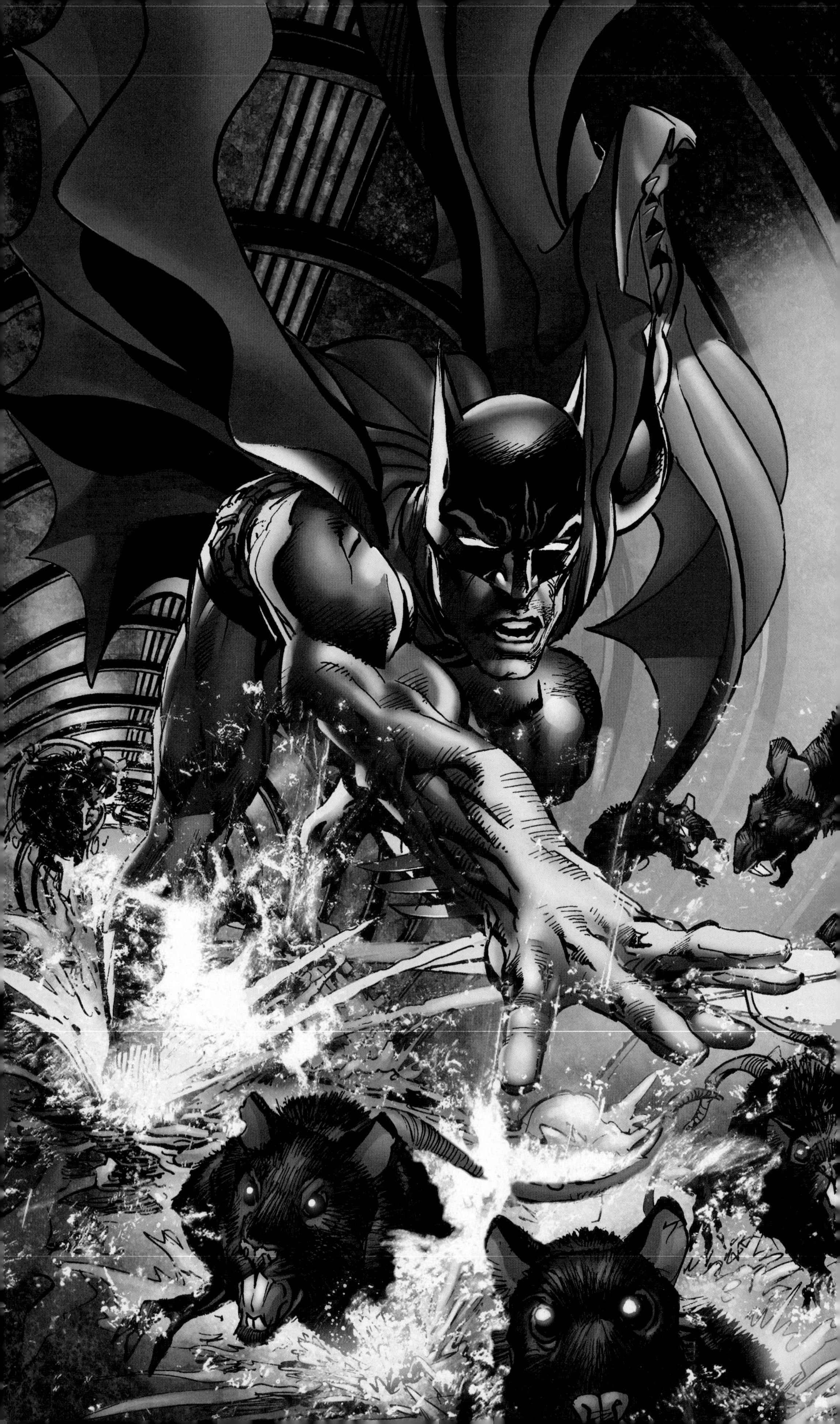

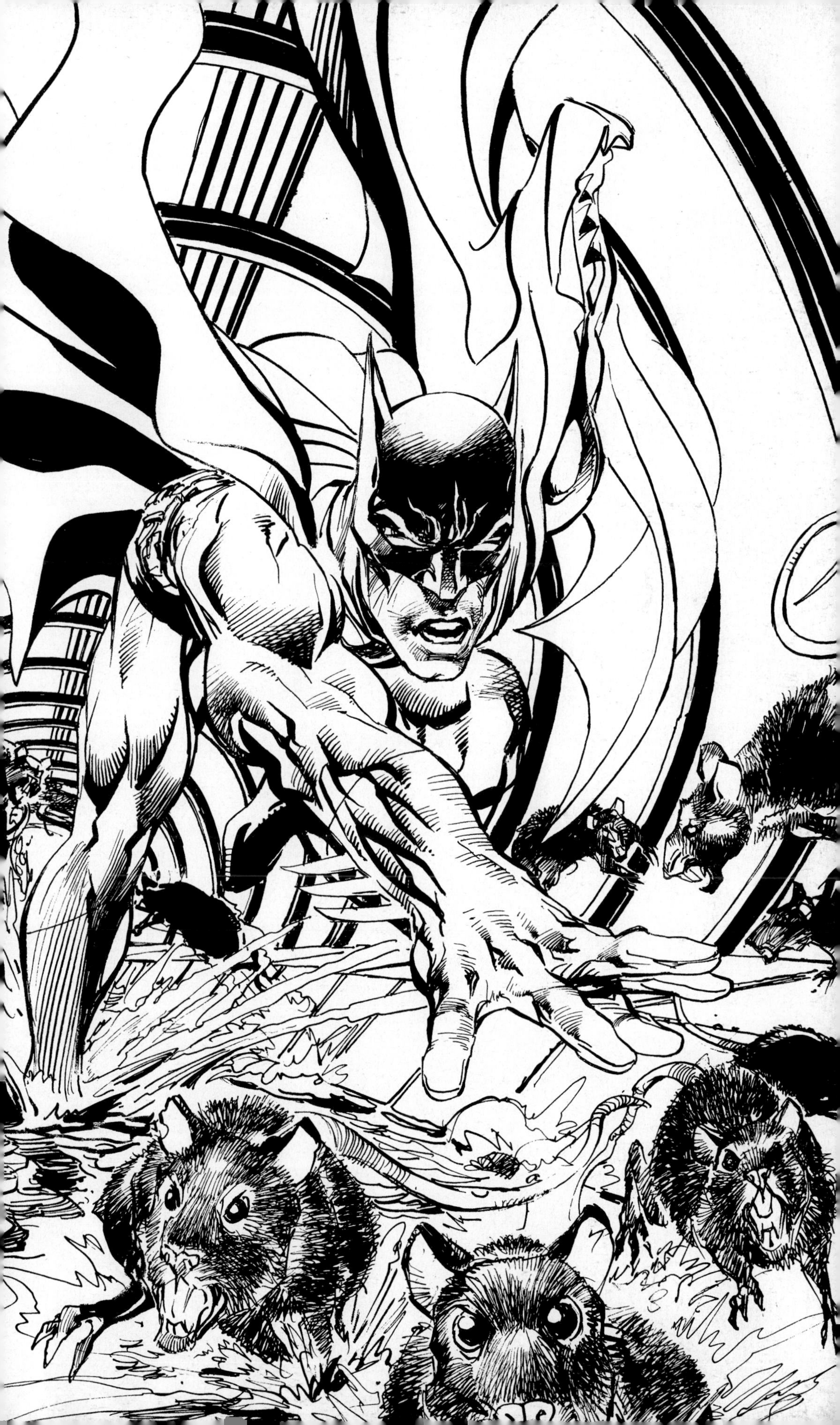

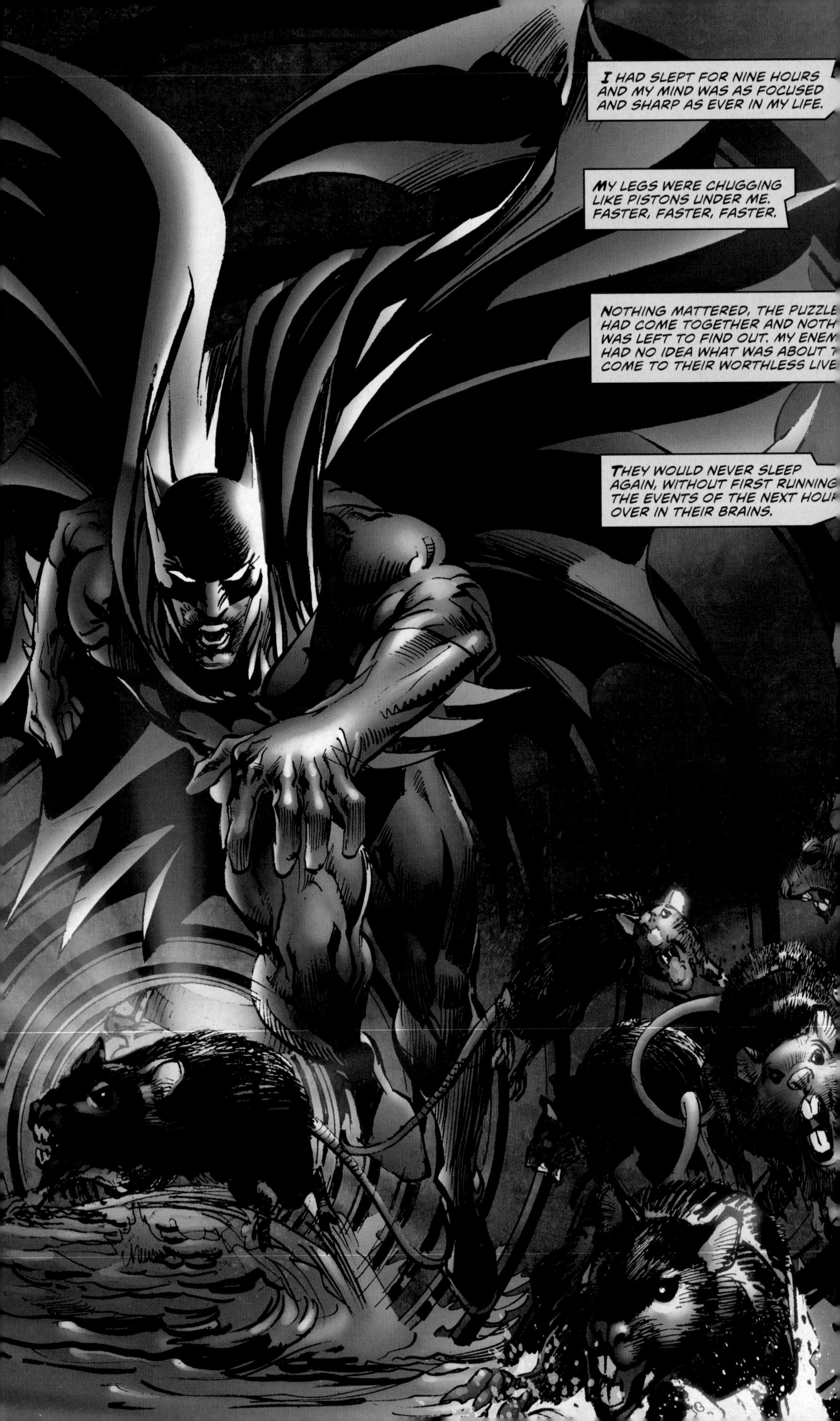
I HAD SLEPT FOR NINE HOURS AND MY MIND WAS AS FOCUSED AND SHARP AS EVER IN MY LIFE.
MY LEGS WERE CHUGGING LIKE PISTONS UNDER ME. FASTER, FASTER, FASTER.
NOTHING MATTERED, THE PUZZLE HAD COME TOGETHER AND NOTH WAS LEFT TO FIND OUT. MY ENEM HAD NO IDEA WHAT WAS ABOUT T COME TO THEIR WORTHLESS LIVE
THEY WOULD NEVER SLEEP AGAIN, WITHOUT FIRST RUNNING THE EVENTS OF THE NEXT HOU OVER IN THEIR BRAINS.

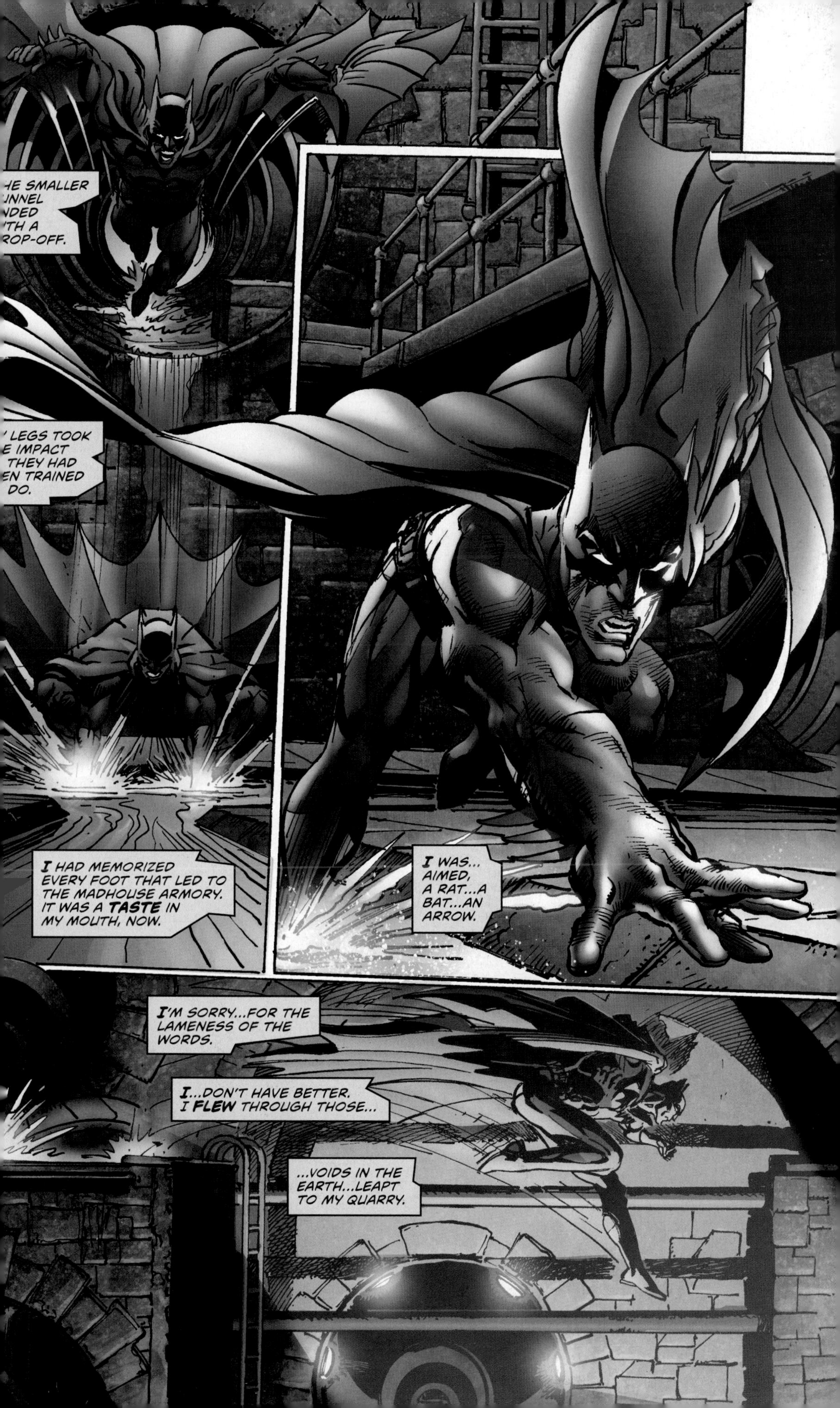
HE SMALLER UNNEL NDED TH A ROP-OFF.
LEGS TOOK E IMPACT THEY HAD EN TRAINED DO.
I HAD MEMORIZED EVERY FOOT THAT LED TO THE MADHOUSE ARMORY. IT WAS A TASTE IN MY MOUTH, NOW.
I WAS... AIMED, A RAT...A BAT...AN ARROW.
I'M SORRY...FOR THE LAMENESS OF THE WORDS.
I...DON'T HAVE BETTER. I FLEW THROUGH THOSE...
...VOIDS IN THE EARTH...LEAPT TO MY QUARRY.

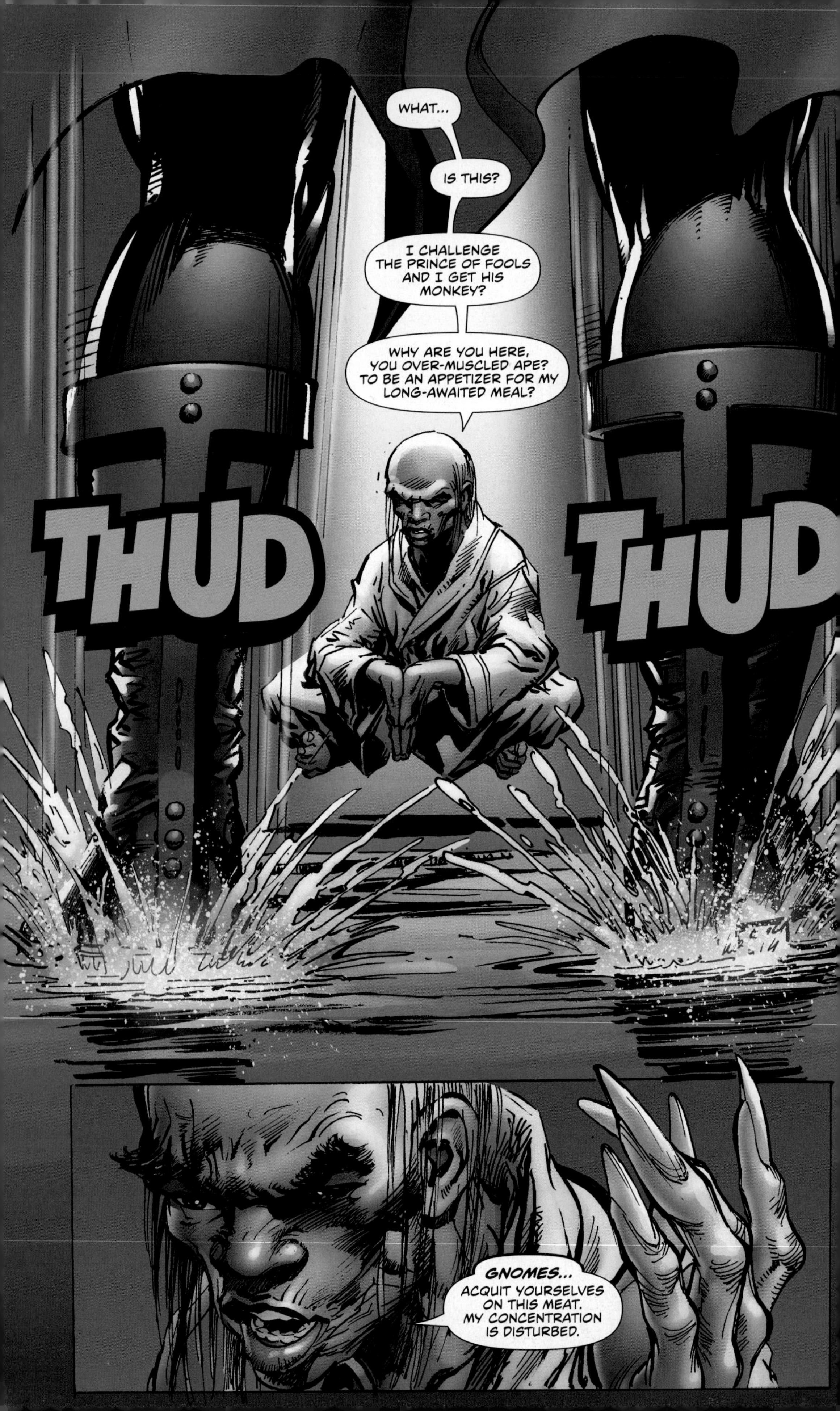
WHAT...
IS THIS?
I CHALLENGE THE PRINCE OF FOOLS AND I GET HIS MONKEY?
WHY ARE YOU HERE, YOU OVER-MUSCLED APE? TO BE AN APPETIZER FOR MY LONG-AWAITED MEAL?
THUD
THUD
GNOMES... ACQUIT YOURSELVES ON THIS MEAT. MY CONCENTRATION IS DISTURBED.

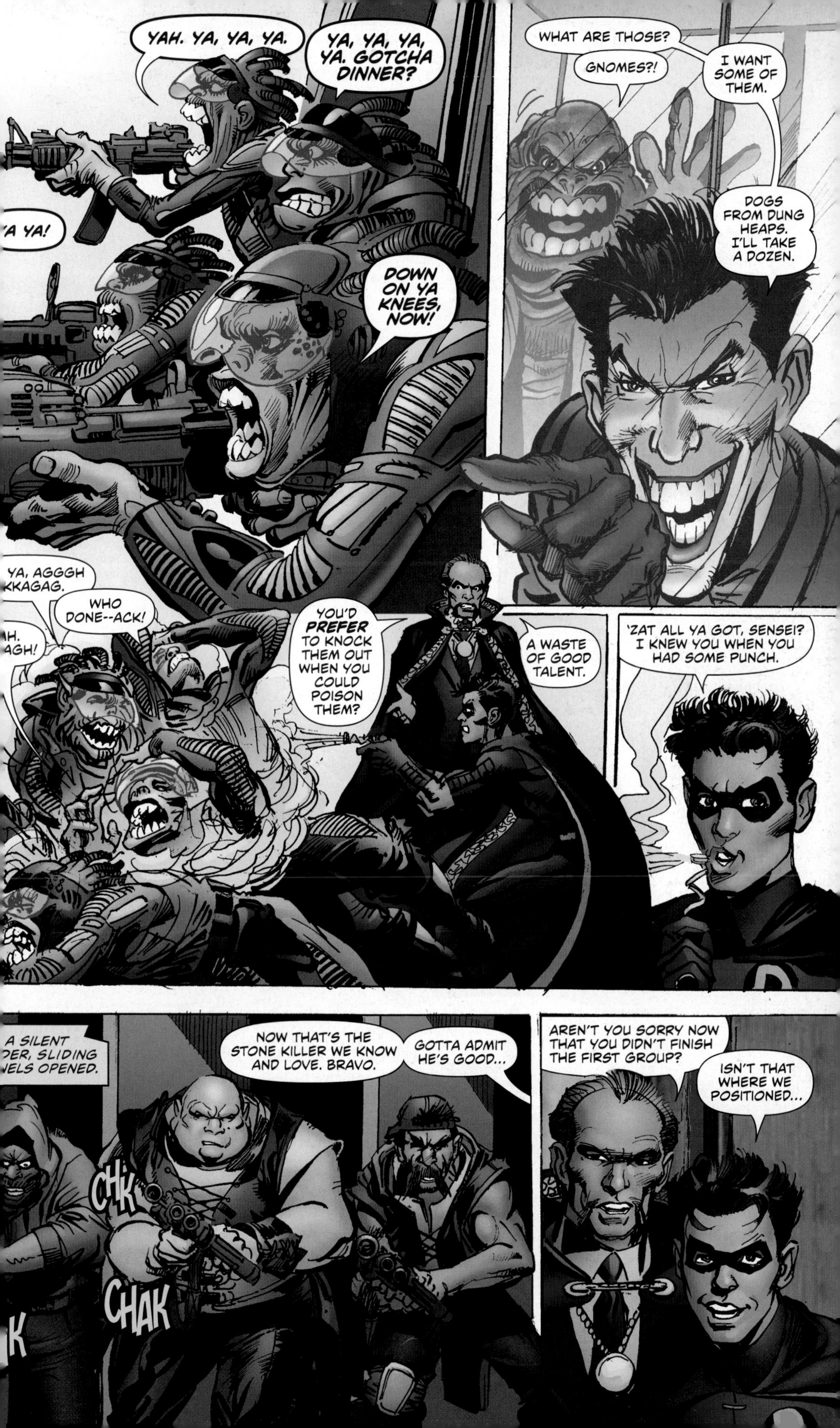
YAH. YA, YA, YA.
YA, YA, YA, YA. GOTCHA DINNER?
A YA!
DOWN ON YA KNEES, NOW!
WHAT ARE THOSE?
GNOMES?!
I WANT SOME OF THEM.
DOGS FROM DUNG HEAPS. I'LL TAKE A DOZEN.
YA, AGGGH KKAGAG.
WHO DONE--ACK!
H. AGH!
YOU'D **PREFER** TO KNOCK THEM OUT WHEN YOU COULD POISON THEM?
A WASTE OF GOOD TALENT.
'ZAT ALL YA GOT, SENSEI? I KNEW YOU WHEN YOU HAD SOME PUNCH.
A SILENT DER, SLIDING NELS OPENED.
NOW THAT'S THE STONE KILLER WE KNOW AND LOVE. BRAVO.
GOTTA ADMIT HE'S GOOD...
CHIK
CHAK
K
AREN'T YOU SORRY NOW THAT YOU DIDN'T FINISH THE FIRST GROUP?
ISN'T THAT WHERE WE POSITIONED...

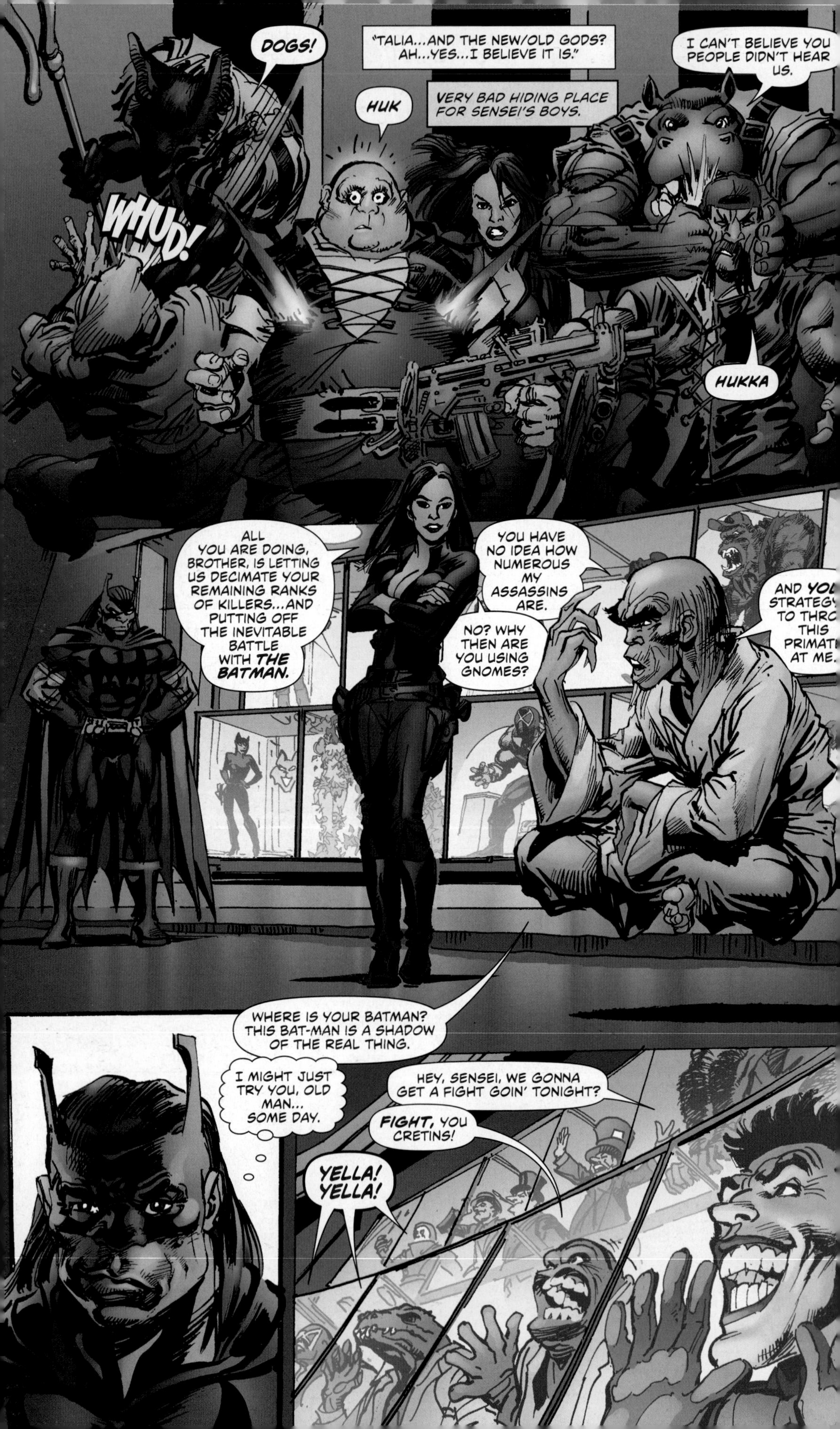
DOGS!
"TALIA...AND THE NEW/OLD GODS? AH...YES...I BELIEVE IT IS."
I CAN'T BELIEVE YOU PEOPLE DIDN'T HEAR US.
HUK
VERY BAD HIDING PLACE FOR SENSEI'S BOYS.
WHUD!
HUKKA
ALL YOU ARE DOING, BROTHER, IS LETTING US DECIMATE YOUR REMAINING RANKS OF KILLERS...AND PUTTING OFF THE INEVITABLE BATTLE WITH THE BATMAN.
YOU HAVE NO IDEA HOW NUMEROUS MY ASSASSINS ARE.
NO? WHY THEN ARE YOU USING GNOMES?
AND YOU STRATEGY TO THRO THIS PRIMAT AT ME.
WHERE IS YOUR BATMAN? THIS BAT-MAN IS A SHADOW OF THE REAL THING.
I MIGHT JUST TRY YOU, OLD MAN... SOME DAY.
HEY, SENSEI, WE GONNA GET A FIGHT GOIN' TONIGHT?
FIGHT, YOU CRETINS!
YELLA! YELLA!

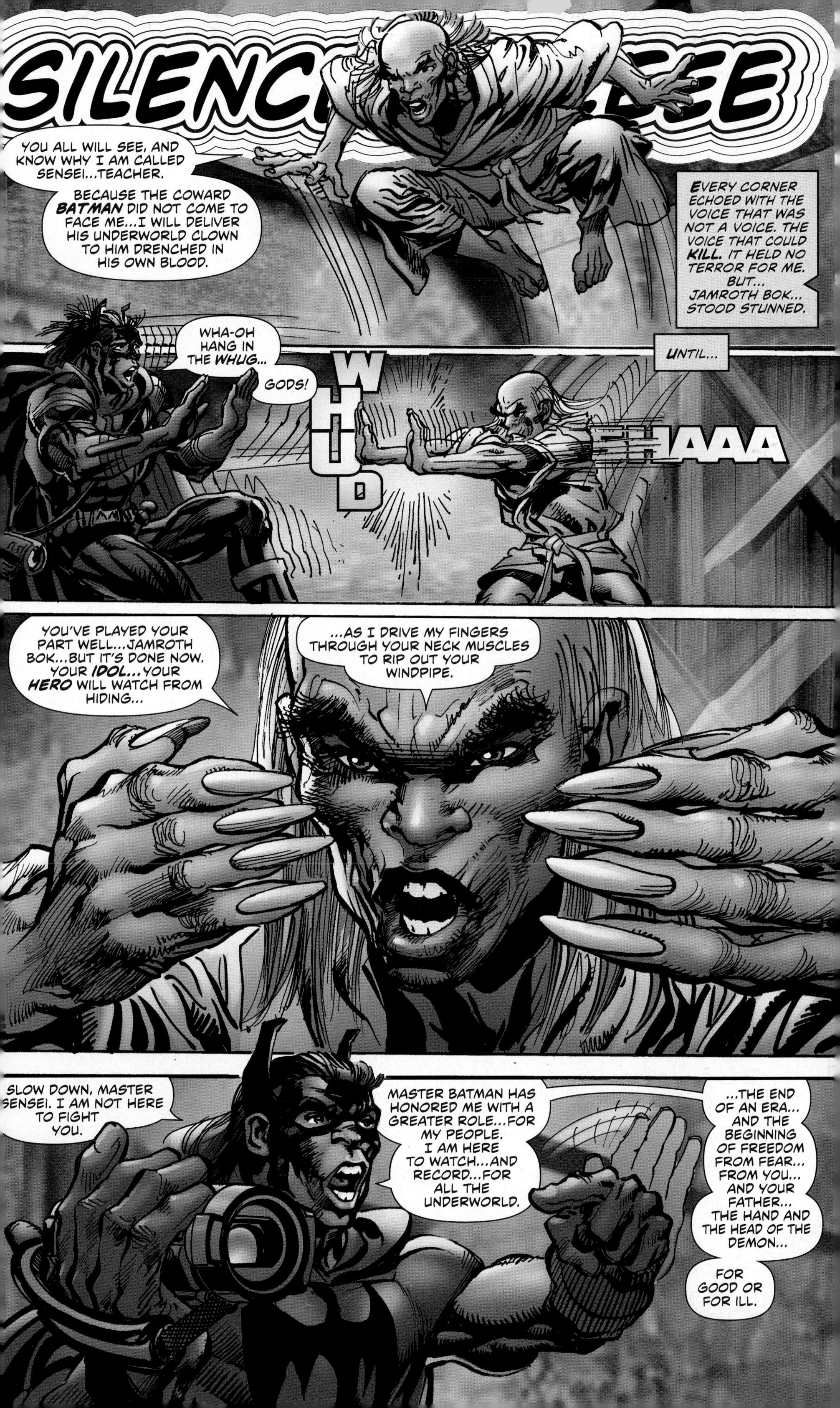
SILENCE ... EEEE
YOU ALL WILL SEE, AND KNOW WHY I AM CALLED SENSEI...TEACHER.
BECAUSE THE COWARD BATMAN DID NOT COME TO FACE ME...I WILL DELIVER HIS UNDERWORLD CLOWN TO HIM DRENCHED IN HIS OWN BLOOD.
EVERY CORNER ECHOED WITH THE VOICE THAT WAS NOT A VOICE. THE VOICE THAT COULD KILL. IT HELD NO TERROR FOR ME. BUT... JAMROTH BOK... STOOD STUNNED.
WHA-OH HANG IN THE WHUG...
GODS!
UNTIL...
WHUD
SHAAA
YOU'VE PLAYED YOUR PART WELL...JAMROTH BOK...BUT IT'S DONE NOW. YOUR IDOL...YOUR HERO WILL WATCH FROM HIDING...
...AS I DRIVE MY FINGERS THROUGH YOUR NECK MUSCLES TO RIP OUT YOUR WINDPIPE.
SLOW DOWN, MASTER SENSEI. I AM NOT HERE TO FIGHT YOU.
MASTER BATMAN HAS HONORED ME WITH A GREATER ROLE...FOR MY PEOPLE. I AM HERE TO WATCH...AND RECORD...FOR ALL THE UNDERWORLD.
...THE END OF AN ERA... AND THE BEGINNING OF FREEDOM FROM FEAR... FROM YOU... AND YOUR FATHER... THE HAND AND THE HEAD OF THE DEMON...
FOR GOOD OR FOR ILL.

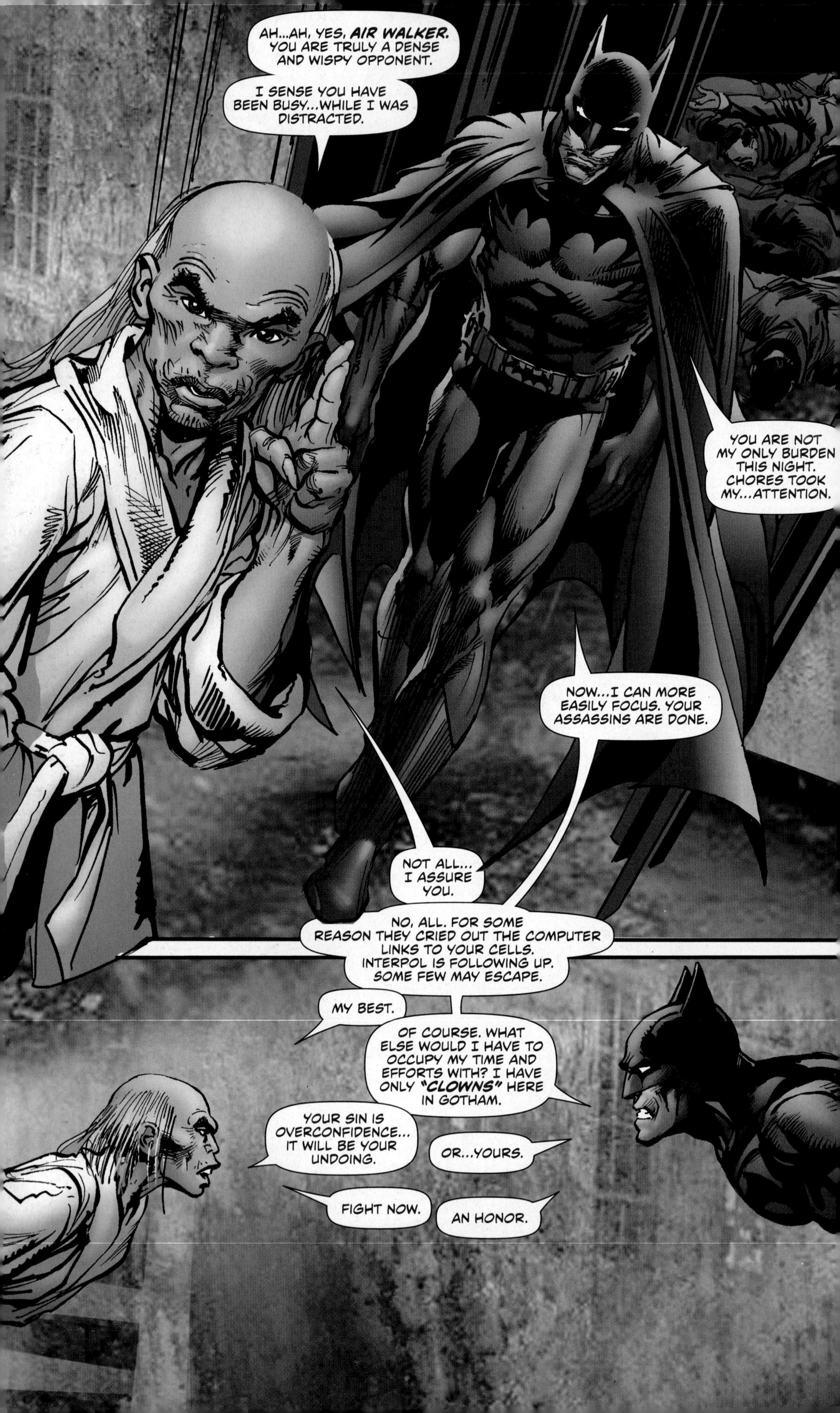
AH...AH, YES, AIR WALKER. YOU ARE TRULY A DENSE AND WISPY OPPONENT.
I SENSE YOU HAVE BEEN BUSY...WHILE I WAS DISTRACTED.
YOU ARE NOT MY ONLY BURDEN THIS NIGHT. CHORES TOOK MY...ATTENTION.
NOW...I CAN MORE EASILY FOCUS. YOUR ASSASSINS ARE DONE.
NOT ALL... I ASSURE YOU.
NO, ALL. FOR SOME REASON THEY CRIED OUT THE COMPUTER LINKS TO YOUR CELLS. INTERPOL IS FOLLOWING UP. SOME FEW MAY ESCAPE.
MY BEST.
OF COURSE. WHAT ELSE WOULD I HAVE TO OCCUPY MY TIME AND EFFORTS WITH? I HAVE ONLY "CLOWNS" HERE IN GOTHAM.
YOUR SIN IS OVERCONFIDENCE... IT WILL BE YOUR UNDOING.
OR...YOURS.
FIGHT NOW.
AN HONOR.

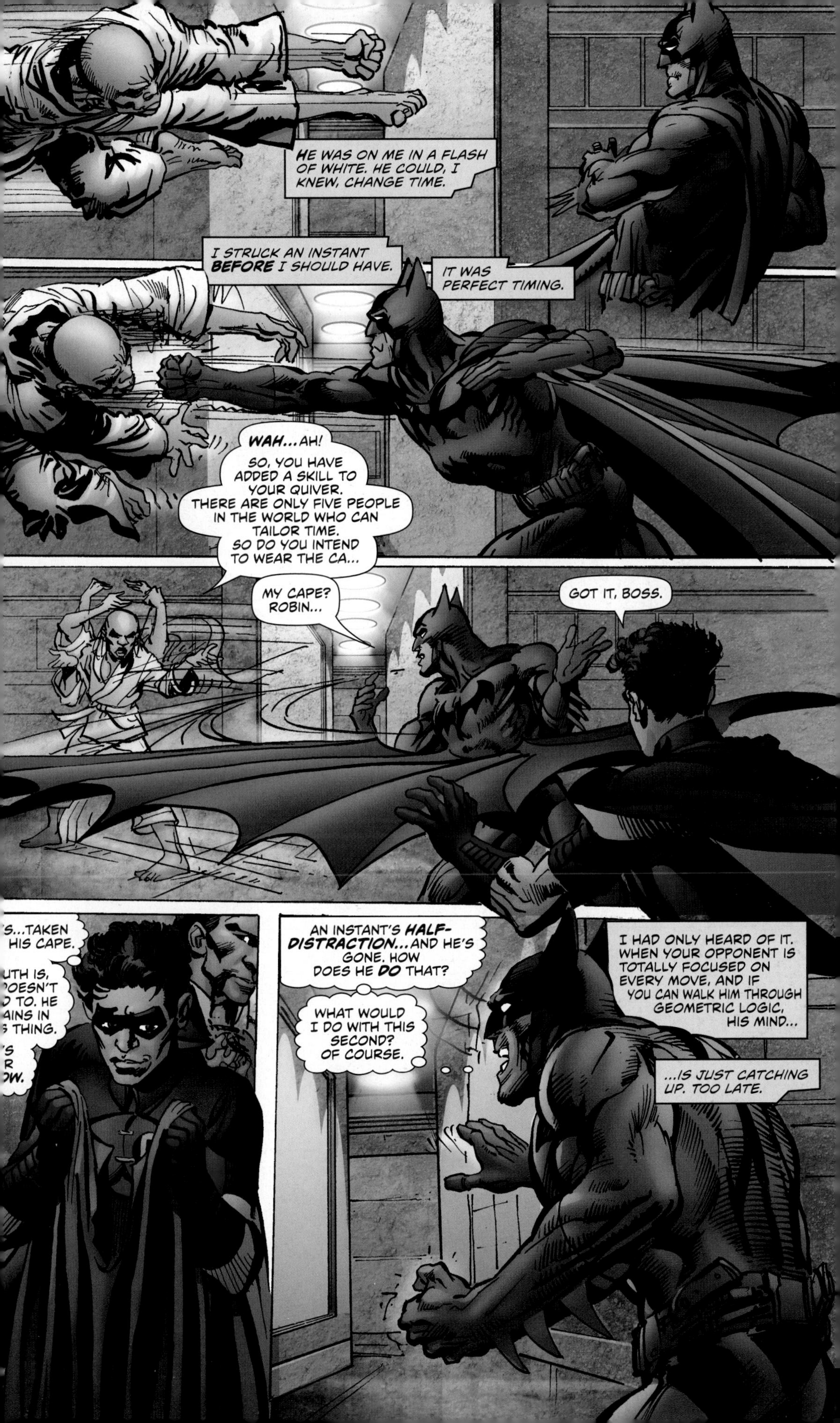

HE WAS ON ME IN A FLASH OF WHITE. HE COULD, I KNEW, CHANGE TIME.
I STRUCK AN INSTANT BEFORE I SHOULD HAVE.
IT WAS PERFECT TIMING.
WAH...AH!
SO, YOU HAVE ADDED A SKILL TO YOUR QUIVER. THERE ARE ONLY FIVE PEOPLE IN THE WORLD WHO CAN TAILOR TIME. SO DO YOU INTEND TO WEAR THE CA...
MY CAPE? ROBIN...
GOT IT, BOSS.
'S...TAKEN HIS CAPE.
UTH IS, OESN'T D TO. HE AINS IN S THING.
'S R OW.
AN INSTANT'S HALF-DISTRACTION...AND HE'S GONE. HOW DOES HE DO THAT?
WHAT WOULD I DO WITH THIS SECOND? OF COURSE.
I HAD ONLY HEARD OF IT. WHEN YOUR OPPONENT IS TOTALLY FOCUSED ON EVERY MOVE, AND IF YOU CAN WALK HIM THROUGH GEOMETRIC LOGIC, HIS MIND...
...IS JUST CATCHING UP. TOO LATE.

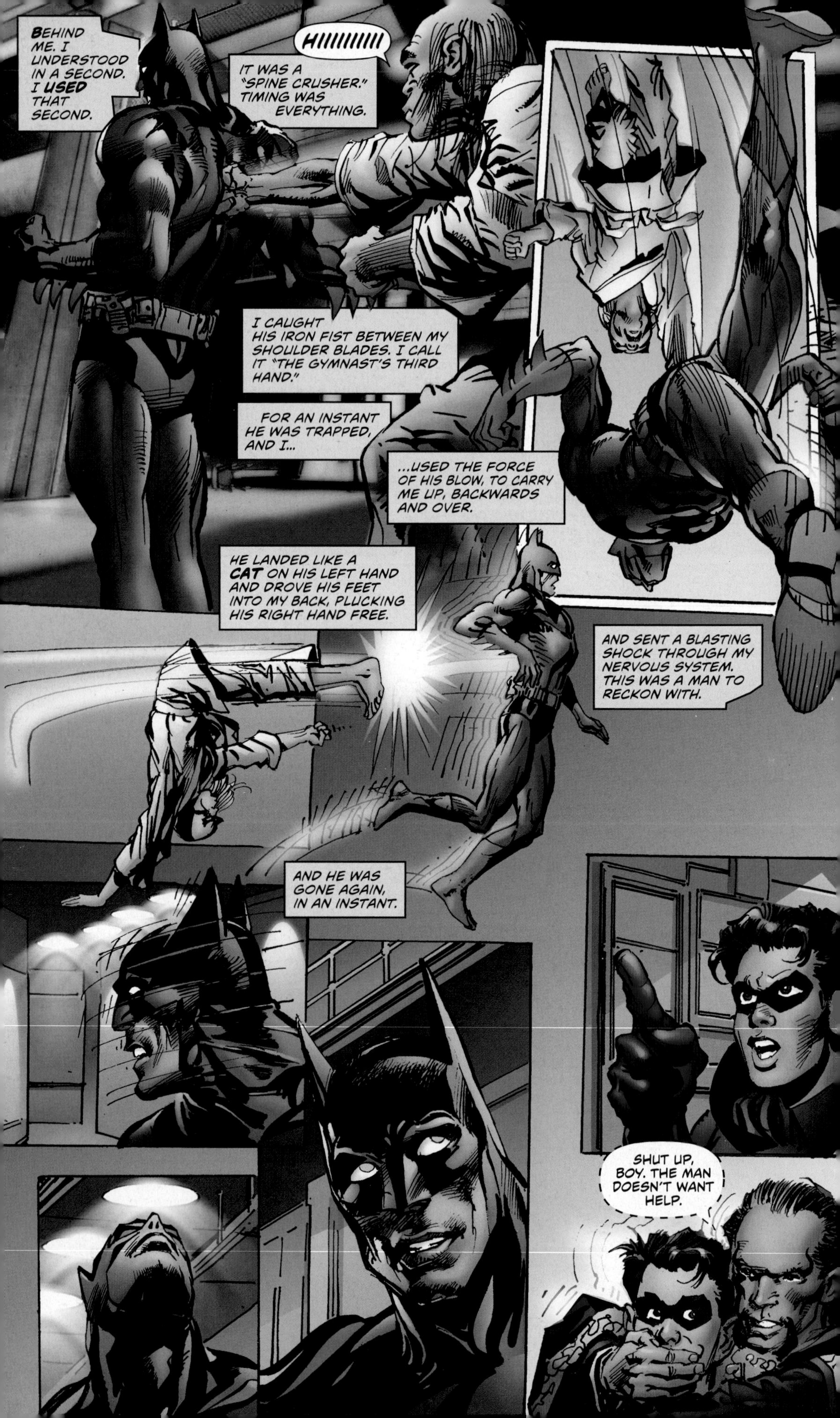
BEHIND ME. I UNDERSTOOD IN A SECOND. I USED THAT SECOND.
HIIIIIIIIII
IT WAS A "SPINE CRUSHER." TIMING WAS EVERYTHING.
I CAUGHT HIS IRON FIST BETWEEN MY SHOULDER BLADES. I CALL IT "THE GYMNAST'S THIRD HAND."
FOR AN INSTANT HE WAS TRAPPED, AND I...
...USED THE FORCE OF HIS BLOW, TO CARRY ME UP, BACKWARDS AND OVER.
HE LANDED LIKE A CAT ON HIS LEFT HAND AND DROVE HIS FEET INTO MY BACK, PLUCKING HIS RIGHT HAND FREE.
AND SENT A BLASTING SHOCK THROUGH MY NERVOUS SYSTEM. THIS WAS A MAN TO RECKON WITH.
AND HE WAS GONE AGAIN, IN AN INSTANT.
SHUT UP, BOY. THE MAN DOESN'T WANT HELP.

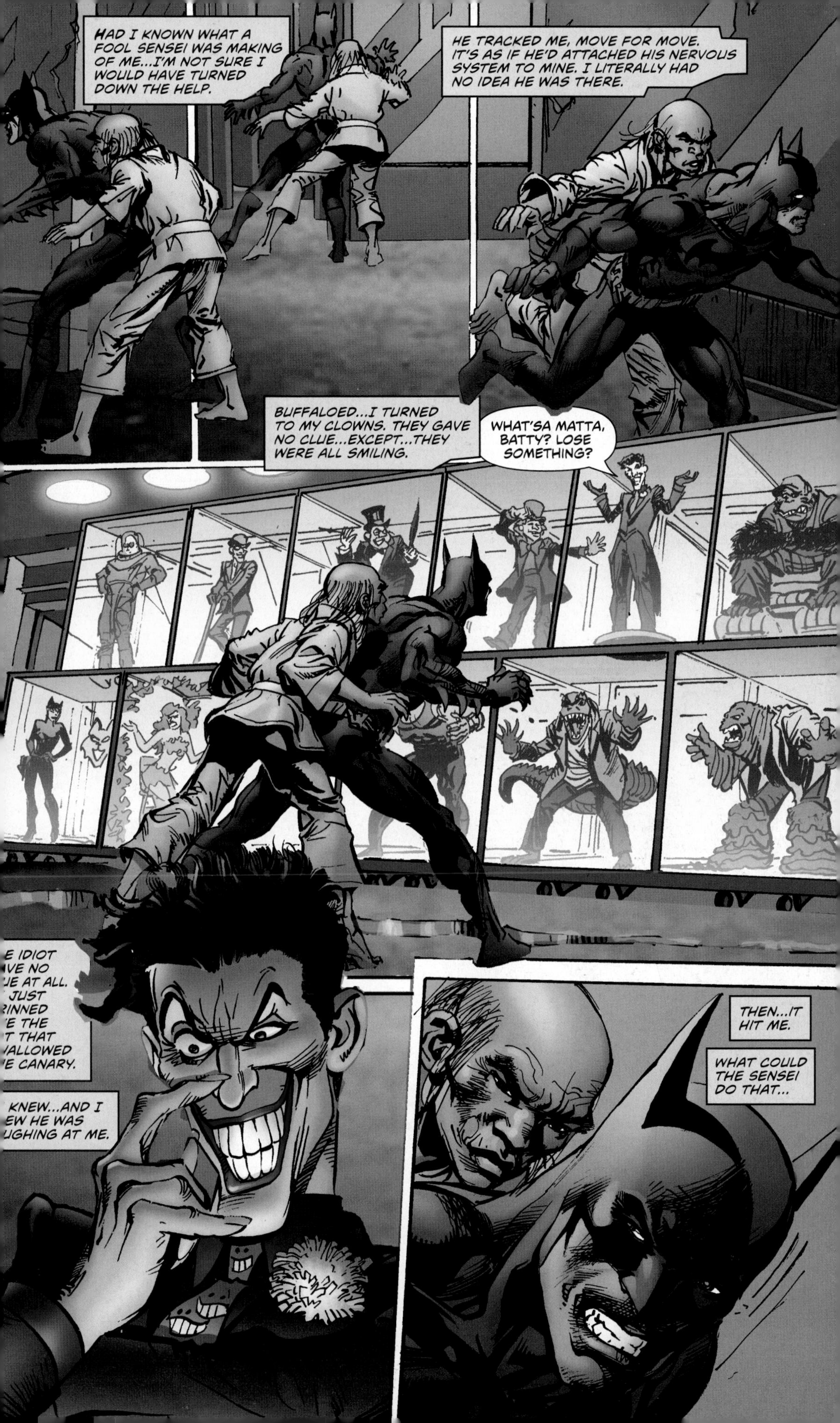

HAD I KNOWN WHAT A FOOL SENSEI WAS MAKING OF ME...I'M NOT SURE I WOULD HAVE TURNED DOWN THE HELP.
HE TRACKED ME, MOVE FOR MOVE. IT'S AS IF HE'D ATTACHED HIS NERVOUS SYSTEM TO MINE. I LITERALLY HAD NO IDEA HE WAS THERE.
BUFFALOED...I TURNED TO MY CLOWNS. THEY GAVE NO CLUE...EXCEPT...THEY WERE ALL SMILING.
WHAT'SA MATTA, BATTY? LOSE SOMETHING?
E IDIOT AVE NO UE AT ALL. JUST RINNED E THE T THAT WALLOWED E CANARY.
KNEW...AND I EW HE WAS UGHING AT ME.
THEN...IT HIT ME.
WHAT COULD THE SENSEI DO THAT...

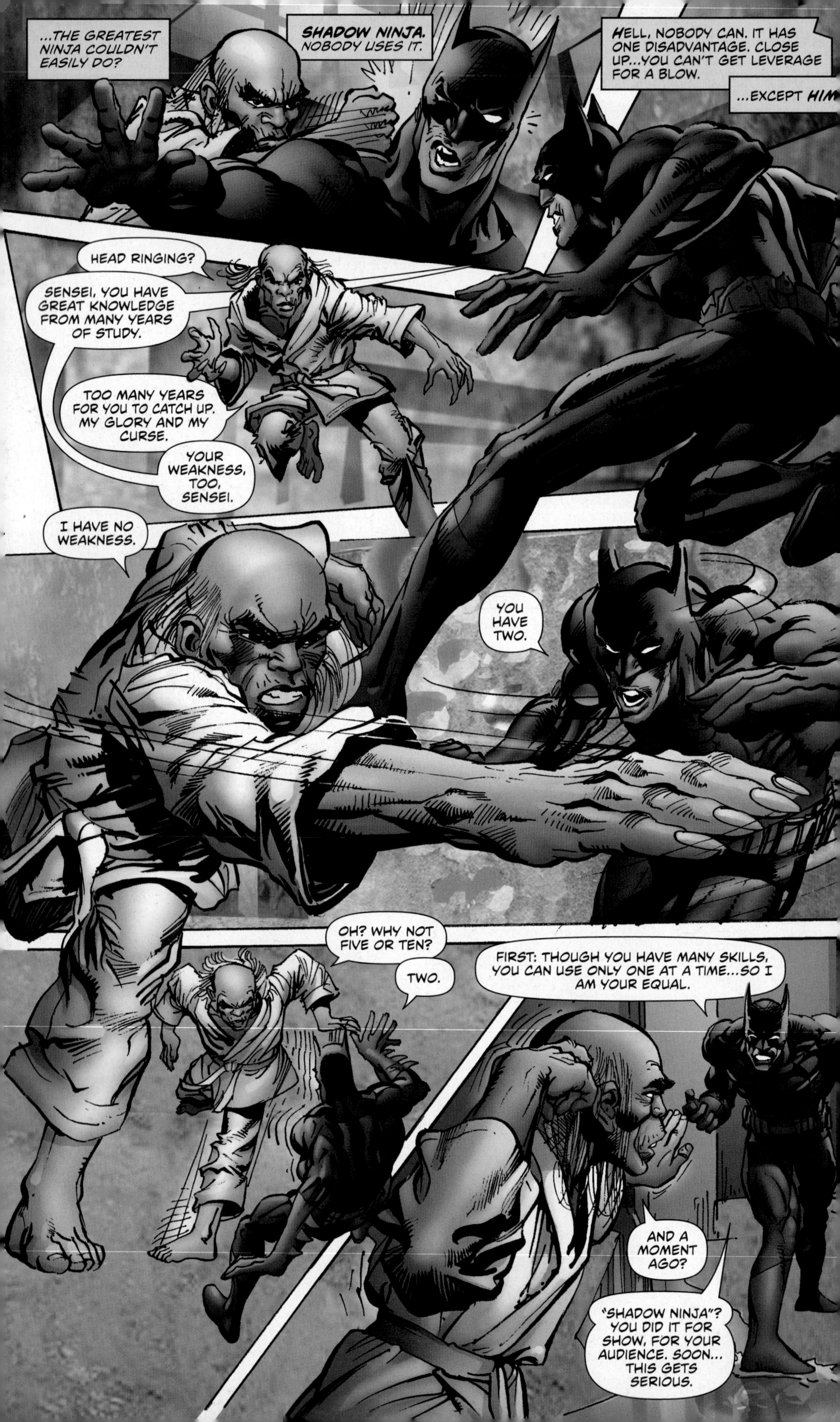
...THE GREATEST NINJA COULDN'T EASILY DO?
SHADOW NINJA. NOBODY USES IT.
HELL, NOBODY CAN. IT HAS ONE DISADVANTAGE. CLOSE UP...YOU CAN'T GET LEVERAGE FOR A BLOW.
...EXCEPT HIM
HEAD RINGING?
SENSEI, YOU HAVE GREAT KNOWLEDGE FROM MANY YEARS OF STUDY.
TOO MANY YEARS FOR YOU TO CATCH UP. MY GLORY AND MY CURSE.
YOUR WEAKNESS, TOO, SENSEI.
I HAVE NO WEAKNESS.
YOU HAVE TWO.
OH? WHY NOT FIVE OR TEN?
TWO.
FIRST: THOUGH YOU HAVE MANY SKILLS, YOU CAN USE ONLY ONE AT A TIME...SO I AM YOUR EQUAL.
AND A MOMENT AGO?
"SHADOW NINJA"? YOU DID IT FOR SHOW, FOR YOUR AUDIENCE. SOON... THIS GETS SERIOUS.

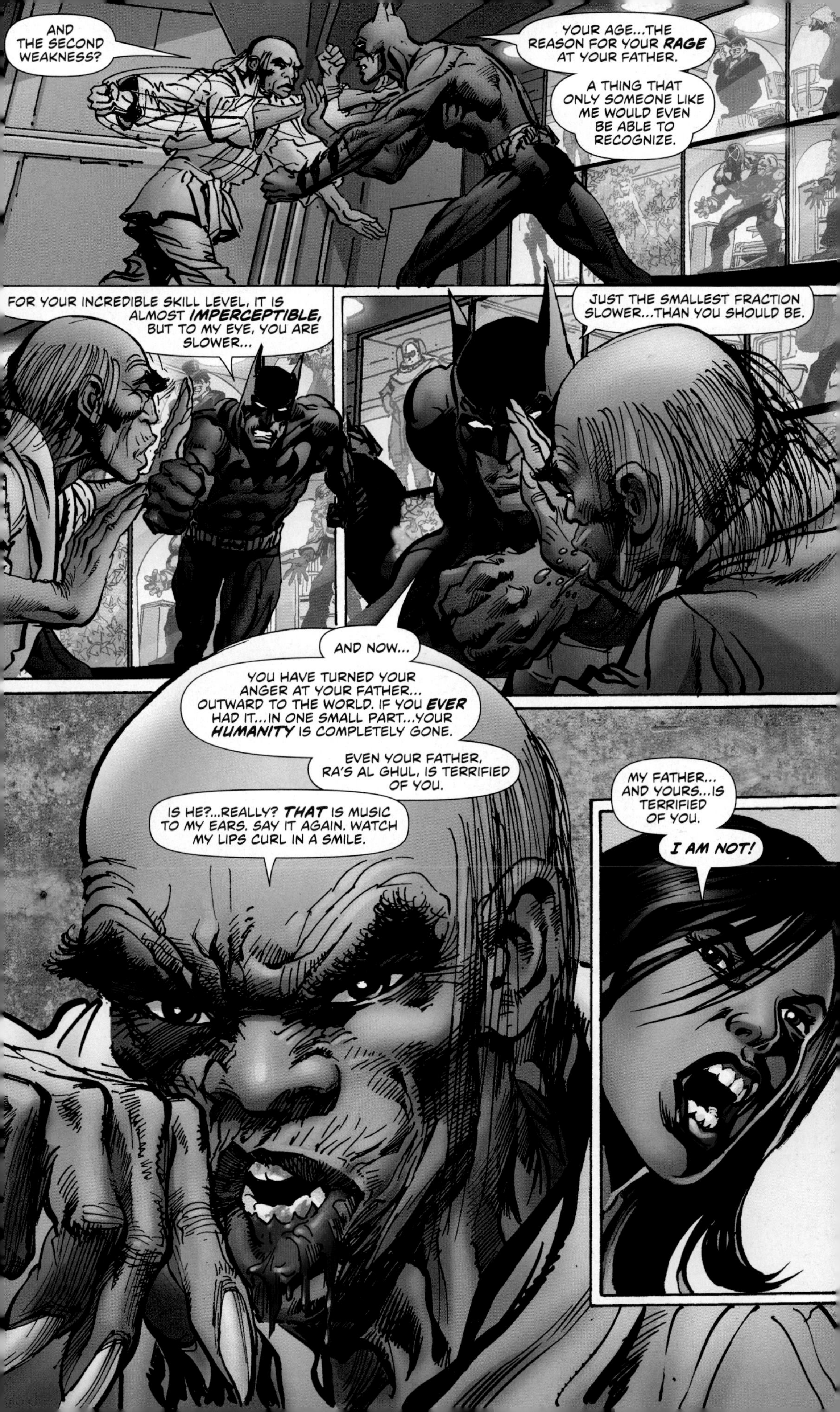
AND THE SECOND WEAKNESS?
YOUR AGE...THE REASON FOR YOUR RAGE AT YOUR FATHER.
A THING THAT ONLY SOMEONE LIKE ME WOULD EVEN BE ABLE TO RECOGNIZE.
FOR YOUR INCREDIBLE SKILL LEVEL, IT IS ALMOST IMPERCEPTIBLE, BUT TO MY EYE, YOU ARE SLOWER...
JUST THE SMALLEST FRACTION SLOWER...THAN YOU SHOULD BE.
AND NOW...
YOU HAVE TURNED YOUR ANGER AT YOUR FATHER... OUTWARD TO THE WORLD. IF YOU EVER HAD IT...IN ONE SMALL PART...YOUR HUMANITY IS COMPLETELY GONE.
EVEN YOUR FATHER, RA'S AL GHUL, IS TERRIFIED OF YOU.
IS HE?...REALLY? THAT IS MUSIC TO MY EARS. SAY IT AGAIN. WATCH MY LIPS CURL IN A SMILE.
MY FATHER... AND YOURS...IS TERRIFIED OF YOU.
I AM NOT!

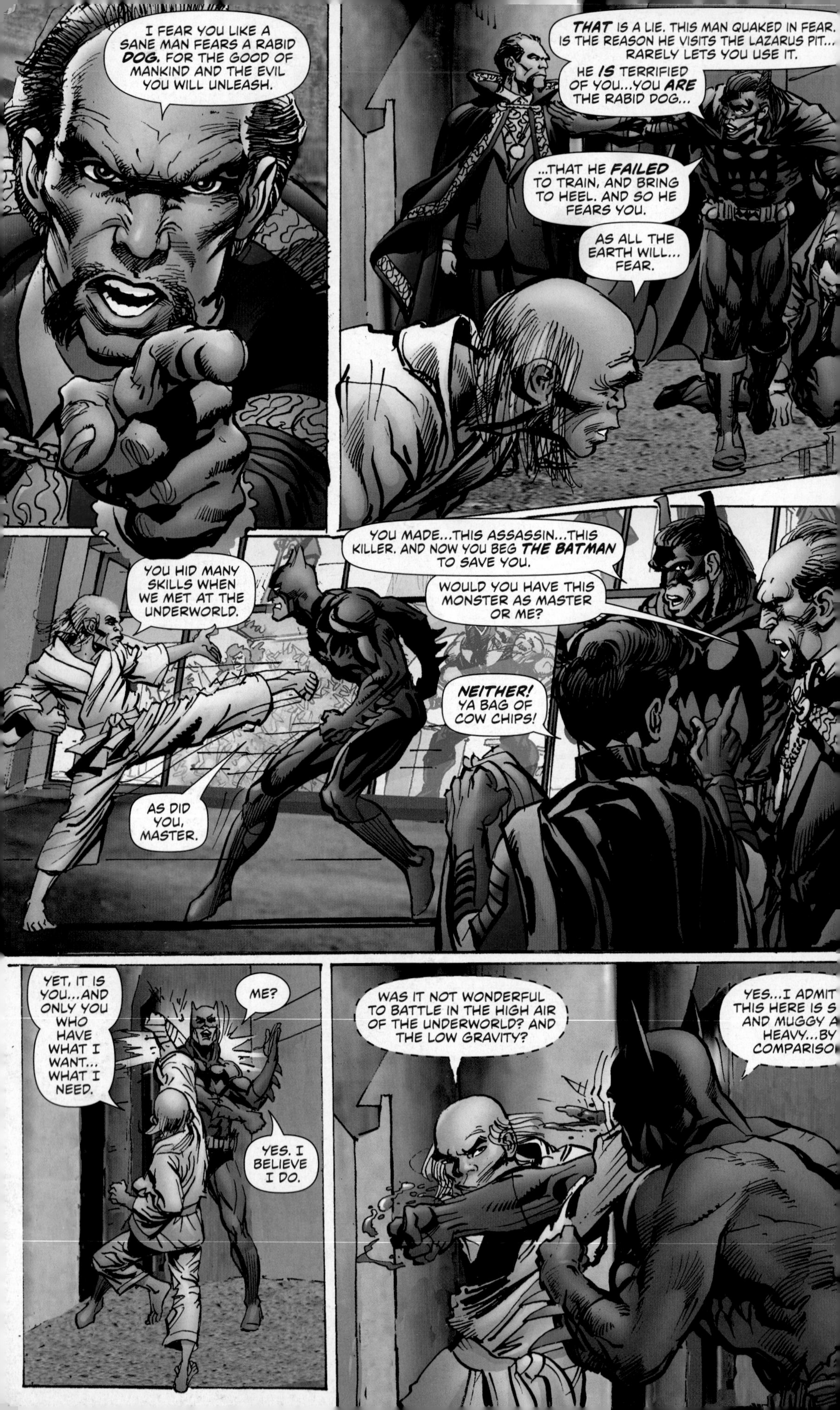
I FEAR YOU LIKE A SANE MAN FEARS A RABID **DOG.** FOR THE GOOD OF MANKIND AND THE EVIL YOU WILL UNLEASH.
THAT IS A LIE. THIS MAN QUAKED IN FEAR. IS THE REASON HE VISITS THE LAZARUS PIT... RARELY LETS YOU USE IT.
HE ***IS*** TERRIFIED OF YOU...YOU ***ARE*** THE RABID DOG...
...THAT HE ***FAILED*** TO TRAIN, AND BRING TO HEEL. AND SO HE FEARS YOU.
AS ALL THE EARTH WILL... FEAR.
YOU HID MANY SKILLS WHEN WE MET AT THE UNDERWORLD.
AS DID YOU, MASTER.
YOU MADE...THIS ASSASSIN...THIS KILLER. AND NOW YOU BEG ***THE BATMAN*** TO SAVE YOU.
WOULD YOU HAVE THIS MONSTER AS MASTER OR ME?
NEITHER! YA BAG OF COW CHIPS!
YET, IT IS YOU...AND ONLY YOU WHO HAVE WHAT I WANT... WHAT I NEED.
ME?
YES. I BELIEVE I DO.
WAS IT NOT WONDERFUL TO BATTLE IN THE HIGH AIR OF THE UNDERWORLD? AND THE LOW GRAVITY?
YES...I ADMIT THIS HERE IS S AND MUGGY A HEAVY...BY COMPARISO

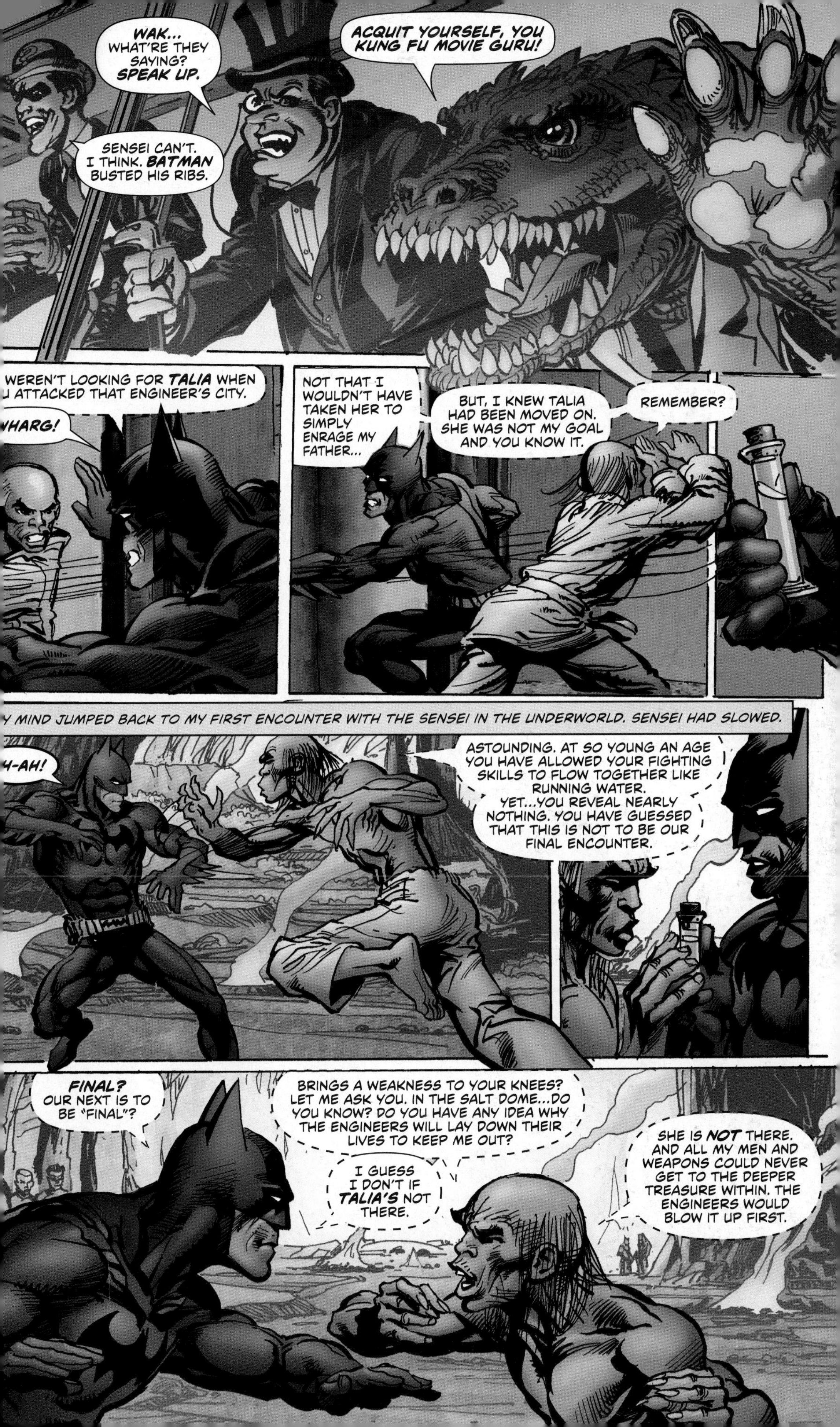
WAK... WHAT'RE THEY SAYING? SPEAK UP.
ACQUIT YOURSELF, YOU KUNG FU MOVIE GURU!
SENSEI CAN'T. I THINK. BATMAN BUSTED HIS RIBS.
WEREN'T LOOKING FOR TALIA WHEN
U ATTACKED THAT ENGINEER'S CITY.
WHARG!
NOT THAT I WOULDN'T HAVE TAKEN HER TO SIMPLY ENRAGE MY FATHER...
BUT, I KNEW TALIA HAD BEEN MOVED ON. SHE WAS NOT MY GOAL AND YOU KNOW IT.
REMEMBER?
Y MIND JUMPED BACK TO MY FIRST ENCOUNTER WITH THE SENSEI IN THE UNDERWORLD. SENSEI HAD SLOWED.
H-AH!
ASTOUNDING. AT SO YOUNG AN AGE YOU HAVE ALLOWED YOUR FIGHTING SKILLS TO FLOW TOGETHER LIKE RUNNING WATER. YET...YOU REVEAL NEARLY NOTHING. YOU HAVE GUESSED THAT THIS IS NOT TO BE OUR FINAL ENCOUNTER.
FINAL? OUR NEXT IS TO BE "FINAL"?
BRINGS A WEAKNESS TO YOUR KNEES? LET ME ASK YOU. IN THE SALT DOME...DO YOU KNOW? DO YOU HAVE ANY IDEA WHY THE ENGINEERS WILL LAY DOWN THEIR LIVES TO KEEP ME OUT?
I GUESS I DON'T IF TALIA'S NOT THERE.
SHE IS NOT THERE. AND ALL MY MEN AND WEAPONS COULD NEVER GET TO THE DEEPER TREASURE WITHIN. THE ENGINEERS WOULD BLOW IT UP FIRST.

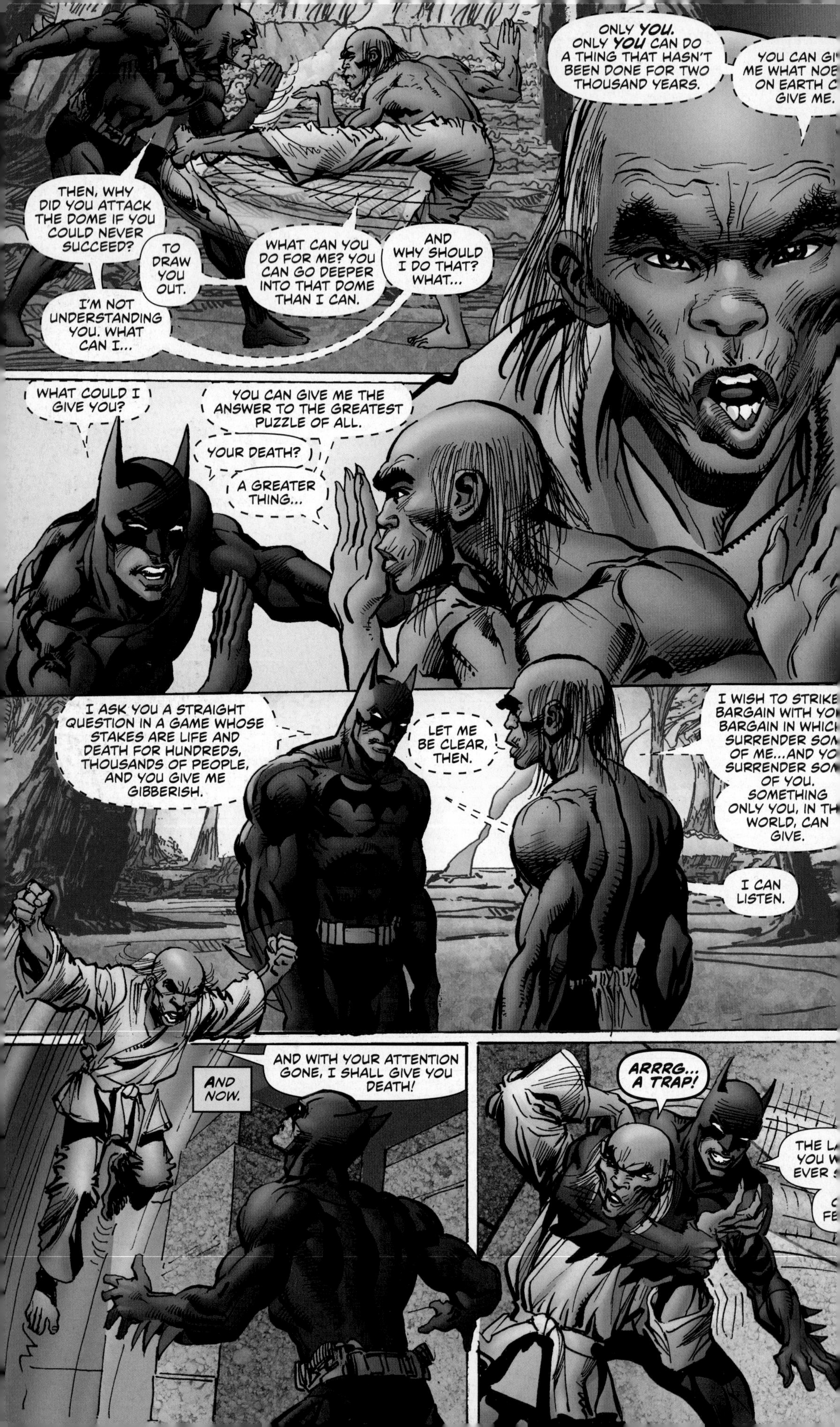
THEN, WHY DID YOU ATTACK THE DOME IF YOU COULD NEVER SUCCEED?
TO DRAW YOU OUT.
I'M NOT UNDERSTANDING YOU. WHAT CAN I...
WHAT CAN YOU DO FOR ME? YOU CAN GO DEEPER INTO THAT DOME THAN I CAN.
AND WHY SHOULD I DO THAT? WHAT...
ONLY YOU. ONLY YOU CAN DO A THING THAT HASN'T BEEN DONE FOR TWO THOUSAND YEARS.
YOU CAN GI ME WHAT NOB ON EARTH C GIVE ME.
WHAT COULD I GIVE YOU?
YOU CAN GIVE ME THE ANSWER TO THE GREATEST PUZZLE OF ALL.
YOUR DEATH?
A GREATER THING...
I ASK YOU A STRAIGHT QUESTION IN A GAME WHOSE STAKES ARE LIFE AND DEATH FOR HUNDREDS, THOUSANDS OF PEOPLE, AND YOU GIVE ME GIBBERISH.
LET ME BE CLEAR, THEN.
I WISH TO STRIKE BARGAIN WITH YO BARGAIN IN WHICH SURRENDER SOM OF ME...AND YO SURRENDER SOM OF YOU. SOMETHING ONLY YOU, IN TH WORLD, CAN GIVE.
I CAN LISTEN.
AND NOW.
AND WITH YOUR ATTENTION GONE, I SHALL GIVE YOU DEATH!
ARRRG... A TRAP!
THE L YOU W EVER S

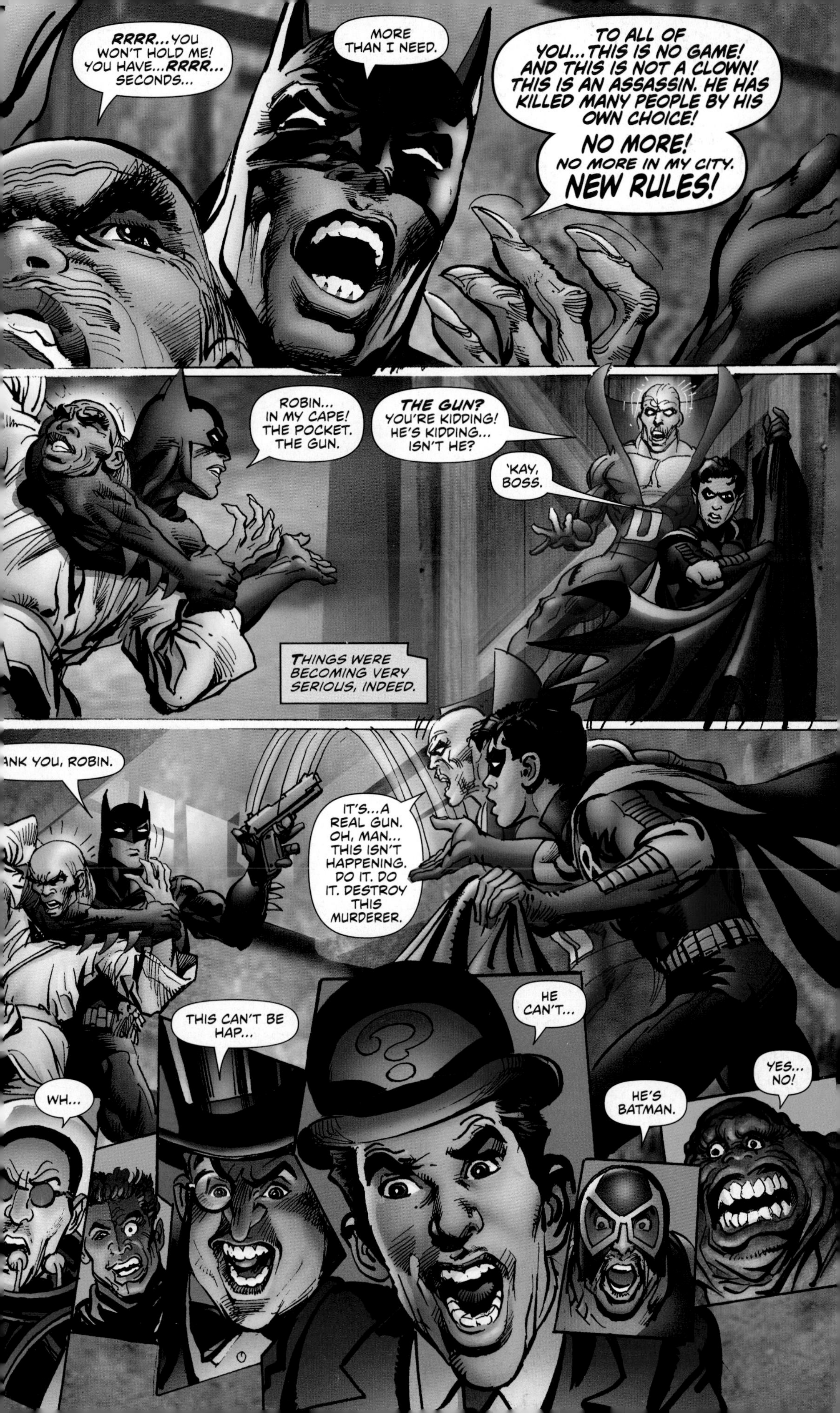
RRRR...YOU WON'T HOLD ME! YOU HAVE...RRRR... SECONDS...
MORE THAN I NEED.
TO ALL OF YOU...THIS IS NO GAME! AND THIS IS NOT A CLOWN! THIS IS AN ASSASSIN. HE HAS KILLED MANY PEOPLE BY HIS OWN CHOICE!
NO MORE! NO MORE IN MY CITY. NEW RULES!
ROBIN... IN MY CAPE! THE POCKET. THE GUN.
THE GUN? YOU'RE KIDDING! HE'S KIDDING... ISN'T HE?
'KAY, BOSS.
THINGS WERE BECOMING VERY SERIOUS, INDEED.
ANK YOU, ROBIN.
IT'S...A REAL GUN. OH, MAN... THIS ISN'T HAPPENING. DO IT. DO IT. DESTROY THIS MURDERER.
WH...
THIS CAN'T BE HAP...
HE CAN'T...
HE'S BATMAN.
YES... NO!

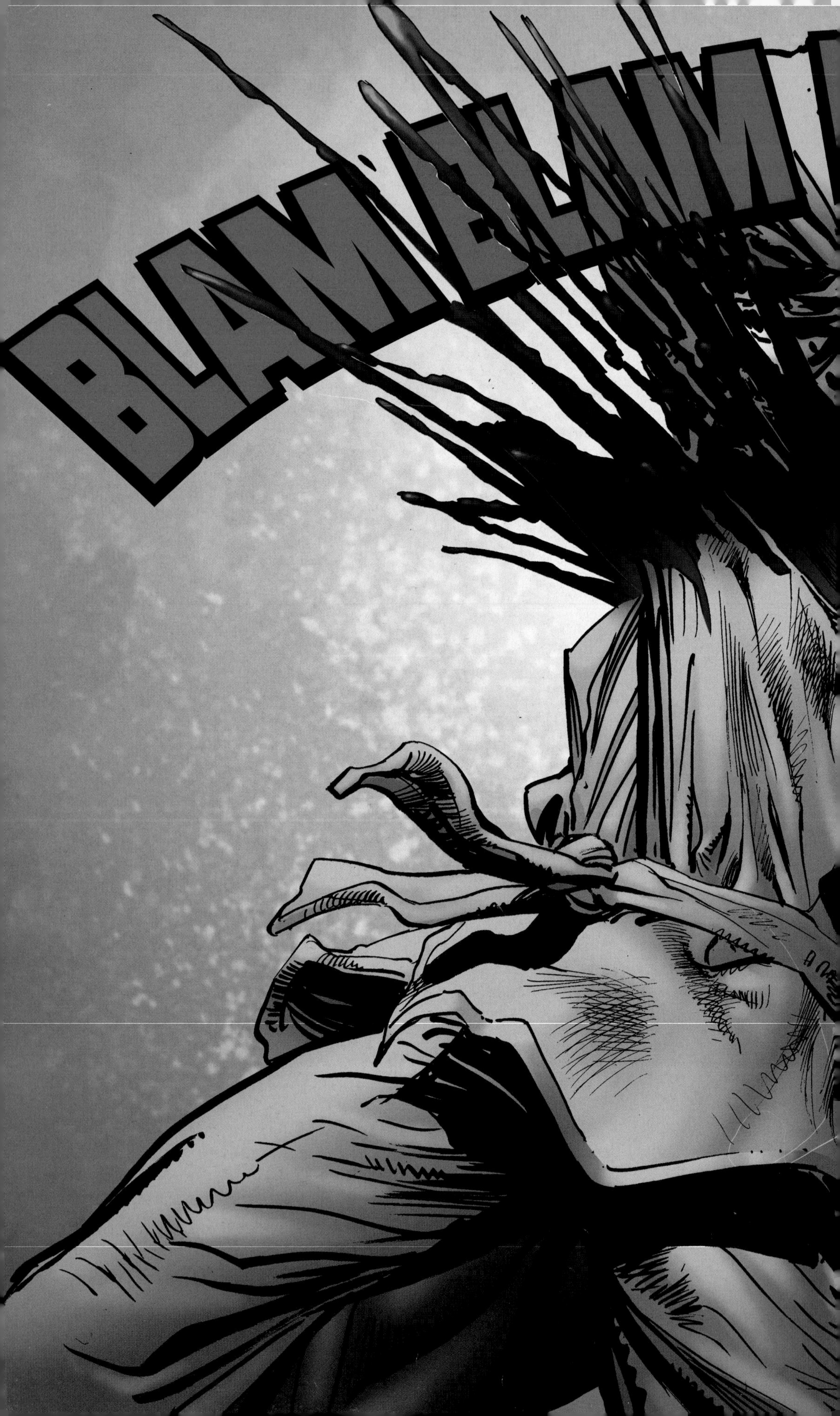
BLAM! BLAM

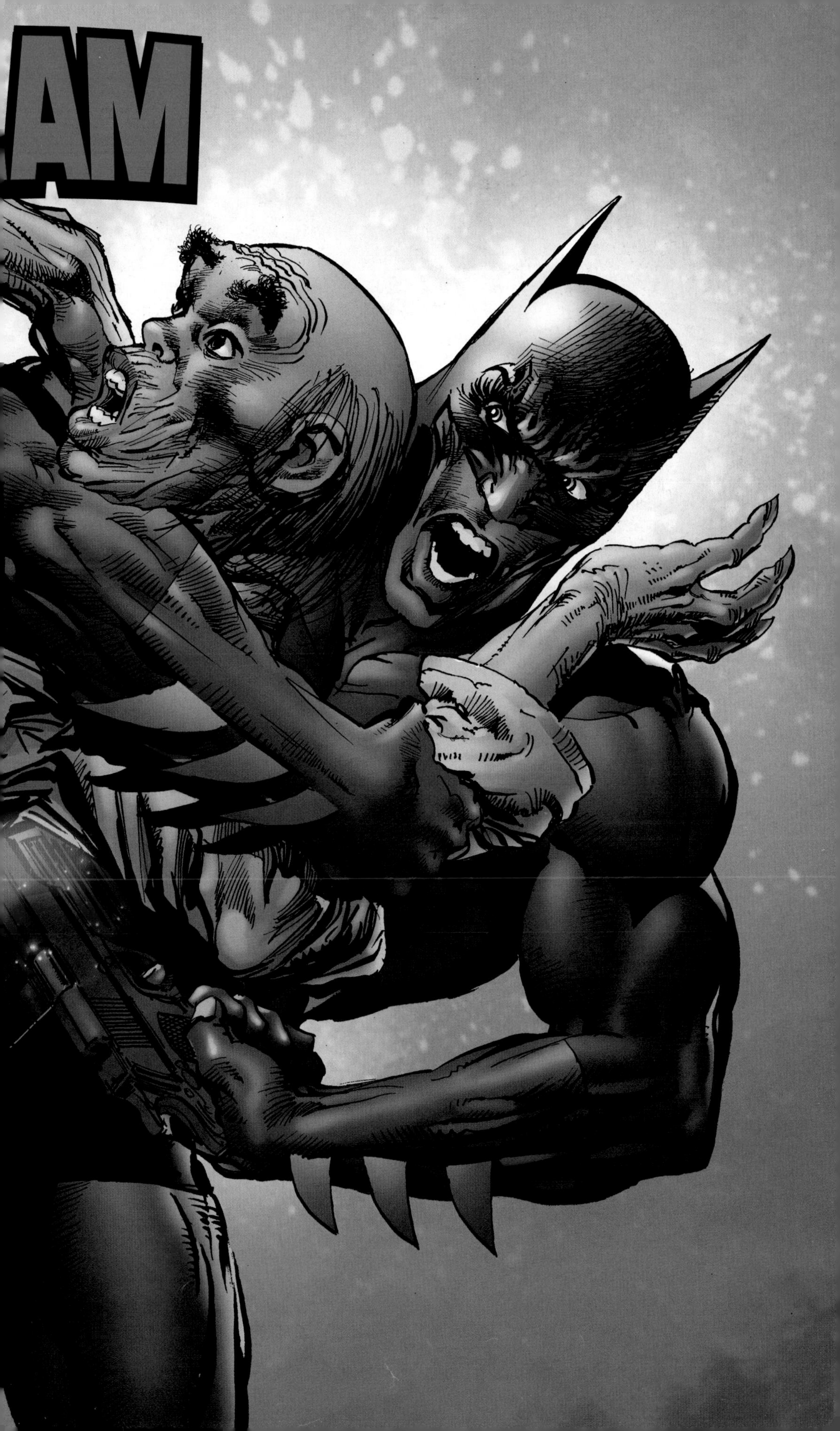
AM

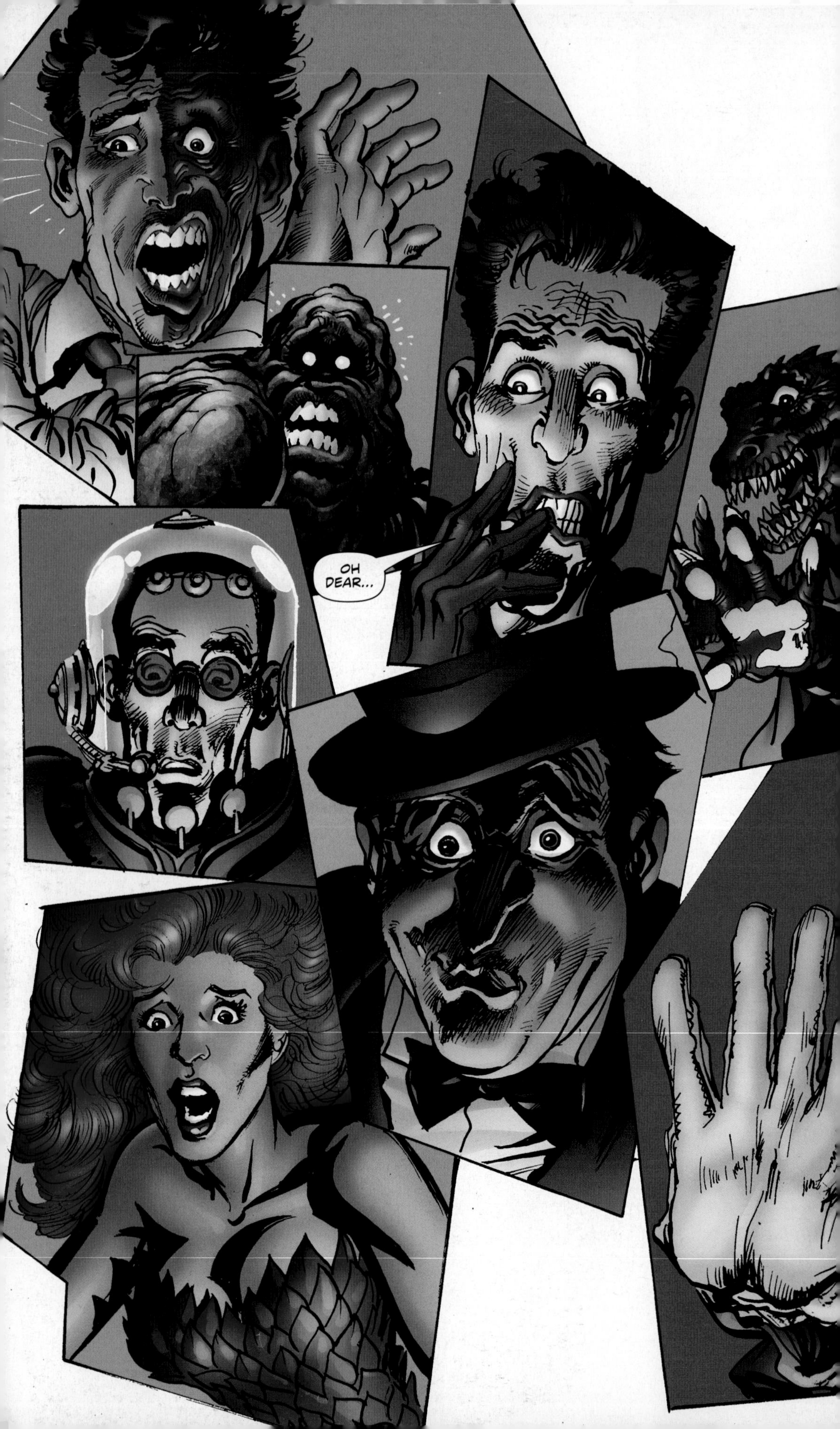
OH DEAR...

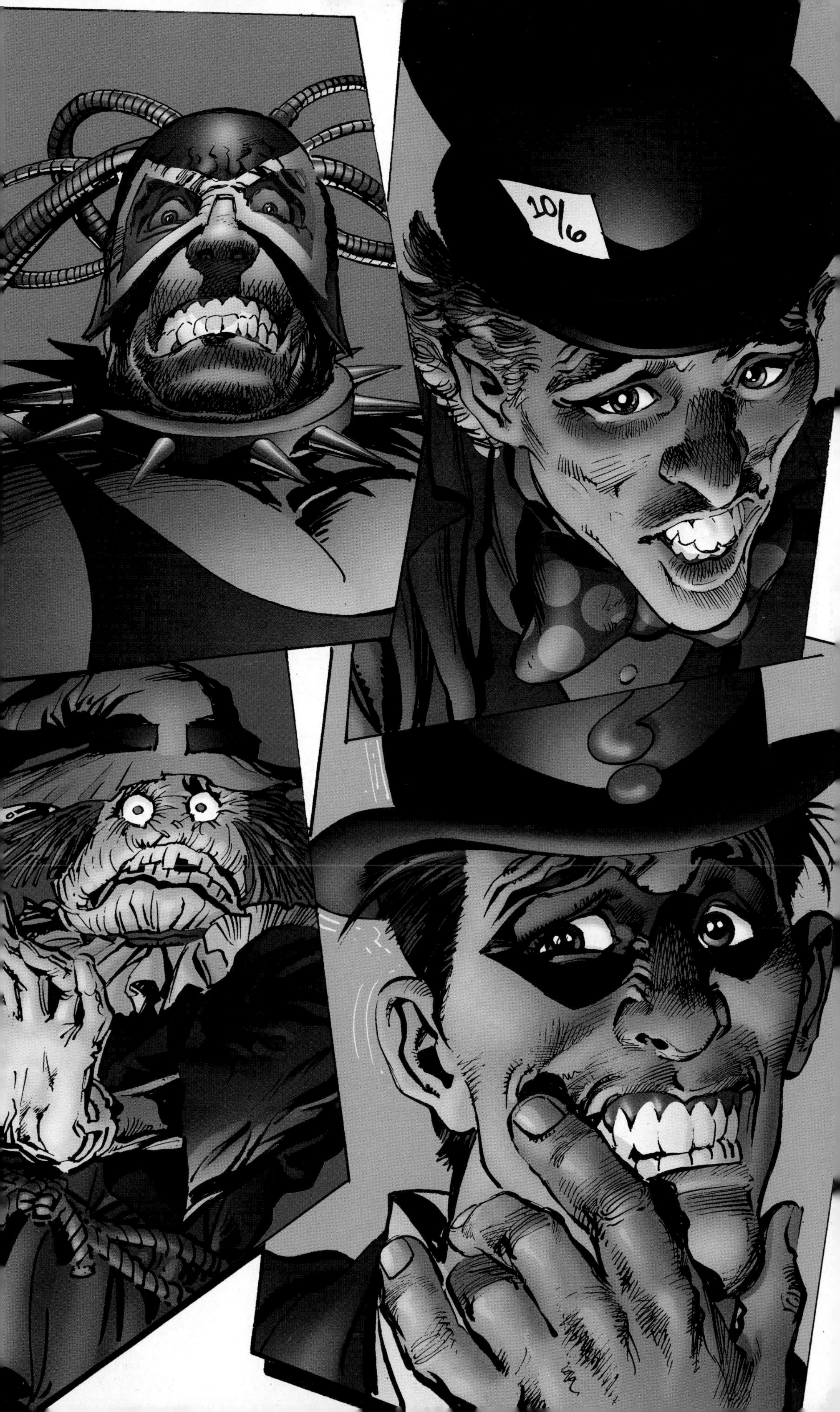
10/6

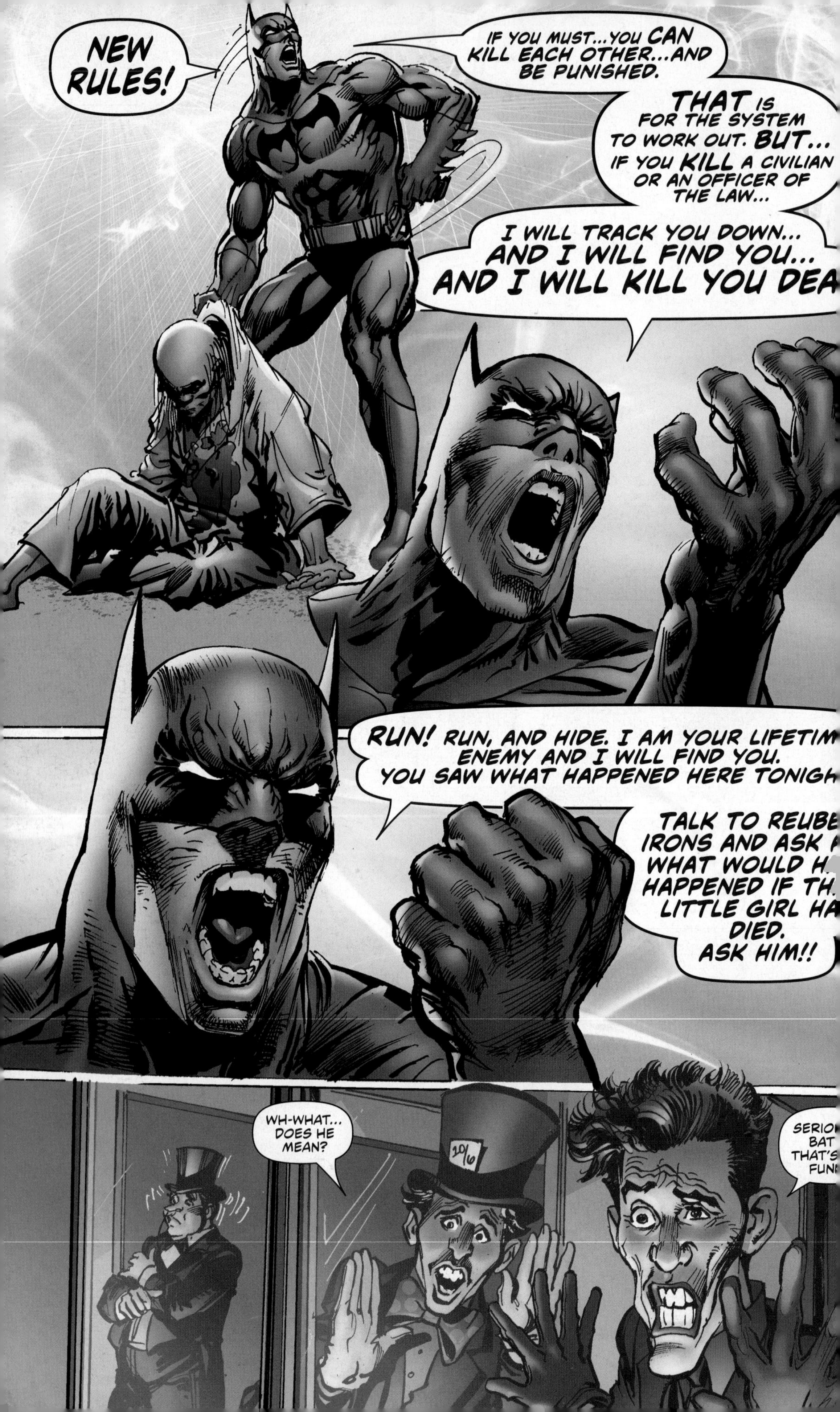
NEW RULES!
IF YOU MUST...YOU CAN KILL EACH OTHER...AND BE PUNISHED.
THAT IS FOR THE SYSTEM TO WORK OUT. BUT... IF YOU KILL A CIVILIAN OR AN OFFICER OF THE LAW...
I WILL TRACK YOU DOWN... AND I WILL FIND YOU... AND I WILL KILL YOU DEA
RUN! RUN, AND HIDE. I AM YOUR LIFETIM ENEMY AND I WILL FIND YOU. YOU SAW WHAT HAPPENED HERE TONIGH
TALK TO REUBE IRONS AND ASK WHAT WOULD H HAPPENED IF TH LITTLE GIRL HA DIED. ASK HIM!!
WH-WHAT... DOES HE MEAN?
SERIO BAT THAT'S FUN

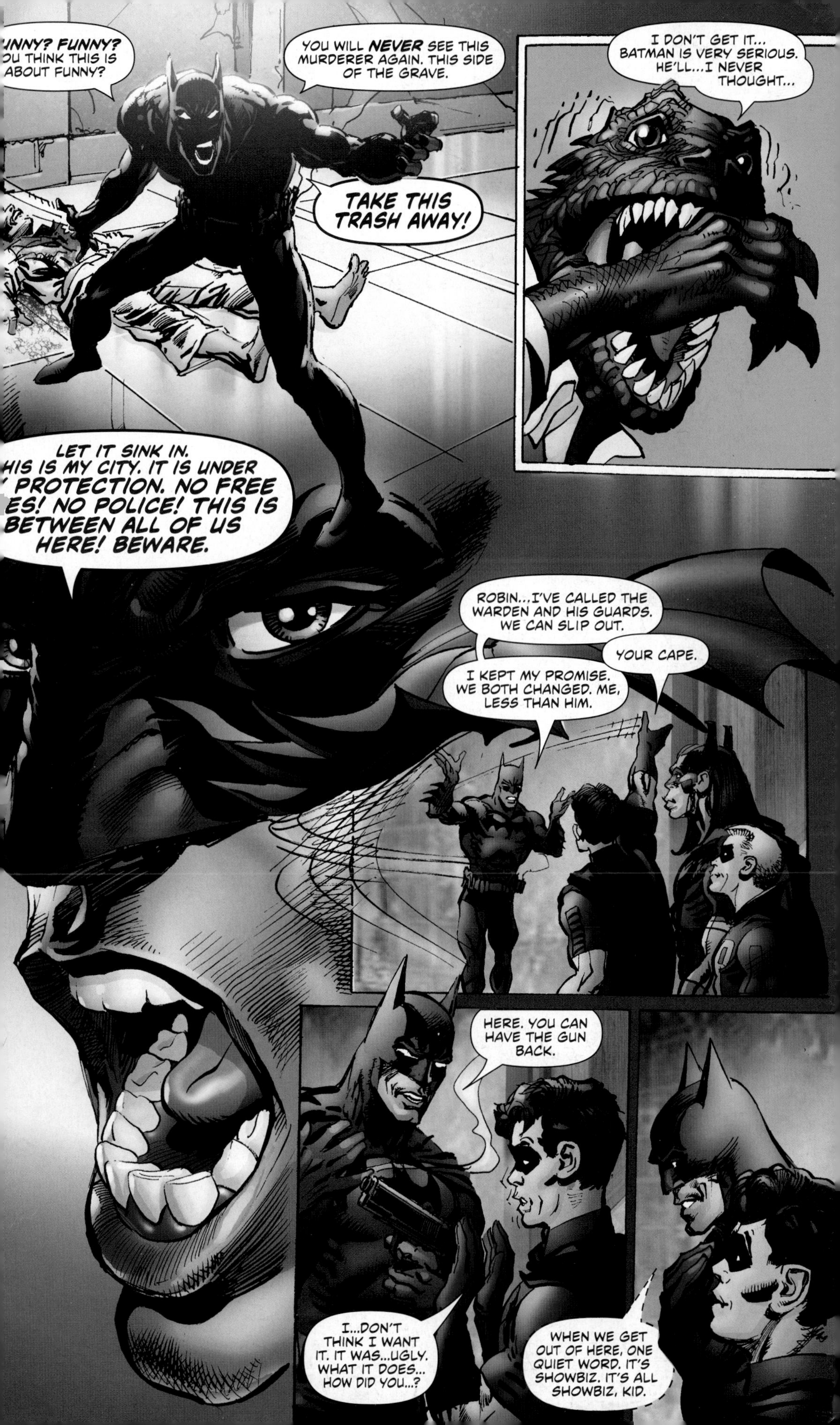

FUNNY? FUNNY? YOU THINK THIS IS ABOUT FUNNY?
YOU WILL NEVER SEE THIS MURDERER AGAIN. THIS SIDE OF THE GRAVE.
TAKE THIS TRASH AWAY!
I DON'T GET IT... BATMAN IS VERY SERIOUS. HE'LL...I NEVER THOUGHT...
LET IT SINK IN. THIS IS MY CITY. IT IS UNDER MY PROTECTION. NO FREE RIDES! NO POLICE! THIS IS BETWEEN ALL OF US HERE! BEWARE.
ROBIN...I'VE CALLED THE WARDEN AND HIS GUARDS. WE CAN SLIP OUT.
YOUR CAPE.
I KEPT MY PROMISE. WE BOTH CHANGED. ME, LESS THAN HIM.
HERE. YOU CAN HAVE THE GUN BACK.
I...DON'T THINK I WANT IT. IT WAS...UGLY. WHAT IT DOES... HOW DID YOU...?
WHEN WE GET OUT OF HERE, ONE QUIET WORD. IT'S SHOWBIZ. IT'S ALL SHOWBIZ, KID.

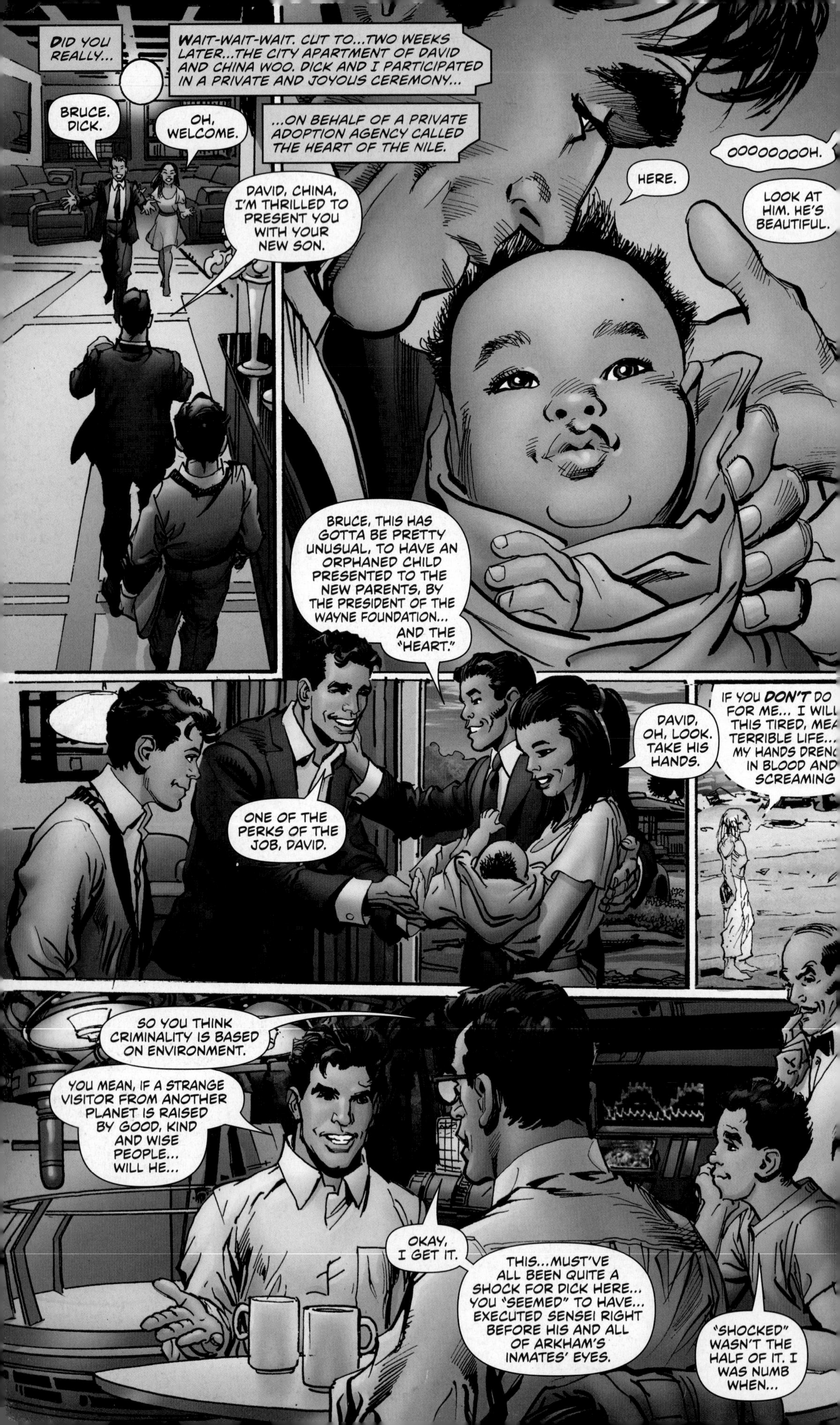
DID YOU REALLY...
WAIT-WAIT-WAIT. CUT TO...TWO WEEKS LATER...THE CITY APARTMENT OF DAVID AND CHINA WOO. DICK AND I PARTICIPATED IN A PRIVATE AND JOYOUS CEREMONY...
...ON BEHALF OF A PRIVATE ADOPTION AGENCY CALLED THE HEART OF THE NILE.
BRUCE. DICK.
OH, WELCOME.
DAVID, CHINA, I'M THRILLED TO PRESENT YOU WITH YOUR NEW SON.
HERE.
OOOOOOOOH.
LOOK AT HIM. HE'S BEAUTIFUL.
BRUCE, THIS HAS GOTTA BE PRETTY UNUSUAL, TO HAVE AN ORPHANED CHILD PRESENTED TO THE NEW PARENTS, BY THE PRESIDENT OF THE WAYNE FOUNDATION... AND THE "HEART."
ONE OF THE PERKS OF THE JOB, DAVID.
DAVID, OH, LOOK. TAKE HIS HANDS.
IF YOU DON'T DO FOR ME... I WILL THIS TIRED, MEA TERRIBLE LIFE... MY HANDS DRENC IN BLOOD AND SCREAMING
SO YOU THINK CRIMINALITY IS BASED ON ENVIRONMENT.
YOU MEAN, IF A STRANGE VISITOR FROM ANOTHER PLANET IS RAISED BY GOOD, KIND AND WISE PEOPLE... WILL HE...
OKAY, I GET IT.
THIS...MUST'VE ALL BEEN QUITE A SHOCK FOR DICK HERE... YOU "SEEMED" TO HAVE... EXECUTED SENSEI RIGHT BEFORE HIS AND ALL OF ARKHAM'S INMATES' EYES.
"SHOCKED" WASN'T THE HALF OF IT. I WAS NUMB WHEN...

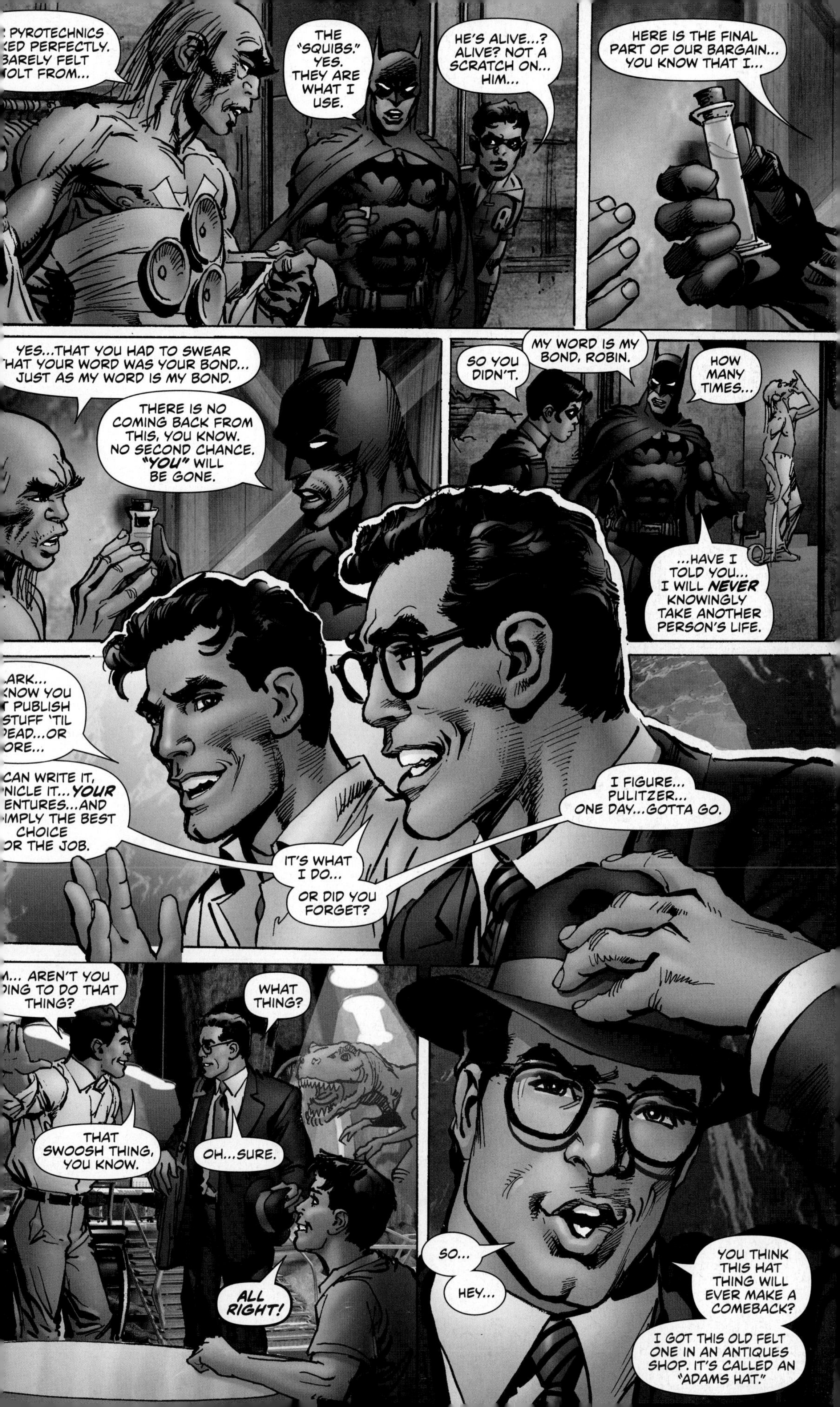

PYROTECHNICS
KED PERFECTLY.
BARELY FELT
OLT FROM...
THE "SQUIBS." YES. THEY ARE WHAT I USE.
HE'S ALIVE...? ALIVE? NOT A SCRATCH ON... HIM...
HERE IS THE FINAL PART OF OUR BARGAIN... YOU KNOW THAT I...
YES...THAT YOU HAD TO SWEAR
HAT YOUR WORD WAS YOUR BOND...
JUST AS MY WORD IS MY BOND.
THERE IS NO COMING BACK FROM THIS, YOU KNOW. NO SECOND CHANCE. "YOU" WILL BE GONE.
SO YOU DIDN'T.
MY WORD IS MY BOND, ROBIN.
HOW MANY TIMES...
...HAVE I TOLD YOU... I WILL NEVER KNOWINGLY TAKE ANOTHER PERSON'S LIFE.
LARK...
KNOW YOU
T PUBLISH
STUFF 'TIL
DEAD...OR
ORE...
CAN WRITE IT,
NICLE IT...YOUR
ENTURES...AND
IMPLY THE BEST
CHOICE
OR THE JOB.
I FIGURE... PULITZER... ONE DAY...GOTTA GO.
IT'S WHAT I DO...
OR DID YOU FORGET?
M... AREN'T YOU
OING TO DO THAT
THING?
WHAT THING?
THAT SWOOSH THING, YOU KNOW.
OH...SURE.
ALL RIGHT!
SO...
HEY...
YOU THINK THIS HAT THING WILL EVER MAKE A COMEBACK?
I GOT THIS OLD FELT ONE IN AN ANTIQUES SHOP. IT'S CALLED AN "ADAMS HAT."

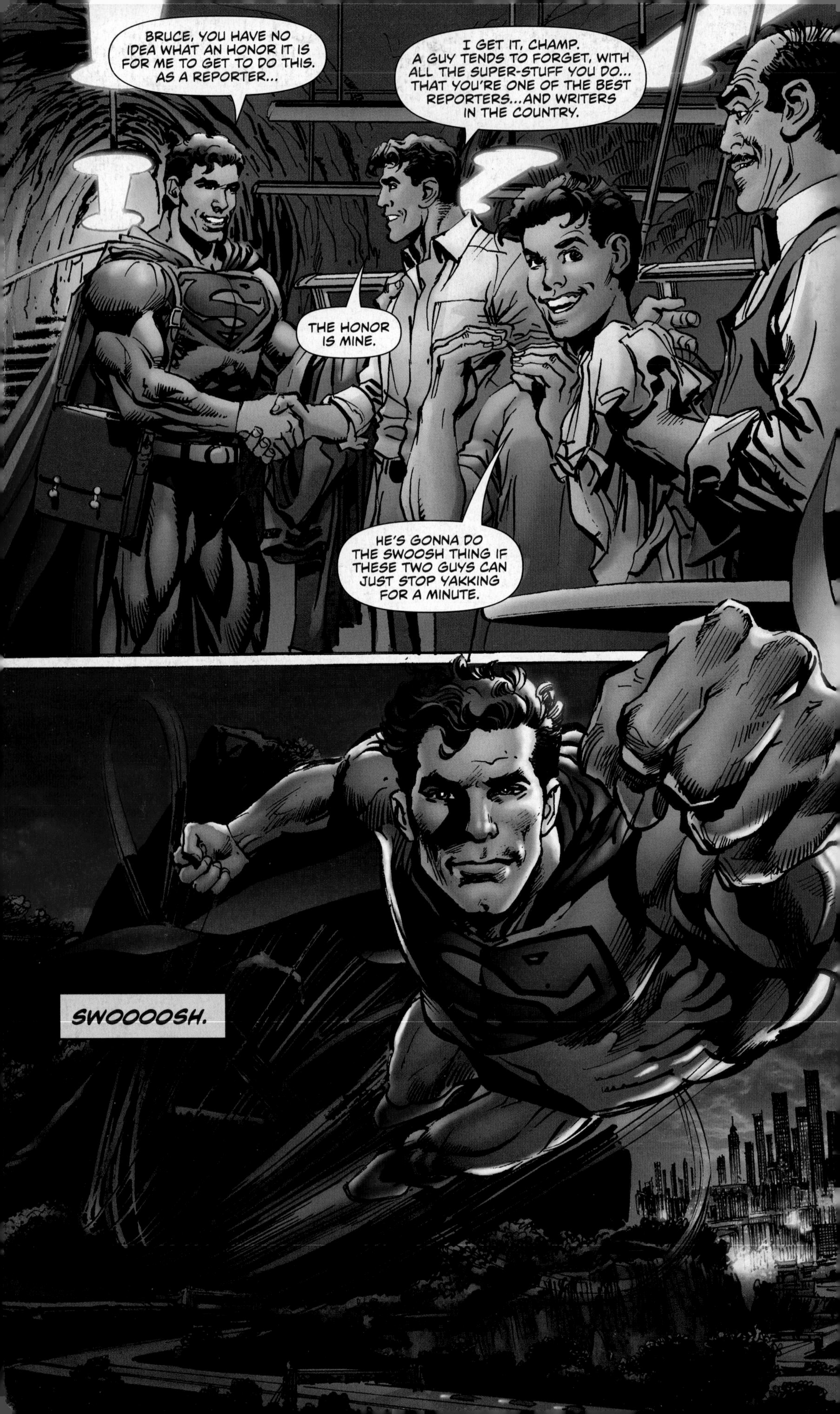
BRUCE, YOU HAVE NO IDEA WHAT AN HONOR IT IS FOR ME TO GET TO DO THIS. AS A REPORTER...
I GET IT, CHAMP. A GUY TENDS TO FORGET, WITH ALL THE SUPER-STUFF YOU DO... THAT YOU'RE ONE OF THE BEST REPORTERS...AND WRITERS IN THE COUNTRY.
THE HONOR IS MINE.
HE'S GONNA DO THE SWOOSH THING IF THESE TWO GUYS CAN JUST STOP YAKKING FOR A MINUTE.
SWOOOOSH.

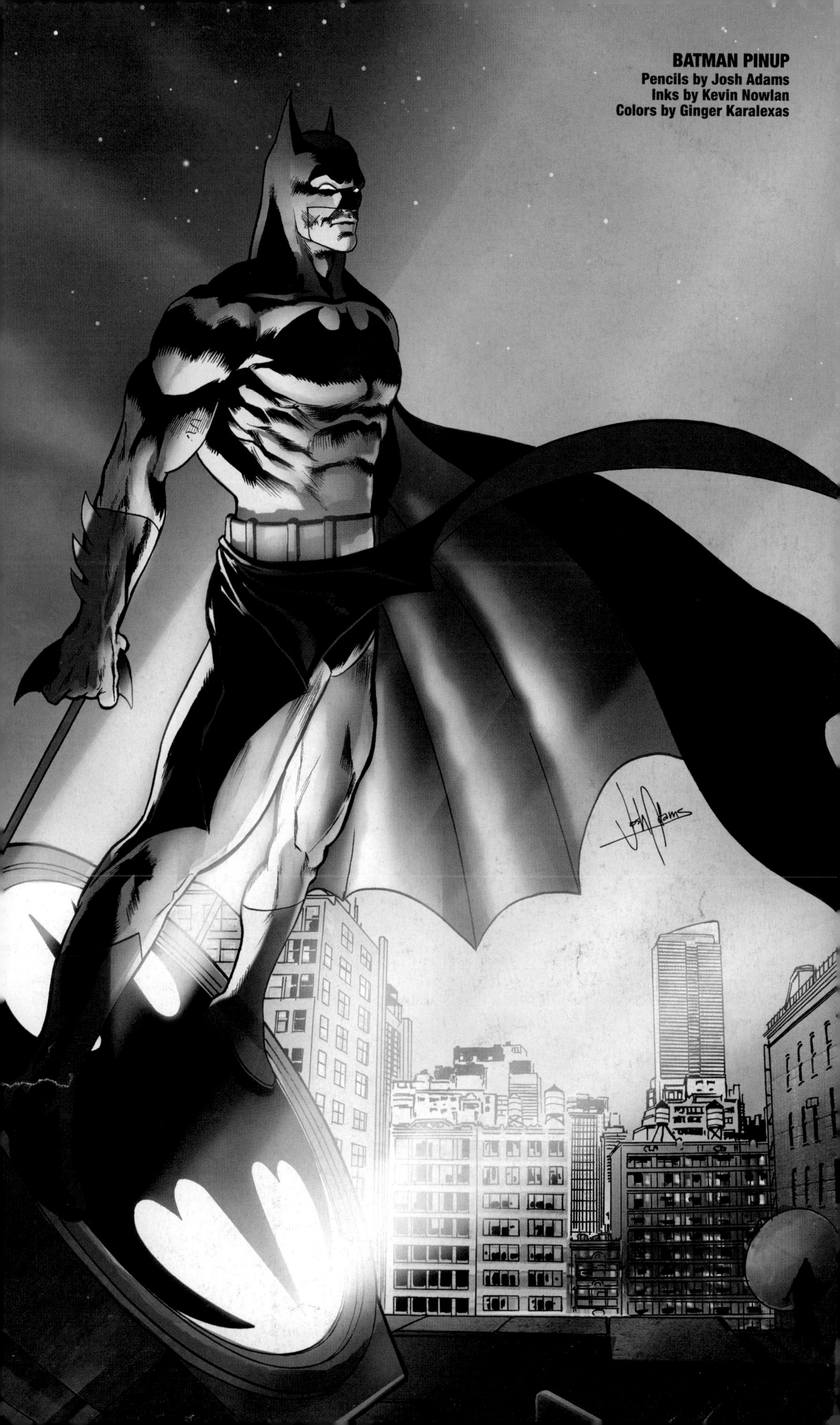

BATMAN PINUP
Pencils by Josh Adams
Inks by Kevin Nowlan
Colors by Ginger Karalexas

DC COMICS™

*"THE LONG HALLOWEEN is more th
a comic book. It's an epic traged*

—*Christopher Nolan (director of Batman Begi
The Dark Knight and The Dark Knight Rise*

*"THE LONG HALLOWEEN is the preemine
influence on both movies [Batman Begi
and The Dark Knight*

—*David Goyer (screenwriter
The Dark Knight Rise*

JEPH LOEB & TIM SAL
BATMAN: THE LONG HALLOWEE

**BATMAN:
DARK VICTORY**

**BATMAN:
HAUNTED KNIGHT**

**CATWOMAN:
WHEN IN ROME**

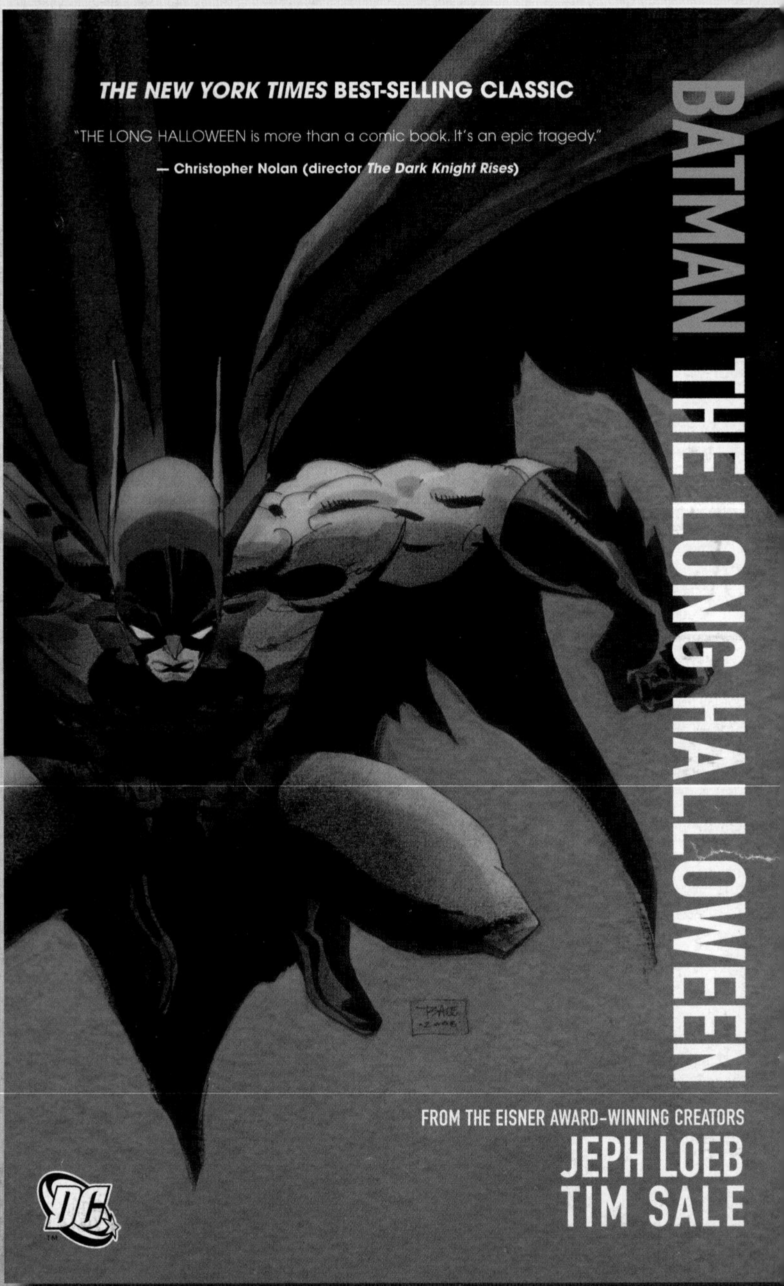

THE NEW YORK TIMES **BEST-SELLING CLASSIC**

"THE LONG HALLOWEEN is more than a comic book. It's an epic tragedy."
— **Christopher Nolan (director** *The Dark Knight Rises***)**

BATMAN THE LONG HALLOWEEN

FROM THE EISNER AWARD–WINNING CREATORS
**JEPH LOEB
TIM SALE**

MICS™

FROM THE EISNER AWARD-WINNING WRITER OF *100 BULLETS*
BRIAN AZZARELLO
with LEE BERMEJO

LUTHOR

with LEE BERMEJO

SUPERMAN: FOR TOMORROW

with JIM LEE

BATMAN: BROKEN CITY

with EDUARDO RISSO

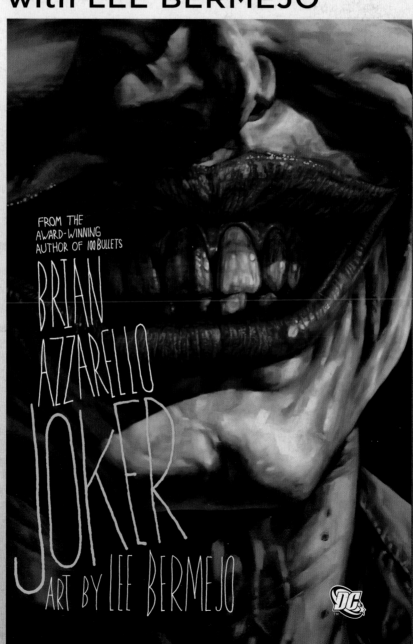

DC COMICS™

FROM THE CREATOR OF *300* & *SIN CITY*

FRANK MILLER

BATMAN: THE DARK KNIGHT
RETURNS with KLAUS JANSON

**BATMAN:
THE DARK KNIGHT
STRIKES AGAIN**

**BATMAN: YEAR ONE
DELUXE EDITION**

with DAVID MAZZUCCHELLI

**ALL-STAR BATMAN
& ROBIN, THE BOY
WONDER VOL. 1**

with JIM LEE

BATMAN: THE DARK KNIGHT® RETURNS

FRANK MILLER

with KLAUS JANSON and LYNN VARLEY